THE DREAM HORSE MYSTERIES

Prequel, 1, 2, and 3

CANDACE CARRABUS

Witting
Woman Works

*These books are dedicated with love
to my fabulous family, killer critique group,
and superb street team.*

---

*A very special thanks to
Dr. Terry E. Newton
of Bowling Green Veterinary Clinic
for veterinary advice.*

THE DREAM HORSE MYSTERIES

CANDACE CARRABUS

COLD

A DREAM HORSE MYSTERY PREQUEL

BACKED

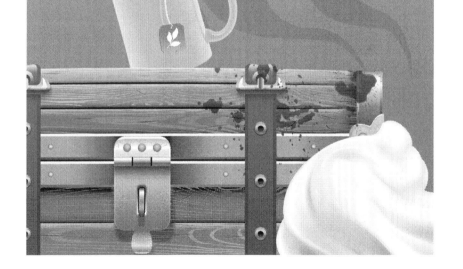

ROUND 1

A HARSH MORNING breeze sang sharp notes of coming winter, steaming horse manure, and dejection—mine.

I'd come to the show hoping to catch a few rides, make a few dollars, but no one needed help. Or no one wanted me. One pervy guy leered, grabbed his crotch, and said he'd like a ride.

Nice as could be, I asked, "And aren't you a quelling rump-fed maggot-pie?"

He stood there collecting flies for a moment then sputtered, "Yeah well, you're...you're..."

"Smarter than you, that's what." I walked away, not feeling particularly virtuous or victorious.

I took my weak horse-show coffee outside and sank to the damp ground against the wheel of a horse trailer out of the wind, letting the feeble sun bathe my face, trying to decide whether to stay or go home and nurse the ferocious hangover pounding my head.

Reason for said hangover chose that moment to appear, looking more dapper than anyone who'd drunk me under the table had a right to. He even had his stock tie pinned in place, complete overkill for a schooling show.

"How you be, V?"

I shot him a look through slitted eyes. "I think you know how I am."

Harry collapsed all six-plus feet of his skinny self next to me. "Crabby and all out of whipped cream?"

That about summed it up. I sipped my coffee, rapidly going cold and stale, but it took a hair off the edge.

A young man led a horse out to the field in front of us. The sleek dark bay wore saddle and bridle, and a lunge line was clipped right to the ring of the snaffle. Idiot. The grass was slick with half-frozen dew. I wouldn't work a horse out here, especially not one vibrating like a thoroughbred being led to the starting gate. She probably was off the track by her looks and conformation. Sweat already darkened her shoulders and flank. She'd been getting ridden in the indoor warm-up ring, I'd bet, and not cooperating, so they'd brought her here to work out the kinks at the end of a lunge.

With my attention riveted on the horse, I asked Harry, "Where've you been?"

Out of the corner of my eye, I saw him swipe a finger under his nose, a habit from his cocaine days. I hoped he wasn't stupid enough to start again. It would explain how he could stay up half the night drinking and still be here at the crack of dawn like the Energizer Bunny.

He grinned like an addle-pate. Not sure why I had Shakespeare on the brain this morning. Probably the tragedy of my current situation.

"Perfection takes time, *petal*, you know that."

I kept my nose to the opening of my cardboard cup of black coffee—one of my vices. Inhaling deeply to block the scent of cologne and cough drops, I wondered how I'd ever been attracted to this person. The fact that he could model for Ralph Lauren might have something to with it. "Perfection," I drawled. "Right."

The boy with the horse jerked the line. The mare's mouth worked, foam dripping, and her ears swiveled to me, to the field, to the indoor, anywhere but to him. He gave her slack, brought the whip behind her, and she moved out into a huge trot, covering tons of ground, tail swishing angrily with each stride. Four white socks and an irregular star. Barely visible dapples slid over her haunches like melted dark chocolate. Flashy. Beautiful didn't cover it. Long sloping shoulders and a well-sprung ribcage. A dream made real. My fingers itched to stroke her neck, comb through her mane, take the reins, gather all that power to me. This one could jump the moon.

Harry swigged his extra large vanilla soy latte out of a designer ceramic go cup and sighed, knowing too well the turn of my mind. "Yes, sweetheart. Perfection."

I let my head fall back against the tire. "Ugh."

"Why Viola Parker, do I smell a particularly sour disposition this fine morn?"

I shrugged. We both knew the truth. Since the fatal wreck with Wastrel, very few trusted their expensive equines to me. They used to beg for my butt on their horse's backs.

We stared at the stunning mare for a few minutes. My mouth felt pasty. I needed whipped cream to soothe my senses. Why had I gone out drinking with Harry? I didn't remember getting home but had woken in my bed at my cousin's house, so somehow I'd gotten there. My truck had been parked half on the curb with the keys still in it, but I'd missed the mailbox. I'd left before Penny got up to find my bra on her kitchen counter again. But as I watched the mare move, warmth spread through me and tingled up my spine. My heart expanded. I could feel the floaty bounce of her step, the intelligence behind her dark eyes, the weightless sense of flying. My heart reached for her, got inside. She wouldn't be easy, never that, but the spark was there. One eye rolled to me as she passed, and I nodded. We belonged to each other. I stood and took a step toward her, wondering if Harry planned to go south for the winter circuit. I could tag along. Depending on who owned her, this mare might be down there. *Harry* was still in everyone's good graces, despite his chronic bad boy behavior. *Harry* never killed a horse.

I huffed, pulling my shredded pride tight. Who was I kidding? I wasn't going to Florida, and I would never ride this mare. It was my day off, but I'd go to work anyway, give the barn a good cleaning, and take Ed Todd to lunch. The old geezer could barely see anymore, but he loved his horses and always gave me a job when I needed it, even if it was only mucking stalls and exercising his retired jumpers.

Yet, I didn't move, couldn't take my eyes off the dark bay. She hunched her back and shook, flopping her short mane from side to side, then raised her neck, hollowed her back, champed the bit, dropped her head, shortened her stride…barely contained energy just waiting to bust free. The handler idly swept the whip along the ground, asleep at the wheel. Dangerous with a horse like this. She slipped a little, squealed and bucked, testing him. The stirrups flopped up and down with a thunk. She shook her head again, wanting to go. He yanked at her. She cut into the circle, ears back. Not flat, but he didn't seem to notice, just waved the whip, and she went out to the end of the line, still trotting, overstepping by a mile, tail stiff. Raw physical talent constrained by stupid people. Something was wrong. They'd either failed to notice, or done something to cause it. My vote was for the latter.

A girl came out of the barn and walked toward them dressed in boots and breeches, a helmet and show coat.

"Oh Christ."

I hadn't noticed Harry getting up, coming to stand beside me and admire perfection on four hooves. He gave a low whistle.

"Yes," I confirmed. "Becca Scissorhands." Who had no business within a mile of this horse, let alone riding her. Becca's boots were sweaty, and she tapped her whip against her leg. She'd already been up on this piece of heaven, and it hadn't gone well. "A crime's about to happen, and they don't even know."

"See?" the boy said, turning to Becca. "She's fine."

Becca crossed her arms, clearly unconvinced. Maybe intelligence lurked behind the sneer after all.

The mare felt the moment of her handler's inattention and stopped. Becca stomped toward her. The mare backed. Becca grabbed the lunge line as if she might pull the horse down to her level and give her what for, but the dark bay continued backpedaling.

"Whoa," I whispered, as if I were at her shoulder, and I began walking without even realizing what I was doing. "Easy now."

Becca advanced, and the mare took one step, two…Becca's whip came up. The mare wheeled her front end to the side nearly jerking the girl off her feet.

"No," I shouted, but before Becca could lay the lash across the mare's silky hide, the horse reared, pulled the line out of the boy's hands, and took off for the other end of the show grounds.

At the far side of the field, not much of a fence separated us from a busy road. The line snapped in the air behind her, but if she slowed, it might get around her feet. I threw down my cup and started running.

"Turn," I telegraphed to her. "Circle back. It'll be all right." I would make it all right. But, oh, God, the running hurt my sore head.

I heard Harry's long strides catching up. Farther back, Becca screamed at the boy, but her words were lost to the bitter wind.

The mare cut loose with a series of irritated leaps and bucks and got one foreleg over the line. I pushed more speed into my legs, ignoring the kettle drum beat of blood in my ears, but the distance between us only lengthened. On foot, I could never catch a galloping horse. Had to try. "Whoa, girl, whoa. Turn."

The fence came closer, and I couldn't tell whether she didn't see it or didn't care. Like Wastrel galloping for that last jump. Fear, raw and overwhelming, seized my gut and nearly took me down.

"Please," I breathed. "Stop."

I could barely see for the watering of my eyes, but she might have slowed. My arms pumped but I felt light-headed and fuzzy and no longer in touch with the ground.

Suddenly, she stopped and faced me, and I nearly ran into her. Quickly, I unsnapped the lunge line and kicked it away, then undid her reins from where they'd been looped under the throat latch. She stood as if we'd done this a hundred times, and I felt like we had. Felt like we knew each other at a soul-deep level. Like I hadn't felt with a horse since Wastrel.

"Good girl," I crooned, and she nudged my shoulder, nostrils flaring, blowing warm air over my cheeks. I loosed a long breath of relief, pressed my forehead to her cheek, stroked her damp neck. Like satin, she was, steel-wrapped satin. With one hand, I unbuckled the girth, shoved the saddle off, and ran my palm over her back. She flinched. Just as I thought.

We stood like that forever, as if she hadn't just nearly killed herself. I felt Harry come up, but he stayed silent. Other footsteps and labored breathing behind me, but I kept my connection with the mare, her with me, our hearts beating as one.

"Well, if it isn't Vi the valkyrie."

Becca.

The beater, the bitch, the heavy-seated bugbear who would ruin this mighty spirit with her whip and sawing hands. If the mare didn't kill her first. A tantalizing image, but not one I would encourage in spite of my reputation as *chooser of the slain*. If only.

"You lost something," I said. "Something valuable." The boy reached for the reins. I didn't relinquish them, kept my focus on Becca. "You shouldn't be so careless."

"Mind your own business *has-been*." The patented Becca sneer was firmly in place. "She's a high-strung cold-backed witch, but her owner wants ribbons, and I'm going to give them to him."

I breathed through my nose, forcing calm. "Whatever it takes?"

Harry's eyebrows shot to his hairline. He cut a warning glance to Becca.

Becca snatched the reins, and the mare stiffened. "Pick up that saddle," she ordered the boy. He scrambled to do her bidding, and they started away.

"Use a different saddle pad and a saddle that fits her," I said. Not that I was interested in helping Becca, but if it helped the horse, I was on it.

Becca flipped me off over her shoulder.

I gritted my teeth until they were out of ear-shot. "Goatish fen-sucked flax-wench."

Harry blinked at me. "You haven't pulled out your epic insults in a while, V. It gives me pleasure and hope to hear you spouting Shakespeare."

I headed for my truck. "You've always been easily entertained."

"That's a low blow." He jogged to catch up. "What crawled up your ass and died?"

I whirled on him. "Seriously, Harry? My life is in the toilet, and the best horse I've met in a good long while just got led away by hell on two feet."

"You haven't ridden her. You don't really know. Maybe she's worthless."

If only he were referring to Becca. But he knew better than to cross me when I was in this mood. Especially when I'm right. "If that's what you think, then you're right up there with Becca Scissorhands. *And* blind." I walked away before the tears clogging my throat escaped.

Again, he caught up, put his hand on my arm. "Vi, I'm sorry. If you say she's the best thing since sliced bread, then I believe you. You've always been better at this than me."

I pulled my arm away but wasn't angry at him. If I'd managed my life better, I'd be in a position to buy that mare. I'd been waiting for a horse like that for years. I didn't know her name or who owned her, not that it mattered. There was nothing I could do.

"You just need to open your eyes, Harry. That's all."

"That's not all. You see with something else, some inner vision I'm not privy to." He gazed over his shoulder for a moment, back in the direction the mare had gone—the indoor arena. It might as well be a torture chamber. "If you'd only—"

"Don't start." He'd been on me to go into business with him for years. In some ways it made sense. He had wealthy parents who loved me like their own, who would happily finance whatever equine-related venture we put together. Only problem was, it would mean being legally tied to Harry. If that also included marriage, his parents would be ecstatic. Drinking buddies was one thing. Saddling myself with a man with worse addictions than me? Uh-uh. Nope.

Once again, I started walking. "I'll be at Todd's if you need me."

He didn't follow, but said, "You're coming to Thanksgiving dinner on Thursday, right? Allie-Baba will be sorely disappointed if you don't show. Two p.m. sharp."

Allie and Baba were his parents, Alcott and Babette Brown.

Without turning, I answered, "Wouldn't miss it."

Half an hour later, I turned into the barn drive knowing I'd have the place to myself. The three boarders—all teenaged girls—had taken their horses to the show I'd just left. They were blonde and sickeningly adorable, with names like Kayla, Kaitlyn, and Kaylee, or maybe one of them was Kylie or Kelsey? I'd be damned if I could remember who was who. I thought of them as grounded, flighty, and spacey, and some days it was all I could do not to shoot them, or myself. But they were good to their horses, so I mustered a handful of tolerance and let them go about their giggly business.

Ed would probably be snoozing in the tack room breathing horse and leather and dreaming of galloping cross country after a fox, or in a stall with one of his retirees, brushing him and talking the horse's ear off. After mucking stalls, we'd go to lunch at his favorite diner where the waitresses knew what he liked and pretended he could still see well enough to read the menu. He'd tell me the same stories he's told me a hundred times, and I'd forget for a while that I was no longer highly sought after by the top owners and trainers, or by anyone. I'd forget it was nearly winter and I didn't have a decent job. I'd forget the amazing horse I just met and would never have. Jesus. I hate frigging pity parties.

First things first. I headed for my stash of canned whipped cream in the tack room fridge. That never failed to adjust my attitude.

The barn was blissfully peaceful. The few horses inside dozed and idly swished their tails. Weak sunlight shone through the windows and dust sparkled in the narrow beams.

"Ed?" I called softly as I opened the door to the tack room. I didn't like to startle him if he was sleeping. His hearing wasn't so great, either.

But Ed Todd wasn't in his chair.

He was sprawled face down on the worn carpet, a wet stain pooled beneath him.

ROUND 2

"Ed!" I dropped to my knees beside him, holding my breath, unsure whether to touch him. His skin was the color of a dead mouse. "Oh, God, Ed. Please, no."

This wasn't the kind of crime I'd been thinking about earlier. The wet spot wasn't blood at least. I poked his shoulder. He groaned.

"Jesus effing Christ, Ed." Hadn't my day already been bad enough?

He looked smaller than usual, crumpled. One knee was bent and his arms were flung out to his sides. His mouth worked. I think he said *goddamned shit*, which reassured me. But how the hell had he gotten on the floor?

Milly the skinny white barn cat stood from where she'd been napping on the couch. She stretched, jumped down, sniffed Ed's ear. In cat years, she was as old as he was. Maybe older. That would make her about a hundred. Satisfied he'd live to feed her another day, she hopped over him and went out the door.

"Ed, what happened?" I stroked his nearly bald head. "Are you hurt? You need to get up. I think you pissed yourself."

He grumbled and got one hand under himself, started to push up. I grabbed his shoulders and together we got him into a sitting position. He leaned against the trunk that served as a coffee table. I wiped dirt from his cheek. He batted my hand away.

"Spilled my tea is all," he slurred.

His favorite mug sat on its side nearby, the teabag a few inches from that.

"That's not all, but at least your mug is intact."

"Well, I didn't piss myself, but I will if you don't get me off this cold floor."

"Hey, it's not my fault you tripped over your shoelaces." I helped him up and he shuffled to the bathroom. I tried to keep hold of his elbow because he was pale and looked like he might keel over again, but he shrugged away.

Cantankerous old cuss. I'd known him since I first started to ride at five. Guess you could say I came by my own orneriness honestly.

I retrieved his cup, put it in the sink, and found a towel to dry the rug, although it appeared Ed's sweatshirt had absorbed most of the liquid. That's when I noticed the coffee table wasn't in its usual spot. It had been moved several inches away from the couch and sideways about a foot. I always made sure everything was in its place. The *same* place. Always. With Ed's eyesight nearly gone, but him not willing to admit it, he could get around so long as he knew where every object in the barn and tack room was and nothing shifted.

Had someone moved it? As usual, I'd double checked before leaving the night before. The only people who might have been here this morning were the K girls, but if I knew them, they'd had the trailer packed the night before and hadn't even come in the tack room. I'd ask them later anyway. Maybe the table moved when Ed fell? Unlikely. The scarred steamer trunk barely closed it was so crammed with old issues of *The Chronicle of the Horse*, *Practical Horseman*, and *Equus* magazines. It weighed more than he did.

A few minutes later, we sat on the couch together. His chipped mug rested in the curved shelter of one roughened hand, steam rising from the freshly steeping cup of Earl Grey. He held an icepack to his forehead where he had a bump. I offered him my can of whipped cream. It's pretty much a cure-all.

"No good for my diabetes."

"A little won't hurt."

He opened his mouth and I squirted some in. He chased it with a swig of tea.

"Did you forget to eat this morning?"

"Had one of those hard-boiled eggs you left. Toast."

It was better than I'd done for myself. So he probably hadn't fainted.

"Do you remember what happened?"

He gave me a sharp look. "'Course I do. I came in here after feeding to get my tea and banged my shin on the dang trunk, lost my balance, and fell down." He glared at the trunk as if it'd tripped him on purpose. "That's not where it belongs."

"I know."

He lowered the ice pack, revealing a knot and the beginnings of a bruise. "Must've hit my head."

I glanced at the clock. He fed about six-thirty when I wasn't there. It was barely eight. He'd been on the floor nearly an hour.

"Want to go to the hospital?" I already knew the answer but had to ask.

"Hell no."

"All righty then. Let's get some pain killers in you. I don't want to listen to you griping about your aches and boo boos."

He smiled. "Okay. But only if you let me take you to lunch later."

I insisted Ed stay in the tack room while I mucked stalls, and I put the TV on his favorite news station. He seemed okay so I didn't harass him about being careful or seeing his doctor. The image of the out-of-place trunk kept dancing through my mind—when that spectacular mare wasn't galloping around. Later, I asked the K girls if they'd been in the tack room that morning, but they swore they hadn't. I doubted all three of them together would have been able to move the thing. It was impossible to know who else had been there. The not knowing frustrated and angered me. It had been deliberate. Someone wanted to hurt Ed. That was not okay. Not at all.

Over the next couple of days, my thoughts pinged from that to the mare, obsessing like a dime novel detective over who would want to hurt a kind, lonely old guy and over the mare like a new crush. I almost called Becca Scissorhands a couple of times, but always stopped myself. No point. It's not like I could make an offer. The chances of the owner hiring me to ride her were about as good as my coming into an inheritance—zero.

On Thursday, I drove out to Allie-Baba's house in East Hampton as ordered to have Thanksgiving with them. Sullen clouds spit freezing rain, but my truck slid only once as I took the exit a little too fast. The warm house welcomed me with a perfect cloud of pumpkin, cinnamon, and roasted bird smells. Fire crackled on the grate, and the windows dripped with steam. Alcott and Babette fawned over me even more than usual, which made me feel wanted and suspicious in equal measure. Harry was unusually subdued— probably because they paid more attention to me than to him—and guzzled his rum and apple cider cocktail like water. They always made such a fuss as if anxious and unsure of my affection. I don't know why Harry insisted I come. But the food was good, so I could ignore his sulkiness for one day, and they'd load me up with leftovers which I'd take to Ed.

Baba wore sparkly chrome nail polish. Her fingertips glittered like razors over the place settings—the help hadn't aligned the forks with the same precision I would a set of cavaletti poles—and making sure all the food got to the table hot. Allie sat in a corner smoking his pipe and working the New York Times crossword puzzle. If I didn't know they were so dysfunctional, I'd think I'd stepped into a Norman Rockwell painting. Well, maybe not the silver nails. And the dysfunction? Made me feel right at home.

The turkey was free-range with grape leaves—flown in from Greece for all I know—garnishing the porcelain platter. Pumpkin risotto came to the table in hollowed out gourds, and Brussel sprouts were grilled still attached to the stalk. There was cheesy cauliflower with a sexy Italian name, more cider in the stuffing along with golden raisins and bacon, celery root puree with toasted hazelnuts, sautéed green beans with caramelized pecans, and cranberry chutney. Mountains of fragrant fresh-baked rolls steamed from beneath embroidered cloths. All brought out by glove-wearing servants. Fancy. I'd think they were trying to impress someone, but it was just us, and this was normal for them. Christmas was an even bigger deal because, you know, gifts. I'd given up trying to procure presents for them. They always made a joke of saying my *presence* was more than enough. God knows why. I could be as sullen and bad-tempered as Harry, or Ed Todd for that matter, but they never seemed to mind.

Harry waved away a hovering servant, snapped his linen napkin to his lap, plunged a silver spoon into his risotto, and directed a seemingly innocuous question to my end of the table. "You hear about Becca?"

My forkful of turkey froze midway to my mouth. "We don't exactly travel in the same circles." I stabbed a few green beens and stuffed them and the turkey in. That would prevent me from saying something I shouldn't, but I doubted it kept my eyebrow from hiking up. Anyway, Harry could read me better than anyone. He'd baited the hook with an irresistible morsel.

He took his time, dumping a dollop of cranberries on his plate while I chewed. To my right, Baba tried to hide a sigh behind the corner of her napkin, and to my left, Allie focused on cutting his food into bite-sized pieces. Bite-sized, that is, if you were a hamster. I caught his barely audible *tsk* when I shoved all that food in my mouth at one time. For all their class, none of them were particularly subtle.

Harry buttered a roll, savoring the moment.

I jumped at the bait. "Well? You're obviously dying to tell me, so spill."

He tilted his head, and one side of his mouth curled up. "That mare bucked her off in the low hunter class."

Many uncharitable thoughts swirled through my mind before I spit out the correct response. "Oh my God, is she okay?"

Harry shrugged. "She will be. I don't think the limp will be permanent."

"You mean Becca, right, not the mare?"

He gave me a look. "I should have known you were more concerned about the horse."

"No, I was asking about Becca, really."

An exaggerated eye roll let me know exactly what he thought of that. "She has just bruises, mostly."

Yeah, to her pride. I knew that feeling but couldn't dredge up any sympathy for her. Whatever the mare had done, cold-backed or not, Becca had most likely driven her to it.

Baba put her hand on Harry's arm. "Michael, dear, you shouldn't take pleasure in another's misfortune."

Harry jerked his shoulder. He hated it when she called him by his first name. She always called him Michael, so he was perpetually mad at her.

"Did I say I took pleasure in it? I'm just reporting. For some reason, Vi liked the horse. I thought she'd want to know."

"It doesn't change anything," I said.

Harry shrugged again, but his shrugs never meant disinterest. If anything, they meant he knew more than he was saying.

"Everything happens for a reason," his mother said with another sigh.

I didn't want to dwell on Becca's bad luck, bad choices, or bad riding, so I changed the subject.

"When I got to Ed's last weekend, he was out cold on the floor."

Baba gasped and pressed her gleaming fingers to her heart. Even Allie looked up with interest. They knew Ed from his heyday, and if they hadn't exactly shunned him since he'd fallen on hard times, they didn't exactly reach out to him, either.

Harry didn't stop slicing a fresh piece of turkey. "You'd think the old guy would know better than to try and keep up with you."

"Harry," I said. "Sometimes you go too far. He fell over the trunk and hit his head. He's lucky he didn't crack his skull open or break his hip or something."

"I doubt it," Allie put in. "He's got strong bones from all the riding. I wouldn't worry about his hips."

"Someone moved the trunk. But I can't figure out who or why. The thing weighs a ton."

"I thought you always kept everything in its place, Vi, so he can get around without tripping." Harry mopped up celery root puree with a hunk of stuffing. "Maybe you should get him a seeing-eye dog."

"Michael, dear, they're called therapy dogs, now."

Harry colored slightly. I knew what he was thinking but not saying. *I don't give a fuck what they're called, Mother.*

And really, Baba could be annoying. We called her *Our Lady of the Platitudes.*

Allie—also known as *Lord of the Pregnant Pause*—brought us back to the point. "Is he...all right?"

"I'll fix a plate for you to take to him." As if that would fix everything. In platitude-speak, that meant Baba would have the servants fix several plates, wrap them in foil, nestle them in season-specific colored tissue in an insulated hamper, and tie it all up with a neat bow. She'd probably have them include a thermos of rum and cider cocktail as well.

"He has a bump on his head, but he's as cantankerous as ever, so I think he'll be all right."

In a rare show of poetic generosity, Harry said, "Clearly, it'll take more than a knot on his noggin to keep Ed Todd down."

Over the next few weeks, I asked around plenty, but no one admitted to being at the barn that morning, let alone moving the guilty trunk. I'd put my entire body into shouldering the heavy box back into place.

The show season was pretty much over. Anyone with the money for it was preparing for the winter circuit in Florida. I helped my cousin, Penny, decorate for Christmas, did a little shopping, and tried, unsuccessfully, to keep that mare out of my mind. I'd even called Harry to see if he'd learned who owned her or where she was stabled, but he hadn't, didn't. He offered to find out, but there simply was no point. What was I going to do? Visit her? That would only make it worse. Especially if Becca was around, limping or otherwise.

On Christmas morning, we opened presents and feasted on cinnamon rolls and waffles. With whipped cream, of course. I was sipping my third cup of coffee, hoping to stave off a carb coma, when the phone rang. I assumed it was Aunt Trudy, Penny's mother, with some last-minute need for us to pick up on our way over for Christmas dinner. But Penny handed the phone to me.

Too brightly, Baba's voice came through the ear piece. "Vi, dear, Merry Christmas."

"Merry Christmas, Babette." I paused, but she didn't add anything, so I asked, "How are you and Alcott?" I'd told them I wasn't coming Christmas day. I'd go out for New Year's. Was something wrong?

"Erm…"

It wasn't like Baba to hesitate or beat around the bush. That was Allie's speciality. Worried that something had happened to Harry, I took the phone down the hall to my room.

"Yes?"

"Santa Claus left something here for you. A…package…was delivered."

"Out there?"

"Yes, dear." A delighted and baffled giggle came through the line. A land line—the only phone Baba uses.

"Okay," I said slowly. "I'll get it when I come next week. If that's okay?" I really didn't feel up to the hour and a half drive out East.

"No, no. You really should come today. If you can."

"I—"

"You must. Whenever it's convenient, but soon would be best."

"Is it something that will spoil if I don't come right away?" I was really looking forward to Christmas dinner with Penny and her husband and Aunt Trudy and Uncle Vic.

"No, dear, not spoil, not exactly. Please come."

I took a deep breath, working through how I'd explain this to my aunt. She liked things how she liked them on Christmas. I glanced at the clock next to my bed. If I left now, I could just about make it back in time for dinner. A dinner that started with cheese ravioli drenched in sauce canned by Aunt Trudy from the bounty of her lovingly tended garden—not something I intended to miss.

"Okay. I'm coming, but I can't stay long."

"Good. Drive carefully. Ta ta."

I took a quick shower, pulled on my new fleece-lined jeans—thank you, Penny—and grabbed a nice pair of slacks for later. Without waiting for my truck to fully warm up, I headed east. Last week's snow had melted and become dirty, but a fresh dusting overnight brightened it and cheerfully stuck to the branches of the dense pines to either side of the highway. Happy kids woke up to a white Christmas. I was one of them.

Two sets of perfectly beaming smiles met me at Allie-Baba's door, and I wondered why Harry hadn't also greeted me. Inside, I stomped slush from my boots and started to take off my coat, but Baba stopped me. "Keep it on, dear, we're going out." She pulled on hers as well. Turning to Allie, she said, "Be a dear and bring some hot chocolate to the barn."

Curious, I followed her through the mud room and out the back. The new snow made their place glow like a Christmas card. But why the barn? It would be just like Harry to order some ridiculous quantity of one of my favorite foods—like several cases of whipped cream—and have it shipped to arrive on Christmas. With enough money, you can arrange stuff like that. I smiled. He'd be wherever the gift was.

A large pine wreath decorated the Brown's red board-and-batten barn. Each white fence post from the barn to the road was topped with a red bow. It wouldn't surprise me to know they'd hired Martha Stewart to consult on the decorations. "Where's Harry? I mean, Michael?"

Allie caught up with us and wrapped my cold fingers around a steaming mug. "He's…away."

I felt my brows draw together and a question form, but I knew I wouldn't get more out of him unless he wanted to tell me, so I didn't ask where or for how long, although I was a little put out Harry hadn't informed me himself.

Baba opened the door and hurried us inside where it was measurably warmer. I love being in a barn on Christmas. The cozy warmth, animal smells, and the sound of horses munching…the first Christmas was in a stable, after all. It made me feel right with the world. Baba stopped at the first stall. The only horses here were Harry's ancient pony, Thelwell, and Baba's retired hunter, Grace. Allie didn't have a horse. He'd been happy to pay the bills but never rode.

The horse in the stall was neither Thelwell nor Grace. She or he had his back to us and head down in a mound of hay. A new green blanket trimmed in red wrapped the horse from shoulder to tail.

Like a Christmas present.

The horse turned to us.

My breath caught in my chest.

The mare.

From the show.

I looked at Baba. She grinned. "Her name is Calypso."

"I…but…who? How?"

Her shoulders hiked to her ears, the grin widened. "There's an envelope pinned to her blanket. Maybe that explains." She replaced the hot cocoa with a leather halter and matching lead, then took Allie's arm and left.

I hung up the halter and quietly entered the stall, slipping to the mare's shoulder. She curled her neck around to sniff me. I ran my knuckles over her cheek, barely making contact, feeling like I'd stepped into a dream, afraid she might poof into nothing if I touched her or spoke. It might be a dream, but tired cliché or not, I never wanted to wake up.

The envelope had my name typed on it. No handwriting for a clue, but Harry must have been behind this.

Inside, the note was also typed. Harry hated writing anything out. And his penmanship sucked. But he'd signed it, confirming my suspicions.

Dear Vi, it started. So formal.

Surprise! Okay, better.

Of course I lied when I told you I knew nothing about the mare. Harry? Lie? Shocking. Not.

But before I get to that, I need to confess that it was me who moved the trunk in Ed's tack room. Son of a bitch.

My favorite tie pin went missing and I thought I might have dropped in Ed's tack room the last time I visited. Which would have been months ago. *I swear I thought I'd gotten that beastly trunk back in place, but I guess not.* Yeah, guess again. *I'm terribly sorry Ed conked his head.* Sorry? That's what you say when you nearly kill someone?

Perhaps the presence of the creature you are standing with right now will help you find forgiveness in your heart for an old fuck up like me. Plus, I wanted to give you something you'd actually value. It was true I rarely appreciated his extravagant gestures.

I know you'll want to pay me back—yes—but after the incident with Becca, I got the mare for a song. Killer price, really, so not necessary. I rescued her for you. Could be the best thing he'd ever done, but I couldn't be in debt to him.

She is cold-backed. And the truth is, so are you. You never let anyone stick, especially me. You deserve each other. Well.

But I've gone away to get better. That's all I'll say about it right now, so don't try to find out more. My parents don't know much, so it's no use bribing them, either. Maybe someday I'll be able to earn more than your disdain. Good Lord.

I don't know when I'll be back. Good luck.

Harry

I didn't know whether to crumple it up and throw it against the wall or mash it into a pile of poop or what. Hot tears pricked my eyes. What the hell was I going to do with her? I couldn't afford rent for myself let alone board for a horse. Then I noticed the postscript.

P.S. She can stay at Allie-Baba's indefinitely.

I sucked in a deep breath. I didn't exactly want to be indebted to Harry's parents, either, no matter how well intentioned their generosity. I folded the note, slid it back in the envelope, tucked it into my pocket, and put my arms around Calypso's neck. I would call her Cali. She kept chewing her mouthful of sweet timothy grass. I breathed in her scent of warm skin, dust, wood shavings, and hay, then stepped back until I could look at her. She picked up her head and regarded me with dark eyes full of intelligence and longing. I understood that longing at a soul-deep level. Perhaps we did deserve each other, but not in the way Harry implied.

"Cold-backed?" I asked her. "Nah. All we need is someone to understand us, right?" I pressed my palm to her forehead. She blinked at me. "Someone who wants to know what's inside." I stroked her ears. "I'll be that someone for you, okay?"

She nudged my hand and blew out a long breath that ruffled her nostrils.

I think she agreed.

End of *Cold Backed*

CANDACE CARRABUS

ON THE

DREAM HORSE MYSTERY #1

BUCKLE

CHAPTER ONE

THE TRUTH IS, my parents are alive. Pretending they're dead makes their absence in my life tolerable. When the letter came from their attorney—crap—who would have guessed they had a lawyer? Anyway, it was like they were dead because it referred to money I might receive, "amount undisclosed." That was just like them. Jesus. Amount undisclosed. What the hell was that supposed to mean? It could be five dollars for cripe's sake.

I tightened my horse's girth from where I sat in the saddle, and she swished her tail in irritation, tossed her head. We both needed a good gallop.

The letter said my parents had "made arrangements." That's a thinly-veiled Dad euphemism for "here's what I want you to do, and I've fixed it so you have to." He always gets his way. I went along like an idiot—hadn't seen or heard from them in years, and I still went along.

I'm like a dog. I can say that because I have a dog—Noire—running alongside. Doesn't matter how I treat her—and I treat her good—she'd be happy to see me.

Always hopeful. That's what it was. I was hoping this time they'd finally come through for me—that it would be more than five dollars.

I can talk myself into anything.

This was the situation: In the next month, on May first, I would be twenty-nine years old. The letter from an attorney said there was this trust fund for me. To get it, I had to keep a job for one year by the time I was thirty—even a job working with horses—and I had to leave with a glowing letter of recommendation. That goes to show they were still keeping tabs on me, probably through my uncle. God forbid I should know where they were or what they were doing.

We hit the straight stretch and I gave Cali her head. She eased into gallop.

My first mistake was telling my cousin, Penny, about the letter. She's more like my sister since my aunt and uncle raised me, and I lived with Pen and her husband, Frank. She'd shifted into gear, scoured the want ads of all my horse magazines, sent out my resume, and came up with a doozy of a job for me.

Penny had sat one wide hip on the edge of the bed and flipped her long, dark hair over her shoulder. "You have to do something, Vi," she said. "You haven't kept a job for more than a few months solid ever."

She didn't have to remind me. The breaks between had become longer. It was getting so I could hardly keep Cali in hay. If it weren't for the tolerance of Penny and Frank, I'd have had to sell the nag.

"Penny," I'd said. "I ride horses, fancy show horses, remember? The kind that jump really big jumps for really big money. I do not give trail rides."

"It'll be a nice break for you. All that competition is stressful."

Stressful. Yeah, right. What was stressful was the owners. All they cared about was winning, not whether their horses were happy or healthy or even ready for the next level. Penny knew all about the blowup with my last client over his horse. He says he fired me, but I walked out because I wouldn't make his horse do something that would get one or both of us hurt. And I don't mean the owner.

I tried a different tack. "Yeah, but Missouri? For cripe's sake, Pen, what do they have out there, corn fields?"

"I'm sure they do have corn fields. But St. Louis is a big city. They have baseball, museums, a good symphony …"

Crap. Penny is thorough. She'd done her homework, and she is always reasonable. I'm not. It's a bad habit. Can you really expect reasonableness from someone with a name like Viola? Jesus. It's the twenty-first century.

"Like I'll have time for the symphony when I'm taking care of twenty hack horses and who knows how many boarders and…I'm not teaching riding lessons, right? You told them I don't teach?"

She nodded, and I continued without taking a breath. "Anyway, you know I don't care about sports, and I'm not going to be anywhere near St. Louis. How could you do this to me?"

"I have not done it *to* you. I've done it *for* you."

She'd raised her voice. She was folding laundry and snapped the life out of a couple of pillowcases by way of calming herself before continuing.

"You'll be a little over an hour from St. Louis. It takes that long to get to

Manhattan, so don't make such a big deal about it. You hardly ever go into the city anyway. Now get going, before they change their minds or you run out of time."

I'd used every excuse I could think of. Penny overrode all of them. She's not usually bossy, but had reached her limit, being pregnant. They needed my room for a nursery. I wouldn't have a home to come back to when the year was up.

So, I made plans to haul myself and Noire and Cali to Winterlight, the Malcolm family's public riding stable out in God's country, for a year of keeping their horses fit for fox hunting, giving trail rides, and "helping out around the farm." That, I knew, could be anything. I hoped they didn't expect me to milk cows or slop hogs or anything like that. Working at a hack barn was low enough.

I ride jumpers, and I'm good at it. When I get in the saddle, some channel opens that is closed to most others. I used to get paid well to jump horses around grand-prix courses with jumps so high it would make your hair stand on end. It put me in a zone of some kind where nothing could touch us —if I was on a horse I knew was ready, a horse that could do it. If I was on a horse that wasn't ready, I'd get a sick feeling in my stomach and do my best to find a way out of it.

When the unthinkable happened because I didn't listen to my gut—a deadly crash at a square oxer in the middle of a difficult triple combination that left a gelding with great heart in a heap and having to be put down, when that happened, and I went to the emergency room with a fractured sternum and more bruises and contusions and sprains than I could count, and I spent several days in intensive care on a respirator, only to hobble out to face a law suit from the irate owner who demanded I push his horse beyond his limits, I quit for a while and tried giving lessons.

Made me wish they had put me down.

Maybe a year of forced trail riding would be a good break. I would do my time and get the glowing letter of recommendation.

Before I left Long Island, Penny made me promise not to "smart off," drink, or get involved with my boss. Maybe she was right, but I only smarted off because the people I worked with were such idiots. The drinking thing I have under control. And Harry, well, who could resist Harry? Apparently no one, male or female. Harry didn't discriminate that way either. I don't like to share, so it was best to move on.

I pulled into the drive of Winterlight toward late afternoon on the last Saturday of April, and stopped. The ground rose and the road topped a hill, blocking my view of the place. A light cloud of dust hovered beyond the hilltop—probably someone riding in a dry arena.

Nothing said I had to do it. Nothing said I had to collect the mysterious trust fund.

The problem was a child. That's why I stopped with the engine idling roughly, Noire eyeing me expectantly, and Cali pawing the floor of the trailer. They wanted to get out and run. I wanted to get out and run the other way.

There was a child at Winterlight. I'd managed to avoid thinking about it all the way there. The girl of eight was just learning to ride. Penny told them I don't teach, and they said that was okay, I didn't have to give her lessons. The point was, she would be around, the child and her pony. I'd have to watch her ride.

I rested my forehead against the steering wheel, but the engine jerked so bad, I feared a bruise, so I leaned back and rubbed my hands over my face. I was road-weary and really needed to stretch my legs, take a shower, go for a ride, anything.

I didn't have to baby-sit; I would find something else to do when she rode. She wouldn't be my responsibility. No, I would not let the dangerous mix of young children and riding get in my way. I would work hard, take good care of the horses, and keep my head down.

Like I said, I can talk myself into anything.

⋯⋯⋯⋯

A long board-and-batten barn stood on the left. A second story at the other end was probably the apartment where I would live. A shed stuck out over a six-horse gooseneck trailer. On the far side stretched the biggest pasture I'd ever seen. Several horses grazed in its four-board confines. Somewhere beyond the barn, over on the other side of my apartment, was the cause of the dust. I couldn't see the riding ring, but could just tell several people were trotting around in a circle, probably taking a lesson.

It wasn't too late to turn around. The New York plates might be a give-away, but maybe no one had noticed. To my right, another field rolled out of sight, this one fenced in wire, with—oh crap—cows. The drive continued another hundred yards up to an old farmhouse. The sun lowered itself behind the two-story, white home, casting shadows in my direction, but I could make out a man and a woman—Mr. and Mrs. Malcolm, I supposed —coming at me, chasing a cow. Have I mentioned I don't like cows?

Nothing personal, they don't strike me as the most intelligent animals ever created.

Mr. Malcolm waved. That was it. I was made, stuck in Missouri for a year. And right in front of me came my first chance to show how helpful I could be. I shut down the hot engine. It wheezed with relief. When I stepped out, Noire bounced off the seat behind me. She'd never seen a cow, but I figured she could handle it.

A gate hung open in the cow field fence, so I assumed that's where they wanted this big, black one. I could block the escape and shoo her in. Couldn't be much different from corralling a loose horse.

Behind me, I heard voices and the sound of steel-shod feet on concrete—the horses being led in to the barn from the ring. With a glance over my shoulder, I counted five horses in need of a bath coming up the aisle and getting clipped onto crossties. Clipped right to their bits. Crap. A disaster waiting to detonate. Grime coated their sweaty necks and filled the crevices above their eyes.

"Hey," yelled a big woman crammed into black jeans, a pink camouflage sports bra, and high-top sneakers, "the new girl's here."

The new girl? Guess that was me. I returned to the bovine situation.

Mr. Malcolm, a short, bow-legged guy swathed in denim, shook a stick at the cow to keep it moving, and Mrs. Malcolm, who was a freaking Amazon in a plaid skirt, shouted something I couldn't hear. Jesus. Am I in the Midwest, or what? Noire barked at the cow, who considered, head lowered. I shouted my dog back and stepped toward the beast. She grunted, I lobbed a clod of dried horse manure at her, and she tossed her head up, thought better of whatever was passing through her pathetic little brain, then shuffled through the opening to join her herd mates. I shut the gate.

Mission accomplished.

"Hope that's where you wanted her," I said as the Malcolms came up. On closer inspection, I saw the person I thought was Mrs. Malcolm was a *man* in a plaid skirt.

"What the hell do you think you're doing?" he yelled at me.

This was a bad start. I swallowed my sarcastic tone and said, "Helping?"

The little guy looked away quick to hide a smile. He had a face like a tattered linen shirt left too long balled up in the bottom of a drawer, but the grin ironed the wrinkles from his cheeks. The big guy's skin tightened like my old trainer's face used to when I didn't ride the way he liked. His light-brown hair picked up the last traces of sunlight in golden sparks.

"Do all Easterners think they walk on water, or do you know something about bulls we don't?"

Out of the corner of my eye I saw a small crowd gathered in front of the barn—five riders and a sixth person I assumed was their instructor. An audience. Was it too late to crawl into my truck and slither away?

The man in the skirt didn't control the sarcasm in his voice, so I really had to breathe deeply to keep from saying something I shouldn't. Did he say bull?

"Did you say bull?"

"Christ," he muttered. He slapped one hand up to his big, square jaw—he needed a shave—fingers on one cheek, thumb on the other, and drew his hand down his face in obvious frustration. He addressed his companion who so far had said nothing. "My new manager doesn't know the difference between a heifer and a bull."

I glanced from one to the other. Obviously, the big guy was Mr. Malcolm. I leaned back to get a better look at him, skirt and all. It was a kilt, actually. I knew that much. A well-worn one. Great legs. Never thought I'd find a man in a skirt attractive, but this guy would look good in a tutu—Pen's third rule came to mind: Don't get involved with the boss.

I stuck out my hand to shake. "Mr. Malcolm?"

He regarded me critically, the way I'd done him, then took my hand. I squeezed hard—my hands are strong—and before he could say anything else, I added, nice as could be, "You hired me to take care of your horses, not your cows."

The little guy snorted, and the beginnings of an appreciative smile played at the corners of Mr. Malcolm's wide mouth.

He shook my hand. "That I did. You'll be Miss Viola Parker, then. Welcome to Winterlight."

A smattering of applause greeted me when I turned around, so I bowed. Sheesh.

At that moment, one of the horses in the aisle squealed like it had been bit, I heard the smack of a hoof connecting with flesh, another squeal. The horses in the field lifted their heads. A couple whinnied, and they all trotted over to see what was up. My radar went on full alert. There was a loose horse in the barn and no one else had noticed.

What was this? A peep show? Jesus. Action, please. It happened so fast; my audience still had all eyes on me, their backs to the impending disaster.

At the other end of the aisle, a chestnut head came up, another horse shifted sideways and the one causing the havoc, a small gray, ducked under one crosstie, then another, coming our way, gaining speed. The little palomino in front flattened her ears and let go with both barrels as the gray snuck by, his reins broken and tangled around one leg, whites of his eyes glowing. The palomino's shot missed and hit a stall door with a bang. Everyone jumped.

"Get back," I yelled to the group, and I ran forward, putting myself between them and the gray. "Whoa," I said for the gray's ears alone. Noire stayed near, blocking the driveway. I dug in my pants pocket—I always have a piece of carrot or some kernels of corn or something in there, and if not, I could fake it to get close enough.

Cali whinnied and shifted in the trailer, catching the gray's attention for a moment. In the next, I had the rein and was at his shoulder. Blood seeped from a hoof-shaped cut on his forearm. "Whoa, whoa now, it's all right," I said, running my hand down his leg to pick up his foot. He answered Cali and danced sideways. I stayed with him, leaning into his shoulder and squeezing his ankle. He bent his knee, and I untangled the rein.

Mr. Malcolm stood behind me. I hadn't seen him move, but I knew he was there. He put his hand on the gray's nose. Long fingers. Dirt under the nails. No wedding ring.

"Okay, Smitty, show's over. Renee, why don't you take Smitty around the back and hose him off? We'll figure out what to do with his bridle later."

A tall black woman with short gray hair took Smitty.

"He'll need that kick hosed for a while to keep it from swelling," I said to Mr. Malcolm. "And horses should always have their bridles removed and their halters put on before they get put in crossties."

He looked at me for a long moment, not smiling, not frowning, sandy brows ever-so-slightly drawn together, questioning maybe—maybe if I knew him better I could tell. I read horses better than I read people.

"You're the boss," he said after a time.

Real soft like. Like a caress, seductive as the velvety down on a horse's muzzle.

Then he turned toward those who remained. "Norman?"

The man I took to be the instructor came forward, and Mr. Malcolm spoke quietly, but not at all the way he'd addressed me. Now, there were sharp nails in his voice.

"Why are the horses cross tied to their bits? Please make sure their bridles are removed and their halters put on first."

Norman slouched off without acknowledging the order. Oh, Malcolm had said "please," but it was an order, no doubt about it. Why hadn't I paid closer attention when Penny described his background? All I knew was that he was a mostly absentee owner, which suited me fine.

CHAPTER TWO

He switched tone again. This time it came out neutral. "The rest of you, get your horses untacked. Trail ride's canceled for tonight. You can make it up next week."

There was grumbling and shuffling, but the riders went to care for their mounts.

Malcolm and the short guy waited while I unloaded Cali. Malcolm helped with the trailer—he had an efficient no-nonsense way about him that said he knew what he was doing. When he lowered the ramp, he didn't drop it, and he waited to unhook the butt bar until I was ready.

My horse stepped over her own pile of poop and backed with measured steps, calm and collected. I knew better. She stopped to look around, and the horses in the field caught her eye. They had gone back to grazing once Smitty had been led away. Cali whinnied, swished her tail and sprang out with a sideways hop, just missing my toes. Malcolm moved back and whistled.

Yep, Cali's a looker—a dark-bay mare with four white socks and a perfectly-centered blaze. *Lots of chrome*, as horse people say. Chocolate-colored dapples melted along her flanks making her irresistible. Malcolm reached out a hand—I knew he wanted to touch her. She had that affect on everyone—horsy and non-horsy alike. But I warned them away. Her temper was barbed as razor wire. She didn't like being touched when her attention was taken by something else, like it was then, by the horses galloping across the pasture to say hello.

"Don't—" Too late. His hand grazed her ribs, and fast as a python strike, her right hind found its mark—Malcolm's leg.

Double crap.

He grabbed his knee and swore.

Shorty said, "Gotdamn! What a shot."

I led Cali forward fast, rattling her halter to keep her from nipping me. The mare didn't mean anything by it—she didn't even look at Malcolm—you just had to know how she was. Should have said something before I brought her out, I guess. She got me once. Just once. But seeing as how she was a thoroughbred I rescued off the racetrack, I explained she should be grateful she wasn't on some Frenchman's plate, and we came to an understanding. I was careful how I touched her, and she didn't let me have it without good reason.

"Where should I put her?" I called over my shoulder. I wanted to make sure Mr. Malcolm was all right, but I couldn't just let my horse go.

Shorty pointed to the first stall on the left. A caustic stench skidded out of the barn and stole tears from my eyes. This was bad. I had a lot of work in front of me.

Pink camouflage lady led the palomino forward, cooing baby talk in the mare's ear, and came straight up to us. "Wittle Fawny want to meet the big new guy—"

"Don't—" Too late *again*. The mare's noses touched and both squealed. Wittle Fawny spun her fat ass into our faces and let loose with her signature double-barreled shot. Fortunately, she missed slamming Cali's knees. Unfortunately, she caught me square in both thighs.

"Shit. Fuck. Piss," I swore through clenched teeth.

I would have kicked both her and pink camouflage over the barn, but it was all I could do to suck in air.

"Get. Away," I gritted out.

With a swirl of plaid skirt, Fawny walked off. I stood with my hands on my knees, eyes squeezed shut. The ringing in my ears prevented sounds from coming through and also, thankfully, coherent thought. I was no stranger to pain, knew the initial shock would wear off. The real pain would hit later, and the bruises, Jesus, I would be purple from crotch to knees. Good thing I didn't plan to model bathing suits on the side.

Noire whimpered and licked my hand, and Cali nudged my head. They were my truest friends, these two critters. Clearly, people were not to be trusted.

I'm not sure how long I stayed like that, but a hand came to my shoulder, a voice asked if I was all right, if I needed anything. The short guy, I think, maybe Malcolm.

I needed to get out of there, that's what I needed. Barely ten minutes on the ground and multiple disasters. What did I have to look forward to? Nowhere to go but up? Pen's mom swears you should never say it couldn't get worse because the one time she said it, it got worse. But really, could this situation be worse? I think I shook my head, straightened, wiped my face on my shoulder. The aisle had cleared and quiet descended. Apparently Malcolm had hustled everyone out because I heard a car door slam, an engine sputtering down the drive.

"Want me to take her?" Shorty asked.

Good God. Hand my horse to one of these maniacs? I shook my head again, focused on the barn, moved. Cali's steel shoes clopped on the concrete aisle before she stepped into a damp stall. I held my breath against the stink and removed her halter. The shipping boots could come off later. I knew she wanted to pee and roll at that moment. As if the place needed more pee. *Stale* and roll, as I learned to say in England. And head collar instead of halter, rug instead of blanket. I needed fresh air, and I could see why the horses were out in the field. The barn was uninhabitable.

Oh yeah, and I got to live upstairs. Great.

"Pretty," Shorty said, then added, "I'm Hank."

We shook. He nodded and pointed his bristled chin toward the door. "The Laird'll be p-oed."

The Laird? Now, the kilt made sense. I didn't hear any Scottish accent when he spoke, and I'm sure Pen would have told me if he had one. As a faithful fan of Romance novels, she would have swooned if he had one. She'd want to visit when I told her the Laird sashayed around in a kilt.

To Hank, I said, "She doesn't usually kick. You just have to know how to be around her." I was trying really hard to ignore the fact that I'd been kicked, too.

"He means you," Malcolm said as he came in.

He had a purple welt across his shin, was working hard not to limp, but didn't sound p-oed. I let out my breath, which meant I had to inhale the fetid smell of the barn. A wave of light-headedness swept over me, and I caught myself on the stall-door frame.

"Are you all right?" Malcolm asked.

"Shoot fire," Shorty said, "she's tough. Can't you see that?"

"Fine," I answered. He'd have to be a complete idiot to believe that, and he didn't strike me as an idiot of any stripe. He had the sense not to comment, just stood there with his arms crossed studying me in silence until I felt better. Weird. The feeling better part.

"I'm not happy you were hurt," he said after a bit, "or that Smitty got loose. We've made a bad impression. Come to the house. You need ice, and I don't think there's any upstairs."

Hank said he'd see me around and headed out the other end of the barn whistling, leaving me with Malcolm.

"I'm sorry," I started, but he cut me off with a wave of his hand. What a man. So typical to act tough. Of course, I was trying to act tough too, so I guess it takes one to know one. And I didn't hear him making any apologies.

"My fault," he said. "It was only a glancing blow."

Oh.

I might have to reassess this guy. I do jump to conclusions about people.

In the steadier light inside the barn, I could see his eyes were sparkling blue and full of humor. The crack about Easterners walking on water must have been a joke.

Cali's stall had a bucket full of what looked like hay and green slime soup. I dumped it outside and Malcolm refilled it from a hose. She'd peed and rolled, and now had some other horse's shit in her mane. She opted to stand with her head out the window and ignore everything else. Smart horse. She'd be all right for a bit.

The worst of the pain had eased, but I was afraid to look at my thighs. Moving would be good, keep me from getting stiff, so I followed Malcolm up the drive that separated the horse pasture from the cow field.

He sat me at a chrome-legged kitchen table and gave me two ice packs and a towel. The cold cut through my jeans, then I went numb. Numb was good.

"Care for a drink?"

He waved a bottle of scotch at me, but liquor was the last thing I needed. I'd done that kind of numb, plenty, and I didn't want to go there at the moment.

I felt like when I'm galloping toward a five-foot jump on a horse that was trying to backpedal. I hate that feeling, like I've made a major mistake. Winterlight was a huge mistake, but I'd agreed to a one-year contract. Screw the trust fund—I keep my word.

"Do you have any crackers?" I asked. The sure-fire cure for icky tummy, whether from a hangover, nerves, or morning sickness—that last from Penny, who was fast rising to the top of my I-hate-your-guts list.

He rifled a cupboard, produced a box of Saltines, opened it, dumped a sleeve out on a plate and put it in front of me.

"Iced tea?"

Pen recommends tea and crackers. I guess iced counts. "Sure," I said.

I nibbled the stale crackers and sipped the too-sweet drink, and he leaned against his tomato-colored Formica countertop. By the looks of it, the kitchen had never been updated. But it was hard to tell what era it aspired to. The floor was a sheet of peeling vinyl made to look like river stones, probably intended not to show dirt tramped in from the farm. If it were a river, it'd be polluted. Okay, so I'm anal about cleanliness. I don't give a rat's ass whether cleanliness is next to Godliness, but it makes things run better. When I can, I strong-arm others to my way of thinking, but not now. This was his kitchen, or his wife's. Her problem. God knows I had enough of my own. The cabinets were dark, distressed wood with hardware that emulated the heavy iron of an old barn. In here it just looked…heavy.

Malcolm crossed his arms and watched me stuffing my face. I hadn't eaten since breakfast, the last of the apples Pen packed. The kilt brushed the tops of his knees, and it was hard to tear my eyes away, wondering what was underneath. Much as I hate to admit it, I guess I can understand why men stare at women. His legs looked strong, like the rest of him, and he had a head's height over me, which put him around six feet. His shin had swelled and gone shiny.

"You should put ice on that," I said.

He glanced down at his leg, but didn't appear to really see the growing bruise.

"After what just happened, I wouldn't blame you if you wanted to turn around and head right back where you came from," he said.

Well, that was getting right to the point. I gulped tea to wash down the crumbs, nearly gagged on the sugar, but he continued before I could comment, which just as well. I would have agreed too readily.

"Winterlight must be a comedown from what you're used to back East."

I mustered my full repertoire of tact, and said, "It's…different."

"All right. It's a mess. I know better. I'm not here most of the time, and it's hard to find someone willing to do what needs to be done."

That sounded ominous. "Why do it at all?" We might as well get our cards on the table. Why would he try to run this kind of business if he couldn't be here? What did he get out of it?

"A question I ask myself all too often. I keep thinking work will slow down and I'll be here more. Look, I need your help. You don't have to stay the year if you don't want. Can you give me a month?"

It would take a month just to get the ammonia fumes out of the barn, but I heard myself agree even though he hadn't answered my question.

He didn't have to know I would stay the year whether I liked it or not.

CHAPTER THREE

"I'LL SHOW YOU AROUND, then leave you to get settled. I have to go out of town tomorrow, but if you're up for an early ride, I can give you a tour of the farm in the morning. We're closed to the public on Sundays."

"I'd like that," I said, not sure what he meant by early. If it wasn't a horse show, I didn't do early.

He led the way into the barn saying, "C'mon, it's time to feed," over his shoulder.

Inside, the stink hit me again. The stalls were bedded deep, but something was not being done right. There were lots of windows and plenty of fresh air. If I was going to sleep upstairs the smell had to go. I wrinkled my nose and wondered who'd been mucking out.

He looked at me. I didn't know what was going through his mind, but I probably had disapproval written all over my face. Trying to rearrange my look to suit him might have made things worse, so I just stared back.

"I know," he said. "The help I've had—you met Norman. I needed help and he needed the job. The other guy…let's just say he's not a horse person."

My right eyebrow arched. I tried to cover it, pretending to swat a fly. I wondered why his wife wasn't doing it, if she had a horse, which was what I remembered. The kid was old enough to help, too. But he kept saying "I," not "we."

There's no excuse for not keeping stalls clean. We ask a lot of our horses. Making them inhale pee vapor and sleep on poop is not how they should be rewarded. That, however, is not a universally shared notion.

He gave a little nod, like he'd read my thoughts. "Do what you must to make it right. There's plenty of straw in the loft with the hay. I've accounts at the elevator and MFA. If you need anything, get it."

I didn't know what an elevator was, and MFA could have stood for More Freaking Assholes for all I knew. "Right." There's much more I would have said, normally, and my tongue was bleeding from my effort to hold it. But I would hold it.

We measured grain. Horses banged the walls. Each stall had a Dutch door opening into the pasture and a sliding door leading to the aisle. It was a fairly new barn, built for horses. Nice. I'd been in too many converted cow barns. Maybe that's why I didn't like cows.

But he didn't bring the horses into the stalls. He scooped grain into two five-gallon pickle buckets and dumped them in a communal feeder in the field. That explained why some of the horses were fat, some not. Poor little Smitty couldn't get his nose in to eat.

Malcolm moved down the line, gently pushing Fawny aside to make room for a strawberry roan. He patted a blood-bay and murmured something in his ear.

"This is Fergus."

Fergus was a gelding past his prime, with deep indentations above his soulful eyes, but those eyes still had a game gleam in them.

"Thoroughbred?" I asked.

He nodded. "My first horse. I don't use him for fox hunting anymore, but he still likes to get out for a hack. He doesn't need as much exercise as the others." He took the horse's muzzle and kissed his nose. "How would you like to go out for a spin in the morning, eh old boy?" He rubbed Fergus' ears and the horse leaned into him.

This was a good sign. He talked to his horse. It brought a soft feeling to my belly. I'm a sucker for men who are kind to animals. I squelched the sensation by imagining him with a neon sign on his forehead that flashed, "Married."

Malcolm pointed out his new mount, Gaston, a chestnut Selle Français with a white star between his eyes. He was a tad long in the back, but had a great neck and nice, sloping shoulder.

Next, he introduced another, darker chestnut, a compact Quarter horse, Ciqala, one of two boarders.

"Ciq belongs to Dex One," he said. At my look, he explained, "Hard to believe, but I know two Dexters, both hunt, and both keep their horses here. Dex One is "

He went to the next horse. "Little Miss Bong here belongs to Humphrey

J. Dexter the third, who doesn't like being called Humphrey, so he goes by Dex too—also. To keep them straight, I call them Dex One and Dex Two."

Little Miss Bong was anything but. She was a huge, raw-boned gray who must have been part draft to have the size she did.

A liver chestnut mare flattened her ears at Smitty, and he shied away. The kick to his forearm was beginning to swell. I made a mental note to dig out my lineament for him. The chestnut was Mrs. Malcolm's, Mr. Malcolm explained. A well-balanced, medium-sized mare with no white, Barbie was fat and out of shape, didn't look like she'd just finished a season of hunting. He said nothing about her—the wife or the mare—except to mention Barbie didn't need exercise. I took that to mean his wife—I couldn't remember her name—rode enough herself.

Last in line was the child's pony, Mike. Mike was a cute black-and-white paint with a blue right eye where the white pigment spilled from his forehead.

"Nicky's with her mother, Brooke, in Chicago. I'm not sure when they'll be back," he said, his tone flat. "Probably this weekend."

Brooke, Brooke. I repeated the name to commit it to memory. And Nicky. Doesn't know when they'll be back? I went to give Cali her grain so he wouldn't see that eyebrow of mine quirk up again. I can't control it. Who needs to speak when you've got a big question mark on your face?

The rest were the hack horses, like Smitty and Fawn. Norman would fill me in on Monday. I could hardly wait to spend a day with Norman, a man who exuded enthusiasm like frozen tar.

Malcolm led the way to the tack room. It measured about twenty by twenty with English and Western saddles resting on racks on the left, bridles opposite, and a sink against the far wall. In the middle of the floor lay a dirty oriental rug surrounded by a tattered love seat, battered coffee table, and a one-armed, upholstered chair that looked like a cat had been using it for a bed. There was also a half-bath over by the sink. With some elbow grease, I could have lived in it.

An old door probably taken from a porch somewhere led upstairs where there was a square living room with two floor-to-ceiling windows overlooking the pasture. Beyond was a bedroom with a tiny window for viewing the stall below in case of a sick horse. A galley kitchen had a drop-leaf table and two chairs at one end. The bathroom completed my digs. It all needed elbow grease too, but the smell wasn't as bad as I'd feared. It was more than I'd ever had to myself.

"I've stocked the fridge to get you started, and here are the phone numbers you'll need." He indicated a pad of paper on the counter with the farmhouse, his cell phone and pager, Hank's number and Norman's, black-smith, vet. Funny, the search and rescue squad I needed weren't listed.

"You won't be able to get hold of me most of tomorrow, but you can leave a message on my voice mail. Only page me if it's an emergency."

I nodded. Noire cozied up to Malcolm, sticking her nose under his kilt. Without looking down, he rubbed her ears. "Haven't had time for a dog. It'll be nice to have one around." He glanced at her and smiled a genuine unguarded smile, then looked at me. "Can I help you bring your stuff in?" He started down the stairs.

"Thanks. I can manage. What time in the morning?"

"Six okay?"

I followed so I could get my suitcase and park the truck and trailer. "Fine." Horse shows require brutal hours and lots of exhaustion; this would be easy.

In the barn, a glossy, fat, black cat wobbled down the aisle and curled around Malcolm's ankle. He picked the cat up and cradled it to his chest, making it purr.

"Old Henry here wandered in a few weeks ago, looking pretty scrawny." He squatted to put the cat down and I averted my eyes in case that kilt rode too far up his thighs. "His food's in the feed room too."

"If you ask me, Henry looks like he needs a diet."

"You're probably right. But he still manages to catch the mice." He gave Henry a final pat. "See you bright and early."

I waited for him to leave, hefted Henry, felt his belly and checked under his tail. I hoped Malcolm liked cats, because the kittens would be along any day.

By 5:45 a.m., I had the horses fed, Cali's stall picked, aisle swept, and Cali and Fergus groomed and tacked up. The stalls were going to take some work. Fresh straw had been piled over layers of wet and manure—a regular shit lasagna. I wiped down Malcolm's saddle and bridle, but it needed serious scraping to remove the ground-in sweat. I did plan to keep the job for a year.

I hadn't had much time for reflection the night before, or even to call Pen. I crashed the second I hit the lumpy mattress, Noire sprawled next to me and Henry—Henrietta—snug behind my knees, and slept like I always do—deeply, soundly, dreamlessly. But I thought this wouldn't be hard. Malcolm gave me free rein and wouldn't be around. Even if he were, he appeared a decent guy to work for.

He walked in, duded up in boots and breeches and a polo shirt; short sleeves straining around hard biceps. I shouldn't say duded up. After all, I wore the same. But men always look duded up when they don boots and breeches. Not all men look quite as good in them as Malcolm did, though. He kept himself in shape—the close knit of riding pants is not forgiving of bodily imperfection. I couldn't find anything to complain about in the outline of his thighs and...the rest.

I was just being objective. If you have to look at someone in what amounts to heavyweight tights, male or female, that person should look good in them.

At five-foot-seven, 130 pounds, and "all leg," as my uncle says, I could model for the tack catalogs. This is not vanity, just fact. The other facts of my appearance are another matter. On a good day, my hair lays in tame, loose waves. Not quite as smooth as my mother's sleek locks, but manageable. On damp or humid days—and most days on Long Island are one or the other—I sprout my dad's wiry mess, which defies all efforts to contain it. No amount of mousse or clips keeps it from sproinging loose.

I did get mom's svelte dancer's body, however, her natural grace and balance—which really pays off in the saddle—and her "elegant" nose—read: long. My dark-brown eyes are too close together, and pretty boring except for their lashes. No need for mascara there. I got the not-quite-red, not-quite-brown color of Dad's hair. Fortunately, my skin has my mother's olive Italian coloring. My father's skin is so white he reflects the sun. When you spend as much time outside as I do, it helps not to have to worry about frying to a crisp. I use sunscreen anyway. I've seen too many seasoned horsewomen who looked like they should use saddle soap on their faces.

Malcolm frowned at Fergus, then directed a hard look at me. His tone, when he spoke, was not nice at all.

"Don't you think I can get my own horse ready?"

I stared at him for a sec, finished buckling Cali's throatlatch, and said, "Of course. Thought you'd be in a hurry."

He jerked the stall door open, grabbed the reins and led Fergus out without a backward glance.

Prick.

I followed, Cali in tow. Malcolm's shirt stretched tight across his shoulders, and I could see they were bunched, tense. What the hell did I do? You could bet I'd never tack up his freaking horse again, that's for sure. Jesus. So much for him being a great guy to work for. And so much for the pleasant morning ride I'd been looking forward to.

Outside, it was cool yet, and still. Malcolm had already mounted. He'd double-checked his girth first and adjusted Fergus' forelock over the brow band. That's good. Always inspect everything when someone else tacks up your horse. He didn't look at me, just waited. I took my time because I'd just realized how gorgeous the moment was. Sunlight streaked through the trees. One bird sang, and that was all I could hear. Between trills, I listened for other sounds, but there were none. No drone of traffic, dogs barking in the distance, hum of high-tension wires, airplanes, voices, radio, television, nothing. It was so quiet I could hear the cows tearing grass forty feet away.

Puffs of mist clinging to the low areas of the fields began to rise and congeal. Thin, high clouds turned pink. I'd seen a lot of sunrises, but none quite as serene and perfect as this. I wanted to be pissed at Malcolm, but I couldn't. Noire jumped up and down and whimpered, eager to be smelling new smells, and Cali champed her bit. The girls were ready for a ride, and I wouldn't let one grumpy guy ruin it for us.

I mounted, bending and unbending carefully so as not to stress my thighs, which were screaming, but only when I moved. The damage wasn't pretty. I could count all eight nails of Fawny-Wawny's shoes in black-and-blue relief on my skin.

I urged Cali next to Fergus. The old thoroughbred flattened his ears. Cali nipped his neck, just missing Malcolm's rein. Fergus jumped, curled his lip, and bellowed.

"Hey." Malcolm smacked Fergus on the neck. "Mind your manners, old man."

We set off up the drive. Cali bared her teeth if Fergus swayed too close. The bird flitted from its perch on the fence to a telephone wire overhead.

"What kind of bird is that?"

"Meadowlark."

I waited a beat. He didn't offer more. So much for that conversation opener.

We followed the drive to the right, then took a cut through the tree line.

On the other side of the trees dense new growth grew verdant in a flat field. We turned left and stayed at the edge.

"This is my main hay field," Malcolm said. "Timothy and brome. Some red clover and orchard grass."

"You bale your own hay?" I really should have paid closer attention to Pen. But I hadn't wanted to know.

"You understand this is a working farm?"

Oh man, he wanted to punish me. I gritted my teeth and nodded. "I saw the herd of cows. You milk them?"

He didn't have to turn for me to know he'd set his jaw.

"Those are beef cattle and they're Hank's. He rents the pasture."

I cast a glance heavenward and there I saw two very large, dark birds circling, gliding on an unseen updraft.

"What are those?" I pointed.

"Vultures."

Oh, my, God. "Vultures." Not twenty-four hours into my year and I already had vultures circling overhead. Not a good sign. "You have vultures?"

"Yes. Turkey vultures, to be precise."

I could see I was in a losing situation conversation-wise, so tried a different tack. We had clear sailing for a couple hundred yards. "Shall we see if the horses want to stretch their legs?"

"All right," he said, his tone going from sarcastic to challenging.

With a sigh, I realized I couldn't do anything right this morning. He gathered Fergus' reins, and the horse leapt with a buck into canter. Cali tossed her head and went after him. If he wanted to race, we would win. Cali was quick, and much younger than Fergus. But I wouldn't take the bait. Not this time, anyway. I held Cali back and let Malcolm take the lead.

We galloped toward a tree line and a shallow creek. Malcolm didn't slow, and Fergus sailed over the narrow band of water, bucking again on landing. Out of the woods along another field planted in neat rows. Cali skipped over the creek and pulled to catch up.

Malcolm kept his weight in his heels, his seat out of the saddle, and didn't hang on the horse's mouth. He checked on me and appeared pleased I was nearly on his tail. We curved around a spit of trees and kept skirting the field, then jumped a low gate and dove into deeper woods. After that, we slowed, then stopped. Sunlight lit a small cloud of dust kicked up by the horses. Malcolm gave Fergus a big pat on the neck, and turned to me, a broad grin on his face.

I smiled and nodded. He didn't have to say anything. There's nothing like a game riding partner—human or equine.

I rubbed Cali's withers. We walked along a trail wide enough for two to ride abreast while the horses caught their breath. "Good," I said. The pleasant aroma of sweat mixed with something sweet carried on the air.

"Yes," he replied. "It is good to have someone to ride with."

Again, I wondered about Brooke. I almost asked, but decided against it. He ran too hot and cold to judge.

"Have you hunted her?" he asked.

For a second, my mind still on Brooke, my brain supplied a juicy mental image. Then I realized he meant Cali. "No, but we've done cross-country work. She's tough despite her delicate appearance."

He nodded. "Thoroughbreds are like that. Surprising."

"That's an understatement."

Malcolm patted Fergus on the neck again. "This one's full of surprises, anyway. Keeps me on my toes. I like that."

Now, there was a valuable piece of information.

"How old is he?"

"Twenty-one. I've had him fifteen years."

"I can see in his eyes that he's a wise old fellow, although twenty isn't so old, really. I've known plenty of horses that were still competing at that age. He likes you, that's for sure." Like I said, I'm better at reading horses than people, and I could always tell when one appreciated his owner.

"He's been good to me."

Fergus snorted, and we both laughed. "Looks like you've been good to him, too."

We stayed under the trees. The creek widened and its shallow depth revealed an inviting sandy bottom. On the other side, a narrow trail held to the curving bank. Malcolm pulled up, inhaled deeply.

"This is my favorite spot on the farm."

Holy mackerel, I thought. We're sharing intimate info on our first ride. I nodded. Tiny purple and blue wildflowers saturated the ground. The creek snuck down a short drop and tinkled over some rocks. Above, light-skinned trees fingered the brightening sky. This was one of those spots that would change but be splendid with each season. I would return.

"It is beautiful," I said. "Peaceful. If there were a spot like this back where I come from, it would either be fenced off to preserve it, or so crowded with others trying to appreciate it, it'd be gone overnight." I took a deep breath. No exhaust fumes or food smells polluted the pure scent of nature. That was different. "You're lucky to have this all to yourself."

"I know it." He looked around at the trees and the creek and the flowers. "And I intend to keep it that way."

Okay, then. The man didn't like to share.

"This is the main trail the riders use," he said as we walked on. "There's another for more experienced riders. It even has a few jumps on it."

"How do you know who's experienced enough?"

"You determine that when you give them their lessons."

I didn't mean to jerk the reins. Cali stopped with an annoyed huff, and I stared at Malcolm, probably looking stupid with my mouth hanging open. The birds still sang, and I could hear Noire splashing in the water, and feel Cali's steady breathing between my legs, but my own had stopped. He didn't just say I would be giving riding lessons, did he? No, no, no. I misunderstood, surely. Pen had said I didn't have to teach riding, right? I couldn't, and that was that. Yes, that was that, and I would not think of it again until I could talk to Penny. Which I would be doing the moment we got back to the barn.

We rode on, and he showed me another hay field, corn, winter wheat, and one patch that would be in soybeans. I scarcely noticed. My hands had grown cold, my neck prickly, my innards soft.

"Hank takes care of the crops and the livestock for the most part," he said. "Everyone pitches in when we do hay."

So, that's what "helping out around the farm" meant. I'd stacked plenty of hay. "Sounds like fun," I mumbled.

In my mind, I kissed the trust fund good-bye. I could not do the job expected, and even if I could, I was sure to die of boredom before the year's end.

CHAPTER FOUR

"I'M IN HELL, Penny, and you sent me here."

I called her the moment I put down my sweaty tack and saw Malcolm leave. It was almost nine o'clock on the east coast. On a Sunday morning at Pen's house that meant fluffing her hair and yelling at Frank to get out of bed so they could go to church. I could hear him grumbling in the background and the toilet flushing and her rifling the bathroom drawers to find the right shade of lipstick.

"Don't even say that. It's Sunday morning."

"Oh for cripe's sake, hell is hell no matter what day of the week it is." I flopped on the bed and cradled the phone with my shoulder. Noire stuck her nose under my hand where it hung over the edge of the mattress, and I rubbed her ears. Wish I had someone to give me a rub.

"You haven't even been there twenty-four hours. Give it more time."

"The place reeks, the horses are mangey—"

"There's always—"

"And vultures. *Vultures* for cripe's sake."

"—whipped cream."

"Did you hear what I said? *Vultures.*"

"Get some whipped cream. Sounds like you'll need it."

"It doesn't fix everything, you know."

"But it does make you feel better, right?"

She was right, but I refused to be put off my tirade. "My boss is a prick—"

"He sounded so nice on the phone. Are you sure?"

"Don't try to distract me. And by the way, you said I would not be teaching riding. Clearly that is expected. Explain."

She hesitated, taking a deep breath as I had, probably using the moment to swipe on her favorite lip-gloss.

"Well?" I prompted.

"Well, so what? You aren't going to be teaching them to ride, just testing their ability before they go on the trail, that's all. That's not teaching. Not the way you teach, anyway, all serious and everything like everyone has to compete at Madison Square Garden or something."

"What's wrong with serious? They should take it serious. Seriously. Riding is serious."

"Does it have to be? All the time? Can't you just ride…what do you call it? On the belt?"

I almost laughed. Penny could do that, and she knew it. But I wasn't taking her off my I-hate-your-guts list yet.

"On the buckle," I said.

"Yeah, on the buckle, that's it. Isn't that when you relax and give your horse his head? Can't you just loosen the reins and relax a little? A little. I'm not saying a lot."

I hate it when she uses horsy metaphors to make a point. Usually she gets it wrong. But this time she was dead on. I couldn't argue that I was wound tight. What she might call heavy-handed, if she knew how to extend the metaphor. The kind of hands that make a horse toss his head, shorten his back, fight the bit. That's how I handle myself.

I let out a ragged breath. "I don't know. This place is a mess."

"Then it won't be hard for you to improve the situation. Look, I gotta go, Frank's in the car. I'll light a candle for you. Call you tomorrow."

Downstairs, I stood at one end of the concrete aisle with my knuckles firmly planted on my hips. The more I looked around, the worse it got. Cobwebs everywhere, dust, the stink, flies. I climbed a built-in ladder to the loft. Must and more dust. Right outside the barn, where the horses congregated, there was a leaky bathtub serving as a water trough. Fawn sloshed her nose in it, playing, making a puddle that the others mashed manure and pee into, turning the entire area into muck pie.

Not only did everything need cleaning, *everything*, but I had to get to know the horses, too. And figure out how to feed them individually rather than family style. He wouldn't blame me if I wanted to leave, huh? We'd see about that.

In the tack room, I'd found a schedule. There was a ride in the morning.

A list of six horse's names had been jotted down with "Norman" written alongside. In the meantime, I had the rest of the day to get done what I could, and maybe do a bit of shopping. Whipped cream, the kind in a can that you squirt straight into your mouth, was at the very top of my shopping list. Only Pen knew I was addicted to the stuff.

The wheelbarrow leaned against a wall with a few other utensils. I retrieved what I needed and got to work.

Hank dropped by around three. He whistled when he came in, stopped outside the stall where I was. "Shit fire," he said.

"No kidding." I didn't know what he meant, but agreed.

A wheelbarrow full of saturated dark-brown straw stood in the stall door. The fumes stung my eyes, I'd been sweating for hours. No telling what my hair looked like where it stuck out from under my baseball cap. I'd made it through half the stalls, found a bag of lime and sprinkled some over the dirt floors to help absorb the smell and also thrown several bales of fresh straw down from the loft in preparation to re-bed. The manure pile had doubled in size, and it was already too big to begin with.

"Looks like alotta work for a Sunday," Hank said. "You make them boys look like they's in reverse." He looked around and whistled again. "How's it goin'?" he asked.

I wiped my arm across my face. "It's fine."

"Need anything?"

I had a list, but didn't think he really wanted to hear it. "Where's the nearest store with pitchforks and stuff?"

To add insult to injury, I hadn't been able to locate a straw fork. No wonder the place was such a mess. Didn't matter today, the stalls needed to be stripped, no finesse involved. A big shovel did the job.

"MFA'd be best. Other side of town. Run you up myself in the morning. Need a couple things too."

"That'd be great, thanks."

"Missus'll have supper ready in about a hour. We're the next place down."

He jerked his thumb past his ear to indicate the direction and was gone before I could protest.

The next morning my back ached when I went down to feed. I brought twelve horses in and rounded up halters and lead lines and tied the remaining six to spots along the fence and gave each one a bucket of feed.

I watched them for a while, then went in to sort through the tack. There were five English saddles and five Western. None were labeled, but Smitty and Fawn were both on the list for the morning's ride, so I started with them and waited for Norman.

He motored in on a four-wheeler at eight-thirty. Talk about duded up. Fake alligator shit kickers with chrome toe guards and skin-tight Levi's hugging a barely-there ass. The pearly snaps of his plaid shirt were left open too far down revealing a totally naked and pale chest, and the straw ten-gallon boater on his head could rescue a family of five. His beady eyes darted around the barn.

"You've been busy," he said.

"Yeah. So, who are Cheyenne, Honey, Oreo, Brownie, and Kismet?" I rattled off the names on the list. "I have Smitty and Fawn groomed, but wasn't sure whether they go English or Western."

He hesitated. "Uh."

Which didn't tell me much. He retrieved the list, moving fast. Maybe Norman had some get-up-and-go after all. Shortly, we had them all ready, although Norman's grooming skills left much to be desired. He went through the motions, but barely removed the sweat marks still left on some horse's backs from Saturday, and although he picked up each hoof, I think all he did was clink the hoof pick against their shoes. When he went to get saddles and bridles, I redid his job.

The tack was serviceable and plain and in need of saddle soap and neats-foot oil. The polyester sheepskin pads were glazed with dried dirty sweat.

"Is there a washing machine around here?" I asked Norman.

"Yeah, sure." He led me to the back of the feed room where he pushed a plaid horse blanket on the floor. I opened the washing machine and closed it just as quick. There was something in there, something that had been there for a while and had mildewed beyond recognition. I thought I caught the flicker of a smile skitter across Norman's narrow face

"Gross," I said. "What's in there?"

He shrugged. "Leg wraps, maybe. Don't remember."

"You don't remember."

His shoulders hitched again and he gave me a "tell it to somebody who gives a shit" face, and turned on his heel. "Gotta make the coffee. Always have coffee when they get here."

I followed him into the tack room where he pulled a Mr. Coffee machine from the cabinet under the sink, then filters and a small can of coffee.

"What, exactly, is your job?" I asked him.

"Head wrangler. This is my last week. I'm moving on, you know, bigger and better things."

Whatever. *Wrangler?* Where did he think we were, Wyoming? "Are there assistant wranglers?"

"A couple kids come after school to help out sometimes."

Oh, boy.

I turned to the washer, twisted the knob to hot, stood back, opened it, dumped in bleach, and dropped the lid.

The riders arrived, one by one. If the half-clean barn, or the lack of cobwebs, or the swept aisle surprised any, not one made a comment. They all rode regularly on Monday so there was no need to assess their ability. We went straight to the trails. Norman led on Captain, a bay gelding, and I followed on Cali. It didn't take much to see they were all beginners, and the ride consisted mostly of walking and butt-numbing trot. A heavy-set woman atop Honey almost slipped off around a turn. Her legs stuck straight out, but she had a death grip on the horn and righted herself before hitting the dirt.

Norman wanted to be John Wayne, but he was shorter and skinnier than me. Cowboy boots and hat didn't get him close to The Duke. He'd waited for everyone else to mount, then swung to Captain's back from the ground.

He'd kneed the horse in the belly and over tightened the girth first to make this stunt practical, since he put all his weight on the saddle horn to hoist himself up. He rode like an idiot—all toes and elbows—and bounced and jerked the reins.

Captain suffered the act with patience, one of many saintly horses I've known. I didn't say anything to Norman right then, and maybe I wouldn't. After all, he'd be gone soon. On the other hand, his show-off style bordered on abuse, and if he were going to be working with horses, I could do them all a favor if I taught him a couple of things in the next week.

When we returned to the barn, Hank was waiting to take me to the MFA. As soon as the horses were settled, we set off in his faded blue pickup. Norman muttered something about things to do, mounted his four-wheeler, and took off in the other direction, up the gravel road past Hank's.

At dinner the night before, Hank had promised to bring his tractor and manure spreader over and start working on the manure pile. But when he dropped me back at the barn after we finished shopping, he had to go till Clara's garden.

I'd stuffed myself the night before with Clara's fried chicken—one that had been alive and pecking that morning. There'd been green beans from last year's garden, scalloped potatoes, salad from this year's garden, iced tea, and some kind of pie so gooey sweet it set my teeth on edge. I ate a piece to be polite. There was no coffee to wash it down, but I managed with the tea. I usually skip dessert, but she insisted.

"What do you mean, you don't want pie?"

The look on her face had been pure astonishment, like I'd landed from another planet. Disappointment and determination twisted her mouth, and there'd been a knife in her hand. She held it loosely, almost carelessly, but I didn't doubt she knew how to use it, or would hesitate, if the need arose. I don't think anyone messes with Clara, especially when it comes to pie.

Hank went to till the garden, his truck leaving behind a billow of dust, and I went upstairs to call Pen. On the way, I mused that the morning had been a resounding success. I hadn't been bitten, stomped on or kicked, and no one had called me "the new girl." Today, I would finish cleaning the stalls.

Pen picked up on the third ring, and I could tell she'd been running.

"Where'd I get you from, the basement?"

"Just the other room."

"Really? Are you okay?"

"It's being pregnant. I'm out of breath all the time."

All the time? She was only five months along, barely showing when I left, but she was a little chubby to begin with. Still, an alarm went off in my head.

"What does your doctor say?"

"I see him tomorrow. Don't worry about me. How's everything there, better?"

I'd drop it for now, check again later. "Today I learned MFA stands for Missouri Farmer's Association," I told her. "And an elevator is where they take the corn and wheat and soybeans after the harvest, and store it in big, round, metal buildings to dry before it gets shipped to Russia, or wherever."

"We use some of that stuff in this country," she said.

I knew that. Don't I eat only whole-grain bread? And tofu? In fact, I'd thrown away what the well-intentioned Mr. Malcolm left in the fridge. White bread. Jesus. Okay, I don't believe in wasting food. I gave it to the birds.

"Both the MFA and the elevator sell feed and supplies and stuff. I bought a straw fork. No wonder the stalls were such a mess. He didn't even have the right equipment." Another part of my brain suggested that his equipment was perfect.

"Well, that's what you're there for. So, it's okay?"

Okay? Hell no it wasn't okay. "The neighbor's a great cook."

"That's not what I mean, and you know it. Do you think you could feel at home there?"

Penny had a theory about "home" which was definitely tied to "where the heart is." In my case, she said the root of all my problems was homesickness —not because I missed it, but because I'd never found my true home. I'm not big on theories.

"I guess it will be all right, except for Mr. Malcolm acting like a dick-head yesterday." Not like I had a choice. Winterlight would be my address for a year, if not my home. "I'm getting the stalls clean, so things smell better.

Hank says he'll teach me to drive the tractor, and I can empty the manure spreader in one of the fields. I'll be a goddamned farmer."

"Sounds great. So, what does he look like?"

That's Penny. Warn me off the guy one minute, then breathlessly insist on his vitals the next. She'd talked to Malcolm on the phone and no doubt formed a vivid opinion of him already.

"Didn't you tell me to stay away from him?"

"You should. That doesn't mean I can't fantasize about him. Now, give it up."

Penny is smart and funny and artistic—though she doesn't do anything with her talent. She fell in love with a plumber. Not that there's anything wrong with plumbers. Frank's nice, a little short, going bald, growing a beer belly, and has no interests beyond football and pork rinds. He supports her, but not in any way that matters.

Anyway, Frank's not exactly the hunk on the cover of the books she reads. She lives vicariously through the guys I know, some of whom could model for book covers. You couldn't necessarily have a conversation with them, and some of them are gay, but I have known some very handsome men.

"He's tall—over six foot, I'm sure."

"Yeah. Go on."

"He's got longish light-brown hair with streaks of gold in it like a life guard." I figured I might as well lay it on thick for her, not that I was exaggerating. "Blue eyes—with humor in them." *When he's not being a prick.* "You've heard his deep voice."

"Yeah, yeah. Go on."

I ticked off the rest. "Broad shoulders, flat stomach, strong jaw, high cheekbones, sexy when he hasn't shaved in a couple of days. Looks great in breeches."

Penny moaned. "Oh my God, Vi, how can you stand it?"

"I'll manage. Pretty is as pretty does, you know. Anyway, he's married." But his wife wasn't around, and I wondered what that meant. Somehow, I thought there was more to it than just visiting family. "Married's off-limits, even for me."

"I know. Anything else?"

"Well," I said, drawing it out. "There is one thing."

"Yeah?" Anticipation laced her voice.

I delivered the kicker. "He wears a kilt."

She dropped the phone.

CHAPTER FIVE

LATER THAT DAY, another Midwestern-farm-grown example of male pulchritude strolled in, and the first thing I thought was, wait till I tell Pen.

He rolled up in a Ford pickup of indeterminate color—might have been green at one time, but it was mostly rust with dashes of primer. The right headlight hung down like a gouged-out eye, and the tailgate had gone missing. Half an antenna stuck up from the hood, duct tape criss-crossed the back window, and the roof looked like an elephant had danced on it. Baling wire held the driver's-side door closed.

The guy who stepped out, after scooting across the bench seat to exit the passenger side, was tall and lanky with straight, dark hair and a smooth, well-trimmed beard. He was in much better shape than his truck.

I squeezed water from the sponge in my hand and rubbed at a persistent spot of sweat on Captain's bridle. My visitor wore a green cap that said, "Nothing runs like a Deere," a plain, white T-shirt with an oil stain on one side and a tear on the other, and unlaced work boots crusted with mud. His jeans were so worn down the fronts of his thighs, they were white, and the knees were blown out. The faded blue fabric looked especially thin over the bulge at the base of his fly.

When he entered the barn, Noire lowered her tail and growled deep in her throat. I trust her instincts. If my dog thinks someone's not quite right, then someone's not quite right. She's better at that than I, but sometimes I ignore her.

He acknowledged me with a sweeping gaze that landed on Noire. "Mac around?"

"Out of town. Can I help you?"

His eyebrows pushed his cap up, then he leaned one elbow on a rung of the ladder leading up to the loft and shook a cigarette out, started to light it.

"There's no smoking in the barn."

"Since when?"

I didn't know him, and he looked great, so I decided not to bite. Noire planted herself between us, clearly less certain this was the right course of action. I smoothed her ears. She kept her eyes on the stranger. "Smoking is never allowed in horse barns," I explained. "It's dangerous."

"Really," he said. He glanced at the cigarette, up toward the loft, then shrugged and shoved the cig back in the pack. "Never thought about it, but I see your point."

He dug a toothpick out of his pants pocket and stuck that in his mouth instead, rolling it with his tongue. Reminded me of a guy I saw careening down the Long Island Expressway once in a Cadillac Eldorado with a toothpick and a cigarette hanging out of his mouth at the same time.

"I'm JJ. You must be my replacement."

I'd replaced two men. That appealed to me. Okay, maybe one and a half, since Norman was the other. JJ must be the non-horse person Malcolm referred to.

"JJ, nice to meet you." I stuck out my hand. "I'm Vi."

He hesitated, wiped his palm on his jeans, then crossed the aisle. Well-defined biceps bulged when he squeezed my hand, and a tingle went right to my belly.

Noire made a quick sideways movement to get out of his way. The sudden motion surprised JJ, and he jumped, jerking my arm.

"Brought your guard dog, huh?"

It was my turn to shrug. I'm not sure what she would do if pressed, but I wasn't above using her image to my advantage. "I wouldn't mess with her."

He stepped back with a smile that amped my tingle to a warm hum.

"Cool," he said with a nod, and added, "Vi." He glanced around the barn, sliding the toothpick from one corner of his mouth to the other. "You've done a lot of work since you got here. Place looks good. Mac'll be pleased."

"It's getting there," I said, trying to fight a feeling of gratification. Anything would have been an improvement. "Still plenty to do."

JJ's eyes moved from my face down to my toes and back. "I've some time this afternoon, especially since Mac's not here. Need any help?"

Interesting question. If he hadn't done his job before, why the sudden interest? The answer didn't really matter since I'd be glad to let him do some heavy lifting—cleaning the stalls he'd let become such a mess in the first place. I wouldn't mind watching those biceps in action for a little while.

"Sure," I said. "I'd appreciate that." I put the shovel in the wheelbarrow and pushed it where it needed to be, pointed to the mass of wet straw and manure. "Everything out. Down to the floor."

His cap moved up again. Whatever he'd had in mind, this wasn't it. Then, a wry smile creased one cheek, and the warm hum in my belly expanded into my chest.

"No problemo," he said. He grabbed the shovel and went to work.

Twenty minutes and three trips to the ever-growing manure pile later, he had the one stall done. Sweat darkened his T-shirt and glossed his skin. The indentation at the base of his throat had a tiny pool of moisture collected in it. The bicep action had been good. Not that I stood there staring. I found things to do that kept me walking past while he worked. Each time, he smiled that wry half-smile at me, and my internal motor revved.

JJ removed his cap and smoothed his short hair. "How's that?" he asked.

I made a show of inspecting the stall. "Nice work," I said, but I wasn't looking at the stall. "Thanks."

He tilted the wheelbarrow against the wall, hung up the shovel, and grabbed the broom. The aisle had been perfectly clean when he arrived. He swept his leavings out the back door, replaced the broom on its hook. Not bad. Maybe Malcolm hadn't given him any instructions about how to keep the stalls clean.

"That's all I got time for, today."

"I appreciate it."

"You had a chance to get out?"

"Hank took me to the MFA."

JJ laughed. "Not what I meant."

I knew what he meant.

"How 'bout dinner?"

I hadn't had a chance to grocery shop yet. Tomorrow was open. I would be schooling horses in the morning, and at some point I needed to finish digging out the stalls. I could shop later. For tonight, dinner out sounded good. Dinner with a good-looking…hang on a sec.

"Are you married?"

He looked startled, like I was proposing rather than gathering information. Then, the grin came on full blast. I suspected there were dimples hiding under his silky beard.

"No, ma'am," he drawled.

JJ gave me directions to Mel's tavern. We agreed to meet there later. JJ was definitely attractive, but I wasn't ready for anything remotely resembling a date. Even if I was, taking my own truck made me feel safer, in control. Anyway, I could handle whatever JJ might dish out. Back home, I'd met some mighty squirrelly guys. He had nothing on them.

I strolled into the bar at seven. There were pool tables toward the back past a wheezy-looking jukebox and open space in the middle could have been a dance floor once, but was now occupied by a few square tables. A hand-written sign advertised karaoke on Thursday nights. Two women sitting at a table scanned me from the neck of my red T-shirt down to my sandals and returned to their pizza. They wore dirty jeans and boots and looked like they'd just come from milking the cows. To them, I must've looked as out of place and useful as a fart in a mitten.

The skirt I'd chosen covered the bruises on my thighs, barely. If I were careful when I sat, no one would notice. I'd tested this before leaving. Should have worn pants, I know, but the skirt was cuter.

JJ was throwing darts at a board beyond the pool tables. When he saw me he waved, threw one more dart and sauntered toward me as I took a seat at the bar. He wore clean work boots and walked with long strides, confident. The sleeves of his faded blue T-shirt grazed those lovely muscular arms of his. He smelled like cologne and filled out his jeans nicely and pulled a bar stool out for me before taking his own. So far, so good.

"What can I get you?" the bartender asked.

He'd been leaning back against the cash register when I came in, sort of in shadow. In more direct light, he looked like he served as the bouncer as well. Burly. No—more like meaty. He had a pleasant round face and curly brown hair, fingers thick as a pitchfork handle and a belly that obscured his belt, but something about the way he held himself warned anyone paying attention not to underestimate him.

I caught JJ getting an eyeful of my legs when I crossed them. Okay, so that's why I wore the skirt. "Water," I said. He ordered a Budweiser.

"Kevie makes the best pizza in town," JJ said.

No place has better pizza than New York, but given that Kevie probably made the *only* pizza in town, I figured this wasn't really an overstatement. I decided to find out just how bad it was and ordered one with everything. We took a table.

"So," I said, "have you worked for Mr. Malcolm long?"

He paused in knocking back his beer and surveyed me over the top of the bottle. Something shifted behind his eyes, like he was trying to decide between many possible answers.

"Just forever."

Hunh. Dutifully, I responded, "Forever? That's a long time."

Another shift, this one more obvious. Bad blood between JJ and Mr. Malcolm?

"Seems that way."

Mucking stalls for even thirty minutes can seem like forever, especially if you have no interest in horses. Ever since I was a little girl, I would have done anything to be around them. Dirty stalls went with the territory and got me the contact I craved. But JJ hadn't really been cleaning the stalls, even if he thought he had, and even if that's what he'd been paid for.

"He needs all the help he can get," JJ added. "What with him being gone most the time and since his Dad moved back to the city. I do what I can."

Something else passed behind his eyes, and this time the inner thought made him smile. I reminded myself I was new to the area and these people had known each other *forever.*

"Were you born here?" I asked.

JJ glanced around the bar. "Not exactly right here."

I forced out a laugh. "That's a relief." Smart-ass.

He leaned his elbows on the table, let the bottle dangle from his fingertips, and hiked up one corner of his mouth. Damn, he had a great smile. And this close, I could see he did have dimples.

"Just messin' with you. I know what you mean. Yeah, born and bred. All my life. Just like my pop, and my grand pop."

"So, you have a lot of family around?"

I'm always curious about other people's families and their relationships since mine are so…odd. My parents left me to pursue their dream of international stardom in the world of competitive ballroom dancing. Guess I looked like excess baggage, and my aunt and uncle were willing to take me in.

Aunt Trudy is my mother's sister. Their parents, who were from Italy, died before I was born. Uncle Victor is as steady as they come—so long as he doesn't drink the wine he makes. He's the only child of Lithuanians who had him late in life then died young. My mother's parents raised him, so for all intents and purposes, he's as Italian as my aunt. Being raised by someone other than his parents is probably why he didn't bat an eye when my mother dumped her child on him just weeks before his own, Penny, was born.

My father grew up in an orphanage and met my mother at his first job— cleaning toilets for a dance instructor. Mom was a promising young student in need of a partner. Sounds romantic till you get to the part about me. They weren't married yet when I was born, so I'm a bastard. Most people assume I'm Vic and Trudy's kid, and I let them.

Kevie brought the pizza. It was much flatter than I expected and cut into little squares instead of big triangles. Weird. How was I supposed to eat the pieces on the inside with no crust to hold?

"Sure you don't want a beer with that?" JJ asked.

"No thanks. So, about your family?"

He tipped his chair until it leaned against the table behind us, cradled a fresh beer against his chest. It looked good. The beer. Okay, his chest, too. And there was that shift behind his eyes again. This time, accompanied by a glance over his shoulder. Maybe he was consulting with an angel. I have a way of stumbling onto the touchy subjects and not knowing when to drop them. And sometimes people resort to prayer when they're talking to me. As in, "Jesus, would you get off my back?"

"My mom's around."

Around, as in wandering around? "Siblings?" I asked.

He stared at me. Maybe it was the beer. I clarified. "Brothers and sisters?"

"Older sister lives in the city. Married a lawyer she met in college."

The way he said it, his sister had betrayed him in some way, like she'd married outside the species. I took my turn looking away and chewing. It was not good. In fact, it was bad enough it really couldn't be considered pizza at all. Thinking that way set up a false expectation. Cheez Whiz on crackers, maybe. Not pizza. The sausages were little crumbles that obviously had been frozen and nuked. These rubbery little delights had been tossed with dried-up olives, onions that looked like they'd been shaken from a spice jar, and tiny bits of green pepper with no flavor at all. I needed a beer to wash it down.

Just one.

I waved to Kevie, pointed at JJ's beer. Kevie gave a very slight bob of his chin, cracked open a cold one and brought it over. JJ helped himself to a square of our meal. A string of cheese stretched all the way from the metal pan to his mouth. He pinched it off at the base and slurped it up like spaghetti without getting a speck on either his beard or his mustache. Impressive.

He smiled as I sipped my long-necked Bud. Only Anheuser-Busch products available, even this far from St. Louis. That was okay. I didn't have a preference. When I drank, anything would do. Which is why I don't drink. For a while, after Wastrel died, I sucked down a lot of alcohol. I figured it was no different from the drugs the doctor prescribed for my pain, and so much more fun than pills. Then, I stopped. Then, I started teaching riding. And I started drinking again. I'd stopped…

"How about you?" JJ asked.

I glanced around the interior. "You can bet your ass I wasn't born here."

He laughed, and I smiled, and it felt good.

"No, really, what brought you here from The Big Apple?"

"Time for a change of scene, you know what I mean?"

He belched, then nodded. "I hear ya," he said.

We clinked bottles, he winked. Charming. I felt the muscles between my shoulder blades begin to unkink. I hadn't realized how tense I'd been. The beer was a good idea. I could like JJ.

He let the chair clunk to the floor. "I've been thinking lately I need a change of scene, too. That's why I quit Mac's place once and for all. There's no future with him, you'll see."

JJ didn't need to know I wasn't looking for a future, not a very long one, anyway.

"Yep, time to broaden my horizons," he said. "Maybe I'll check out New York."

"If you do, let me know, I'll give you the names of some people." And who, exactly, would that be?

"Then again," he continued with a blatant perusal of my legs, "the scenery here has improved lately, so maybe I'll stick around, see what comes up."

He clinked my bottle again.

See what comes up, indeed.

Half an hour and most of that nasty excuse for a pizza later, JJ demonstrated how to throw darts. He stood right behind me to do it, and I noticed how good he smelled and heard myself giggle and suspected I'd downed another beer—to chase the two shots of vodka. I felt relaxed, moving toward tired, and figured I'd better call it a night before I couldn't find my way to Winterlight. Two beers and two shots was beyond the limit, I knew that. I can't drink at all. And I definitely shouldn't mix. I start saying stupid things, then doing stupid things. That's why I usually drink alone at home, just like an alcoholic.

But JJ's left hand was on my hip. He held my throwing arm, cradled my right hand in his, and maybe, just maybe did something suggestive with his fingers against mine where he wrapped them round the shaft of the dart. A little more time with him wouldn't hurt. I had my truck.

I giggled again and leaned into him. I hate it when I giggle. It's a clear indication I've had too much to drink. He was solid muscle and took my weight easily, pulling me back so I could feel exactly what had come up.

I tossed my dart at the board, but exaggerated my windup and nearly poked out JJ's eye. This elicited a snort. From me. Jesus.

"Whoa, sorry. Listen, thanks, but I need to get going." I swayed enough to have to sidestep when I went to the table to get my purse. Tired. I was tired, that's all.

He hooked my elbow. "Hey, no problem. I'll walk you to your truck."

What a gentleman.

I felt Kevie's watchful eyes on us all the way to the door. I glanced over my shoulder at him, but between the shadows and my stupid state, could not read his face.

Outside, a dingy light above the door did little to keep the dark at bay. A full moon hung over the treetops and the quiet made me sigh. The quiet was nice, I had to admit. Very different. So much background noise in my life. I took a deep breath of the night air. My head cleared some. JJ led me to my truck.

"You sure you're okay?" He flattened his hands against the driver's side window to either side of my head.

I leaned against the door and looked at him, but couldn't make out his eyes with the moonlight behind him. He wasn't too much taller than me. The clean, fresh scent was tinged with cigarette smoke, but he hadn't lit one up all night. Couldn't be a very serious smoker if he could be in a bar, eat bad pizza, drink beer, and not smoke. Or had he done it just for me?

"Fine," I said. "Just point me in the right direction."

His thumbs caught in my hair, twirled a few strands. "I'll do better than that. I'll lead, you follow."

He slid one hand toward my door handle, drawing his fingertips along my neck and shoulder on the way. My tummy did that curly thing it does when I get turned on. I suspect it's really my uterus doing a mating dance.

"A shame to waste this moonlight," he said.

I agreed. The moon was amazing. "Whad'ya have in mind?" My head tilted to one side and my lashes lowered.

For cripe's sake. No. Go home. Go to bed. Alone. You haven't even been here a week. You know nothing about this guy.

Nothing.

Nothing except that the thought of getting laid by all that good-smelling hunk of lean body had my crotch damp. He must have been able to sense my hesitation.

He brushed his lips over mine. "Follow me."

JJ loped to his truck, and I hopped in mine and followed his taillights into the dark. We turned near Winterlight. Good, I thought, close to the farm. We meandered along a gravel road first through fields, then woods, but it wasn't far. Off to the right, a river rippled the moon's light. We stopped at a narrow spot where trees and brush had been cleared to the water's edge.

"Nice," I said when I got out. I took another deep breath. Back on the Island, I'd gone to the beach plenty of times after a night out. Even watched the sun rise there once in a while. I wouldn't last that long tonight. But a few more minutes wouldn't hurt. "I need to get back soon," I said.

"Sure."

I slipped my sandals off and stepped into the cool water. It was shallow and sandy, a gravel bar just a few feet away. It had been hot during the day, and dry. The water felt good, the silky lap of current against my knees slackening me further.

Dimly, the chirp and gurgle of frog song registered—they sounded like they were laughing. Somewhere nearby, a splash. A turtle maybe. And everywhere, the moist scent of earth and wet vegetation. So unlike the tang of the ocean, beached seaweed, and drying shells.

JJ came up behind and pulled me against him like we had been lovers before. His erection nestled against me—a totally naked erection. My hand grazed his thigh to make sure. Yep, he'd shucked his clothes on the bank.

"No rush," he whispered in my ear. "You and me will find a change of scene together."

"I just got here."

"You shouldn't stay. I'm telling you, there's no future here. But right now…"

He pressed his palms against my hips, then slowly moved them across my belly.

I wasn't sure we were about to become lovers and supposed that was not really fair because he probably expected just that. Especially when he dipped his hands in the water and trailed wet fingertips up my inner thigh. Very nice. I shivered against him.

"Listen," I said. "I think—"

He shushed me and kissed my neck and reached beneath my shirt with one hand at the same time his other found my panties.

Now, why, I wondered, had I worn my red, lace panties if I didn't expect to get laid?

I spun to face him right as he squeezed my nipple and hauled me against his chest. I'd meant to push away from him, but that move knocked the breath out of me and twisted my panties to my knees, seeing as how he had a fistful of them. Easier to step out of them at that point than fuss. I'd only fall in the water. His arm encircled my waist like a vice. Yeah, he was strong all right, and sometimes that is not a good thing.

He put his lips to mine and his tongue touched my tongue. As if it had a mind of its own, one of my legs hitched toward his hip, riding my skirt above my thighs. Any self-consciousness about the dark-blue splotches on my skin wafted into the night air. My hands splayed over his ribs, found his waist, slipped between us. He made a low noise in his throat and slid a finger along the wetness at the top of my thighs.

"Girl, you are slicker'n a hound's tooth."

I froze. *Slicker'n*—had I heard him right? My head cleared in a whoosh like I'd fallen in the water. What the hell was I doing?

I dug my fingernails into his balls—not too hard—but enough to tear a surprised, "hey!" from him. He loosed his grip on me. I broke away, lurched for my truck, climbed in, and started it without closing the door. To hell with a seat belt.

I'd gunned it down the road and left him and his hard-on in a cloud of dust before I realized my sandals were still parked under a bit of brush and my panties had drifted downstream.

CHAPTER SIX

MY HEAD HURT.

No. It was a bowling ball attached to my neck. Impossible to lift. I cracked one eyelid. Light and memory invaded, painful recognition of this feeling, disgusted memory.

I'd thrown a gutter ball.

The frogs had been right to laugh.

I pulled the pillow over my head and dozed.

That's when I had the dream. I know everyone has dreams, but I never remember mine. Not a feeling about what I dreamed, not a glimpse, not anything. This one came to me so vividly, I sat up. That was a mistake. The pounding in my head made me cover my eyes and drop back to the mattress.

Wastrel trotted to me out of a bright mist, whole and sound, not broken and bleeding like the last time I saw him moments before he was put down and I was put in an ambulance. The big bay snorted and shook his head and nuzzled my side. I felt his warm breath, the tickle of his whiskers. He didn't smell like the usual clean wood shavings and liniment; he smelled like heaven.

Okay, so who knows what heaven smells like? For some, it might be bacon frying or a chocolate milk shake, lilacs, freshly-turned earth or new-mown grass, a just-washed baby, the air on top of a mountain or the sea. What Wastrel smelled like in my dream was all those things rolled into one. So, that's what heaven smells like.

He danced around me. I reached for him and he moved away, just as we had always played together out in the paddock before I'd bring him in to work. He swished his tail and returned, almost within reach, but not quite.

Wastrel had been my favorite ride of all time. On him, my connection was pure and open, and we could do anything. Only thing was, Wastrel didn't enjoy jumping. Not the man-made competition jumps, anyway. A fence across a field, a log out on the trail, a ditch along the road, he sailed over all. But point him at a course in a ring, and he balked. Observers couldn't see it. Only he and I knew. I tried to explain to his owner, but he pushed and pushed for the grand-prix prize. Wastrel could do it, and he did do it for me. Many times. But he'd grown tired of it.

That day, our ride was going smoothly, well under time and no faults, until he launched himself at the square oxer in the middle of the triple combination. It was perfect, we'd hit the ideal take-off point. The next moment, all I knew was splintering wood, and the muted roar of the crowd, and the ground coming up, and the shock of it going wrong. He tried to keep me from getting hurt; I tried to help him get free. His freedom was hard won. He never got up again. I often wondered if it had been deliberate.

In the dream, I sensed I'd been right. He was happy and intact and never had to jump unless he wanted to. In heaven, the fields were always green and the ponds clear and the trees shady. Somehow, he communicated that.

Wastrel led me to a wooded hillside. There was Winterlight's manure pile. It didn't smell like heaven, not at all.

"Yes," I said. "We're going to clean that up today."

He climbed to the top and whinnied, then struck and dug at the heavy pile with his forefoot, spewing wet straw and manure through the crystal air.

"Okay, yes, I get it."

Why would a dead horse be worried about an oversized manure pile at a farm he'd never visited while living?

Dreams are weird.

Once I'd showered and gargled the pasty remnants of beer from my throat with four cups of strong coffee, I concluded I had not had sex with JJ.

Relief left me boneless where I sprawled on the tack-room love seat after feeding the horses. Its musty smell reminded me I should check the mysterious contents of the washing machine, but I wasn't up to it. And that got me wondering where Norman was. I thought he'd said this was his last week, but I didn't know what his hours were supposed to be. Maybe he figured since I lived here he didn't need to arrive any time in particular.

I didn't waste time with self-recrimination. I knew perfectly well what I'd been thinking the night before. More precisely, I hadn't been thinking at all. I'd been tired and feeling unappreciated. JJ happened along at the right time.

With any luck, his change of scene would happen soon, and I wouldn't have to deal with him again.

Henrietta jumped to my lap and purred when I stroked her back. Her belly stuck out like she'd swallowed a football. Probably have her kittens today. When I rose, she made a beeline for my apartment. Great. She might even have her kittens in my closet.

There'd been a message on the answering machine from Malcolm that he'd finished his job early and would be home tonight. Crap. I'd wanted to have so much more done before he got back. He'd sounded surprised not to find me in when he called at nine at night. Surprised or disappointed? Hard to say, especially in my fuzzyheaded state. After our last encounter, I'd just as soon he stayed away. Unless, of course, he was wearing his kilt.

And that was just the sort of sentiment that got me in trouble last night.

If I hustled, I could get the horses worked, clean out a couple more stalls, and do my grocery shopping before Hank showed up with his front loader and manure spreader to start moving the big pile. That thing had been building for months and achieved a height of at least ten feet and probably double that in width and length. It was down a hillside and out of sight—just like in my dream. Out of sight, out of mind, for the people around here. Not for Wastrel.

The dream followed me through the morning. Every detail stuck with me. What it meant, I had no idea.

The nearest grocery store was fairly new—a testament to civilization inching into the country. Progress, some people would call it. It was also small and limited in its offering. No organic anything. I wheeled a cart down the canned goods aisle. Good selection of baked beans.

I felt more clear-headed since riding, and my sense of purpose grew as I got to know the horses. Gaston, Malcolm's new mount, had a big trot and a rolling canter but was lazy to the jumps. We'd work on that. He'd be bolder going cross-country than in the ring. Ciqala knew his job and moved efficiently. Miss Bong should have been called Miss Boing. She did everything with lots of bounce.

Cali had lugged on the bit, swished her tail, and called to the horses in the pasture. Fergus answered, Smitty raised his head, and the rest kept to cropping grass. She wanted out with them, but I was cautious. No sense endangering Winterlight's other occupants unnecessarily. So far, I'd let her out in the riding ring only. I rode her on the buckle, let her stretch her topline through trot and some canter, very relaxing for us both.

I'd taken some aspirin. Still, my head had a persistent, throbbing ache, and I had to keep consulting my shopping list to remember what I needed. What had I come down this aisle for? There it was, green beans.

Wastrel kept edging into my thoughts. After the accident that left him dead and me on a respirator for a few days while my fractured sternum popped back into the correct position, I tried to put the memory behind me, drowned it in alcohol, but the dream brought it all back. So, on top of being hung over, feeling stupid for getting drunk and nearly having sex in a river, I had to contend with a dream horse intruding on my ride time. At least the old feelings of grief and remorse, guilt and anger weren't as strong as in the past. Seeing Wastrel in one piece and not upset with me helped.

I was choosing between regular and French cut beans when a cart careened into mine and pushed it over my foot.

"Oops, sorry," the other woman said.

Pink-camouflaged lady smiled in recognition. Was I doomed to injury every time she got close? Her hair hung over her shoulders in ratty waves that had been bleached and permed so many times it looked like it might break. Now that I had a moment to study her, I realized she was younger than I thought, maybe early twenties. Her clothes today were relatively respectable —plain T-shirt and baggy shorts. Still, there was no hiding her size-D chest.

"Hey, you're—" she started.

"The new girl," we both said together.

"How's it going?" she asked. "I'm Sandy Houseman, by the way. Sorry about what happened." She hunkered down a bit. "How's my wittle Fawny-Wawny?" she asked in a little-girl voice. "She being a good girly?"

"Uh…yeah. It's going okay." I glanced down at her bare legs. "But I won't be wearing shorts anytime soon."

She straightened and spoke in a normal tone. "That bad, huh?"

"I've had worse." Before she could ask for details, I changed the subject. "Fawn could use a little more exercise. How often do you ride?"

"As often as I can. But I have to work to support it. I'm on break from the vet's office right now. Can I come over later?"

Sandy worked for a vet. Always a good person to know, but I almost said no anyway. The baby talk made me grind my teeth. Maybe if she didn't direct it at me, I'd survive.

At my hesitation, she added, "I need to see Norman about something anyway."

"Sure. Hank and I will be moving manure all afternoon. After that will be good."

Two older ladies walked toward us, each carrying a small basket rather than pushing a cart. They were deep in conversation, heads tilted toward each other, so we moved over until they went on, but they stopped at the canned gravy. Sandy did an eye roll that had me afraid her eyes would get stuck inside her head, then picked out a can of corn niblets and one of creamed, and appeared to consider.

"Well," the first lady said, "when Fred went down to the bottom to count head this morning, some of them was in the river. He almost had an apoplexy when he seen his prize bull."

"What'd he do, Melba, get himself stuck in a hole again?"

I started to back my cart. Without looking away from the corn, Sandy put one foot on it to keep me from moving off. I returned my attention to the green beans.

"Oh goodness, no. Fred thought he'd gashed his face open or tore off an ear. Lordy, his whole head looked bloody."

"Oh dear, it wasn't one of the cows, was it?"

"No, no, no. Now, just let me tell it."

Melba wore a striped dress, pantyhose, and faded Keds with the toes cut out. Support-hose clad toes showed through the openings. She had short, white hair and Delft blue eyes. Edna looked like her twin except she wore green polyester pants and black slip-on shoes with her plaid cotton blouse. Her swollen ankles and feet overflowed the top edges of the shoes.

"Look, Fred's favorite gravy is on sale," Melba said. "Buy two get one free. Oh, but I can't use that many."

"I'll take the free one," Edna said. "Even though it's only me, sometimes I invite Herbert over."

I sighed in exasperation, exchanged a look with Sandy. What in heck happened to Fred's bull? She put a can of creamed corn in my basket.

At my squinty-eyed stare, she whispered, "Try it, you'll like it."

Melba gently elbowed Edna. "I think Herbert's sweet on you."

Edna hid a giggle behind an embroidered hanky. "Now, tell me about that silly bull of yours."

"Yes, well," Melba cleared her throat and leaned closer. "You won't believe it. Turns out it was a pair of red lace underpants stuck on his horn."

CHAPTER SEVEN

SANDY BURST out laughing when Melba made her announcement, and I stared at them, dumbstruck.

"Was they Fred's?" Sandy asked. "Or one of the cows'?"

Melba and Edna lowered their identical gray brows at us and moved along without another word. Sandy turned to me, still laughing.

"If that don't beat all." She wiped a tear on her shoulder. "You see the looks on their faces?"

"Yeah. Hilarious." I headed for the checkout.

"Tell Fawny-Wawny I said hi, okay?"

I'd put my three bags on the seat of the truck before I began to see the humor in the situation. So long, that is, as no one ever found out the panties were mine.

Back at the ranch, I put groceries away quickly, loading the two cans of Reddi-Wip into the door of the fridge. I'd gotten one plain, one chocolate. The chocolate was for extreme stress. Emergency provision only. I took a hit of the creamy white stuff, closed my mouth, then swept my tongue through it a little at a time, letting it dissolve at its own pace. Tension slipped away like water from a leaking trough. After a deep breath, I took another quick squirt and headed outside, feeling renewed. Who needs yoga and meditation when there's whipped cream in a can?

I grabbed my baseball cap and pulled my hair through the opening in the back.

Henrietta was nowhere in sight, which made me nervous, but I didn't have time to look for her. Hank had parked the manure spreader at the top of the hill. His tractor looked more like a jolly green bulldozer with four back wheels taller than me and a scoop on the front-loader big enough to pick up a car. He shut the giant down when he saw me.

"We'll hitch the spreader to the Laird's Ford, and I'll show you how to run it."

"Sure," I said, wondering about ear protection. Hadn't anyone in the tractor business heard of mufflers? "Does everyone call him the Laird? Should I?"

"Hell no. He hates it. That's why's I does it. Ever since he came back from that school in Scotland. He was tellin' me and Clara about it one night and the history and whatnot and I took to callin' him that after. Pisses him off right royal, it does."

"Why do you do it, then?"

"I known him since he was born. No need of him to start puttin' on airs thirty-two years later. Just remindin' him where he came from, is all."

Made sense, in a convoluted way. Either that, or the fumes from the manure pile were getting to me.

"How often does he wear that kilt?"

Hank gave me a look, like he was trying to figure out why I asked. I knew the moment he found an answer he liked because it made him smile.

"Most the time."

I could get used to most of the time. No, less distracting if he didn't. Better to remember Malcolm was a prick the last time I saw him.

"We gonna get this shit moved today, or stand out here yammerin' or what?"

"Let's go," I said.

Mr. Malcolm's tractor sat under the shed along the north side of the barn. I hadn't ventured over there yet. The gooseneck horse trailer was backed into the front of the shed, and in between sat a square baler. Or so Hank explained. Okay, so I'm a typical consumer. I've fed hay to horses all my life —bought, unloaded, and stacked it. I've never seen it baled and cannot figure out how this contraption does it. Hank pointed out a hay rake, too, which didn't look anything like any rake I'd ever seen before.

He showed me how to start the tractor and pointed out the clutch, gas, and brake. My truck was a stick, so I eased out the clutch and backed clear of the shed. Attached to long arms on the front of the tractor there was some other mean-looking farm implement with three, thick metal spikes—two short and one long—each with sharp points. I pointed at them.

"What's that for?"

"Bale spear," Hank answered. At my blank look he added, "To pick up them big round bales."

I don't know what I'd expected, but doing hay on the farm was not going to be it. I made a mental note to stay far away from the bale spear. That thing could skewer a person or two and never know the difference.

Hank jumped on the back, rode to where he'd left the manure spreader, and hitched it up when I got close enough.

"Okay," he yelled.

I turned the gas down to lower the noise and cupped my ear to hear him better.

"Wait a minute, and I'll bring up a scoop. Then, I'll show you where to empty it."

I nodded and gave him a thumbs up. For an old guy, he moved easily, swinging into the seat of his green John Deere with the flexibility of a much younger man. The diesel engine roared, and smoke poured from the stack.

I looked the spreader over while I waited. It had two long handles sticking up at the front that connected via cables to gears at the back. A chain connected the rear axle and gears. Three bars crossed the open back end—two with eight-inch rods along their length—a third had fan-like blades. I couldn't wait to see the thing in action.

In a minute, Hank came up with a scoop full of steaming compost—the kind of stuff people back East pay gobs of money for. I'd read once that a pile like this could get as hot as one-hundred-seventy-five degrees. He dumped it, and the weight pushed down on the hitch, lowering the tractor an inch or so. I squeezed my eyes shut and pulled the neck of my T-shirt over my nose.

Hank climbed onto the hitch behind me, and pointed toward the road between the riding ring and pasture. Now, I saw a trail of dark-brown straw and a few horse turds he'd left on the previous run. I stood to jam the tractor into second gear and followed the road through an opening in a barbed wire fence to a field. On the far side, I could see the roof of Hank's house, over half a mile away. He told me to shut the engine off, and we both went to look at the spreader.

"Squeeze this handle and pull this lever back to here, see?"

When I nodded, he continued, "Make sure it hits this notch." He pointed to a knobby half-circle then led me to the back. Somewhere between the front and back, I zoned out while he explained the machine's intricacies. He showed me how to set the lever that engaged the axle, then glanced at the sky. The day had turned cool.

"Be good to get some rain over top of this. Let's get it spread before it starts."

I hopped onto the tractor and fired it up.

"Slow and steady," Hank yelled.

The spreader started as soon as I moved forward. I thought the tractor was loud. This thing clanged and clanked and thumped and jangled like an army of one-man-bands trying to outdo each other. The pile inside slowly moved to the back, and then, the shit hit the fan. Literally. Manure flew through the air and out to either side for twenty feet. It was fabulous. I laughed, then had to jerk the wheel before I drove into a ditch on the side of the field.

Off to the west, a heavy gray line of clouds edged over the tops of the trees. Maybe Hank was right. I hadn't turned on a television since I arrived, had no idea what the weatherman was calling for.

I'd never been so out of touch, but rather than being nervous, I felt calm. The drone and vibration of the tractor were mesmerizing. And the slow but steady pace—was this the right speed to take life? I could easily view my surroundings at this rate, and still think…once I got earplugs.

I made a wide turn at the far end and headed toward Hank again. That's when the spreader shuddered and screeched like a blender trying to puree wet wood. The whole mechanism stopped.

"Something's stuck," I shouted to Hank.

He jogged across the field. "Shut it off."

I did and climbed down to inspect it hoping no one had ditched something stupid into the mix. Good, hot, compost can decompose almost anything. Which is great, but it doesn't necessarily mean you'd want it spread on a field used to grow food.

Hank joined me. He lifted his MFA cap, stroked his bald head, scratched his neck, then dropped the cap into place. "Probly a gotdamned chain broke."

I flicked bits of straw and manure from the spreader's edge with the back of my hand, wishing I'd put on gloves. Nothing obvious showed in the large hump of compost still inside the box. I continued around the back. Sunlight flashed on something shiny beneath the bottom row of blades. My eyes registered the image before me, but my brain refused to process it.

It was a toe guard.

The kind found on the point of a western boot.

Like the ones Norman wore.

This toe guard was still attached to a western boot.

A black fake alligator western boot like Norman had been wearing the last time I saw him that now had one of the spreader blades cutting into it.

Beyond the top of the boot, I could see an inch of blue jeans, a leg that disappeared beneath the ponderous load, nothing else. The fine hairs on the back of my neck lifted, and the air crossing my sweaty skin suddenly felt icy.

Hank edged over, picking up on my vibe. He did what I should have, but couldn't. He poked it—with a big screwdriver he pulled from his belt. Like you would poke a snake or anything else you didn't want to touch. There wasn't a screwdriver in the world big enough to make me willing to poke a boot sticking out the back of a manure spreader.

Hank's voice, when he spoke, sounded like two emery boards scraping together. "Still attached," he said.

I covered my mouth and forced myself to breathe, took a step back. "You think—"

"I think there's a foot in there, but that's all I'm willin' to specalate on. Stay here. I'm callin' the sheriff."

"Oh, no. I'm not staying alone with…could he be…?" *Alive* was what I was thinking. That seemed impossible.

Hank went to the spreader's box, paused a moment, scooped a handful of compost away, then another. He turned to me, and I saw his age on him for the first time. His eyes lacked their usual spark, and his tattered-linen-shirt-face was more threadbare than ever. He shook his head.

"He ain't goin' nowhere."

I stumbled after him. We left both tractor and spreader where I'd stopped. The breeze picked up behind us, bringing the clouds closer, but for the moment, the sun still cast our shadows to the side.

Shit. Norman did not burrow into the manure pile on purpose. Someone put him there. Some time since the day before. Some time…while I'd been out? It had to have been. Noire would have barked if she'd heard anyone. Then again, given the stupor I was in, I might not have heard her.

Inside the tack room, Hank dragged a rotary phone from under a pile of notebooks and magazines. I hadn't had a chance to tidy or dust this area yet. I grabbed the stack from him and realized what I held were ledgers and records for Winterlight. They felt real and substantial, and I hugged them to my chest. But it didn't help. I dropped onto the loveseat, then stood. I just couldn't get past imagining Norman cooked in the manure pile. Imagining what had happened and why and who. And knowing it had all gone on right outside my window. Jesus, why was I spooking myself like this?

"That's right," Hank said into the phone. "The Malcolm place. We'll be here."

He put the receiver down. "You okay over there?"

Through the window, I could see three vultures circling the field. "No."

He dialed the phone again. "Clara? Get over here, pronto. Huh? Hell no, I ain't hurt. I'll explain later. Bring some tea."

Hank and Clara were crazy if they thought a glass of iced tea could fix this. Unless it was a Long Island Iced Tea.

He hung up, dialed more numbers—long distance. "That you Dex? We got a sit-ee-ation here. You catch it on the scanner? Might could help if you come on out. Figured you'd already be on your way, anyways. Sure, call him, that'd be good." He paused, listening. "Huh? How the hell should I know if she's freaked?" He spat the word like it tasted bad, pressed the receiver to his chest, and addressed me. "You freaked?"

Freaked didn't begin to cover it. This was going to take a whole case of chocolate whipped cream. Maybe two. I shook my head no.

"No, she ain't freaked. Not yet, anyways. But hurry."

CHAPTER EIGHT

FOR A FEW MINUTES, light streaked through the barn windows and lit dust motes floating in the air. Then, the lowering clouds swallowed the sun, and the interior of the barn dimmed. First, I found Noire and held her close. That helped ease the tightness in my chest, but I longed for Penny to put my arms around, or, more specifically, to put her arms around me.

I began cleaning a stall, shoveling dirty bedding as hard as I could pump my arms until I was so out of breath, I had to stop and lean on the shovel. Noire stayed near and thumped her tail each time I looked at her.

Clara appeared and handed me a plastic cup of iced tea. She wore sweat pants that showed off her cellulite and bulges. Despite that, for a woman of at least seventy years, she looked in good shape, not unlike her husband, Hank. By the dirt on her knees, she must have been digging in the garden when he called her to my rescue. I forced the drink past my dry tongue so fast it dribbled over my chin. It had too much sugar, and it didn't fix anything, but it hit the spot. Only then did I realize the futility of my frenzy. No way was I going to push the wheelbarrow outside or anywhere near the manure pile.

I handed Clara the empty cup. "Thanks. You think it's okay if I go upstairs?"

She smiled a motherly smile. "Of course, sweetie." She patted my arm. "You've had a terrible shock." She shook her head, glanced in the direction of the…situation. "Terrible. We'll let ya know if we need you. I brought some pie. You want and take a piece up with you?"

The thought of Clara's sickly-sweet pie made my head spin. What I needed was to lie down. "I don't think I could eat just now. Maybe later."

"You sure you want to be alone?"

"Just for a while. I'll be all right. Thanks."

Numb, that's what I was. I'd never seen a dead body before. Not a human, anyway. Okay, so all I'd seen was a foot—boot—but that was enough. A dead boot. I hadn't even tried to see what Hank uncovered. Later it'd sink in, and I'd have some other reaction, but right then, I didn't feel a thing. I trudged up the steps to my apartment, went straight to the refrigerator, grabbed the chocolate Reddi-wip, and filled my mouth.

A short time after, a car came up the drive, and I went downstairs. Two uniformed sheriff's deputies ambled into the barn, found Hank, spoke for a moment, went outside. I stayed inside, armed with my canned cream.

Another car pulled up—a long, dark-blue sedan. An older man unfolded himself from the front seat. He was tall and all angles with brown hair graying at the temples. I squirted myself another mouthful of chocolate cream while he walked toward us. Clara met him halfway.

"Howdy, Frank." She pulled him into a hug. "Terrible business about little Norman. He's in the next field." Clara pointed him to the manure spreader.

"That there's my cousin Frank," she said, pride filling her voice. "County Coroner. Postmaster, too."

"Oh," I said with a nod. "You want some whipped cream?" I showed her my can. Sometimes I thought it would be neat to have a holster for it.

She looked at me real concerned like. Like I was freaked. Well, I was.

Rain started to tap the tin roof. A state trooper tore in, lights flashing, and skidded to a halt next to the sheriff car, spitting a shower of gravel onto their fender.

"It's chocolate," I offered. "I have plain, if you prefer."

She looked sideways at me. "Don't ya need some pie to go under it?"

I took a shot of cream. "Nope," I said after I'd swallowed, "I like it straight."

She watched the trooper striding past the barn windows on his way to join the rest. "Yeah, sometimes you just gotta take it straight."

Noire followed the trooper for a minute, just as she had the deputies and the coroner, sniffing their heels, hoping for a pat. Until the next vehicle arrived, then she went to the front of the barn again. A truck pulled up, and she wheeled to run toward it. This one a small, red Nissan.

"There's Dex One," Clara said. She set off to greet him at a fast waddle.

I swear, she was enjoying all the activity. I wondered how well she knew "little Norman." I'd met him only twice and was having trouble keeping my whipped cream down at the thought of what might have happened.

Clara brought the man to me. "Dexter Hamill, this is Viola Parker."

I winced at the use of my full name. "Vi" would have done. Of medium build with buzz-cut blond hair and matching mustache, Dexter One's most distinguishing feature was a pronounced limp. The way he moved, it was an old injury to which he'd adapted long ago. How he rode with it, I could not imagine. I stood to shake his hand.

His grip was strong. The look in his eye was all warm molasses, but there was a hint of determination behind the softness, and I knew that whatever caused the limp kept Dex from very little.

"Let me talk to these fellers outside for a minute, see what's up. I'll be back."

He hobbled out into the drizzle. Clara's heavy body heaved a great sigh.

"That man can park his boots under my bed any time," she whispered.

I blinked at her. Her and Hank looked like they'd been together forever, but he was a bit of a bow-legged little gnome. Dex was fairly ordinary looking until you noticed his eyes. Even with the limp, I could see how she'd find him attractive.

"You sure you don't want a hit?" I brandished my can.

Clara plopped beside me. "Maybe I will," she said.

She sprayed a generous dollop of chocolate whipped cream straight into her nose. It takes practice to get the technique right. She jumped to her feet and snorted it into the aisle with a flurry of waving hands, coughing and spitting. Good thing this wasn't the crime scene. I'd call it compromised.

An emergency medical service truck pulled in and behind it a beat-up white compact. Sandy slammed her car door and hustled into the barn before the EMTs could disembark. Noire gave her a quick sniff and decided to ignore the others. Sandy probably reeked of all sorts of animal smells from the vet's office. She wore her riding togs. Stretch black jeans and high-top sneakers. A red, checkered sports bra zipped up the front and didn't look like it offered much in the way of support given the amount of bounce and sway coming our way.

Clara opened her mouth like she was receiving communion. "Hit me," she said.

"What the hell's going on here?" Sandy asked when she reached us.

I gave Clara a squirt while Sandy bent over backwards to get a glimpse of the crowd in the next field. Her breasts rolled to either side, and I wondered how she kept her balance. The sheriff himself had arrived and drove straight to the field. Now, the EMTs were aiming their truck in that direction, too.

"Jesus effing Christ on a hot, brown shingle," Sandy said. "Is that Norman?"

She started for the door, but Clara laid a restraining hand on her arm. "You'd better sit down, honey," Clara said. She patted the step next to her.

Sandy lowered herself without taking her gaze from the scene outside. I didn't look. Instead, I shook my can and took a squirt.

"Can I have some of that?" Sandy asked.

Splotches of bright pink bloomed on Sandy's cheeks and her eyes filled with tears.

"Helps if you tilt your head back," Clara said. She rubbed her nose.

Sandy had clearly used this form of nourishment before. She injected the stuff with a flourish, moving the can up and down for effect, and her face cleared. I went upstairs for my spare. Plain would have to do. But I'd need to get to the store soon for reinforcements.

"How bad is it?" Sandy asked when I returned.

She seemed to have regained her composure. Whipped cream is good that way.

"What happened?"

"I don't know," I said. "Hank and I were cleaning up the manure pile. I was spreading it, and…" my voice broke.

Clara patted my arm.

"Don't know more than that," I said. "He was fine yesterday."

"Dang," Sandy whispered. "What a way to go."

She was making light, but her voice sounded tight.

"He didn't go thataway," Clara said. "You don't fall into the middle of a manure pile like that and accidentally get buried. Stuff's too…you know, firm-like. You might fall on top of it, get overcome by the smell, roll to the base. He had to be dead already."

That was the first time anyone had said *dead*.

Clara continued, "Yep. Somebody put him there."

We all looked at each other, then away.

"Anybody want pie?" Clara asked. "There's tea, too."

We agreed we all needed tea and walked up the step into the tack room.

When we went out again, Renee, the tall black woman who had taken care of Smitty the day I arrived, stood in the aisle looking through the back door. Near the fence line, an old couple walked arm-and-arm under an umbrella. I recognized Melba from the grocery store. The man must have been Fred. Yellow police tape flapped in the breeze now, and all the horses stood staring, heads high, ears twitching. Cali trotted up and down inside the riding ring. She kicked out, and broke the top fence rail. The loud snap sent her off at a dead run to the other end, bucking and farting the whole way.

Renee turned to look at us. "What on earth?"

"Hey, Renee," Sandy said. She'd been sniffling and dabbed at her eyes with a tissue. "Vi, remember Renee?"

"I remember," I said. "You took care of Smitty. Good to see you again."

Renee raised an eyebrow at me, turned away. I looked to Sandy, who shrugged. "Were you coming over to ride this afternoon?" I asked Renee.

"You expecting points because you remembered the only black woman within fifty miles of this place?"

Okay, fine. Everybody handles stress differently. There was no reason to get snooty, but I get that maybe she was upset and decided to take it out on me.

Renee murmured to no one in particular, "Um, um, um. Norman, Norman, Norman. What kinda mess you get yourself into, boy?"

I turned on my heel. "If anyone's looking for me, I'll be right back."

"Where you gonna be at?" Sandy asked.

I held up my can of Reddi-Wip. "We're going to need a couple of cases."

A man's voice called to me before I reached the end of the barn aisle. Dex. I stopped.

"Miss Parker, these gentlemen need to ask you some questions."

I turned in time to see him indicate the deputies. Crap.

We went into the tack room where they both helped themselves to tea and one grabbed a piece of Clara's pie without using a plate. He crammed most of it in his mouth at one time. Crumbs sprinkled his chest and caught around his shiny badge.

"Miss Parker, where were you last night?" the other asked.

I narrowed my eyes. Was he questioning me like I was a suspect? At my hesitation they exchanged a look. Dex sat next to me on the love seat. He smelled like freshly-baked bread, and I wondered if that was why Clara wanted his boots under her bed. He patted my knee as if we'd known each other longer than a minute.

"It's routine, Vi. Just answer them." I stared at the back of his hand. He removed it from my leg, lowered his head, and rubbed his temples. If his headache was anything like mine, it was going to take more than that to fix it.

The deputy hadn't specified a time. Which meant they didn't have a fix on time of death. "I was here until six-forty-five, then I went to Mel's."

"Can anyone verify that?"

"JJ…" Crap. I didn't know the guy's name, but at the mention of him,

Dex's head came up.

"John Jenson?" the deputy asked.

Figures they'd know. I glanced at Dex. "Is he the guy who used to work here?"

Dex nodded, closed his eyes, and breathed deeply, as if this was bad news.

"That's him," I said. "He was here in the afternoon. Then, he left, and I met him at Mel's at seven. We were there until around ten." I'd noticed the time when I got in my truck. I get stupid when I drink, but not unable-to-tell-time stupid.

"And what transpired while you were at Mel's? Did either of you leave and return during that time?"

What *transpired*? Sheesh. "We ate pizza and played darts and talked, and we were both there the whole time."

"Did you imbibe liquor?"

"I had a couple of drinks, yes."

"One, or two, or more?"

"Two." This much I knew for sure. I really didn't think there was a third. Beer didn't count.

"Miss Parker arrived at Winterlight for the first time on Saturday evening, officer," Dex said. "She's been working almost non-stop since."

The deputy eating pie crammed in the last crumbs, licked his fingers, cut his gaze to Dex, then to the other deputy. I glanced around for the security camera I must have missed. How the hell did Dex know what I'd been doing? Did I ask him to defend me? Did I need defending?

"Do I need an attorney?" I asked. I thought of my parents' lawyer in Connecticut. He might not be the best one to call, but I didn't know any others.

"Like Mr. Hamill said, routine. When was the last time you saw the deceased?"

When do people go from being persons with names to *the deceased*? How did that make it easier? My stubborn streak, which has a habit of raising its ugly head at the most inappropriate times, chose that moment to make an appearance.

"You mean Norman?" I asked. I didn't know Norman and didn't care for him the little I did know. Didn't know his last name either, but he'd had one. He'd been a person who thought he was "moving on to bigger and better things." A person with hope.

They exchanged a look. I'd seen that look before. I took a turn rubbing my temples. When was the last time I'd taken any pain pills? Surely it was time for more—with a whipped cream chaser—which even I knew wasn't appropriate during a questioning. My tummy started an uncomfortable roiling at the thought. Maybe I'd already had enough.

Dex squeezed my shoulder. "Take your time," he said.

Either he mistook my manner for grief, or he knew I was getting pissed. I voted for the latter. I remembered then Malcolm saying Dex One was a retired-mounted-cop-sometime-private-investigator. I'd bet nothing much got by Dex.

"Monday morning around ten-thirty," I answered. "He rode his four-wheeler up the road." Hank had probably already given this information as well.

The deputy made notes and nodded. "And after ten p.m. last night? Where did you go when you left Mel's?"

I'd so hoped he would not return to that timeline. But I don't lie, and there was no point in it I could think of. Except for my pride. Except I'd already sunk so low by coming to work at a hack barn, pride hardly figured in.

"We went down to the river for a little while, no more than fifteen minutes. I'm not sure where, but not far from here."

"You don't know where?"

"It was dark. I followed JJ, but I don't exactly know my way around yet."

"Mr. Jenson was with you?"

For cripe's sake. "Yes. At the river. He drove his truck, I drove mine. I left after fifteen minutes or so. I don't know if he stayed there, or what."

"I see. Did you quarrel?"

I'd been leaning forward, my elbows on my knees, my head hanging down. I raised it to look at the deputy. "What does that have to do with anything?"

"I'm asking the questions, here, ma'am."

"No, I wouldn't say we quarreled."

"What would you say?"

I noticed Dex watching me closely. His eyes had turned dark as stout, unreadable.

"I'd say Mr. Jenson and I had a difference of opinion about what was to transpire between us at the river, and I left him there before anything he might have been hoping to transpire between us but that I was not interested in having transpire did so transpire. Does that answer your question?"

The deputy blinked several times, then wrote in his notebook.

Dexter's shoulders shook. He acted like he was coughing, but he was laughing.

CHAPTER NINE

THE DEPUTIES ASKED whether I remembered hearing any noises outside after I got home the night before. I didn't. They went to question everyone else. I went in the bathroom and threw up.

I ventured to look outside after I felt better. The rain had slowed, but spongy looking black clouds hovered out past the house just waiting for a good squeeze. The EMTs had gone, and I could see Frank, the coroner, had moved his sedan next to the manure spreader and popped the trunk. Hank moved a couple of bags of feed to the back seat. Then, the sheriff and Frank put a body bag into the trunk. The sheriff wiped his hands on a rag, and the coroner brushed his against his pants legs. They shook, Frank nodded at Hank and slammed the lid. Heck of a way to transport *the deceased*.

Deputies picked through the manure pile for evidence. They'd shoveled it into miniature pyramids, leaving messy piles of straw and poop all over. For a brief moment, resentment tumbled my gut. More work. Then, I let it go. I can be selfish, but even I could admit this wasn't about me.

Dex sidled up, peered past my shoulder. As if reading my mind, he said, "We'll get it cleaned up. Don't worry. But it will have to stay like this a little while. Till they decide they've gotten everything they can out of it."

"What are they looking for?"

"Hard to say. Norman didn't bury himself in there."

"Was he…?"

"Dead before he got put in there? Maybe."

And maybe not.

"I thought he'd cleaned up his act," Dex said.

"Meaning?"

He shrugged. "He had a little history with drugs. Nothing too serious. But it's hard to shake no matter what."

I'd never done drugs but could relate to the difficulty of shaking addiction. Did Dex have personal experience with that too? He put his hands on my shoulders and kneaded the muscles at the base of my neck. It felt great and weird all at once. He didn't know me well enough to do that, but I didn't want him to stop, either. So, I just stood there, letting him make me feel better. It was the first time I'd let someone touch me uninvited. Actually, it was the first anyone attempted such a thing.

"Do they know how?" I asked.

"How he died? Coroner wouldn't speculate. That's for the medical examiner in St. Louis to determine."

Clara knocked, and let herself in without waiting for a reply. Dex released me. She glanced from him to me, her face unreadable.

"Let Hank know I'm gonna go get supper ready," she said to me. "You want to come down now or later?"

The assumption being that I was eating dinner with them. I sighed inwardly. I wanted to be alone, and I didn't want to be alone. I didn't know what I wanted. Clara smiled at Dex.

"You're welcome, too, Dex. How 'bout it? I got pork chops and chess pie."

"Wouldn't miss it, Clara, you know that. We'll be down," he glanced at his watch, "in about an hour, okay?"

She went out with a wave.

"That enough time for you to shower and nap?" Dex asked.

Dex assumed a lot, but right then I needed someone to take over. No doubt, the numbness I felt was written all over my face, and he'd probably dealt with this sort of thing before. His manner would have really, really irked me yesterday, especially since he wasn't coming on to me.

Today, I lived in a whole new world.

CHAPTER TEN

As I went upstairs, the tack-room phone rang. "Winterlight's closed," Dex said by way of answering.

Pause.

"Check back after the weekend." A note of impatience tinged his voice. Then, "We're doing inventory!" He slammed the receiver down.

I let myself smile. I liked Dex. I called Penny to see how her doctor's appointment went and told her everything was fine with me. No reason to add to her burden. Her doctor said she should rest more. Fat chance of that happening.

After a long, hot, shower, I found Renee and Sandy feeding too much and letting the horses fight over it. I explained how I was organizing it, and they exchanged one of those looks, like they were thinking, oh, here we go, we're trying to help, and the bitch from New York is complaining.

I told them if they really wanted to help, they could groom everybody and pick out their feet. Smitty and Fawn had thrush, and they weren't the only ones. I showed Renee and Sandy the bottle of treatment to use on the soles of the horses' hooves. If they couldn't handle that, I asked them not to bother.

Yeah, I was feeling a little bitchy.

Now, it was pouring rain. I turned my face up to it before getting in Dex's truck to go to Clara and Hank's, letting moisture pelt my open eyes and my cheeks and run into my mouth. Would have stayed like that, but Dex grabbed my sleeve and yanked me onto the seat next to him.

Finally, Dex dropped me at the farm, everyone had gone home, and I had the place to myself. Well, not entirely. Henrietta had delivered four kittens in the laundry basket in my closet. At least she'd chosen to labor on the clothes that were already dirty. Noire sniffed at the new cat family, looked at me. I said, "Surprise!" and she wagged her tail, then jumped on the bed and went to sleep.

The kittens—one black like his mom, two brown tabbies, and one white with orange splotches—mewed and squirmed at Henrietta's belly, and she had that contented purry look about her, like she was exhausted, but elated.

I was exhausted, but not elated.

The worst of the bitchiness had worn off, and having four kittens in my closet made it hard to maintain any level of anger. I'd no one to be angry with, wasn't even sure if that was my main feeling. Mainly, I needed to sleep.

Dex told me he'd gotten a call from Malcolm. His flight had been delayed, and he wouldn't be at the farm until after eight p.m. It was close to nine. I didn't know whether he'd returned, and I really didn't care. I was out of whipped cream, and all I wanted was to be horizontal, like my dog.

I took another shower, lay down, and the phone rang. I considered not answering, let it ring once more, picked it up. There was a slight pause after my hello.

"Malcolm here."

Serious and business-like. So much so that I almost laughed. I lowered my voice and tried to match his tone.

"Parker here."

Another pause on his end, and I could hear his brain whirring and clicking. Then, a soft, relieved chuckle.

"You okay down there? You've had quite a day."

I should not try to hold a conversation when I'm that tired. It's almost as bad as being drunk. Except that I'm not stupid when I'm tired, just vulnerable and honest. I most definitely should not talk to a man who has a chuckle like velvet, not after the kind of day I'd had.

"Yes," I said. "But, it couldn't have been easy for you, either." I knew from Hank and Clara that Norman had worked at Winterlight only for a few months. Malcolm had hired him on Sandy's recommendation. Before that, he and Malcolm hadn't met. Still. He was human. "I'm sorry."

"Thanks. But I'm the one who should be apologizing. This is a mess. I would understand if you wanted to—"

"I'm fine, really." Like hell, but if he thought I was so easily gotten rid of, he had another think coming.

Another pause, then, "Well, if you need anything…are you sure you're okay alone? You can stay up here or over at Hank's."

Being alone wasn't something I worried over. But I'd never been alone in a strange place where someone had been murdered and the body disposed of under my nose.

"Seems to me I'm not the one who's alone," I said in a not-intentionally throaty tone. It's how I sound when I'm running on empty.

Silence. Poor guy. He was surely questioning the wisdom of checking on me, maybe even wondering what he'd been thinking when he made the job offer via my cousin. Which, now I thought about it, said as much about him as my accepting the job via Pen did about me.

"Beg pardon?"

Ah, the pull back to business-like. As it should be. At least one of us was operating on full. "I have the horses," I said, "And Noire. And—"

"Good point."

I wanted him to see Henrietta's kittens, but in truth, that could wait until morning. I let the silence stretch, then said, "Maybe you should come down here."

Ten minutes later, he knocked on my door. I'd dozed off, and stumbled down the stairs to answer in bare feet and pajamas—baggy flannel pants, loose tank-top, and no underwear—before I realized what I must look like. My hair straight out of the shower—especially if I lie down while it's wet—not pretty.

I pushed it away from my face and fumbled with the lock before swinging open the door to the tack room. He stood leaning against the frame with one hand. In the other, he grasped that tempting bottle of scotch he'd offered the day I arrived. He wore dressy khakis and a blue, button-down shirt with the top button undone, like he'd just taken off his tie. On his feet were leather barn clogs. I doubted he'd worn those on the plane, but otherwise, it looked like he'd just gotten home and hadn't changed. Maybe *he* didn't like to be alone.

"You've tidied up a bit," he said.

I wasn't awake yet and glanced down at my disheveled self before realizing he meant the barn. "Not as much as I wanted to," I said when I returned my gaze to his face.

He looked tired. His clothes were rumpled, and his hair mussed, like he'd been running his hands through it. I remembered how the sun had shot sparks out of it the first time I saw him. That made me picture him in his kilt. And I realized right then I should never have invited him. If he turned out to be a nice guy, I was in deep shit.

"Come in," I said. "There's something I want you to see."

He followed me up the stairs, and I had the sense he was eye-level with my ass, and he knew I didn't have underwear on. Men are like that. Even when you're wearing something baggy, they just know. Made me wonder if he wore nothing under his kilt, like a true Scotsman.

Noire slid off the bed and trotted up to him, wagging her whole body hello. I considered the difference between this and how she'd reacted to JJ and vowed to try and see her side of things in the future.

Malcolm squatted and ruffled her ears. She licked his chin, then my hand, and went back to bed. Smug little bitch. Of course, she couldn't know he was married.

"You said you had something you wanted me to see?"

"Yeah," I said, "in here."

He followed me toward the bedroom, then hesitated. I stopped halfway across the room. Technically, the place was his and he could go anywhere he wanted. But this was my bedroom for the time being, and that meant a barrier he evidently intended to respect, even if it hadn't crossed my mind.

"It's okay," I said. "They're in the closet."

That sent such a confusion of emotions flying across his face, I did laugh. I thought my eyebrows were expressive. Nothing like stress and fatigue for making it hard to conceal what you're feeling. He edged in, keeping distance between his body and my bed, then peered into the closet where I pointed.

The relieved and amazed smile that creased his face when he saw Henrietta and her kittens gave my stomach a pleasant roll and brought tears too close to the surface. I turned away, but not before noticing the return of his confusion.

"Who is that?" he asked.

I grabbed a few pieces of laundry off the floor to hide my mix of feelings. Really, what had I been thinking when I suggested he come down here? I was much too raw. I sat on the edge of my bed with my clothes wadded in my lap and pressed my fists into my eyes. "That's your Henry," I said. "I've been calling her Henrietta."

Malcolm eased himself cross-legged to the floor, the muscles of his thighs showing through the fabric of his pants. "You knew?"

"The moment I met her."

He chuckled, like he had on the phone, and tapped his forehead with the palm of one hand. "You must think I'm an idiot."

I didn't think he was an idiot, and he wasn't a prick, either. "No, I don't think that." This came out a whisper. I turned and threw my dirty clothes in the corner, but I wasn't fast enough.

"Hey, you all right?" He stood. "Come here." He took my elbow and tugged me to the living room, sat me on the couch, put the scotch on the coffee table. "Want a drink?"

It caught up with me, and his being there and being kind, just made it worse. It was my whole life—and how stupid I'd been the night before with JJ, and everything that had happened today, and Wastrel and…the list went on. I shook my head.

He tilted his to one side. "Can't, or won't?"

"Shouldn't."

He nodded, went to the kitchen, got himself a tumbler and me a glass of water. I took a few sips while he sat in the easy chair, poured a couple of fingers of scotch into the glass, swirled and sniffed it, set it down, looked at me.

I wouldn't cry in front of him. I wouldn't. I wanted him to leave, and to stay, and that was perfectly in keeping with how confused I'd been all day starting with that stupid dream. I couldn't ask him to go because I was afraid if I tried to speak, tears would come and not stop. Why his presence was so soothing, I don't know. Jesus.

"Mind if I look at the kittens again?" he asked.

"Course not," I managed to say.

When I awoke in my bed, I had one of those moments of true blissful ignorance. I didn't know where I was, or what day it might be. The bed was familiar, but not. Without opening my eyes, I knew that if I was supposed to have fed horses, it was late. Too much light bathed the room. I imagined the hiss and smell of bacon cooking and other puttering sounds coming from the kitchen. Ah, the weekend at Aunt Trudy and Uncle Vic's house.

All this fluttered in the place between sleep and wakefulness in a heart-beat. In the next, I sank into the dream I'd been having of galloping Wastrel through endless green fields. Then, my feet hit the floor, and I headed for the bathroom, knowing exactly where I was and what I was supposed to be doing. Shit, what happened to my alarm?

Just beyond the opening to my kitchen, I stopped. Out of the corner of my eye, I'd seen a man standing over the stove where a pan of bacon sizzled. I forced air into my lungs, hoping that would pump enough blood to my brain for me to think straight.

Getting my privacy invaded was my all-time least favorite thing. I'd had precious little of it because I rarely lived alone. I guarded what I had, and in only three days at Winterlight, had become possessive about my solitude, such as it was.

If Malcolm thought he could waltz in here any time…I was pretty sure it was he. Who else could it be? I swiveled on one heel and squinted toward my bed. The last thing I remembered was sitting on the couch.

Noire strolled out of the kitchen, licking her lips. That eliminated JJ—unless she'd eaten him. Not that I thought he would break in. Had I even locked the door last night? Of course not, because I'd expected Malcolm to leave. Had he left?

Dex was a possibility. He was presumptuous enough, and I wouldn't be surprised if he had his own key. I tiptoed to the kitchen door, hands on hips.

Malcolm stood turned slightly away, pouring coffee into a cup. He had his nerve. Surely, in this circumstance, smarting off to the boss could be expected? I took another deep breath. Since I couldn't smart off, I'd no idea what to say.

"Don't you think I can get my own breakfast?" is what came out.

He jumped and poured hot coffee on his hand.

"God damn it," he said.

"Oh, shit." I grabbed his arm and shoved it under the tap, turning on the cold water at the same time. "I'm sorry." Served him right. "I didn't mean to startle you."

"What are you doing sneaking up on me like that?"

"What am *I* doing? What are *you* doing in here?"

My fingers didn't reach all the way around his wrist, but I could feel the bones, and his blood pumping under my thumb. Against my palm, the fine hairs on the back of his arm felt rough. He flexed his fingers, moving tendons and ligaments, and I released him, stepped away. I never, ever should have touched him. Shit.

The night before flooded back, and my face went hot. I must have been as red as his hand. He'd sat with me, that was all. He'd touched my elbow to lead me into the living room. At some point, though, he'd lifted me off the couch and put me in bed. I was asleep, but my body remembered the strength of his arms, the hardness of his chest under my cheek, the few steps he held me against him, how he'd gently lowered me to my mattress, covered me. His fingertips had stroked a few stray hairs off my face.

"Excuse me," I said. I retreated to the bathroom, heart pounding. There, I filled the sink with cold water and submerged my face for as long as I could. Drowning held a certain appeal, but I'd lived through worse than this. I pulled on the jeans and shirt I'd worn the day before, hauled a brush through my hair, and ran wet fingers through it. Today had low humidity. My brown locks flowed past my shoulders in smooth waves, as if I'd done something to make them look good.

I returned to the kitchen where Malcolm had cleaned the coffee from the counter and floor, and put the bacon on paper towels. "Okay," I said. "Where were we? Oh yes, you were going to explain what the hell you are doing in my apartment at…" I glared at the clock on the microwave. Holy cow. It was past nine.

Malcolm stirred the scrambled eggs. "How do you like your coffee?"

He leaned against the counter, too relaxed. He filled all available space and sucked the oxygen out of the room too, or so it felt to my lungs. He must have gone home, because he wore jeans and a navy, long-sleeved polo shirt, the sleeves pushed up to his elbows. His feet were bare. The clogs were at the top of my stairs. If he was pissed I'd overslept, I couldn't tell.

"What?" I asked.

His gaze slid down to my feet. So, we were both barefoot, what of it? What of it was an intimacy that didn't belong. When his eyes returned to my face, he smiled a little, enjoying my uncertainty, the bastard.

"You drink coffee, right?"

I pursed my lips, unsure of how to approach this situation. I had a right to be mad he'd let himself in. I invited him the night before, but that wasn't a carte blanche, why-don't-you-come-up-and-see-me-any-time kind of invite.

I noticed fresh flowers on my kitchen table, and it hit me that the horses weren't whinnying for their breakfast. I pressed my fingers to my temples. The coffee smelled good. "Yes," I answered. "With cream. But…" my eyes strayed to the stairs.

"I've already fed them," he said.

Oh great. Again, my plan to get the skinny ones fat and the fat ones slim had been thwarted. Wait, how had I slept through that? It was a noisy activity, what with the horses banging their hooves on stall doors, and buckets of feed knocking into each other, and the metal scoop clanging. And, why were there flowers on the table?

"I found your feeding schedule." He opened the fridge, pulled out the cream, poured some in a cup. "Good idea about separating them. Wish I'd thought of it."

The night before I'd written feeding instructions on a white board in the tack room.

He caught me staring at the flowers, handed me the coffee. "Happy Birthday, Miss Parker."

CHAPTER ELEVEN

I JERKED my head around to look at what I called The Thing—an amalgamation of calendar, almanac, horoscope, and housekeeping hints. It included livestock gestation tables, weight and measurement conversions, and instructions on how to plant by the phases of the moon. It had been hanging on the wall when I arrived and was so fascinating, I didn't replace it. In any case, I hadn't turned it from April to May, what with all the excitement the day before. I took it down, flipped the page, and tacked it back in place. Sure enough, it was May first, and I'd forgotten my own birthday.

Malcolm used this lull to load two plates with bacon and eggs and put them on the small table. The only way he knew it was my birthday was if Penny told him. And the only reason she would tell him that was if she told him everything. Crapola. To think I'd been feeling sorry for her, even taken her off my "I hate your guts" list.

I sat at the table and considered giving Malcolm an earful of what I thought of his breaking and breakfast making. But the food smelled terrific, even if it wasn't my usual fare. I decided to give him the benefit of the doubt. After all, he'd brought a posy, and as much as I disliked having my privacy invaded, I rarely received flowers.

They were small and delicate and fresh. Purple, white, and blue, with tiny bugs crawling on the stems.

"Where'd you get the flowers?"

Malcolm swallowed a bite of his eggs. "In the woods."

"You went down to the woods this morning and picked flowers?"

"Figured you could use cheering up." He gently flicked the deep blue blossoms. "Bluebells. Dutchman's Breeches." He pointed to several rows of a white flower that did look like poofy little breeches. "Violets, and wild hyacinth."

"Okay, okay. I'm impressed." He could identify birds and flowers. "So, do you often let yourself into your employee's living quarters and cook breakfast?"

"First time offender, your honor." He put one hand over his heart. "I throw myself on the mercy of the court."

He had an engaging grin, and I liked sitting at the table with him. I bit off a piece of bacon, narrowed my eyes. "Perhaps a short parole would be best, with time off for good behavior…if there is any."

He hung his head and pretended to look repentant. "I accept your decision."

I chewed and stared out the window for a while. The bacon was thick-sliced and peppered, greasy and good.

"Do you have any ideas about what happened to Norman, or why?" I asked.

The grin faded. I realized this whole breaking and breakfast making birthday surprise was as much a distraction for him as it was for me, and I regretted spoiling the mood by bringing up *the situation*.

He shook his head. "I didn't know Norman very well. I hired him as a favor to Sandy. Dex One was against it, said he had a history of drug abuse. But Sandy promised he was clean. And there weren't any problems."

"Until yesterday."

"Right. Until yesterday. I don't know what he was into, but I guess he got in over his head."

Yeah, in shit. "But whatever it was, who would want to put him in your manure pile?"

"I was up all night wondering the same thing. But I intend to find out. Whoever did this will pay."

It was hard to tell what he was more enraged about—Norman's death or the fact that whoever did it put him in his manure pile—but I think that last statement came out way stronger than he intended. He ran his hand over his unshaven cheek. He didn't seem to bother with shaving when he wasn't working.

"Look," he said, "let's avoid that subject for now. I propose we take the day off. Get out of here for a while."

"You haven't been here."

"Another good point."

"I'm not trying to make points."

He stabbed at his eggs. "Look—"

"How did you know it was my birthday?"

He took a moment to stare out the window. The view was mostly of the north roof of the barn.

"Your cousin," he said. "Tell you what. Why don't you get ready to go while I finish up with the horses. Meet me out front in ten minutes. We can talk in the car." He rose and took his dishes to the sink, rinsed them off. Considerate.

I followed with my plate and cup. "Where are we going?" It might make a difference in what I wore, I told myself.

He left the kitchen, and I could hear him stepping into his clogs. "You're new here," he called back to me. "You decide. Zoo, art museum, brewery, the Arch…"

I kept the water running while I dumped the rest of the coffee. I shouldn't spend the day with him, should I? I raised my voice to be heard over the water. "I can't go with you. You're the boss, and…what about your wife?"

During the silence that followed, I shut off the tap and dried my hands, then poked my head around the corner. He stood at the top of the stairs with his back to me. In a rare moment of self-restraint, I kept my mouth shut and waited.

After what felt like five minutes during which I was glad to have the dish-towel to twist, he said, "My soon-to-be ex-wife doesn't give a rat's ass what I do with my time."

In his voice, I heard old resentment and hurt, disappointment and relief.

"We sign the papers next week," he continued, and faced me. "I can't do anything about being boss, but I'd like you to consider a working partner-ship." He headed down the stairs. "Ten minutes," he said as he reached the bottom.

Ten minutes later I shut the door of a 1972 British racing green Jaguar XJ6 and strapped myself in. I'd seen a few when I'd been at school in England, and some still cruised Long Island, too, mostly on the East End. While I consider cars merely a means of getting from point A to point B, I had to admit to a long-held yearning to ride in one of these. I stroked the walnut dash.

"Glad you like it," he said.

We sat there a moment, and I remembered the rest of my dream with Wastrel. We'd been galloping, bareback, no bridle, like you see sometimes in the movies. But there were other horses as well, loose and running and scared.

Some of them looked vaguely familiar. I'd wondered about my first dream—Wastrel pawing the manure pile, then us finding Norman. No connection, I'm sure. Malcolm put the car in gear.

"Wait," I said. I got out and checked the latches on all the gates, then did a quick run-through of the barn to make sure all was secure.

"Don't trust me?" he asked when I'd clicked my seatbelt again.

"It's not that," I said.

He accepted this without comment and drove out, took it easy for the twisty hilly miles, and let the engine stretch when we reached the highway.

"So," I said, "exactly what do you mean by partnership? As I see it, you own everything, and I do all the work."

"You have a p—"

"Don't say it."

"Okay. Ever heard of sweat equity?"

I got a funny feeling in the pit of my stomach. Coming on the heels of *the situation*, I was afraid to think anything. But that feeling, it was the thrill of hope. I quashed it before it became expectation. "Are you offering something?" I watched him with my peripheral vision. He kept his eyes on the road and didn't answer for a few breaths.

Finally, he said, "Maybe. A year is a long time."

"I'll be happy to get out of here alive with my letter of recommendation."

Self-restraint remained an elusive virtue for me. Sometimes, I thought I should wear a shirt that said, "Help me, I'm talking, and I can't shut up."

Malcolm, on the other hand, said nothing. For miles. That gave me time to consider the implications of his maybe offer, and of his impending divorce.

My thoughts ran in circles, though, raising dust and little else. Without more information, I couldn't weigh the pros and cons of a partnership. As for his divorce, that complicated matters. Sitting so close to him set my skin tingling, like an itch I couldn't scratch.

After about half an hour of letting me stew, Malcolm piped up. "Given that Penny explained what you are doing here, it's only fair you know I have a one-year deadline, too."

"I'm sorry about what I said before."

"Okay," he said, and he gave my wrist a reassuring touch.

I fought the urge to yank my hand away and rub it, like I'd been scorched. He released me. He felt it too? What were we doing shut in this car for over an hour, anyway? How had things gotten so out of control? Oh, yeah. Norman. The little twerp. He'd ruined everything.

We decided on the art museum. By the time we arrived, I knew Malcolm's father wanted to sell the land to developers. He'd given his son a year to prove the farm could make money. Otherwise, he was cashing in. Now, I understood the comment Malcolm had made about keeping the land to himself. He wanted to preserve it, not have hundreds of houses built on it. That was a sentiment I understood. Much of Long Island's farmland had long ago been bulldozed into suburban sprawl and strip malls, and it wasn't pretty.

Renting horses to the public brought in much-needed income. But it wasn't in Malcolm's long-term plan. He had many ideas. Many of these ideas relied on my abilities, or those of someone like me. Short-term, boarding and riding lessons seemed the best option. To me, the fewer lessons, the better. But liability was high renting horses for people to tootle around the trails, too.

He tossed out the possibilities of a boarding-bed-and-breakfast, a retirement farm, a rehab facility, and even holding equine spirituality seminars. For the time being, he'd consider anything that would pay the bills, and he was open to suggestions.

We walked in silence after passing through the high-ceilinged, marbled entrance hall of the museum. We went through three galleries before he said anything.

"You're quiet," he said.

"You're supposed to be quiet in here," I whispered. "It's like a library."

"In that case, think they'd mind if we checked out one of the collection? This one would look good over my fireplace."

He indicated a pastoral landscape I thought would do better in the fireplace.

"They would frown on that most severely. Remember your parole status. You don't want to jeopardize that further."

"Further?"

"Shush."

He steered me to the restaurant.

"Enough whispering," he said when we were seated.

I glanced at the menu. Malcolm's breakfast had left me full. Especially since I hadn't ridden or done anything to work it off. I ordered salad and snuck a peek in my wallet. Empty.

"I'm buying," he said.

Did he have x-ray vision or something? He did have that square Superman kind of jaw. "No," I said.

He sighed. "It's your birthday, remember? My treat."

"Okay," I said. "Just this once."

He smiled.

I was doomed.

After the waitress took our order, he asked, "Why don't you teach riding? With your experience and training—"

"I thought Penny told you everything?"

"I don't know what you mean by *everything*. She said you needed a year's contract, and that was fine with me. Although, I hope it will turn out to be longer."

"It's a little soon—"

"I mean I hope the farm is doing well enough to offer more, if you want it. That's what I meant."

He'd fallen over himself pretty quickly to make that explanation. Which meant it wasn't what he meant. Maybe. Oh, hell, I didn't even know what I meant. But I was glad to learn Penny hadn't revealed all my secrets.

"I prefer not to teach," I said. "I'm not very good at it."

I must have had a neon sign on my forehead flashing "big fat lie." I hate lying, really I do. But I didn't want to talk about this. It hurt too much.

"Have you tried?"

"Yes. It didn't work out."

"I see."

He saw. Yeah, right. I felt myself squirm inwardly. But *at the length truth will out*. Shakespeare knew. I took one more stab at putting him off. "You wouldn't understand."

"Try me."

He wanted to know about me. Had a right to, I supposed. Fair enough. And he *would* understand. I could see it in his eyes. There was softness there, a safe place to land.

"Someone got hurt. A girl. Heidi. She was getting ready for a lesson. The others were already in the ring with me. They were taunting her, the others. They were mean. Heidi was always running late." I reached back, smelled the barn and the soft, slightly damp footing of the indoor arena. Saw Heidi's ready smile. "She hurried her pony in and didn't double check the girth. Another rider...I had my back turned for just a moment."

"The world can change in a moment," he said.

I nodded. He did understand, but I hadn't shared this with anyone who didn't already know about it before.

"This other rider, she smacked Heidi's pony on the back with her riding crop just as Heidi put her foot in the stirrup."

I drifted away, my gaze on nothing in particular, the saltshaker, maybe. But the hot sting of tears brought me up short. I wiped at them and looked at him. No judgment, only compassion. It was okay to tell him.

"He jumped forward," Malcolm said softly. "Her pony. And the saddle slipped."

I nodded. "She fell…and got all tangled…and dragged…and her pony. He panicked. I stopped him as soon as I could." I looked around the restaurant. It was a weekday. Slow. Only an older couple near the window. "I'm sorry," I said.

"I'm sorry I asked about it. But it wasn't your fault."

"She died." I said. "She had on a helmet, so her head was okay, but there were internal injuries. Liver, spleen, lungs, everything got all mangled."

I found myself twisting the cloth napkin like I had the dish towel earlier.

"I knew those other girls were out to get her. Well, they did." I stood. "Excuse me."

I went to the bathroom and sat on a toilet and dabbed at tears, trying to keep from getting mascara all over my face. I'd managed to not think about Heidi for some time. The memory had been on the periphery since the day before, though, and I'd kept it out there.

Until now.

Damn Malcolm.

He touched my hand when I returned to the table. My salad had been delivered.

"You okay?"

I shrugged. "She was nine years old. Heidi. She was one of the good ones."

"It wasn't your fault, Vi. Sometimes, bad things just happen."

"That's what her parents said, too. But I'll never forgive myself. And I won't teach, especially kids. Okay?"

I picked at the greens on my plate. They tasted like cardboard.

"Tell me about your time at the British Horse Society school," he said a little while later.

Jesus. What was this? Twenty questions in twenty minutes?

"It was great. I learned a lot."

"Did you go there straight out of high school?"

"No. I tried college for a couple of years, first."

"Then we were over there at about the same time."

"You went to school in England?"

"University of Edinburgh. Freshman year abroad program."

So that was what Hank was talking about when he mentioned Malcolm being at school in Scotland. Good. Now the subject was him instead of me.

"Malcolm's a Scottish name, right?"

"Yes. My father is Scottish through and through."

"And your mother?"

"She was more enigmatic about her ancestry. But her maiden name was Pinozzi."

"Ah, now that's some blood I can relate to. Is she—?"

"Died of cancer a few years ago."

"I'm sorry."

"She was enigmatic in general, kept her distance emotionally. I miss her, but we were never close."

And I thought my parents were bad. "So, what did you study your freshman year abroad at the University of Edinburgh?"

"Computer systems. Finished my undergrad at Mizzou, then got a masters from Wash U in St. Louis."

Sounded expensive. I hadn't been able to finish a bachelor's.

"I'm still paying off my student loans." He took a bite of his turkey club and chewed, looking thoughtful. "I took a year off in between. I wanted to work for a while. Went back to Scotland for part of the time."

There was more to it than wanting to work for a while, I could tell. "Between schools? Why?" If I kept him talking about himself, we wouldn't return to the subject of me.

"Something happened in my senior year...I needed time to think."

I gave him a look that said, I spilled my guts, now it's your turn.

"Someone I knew, a friend, was killed. Mugged. Murdered for her purse, which contained little more than twenty dollars. Right outside her dorm. Shortly after I dropped her off."

Yikes. "Girlfriend?"

He hitched his shoulders up. "Friend. Girl—woman—I cared about her. They never found him, the bastard."

We sat in silence for some moments, and I'm guessing his food suddenly tasted like cardboard, too, because he pushed his plate away. Where's the whipped cream when you need it?

"We'd gone to the movies. A Bergman retrospective. Depressing. Usually, we found a place for coffee afterwards, but she had a test to study for, so I took her home."

I longed for the courage to touch his hand like he had mine. But I just sat there, watching his face, watching him replay what he knew of it—or imagined—behind his eyes.

"If we'd gone for coffee..."

He didn't cry, of course, but he looked like he wanted to.

"Makes you feel helpless, doesn't it?" I said. "Sucks."

He met my eyes. "Sucks doesn't begin to cover it." He straightened his cutlery. "How did we get on this subject?"

"Taking turns baring our souls?"

He let out a huff of air. "Yeah. I think it's my fault."

I did touch his wrist then. With just one finger. "I'm kind of glad you brought it up. I feel better, now. You should try crying. It helps, really."

He exhaled again and much of the tension went out of him. "Believe me, I have. Plenty. Knowing someone who understands helps, though."

He smiled at me, a full-on, genuine, unguarded smile, the kind one rarely sees, and I felt that scared-thrilled-fluttery feeling like I'd gone over a cliff edge.

His cell phone rang. He answered, then mouthed "Hank" to me. I watched his face go from relaxed to tense.

"What? Slow down." He listened for a minute. "We'll be there as soon as we can." He disconnected, dug out his wallet and threw money on the table. "We have to go," he said, and grabbed my arm, dragging me from my seat.

I'd been on edge since my dream, and now a sense of inevitability settled over me. Outside the restaurant, he took off at a run to the nearest exit. I raced after him.

"What happened?"

"The horses are out," he sailed over his shoulder.

I didn't ask the obvious question—all of them? If only some of them were out, he'd have said so. From the conversation we'd just had, I'd learned he spoke with an economy of words. If he said the horses were out, he meant all of them.

We reached his car, and he had it started and in reverse before I'd gotten my door shut. That many loose horses in open country, I thought, anything could happen. I held tight while he alternately whipped around turns and slammed the brakes until we were on the highway. By then, I'd learned a couple of colorful new combinations of swear words.

"Hank's got some of them rounded up. Renee's the only other person there. Captain and several others are still missing."

I had a feeling there was more. "What else?"

"Gaston was last seen heading toward the highway. That horse hasn't got a lick o' sense."

The highway was miles from the farm, but a horse without sense could get himself in trouble anywhere.

"Hank couldn't go after them all." He tossed his cell phone in my lap. "Both Dex's are programmed in. Call Sandy, too. We're going to need veterinary help."

I swallowed hard against what he wasn't telling me and concentrated on the phone. Sandy said she'd go right away. I called Dex Hamill next. He said he was on his way and offered to call Dex Two.

We were out of the worst of the traffic and zooming past the rest. But it was a long drive from the city to the farm.

"And?" I asked.

He glanced at me, my own worry mirrored in his eyes, and sympathy too. My heart jumped to my throat. He returned his gaze to the road.

"Cali's hurt."

CHAPTER TWELVE

MALCOLM REACHED for the radio knob. "Music? I had a CD player installed. You can see what's in there." He pointed at the glove box.

"Will it help?"

"I doubt it."

We didn't put music on. He didn't try to reassure me. No sense in saying everything would be okay if you didn't actually know. I hated false sentiment. He didn't try to distract me with inane conversation, either, which I also appreciated. He focused on getting us back quickly and safely. I tried to keep my hands in my lap and not make fists, but found myself staring out the window and gnawing my knuckles.

When we turned off the highway, I noticed him glancing out his side window. I began to do the same, keeping my eyes peeled for a glimpse of copper coat.

About a mile from Winterlight, I said, "Stop," then braced against the dash when he slammed on the brakes. I gave him a look, then said, "Back up to that dirt road."

Malcolm shifted into reverse and slung his arm behind my head, grazing my hair. Our eyes met for a just a moment before he concentrated on the road and skidded to a halt at the opening to a field. He craned his neck to see past me.

"Could be Gaston," I said. "Beyond those bushes."

We got out and didn't shut the doors. He found a couple of bungee cords in the trunk. The sound of a horse munching grass greeted us, and Gaston lifted his head when he heard us approach.

"I'll be damned," Malcolm said. He squeezed my shoulder. "I'll take it from here. You get back to the farm."

Gaston had found a patch of alfalfa. Purple flowers wobbled on the ends of the stems sticking out either side of his mouth. Sunlight turned his back golden, and a casual observer might think he looked content, but everything in his stance said he'd be gone in a second if we made a wrong move.

"You think he'll let you lead him home with a bungee cord?"

"It's all I've got. It'll have to do."

I was not convinced. My connection with a horse usually lasted only until I dismounted, but a bit of mental persuasion might be worth a try anyway. Malcolm walked forward, and Gaston stopped chewing, his ears coming fully alert. I put my hand on Malcolm's arm. "Wait."

With my eyes closed, I pictured Gaston staying still as Malcolm walked up to him and put a bungee cord…no, that was not going to work. "Take off your belt," I said.

"Excuse me?"

"Your belt'll work better. Put it around his neck, behind his ears like a halter. I'll tell you what to do next."

Malcolm looked as frustrated as I felt, but he unbuckled his belt and slid it off.

"And don't act all mad. That will just make him bolt."

He tried to smile, but his body language said something different. The moment he stepped toward his horse, Gaston moved back and swished his tail.

"Damn it," Malcolm whispered.

"Can I try?" We didn't have time to chase this horse all over the countryside. He handed me the belt and bungee cords. I stuffed the cords in the back of my pants, held the belt behind me, and walked toward Gaston, hand out like I had a treat.

"Come 'ere. Good boy. Had a fun day? Found something yummy?"

Gaston swished his tail again, but didn't move. He couldn't reach the alfalfa anymore, so I grabbed a handful and held it toward him. "Come on." He craned his neck to reach for my hand. I made it to his shoulder. While he snuffled up the grass, I looped Malcolm's belt around his neck. I put one bungee cord around his face like a noseband, hooked the other to the belt under his jaw, and ran it through the loop around his nose forming a makeshift lead line.

Malcolm came up and I put it in his hand. "Good luck."

I didn't give him time to respond, just raced to the car, shut the trunk and doors, and took off.

The farm looked too peaceful when I pulled up. I recognized Sandy's white compact and Renee's blue Beetle. Next to that were Hank's four-by-four and a red SUV I hadn't seen before. Horses were in the pasture, but Mike the pony was either still at large or in the barn. Fawn was missing too, but I didn't take a complete inventory.

Smitty stood toward the back of the first stall on the right with a bandage covering one front leg. Cheyenne was next, but I couldn't see any injuries. I kept moving to the stall I knew Cali would be in. Noire hadn't greeted me, and I figured Sandy must be out on Fawn, looking for stragglers, and my dog had gone, unable to resist a chance to run through the woods.

That's when I noticed the smell. Like someone'd been smoking pot. Near the tack room, Renee walked in a small circle, waving what was either a very fat cigar, or the biggest joint in the history of the world. Sounded like she'd been smoking dope, too—she was chanting.

"What the—" I started.

She held up one hand to stop me, and continued her chant.

"Sacred sage, drive out the negativity, take away the dark energy."

Even though I was still tired from the day before, my morning had been nice—until the phone call. Now the tension that had built since then collided with my fatigue.

"Oh, for cripe's sake, Renee. Can't you find anything better to do than this?"

I didn't know what she was doing, but if she wasn't tending to or looking for a horse, then it didn't need to be done.

She wafted the smoke toward me. "I am cleansing this place, inviting balance to return. Your aura has dark patches. You need to be cleansed."

I've never tried pot myself, but right then, the mellow mood it was supposed to bring sounded appealing. Especially since I was out of whipped cream. I waved the smoke out of my face. "What needs cleansing are these horse's injuries." I gestured down the aisle.

"Don't stink the place up with this crap."

She lifted her chin, but otherwise ignored me, and went out the back door, still chanting. I didn't dare wonder if my day could get any worse because that just seemed to be a given. Instead, I turned to Cali's stall.

Her ears drooped to either side, a sure sign she'd been drugged. Sandy'd left a note on her door confirming what I thought—she was out looking for Mike, and Noire had gone with her. Dex Two had ridden out on Little Miss Bong in the opposite direction. Hank and Dex One were looking for Gaston.

Cali needed stitches for a gash across her chest and might have a torn ligament in her right front leg. A puncture wound near her left knee had been flushed, but probably needed more work, the note said. The vet would be there later. The plastic bucket outside the stall held a vial of painkiller, and Sandy'd already administered ten CCs.

I sent out a mental thanks to Sandy, ran upstairs to swap my skirt for a pair of jeans, and went into Cali's stall. She barely responded. She always had been a cheap date, easily subdued by the minimum dose. I stroked her neck and inspected the eight-inch flap of skin hanging from her chest. It looked nasty, but would heal and not affect her soundness. The leg injuries concerned me. Puncture wounds to joints were especially dangerous, and torn ligaments could become a lifelong issue if the recovery was rushed. I wouldn't be riding her soon.

I stood back and looked over the rest of her, then slowly rubbed the flat of my hands over every inch, starting behind her ears, working my way to her tail, picking up her hind feet, then returned to her face. She had a few other nicks and cuts.

"Poor baby," I whispered to her. "I'm so sorry. We never should have come here."

Her lower lip hung loose, and her eyelids were as droopy as her ears. She had no idea what I was saying. I pressed my cheek to hers.

We'd been together less than a year. Her lackluster racing career had ended after several starts where she finished dead last. Unfortunately, her bloodline wasn't good enough for breeding, and I'd been lucky to hear about her before they sold her to the killers. She was pretty and had good conformation. What she lacked in speed she made up in an aptitude for jumping.

My own lackluster career had forced me to move her several times, and I'd always managed to keep her safe, until now. *Stupid*, I thought. Moving all the way out here for the money. That was always the wrong reason.

Several deep breaths later, I had myself under control. I knelt beside Cali's leg. The loose bandage around her knee came away easily, and I tossed the blood-soaked gauze pads out in the aisle. Blood in this case was good, flushing the wound of anything left behind by whatever punched the hole— probably a nail from the fence around the riding ring. I left for a moment to look outside. Sure enough, splintered rails and a smashed post marked the place where she broke out. Did something spook her? The loose horses? Impossible to know. It seemed unlikely the whole herd would escape the same day Cali broke through a fence—an extreme and uncharacteristic act of fear.

I heard the sound of my dog, and a second later, she bounded up to me, wet from the creek, tail wagging her whole body. She cleaned my face with her tongue as long as I let her, then she made a brief stop in Cali's stall, sniffing her knee and the used bandages, then went and took a long drink from her water bowl.

Sandy appeared in the back doorway a moment later, slid off Fawn's back, and led her into the barn. She didn't have Mike.

"No luck?" I asked.

"No, but he's a pony. They're tough, right? Dex Two'll find him. How's Cali?"

"Thanks for doing the initial patch up. I really appreciate it. Is Renee still out there doing whatever it is she's doing? What the hell is she doing, anyway?"

"She's just smudgin' the place. Some kinda ancient Indian ritual or some-thin'. Supposed to clear out our dark thoughts. Hell, I don't know. But I think she's harmless."

"Maybe, but I'd rather she help with the injuries."

"Now that's where you're wrong. She can't stand the sight of blood, gets to shaking if one of the horses gets so much as a stone bruise. Nope, she's pretty much useless thataway. What she's doin' is the best she can do."

Hunh. "Anyone missing or hurt besides Smitty and Cheyenne?"

"Mikey and Gaston are the last ones we need to find. Cheyenne near tore off a shoe and a good part of his hoof. I haven't done nothin' with that yet. Cali's knee should be hosed, and Smitty's leg, but I wanted to see if I could find Mikey. Nicky'll be awful upset if anything happens to her pony-oney."

Sandy took Fawn to the pasture.

"We found Gaston," I said when she came in. "Malcolm's leading him back. He's not hurt."

"Gaston or the Laird? I'm thinkin' Malcolm's gonna be pissed at all this. There's a few other bumps and bruises, nothing major. But I think the fence got cut. Hank and Malcolm keep that fence in tip-top shape"

I got a prickly feeling on the back of my neck. And it wasn't because I had dark patches in my aura, whatever the hell that meant.

"You think someone did this on purpose?"

CHAPTER THIRTEEN

COMING on the heels of Norman's murder, the horses getting loose was a weird coincidence. Bad weird. Knowing there was someone out there who would do this—who could let loose this many horses knowing some of them would get hurt? Then again, it wasn't much of a stretch after murder. I forced my thoughts to the present, haltered Cali, and led her into the aisle.

I adjusted the water pressure to little more than a trickle and stood with one arm lightly draping her shoulder, my forehead against her neck. I didn't think, just kept water running over her leg, hoping to get ahead of the swelling. Sandy took Smitty to the hose out front. I wanted to check everyone. We needed more hands.

The sound of flowing water soothed, like a waterfall in a Japanese garden. The act of standing next to a horse with a hose in my hand, something I'd done countless times since I was a kid, brought a sense of normalcy to what had been an exceedingly odd few days. If I closed my eyes, I could be anywhere. Anywhere but Winterlight.

Outside, I heard Sandy greet someone. A moment later, Little Miss Bong came into view. The dark-haired man on her back must be Dex Two. He rode up with Mike the pony on a lead line next to Miss Bong. She had briars stuck in her mane, Mike was soaking wet, and Humphrey J. Dexter the third looked like he'd had it out with a pack of drenched cats.

He swung his right leg over his horse's neck, slid to the ground, and led both animals into stalls. Miss Bong shook herself as he unbuckled the girth.

He scarcely got her bridle off before she lay down to roll. She probably had thorns under the saddle as well.

The top of Dex Two's head barely reached my nose, and I wondered how he got his foot in the stirrup to mount his very tall horse. He wore jeans and half-chaps, muddy paddock boots, a St. Louis University T-shirt, and no hat.

"Sandy informs me you are Miss Parker," he said. "Humphrey J. Dexter the third, Esquire, at your service. I would rather we met at a garden party, where I could be sure not to have blood caked on my cheek and mud in my teeth." He put his tack down and removed his leather riding gloves, one finger at a time. "Be that as it may, I am honored to make your acquaintance."

He took my free hand, bowed over it, and kissed the back of it. I squelched an urge to curtsy and bob my head. Dex Two had thick, black hair cut short, a narrow face, and a stocky build. He carried himself with an air of formality that matched the way he talked. That was no reason for me to feel better, yet I felt my mood lifting.

"You can forgive my disheveled appearance, I hope, under the circumstances?"

"Of course," I said. "Miss Bong's all right?"

"Fit as a fiddle, if a very itchy one. And Mike, the good pony, apparently intended trekking to the Mississippi. He did not look kindly upon my efforts to rescue him from a dense stand of wild blackberry. Once he ascertained I was determined in my commitment to bring him home, he used every trick in that wily little head of his to get away."

If we were having this conversation a week before, in nearly any other place I'd worked, I would have instantly written off Dex Two as a hopeless, condescending snob. But he struck me as entirely sincere and unaffected, despite his style. I liked him as well as I liked Dex One, even if they were completely different from one another.

I teased a short thorn branch out of his black hair. "Including dragging you through the blackberries?"

"Precisely."

"And the creek?"

"Twice."

I stifled a giggle. "How very inconsiderate of him."

"He is a pony," Dex Two said. "Poor manners seem to go hand-in-hand, or should I say, hoof-in-hoof, with poniness."

"That has been my experience."

"To put it quite plainly, he is a little shit." Dex stomped up the steps to the tack room, paused at the door and let his gaze fall to Cali's leg. "But an unhurt little shit."

"What about you?" I asked.

He turned a blazing smile full of perfect teeth toward me. "Catching the little shit was the most fun I have had since the end of the hunting season."

The door closed behind him. Cali shifted her weight from one hind leg to another, lifted her tail and emitted a long fart. I moved the hose up to her chest.

Dex One and Hank came in.

"Saw Mac comin' up the road on that useless beastie of his," Hank said.

"He's riding him?" I asked.

"Ain't neither of 'em got a lick o' sense."

"It is faster to ride than lead a horse," Dex One said. He winked at me.

Dex Two came out of the tack room. He'd washed off his face. "That's everyone accounted for, then," he said.

"I see you've met the other Dex," Dex One said.

"Who is to say you are not *the other*?" Dex Two asked.

"I was here first," Dex One said. "Hence the designation as Numero Uno. Comprende?"

"In point of fact, as I descend from a long and illustrious line of Dexters, I must assert that regardless of your method, I am Numero Uno as you so aptly say."

Dex One shot me a helpless look. "Lawyers," he said to me. "I'm older," he said to Dex Two.

I hoped they weren't going to unzip their flies and whip out their wing-wangs.

"There is that," said Dex Two. "Age before beauty."

"You two idiots shut up and make yourselfs useful," Sandy bellowed from the other end of the barn. "I'm done with Smitty. One of you take over hosin' that mare while Vi helps me with Cheyenne."

Dex One saluted and took the hose from me. Sandy held Cheyenne while I picked up his hoof. He didn't like to be cross-tied. He'd feel the tension in the ropes and rocket all his weight into his hind end until hardware snapped or the rope gave out. I'd met his type many times. Norman had warned me about him the other morning. Jesus. What day was it? That had been Monday. Was it only Wednesday?

The heavy metal shoe had twisted into an S-shape. Probably he'd been galloping and caught his front heel with a hind toe, shearing off much of the flesh and bending the steel all at once. I'd seen it happen before.

"I think a bucket of water to wash this would be best."

Dex Two hovered nearby. "I'll get it," he said.

In the meantime, I slowly worked the shoe loose. It barely hung by one nail, so it wasn't hard.

Malcolm rode up and put Gaston in a stall. He barely acknowledged everyone before walking to the pasture to check the other horses. After three tries, I got Cheyenne's foot settled in the bucket of water, instructed Dex Two to make sure it stayed there, and followed.

Malcolm inspected Fergus first. I watched him lovingly run his hands over every inch of the old horse's skin and pick up each hoof in turn, just as I had with Cali. Then, he caressed the old horse's neck. Fergus was okay.

I did the same with Captain, and we worked our way through the herd silently, meeting in the middle at Barbie, Brooke's mare. A three-inch lump crossed diagonally between her eyes. She'd ran into something solid.

Malcolm brushed Barbie's forelock away from the swelling. "Brooke won't be happy about this."

"I don't think it's serious."

"Doesn't matter." He dropped his hand to his side.

I patted the mare's neck, trying to ignore the welter of emotions rising off of him, dismissing my own. "She's perfectly ridable."

"Brooke doesn't care about riding."

So, why does she have a horse? None of my business.

"Sandy thinks someone might have messed with the fence or something. Said you keep it in tip-top shape. Any reason why someone would want your horses out?"

"No more reason for that than killing Norman and putting him in my manure pile," he said with disgust.

Which meant there might be a connection. "You sure about that?"

"You were concerned about them getting loose this morning."

"I was?" I hadn't said anything to him about it.

"You made me stop so you could come back and double check all the gates."

That dream. Damn Wastrel. "Habit."

He gave me a "yeah, right" look. "I'm going to walk the fence. Want to come?"

I glanced toward the barn.

"Can you do anything until the vet gets here?"

"Guess not," I answered on a sigh. I didn't want to leave Cali, but there really wasn't anything that would help.

"Is there anything I can do for you?" he asked.

"Not unless you have a can of whipped cream in your pocket."

He gave me a curious look, but didn't respond except to shake his head. "Dr. Hurt is in emergency colic surgery on one of Busch's Clydesdales."

He began to walk down the fence line.

"Dr. Hurt? Is that his real name?"

"Yes. Lynette Hurt. And don't tease her. She's heard it all."

The fence marched straight ahead past a row of trees and up a low hill. I couldn't see where it stopped. The thought of following it to the end and beyond drew me forward, as if there might be an answer for me there. An answer to a question I hadn't posed yet, a question I hadn't formed.

Instead, I asked, "Is Dr. Hurt the vet Sandy works for? Is her clinic around here? How do you know about the surgery?" Easy questions with answers that didn't matter.

"No, and no, and I called her while I was riding." He produced his cell phone.

He was maddeningly calm. "You rode your horse down a road bareback, with nothing more than a belt and bungee cords for a bridle, and called your vet at the same time?" I heard the edge in my voice, felt a tightening in my throat, as if the question I needed to ask was trying to escape.

If only I knew what it was.

He gave me a sideways smile as we walked along. Here, there were deep divots gouged out of the soil, like the horses had been running. But the ground was soft from the rain. They could have simply been playing.

"Gaston is a good horse," Malcolm said.

"You said he hasn't got a lick of sense."

"He doesn't. That makes him predictable and easy to get along with."

"Ohhhh. I see. Predictable and easy to get along with—that's what you like, huh? If I remember correctly, you like Fergus because he's full of surprises and keeps you on your toes."

He snorted and the tension in my throat eased.

"Guess I like a little of both."

We shared a smile that reached my toes. "Wouldn't another vet be able to get here sooner?"

"None that I'd want sewing on my horses."

"Gotcha."

We reached the trees. They bordered a different stretch of the same creek we'd ridden to Sunday morning. Back when I thought I would die of boredom and my number-one problem was vultures.

"How big is this pasture?"

"Almost eighty acres. It's over half a mile along this side. We won't walk the whole thing right now. I'll come out in the truck later."

"Is it all fenced like this?"

Some of the posts were a foot across at the base, spaced no more than eight feet apart, and each of the four rails measured two by six. I gripped the top rail and pushed. Very solid.

"It switches to wire at the far end where the fence is in the woods. That's the most likely weak spot. It's on my to-do list to get that section replaced this year." He took my hand off the fence and tugged me along. "Come on."

Something rose up from my belly when he mentioned replacing the fence. Not hysteria, I'm sure. I don't get hysterical.

"Oh, goody. Will that be before or after we bale hay?"

I made a feeble attempt to pull away from him, but he kept a tight hold on me, lacing his fingers with mine. We were under the trees, now, near the creek and out of sight of the barn. The creek burbled, plump from the recent rain. I babbled right along with it, trying to keep whatever it was that was inside of me from getting out.

"Because I can't wait. Can't wait to start building up that sweat equity. I mean, it would be too mundane to just spend a whole day working, wouldn't it? A day when no dead bodies showed up, and the horses are well, and…and we could ride like we did on Sunday—"

He pulled me against him, and I didn't fight him. I gripped his shoulders and beat my forehead against his chest, wadding his shirt in my fists. I wouldn't have thought I had it in me, but this was what I needed, body-wracking sobs. He held me tight, and through my storm of emotion, I felt him take a measure of solace from the contact, too.

"Stop," he said after a while, rubbing my back. "It will be all right. I swear to God. Every day *was* like that—"

"Until I got here? Is that what you were going to say?" I pushed away, too confused to know what was right or what I wanted. But by God, he felt good. The moment I was away from him, I regretted it.

He had the decency to look embarrassed, or maybe he was confused. After all, it was his farm where the body had been found, his fence that had been cut. His horses had been hurt, too. Yet, he was being helpful and kind to me, and I was acting like an idiot.

I turned away and pressed fists against my eyes to stop the tears. Stupid tears. What was I crying for, anyway? Then, I sat on a log, and a moment later, I laughed. Maybe I'd been too quick to dismiss the possibility of hysteria.

"Jesus. Is this the biggest freaking cosmic joke of all time, or what?" I faced him. "Some birthday, huh?"

CHAPTER FOURTEEN

WHEN WE GOT BACK to the barn, Renee, Sandy, and Dex Two were gone. Dex One had kept water on my horse's leg, and Hank stood with Cheyenne. Clara arrived with iced tea, pie, and, God bless her, half a dozen cans of whipped cream—three plain and three chocolate.

"A little birdie told me it was your birthday," she said, presenting me with the bag. "I made a roast for supper, but it looks like you're gonna be tied up here for a spell, so I brought sandwiches."

"You're a life-saver," I said. "Thank you."

I cleaned Cali's stall and put her in it, globbed ointment on Cheyenne's foot, wrapped a bandage around it, and returned him to a clean stall. We all went in the tack room to eat and wait for Dr. Hurt. I ran the whipped cream up to my fridge, taking a big hit off a plain one on the way.

"I heard from Frank," Clara said when I reentered the tack room. "He's my cousin, you know—the county coroner. That there city guy ain't even looked at Norman, yet." She turned to me. "Got some unsweetened tea for you, Vi."

No way to know how she guessed I didn't like sweet tea, but Clara was growing on me. At home, I enjoyed a comfortable anonymity. I could be aloof. Here, that was impossible. Was it what I still wanted? Sure, back home no one knew anything about me, and that made it impossible for them to help. I'd thought I didn't need or want help.

"You mean the St. Louis Medical Examiner?" Malcolm asked.

"He's the one," she said. "Can't believe it."

"It can take days," Dex One said. "But I'm going to make a few calls, see if they can hurry it up."

"T'ain't right," Hank said. "Keepin' the family waitin' like that. Can't plan the funeral or nothin'." He pushed his MFA cap to the back of his head. "T'ain't right."

"His poor mother," Clara said with a shake of her head.

Poor Norman, I thought. I crammed half of a roast-beef sandwich slathered with mayonnaise in my mouth and washed it down with tea.

"Sheriff don't want us movin' nothin' neither," Hank said to me. "Not the manure pile or the spreader."

"Okay," I said. "Guess I'll start a new pile." It's not like I wanted to go near the old one. And if I never emptied the spreader again, that would be soon enough. Yellow police tape still surrounded it all anyway.

Noire barked. Malcolm poked his head out the door and peered down the barn aisle. "Lynette's here."

We filed behind him. The woman coming toward us matched Malcolm in height, was skinny as a number-two pencil, had red hair pulled into an untidy ponytail, and freckles on her tired face.

"Dr. Hurt," Malcolm said, "this is Vi Parker. Can you look at her mare first?"

"Call me Lynette," she said to me. "Nice to meet you." We shook hands. Hers were strong and slightly chapped, like most vets'. "Sorry it took me so long to get here."

I led the way and Malcolm filled her in on what had happened.

Clara said the food was in the tack room and she and Hank would see us later. A second after, Dex One's beeper went off, and he said goodbye, too.

Lynette and I went into Cali's stall.

"Bring her into the aisle where the light's better. I'll get my sewing kit."

Lynette administered local anesthetic, then cleaned and sewed up the chest wound. She glanced at the knee, and said, "We'll need a picture of that."

Malcolm listed everyone else's injuries, and brought in Barbie.

Lynette probed all around the lump. The mare tried tossing her head, but the vet held her still. A sound like popping Bubble Wrap came from the mare's head. "Probably a slight fracture of the sinus," she said. "She might have an indentation after it's healed."

"What was that sound?" I asked.

"Air," Lynette answered. "With a wound like this, air escapes from the sinus cavities and gets under the skin. The air will work its way out as it heals."

That was a new one on me. My days were going to be full with all the boo-boos. Several horses would be stall-bound for a while and need to be hand-walked for exercise rather than turned out with the others.

Lynette lugged in the x-ray machine and began to set it up. I'd done this before with other horses. The vet would take a picture while I held a rectangular "plate" that contained the film. We'd all hold our breath hoping the horse didn't move. They could be uncooperative, and I was unsure what my mare's response would be. The drugs were wearing off, and she didn't want to put any weight on the bad leg.

Cali shifted the moment the vet approached. Horses always knew, it seemed. Lynette spoke in soothing tones and stroked her shoulder. I stood at her head, talking, trying to distract her. Malcolm positioned himself near the opposite hip, but I noticed him hesitate before putting a hand on her. My gaze dropped to his shin, covered by the same slacks he'd worn to the museum. The last time he'd touched this horse, she'd nailed him, so I could understand his reticence.

"Why don't you take the front end?" I suggested.

He smiled his most engaging smile, and we switched places. He gave my hand a reassuring squeeze as we passed each other. I jumped. Cali jumped and banged into the machine which tipped onto Lynette's toe.

"God damn it," she said.

"Oh, shit," I said at that same time. "Sorry."

"My fault," Malcolm said.

He stooped to right the machine, and I returned to Cali's head.

"What were you two doing over there, dancing?"

Malcolm caught my eye. "You could say that."

I couldn't help smiling. "Yeah, but he doesn't like it when I lead."

Lynette snorted. "I have that problem with men all the time." After a moment of fiddling with the dials, she said, "Okay, who's going to hold the plate?"

"I will," Malcolm said.

Maybe he moved too fast, I don't know, but Cali tossed her head and caught me in the chin. I reeled back and felt my lip, tasted blood. Malcolm pulled out a handkerchief. I don't know any man except my uncle who still carries a perfect square of soft white cloth in his pocket. I tried to take it from him, but he held it out of my reach.

"I'm leading, okay?"

I rolled my eyes and let him dab the blood off my lip.

"You okay?" Lynette asked.

I nodded.

"One more try, and I'm knocking her out. Robert, you get this mare's other front leg off the ground and keep it there."

I picked up the plate, but Lynette and I collided.

"Maybe try it from the other side?" she asked.

I went to where Malcolm stood holding my horse's bent leg. She was leaning most of her weight into his hands, and he had his shoulder set against hers.

I had to crouch and nearly touch my head to her steel-shod foot to position the plate. If Malcolm let go, I'd have a hoof print over my ear, a monster headache, and maybe even get to suck my whipped cream through a straw for the rest of my life.

"You got her?" I whispered.

"You bet," he said.

"Where do you want me?" I asked Lynette.

Malcolm grunted and said something under is breath. I could swear it sounded like "Everywhere," but must have heard wrong. Lynette got the plate where she wanted it, and I tried not to move.

"Okay," she said. "Here we go. No dancing over there."

I held my breath and heard the little buzz of the x-ray. We all exhaled. I stood, and Malcolm gently released Cali's leg.

"How many more?" I asked.

"There's more?" Malcolm asked, lacing his fingers together and stretching his arms.

"Three or four," Lynette answered.

"No problem," he said.

A minute later, we prepared to do it again. My horse refused to pick up her foot for Malcolm, so I did it, and waited while he got in a good position for us to switch places. He hesitated a moment, but there was only one way to do it. I'm sure he tried to keep space between us. Just the same, his hips came against my rear end, his chest along my back, and his arms around me. Just for a moment. Then, I wriggled out from under him.

"She's going to be okay," he whispered to me as I picked up the plate and crouched.

I smiled. "You are entirely too nice for your own good," I said. "I hope you're right."

"I've been telling Robert that for years," Lynette said from Cali's other side. "I'm glad to hear someone agree."

"I don't know what you're talking about," Malcolm said.

Lynette made a disgusted sound and muttered, "He's hopeless."

"How do you want me this time?" I asked her. If I'd had a free hand, I would have smacked myself for asking the same stupid question. I heard Malcolm's response clearly this time, but I'm not sure he meant me to.

"You can't imagine," he muttered.

CHAPTER FIFTEEN

LATER, I stood in Malcolm's mudroom, which was off to one side of his kitchen. He'd insisted on making me something to eat, and I hadn't taken much convincing. When Lynette finally left, it was dark. We returned to the tack room to find Noire had gorged herself on the rest of Clara's roast beef.

I stared into a small mirror, turning my head from side to side to look behind me. Couldn't tell about my aura, but I looked like crap. "Can you see dark spots in my aura?"

"Christ. Did Renee tell you that?"

"Yeah, why?"

"Apparently, I have the same problem."

"It's a freaking epidemic," I said, returning to the kitchen.

He chuckled and put a plate of spaghetti in front of me.

"What's an aura, anyway?" I asked as I dug in.

"It's your...you know." He sat across from me and waved his hands around in a vague outline of my body. "Your light, your energy. Hell, I haven't a clue."

I don't know why I was so intrigued by the idea. Maybe if I understood my aura, the big *it* that was my life would straighten itself out. "Can she really see auras?"

Malcolm twirled a big forkful of pasta. "Damned if I know."

It was the second time that day, no, the third, that we'd sat down to a meal together. Fourth, if you counted the quick sandwich in the tack room. And I was damned if I could point to the one thing that had happened over the course of the day to make me feel so at home in his presence. That's not to say I was comfortable. I was too aware of him, too disconcerted by the slow smile that said he felt the same heat coiling in his belly I did.

I could have hung out in his dingy kitchen with him all night. But I wanted to make a last check on Cali and the others and get to bed. The next few days would be long enough. I ate quickly, said I was tired—which was true—and went out.

Malcolm walked with me to the barn. The moon was bright enough in the inky sky to cast shadows. It had been nearly full on Monday. Not that I wanted to remember the events of that night.

A howling came from behind the house and stopped me in my tracks. Noire was at my leg, so it wasn't her, not that I'd ever known her to bay at the moon. Several sharp yips followed, then more howls that lifted the hair on my neck. I grabbed Malcolm.

"What the hell is that?"

He put his warm hand over mine, and I nearly forgot the Hounds of the Baskervilles.

"Coyotes."

"Coyotes?" First vultures, now coyotes. Jesus. I thought I'd come to the Midwest, not the Old West.

Noire's ears had come up at the first note. She had a belly full of roast beef topped with spaghetti, so I thought she might not react, but then she stuck her nose in the air and let loose a plaintive wail. Yep, we were both going crazy. I might start howling at the moon myself at the rate things were going.

I raised my voice to be heard over the chorus. "You got a lot of dead stuff needing to be cleaned up around here?" The moment the words left my mouth, I clapped my hand over my lips. "Sorry." I was glad for the near dark. If the heat in my cheeks was any indication, I'd turned bright red. "That was a terrible thing to say."

The corners of his mouth twitched. "Yes, terrible." He pressed his fist against his mouth and faked a cough. I felt him shake with laughter before any sound escaped, then he let go.

And I joined him. We were both tired and stressed, and we laughed long and hard. Noire looked at us like, well, like we were howling at the moon.

Malcolm collected himself first, patted my hand where it still clung to his arm, and said, "Yes, I suppose we do."

"Stop."

He wiped a tear from my cheek. "Things were so boring before you arrived."

"That's enough." I shoved him away from me, feeling drained but better, even though I knew death was no laughing matter.

He just smiled and took my hand and held it all the way to the barn. These small intimacies—laughing together, walking hand-in-hand under the blazing moonlight, not to mention literally crying on his shoulder—made my heart swell in an unfamiliar way. As soon as we reached the first stall, I used the excuse of opening the door to pull away from him, and he let me.

We looked in on all the patients, and Malcolm came as far as the tack room.

"I'll be in town through the weekend," he said. "I'll help with the extra work."

"Thanks."

"You've already done a lot. The place looks great. I just wish…" he trailed off and glanced out the window into the dark, toward the pasture and beyond.

I couldn't see whatever he saw in his mind, but I think that's when I fell in love with him a little. Because what I could see was the passion he had for the land. His heart was in it. And I didn't want to let him down. I had no idea what he really expected from me, but somehow I would help him keep this place the way he wanted it.

"Vi, I wish…I'd understand if—"

"Don't say it." I almost put my fingertips to his lips, but stopped short of touching him. "It's okay. It will be okay."

He looked me very steadily in the eyes for some moments. Whether assessing the truth of those words, or simply trying to believe them, I don't know. Then he grazed his knuckles over my swollen lip, barely touching, just the fine hairs on his fingers tickling my skin.

"Should have put ice on that," he said.

I about melted on the spot. "It'll be okay." Maybe, maybe not. I don't think either of us thought I was talking about my fat lip. Tomorrow, I would get more information from him on the working partnership.

"I'm glad you came here," he said in that velvety voice he'd used with me a couple of times.

I nodded, because if I said anything it would probably sound like, *Please join me upstairs*, and I might drool into the bargain, so I turned to go up, alone, then stopped and faced him.

"By the way," I said, returning to what he'd murmured when we'd been helping the vet. "I have a very good imagination."

CHAPTER SIXTEEN

NOIRE CEASED HOWLING when the coyotes quit. I slept deeply, and I wish I'd slept without dreaming, but there was nothing new in Wastrel's visit. He was back in the manure heap, pawing like he had the first time. It nagged at me come morning, but I shoved it aside in favor of watching Henrietta nurse her kittens and purr while I massaged liniment into my bruises. The kittens still had their eyes closed, but they were starting to wiggle around. Soon, I'd begin picking them up.

All was peaceful in my world.

Then, just as I finished feeding the horses, Malcolm strolled in. Wearing his kilt. I watched him approach while I filled Cali's water bucket. I needed to call Penny so she could remind me why I shouldn't mess with the boss. Right at that moment, as the morning sun caught in his hair and that skirt slapped his thighs, I couldn't for the life of me think of one reason why I shouldn't drag him upstairs right then and there. Heck, we wouldn't even have to worry about getting him out of his trousers.

Damn, I had it bad. Icy water splashed my feet, and I quick kinked the hose to keep from flooding the stall.

"Are you going to hang around here all day dressed like that?"

He glanced down at the kilt. "What's wrong with this? It's comfortable."

I moved to the next stall, put the hose in the bucket. "It's distracting."

He smiled a too-satisfied smile. "You think that pink skirt you had on yesterday wasn't distracting? Nice legs, by the way."

I overflowed the water bucket again. See? I already wasn't concentrating.

"Why don't you let me do that." He took the hose and hummed the chorus of the Rolling Stones' "You Can't Always Get What You Want" as he went to the next stall.

"Not funny," I said. I brought Cali into the aisle to change her bandages.

"*You can try sometimes…*" he sang, not in tune.

Sheesh. I decided to ignore him. Lynette was supposed to call first thing with the results of the x-rays. If Cali's knee was messed up, I didn't know what would happen. I couldn't afford surgery. Would Lynette take monthly payments on the bill? Veterinary care was expensive. I didn't even have medical coverage for myself.

"*You just might find…*" drifted from the other end of the barn.

The tune caught in my head, and I found myself humming, *you get what you need.*

"What do you say we get everything done and go for a ride?" Malcolm asked when he finished watering. "You can ride Gaston, or whoever you want."

"Will you stop singing?"

"Maybe."

I sat on my haunches and looked at him. He'd change out of the kilt if we went riding, so it was a good idea. Then again, he'd put on breeches that hugged his muscled…body. On the other hand, I could use a long gallop. "Sure."

"We'll pack a lunch. I'll show you the sights."

"What does that mean, the best corn fields in the county?"

"No, I'll give you the deluxe tour. Take you to see milo."

Before I could ask who Milo was, a truck pulled up. An older man waved and got out.

"There's Fred," Malcolm said. "He's bringing me some lumber." He walked to the front of the barn.

"Got it right here," Fred said, gesturing toward the back of his truck. He peered down the aisle. "Who you hidin' in there? That Brooke?"

I brushed off my hands and went out. In the past, I would have ignored him, but that didn't seem right anymore.

"I'm Vi," I said. "Nice to meet you."

"You're the New Yorker. Melba said she saw you in the store the other mornin'." He turned to Malcolm, who looked amused. "Where you want it?"

They walked to the back of the truck, and I followed. As if I cared about a load of lumber, but I was curious what it was for, especially if the work might involve me. There were long pieces that looked like fence rails hanging well beyond the tailgate.

"Nice flag, Fred. Those Melba's?" Malcolm asked. He pointed at something on the back of the load.

Fred chuckled. "No. Found them down by the creek. My bull was wearing 'em."

The granola I'd had for breakfast threatened to recycle itself.

Fred yanked my red panties off the end of a two by six. "Nice, huh? Can't imagine how they got there. Kids, I guess."

Malcolm crooked a skeptical brow. He didn't look at me, thankfully, and I went back to work before they could see I'd turned as red as my panties.

No sooner had I snapped a lead line on Cali to take her out the back door to stretch her legs, than another truck pulled up. Malcolm and Fred were unloading the lumber near the shed on the other side of the barn. A moment later, I recognized JJ's voice talking to them, laughing. Shit. There was nowhere to go except the riding arena or the field where the manure spreader still sat. Instead, I led her out the front and up the driveway toward the house. There, I stopped and let her pick at grass along the edge of the lawn. I couldn't see JJ's truck, so after a while decided it must be safe to go back to the barn.

Wrong. Malcolm and JJ walked out to meet me. Malcolm looked stiff, unhappy. JJ ambled, all loose-limbed confidence. And there was no escape for me. I should have anticipated this.

"I was going to introduce JJ," Malcolm said, "but it appears you've already met."

Every swear word I knew whipped through my head, but I couldn't form a coherent thought or statement out of them. I already knew going out with JJ had been a huge mistake, but I hadn't come close to thinking through the implications.

"Yeah," I said, and kept Cali walking. Not very intelligent, but all I wanted was to get away, to not get caught in the crossfire between the two men. I'd been right to suspect bad blood between them. The tension in the air might have been sparked by my unwise choice, but it clearly had existed long before I showed up.

JJ rocked back on his heels. "Oh, yeah," he said as I walked away. "We've met. Mac, you want to have some fun, just get a few drinks into this one. She'll be slicker'n a hound's tooth in no time."

I stopped.

"Ain't that right, *Slick*?"

I felt my spine straighten and shoulders square as I turned to face him.

He lit a cigarette, and I wondered how I'd missed the menace in him before. Noire had known. She came trotting across the cow pasture just then, slathered in creek muck. The moment she became aware of JJ, she stopped, lowered her head, and quit wagging her tail.

Malcolm's face was unreadable. Pissed probably didn't cover what he felt. I wasn't sure whether the low growl I heard came from him or my dog.

"Too bad about your horse," JJ said, flicking ash off to the side. "Nothin' like that ever happened on my watch. Guess you been distracted." He took a deep pull from the cigarette and let his gaze fall on Malcolm. "What with Norman, and all."

"We have nothing to talk about," I said. Pretty lame, but it was all I could think of—besides screaming—and that wouldn't help.

"Ain't interested in talking," JJ said. "None of us are." He punched Malcolm in the shoulder. "Us boys all want the same thing from a pretty girl, right Mac? Never had nothin' to do with talking." He grinned, but there was no smile on his face.

Malcolm said nothing. He stared at me, hands curled into fists at his sides. I could have sunk into the ground. God, I was stupid. Stupid, dim, brainless.

"Yep, we're all the same," JJ rambled. "You give ol' Mac here half a chance, and he'll take you for a nice ride, too. That's a promise. Maybe even down to the river, 'cept I don't think that's his style."

Could this get any worse?

Malcolm finally forced sound past his clenched jaw. "I think it's time for you to leave, JJ."

JJ's smirk faded. "You kickin' me off this land?"

Malcolm's nostrils flared, he took a deep, calming breath, and slowly unclenched his fists. "I'm asking you to leave. We can continue this conversation another time."

JJ shrugged. "Sure. Whatever you say, *Mr.* Malcolm."

He fished something out of his back pocket. My stained and torn panties.

Okay, it could get worse. Much worse.

He twirled them on his index finger.

"You and me got unfinished business, Vi."

As soon as JJ rounded the corner of the barn, I said, "Nothing happened."

Malcolm had stayed in the drive with me, watching JJ, hands twitching like he wanted to punch something.

When he looked at me, I couldn't tell what he was thinking. "That's none of my business," he said.

"I want you to know," I said. "I met him at Mel's Monday night, and I did have too much to drink, and we went down to the river, but nothing happened."

Except for my panties going on an extended trip without me. Which was at odds with my assertion nothing had happened, even I could see that. Malcolm would believe what he wanted. JJ's truck sputtered into view, going up the road past Hank's. A flash of red flapped on the tip of his broken antenna. We watched until he was gone, then Malcolm's eyes cut to me.

"You interested in seeing him again?"

"What? No. Definitely not." Not him or the damn panties. I'd never wear red lace underwear again. "No." I toed the dirt at my feet. "I made a mistake, okay?"

"It would be in your best interests not to repeat it."

That made me mad. But since it coincided with my own feelings, I didn't argue.

"What you do on your own time is none of my business," he said.

It was obvious he was making a great effort to keep his voice even, but it had that hard edge to it I'd heard the first day when Norman let Smitty get hurt. It sliced into me as surely as a farrier's blade carves hard hoof wall.

"Your best interests," he continued, "however, are my business."

"Maybe," I said slowly. Where the hell was this going? He wasn't the boss of me. Well, he was, but not of my personal life. Oh, hell, who was I kidding? Jesus, was I conflicted, or what?

"JJ may be right about him and me being alike," he said. "But he's wrong about one thing." He glanced in the direction JJ had gone. "I'll want you sober."

CHAPTER SEVENTEEN

WE DIDN'T GO for a ride. But I wanted to. I needed to get away from the place, to think, to try and clear up all the contradictory emotions and information. Not that there was anything I could do to figure out what happened to poor Norman, or change whatever was between JJ and Malcolm. But I wanted to get on with my year, and this mess made it harder.

He'd want me sober? Damn him. He sounded pretty sure about that.

Maybe a horse ride wasn't the answer. I wanted more distance. Like the nearest mall. I hated malls. They were all the same, and that's what I wanted. I could pretend I was back on the Island. I could slip into my comfort zone of anonymity and forget Winterlight for a while.

I couldn't forget it. If there was anything I could do to help solve the murder...a clean slate going forward would be good. But where to start?

There were five messages on voice mail. Lynette said Cali's knee joint was fine. I sagged onto the tack room loveseat in relief. Henrietta had left her kittens, and she jumped into my lap. I petted her and listened to the rest. Dex One wanted to know if we needed anything, if I was available to join him for a ride in the morning, and he wanted me to call him. Dex Two wanted to know if he could bring me anything when he came out on Saturday, and would I have time for a ride, and he wanted me to call him. Sandy planned to swing by after work to help out and ride, and would I ride with her? Clara had pork chops cooking for dinner, they'd be ready at noon, bring Robert. That would be Malcolm.

Fat chance.

It was already past nine, and I still had three injured horses to look after, stalls to clean, and sound horses to exercise before I started over with the evening chores. Assuming Malcolm was not going to help, the mall was out for today, but if I worked without a break, maybe I could go later. That would be better than sitting alone in my apartment all night.

Right at noon, my stomach reminded me about the pork chops. I didn't want to have to face Clara and her carving knife and try to explain why I hadn't come over, so I took a break and walked to their place.

"Where's Robert?" Clara asked.

"Haven't seen him," I said.

She gave me a curious look and called him at the house, but evidently he was too busy to join us. Good. I ate quickly. Clara packed leftovers and pie for me, and Hank gave me directions to the mall. It was an hour away, but that was even better as far as I was concerned. The drive would be good, too.

I took the leftovers to my apartment and returned Dex One's call. I got an answering machine so left a message saying I could ride between ten and eleven if that would work for him. Dex Two had a secretary. She put me through.

"Miss Parker, how delightful to hear your voice. Thank you for returning my call."

"You're welcome. Thanks for offering to bring something, but I'm pretty well set. What time will you be here?"

"Will you be able to join me for a ride?"

"If you can come in the late morning, yes."

"Perfect. In the meantime, what are you doing Friday night?"

Crap. Was he asking me on a date? I was done with men for a while. Going on trail rides didn't count.

"My partner is out of town, and I have an extra ticket to the symphony."

Now, was that his law partner, his way of referring to his girlfriend, or was he gay? Didn't matter, I decided. He had a partner, that was the important thing.

"Do you like the symphony, Miss Parker?"

"Yes, I do. What are they playing?"

I heard papers shuffling. "Ah, here we are. They are opening with Rossini, then performing Beethoven's Ninth. The concert begins at eight. Can you get away in time for dinner?"

"The Ode to Joy?" I didn't know much classical music, but I'd loved this one since childhood, especially the singing.

"You know it?"

"It's my favorite." At that point, I would have said anything to get away from the farm for a while.

"Then you will come? I can pick you up."

"No need to drive all the way out here." Just in case. That made it too date-like. "I'll meet you someplace for dinner. "

We decided on a restaurant—Indian—and he gave me directions.

When Sandy showed up at four, Malcolm still hadn't appeared. Guess he was too pissed to even come down and help like he'd said he would, or maybe it was something else altogether. Penny was fond of saying not everything had to do with me. But I had my doubts.

I'd finished work except for the evening feeding, so Sandy groomed and saddled Fawn, and I decided to try out Captain.

We went down the road past Hank and Clara's rather than up past Malcolm's house. Sandy wanted to show me some trails the paying customers didn't know about. I'd assumed she was a paying customer, but she came and went as she pleased and appeared to ride Fawn whenever she wanted, even though I knew Winterlight owned the mare.

True to his upright shoulder and short-necked conformation, Captain's gait was as bone-jarring as sliding down a flight of stairs on your butt—a favorite pastime of mine and Pen's when we were kids, one that guaranteed a scolding from Aunt Trudy. That never stopped us, though.

Sandy exchanged work for riding privileges, she explained, including acting as guide to the trail riders on the weekends, so she knew the land well. We rode for over an hour, and though not the deluxe tour with boxed lunch I'd been anticipating that morning, the scenery was pleasant, the company tolerable, and the gallops satisfying. I felt more relaxed than I had in days by the time we returned. She helped me feed, and while I topped off the water buckets, she swept the aisle.

When we were done, we sat on the tack-room steps to watch the sun set. She brought a couple of beers from a cooler in her car, and I had one.

Just one.

The sky went from golden to orange to crimson to purple. The farm sat on a ridge and was higher than much of the surrounding land providing a good view.

Sandy was quiet for a change. I sensed she had something she wanted to ask me, or tell me, maybe. In the light I noticed a bruise on her forehead, right at her hairline. It looked fresh; there was a bump, too. She'd been wearing a baseball cap when we rode, but had taken it off when we sat.

"What happened to you?" I asked. "Walk into a door?" I chuckled.

Her eyes went wide and her hand flew to her head. "Dang it. Forgot about that." She touched the spot with her fingertips. "No…" she gave her head a little shake. "It don't matter."

"Are you okay?" I knocked back the rest of my beer.

She laughed, but it had a bitter sound. "Truth is, my boyfriend gets a little rough sometimes."

I froze with my head tilted back, the bottle still to my lips, then slowly lowered it and looked at her. Boyfriends being a little rough are forbidden.

"You don't have to put up with that, you know."

It grew dark. The light from inside played over her face, and I noticed the same high color and watery eyes she'd had the day we found Norman. She didn't say anything for some time, but her breathing quickened.

Finally, she blurted, "I miss Norman," dropped her beer and sobbed into her hands.

Jesus.

This was not a good area for me. Emotions, that is. They left me feeling helpless—I'd no idea what to say, no way of knowing she and Norman had been friends. It didn't seem like the appropriate time to lecture her about why it's wrong for a man to hit a woman. So, I put my arm around her, and for a change, said nothing.

My muscles slackened with fatigue, and I abandoned the plan for going to the mall. I'd have my chance to get out of Dodge the next night.

We sat like that till she got herself under control. She wiped her nose on her sleeve, mumbled thanks and goodbye, and left without a backward glance.

I tossed the beer bottles, took a shower, ate leftover mashed potatoes, and went to bed.

Wastrel galloped up behind me, slid to a stop, and punched the center of my back with his nose, nearly knocking me to my knees. It had been dark and quiet and he'd come out of nowhere. It startled me awake, my hands thrust forward to break my fall. I lay in bed staring at the ceiling wondering what in the world that meant. Not that I'd gleaned any meaning from the previous dreams, not at least, until after the fact. But I hadn't tried to analyze them ahead of time.

Alive, he'd been a gentle horse. Until now, death hadn't changed this. Good God. A dead horse was communicating with me. No. It was just weird dreams. I was under a lot of stress. Weird dreams and stress go together, right?

Yes. But. Was it only a coincidence that Wastrel had been digging at the manure pile where a dead body lay buried? Or that I'd dreamed of running, frightened horses the night before Winterlight's entire herd got loose? Why the recurring dream of the manure pile? Could there be something there—something the police had missed?

If I could help solve Norman's murder, things would settle down. Maybe the dreams would stop. Much as I hated the idea, I would look in the manure pile. But for what?

I was missing something, that much was sure, and it wasn't just a peaceful night's rest. Did this latest vision mean I should pay closer attention, or was it a warning to watch my back?

CHAPTER EIGHTEEN

"LOSE YOUR WAY?"

The voice belonged to Dex One. He stood on the other side of the police tape, mirrored glasses reflecting the morning sun.

He'd caught me standing in the middle of the old manure pile, hands on hips, peering into the decaying mass of straw and dung. I didn't know what I was looking for but hadn't been able to concentrate on work.

"Yeah," I said, "looks like that, doesn't it?"

"Looks to me like you're knee-deep in shit, but that's just my opinion."

More like up to my neck. "Truer words were never spoken."

I certainly wasn't going to tell him about my dreams. If Wastrel wanted to pass along a little postmortem equine intel to Dex—well, Dex slept, too, though no better than I did, from the look of him. He probably had his own demons setting him to ponder his sanity.

I kicked the debris at my feet in frustration. Maybe I needed to walk the field where I'd been driving the tractor before poor Norman got stuck. If I hadn't decided to dispose of the manure heap, he'd still be in it. I shuddered at the thought. Whoever buried him must have thought he'd stay there until he was gone, or there was too little of him left to notice.

A big pile of manure and straw like this got awfully hot on the inside. Warmth seeped through the soles of my boots now. The heat broke things down quickly. Whoever disposed of Norman's body knew about the pile, knew it had been there for some time, and expected it to stay there even longer.

They hadn't anticipated a clean freak from New York showing up.

"I said, do you need help?"

I'd forgotten Dex was there. "Oh. Um—no. It was just an old hoof pick. No big deal." He lifted the yellow strip of plastic for me to duck under. With his eyes hidden, I couldn't tell whether he believed me or not.

"I pulled in a favor with the medical examiner," he said.

I shortened my stride to keep pace with his limp, wondering when I'd find time to walk the field, wondering what the hell I thought I was doing.

He waved a hand in front of my face. "Where are you?"

"Sorry," I said. "Lost in thought. What did you say?"

"Must've been a hell of a hoof pick."

I focused on him. "You know how it is. It was a gift."

We entered the barn, and he shoved the dark glasses in his breast pocket. "They're going to have a look at Norman today. Should know something by Monday."

"Good. I'm sure his family will be relieved."

"His family's not who I'm worried about." He pointed his chin in the direction of Malcolm's house. "Looks kind of bad for him, don't you think?"

"But he was out of town. Surely people don't think—"

"People think all kinds of crazy stuff. The sooner it gets cleared up the better, that's all."

"Do you have any idea who—"

"I'm trying to figure out *why*, Miss Parker. When I know that, the who will be easy."

He limped along to his mare, Ciqala. He wore jeans and short boots, zipped on chaps before mounting, and strapped a helmet over his blond crew cut, too, I was glad to see. Sandy hadn't worn one, and I knew I would be posting a sign and enforcing the rule to always wear a helmet when riding.

I shook off all thoughts of dead bodies turning to compost and decided to try out Honey. The two mares were well matched in size, and I anticipated a more comfortable ride on the palomino's broad back than I'd had the day before on Captain. I wasn't disappointed.

We jogged past Malcolm's house. Almost no energy made it from Honey's legs to the saddle, which made her easy to sit. I kicked free of the stirrups and let my legs hang, using my rear end and hips to follow the minimal movement. She'd have a rocking-chair canter, the kind you could ride all day. She'd never cut it in my world as a show horse, but for a hack, one couldn't go wrong riding her type. With more-whoa-than-go, Honey suited me perfectly that morning.

The white farmhouse receded from view, but I'd no doubt we were being watched, and I couldn't help a quick glance over my shoulder to see if I would catch him looking out a window. Unfortunately, Dex saw me looking.

"He's not pissed at you."

I jerked my head to look at him. "Who?"

"Malcolm."

He'd read my mind too easily. I'm sure he could tell by the look on my face that he'd hit the mark.

"More like upset with himself for bringing you here right when all this erupted."

"What, exactly, is *all this*?"

"Exactly what I'm trying to find out."

"And?"

"I have some leads. Norman had a history, and some not-so-great associates. You don't need to worry about that."

"I'm not worried." The neon sign on my forehead started flashing.

"Yeah, right."

"You don't know anything about me."

"You'd be surprised."

I wasn't sure I'd be surprised at anything. My first week at Winterlight was coming to a close, and I'd already been hit upside the head more times than I could count.

Dex smiled. "You're twenty-nine years old and have had eighteen different jobs since you were fifteen—those are just the ones on the books. You've used only two addresses your whole life up until this week, but I suspect you've laid your head in more than a few others."

"Hey," I groaned in protest.

"I mean that in the nicest way."

Yeah, right. Why did I keep forgetting he was an ex-cop-sometime-PI?

We rode past the wheat field toward the creek. Whatever it was that caused him to limp when walking scarcely registered with him in the saddle. His left foot rested in the stirrup, as if he couldn't put weight in it. His seat was solid, though, his balance strong. He was an efficient rider, no finesse, but he stayed out of his horse's way.

"In addition to your training at a British Horse Society school," he continued, "you've completed seventy-two hours toward a bachelor's degree of nothing in particular, never owned real estate, never been arrested or in drug rehab, never even had a utility bill in your name, let alone a loan. No credit cards."

I resigned myself to the knowledge he'd done a background check. Whether before or since Malcolm hired me was the question.

"You're damn close to off the grid for someone who has nothing to hide."

I took a deep breath, let it out loudly, but I was only mildly annoyed. "I don't have anything to hide." Sometimes, I wished I did. Sometimes, I wish I had what others called assets, besides my truck and trailer.

"You have a checking account, that's something. But you have only four-hundred eighty-three dollars and thirty-five cents to your name."

There was no point in denial. It was true. That was all the money I had. "Yep. Pitiful." But I had Noire and Cali. Critter rich, cash poor.

"You don't feel sorry for yourself."

"Only sometimes. But you didn't learn that from looking at my bank account."

Dex reined in Ciqala. She tossed her head in protest, then made the most of the moment by tearing at the leaves on a branch next to her head. He gave me a clear-eyed look of assessment. "No. I learned that from watching you." He patted his mare's neck. "That's how you get the important stuff."

I nodded, having no argument or comeback, wishing I had his abilities, and rode on. I'd have better luck choosing jobs if I were a better judge of people. Malcolm was the first boss I'd had in a long time who appeared to be a genuine straight arrow. And Penny had found this position for me. It sucked in every other way, though, so that made us even.

When he trotted Ciqala forward, I asked, "What is the important stuff?"

"You haven't opened a checking account here. You're still using the one at a bank on Long Island."

"That's the important stuff?"

"You plan on staying, or not?"

It was my turn to pull up. We were in that pretty area under the river birch. Malcolm's favorite spot on the farm. I looked around me, maybe seeing some of what Malcolm had been picturing in his mind when he stared out the tack-room window the other night.

But what business was it of Dex? My annoyance level ratcheted up a notch. I hadn't promised not to smart off to the boarders. "Don't you know?"

"I don't know everything."

"What would you guess from watching me? Is that the important stuff you were talking about?"

"Partly."

"Why do you care?"

He took a moment to study the trees and the creek and Noire bounding through the water, pouncing on some unsuspecting frog or crayfish.

"I love him like a brother."

Jesus. What was it about this spot that encouraged men to reveal intimate details? Did I need to know this? I'd hoped to get through the week without any more slaps upside the head.

A bluebird caught my eye, a flash of azure against a light-skinned tree. It flitted to a twig, then flew out of sight.

Dex booted Ciqala into my line of vision. "He's been good to me. He's a good man. Too trusting maybe, and too high a boiling point to suit me, but that's why I watch his back."

"When did he ask you to check up on me? Did you warn him not to hire me, like with Norman?"

"He didn't. I did it on my own as soon as I got your name from him. And no. I told him he should hire you, but he'd already decided."

Hunh. "So, what did you tell him?"

"Nothing to tell he didn't already know from your cousin."

I urged Honey forward, across the creek and along the trail on the other side. Dex came up next to me, quiet for the moment, letting me absorb that last piece of information. Noire trotted after us, then spotted a squirrel and rushed into the underbrush. The squirrel scurried up a broad trunk, along a branch, soared to another tree, and kept going.

That Malcolm was a good man was not news to me. I'd already figured that one out for myself. Now, I knew he had devoted friends, too. Loyalty, I understood. And honesty was something I valued.

"You don't want him to get hurt," I said.

"Now you're reading my mind."

I smiled at him, and he gave me a helpless shrug.

"Busted," I said. "How about a canter?"

He didn't wait, just kicked Ciqala into gallop. True to her quarter-horse breeding, she sped out like a sports car, zero-to-sixty in two strides. Honey barely reacted. I had to slap her neck with the reins to get a response, and that was the rocking-chair canter I'd expected, nothing more. She slowed to walk long before we caught up with Dex, who was waiting at the next turn, grinning.

"Sorry," he said. "That wasn't fair. I forgot who you were riding."

We fell into step next to each other again. "Do you usually play fair?"

"Depends on who I'm playing with," he said with a drawl.

"I'll keep that in mind."

He turned serious, his coffee-colored eyes soft. "You can count on fairness and honesty from me, Miss Parker. You've earned at least that much."

"Likewise," I said. "And just for the record, I'm staying." Crap. Now I'd done it. I'd said it out loud.

"Because you have to."

"Because I want to."

We talked little more. Yet, half an hour later when we rode into the stable yard, I understood we had tacitly agreed to be honest and trust one another, and to help Malcolm. We untacked, and walked the horses down the drive together to give them a few minutes to cool before putting them in the pasture. If they drank a belly full of water when they were hot, they'd colic.

"What are you doing tonight?" Dex asked. "It's Friday."

"Oh, big doings," I said. "I'm going to dinner and the symphony with your rival in Dexterness."

"Oh ho! So he beat me to the punch, the little rascal."

"You were going to invite me to the symphony?"

"Heck no. Baseball game."

I admit I wasn't really listening. I wanted to ask him about Dex Two, but when I hesitated, he said, "Don't you like baseball?"

"Oh, no, I mean, well, I'm not a huge sports fan, but I don't mind going to a game once in a while." I considered not pursuing what I wanted to know, but curiosity got the better of me. "Is the other Dex—"

"Gay?"

"How'd you know that's what I was going to ask?"

"That's what everyone wants to know."

We turned the horses at the bottom of the drive and headed back toward the barn. Honey rubbed her itchy head against my shoulder. I braced myself so she didn't knock me over.

"You don't know?" I asked.

"I don't think he knows."

"You mean he's bisexual."

Dex unbuckled his helmet, slid it off, and wiped his gloved hand over the top of his head. "I mean he's asexual—doesn't know whether he's interested at all. Building his law firm's all he thinks about. Becoming a judge."

"He said his partner was out of town."

"Smoke screen. Now me, on the other hand—"

"I wasn't asking about you."

He put his free hand over his heart. "You cut me to the quick, Miss Parker."

"I didn't mean it like that. What I meant was I feel pretty sure…"

"Have no doubt, my dear."

He waggled his eyebrows and gave my chest a lustful leer that left no doubt whatsoever.

CHAPTER NINETEEN

TOWARD THE END of the symphony, right as the chorale reached a crescendo, I fell asleep on Dex Two's shoulder. My curfew is ten p.m., and that's pushing it after the kind of week I'd had. The need to get away from the farm had outweighed common sense. As if that were a rare occurrence.

Dinner had been delicious and Humphrey J. Dexter the Third, Esquire, the perfect gentleman. Despite his alleged lack of preference, he'd beamed a wide-eyed look of appreciation from my head to my pump-clad toes and back again when I walked into the restaurant. He'd stood and kissed the back of my hand, held my chair for me, told me how beautiful I looked.

He wore an elegantly tailored navy-blue suit and smelled like spicy after-shave. I'd worn my only little black dress, a simple, sleeveless crepe number with flattering princess seams. It felt good to dress up, wear a little makeup, and twist my hair into the only 'do I could do—a simple chignon.

My mother had showed me how to pin up my hair during one of their rare visits stateside. She said it was required knowledge for ladies. I'd resisted, preferring ponytails and hats, knowing, even at age eight, that I was not a lady, not like her, anyway. She'd insisted, and made me practice until I got it right. It's the only thing she ever taught me.

Before we took our seats, I had a bottle of water, and Dex Two had a glass of champagne. We stood in the opulent lobby of the symphony hall while he introduced me to everyone he knew, which seemed to be everyone. Most of the conversation centered on land conservation. He was a member or on the board of several local and national nature, river, or prairie conservancy organizations, trusts, or foundations. The names all ran into each other after the first few.

I listened and nodded a lot. I agreed with conserving land, but had never done anything about it. If I helped Malcolm keep the farm, that would be a start. The thought made me feel more grown up than I had in some time.

Now, I faced the drive to Winterlight armed with a Venti black coffee from Starbucks, the symphony's bass notes still thrumming my blood.

Keeping my eyes open all the way was tough. I stuck my head out the window, turned the radio up, and gulped caffeine. I talked to myself and finally pulled in at nearly midnight, needing to pee like the proverbial racehorse.

I rushed to the nearest unoccupied stall, shimmied my panties and hose to my knees, squatted, and relieved myself. I didn't know many women in the horse business who hadn't learned to empty their bladders quickly and efficiently in horse trailers, stalls, or woods. Usually, however, I wasn't wearing high heels. They sank into the deep bedding. The moment I tried to stand and pull myself together, I toppled over backwards, getting straw up my skirt.

The horse next to me snorted in surprise when I swore quietly and scrambled to my knees. In the moonlight slicing through the stall window, I picked the worst of the straw from the most sensitive areas, hastily pulled up my panties, and my skirt down. Even in the private darkness of a deserted barn, I didn't like leaving myself exposed for too long.

Noire wiggled through the nearly-closed stall door, sniffed me, and wagged her tail. She didn't bark when I pulled up; she knew the sound of our truck, and I could tell she'd been asleep. She yawned but followed me to retrieve my purse, then perked up when she saw I had a doggie bag.

"It's not for you, sweetie. You don't like chicken curry, remember?"

She looked like she'd reconsider if I would just give her the to-go box. I flipped on a couple of lights and looked in on each horse. A few needed water, so I began to top off buckets, pulling down my hair as I went. I held the hairpins between my teeth and shook my head.

When I moved from one stall to the next, Noire growled the low menacing sound reserved for whatever she considered a true threat. We were not alone in the barn. I froze and listened, but someone was already behind me.

He grabbed me, one arm pinning my arms at my sides, the other over my mouth. The hose spun free, spraying us both with water, and I think I swallowed a hairpin.

He dragged me across the aisle and smashed me against the opposite wall.

It knocked the wind out of me. I flailed with my hands, but couldn't get a grip on anything.

"Nice show back there, Slick," JJ hissed in my ear. "I want more of that."

Noire barked and snarled at his shin, and I tried to stomp one of my sharp heels onto his instep, but he kept moving, pulling me toward an empty stall. Freaking pumps. Why couldn't I be in jeans and boots? He kicked Noire in the ribs. She yelped and backed off for a second, then started in again.

"Call her off or I'll kill her, you hear me?"

I tried to jab him with my elbows, but he held me tight as a vise.

He kicked Noire again. "Now." He released my mouth.

"It's okay baby," I sputtered, spitting hairpins.

She latched onto JJ's pants leg. He punted her away. She came back. She was a dumb and persistent Lab, and although I'd never seen her tested, I knew she wouldn't give up while I was in danger. Unless she was dead.

"Let me put her in the tack room." That wouldn't shut her up, but it would keep her from tearing his leg off.

He lifted me off the floor, carried me to the tack-room door and opened it without loosening his grip.

"Come on, girl. Good girl." My voice was tight with fear, and she looked from me to JJ, unsure. "Just let me grab her collar."

He bent me over, let loose one of my arms. She started to snap at me, stopped herself. I forced her through the opening. JJ slammed the door, pinned my arm again and kept me in the awkward pose.

"Alone at last," he said slowly. "Speaking of dogs, I like this position." He humped his hips against me.

Noire dug at the inside of the door, whimpered, barked. I tried to see where the nearest pitchfork was. Right where it was supposed to be—hanging with the rest of the utensils a few feet away. Might as well have been a mile.

JJ's hot breath fanned my neck. He reeked of cigarettes and alcohol. "Hope you like this position. When I saw you on your knees with your panties around your ankles, I knew this was the first way we would do it."

He thrust his fingers into my hair, grabbed a fistful. "Nice outfit. I liked watching you take your hair down."

He carried me to a stall, slid the door open. My heart pounded in my chest, in my throat. I couldn't move, except for my legs, could barely breathe.

"No!" I forced out. I lifted from the waist and twisted, got one arm free, and bashed the back of my fist into his face.

"Bitch!" He dropped me, but only for a moment. Like a python, he struck out and caught the front of my dress, hauling me to my feet. Blood trickled from his nose.

"I warned you," he said. "You should've taken me up on my offer of a change of scene." His open palm sent me reeling to the back of the stall. I landed face down, ears ringing, out of breath again.

"That's where you belong."

I got my hands under me, then my legs up, started to turn over, but he pounced, braced his forearm across my neck, and forced me down with his chest. He shoved my dress up. His dirty fingers found my waistband, jerked. I thrashed, but he was bigger and stronger.

"Knock it off, Slick, or this will hurt even more."

He leaned into the arm across my neck, mashing my face almost to the cold floor. I tried to yell, for all the good it would do me. Maybe Malcolm would hear. I flung straw, rocked back and forth, tried to dislodge him.

"No," I said again. "No, no, no."

With his weight on my back, and my mouth crunched into the ground, I couldn't breathe, let alone scream. He laughed, the bastard, shifting into position. The bitter realization he'd done this before thumped through me. I was not going to escape. There was a roaring in my ears I was grateful for. I wouldn't hear the satisfied grunts he was sure to make.

Then he lifted off me, slammed into the wall, and slid to the floor, limp as a dust rag. I scrambled around and swung blindly, hitting only air. Someone else's hands banged JJ's head against the wall, yanked him to his feet, punched him in the gut, and threw him on the floor. I pushed to my feet and collided with Malcolm. He stood over JJ in a half crouch, hands balled into tight fists, but JJ wasn't moving. He was breathing, but he was out.

CHAPTER TWENTY

I SLUMPED to the floor and pushed a shaking hand against my lips. Then, I was in Malcolm's arms, and he carried me into the tack room. Noire frantically checked me over, sniffed at him, and ran to JJ's prone form.

Malcolm hesitated at the love seat, as if he might set me down, but I clung to him with all I had, so he took me to the phone, keeping a protective arm around me

He dialed 911, explained what he needed, and gave the address. Noire barked. He pushed me behind him, tucking my fingertips into his back pocket, but I was frozen, couldn't force my legs to do more, and I couldn't make myself go anywhere near JJ. Malcolm circled my waist with one arm and picked up a shotgun with the other. We moved across the floor without a sound.

JJ was up on all fours, his head hanging down, with Noire barking at him like he was a loose cow.

"Don't even think about it," Malcolm said in a voice that reminded me of that low growl Noire made when she noticed JJ sneaking up on me.

Malcolm racked a shell into the chamber one-handed and shouldered the weapon. I snapped my fingers near my thigh, and for once, the dog heeled.

JJ collapsed into the straw, holding his head, groaning. Malcolm kept the gun on him; I closed my eyes, tried to control the shaking, and stayed glued to his side. Noire sat next to me.

The roar I'd heard, the one I thought came from inside me, had been Malcolm. He'd reached that boiling point Dex One mentioned.

Two sheriff's cars rolled in—no flashing lights or sirens—just as Malcolm requested. No need to rouse the entire county. That was good. I didn't need anyone's prying eyes or well-meant sympathy, not for this. I'd have to face them soon enough.

As soon as a deputy had JJ cuffed, Malcolm phoned Dex One. He asked him to come down and run interference in case any of the curious souls who heard dispatch on their scanners decided to see for themselves what was going on.

I remained in the protective corral of Malcolm's arm, unwilling to leave his warmth. But I couldn't stop shaking. "He lives that close?" I asked. This felt like safe conversation. The other deputy would be in soon to question me. I wanted to put that off as long as possible. And I wanted it over with.

"Close enough. He was already on his way."

He was still on high alert, the tang of testosterone and adrenaline lifting off his skin like mist off a pond. The fury that brought with it a certain tunnel vision hadn't left his eyes, nor had his muscles began to uncoil. I knew exactly what he felt, except I'd already bypassed that stage for jelly-kneed weakness.

A few moments later, I knew he'd begun to come down, because he took a shuddering breath, turned me into him, and grasped my shoulders.

"Jesus effing Christ, Vi. Are you all right?"

His voice had a tremor in it. The reality of what had almost happened surfaced, bringing a redoubled bout of shivering that seized my whole body. Malcolm snatched the wool throw from the chair and put it around my shoulders. My legs gave out. I dropped to the loveseat and gave a small nod.

"What in God's name are you doing in the barn in the middle of the night dressed like that?"

I narrowed my eyes at him. There was just enough anger and accusation in his tone to get the adrenaline pumping in my system again.

"I didn't…" He scrubbed his hands through his hair. "I don't mean that the way it sounds." He sat next to me and drew his hand down his face. By the look of him, he hadn't shaved in a couple days. "Are you all right?" he asked again, his voice steadier. "Did he…hurt you?"

His real concern went unsaid.

"He shoved me around," I said, "you got here before he could do what he intended." Guess neither of us could voice it. "What are you doing down here at this time of night?"

The deputies came in, so neither of us got our question answered.

CHAPTER TWENTY-ONE

WHEN THE DOOR closed behind the deputy, I rested my elbows on my knees and put my face in my hands. I thought I would cry, but my mind had closed in on itself, shut down to the essentials. The rest of me followed suit. I felt compressed, as if I'd managed to shrink. As if that would help.

"I was checking the horses before going to bed. There's no law against wearing a dress in a barn. I went to the symphony with Dex Two."

He touched my back. I flinched. Couldn't help it.

"I know," he said.

I lifted my head to look at him, rustling up a thimbleful of indignation out of long habit. "You said what I do in my off time is none of your business."

"I did say that. Dex Two called me. He wanted me to know you would be with him, so I wouldn't worry. He let me know you were on your way home, too." He scrubbed his face again. "I was waiting up for you."

I felt a subtle stirring inside me.

He would have worried? I tried to see what loitered beneath his cool exterior. All traces of the avenging angel from an hour before had vanished, but layers of concern still smoldered behind his eyes.

The release of tears washed near then drifted out of reach, like waves going out with the tide. For once, I wished for them, knew my body and soul needed them. But I wasn't an actress. I couldn't cry on demand.

"Do you want to get some things from upstairs and come to the house for the rest of the night? I have a guest room. Or I can call Hank and Clara."

I wanted to be alone, knew I shouldn't. And I couldn't stay upstairs, either. "If you really don't mind," I said. "We shouldn't bother them."

A very slight nod. "Want me to go with you?"

The stiffness of his movements and tone of voice told me he'd scarcely bottled his anger and was concentrating on handling me with care. The effort had him stretched taut.

"I can manage."

I got to my stocking feet—my shoes were tangled in that stall somewhere, and I didn't know when I would retrieve them. Noire trailed me to the landing where we both stopped.

"Malcolm?" No sound came past my throat. I cleared it, tried again. "I think you should come up here."

My apartment had been trashed, and in that instant, it registered that things were out of place downstairs as well. If it were possible, I closed in on myself a little more. The space I'd begun to think of as my own had been invaded. I didn't like to think by whom. But at my core, I knew.

Malcolm joined me, took in the mess with a sweeping gaze, and swore with depth and richness. Noire went in, started sniffing things.

"Was he looking for something, you think?" I asked.

"Could be. He used to stay here once in a while, but it's been years."

"You let..." I couldn't even say his name. "He used to..." The thought that I'd been sleeping in the same bed he had...made me want to puke.

"Oh, God, the kittens."

I rushed to the bedroom. Every drawer had been dumped, the bed stripped, and one closet door hung off its hinge. I was pretty sure I was coming unhinged myself. Henrietta and her kittens were nowhere to be seen. I could only hope she'd taken them somewhere safe.

I sat on the edge of the bed. Malcolm came in.

"Can you tell if anything is missing?"

I shook my head. "Most of the stuff here is yours, anyway. I just brought my clothes and some books."

"Did you take down that photo by the bookcase?"

I knew the one he meant. It was an aerial shot of Winterlight, though why that should matter at this moment was beyond me. "No. Why, is it gone?"

He nodded. "Here," he handed me a plastic grocery bag. "Get what you need, but try not to disturb too much. I'll call the sheriff in the morning."

I slipped into my boots, and first went to the kitchen and grabbed all the whipped cream. Then, I found socks, jeans and a couple of T-shirts.

That was when I realized there was something missing.

"My underwear is gone," I said. "He took all my underwear."

"JJ wants everything that's mine," Malcolm told me later. "Or anything he thinks I want."

Did my underwear fall into that category, or me, or what?

We were in his living room, sitting in front of a fire. I watched him from my perch on the couch where I sat Indian style, a heavy tartan blanket around me like a teepee. He'd changed into shorts and had a well-worn easy chair pushed back with his bare feet up.

When we'd gotten to the house, he'd showed me where the shower was and brought me a set of his own sweats. Way too big, but comfortable and comforting all at once.

I sipped warm brandy. Topped with a generous dollop of whipped cream, it would do. Between that and the fire and the fact that it was three in the morning, the edge was beginning to wear off. I'd finally stopped shaking after standing under a steaming shower for forty minutes, but I liked the fire's cheery crackle, even if Malcolm had a sheen of sweat on his brow.

"But why you? Why does he want what you have?"

Malcolm lowered the footrest and turned his scotch glass between his palms. "He thinks we owe him. His father took off one day. He'd been mowing hay with my father down in the south end of the farm, and said he needed to go home for a while. Their place wasn't far, so he left his truck and headed into the woods. He was never seen again. Ever since…Dad thought we should take care of JJ."

He took a moment to stare into the fire. "Dad would give him money, but he'd spend it on beer, and later, drugs. He gets in fights."

I touched the side of my head where JJ had hit me. My fingertips played over a bump at my hairline. It was similar in size and location to Sandy's bruise. "Does he wear a ring on his right hand?"

Malcolm narrowed his gaze. "Something that was his father's. Why?"

"No reason. Go on."

"For the last couple of years, I've tried to help him out by giving him odd jobs."

That was a misplaced sense of loyalty if I'd ever heard one. Yep, Malcolm was too damned nice for his own good.

He shook his head, looked at me. "If I'd had any idea this would happen—"

"Forget it," I said. "It wasn't your fault. Nothing happened."

He took a big swig of his scotch. "That's not true, Vi. He hurt you. You should get an order of protection."

"No thanks. I'm okay, really." Was the "Big Fat Lie" sign blinking on my forehead again?

He shook his head again, whether in frustration with me or his history with JJ, I couldn't tell.

"I'd hoped with time…nothing's changed. Nothing. He belongs in prison, but I doubt they'll hold him long. Even if you pressed charges, his mother or some stupid girl would bail him out."

I felt the bruise on the side of my head again. Some stupid girl all right.

CHAPTER TWENTY-TWO

I SLEPT for a couple of hours on the couch. Noire woke me at dawn with a damp snuffling nose and a few well-placed licks. Malcolm snored in the easy chair. Great, now we'd slept together. I gathered my things, including my whipped cream from the fridge, and started the day. I wanted to lose myself in work. That way, I wouldn't think too much. If I did, I might get in my truck, start driving, and never come back. What would it take for me to say *enough already?*

Malcolm brought me a cup of coffee and a ham, egg, and cheese sandwich around seven. He took over walking Barbie. Watching him move away from me—his stride covered ground without making him look like he was in a hurry—I knew the idea of driving off and not returning was a joke. I was a long way from *enough already*. After all, he'd waited up for me. No one had ever done that. Not to mention charging to my rescue loaded for bear. I owed him one. Or two.

I took my sandwich and drink to Cali's stall. Strange place to eat, a horse's stall, I know, but I liked being around her. She dozed with one hind leg hooked behind the other, eyes at half-mast, and I admired the glossy darkness of her coat. Hours of grooming went into making her look like a just-poured cup of hot cocoa. Sometimes I thought I could smell chocolate when I was around her.

I sat on the floor where I could feel her warm breath glide over my hair. My body ached from being tossed and whatever chemical was left after the adrenaline had done its job.

Cali sniffed what I had and turned her lip up—she didn't like coffee. Noire didn't either, so she sat with her back to me, but kept darting hopeful glances at my sandwich. The horse and the dog smelled each other. They got along, and seemed to agree on most things—like the worth of coffee—though I had no real idea what they communicated to each other with those noses. Maybe I should take up sniffing people. Not their crotches, of course, but the animals seemed to glean a great deal of information that way. Cali liked to smell my neck for some reason, but it was hard to stay still while her whiskers tickled my earlobe.

Malcolm brought Barbie into the barn. She liked to pause just inside the doors, as if taking the measure of the interior before agreeing to enter. More likely letting her eyes adjust to the difference in light from outside. I heard him mutter an irritated "C'mon," and she continued.

Me and my buddies, the deputies, got to chat yet again. They managed, just, to not smile when I listed the missing five bras and eight pairs of panties. They dusted for prints—but everyone knew whose they'd find—and said I could clean the place up.

Hank and Clara showed up shortly after to do just that. She put a plate with a slice of apple pie on it in my hands and insisted on taking home everything that could be put in a washing machine.

"I can do that," I told her.

"Suppose you could, but I'm going to." She sat next to me on the tackroom steps while I ate the pie. "You okay?"

I shrugged.

"You want and come stay with us tonight? We got room."

I gave that a minute while I tried to imagine getting comfortable in the upstairs bed. "I will. Thanks."

Dex Two arrived and busied himself grooming Miss Bong while I finished cleaning stalls. Sandy called to see if I was all right. She said she had a few things to take care of, and since we were closed anyway, did I mind if she didn't come in? Of course I didn't. She sounded distracted, so I let her go, but I did want to find out more about her "boyfriend," to compare bruises.

While I adjusted the girth on Anna, the only horse in the barn besides Gaston or Cali who had a prayer of keeping pace with Miss Bong, another car drove in. This one, a champagne-colored Caddy. A young girl bounded out of the back seat before the driver stepped out.

"Daddy, daddy!" the girl called, running down the aisle.

Malcolm stepped out of a stall and scooped her into his arms. She whooped with delight, and buried her face against his shoulder. That was a fine place to be, I knew. And he smelled good too. Like soap and starch, and manly sweat. Sweat, but not fear.

My own fear the night before had been palpable, to me, anyway. If I didn't guard my thoughts, it would ooze through my pores again, and I could pluck it off my bare skin with two fingers.

"Nicky, my girl," Malcolm said on a sigh. He hugged her tight, and I think he took a big gulp of her little-girl scent.

Nicky, his daughter. I got that unfamiliar rising feeling in my chest again, seeing them together.

"Look what I have!" she said. She started to give him something, then snatched it back. "Close your eyes."

He put her down, did as she said, and held out his hands, palms up. She put the item in them, and he looked at what lay there. A shadow crossed his face. It was gone in a blink.

Nicky jumped up and down. "It's a cell phone. My own cell phone."

He glanced to the front of the barn where a woman had emerged from the car. She was petite with severely coifed blonde hair that was too yellow to be real and shellacked to a bulletproof sheen. She must be Brooke. She wore cinnamon-colored jodhpurs, expensive and highly polished black paddock boots, and a gauzy, pale-green, sleeveless ratcatcher. Her arms were tan and toned, and her butt looked like she spent most of her time on a stair-stepper —when she wasn't at the hairdresser.

"Why don't you go find Mike, Nicky," Malcolm said. "I'll catch up."

"But Daddy—"

"Go on."

She made a face, but did as she was told, walking my way with her head down, the cell phone hanging from her wrist by a pink strap. Malcolm intercepted Brooke.

"A cell phone?" I heard him say to her.

"Hey there," I said to Nicky before she ran into me.

She stopped and stared at me. She must have her mother's eyes, I thought. They were dark, and she had glossy brown hair that reminded me of Cali's shiny coat. It was pulled into a ponytail with a purple ribbon. She wore jods and paddock boots and a ratcatcher, just like her mother.

"Who are you?"

"Viola Parker. I work here." I put out my hand.

"Oh, your name rhymes with—"

She stopped herself for some reason, and did not return my shake. Instead, she just stood there, looking lost. I glanced at her parents. Brooke had her arms crossed. I could hear bits of their conversation.

Malcolm said, "A cell phone—for an eight-year-old?"

Brooke asked, "What do you care?"

"I'd like to see your phone." I said. If I could hear them, she could too. "Mine's in the tack room. Let's see if they're the same."

With a glance over her shoulder toward the other end of the barn aisle, Nicky shrugged and followed me.

We sat on the loveseat. I opened my phone and held it next to hers. "Wow," I said, "yours is way better than mine. Look at how big the buttons are."

She nodded. "I can make it ring like a horse's whinny."

I widened my eyes. "Seriously? Coolio." Mine rang when I got a call. That's all I expected.

"None of my friends have phones, though, so I can only call Mommy."

"Oh," I said. "Let me see it for a minute." She gave it to me, and I poked around the menus for a moment, pushed a few keys.

"What are you doing?"

"Programming in some numbers. Here, let me show you." I put it back in her hands. "Push and hold the number two like this, and that will dial your daddy's house, okay? And on the number three, I put his cell phone."

She looked at it like it had turned into a pink lollipop. "Thanks, um—"

"Vi. Just call me Vi."

She stared at the phone, looked at mine, then at me, and back at her phone. "Can you put in your number?"

"My number?" This is why I don't mess with kids. They're always one step ahead of me. "What would you want my number for?"

She shrugged. No reason. But somehow, more numbers made it better. It wasn't that long since I'd been a kid.

"Okay." She handed the phone back to me. I put in my cell number. "Now, what if one of your friends is going to call, but you don't want anybody else to know?"

"What do you mean?"

"See this?" I pointed to a button on the side. "Watch." I lowered the volume until the screen indicated the phone was on vibrate. "Give me your number." She did, and out of habit, I added it to my address book. "Put your phone in your pocket."

She cast me a skeptical look—no one can do skeptical like an eight-year-old—but did as I suggested.

"Stay here."

I went into the barn aisle, stood where I could see through the tack-room door window, and dialed her number. When her phone started vibrating in her pocket, she nearly jumped out of her skin. Her face went from shocked surprise to delight in a breath. She smiled, pulled out the phone and answered.

"Is this Miss Nicola Malcolm?" I asked.

She put her hand over her mouth and giggled. This is why parents don't like me to mess with their kids.

"How'd you know my real name?"

Good guess. I made my voice very serious. "Miss Malcolm?"

"Yes?" she squeaked.

I heard a shuffle not far away, shot a quick look—Malcolm was headed toward me. "Shit."

"What?" Nicky shouted at her end.

"Gotta go. Later, kiddo." I clicked off.

She pointed at me. "You said the "*S*" word."

"Quiet." I made a cutting motion across my throat.

She closed the phone and busied herself near the bridles.

"How are you doing?" Malcolm asked.

He managed to convey more than one meaning with his question—how was I doing with what had happened the night before? How was I doing with Brooke and Nicky there?

"Okay," I said. "Keeping busy."

He tried to see past me into the tack room. "What are you doing?"

I moved to block his view. "Getting ready to exercise Anna." I held the phone behind my back. I was poured into riding tights, so there was nowhere to hide the thing.

I looked over his shoulder in case Dex was ready, and also to see if Brooke was loitering nearby. She stood outside Barbie's stall, staring at her horse. Dex led Miss Bong through the door and waved to me.

"You look guilty as hell," Malcolm said.

"You don't know me well enough to know that."

He leaned close. "Yes I do," he whispered. "You're up to something, but I'll let it go for now because you smell good enough to eat."

My mid-morning snack had been half a can of chocolate whipped cream. I leaned away from him a little and cut my eyes into the tack room where Nicky watched us with great interest. "Hold that thought," I said.

He followed my gaze, then smiled at me. "I will."

I hurried to finish getting Anna ready. I wanted out of the barn and into the sunlight. I liked Malcolm—okay, I more than liked him—but the channel between my head and heart was jumpy with interference from

Norman's unsolved murder, Malcolm's pending divorce, and JJ's violence. I just plain didn't want to be around Brooke. She radiated bad vibes.

After he was single again, Malcolm and I would discuss the partnership—and who knows what else—but for now, I needed air.

"What happened to my horse?" Brooke snapped in Malcolm's direction.

I started to lead Anna past her.

"And who the hell is that?" She pointed at me.

I kept moving. Out under the sun's warmth, I took a deep, deep breath. Dex smiled at me, but said nothing. I swung into the saddle.

"Get rid of her," I heard from inside. "Just get rid of the ugly thing."

I couldn't help wondering if she meant Barbie, or me.

CHAPTER TWENTY-THREE

Dᴇx Two and I rode to the river and let our mounts stand in the cool water.

A dark gray sheet began to hide the western horizon, embroidered occasionally with a delicate thread of lightning. The storm was hours away, but I expected it would hit by nightfall and anticipated a quiet evening cuddled with my dog and a good book, rain pelting the windows.

"It's not too late to press charges, Miss Parker. You were assaulted."

I'd been through this with the sheriff and Malcolm. I didn't have the courage to press charges against JJ. He deserved it, if not for what he did to me, then what he'd probably done to others—particularly women—maybe even Sandy.

"No thanks."

"I respect your choice in this, but as an attorney—"

Malcolm wanted me to press charges *and* get an order of protection.

"I appreciate your concern. Shall we ride?"

We rode in silence, but it took an effort on his part.

Before he left the farm, he pressed his card into my hand.

"Call me at any time for anything, Miss Parker. I mean it."

I put his card upstairs near the phone along with Dex One's.

Supper with Hank and Clara consisted of grilled sirloin steaks, au-gratin potatoes, green beans, and cheesecake. That was a pie I could sink my teeth into.

"I suppose this meat was walking around here not too long ago?" I asked.

"Not for a couple of months," Hank said.

"Did you grow the beans and potatoes?"

"Of course," Clara said, clearly miffed at the suggestion she might use store-bought.

"I suppose you made the cheese for the cheesecake?"

She put her hands on her wide hips. "Do I look like a milkmaid to you?"

I shook my head. "Far from it." Not that I know what a milkmaid looks like. "Nice to know where you draw the line."

Hank sawed his meat into little pieces and cut in the potatoes and beans to make a lumpy hash. "Heard you had a little run-in with our neighbor," he said.

Clara took a seat. "JJ," she clarified.

"You could say that." I shoveled a large bite of the cheesy potatoes into my mouth. I hadn't eaten so many fats and carbs all at once in a long time. I'd forgotten what I'd been missing. If I overloaded fast enough, I'd faint and avoid the coming conversation. I suppose I could say I didn't want to talk about it, and they'd probably respect that. They'd be hurt, too, so I decided to go with the flow.

"He was a sweet boy," Clara said.

"Yeah," Hank said. "Then he growed up."

"What would you be like if your pa just up and disappeared one day?" Clara asked.

"Pass the salt," Hank said in answer.

I braced myself, but Clara didn't go for her carving knife.

"Robert and John Jr. grew up together," she said to me.

"You mean Malcolm and JJ?"

"After the Malcolms moved out here full time," Hank said. "Me and John Sr. took care of the farm for 'em afore that. Best piece of land around."

"Be a terrible shame to lose it," Clara said. "But everybody's got to do what they thinks best, I guess."

"Ain't best to build a hunderd houses on it. What'd we do? We'd have to sell most the herd."

"We'd manage."

"He ain't asked me, anyway," Hank groused. "Never did care what anybody else thought."

"Malcolm's father?" He gestured with his fork and grunted. I took this as a *yes*. "Did JJ's family have a farm around here?"

"Their place is south of here, near the river," Clara said.

So close. "That's where he lives?"

"Ain't nothin' there no more 'cept the old trailer," Hank said. "Clara, I need some bread."

She thunked down a plate of homemade bread in front of him.

"Just a little spit of timber, anyways," Hank said as he buttered a thick slice. "His ma moved to town. He stays with her when he c'ain't find some girl to put up with him."

"His ma weren't never the same after John Sr. went away," Clara said. "But she was always fond of Robert. Used to bake him cookies."

"That was a big help with JJ, wasn't it?" Hank asked.

"You leave her alone, Hank Davis. She's been through enough. John Sr. was no better than JJ. But there wasn't nothin' nobody could do with JJ."

Hank muttered something that I swore sounded like *a bullet to the head would do it*, but I didn't dare ask him to repeat it. He sopped up the mess on his plate with another piece of bread. "Somebody'll do us all a favor and kill him afore long. C'ain't believe the Laird ain't done it already."

"Doesn't JJ have any job skills? What does he do for a living?"

"Odd jobs," Clara said.

"He's a fair mechanic," Hank said, "but he don't want to do nothin'."

"He's took or ruined everything of Robert's he could. Ever since they was kids," Clara said with a shake of her head. "They's like night and day. Robert's an angel and JJ's the devil himself. I don't know why Robert tries to help him."

"I'm sure Malcolm isn't perfect," I said.

Hank snorted. "If JJ ain't careful, he'll be seein' another side of the Laird. I ain't never seen him really mad, and I ain't in no hurry to, neither."

"You think?" I asked. I was pretty sure I'd seen a hint of that other side of Malcolm, and I was damn sure I didn't want to see the full force of it. At least, not directed at me.

Clara laid a reassuring hand on my arm. "Ain't nobody's perfect, that's for sure. Everbody's got their limit."

Later, from the privacy of Hank and Clara's tiny guest room, I called Penny. She'd left a message on my birthday, and I hadn't returned her call. Malcolm and Nicky were at their house having pizza and a princess movie marathon. They'd invited me, but I'd already accepted Clara's offer, and princesses, whether singing, swimming, or dancing, are not my cup of tea. I couldn't help admiring Malcolm for being such a good daddy, though.

"You're going to press charges against that SOB, right?" Penny said.

"No. How can you say that?"

She'd had to do it to an ex-boyfriend-stalker once. I knew exactly what she went through with the unending hearings and court dates because I'd been her only witness. In the end, the prick'd gotten off. He defied the restraining order and came after her with a stolen gun. By then she was with

Frank, and Frank, being a plumber, whacked the guy over the head with a pipe wrench, and he'd bled to death all over their new carpet. That had pissed her off more than anything.

"It's the right thing to do, Vi. At least a restraining order."

"That's a useless piece of paper, and you know it."

"You should get a gun."

"I hate guns."

Penny kept a handgun in her bedside table. Frank kept the pipe wrench between the mattresses on his side of the bed.

My gaze fell on my sleeping dog "Anyway, I have Noire."

"Forget the dog. You got Willy with you, right?"

"Willy's right by my pillow where he always is." Willy's my baseball bat. Penny and I played softball all through high school. I was a lousy fielder, but hit a homer almost every time I connected with the ball. If I'd been able to get to Willy the night before, JJ wouldn't have had a chance.

"You'll keep Willy close if you need to go to the barn at night, right?"

"Yes, Penny."

"You going to Mass in the morning?"

"Are you kidding?" Sundays, if I wasn't gone by four a.m. for a horse show, or due to feed, I slept in. The couple of times I'd gone with her in the last few years, she'd had to elbow me awake during the homily.

"Would I kid about that? It'd be good for you. Light a candle for yourself. God listens."

Not to me. "Gimme a break, Pen."

"But don't go to communion, Vi. Not without going to confession, first. You haven't been in years."

"How do you know?" I asked on a yawn. "Me and God talk all the time."

The dubious minute of silence that followed was answer enough. She was a stickler for the rules. She broke them, too, if it suited her purposes.

"Listen Vi, I know you need to keep this job and all, but are you sure you want to stay? We'd make room for you here, you know what I mean?"

I knew what she meant. On the couch. With a screaming puking baby up all hours of the night. "Thanks Pen, but—"

"You already got something going on with him?"

"Who?" As if I didn't know.

"You haven't shut up about him for twenty minutes."

"There's nothing going on, Pen. At least, I don't think so."

"Not yet, you mean."

"I don't know what I mean. Except…he's just so freaking nice." And nice, I realized, was something I'd had precious little of in my life. That made him perilously alluring and seductive. His physical attributes added to his appeal, but pretty is as pretty does in my book.

Penny didn't attempt to hide the sarcasm when she said, "You're going to stay there for the whole year."

"I'm flattered by your confidence."

"It's not that." She hesitated. I could tell she was cupping her hand over the phone to make sure Frank couldn't hear her end of the conversation. "He's that good, huh?" she whispered.

God love her. "Let's just say it's the right thing to do."

She let loose a snort of laughter. "Sis, you got it bad."

After we hung up, I lay in bed thinking. If I'd been willing to consider what I didn't know, I would have been up all night. And I wouldn't be thinking at all if Wastrel weren't invading my sleep. As it was, someone had killed Norman and disposed of the body in Malcolm's manure pile.

Convenience or intention? Either way, it looked bad. The next day the horses had gotten loose. Sandy suggested someone did that on purpose, and Malcolm confirmed the fence looked like it had been cut. I couldn't exactly connect that dot with Norman's murder, but between the two, Winterlight was closed.

Dex One said to concentrate on *why*, not *who*.

Motive.

Did someone benefit from things being messed up at Winterlight? Or was this only about Norman? How could I learn more about Norman? Sandy.

Of course, I wanted JJ to be guilty, the rat bastard. He was surely guilty of something, that was certain. And plenty capable of violence. He had a grudge against the Malcolms and a chip on his shoulder the size of a redwood. Everyone agreed he was bad news. And there was something going on between him and Sandy. He'd hit her, just like he'd hit me. I was sure of it. But did I want to try and find out more about him?

Not really.

Then there was Brooke. How did she fit into the equation? She obviously had no use for Malcolm, the stupid woman. So far, stupidity wasn't a crime. Which was a shame if you asked me.

I wondered what their divorce settlement looked like. The farm was paid for, but it was Malcolm senior who owned it, so she wouldn't be getting a piece of that. Malcolm junior made good money by the looks of things, and Brooke had expensive taste, if the Caddy and riding togs were any indication. She looked the type to suck him dry in alimony and child support and every other asset she could get her claws into. Could he buy the farm, keep it afloat, pay her, and take care of Nicky? What about custody?

What did I know about any of these people? Malcolm seemed to inspire devotion or loathing. Although more were in favor of devotion. The only two I knew who didn't like him were JJ and Brooke.

JJ and Brooke? Could there be a connection there?

What had he been looking for in the apartment?

I sat up, switched on the light, found a pad of paper in the bedside table drawer and dug a pen out of my purse. There were too many questions to keep track of, so I wrote them down. I made a note of everyone I'd met in the past week—Jesus, had it been only a week? I added what connections and motives I could until the page looked like one of those flight maps for a major airline.

It was possible I was thinking about this backwards. Maybe Norman hadn't been killed so that Winterlight would fail but to shut him up about something so that Winterlight would succeed. Besides Malcolm's personal desires, Dex One and Two both had a stake in keeping the farm undeveloped. Dex One loved Malcolm like a brother, so he'd probably do anything to help him. He'd been not-too-subtly persuasive about getting me on board with helping Malcolm.

Dex Two had made it clear he had a rabid love of all pristine nature. He'd even made passing mention of people like Norman who destroyed the river banks and beds with their four-wheelers.

I didn't know about Renee, but Hank and Clara certainly didn't want to see anything happen to the farm, especially because they lived next door. They hadn't mentioned any children or grandchildren, but it was possible they had heirs who were keeping their eyes on the local property values.

Then, there was Malcolm himself. He was too nice to believe. Maybe I shouldn't let myself be charmed. I'd had a glimpse of his other side, the not-so-patient-and-kind part.

I tossed the pad and pen down and lay back against the pillows. Why was I torturing myself about this? There was too much I didn't know.

A minute later, I snapped on the light again. I picked up the pen and added to my list the names of those I'd heard of but not met.

Like Malcolm senior.

He wanted to sell the land to developers for a butt-load of money. Money, I knew, could be a powerful motivator. But murdering an innocent bystander to make your own son look bad so you could pocket some cash?

That was evil.

And falling asleep with evil on your mind is a bad idea.

CHAPTER TWENTY-FOUR

FIRST THING after feeding the horses—which I did while squirting a can of plain whipped cream down my throat—I called Clara to ask where the church was and if she knew when they held their services. The whipped cream helped relieve the worst of the tension left from my dreams, but I needed a higher power that morning.

While I dialed her number, I thumbed the local phone book. It consisted of precisely thirty-four, five-by-eight-sized pages from A to Z and was little more than a quarter-inch thick. I was used to something the size of a restaurant booster seat.

"You want Baptist, Methodist, Lutheran, or what?"

"Oh, I'm Catholic," I said.

"That's okay, honey, some of my best friends is Catholic."

She gave me the name and number but said I'd have to call to find out the time.

I did, and learned I had less then twenty minutes to finish in the barn, get a shower, and drive ten miles. The apartment was clean as a whistle, not a sign anyone had been there. Except for my empty underwear drawer, I thought I could stay there that night. Henrietta had even brought her kittens back.

I was in my truck in eight minutes, a record, but my hair was still wet. If I drove with the window open, at least one side would be dry by the time I got there. I'd sit in a back pew. It's not like I was going to communion.

I turned the key in the ignition. Nothing. Dead.

I leaned my head on the steering wheel, thinking I'd have been better off having a second cup of coffee and another can of whipped cream then rushing out here like this.

But Wastrel'd been at me all night. First the manure pile, then frantic digging at leaves in the forest. We'd galloped through heavy rain, my cheek against his neck, his wet mane clinging to my skin. I'd felt a driving sense of urgency, as if we were being chased. We'd clattered through the city, though whether St. Louis or New York, I couldn't say. There had been a house. Two stories, brick, white trim. Wastrel left me there. I needed to go inside, but bones had drifted out of the dark windows, and I ran away.

I'd awakened exhausted, and determined that Penny was right, I should go to church. If nothing else, I could talk to the priest about an exorcism. Or maybe, like she'd suggested, I needed penance and absolution.

Pumping the gas pedal and turning the key on and off a few times did nothing. I popped the hood, got out, kicked at the front tire as I went by, and stared at my truck's crusty battery. That's where Malcolm and Nicky found me. They were on their way out in an SUV. He had the Jag, the big pickup, and now this. They were all dark green, and they all worked. I hated him.

Malcolm put the window down. "Going to church?"

Jesus. I couldn't catch a freaking break. Nicky waved from the back seat. I waved to her.

"Do I look like someone who goes to church?"

"Where else would you be going dressed like that?"

I wore a longish linen skirt with an old pair of bike shorts underneath, low-heeled leather sandals, and a brown silk tank over a snug camisole that would have to do until I could get to the local underwear store. He got out and perused my engine compartment.

"Sounds like a dead battery," I said.

"Your terminals look like a root-beer float. You want a lift? I can charge your battery later—if there's anything left to take a charge."

"Very funny." Guess I'd be skipping Mass. I wasn't sure I should go anywhere with him. Look what'd happened when we went to the art museum. "No thanks. It's not important."

Nicky lowered the back window. "We're going to church. Don't you want to go? I can have communion now. I did my reconciliation."

I didn't want to go. I needed to go.

"It's the Catholic Church…" Malcolm said, looking hopeful.

I'd been anticipating a little alone time with God, looking forward to the quiet serenity of solitary meditation, hoping for insight into my poor excuse for a life. If I went with them, I'd be conscious only of sitting side-by-side with Malcolm, reciting the ancient prayers together, and being part of a family unit to which I didn't belong.

But if I didn't go with them, I didn't go at all.

"That's okay," I said, resigned. "Some of my best friends are Catholic."

He smiled. "What a coincidence. Get in."

Nicky clapped and said, "Yay!"

We turned left out of the drive, went a short distance, and cut down a gravel road past a muddy fenced area that looked like a bomb had hit it. No underbrush grew beneath the mostly-dead trees. A ditch ran through the middle of the mess with a trickle of dirty water in the bottom of it. There were even three vultures perched high on a bare limb.

"What happened there?" I asked.

"What do you mean?"

"Look at it—the trees are dead, it's all dug up…" Then I saw the cause. Pigs.

"Hogs," Malcolm said. "They root around and make a mess."

"And they're stinky," Nicky said. She oinked at them.

"You're right about that, sweetie," Malcolm said with a glance in his rear-view mirror. He oinked. She giggled.

"What's the difference between a hog and a pig, anyway?" I asked.

He looked at me like he was trying to determine if I were serious. I just looked back, waiting for an answer. Surely I'm not the only person in the world who doesn't know. We came out on a paved road, and he turned right. I was keeping track so I could find my way again, just in case.

"Technically," he said, "a pig weighs less than one-hundred-twenty pounds, and a hog weighs more."

"Ohhh," I said. "That's good to know." Technically, that made JJ a hog. Although I could think of a few other choice names to call him as well.

"They're all fat," Nicky said.

After a moment, Malcolm added, "Yes, and they're all swine."

Amen.

A few minutes later, we turned off the blacktop into a dirt parking lot filled with pickup trucks, SUVs, a few cars, and one tractor. The church was rosy-pink brick, small and old, but each side contained tall stained-glass windows as colorful as any I'd ever seen. A stone's throw to one side was a field of cattle, and in the back, a cemetery. Most of the others hurrying through the heavy wooden doors were either senior citizens or families with small children. Nicky and Malcolm held hands, and I followed. The walkway was cracked, and we had to hop over a few puddles left by the rain.

Malcolm acknowledged other parishioners with a nod, and we slid into a pew about halfway down on the left. Nicky genuflected to the floor, as only the young and those who have recently received First Communion do, and I followed. Malcolm's fingertips lightly brushed my side as he guided me in, sending a jolt of heat to my core.

I knelt. Malcolm did the same. Our elbows touched where they rested on the back of the pew in front of us. *God*, I prayed most fervently, *a little help here, please?*

Shortly after the first song, Nicky asked to switch places so she could sit next to her father. Perhaps God listened to me after all. I revised that thought the moment she slipped up the aisle to attend the children's liturgy, and Malcolm slid closer to me. I spent the rest of the time admiring the rainbow of sunlight coming through the windows, deluding myself I was contemplating the images portrayed. The artist had a remarkable imagination for halos. Each one was an exquisite work of art of its own.

As we filed out, several folks stopped to extend their sympathy to Malcolm over Norman, or ask if there was any news, and exclaim over how tall Nicky was getting. A few old ladies introduced themselves to me—but I could tell they already knew who I was. And I'm sure they all knew and disapproved of my not wearing proper undergarments.

By the time we reached the truck, I thought I would faint from the strain of maintaining a smile for so long. Malcolm took it all in stride, graciously pressing the flesh like a seasoned politician, alternating between asking about absent family members and promising to be in town for the next parish council meeting.

He was clearly a well-liked and respected member of the community. If any local sentiment supported the sale of Winterlight to developers, it was not evident in this crowd.

With Nicky strapped into the back seat, Malcolm asked, "How about breakfast?"

"Can we go to The Brick?" she asked.

"Of course. But we'll have to help Miss Parker with the work when we get home, okay?" She nodded. He looked at me. "Okay?"

God wasn't listening to me at all. He was too busy laughing. I'm sure He loves it when humans get themselves in uncomfortable situations like this. I don't know what Malcolm prayed for, but the look in his eyes when he said, okay? was hungry, and his appetite was definitely not for scrambled eggs.

The Brick was a little café five miles south. As its name implied, it was red and had the squat proportions of a big brick lying on its side.

The hostess seated us and brought coffee while we looked at the menu. A waitress gave Nicky crayons. She sat next to her dad, flipped over the place-mat, and began coloring. I had taken the seat across from him.

"They have a decent buffet, if you don't like the menu."

"Can I have French toast?" Nicky asked.

"If you have a bowl of fruit," he answered.

She frowned.

"I'll split one with you," I offered.

She nodded vigorously. "Okay."

Malcolm smiled at her. He did that a lot.

"So, have you talked to your father lately?" I asked. I'd meant that to sound nonchalant, but it was apropos of nothing in our conversation. No future in detective work for me. I'd have to ask Dex how he did it.

He didn't look up from his menu. "Why do you ask?"

I sipped my coffee and smiled at the waitress while she poured more for him. "Just curious. You know, I never talk to my parents, so I like to see how adults with normal relationships do it." If it were someone else acting so ridiculous, I would have laughed.

He looked at me then, and didn't smile, exactly, but there was a sparkle of challenge in his eyes. "Define *normal*."

"Anything other than what I have with my parents would qualify."

He closed his menu. "Don't be so sure."

The waitress swung by and took our order. I decided to drop the subject. Maybe I could get something useful out of Hank and Clara.

"Are we going to see Grandpa today?" Nicky asked.

Malcolm took her hand and kissed it. "Not today, Pumpkin. Your mom will be by later so you can go back to Chicago."

"I want to stay here."

"I want you to stay too, but summer vacation starts in a few weeks. Then, we'll be together so much, you'll be sick of me."

"Oh, Daddy, I could never be sick of you." She circled his neck with her arms, pulled him toward her, and kissed him.

I looked away, thinking a trip to the restroom was in order, and that's when I spotted JJ.

CHAPTER TWENTY-FIVE

I KNOW the color fled my face, because I'm sure all the blood drained from my body at that point. It hadn't occurred to me I might see him again, let alone so soon, but I should have prepared myself. As it was, I felt something I'd never felt before. Frozen. Not angry or scared, just witlessly rooted to the spot. Malcolm took one look at me, extricated himself from Nicky's embrace, and followed my stare over his shoulder.

Either JJ didn't see us or he was ignoring us. He went to the register, paid, and didn't look our way. I darted a glance at Nicky. She'd gone back to her drawing. My wits began to return, and with them, an overwhelming urge to hide.

"I'll take Nicky to wash up," I said.

I thought I was dealing with it, but I'd only been ignoring it. I'd been attacked. The man who did it was in the same room with me. I was afraid. Malcolm's hand came down on mine before I could get out of my chair.

"Stay," he said. "No matter what happens."

He held my gaze with his, willing me to feel protected. I'd never depended on someone else and wasn't sure I could start now. Running away was a much better solution. But I left my hand in his grip, kept my eyes on his, and took a deep breath. I'd rather be galloping downhill toward a bottomless ditch on a scared horse, but I remained still. I thought of how I would steady that animal, what I would do to convince her she was brave and powerful, that she could handle it. I pretended to be her. I let Malcolm's strength pervade my senses, and tried to believe that whatever happened, it would be okay.

He drank his coffee. I drank my coffee. Nicky colored. JJ saw us just before he slipped out the door. He paused to allow a couple to enter, and appeared to consider his next move. The background hubbub of people talking and dishes clattering receded to a fizz of white noise. He had a Band-Aid over the bridge of his nose and a black eye. I hoped it was from my punch. I hoped it hurt like hell. He looked me right in the face, then locked his gaze on the back of Malcolm's head. If JJ had a gun, Malcolm would be in the crosshairs. An easy shot. No more than twenty feet separated us.

Malcolm studied my face, and I'm sure he could tell exactly what was going on. I've never been a good poker player.

"Look at me," he whispered in that warm tone that usually made me go all soft and moist. When I didn't respond, he squeezed my forearm. "Vi."

I blinked and looked at him. The waitress brought our food. He kept hold of me, his thumb lightly rubbing the underside of my wrist, looking for all the world like a man with no more on his mind than enjoying breakfast.

JJ started toward us.

"He's coming over," I whispered. I took a long drink of water.

"He's not important," Malcolm said for my ears alone. "He's a scum-sucking pig who doesn't deserve to live."

I gagged on my water and almost spit it across at him.

A feral smile touched the corners of Malcolm's mouth. JJ stopped at the edge of our table. Neither of us looked up, but Nicky did, and I wished she wasn't there. I tried to draw her attention by rattling the ice in my water glass.

"Ain't this a pretty picture," JJ said.

"It was, until you showed up," Malcolm said.

"Yeah, well, I'm gonna get what's mine, Mac, and soon."

"You have what's yours, JJ, and then some." Malcolm ran the index finger of his free hand down the handle of his fork, then along the knife's edge. His eyes had hardened to the same shade of cold silver as the utensils. "If you know what's good for you, you will go far away, and you will stay there."

My eyes strayed to JJ's belt buckle, then wandered up to his face. It had turned an unflattering shade of dark red.

"Or, what?" he asked on a derisive snort.

"You've gotten off easy so far. That'll change."

JJ leaned close. He smelled of engine oil.

"Don't get in my way, Mac. I've had everything that's yours already, one way or another." He raised his hand toward me. "This one—"

Malcolm rocketed out of his seat. I flinched and clamped my hand on his arm before a piece of cutlery became embedded in JJ's chest.

Nicky yelped, "Daddy!"

People at nearby tables stopped eating to stare.

Malcolm stood nose-to-nose with JJ. "Your time is coming," he hissed, "but lucky for you, this isn't it. Get out."

I tugged on Malcolm, and he eased back into his seat. A war of words was one thing, but they were close to blows. And I'm pretty sure my hair was literally standing on end.

"This ain't over," JJ said, and he walked away.

"No," Malcolm said to JJ's receding form, "no, it isn't."

He kept his eyes on JJ until his dilapidated truck pulled onto the highway. In the set of Malcolm's jaw and coldness of his gaze, I could see that long-buried antipathy had risen to churn just below the surface. And I could almost read his mind. JJ was a dead man walking. A feeling like icy fingers walking up my spine gave me a shiver. What the hell had I gotten myself into?

Malcolm turned his attention to us, composed and unruffled. I felt like I'd been through the spin cycle a couple of times.

"Daddy, why are you having an argument with JJ?"

"We're not having an argument, sweetie."

She gave him a look. She knew an argument when she heard one.

"Maybe a little disagreement," he said. "Grownups have them."

She mulled that over, and then asked, "Like you and Mommy?"

Holy shit. Maybe now I could hit the bathroom?

He took a deep breath before answering. "Yes. Like me and Mommy." He laid his arm on the table. "You poked me," he said to me. A row of four crescents showed where I'd dug my nails into his flesh. "Look at that." He showed his arm to Nicky.

Nicky giggled. "Vi, why did you poke Daddy?"

"He needed a good poke." I forced myself to smile at her. "Everyone does once in a while."

"I'll give you a poke," Malcolm said to me with a wink.

I widened my eyes in mock horror and took a bite of salad thinking I should have ordered waffles with extra whipped cream. Surely I could get a side order.

How did he set the anger away? Where could I get a side order of that level of emotional restraint?

"By the way," I said, "you should have said hog."

"I beg your pardon?"

"When you called him a scum-sucking pig. Technically, he's a hog."

He leaned back from the table. "By God, you're right."

"Yes," Nicky said in a very good impersonation of her father, "and they're all swine."

CHAPTER TWENTY-SIX

BACK AT THE RANCH, Malcolm removed and cleaned my truck's battery, and hooked it to a charger. He said he didn't have a great deal of hope for it.

"You think I need a new one?"

I hated to spend the money, but he'd paid me the day before, so I could afford it. He'd overpaid me, actually. Said to consider it a signing bonus. The problem was, as Dex One had pointed out, I hadn't opened a local checking account yet. I could do that after the morning chores, but I didn't have anything to drive.

"Tomorrow, I have to go to a client site in the city. I'll be there most of the day, but I can pick one up for you on my way home."

"That'll work." It would have to. But I didn't like the idea of being alone at the farm without a vehicle.

"Just in case, take these." He gave me the keys to the SUV. "I can use the Jag." He dusted off his hands. "I'm going to help Nicky with Mike."

We walked into the barn together.

"You know how to use a shotgun?" he asked.

I stopped. I hated guns. I'd never held one and had no interest in learning how to shoot one.

"No."

"There's nothing to it—"

"No." I walked away.

He caught up with me. "Vi, this is no time to be stubborn."

My stomach began to knot. "It's not open for discussion. I said no. I mean *no*."

"Why not?"

Hadn't I just said it wasn't open for discussion? The funny thing was, I didn't have a reason. I didn't know anyone who had been killed with a gun. I'd never been shot. Maybe it was irrational. I didn't like them.

"They're…loud." I went into the tack room and shut the door. He didn't pursue it.

A few minutes later, Nicky came in. She'd changed from her church clothes into the jods and boots from the day before. I assumed she wanted Mike's tack, but she didn't go to the bridles or saddles. She didn't appear to have any purpose.

"Going riding?" I asked.

She shrugged.

"Don't forget your helmet," I said.

She frowned. I looked into the barn. Mike was on crossties, but Malcolm wasn't there.

"Did you already brush him?"

"A little."

"Pick out his feet?"

"I forgot that."

"Do you need help?"

She hesitated, then flopped into the chair. I sighed. After the scene at The Brick, I didn't have the energy to play a guessing game with an eight-year-old.

"Mommy says I have to."

Crap. Here we go. I gritted my teeth. "Have to what?"

"Ride."

"Don't you like to ride?"

Another shrug.

I'd dealt with kids before who had been "gifted" with the expensive pony and thousands of dollars worth of tack, riding clothes, and all the other paraphernalia that goes with competing in horse shows. As often as not, it was the parents' show, and their approach usually ran along the lines of 'I spent all this money on you, now you damn well better ride, and you damn well better win.'

Then they'd traipse down to the country club to brag about their kids' blue ribbons. The kids had little or no interest, or they just wanted to bang around the trails, not practice posting without stirrups for hours on end.

I couldn't be sure where Malcolm weighed in on this subject, and I didn't mean to be subversive, but I couldn't help myself.

"How will your mother know whether or not you've ridden?"

She looked at me. Clearly, this possibility had never occurred to her. I decided not to encourage her one way or the other. But if she took matters into her own hands, well...

"Have you ever ridden bareback?"

She shook her head and did not appear intrigued.

"Do you want to see some kittens?"

"Yes!"

Bingo. I led her upstairs.

After half an hour of playing with the kittens, during which time she named them Snowball, Night, Tiger, and Tigress, I asked, "What do you say we put Mike away, and you help me change Cali's bandages?"

"Okay."

I made a quick stop in the kitchen. "First, a little snack," I said. "You like whipped cream?"

"Sure."

She followed me. I brandished two cans. "Plain or chocolate?"

"Chocolate? Okay. No, plain. No, chocolate. No, wait."

"You must make up your mind," I sang and waved the cans in circles, then made a show of squirting some plain into my mouth.

"Oh, me, me, me!" She opened her mouth.

I gave her a squirt. She started to laugh.

"No laughing. You'll choke."

Malcolm's voice reached us from downstairs. "Nicky?"

Nicky snorted whipped cream out her nose. I was laughing so hard, I had to sit on the floor.

Malcolm bellowed, "Nicky!" This time, with a note of worry.

"We're up here," I yelled.

A few moments of silence followed, punctuated by our coughing attempts to stop laughing.

"Can I come up?"

Nicky and I looked at each other. We each took another hit, but she couldn't control herself. She giggled most of it down her chin.

"Should we let him?" I whispered.

"I think I peed my pants," Nicky squeaked.

That's when I snorted whipped cream through my nose.

Malcolm found us sitting on the kitchen floor, holding our stomachs, faces red, crying from laughter, dribbles of whipped cream on the floor and the backs of our hands and dripping down our shirts.

"What the—?"

Which only made us laugh more.

When Nicky could talk, she said, "Daddy, Vi had kittens!"

He joined us on the floor.

A little while later, we had ourselves cleaned up and under control, and Cali on crossties. I explained about her injuries and the finer points of bandaging wounds. Nicky watched with keen interest and asked a lot of questions. She was a good kid.

On impulse, I said, "Next time, you can ride her."

Her eyes widened, she shook her head and backed away. "Oh, no. She's too big."

"I would hold her. You could just sit on her." Why was I even suggesting this? I didn't want anything to do with kids and riding.

"I couldn't."

Fear made her dart her eyes around as if looking for an escape route. "How about Gaston or Fergus?" I asked. "They're nice."

Again, the adamant shake of the head. "No." She moved a little farther from Cali.

Something had spooked her. I hated to see her afraid, but I wasn't about to push her, and anyway, this was none of my business. "Well, Mike isn't so big. He looks like he'd be fun."

"I guess."

No matter what my personal feelings were with regard to kids and riding, it sucked that someone had ruined it for her. I could guess who the guilty party was, and she pulled in a moment later. Nicky's shoulders slumped.

"It's time for me to go."

"It's been really nice meeting you," I said. "Thanks for your help."

"You're welcome." She took the handle of a small suitcase with a big Winnie-the-Pooh on the side and began to roll it down the aisle.

Malcolm, who had been grooming Gaston, took her free hand.

"Nicky," I called. "Keep that cell phone on vibrate, okay? You never know when you might get a call from a secret friend."

"Okay," she said. "Bye."

I waved, and they went out. After the Caddy had disappeared, leaving a small dust cloud in its wake, Malcolm said he and Hank would be working on the new fence at the far end of the pasture. They'd already fixed the broken rails of the riding arena.

He'd changed into his kilt. I couldn't fathom why he liked to work in it, but it must have been comfortable, like he said. The faded plaid consisted of large blocks of dark green and navy with narrow stripes of red, yellow, and pale blue. A tarnished blanket pin held it together.

I opened the gate so he could drive his truck into the horse pasture. He stopped and powered his window down.

"Sure you don't want to help?"

My eyes strayed to his bare knees. The kilt's frayed hem rested a few inches above them. "Tempting, but I have quite a bit left to do in the barn."

He followed my gaze and quirked an inquiring brow at me. "Holler if you need anything, okay? We'll hear."

"Hank thinks that kilt's pretty silly, you know."

"Hank's opinion has been noted on more than one occasion."

"What does Brooke think of it?"

"Hates it." He grinned and leaned his arm out the window. "What do you think of it?"

I bit my lip against a growing smile. "I could get used to it," I said.

He gave me a satisfied nod, and I watched him drive over the bumpy field, fencing materials rattling in the bed.

The moment he was out of sight, I jogged over to where the manure spreader sat. I slowed and followed the path I'd steered the day we found Norman, scanning the ground, looking for something that didn't belong. That could be anything. All I could see was what was supposed to be there—dirt and grass, straw and manure. If there were anything else to find, the deputies would have taken it that day. It'd rained more than once since then, so I didn't know why I was wasting my time hunting for the famous needle in the haystack. Oh, yeah, the crazy dreams.

Crazy, all right. And persistent. And, I don't know. I couldn't explain it, but I was beginning to believe Wastrel was trying to tell me something. And I needed to hurry up and figure it out.

While I kept my eyes focused on the ground before me, I listened for the sound of an approaching truck. I didn't want to have to explain what I was doing. It was a quiet afternoon. I could hear Malcolm and Hank hammering. The breeze brought a few snatches of their conversation, although I couldn't make out any words. Then, they were silent.

I closed my eyes and tried to remember details from my dreams. The day's heat lifted the smell of rain-soaked earth to my nose. I turned my face to the sun to feel its warmth. I'd seen Hank go by earlier with his tractor. A big screw-like thing hung off the back that they must use to dig holes. At the moment, though, it had become quiet. The horses in the field were too busy munching grass to make any other noise. A meadowlark sang from its perch on the electrical wires along the road. Noire watched me from a patch of shade under the spreader.

Just as on that first morning when Malcolm and I went riding together, I detected no human sound. I liked it.

I continued my search down the length of the field and made the turn at the far end just as I had when I'd been on the tractor. Nothing, damn it. There simply was nothing beneath my feet except dirt. If I wasn't supposed to be looking, then what the heck was Wastrel trying to tell me? And what if I did find something? Then what? I stopped about ten feet from the spreader and closed my eyes again.

Yes!

Wastrel had been circling it. I did the same. There was no reason not to go right up to it. My dog was under it. Norman's body was gone. Still, it was hard to make my feet go there. The deputies had dumped most of the compost out. I kicked through some of the piles and finally stood next to the big scary farm implement. Should have brought a pitchfork or something to sift through the stuff inside the box. I crouched to look underneath. Noire rolled to her back for a belly rub, and that's when I saw it—something shiny half hidden in a clump of grass.

"Com'ere, you silly dog."

She wormed her way over to me. I had to get on my hands and knees and reach blindly. My fingers closed on a small, hard…I brought it out and opened my palm. It was a micro-cassette tape, the kind used in answering machines. I stuck it in my pocket and hustled to the barn before anyone saw me.

CHAPTER TWENTY-SEVEN

WITH EVERYTHING except the evening feeding finished for the day, I went upstairs. I could have ridden a couple of horses, but I was beat. A short nap would revive me.

Malcolm had an electronic voice-mail setup, so there were no answering machines available to check out the tape. Could it be what JJ had been looking for in the apartment? If JJ killed Norman, what was his motive?

The answer might be on the tape. I wrapped it in tissue and tucked it inside the brim of my competition helmet, which I kept stored in a box on the top shelf of the closet. I flopped on the bed and promptly fell asleep.

The dream came quickly. Wastrel nudged me toward the tangled underbrush of a dark wood. I didn't want to go. He pushed me again, and I stumbled into someone's living room. Nothing was familiar, and the only thing I could clearly see was a small, white dog gnawing a bone.

Bones again.

It was a little Westie, well groomed with a blue collar. It looked at me, got up and walked to the other side of the room. I followed it through a doorway and stood in the dilapidated kitchen of an old house trailer.

A horse whinnied.

I awoke in darkness and bolted downstairs to feed. A glance at my watch told me it was two hours past the usual time. The moment I stepped into the barn, I turned on my heel and went right back up the stairs to retrieve Willy. I wasn't interested in toting a shotgun, but there was no need to be careless about self-protection. While I was at it, I grabbed a quick hit of whipped cream to bolster my courage, wondering if Malcolm and Hank were working in the dark or if they'd come in while I'd slept.

Feeding the horses took three trips to the grain bin. It was awkward keeping Willy in one hand, but why take chances? I rushed through my routine, glancing over my shoulder more than once when a horse huffed or banged a hoof against the wall. Help might be within shouting distance, but my heart beat faster than usual every time I passed an open doorway, wondering who lurked in the primeval dark.

Or in the loft, I thought as I hurried past the ladder.

Worst of all, Noire had taken off. She was probably with Malcolm and Hank.

I was watering when I heard someone come up behind me, and my first thought was, this can't be happening again. Every time someone believes that in a movie, they end up with a knife between their shoulders…or worse.

I put my left thumb over the end of the hose to squirt it with maximum force, and spun around, swinging Willy as hard as I could.

It was already too late when I realized it was Malcolm. The man had fast reflexes. He ducked. Good thing, or I would have knocked him out. I did soak him, though.

I stood there, unable to do anything but stare at him, breathing hard, hearing only the blood pounding in my ears. I dropped the hose.

"It's just me, Vi," he said quietly.

He stripped his sopping shirt over his head, wrung it out, and slung it over a rung of the loft ladder. Willy clattered to the floor. Malcolm shook water from his hair. I moved back a pace, fear replaced by another emotion that elevated my heart rate.

"It's just me," he said again, coming forward.

He had broad shoulders and a well-muscled chest, just enough hair to run my fingers through, smooth skin highlighted by sunburn. The kilt rested on his hipbones, exposing his navel and flat abs. I moved away until I hit the wall. He came right up to me, his blue eyes pinning me in place. I could smell sweat and dirt on his skin.

"Just me," he whispered.

His arm snaked around me to turn off the water. We stood like that a long moment, and I held my breath.

"You startled me," I said.

"I know. I'm sorry. Good thing you didn't take the shotgun."

I let my forehead touch his collarbone, felt his heart beating as wildly as mine. My nipples strained against my T-shirt to make contact with his bare chest.

"I nearly took your head off." I looked up at him.

"You have a hell of a swing. Would have been ugly if you'd had the gun."

His voice was low and slow, a soothing caress, but calm was far from what I felt. He leaned one hand against the wall near my right shoulder and rested his cheek against my hair.

"What were you doing sneaking up on me like that, anyway?" I asked, trying for nonchalance and failing. All at once, I felt stretched and enveloped, as if he were pulling me inside him.

"I didn't mean to." He kissed the bruise on my forehead. "I decided to leave the truck at the other end of the field and walk back. It's a beautiful night. I was about to say something, but you were too quick."

His breath tickled my ear, sending little tremors straight to my lower belly. If I didn't get away from him, my personal volcano would erupt. I shifted to the left. He brought his other arm up on that side.

"How about a walk?" he asked. "We need to talk."

"I need to get to bed." But first I needed to smack myself for saying that.

A leisurely smile curled his lips. "Okay."

"That's not what I meant, and you know it."

I didn't think that's what he intended, either. But there were times like this in my past when I wouldn't have hesitated. He was still married, and that was reason enough to pause. It was also the potential. If I started a relationship with this man, I wouldn't be able to walk away from it without a backward glance like I usually did. That terrified me. More than anything, I didn't want to screw it up.

But at the moment, I could scarcely breathe. After what happened with JJ, I needed more space then he'd been giving me.

"I feel a little trapped here."

His face looked stricken, and he backed off. "You're safe with me, Vi."

"That's debatable." He gave me a narrow look, and I amended, "I mean, I know I'm safe, but..." Physically safe, yes, but emotionally? No.

He nudged my knee with one of his, moving my leg slightly to the side, closing the space between us again.

"I think I know exactly what you mean," he said.

I was sure he was safe, but I still felt scared. "I didn't thank you for the other night," I said. Not much of a delay tactic.

"For what?"

"For saving me."

My hands had been flat to the wall behind me. I moved them to his lower ribs. Big mistake. I'd thought to ease him away a little. His nearness made it hard to think. But he simply felt too right, and his sharp intake of breath when I touched him discouraged any thought of separation.

Thinking was highly overrated.

"I should have been there sooner. If he ever goes near you again, I'll kill him."

I blinked and took a gulp of air at the force of his tone. That was as unambiguous as it gets.

"About that kilt—"

He prodded my legs wider. "What about it?"

"It doesn't do much to…er—" He touched my neck with his tongue, and I forgot what I was saying.

"Doesn't what?"

"Doesn't hide what you're feeling very well," I whispered. What I was feeling was a rush of heat that would soon be out of my control. I wanted that heat, wanted him right then, and more, but…surely we should stop.

I felt him smile against my jaw. "I haven't been trying to hide my feelings." He brushed my lips with his.

I did push against him then, for all the good it did. It was like trying to move a horse that'd stepped on your foot. It was a half-hearted attempt on my part, anyway. I didn't want him farther away, I wanted him closer.

He moved back so he could look at me. His eyes were no more than a couple of inches from mine. I could barely endure the intensity, but I couldn't look away, either.

"Am I making you uncomfortable?" he asked.

Now, how the hell was I supposed to answer that? Of course he was making me uncomfortable. He leaned a little farther back when I didn't say anything. It didn't help.

"Vi?"

"Yes," I said. "And no. I'm not uncomfortable the way you think."

I should have told him to stop, to go home. But, God help me, I didn't want him to. What was the neon sign on my head flashing now? Stop? Go? Alternating between the two?

He watched me for a sec, probably trying to figure out which it was for himself. Must have been Go, because he came close again and made a yummy sound.

"Why do you always smell so good?"

"I'm as sweaty and dirty as you, so it must be the whipped cream."

He kissed me. It took me off-guard at first, the contact was so gentle. I was afraid to move. He deepened it, took my shoulders, and pulled me against him. The rush of heat detonated. I wrapped my legs around his hips, and he pushed me into the wall, his hands taking my hips to support me.

I lost track of time, of myself, knew only the feel of him against me, and nothing else mattered. I'm fairly certain some very un-ladylike groans escaped my throat.

At some point, we stopped kissing, but stayed where we were, holding each other, breathing like we'd run a marathon. I still had my pants on tight, but my volcano had erupted. His, too.

"Vi, I'm sorry, I shouldn't have—"

"Please don't apologize. I…that's never happened to me before."

"Me neither," he said on a relieved chuckle.

"But we probably shouldn't let it happen again."

"I'm not making any promises, but you're probably right. We shouldn't. At least not until…what are you doing Wednesday starting at about two in the afternoon?"

I furrowed my brow at him. "I'll be here."

"Can you clear your schedule?"

"I guess, why?"

"That's when I'll be back from my lawyer's office."

"Your lawyer?"

"I'll be a free man again."

CHAPTER TWENTY-EIGHT

ON THAT NOTE, he kissed my forehead, and eased my feet to the floor. He kept his hands on my hips while I got my legs under me and sorted out my shirt, which somehow had gotten shoved up to my armpits. His thumbs grazed the bare skin of my sides, sending shivers through me. I didn't know what to do or say. I wanted him to stay with me, knew he shouldn't.

He took my hands and kissed my fingers. "I don't want to leave you, but Dex One will be here soon. I wouldn't want him to get the wrong idea."

"Dex?"

He retrieved his wet shirt and curled one arm around my neck—a gesture both casual and intimate. We walked to the front of the barn.

"I assumed you wouldn't consider sleeping in my guest room, especially if Nicky isn't home. You won't stay at Clara's, I can't be here all the time, and I can't allow you to be alone. He's been keeping an eye on things."

"You mean keeping an eye on me."

He turned me toward him. "I mean keeping watch for JJ, Vi. If anything happened to you—"

"Of course." I pressed my fingertips to my eyes. Jesus. I was so tired. "I'm sorry."

He hugged me. "Don't be. I'm sorry all this has happened…" He stopped, squeezed me closer. "All I've done since you arrived is apologize."

Brooke, I thought. She must have blamed him for everything. "Mr. Malcolm—"

He set me away from him. "Call me Robert?"

His smile looked uncertain, as if he regretted asking the second the words left his mouth.

There was a moment then, just a moment, when I knew exactly what he looked like when he was a boy. I yearned to know that side of him. The side he kept hidden. And share that part of myself with him. He must have recognized the expression on my face, because the smile became more confident.

"I can do that," I said, "but it makes it harder to say what I was going to say." It was difficult enough with the soft night air flowing around us, and him with no shirt, and the memory of his kisses fresh on my skin.

He quirked one eyebrow.

I tried saying his name. "Robert." Yep, way more intimate than calling him Malcolm, like everyone else. But he'd asked me to call him by his first name, and I would. And his face lit up when I said it. I took a deep breath and continued. "You are the nicest man I've ever met."

He tried to keep the smile on, but I could tell that was not what he wanted to hear.

"That didn't come out right."

His brows drew together. I was confusing him again.

"You are nice, and many other things as well, but I think what I mean is kind. You are truly kind and not afraid to show it. That's rare. At least, it has been in my experience. And you're generous, too."

I didn't know how to say I didn't want to screw this up. I'd had no practice honestly expressing my emotions. There'd never been the need. And there was this other niggling thought that kept bugging me—that I wasn't good enough for the likes of him.

"You don't really know me very well," he said.

"It's true we haven't known each other long, but it's been…"

"Intense?"

"Yeah, that's one word for it. But, you don't need to apologize to me for anything. I'm a big girl. Everything isn't your fault."

He let out a long breath, as if hearing that was a relief. He looked around at the horses and the barn, and got that faraway look again. Then, he pulled me against him, a quick, hard embrace.

"When things calm down," he said, "I want to talk about that partnership. I don't guess you've had much time to think about it."

"I'm not sure I know what to think about it. I need a little more information. Next week?"

"Yes, next week. Now, I won't say I'm sorry again, but I shouldn't have forced myself on you so soon on top of everything else. It's just that…"

"You didn't force yourself on me. I feel…"

"…I've never felt this way about anyone."

"…the same."

We pushed apart and both said, "What?"

He found a bit of dirt on the floor to stare at, and I studied cobwebs in the rafters.

"I think we should go ahead and have the Monday ride, if you're up to it," he said.

"Yes," I agreed, "the sooner everyone gets back in the routine, the better. There are enough sound horses to do it."

"I'll give you the schedule for the rest of the week as soon as I can."

"Good. Thanks."

We said a good night as if nothing had happened.

But it had. Even if whatever had transpired between us—and I wasn't sure what that was—hadn't, my feelings would be the same, and I tossed and tangled my sheets for some time trying to sort those out.

I thought I knew what love felt like, but nothing I'd experienced in the past resembled what had grabbed hold of me almost from the first moment I set foot on Winterlight. Before, I'd known infatuation, lust, even affection. But this—this was an overwhelming sense of connection, the irresistible pull of belonging, and a devastating awareness of inevitability.

It scared the crap out of me.

I'd never belonged anywhere. My aunt and uncle raised me and never treated me any differently than they did Penny, but I knew I wasn't theirs. Penny had given me a place to live, but I'd always been a well-tolerated temporary guest.

I didn't feel connected to anyone or anything, except the horses I rode. I'd always assumed that was just how I was. Now, I wasn't so sure. Is this what Penny meant when she said I'd never found my home? Maybe she was on to something after all.

My instinct was to run away. That was precisely what I'd done all my life when the emotional going got tough. That scared feeling would bloom in my gut, and my head would tell me to run. I'd create a reason to leave, whether it was a job or a relationship.

Never would I admit my fear—of caring, of getting hurt—and worse—being cared for, and having the capacity to hurt others. I never wanted to feel *at home*. But now, I couldn't leave, no matter what my head said. I was stuck. I had to face this.

Or did I? I'd agreed to stay at Winterlight for a year. But if I wanted to leave badly enough, I already had plenty of reasons to make an excuse to run along. At this point, the stupid trust fund didn't even figure into my thinking. I flipped onto my stomach and punched my pillow. Noire pushed her feet against my side and stretched.

I could blame my father for the situation, but the truth was, I had arrived here thanks to my own damn choices.

The problem was that this time, there was something new between my gut and my head, an organ I was thoroughly unacquainted with.

And that was my heart.

CHAPTER TWENTY-NINE

IN THE MORNING, I made coffee, groomed horses for the ride, and tried not to think about the latest dream. It was very similar to the previous one. The woods, the living room, the Westie with the bone, the derelict trailer. Wastrel was consistent, if not clear.

Malcolm left at eight, but not before Dex One pulled in. They talked before Dex came in, and Malcolm drove off with a wave. Warring feelings of disappointment and relief formed a knot in my chest. It was just as well, I told myself, that he left without coming in.

"Changing of the guard?" I asked.

"Guilty as charged. I won't kid you about it. Hank and Clara are taking some steers to the sale barn today."

"So, you're my babysitter."

"Think of me more as a paid companion."

"He's paying you?"

"Not in the way you think. Anyway, no one would have to pay me to spend the day with you, Miss Parker."

It was hard to stay mad at Dex, and I wasn't angry with him, anyway. I'd awakened with tension perched in my body like a hawk too long without a meal and apprehension roosting in my brain like a sparrow too far from its nest. I couldn't wait to mount up and work out the kinks. Riding through long dreams with Wastrel had only added to my anxiety.

"Got a present for you," Dex said.

I'd been busy combing Smitty's tail, so hadn't noticed he held something behind his back. He produced a Mason jar with a bunch of wildflowers in it.

"Oh, I—"

"They're from him." He pointed over his shoulder with his thumb indicating the direction Malcolm—Robert—had gone. He didn't try to hide his disapproval of such nonsense.

I put the bouquet in the tack room. The knot in my chest unraveled.

"Weren't you already here all night?" I asked when I returned to the barn.

"I see there are no secrets with you."

"Where'd you sleep, in your truck?"

"Sleeping would defeat the purpose of keeping watch, now, wouldn't it?"

"Okay," I said. "Are you coming along on this ride, or staying here?"

"I have my orders. Riding shotgun, Ma'am."

"Oh, please, not literally?"

"Hell no. Shotguns are for folks who don't know how to shoot." He sat on the tack-room steps. "No offense to Mac. I know he likes the cannon, and it's a good choice for home defense." He hiked up one pants leg to reveal a holster with a shiny handgun strapped in.

"Fine," I said. "Just don't shoot yourself in the foot."

"Miss Parker, I will have you know—"

I held up my hand. "Save it. Let's get the horses tacked up."

After the blessedly uneventful ride, Dex said he'd clean stalls while I took care of the injury list. He grabbed the wheelbarrow and the tools he needed.

"I'm glad you're here," I said before he went very far.

He turned and leaned on the pitchfork. "My pleasure, Miss Parker."

"You can call me Vi, you know."

He chuckled at what appeared to be a private joke. "If it's all the same to you, I'll stick with Miss Parker."

"Then if it's all the same to you, Mr. Hamill, let's get to work."

He laughed and started to push the wheelbarrow to the first stall, stopped and turned. "By the way. I have news about Norman."

I don't know why I went cold. I wasn't sure I wanted to hear the details.

"He suffocated."

I tried to let that sink in, but my brain refused to process it. "So, he wasn't dead when he was put in the manure pile?"

Dex shook his head slowly. "Very likely unconscious. He had enough cat valium in his blood to drop a horse."

"Cat valium?"

"Ketamine hydrochloride."

"Never heard of it."

"Veterinary anesthetic."

"Still never heard of it, and I've been around vets and drugs plenty."

"They don't dispense it, so there's no reason you'd know what it was. It's used for surgery. People take it, sometimes."

"Norman was taking an animal anesthetic?"

"It's also a psychedelic. You've heard of date-rape drugs?"

"I'm not that out of touch."

"This is one of them."

I had no idea what to make of this information or how to fit it in with the rest of my half-baked ideas. "So, he might have been taking it for recreational purposes, or he might have been given it?"

"Right."

"Wouldn't there be a needle mark?"

"Not necessarily. When a guy gives it to a girl in a club, he dumps it in her drink."

I sank down onto the tack-room steps thinking that sounded like JJ's style. Then again, he probably liked having an excuse to hit his victims. "But—"

"Think *motive*, Miss Parker."

"They teach that in Detective Work 101? Why do you think someone would want to murder Norman?"

"And hide his body at Winterlight. That's the question."

Hadn't he just said motive was the question? I had my theories about Norman's murderer, but I wasn't ready to share. Without knowing more about Malcolm's father, that one didn't hold much water. JJ was a more likely culprit, if I could determine his motive. I'd have to do some digging for that, and I didn't want to soil my hands with that dirt.

Clearly, Dex wasn't interested in sharing his theories, either.

"Where do people get this cat valium?"

"Steal it, usually, from veterinarians. Or buy it from someone who has."

"Have any of the local vets reported a robbery?"

He shrugged. "No way of knowing where it came from."

I couldn't remember anything from my dreams that pointed to a drug overdose. Maybe if I got off the farm for a while, that would help me think. And a good, long ride by myself would be great.

"I need to run an errand," I said. "I think I'll go do that."

"Heard your truck was out of commission."

"Malcolm lent me his SUV. Come on. We'll get lunch in town." I ran upstairs for my purse. Back in the barn, I asked Dex, "Does town even have a place where you can get lunch?"

"Town has a place, but I need to stay here. And you can't go alone."

Oh, for cripe's sake. "You've got to be kidding."

"I have some discretion. What's the nature of your errand? Do you have a cell phone?"

"You'll be happy to know I'm opening a checking account at the local bank. If you're like most men, you're also happy to know I'm without under-garments and need to buy some. And, yes, I have a cell phone."

His glance scanned my chest and continued on down. Men. Sheesh.

"Since you brought it up, I prefer my women to wear underwear…so I can have the pleasure of taking it off of them. But I'm not sure you'll find anything you like nearby."

I'm sure what he meant was he didn't think I'd find anything he'd like nearby. He made me program his cell number into my phone, said he'd call an order in for lunch, insisted I stop only at the bank and to pick up our sandwiches, and wanted me back in half an hour. And, I had to call and check-in every five minutes.

"Sure you don't have one of those nifty little electronic ankle bracelets I could borrow?"

"Don't tempt me."

I walked to the house where Malcolm's SUV was parked in a garage around back, hopped in, adjusted the seat and mirrors, and took off. Evidently, town had a general store that made sandwiches. I would have given anything for a pepper-and-egg hero from a New-York deli, but I'd have to settle for ham and cheese on potato bread, the same as Dex ordered.

I settled into the SUV's leather seat and turned onto the blacktop. It felt good to be out and about on my own, even if only for a short time. Not to mention being out and about in style. The SUV had bells and whistles I didn't know existed. My truck was over ten years old, and if I hadn't dated a mechanic off and on over the past three, it would have gone to the junkyard long ago. The torn bench seat was convenient for naps at horse shows, but that was about it. Comfort wasn't on its list of attributes. Except for getting me from point A to point B—most of the time—it didn't have any attributes.

I cranked up the stereo and enjoyed the scenery. Malcolm—Robert—had radio stations pre-programmed for classic rock, jazz, classical, oldies, and NPR. The six-CD player contained Jethro Tull, Sting, Handel, Patsy Cline, Tony Bennett, and, *good lord,* bagpipes. Except for that, I couldn't argue with his taste.

I allowed myself a warm memory from the night before, and felt my body softening at the thought of him against me. Robert. For a split second, my thoughts wandered to a place I never allowed—the future. I reined them in sharply.

For music, I chose the tried and true—Jethro Tull. It was one of my favorites, *Heavy Horses*. Listening to the news didn't interest me; I'd had quite enough from Dex already. I jabbed at the stereo's buttons, glanced at the road, negotiated a sharp turn with one hand, and continued trying to get to the right CD.

To either side, the sun shown on grazing cows, casting their shadows over impossibly green grass. Almost every cow had a calf nearby, either sleeping or nursing. In the congestion of my former life, I'd forgotten there must still be places like this in the world. Like the quiet I'd begun to enjoy, I liked the open vistas, the unhampered view to the horizon.

A little farther along, I plunged into the shade of woods. I'd been this way when I went grocery shopping, but didn't know the road well. Still, there was no other traffic to worry about. I topped a small rise and headed downhill toward a rickety-looking, narrow bridge over the rushing creek, light glinting off its swiftly changing surface.

Out of the corner of my eye, I saw movement and let off the gas. A doe and two fawns hopped onto the road from the ditch. Shit. I jammed my foot on the brakes. They caught and the SUV skidded sideways. I steered into it, fishtailed, and overcorrected. Suddenly, the pedal met the floor, and the brakes went out. I lost sight of the doe. The wheels caught the opposite shoulder. The SUV tipped, landed on the roof, slid backwards toward the creek, and came to a scraping halt.

I hung upside down in the seat belt and caught my breath for a few moments, then ran down my body checklist out of long habit. This was a piece of cake compared with getting dumped by a galloping horse. All those falls had taught me not to panic, but to get up quickly, and secure the horse. I wasn't hurt, but a touch disoriented—I didn't usually land head down, feet up. In the rearview mirror, I could see water lapping along the back windows.

First, I hoped I hadn't squished any deer. Second, I was glad I hadn't opened the sunroof, which I'd been about to do. Third, I figured I'd better get the hell out of there because the SUV was slowly shifting farther into the creek.

Ian Anderson still blared from the speakers. The engine had stalled. I turned the key and removed it, pushed against the ceiling to lessen the pressure on the belt, unbuckled, and maneuvered myself upright. The driver's door wouldn't budge. It was against the embankment. I crab-walked to the passenger side, released the handle with my foot, kicked the door open, and climbed out.

I shook myself and noticed that each blade of grass appeared individually illuminated. The thousand ripples and purls of the creek mixed with bird song and the sigh of leaves moved by a breeze. The stench of oil and gas rose from the engine. It pinged, and fluid dripped somewhere.

The hyper-vigilance of adrenaline had me in its grip again. Looking at the dirty bottom of the truck with its wheels in the air made me dizzy. I pushed the strap of my purse onto my shoulder and walked away from it, fishing my phone out of my purse at the same time.

No signal down here in the little river valley.

A blue Beetle came from the direction of town. Renee. I scrambled up to the road and waved. She stopped, leaned across the seat, and rolled down the passenger window.

"Vi?"

"Renee, am I glad to see you. Can you give me a lift?"

She looked from me to the SUV. "What happened? Are you all right?" She flicked on her car's emergency flashers, got out, and came over.

"You think he'll be upset?" I asked, gesturing lamely toward the overturned vehicle.

"Honey, you're looking a might peaked. You better sit down. Here." She opened her car door. "Get in."

I got in. She put a bottle of water in my hand.

"I'll be right back." She went down to look at the wreck.

I couldn't believe Malcolm had lent me his truck when it had faulty brakes. He was the type to keep everything in good working order.

Renee returned and sat behind the steering wheel. "Let's get you home."

"You didn't see any dead deer underneath it, did you?"

"Girl, did you hit your head?"

"I don't think so." But the temptation to bang my head against the wall had come over me all too often of late.

"Let me look at you." She took my face in her hands. They were cool. She had long fingers that she used to gently probe my scalp, then hold my jaw and move my head. "Neck feel okay? Dizzy? Vision blurred?"

I resisted the urge to slap her hands away. "Too many questions. What about the deer?"

"What deer?" She pulled my lower lids down and peered into my eyes. "Have you been drinking or something?"

"No, I haven't been drinking." I removed her hands from my face. "I was going to the bank. A freaking deer family jumped in front of me. I slammed on the brakes, but…" They'd caught at first, then went out completely. Malcolm would keep his truck serviced. Could someone have…

"But what?"

"They didn't work."

CHAPTER THIRTY

"Peaked?" I asked as we drove to Winterlight. "Is that a reference to my aura?"

"You better stop that," she said, but with a smile. "No, 'peaked' would be a reference to you looking whiter than even white people are supposed to look. And you're not usually so white to begin with."

"Um…thank you?"

"Welcome."

"And I'm sorry I was so unpleasant about your smudging."

"I guess it is kinda weird if you've never seen it before."

"That doesn't make it okay to be like that."

"Forget it," she said with a wave of her hand. "That was Malcolm's SUV, wasn't it?"

"He lent it to me. My truck has a dead battery."

She shook her head and said nothing other than, "Um, um, um," until we pulled in. "I see Dex One is here."

I mimicked her tone. "Um-hm."

"He's fine for a white boy, isn't he? But then, so's Malcolm."

I hesitated, unsure of my footing with her. "They both seem like good guys…"

She flashed a grin full of perfect, white teeth. "I'm just messing with you. My husband was white."

Before what, she dyed him black? "Was?"

"He passed on last year."

"I'm sorry."

"Why, you didn't make him dead, did you?" She looked at me with raised eyebrows, as if she suspected I might have had something to do with it.

"Eh...no."

"I didn't think so. Let's give Mr. Goody-Gum-Shoe the news. Is Malcolm here?"

"No, he went to a client's in the city," I said. "Do you know what he does?"

"Something with computers. Programming, I guess."

I had a hard time picturing him hunched over a keyboard. "He doesn't strike me as the computer geek type."

"Dex says he was a jock when he was in school. Baseball, football, whatever. And that sport where you do five things—pentathlon?"

"The one where you ride, shoot and...?"

"Fence, run, and swim," she finished for me. "Yeah. Guess you have to be in good shape to do all that. He's still got that athletic build. Keeps himself fit."

"Athletic. Yeah. That's what I'd call it, too."

"Hah." She poked me in the shoulder. "Good one, New York. Just admit it, you think he's fine."

There was no point denying it. An image of him after he stripped off his shirt the night before popped into my brain. "Yes, I'd have to say he's mighty fine."

Dex One gave Renee's car and me getting out of it a very thorough once-over. Not the kind that expresses admiration.

"What happened?"

I looked to Renee, let her explain.

"Vi swerved to avoid Bambi and flipped Mr. Malcolm's SUV near into the river. You got a problem with that?"

He jerked his head around and gave me a different kind of once-over. "Are you all right?"

"I think so. I had my seat belt on."

"Don't she look kinda pale to you?" Renee said.

He took my arm and started toward the barn. "Come inside and sit down."

"The brakes went out."

He stopped and turned very slowly. "Say that again."

"She said the brakes went out," Renee said. "You losing your hearing now too, Dex?"

He gave her a look I couldn't read. "Have you told anyone?"

"No," I said. "It just happened. Renee came by right after."

"Good. I'm going to have a look. You sit tight. I'll call Malcolm and a tow truck when I get back."

We watched him get in his truck and drive off.

"Sit tight," Renee spat. "Who does he think he is, anyway, telling us to sit tight? He might as well have said, 'Now don't you worry your pretty little head about it, darlin', I'll take care of everything.'"

"It's fine with me." I went to the tack-room. This was my chance to get out of Dodge, and I wasn't going to miss it.

She followed. "You sure you're okay?"

"Yes. Just a little shaky." I considered running upstairs for a shot of whipped cream or some sort of snack, but decided it could wait. "Let's go for a ride."

"You sure you're up to it?"

I did a neck roll, stretched, and cracked a few joints. "Oh, yeah. The real question is how fast can you be ready?"

A little light lit behind Renee's eyes. She ran to get Smitty, who hadn't been badly injured after all when all the horses got out, and I grabbed Gaston.

Two minutes later, we were on a trail, and I breathed a sigh of relief. Finally. Not quite alone, but I was fairly certain Renee was sane, she wouldn't chat my ear off, and she wouldn't give me the third degree. I hadn't seen her ride, but I had a feeling she could keep up.

"Now, you want to tell me what the rush was, New York?"

I tilted my head in the general direction of the barn. "That fine piece of white flesh back there was on the job, and his job was keeping an eye on me."

"You in some kind of trouble?"

I explained about JJ.

"Ohhhh, I see." She shook her head. "Never did like that boy."

"Bad aura?"

"Um," she said with emphasis. "Bad news all the way round."

We trotted side-by-side along a field. She was slim and had a strong leg and soft hands. Smitty mouthed the bit, but didn't fight. They presented a pleasant picture, and Renee was a good rider. Smitty wasn't as big as Gaston, but he was fit. She looked to be, too, though I couldn't tell her age. She had graying hair, but her skin, which was the rich brown of a well-oiled bridle, was as smooth as mine. She could be anywhere from my age on up to fifty.

"What about Norman?" I asked.

"He was okay," she said. "Nothing like JJ. But I worried anyway."

We took a path into the woods that might have been a dirt road at one time, now overgrown with disuse, but still wide enough for us to ride abreast.

"Worried about Norman, or you worried when he was around?"

"Neither, exactly. I worried he wasn't good for Winterlight, you know? He just didn't have the kind of image I think Malcolm wants to present to the public."

I thought of Norman's over-the-top cowboy routine.

"I wouldn't want anything to happen to this place," she said.

She might know of Robert's dilemma, but not necessarily.

"Why would anything happen to this place?"

She brought Smitty to walk, and we let the horses stretch their necks. There, Penny, I thought, I'm riding on the buckle. Happy now?

"I don't know," Renee said. "I just wouldn't want to lose it." She stroked Smitty's neck. "He was my husband's horse, you know. After Leroy died, I had to sell him to pay some debts. Malcolm bought him for a fair price and promised he'd keep him until I could buy him back."

Was the man a freaking saint?

"I didn't ride when Leroy and I first met. Took it up to please him. Loved it. He bought me a pack of lessons for my birthday last July. Then he up and had a heart attack." She shook her head and sighed. "Not that Norman was much of an instructor. But if something happened to Winterlight…it's my connection with Leroy, see?"

I saw. And I added Renee to my list of potential suspects. Maybe they all did it, like Murder on the Orient Express. I didn't like being suspicious of everyone, though. And I still didn't know what Norman had done to get himself killed in the first place. I needed to find a way to listen to that tape. Sandy would probably know if Norman had an answering machine it fit. Not that that would mean anything. Maybe she had an answering machine that took a little tape like that. Did I want to involve her? No, I decided. But I did wonder where she'd been.

I put it out of my mind. It was a glorious day, not too hot, not too cold. Gaston could feel the current of eagerness running through me and tossed his head in anticipation.

I pointed to the trail ahead. "Where does this go?"

"Never followed it to the end, but it runs like this for quite a ways. Probably goes to the river. I don't care for water, so I don't go down there."

"Clear and level, no sudden ravines or sharp turns or low branches?"

She got that gleam in her eye again. "You have something you want to do, New York? Something that involves speed?"

"You read my mind."

She smiled and dropped back a length. "Lead on, you wild white woman, lead on."

"Yell when we get beyond the area you're familiar with, okay?"

She nodded.

I set off in canter and after a few strides, took a glance over my shoulder to make sure she was okay. She gave me a thumbs-up, and I let Gaston flatten down into gallop. He cut loose with a few bucks, and I heard Renee whoop.

"Yeehaw," I yelled.

I hunkered down over his neck and felt at home for the first time since coming to Winterlight. The only way it could have been better was if I'd been aboard Cali...or Wastrel. But Gaston was smooth and sure and strong. He reveled in the freedom of the full-out run just as much as I did.

We rounded several turns, went down an incline, then up again and through a small clearing. Beyond that, a log crossed the path, but we jumped it easily, and so did Renee and Smitty. She laughed. Smitty must've done something silly. After another minute, Gaston began to slow on his own, and I let him. We cantered, then trotted, and Renee brought Smitty alongside. They were both breathing hard, but she grinned.

"That was great, New York! Wow. Don't know if I've ever galloped that long at one time before. Whew. Thanks." She wiped a small clod of dirt off her cheek.

"Felt good, didn't it? It's great to just blow it out every now and then. Good for the engine, just like a car." My head felt clearer than it had in days. I thought I'd never get out of that place.

"I think the horses liked it, too." She rubbed Smitty's sweaty shoulder. "Didn't you, boy?"

We were still on the overgrown road, in dense woods, but I thought I could see it clearing up ahead.

"Do you know where we are?"

She looked around. "No, this is way past where I usually turn around. I'm not even sure we're still on Winterlight."

"How big is the farm, anyway? Do you know?"

"Not exactly, but it's over five-hundred acres."

I couldn't imagine how big that was, or how you'd know when you had crossed the border onto someone else's property. I'd have to ask Malcolm for a map. It was certainly big enough to get lost on. Or to hide something.

The trees thinned up ahead, and I could make out the shape of a structure of some kind.

"Looks like we might be coming to someone's else's ground," Renee said. "Maybe we should go back."

Maybe, but something drew me forward. "What direction have we been going?" I was pretty sure we'd headed south away from the barn, but we'd made so many turns since then, I'd lost track.

"Mostly south, I think, why?"

"Does that look like a trailer to you?"

She looked where I pointed.

"My eyes aren't as good as they used to be, but I think you're right." As we got closer, she said, "Windows are busted out, and a tree's growing in front of the door. Looks deserted. But I've seen people live in worse."

We entered the tiny clearing and rode around the trailer.

"Yeah, me too."

The road leading away hadn't seen traffic in years. Debris littered the area —a broken bucket half filled with water, a box spring, a gas stove, beer cans, shards of glass, bald tires, an old television missing its guts. Over in the woods to one side, a faded pickup truck up on blocks and more trash. All of it was overgrown with grass and weeds. Yellow wildflowers bloomed inside the TV, and honeysuckle vines climbed over the truck's bed.

The window on one short end of the trailer was intact and had a Confederate flag painted on the glass instead of a curtain.

We came full circle to the back, where the door was missing. I dismounted.

"What are you doing?" Renee asked.

"I'm just curious. Hold him a minute, will you?" I handed her Gaston's reins.

"Good thing you're not a cat," she muttered.

I went up the steps and inside. A sour smell hit me first. In front of me was a tiny laundry room with a stained pair of overalls on the floor, but no appliances. I turned right and stood in the kitchen from my dream. The little white Westie wasn't there, but he'd vanished both times when I followed him from the first room to this. I hadn't noticed the smells when I'd been sleeping, but it was dank with mildew and felt cold. Glass and torn linoleum crunched under my feet. I went into the trailer's living room, but it was not the one from my dreams. A painting of the ocean hung crookedly over a stained green couch whose stuffing was mostly on the carpeted floor.

I glanced down a dark hallway that must've led to a bathroom and a couple of bedrooms. Probably the farthest room was the one with the flag on the window. I saw no reason to explore in that direction.

Was I supposed to look for something here? Wastrel had never been in these places, only brought me to them. There wasn't room for him inside, but what did that matter? The laws of physics didn't apply in dreams, did they?

Because the kitchen was where the dog always led me, I returned to it. The little room had a wooden table and damp leaves on the floor. Cabinet doors gaped. Inside one, a box of baking soda lying on its side had spilled its contents long ago in a white waterfall to the green counter. Sunlight came through the window over the sink, and I could imagine a plant thriving there, a woman tending it. A woman who baked cookies. I didn't need Renee's abilities to know the whole place held deep sadness. I shivered and went outside.

This was JJ's parents' place, I was sure of it. It fit Hank's description. Why else would I have dreamed about it? But what did it mean?

I took Gaston's reins from Renee without a word and mounted. She didn't say anything, probably reading something in my face—or my aura—that told her now was not the time for conversation. I probably wouldn't have heard her if she'd spoken.

We walked the horses back the way we'd come. I peered into the trees on either side of the road. Somewhere north of here was Winterlight's property line. And between here and there was where JJ's father disappeared. Had he run off like people said? Or had something happened to him?

"Wow," Renee said, "look at the time. I hate to rush you, but I need to be getting back. You mind, New York?"

"No, I don't mind," I answered without taking my eyes from the surrounding woods.

I couldn't see any open land, but that didn't mean anything.

Hank had said the "little spit of woods" wasn't far from Malcolm's hay field, but that could be a stone's throw or a mile. We continued, and I sensed Renee's growing agitation with my silence, but couldn't stop studying the woods, wondering about the trailer, and reconsidering my dreams.

"Vi!" she yelled after a several minutes.

I twisted in the saddle and faced her. "What?"

"You're creeping me out. What's wrong with you? You sure you didn't hit your head in that car accident? I should not have let you ride."

"Sorry. Nothing's wrong. Just thinking." I gathered up the reins. "You're right. Let's go." I sent Gaston into a brisk trot.

I looked behind us, but the thick woods already concealed the trailer. It was easy enough to find. As soon as possible, I'd return.

Alone.

CHAPTER THIRTY-ONE

RENEE SHOWED me another way back to the barn along a narrow track following an old barbed-wire fence until we picked up one of the public riding trails. That would bring us out near the cow field on the west side. Between her and Sandy, I was beginning to feel like I knew my way around.

She pointed to the advanced trail, the one with a few jumps, and we took it, cantered over the fences, and then walked for some time in quiet.

"How long have you been riding at Winterlight?" I asked.

"A couple of years, I guess. Leroy'd been coming around longer."

"You ever think of getting your own horse?"

"We were thinking about it, but Malcolm always had one for me to ride. Eventually, I'll buy Smitty back. It's what Leroy would have wanted. And he's a good ride." She combed her fingers through his silvery mane.

"Do you go by yourself most of the time, or with…"

"Oh, I go out with Dex One sometimes."

"I meant, riding."

"Yeah, me too." She grinned, then said, "I told you he was fine, didn't I? Don't let that limp fool you. Anyway, him and Leroy were best buds."

I laughed. Dex One and Renee? Why not?

"Leroy used to say that people are like horses—herd animals—not meant to be alone. They need to rub up against each other to really be happy. So, me and Dex, we rub up against each other."

"And you're happy."

She smiled. "If you ask me, New York, you're overdue to join the herd, know what I mean? You've been out on your own too long."

Was it that obvious? "Guess I haven't found the right herd. Anyway, I like being boss mare."

"You can pretend to be boss mare all you want, but if you haven't got a herd, you haven't got anything to be boss of. Except yourself. And that gets old fast." She shook her head. "Um, um, um. Real fast."

The idea of having a herd mate to rub up against was very appealing, but I didn't know how to join a herd. Nor did I know of any herd that would have me. Maybe after we knew each other better, I'd ask her to smudge me past all my stupid fears. In the meantime, I steered the conversation in a different direction.

"Where'd Dex get the limp?"

"Down by the river. That's another reason I don't go there. His squirrelly horse named Genius reared up and fell over. The saddle horn smashed Dex's leg real bad."

"Ouch. So, what happened?"

"Well, luckily, Malcolm was with him, and he saved him. Made a tourniquet, hauled him up on Fergus, called for an ambulance from his cell as soon as he could get a signal, and got Dex home quick as he could."

Jesus. The man was a saint and a superhero. I knew I recognized that square jaw from somewhere.

"They couldn't save his leg, not all of it anyway. It's fake from the knee down. Malcolm helped take care of him afterwards."

Dex said Malcolm had been good to him.

"What happened to Genius?"

"When he flipped over, he cracked his skull open, and never got up. I don't know how Malcolm got Dex out from under that stupid horse. Guess you do what you got to do when you got to do it, right?"

"Um."

"I think Dex would have put a bullet in Genius right there if he weren't already dead."

"Carried a gun then, too, huh?"

"Always."

We came in view of the house, and I could see Malcolm's Jag parked in the drive.

"Um, um, um," she muttered. "We got ourselves a welcoming committee."

I loved how she could infuse those three simple syllables with so many different meanings.

"Um, um, um," I said.

She slid me a sideways glance. "You're getting it. Keep practicing."

Robert and Dex One stood outside the barn, watching our approach. Neither of them looked happy.

"I'll handle Dex," Renee said.

"I guess you will."

She laughed. "Yeah, but that means you've got to handle the big one. And he looks fit to bust."

Robert's face had that stiff, barely-contained fury look about it, kind of like it did the first time I saw him when I helped corral Hank's bull. I rode right up to him, leaned down, and said, "It was an accident."

He grabbed Gaston's reins and stroked the horse's neck, didn't even look at me.

"It wasn't," Dex said.

Robert put his hand on my thigh and squeezed. He wasn't angry with me at all.

"Wasn't what?" Renee asked.

"An accident," Robert answered.

"What?" Renee and I both said.

"The brake lines were cut," Dex said.

I put my hand over Robert's. He finally looked at me.

"I'm okay," I said.

He let out a long breath.

"Oh, crap," I whispered. "That accident was meant for you."

The four of us sat in the tack room a little while later.

"I'm calling in reinforcements," Dex said. "You won't see most of them, but they'll be around. I can't be everywhere at once. Whoever cut the SUV's brake lines managed to do it while I was on the property."

"It's a big piece of property," I said.

"Exactly. Keep your vehicle parked where you can see it all times, or lock it up." He directed this last at Renee.

"What are you looking at me for?"

"You have a garage. Use it."

"What does this have to do with me?"

Dex scrubbed his hands over his head. "I don't know what or who it has to do with. Be careful, you got it?"

We all nodded. Renee stuck her tongue out at him. He ignored her.

"We're closed again until further notice," Robert said, a note of weariness in his voice. "And you," he touched my knee, "No more riding without one of us with you."

"I had Renee with me."

"He means one of them," Renee explained. "A man."

"I'd suggest no more riding out at all," Dex said.

"Oh, for cripe's sake," I griped to no one in particular.

"I agree with Dex," Robert said. "Tomorrow, I have to return to my client site. I'll help you in the morning, then you'll come with me."

"Now, wait a minute, if Dex has people keeping an eye on things—"

"No," Dex said, "that's good. One less for them to worry about."

"What about the horses?" I asked.

"We'll take care of it."

I stood. "This is ridiculous." I couldn't get anything done if I was under armed guard. "I'm going upstairs. Call me if you need me."

Robert wrapped his hand around my wrist. "The only thing you're going upstairs for is a change of clothes. You're staying at my house."

Crap. How to go from super-hero-saint to macho-alpha-male in one easy breath. I peeled his fingers off one at a time. "No."

"One of my men will be camped out in the apartment, Miss Parker. I'm sure he'd enjoy your company…"

I shot Dex a dirty look. The men had obviously worked this out while Renee and I were riding.

"She can stay with me," Renee offered.

I huffed. "No, thanks. I need to be close to the horses. There's too much work to do." And I wouldn't risk something else happening to Cali. "How about if I stay with Hank and Clara?"

Both men shook their heads. "Hank sleeps like a rock," Robert said. "His entire flock of chickens could be killed in his front room, and he wouldn't wake up."

"And Clara can't shoot a gun to save her life," Dex said.

Nice time to talk about killing, I thought. "What the hell do you think is going to happen around here?"

"Miss Parker," Dex drawled with exaggerated patience, "need I remind you a man was murdered? The horses were let loose. You were attacked. Someone attempted to kill Malcolm, and, by the way, nearly killed you instead. In my book, that's reason enough to take a few simple precautions."

And I was worried I'd die of boredom in the Midwest.

CHAPTER THIRTY-TWO

WE WORKED to get everything done so we could attend Norman's wake that evening. I would pay my respects, and I hoped to run into Sandy, too.

Robert and Dex allowed Renee to take me to the bank. She found it highly amusing that JJ had stolen all my underwear, and a great excuse to buy new. She drove like a maniac to the nearest store that sold what she termed real women's underwear. Which meant the mall.

The mall. Jesus. They are all the same. What a freaking relief. That is, until Renee dragged me into the lingerie section of a department store. By the time we left, I had more under thingies than ever before, in more colors and styles than I knew were available. All except red lace. Renee laughed for over half an hour when I told why I didn't want any. She promised to smudge me soon and rid me of all negativity regarding my underwear.

We pointed her Beetle north after gorging on ice cream and big, salty soft pretzels, and between that and our ride earlier, I was beginning to feel human again, despite Winterlight being under an apparent siege. I half-expected to encounter a guard tower and gate when we returned.

But all was at peace.

That should have made me suspicious.

Robert and Dex leaned back in rockers on the farmhouse's long front porch, with their feet on the railing, smoking cigars. You'd think they'd both just won a high-stakes poker game instead of cleaning stalls for an afternoon. Noire lazed between them, her pink tongue lolling out one side of her mouth.

I went to the apartment to get what I needed. As promised, one of Dex's reinforcements sat in a chair he'd turned to face the window overlooking the pasture. He rested a black rifle with a scope across his lap and nodded to me when I came in.

I grabbed what I'd worn to church on Sunday and work clothes for the morning. Henrietta had taken the kittens to the loft, a move I approved of. Not that she'd checked with me first. From the hatbox on the closet shelf I retrieved the tape and stuffed it in the bottom of my purse.

Armed with fresh cans of whipped cream, I walked to the house. Robert showed me the guest room and left me to my ablutions.

When I entered the kitchen an hour later, I said, "If it's all the same to you, I'm going back to calling you Malcolm." I hadn't been comfortable calling him Robert, and if I had to be in close physical proximity, I needed every ounce of emotional distance available.

He nodded. I didn't know what that meant, and I wasn't about to try and figure it out. We ate ham sandwiches and washed them down with iced tea and rode in the Jag to the funeral home without a word. He didn't appear to be fuming, but he did look deep in thought. I guess if someone had used my manure pile as a murder weapon, let loose my horses, and cut my brake lines, I'd be deep in thought, too.

The funeral home was no more than a cinder block building with a tin roof, but cars filled the adjoining lot and lined both sides of Main Street. People stood around in small groups, smoking and speaking in hushed tones. Some nodded as we walked by. I didn't see Sandy or her car.

Malcolm kept a firm grip on my elbow to guide me through the crowd in the hall. We found the viewing room. Wasn't hard. There was only one. What would happen if two people died at the same time?

I saw a few familiar faces. The coroner, and Fred and Melba. Clara and Hank stood with them. Malcolm released me to shake someone's hand, and I slipped away.

I glanced at Norman on my way past. He looked good—not like I'd expect someone to look who got cooked in a compost pile—had more color than I remembered. The undertaker must have a good makeup artist. A new black cowboy hat rested on his chest. I kept moving, but my Catholic upbringing insisted I get up close and say a short prayer before leaving.

"You bring any of that whipped cream?" Clara asked in a whisper when I reached her side.

"I don't think they'd approve of us shooting up in here."

She shrugged. "They've got butter cookies in the other room. Not bad for store-bought. You see the pictures?"

There were easels with photos of Norman.

"In a minute. Have you seen Sandy?"

"Why, no. You'd think she'd be here, too. Lots of others. We don't get many murders round here. Most of 'em didn't know Norman when he was alive, but they're curious."

"Miss Parker?"

I turned to the unfamiliar baritone voice.

"Oh, Vi," Clara said, beaming, "this here's my cousin Frank, the coroner. Frank, Miss Viola Parker."

"I understand you found the deceased," he said.

I gestured with my head toward Hank. "We both did."

"Dirty business," said the coroner.

Hank nodded. "Time was, somebody wanted a body dead, they just shot 'em. Nice and clean."

"Or used a knife," Clara added.

She would favor a knife.

I felt someone sidle behind me, then Malcolm's voice whispered in my ear, "The good old days."

This was an exceedingly odd way to reminisce, but I could see how the coroner would appreciate a body with a straightforward gunshot or stabbing wound over one cooked by compost. And I understood that weird subjects came up when people stood around at a wake, and they laughed at things they didn't usually find funny.

Over Frank's shoulder, I spotted Kevie the bartender-bouncer-pizza maker from Mel's. He made eye contact and started working my way.

"Glad to see you're okay," he said. He very deliberately cut his eyes to Malcolm, then back to me.

I narrowed my eyes at him.

"You didn't end up with that bastard, JJ," he clarified.

"Oh. No. I didn't."

"I tried to warn you that night, but you were already too far gone by the time you left."

There was a shriek from near the casket. A short, heavy woman with pale skin and stringy black hair lumbered toward us. She wore a vintage purple polyester suit with a brown turtleneck beneath, support hose, and mean-looking black stilettos.

Clara put her hand on my arm. "Tighten your girdle, Vi," she murmured. "That there's Bertha, Norman's mother."

Bertha pointed a finger in our direction and screeched like a drunken tropical bird. Heads turned her way. I slid behind the relative protection of

Kevie's stalwart form.

"Why is she coming over here?" I scanned the room for Malcolm and saw him glance up from his conversation at the same time.

"You!" Bertha howled and aimed her plump index finger at my face.

Crap. There was nowhere to go except into a four-foot horseshoe of blue carnations.

Bertha sidestepped around a wing chair and tottered to the right. Her thick ankles buckled, unable to sustain any lateral stability with only the two tiny points of support provided by the five-inch heels. She listed farther right, arms pin-wheeling for anything to grab onto, her fake alligator purse coming loose at the top of one swing sending it spinning in a long arc over the assembly like a quarter-back's pass to the end zone. It landed smack in the middle of one of the picture boards. That tipped over onto a colorful flower arrangement balanced atop a fake ionic column. It began to lean.

Counter to all rules of physics, Bertha found her balance, and then zigged to the left. She bounced off Frank, who had his arms out and ready, but whether to catch her or push her away, I couldn't tell.

"Your fault," Bertha said to me. She zagged right again. "This is all your fault." She overcorrected and began to slip backwards.

The ionic column toppled and the flowers plunged into the casket.

Bertha spun like a buoy in a hurricane. "Nooo," she cried. "Those were expensive." She swung back to me, seeming unable to stop moving once launched. "Norman's dead because of you!" She pointed the chubby finger again. "You! Get out. How dare you? Get out." She swayed.

Kevie grabbed her arm and she plopped into the wing chair.

"Now Auntie, you don't mean that," he soothed.

She blubbered into her hands.

Everyone stared. The only movement came from Malcolm, who pushed his way to my side and hustled me out through a miraculous parting in the sea of onlookers.

Outside, we ran into Dex and Renee.

"Leaving so soon?" Dex asked.

"Vi caused a scene," Malcolm said.

"Sorry I missed it," Renee said.

"Norman's mother asked me to leave."

"I'll bet," Dex said.

When did they become such masters of understatement? We stood there for a minute.

"Anybody know where Sandy lives, or her phone number?"

"Not far from here, I don't think," Renee said.

"I don't have her number with me," Malcolm said.

We were silent again, then Renee asked, "You want to go over there?"

"Don't you think it's odd she's not here?"

"Maybe she's coming later."

"Vi's right," Malcolm said. "Sandy would have been here early and stayed until the end. We can swing by, knock on her door. I don't think she has anyone else to check on her, now that Norman's gone."

The return of St. Malcolm.

Dex said they'd go inside for a visit, and catch up with us later. We agreed to meet at The Brick in an hour, and Malcolm and I walked to the Jag.

He started it, put it in drive, and then shoved the gear shifter back to park. The engine hummed eagerly beneath the hood.

"You sure do make life interesting," he said.

I didn't take that as a compliment. "Guess I'm the keep-you-on-your-toes-and-guessing side of the equation. Anyway, I didn't ask for any of this."

He gave my knee a squeeze, as good at communicating with touch as with words. Small wonder the horses liked him so well. Small wonder I did, too.

"She doesn't really hold me responsible for Norman's death, does she?"

"Probably, but no one else does."

"Do the police have any leads?"

"They've questioned a few persons of interest."

"Who wants to hurt you?" I asked. He didn't answer. "I think I have a right to know what's going on."

"You know just about as much as I do. JJ's the only person I know of who has a grudge against me."

Brooke clutched no small amount of resentment toward him. I thought I'd decline bringing that up right then.

"What does the sheriff make of JJ's history?" I asked.

"He's disappeared for the moment."

"Guess he took your advice."

He grunted. "That would be a first."

"What about the drug Norman took? Any ideas about that?"

"I don't believe he took it," he said with a shake of his head.

"Dex said—"

"I know Norman's history. He was a fuck-up in a lot of ways, but I still don't believe he took that stuff. Not that much of it, anyway."

"Look I'm best friends with denial, too, but—"

He gave me a sharp look and pulled away from the curb.

"Sorry about your SUV," I said.

"Don't mention it."

I got the feeling he really meant that, so I shut up until we reached Sandy's. She lived in a small frame house about two miles outside of town down a dead-end gravel road.

The setting sun soaked the white-shingled cottage in pink, but it didn't hide the peeling paint, sagging gutters, or rotten porch steps. It was hard to tell whether anyone was home, but her car sat in the driveway. Clouds had begun to bunch along the western horizon during the afternoon. They converged at that moment like a shade being pulled shut, and it was obvious there were no lights on inside.

Malcolm knocked. I called her name. No response. We frowned at each other. He pounded and yelled, "Sandy! It's Malcolm and Vi. Are you in there?"

I walked to the side and hopped like a bunny to peer in the windows. Couldn't see much. The condition of the back porch was worse than the front, but the door was open a crack, so I took my chances and went up the three steps. They creaked but held. I shouted to Malcolm, and he came around.

He put one hand on the railing. It swayed. "Go in," he said. "I don't trust this to support both of us."

Crap. Why did I have to be the first one in? Did I look like a brave person? Let me answer that. *No.*

My stomach clenched, and little beads of cold sweat broke out on my upper lip. The last time I'd seen Sandy, she'd been in tears over Norman's death. I'd talked to her Saturday. I wondered if anyone else had seen her since then.

At my hesitation, he said, "Just step in far enough to get off the steps. I'll be right behind you."

That's what they always say.

CHAPTER THIRTY-THREE

I TOOK a bracing breath and did as he said. The door swung in to the kitchen. It smelled like rotten fruit, but in the dim shadows, I saw nothing more than the usual appliances, cabinets and sink. A few drawers hung open.

Malcolm came in and poked me in the back to prod me forward.

"This doesn't feel right," I said.

"We're not breaking and entering. The door was open."

"That's not what I mean."

He moved in front of me, looked around, sniffed. "I think I know what you mean." He took my hand. "Come on."

The kitchen opened to a living room. A worn sofa faced a television. The coffee table in between had several empty soda cans on it. Newspapers and magazines scattered across the floor, and a set of bookshelves had been emptied of its paperbacks, but I didn't get the impression Sandy was a slob.

"He was here," I said. "Whatever he was looking for in the apartment, he came here to look for, too."

"You don't know that."

He didn't sound convinced of his assertion. The place was isolated. No nearby neighbors. JJ could have ripped the sheetrock off the framing and no one would have noticed.

Malcolm nodded toward a doorway in one wall. "You better go in first."

"What? Why me?" But I knew why—in case Sandy was in there and she wasn't decent. The man had boundaries. Respect. Had to admire that. And I would. Some other time. At the moment, I'd prefer he toss his deference out the nearest window.

I stood as far as I could from the closed door and touched it with my fingertips. It creaked open enough for me to poke my head in.

The room on the other side of it barely contained the full-sized bed, dresser, and side table. The closet door was open as well as the drawers in the dresser, and clothes littered the floor. It smelled like the breath of a hangover laced with sex.

Sandy sprawled across the bed, naked, arms flung to the sides, legs and mouth spread wide. Fear jolted through me, and my breath hitched in my chest. Then, I realized she was snoring slightly. Not dead. Jesus. Thank you.

I was met with a view no one but a gynecologist should have. "Hang on," I said to Malcolm. "She's in here, but…" I moved all the way into the room. Evidence be damned. I pulled a sheet up to her chin, then said, "Coast is clear."

He came in. "Is she all right?"

She was pale and sweaty, drooling slightly and taking shallow breaths, not the deep inhalations of someone in a normal sleep. A new bruise spread across her left cheekbone. Her eye looked swollen. I nudged her shoulder.

"Sandy?" I pushed harder and raised my voice. "Sandy!" She didn't move. "Out cold."

Malcolm laid the back of his hand on her forehead, then gently slapped her cheek. "Sandy?"

He used her phone to dial 911. As soon as he hung up, he speed-dialed a number on his cell, probably Dex One.

I looked around the room. Crammed on the tiny table next to the bed were a lamp, an alarm clock, a paperback, a glass with about a half inch of brown liquid in the bottom, and an empty tissue box, all partly buried in used tissues. They overflowed a wicker wastebasket on the floor, too. The trash also held an empty rum bottle.

I sniffed the glass.

"What is it?" Malcolm asked from the other side of the bed.

"If I had to guess, I'd say it was rum and Coke."

"You have experience identifying liquor by smell?"

That was a halfway loaded question. "Some."

I picked up the book. Wadded tissues tumbled to the floor.

"Don't touch anything." He planted his hands on his hips and glanced around. The walls were as bare as Sandy. "Was she covered with this sheet when you came in?"

"No."

"Don't touch anything else."

I gave him a look. The book was a Romance—the kind Penny read. This one featured a fierce-looking, bare-chested highlander holding a sword with one hand and a buxom, red-haired lass with the other. They were framed by a forbidding sky. Wind blew his kilt up and her hair across his chest. Her buxomness looked about to spill out of her thin, lacy chemise. What she was doing running around the highlands dressed like that, I just don't know.

I put it back on the table, and more tissues fell to the floor, exposing what looked like a prescription bottle.

"Uh-oh," I said. "Look at this." I picked it up thinking that in her despair over Norman, Sandy must have overdosed on something.

Malcolm came around the bed. "Didn't I just say—"

"Holy shit. It's ketamine—that stuff Dex said they found in Norman." The small—empty—vial was the kind you use a syringe to extract liquid from. I'd used them plenty with horses. "You think she took it?"

"Put it down. It might have fingerprints on it." He shook out his hand-kerchief and used it to take the bottle and put it on the table. "Let the sheriff figure out what happened, okay?"

"Don't you wonder why this stuff is here, or if she and Norman were using it, or where it came from, or if JJ—?"

"Vi." He squeezed my hand. "No. I don't." He sighed. "Okay. I do, but there's no point. Until she's okay enough to answer some questions—"

"She will be okay?"

"From what I understand, she should be fine once she comes out of it."

Not for the first time since arriving in Missouri, I felt the rise of panic— the roiling of my innards, the inability to take a full breath, the tickle of sweat tripping down my spine.

"If you don't think Norman took the drug, do you think Sandy gave it to him?" I paced around the bed, stopped by the front window and looked out, trying to calm myself. "That bruise—I know JJ was here. Probably raped her, too." I pressed my fist against my lips. "Oh, God."

I turned to face Malcolm, but he'd come up behind me. He put his hands on my shoulders. "This is my fault," I said. "If I'd pressed charges like you wanted me to, he'd be in jail, right? I should have listened. I could have stopped this."

He looked at me, his blue eyes soft and clear as a tidal pool reflecting a cloud-free sky. Very slowly, he folded me against his chest, wrapped his arms around me, laid his cheek against the top of my head, and breathed into my hair. I was reminded of how soothing it is to feel the warm exhalation of a horse slide over me like the caress of an angel's wing. I put my arms around his neck, closed my eyes, and rested against the rhythm of his heartbeat and the steady rise and fall of his chest.

"Remember last night when you told me everything isn't my fault?"

I nodded.

"I'll concede that everything isn't my responsibility, if you'll do the same."

"By everything, I'm guessing you mean, like, global warming?"

He laughed. "Yeah, like that."

"Don't be so sure. My truck—when it runs—emits more greenhouse gas than a coal-driven factory."

"I mean all of this. Even if you had pressed charges, he would've made bail. He would've found a way to do this, if that's what he wanted."

Dex and Renee arrived a few minutes later. Renee and I ended up in Sandy's room, while Malcolm and Dex went outside.

"How come we get the fun part?" I asked.

Renee sighed. "Because we're women, and this is what women do."

"I guess I skipped that chapter of the rule book."

"Sometimes, I wish I'd skipped the rule book altogether."

She sat next to Sandy on one side of the bed, and I sat on the other. We wiped the spit off her cheek, watched her, and took turns saying her name. She began to moan, and never moved, but she kept breathing.

It took half an hour for the ambulance to arrive. A deputy got there first. Joe, if I remembered correctly. He had to clear the scene before the emergency medical folks could go in.

"Figured you'd be here," he said, but in a friendly way.

Not two weeks in the state, and I was on a first-name basis with local law enforcement. Malcolm and Dex thought it was funny. I didn't see the humor in it at all.

One of the emergency techs nodded hello when they went past with the gurney. This was the downside of living in such a sparsely populated area. Or, maybe an upside, I don't know. The concept was so foreign to me, I had to let it sink in for a while before I could decide.

They intubated Sandy, put her on oxygen, and started an IV before loading her in the ambulance. I was still worried but began to relax knowing she was getting medical attention. I felt sad too, because it made me think how no one had been there for Norman.

And then, I got mad. Because I was sure the events of the past week were all tied together. But how? I needed answers.

I only wished I didn't have to ask a dead horse to get them.

CHAPTER THIRTY-FOUR

DEX TOOK Renee home then went to Winterlight. Malcolm and I followed the ambulance to the hospital. Sandy had no family locally, he said. She was an only child, and both her parents had died a few years back. They'd moved to the area when she was a kid, so no extended family nearby, either. The next closest person to her was the veterinarian she worked for. Malcolm said he'd call him later when we knew more.

Shortly after arriving at the hospital and seeing Sandy wheeled into the emergency room, we sat on a waiting-room couch together. A television hung from the ceiling, the volume low. The Cardinals were playing at Houston. It was the bottom of the eighth.

Malcolm watched the screen until the score popped up. St. Louis was ahead by one, but Houston had a man on second. "You want something to eat?" he asked without looking away from the game.

"Yeah," I said, "a bag of peanuts and a beer."

"Very funny." He stood. "Why don't you come with me, and we'll see what they have?"

"No thanks. Just get me whatever looks good."

He grinned. "Jell-O, perhaps?"

"Only if it's topped with whipped cream."

"I'd like to talk about your addiction to that stuff."

I'll bet. Most men have something else in mind when it comes to whipped cream. "Go away," I said.

The moment he rounded the corner, I lay on the hard couch. Just a short snooze for Wastrel to show me something useful. I was ready to pay attention. Maybe with the pieces I had, I could make enough sense out of a dream to see the big picture.

The couch was not made for reclining, but it didn't matter. I could sleep in a mud puddle. In a few moments, I drifted off, the sounds of the crack of a bat and a cheering crowd fading quickly. My last thoughts were of Wastrel.

Wastrel must have been digging for clues in someone else's head. I found myself in the loft at Winterlight, dust floating in the air. I'd been sweeping, getting ready for the new hay crop. Light slanted through high windows, and a big door stood open at one end, letting fresh air blow out last season's mustiness. It was hot. I wore shorts and a tank top. I pulled the top away from my damp skin to allow a little air to cool it, and took a long drink from a water bottle.

Someone came up the ladder. At first, I was afraid because I thought it might be JJ. But Malcolm's head appeared through the opening, then the rest of him. He wore his kilt and work boots. Nothing else.

His body was strong and well formed, but I already knew that. Sweat streaked his torso and dirt smudged his arms from whatever work he'd been doing. He stood for a moment in a shadow, filling the space with masculine intensity. He looked at me, and his eyes darkened.

He walked toward me slowly, the front of the kilt tented with his erection. Desire pooled in my lower body. He took the bottle from me, drank, and poured water over his shoulders, then over mine. My breath caught in my chest, and moisture seeped into my shorts.

He tossed the empty bottle away and circled, looking me up and down. I started to run my hands over his chest to follow the soft trail of hair down his belly, and farther, but he took them, put them behind my back and held them there. His warm mouth covered one breast, sucking through the thin cotton of my shirt. I arched toward him, my hips flexing to reach his.

He moved to the other breast. I moaned and kissed the top of his head, struggling to free myself, to touch him, to bring him closer, but he held me, drawing my nipple deeper into his mouth.

I got one hand loose, shoved it under his kilt, and groped for his penis. It was long and hard and thick. I stroked it from base to tip. He groaned and pinned my arm behind me again holding my wrists in one hand and used the other to loosen my shorts. He pushed them to my thighs and slipped the thin T-shirt above my breasts. They ached with need.

He kissed and licked my belly and knelt before me. I couldn't separate my legs with my shorts tight around them. I needed to spread them, needed him inside me, but he kept me stretched taut and exposed only what he wanted.

Sizzling need coursed through me, zinging straight from my breasts down to my personal volcano. Heat and pressure built inside me.

His tongue flicked lower, slipped between my legs. I opened my legs as wide as I could. He slid a finger inside me. Muscles contracted; my whole body rocked and bucked.

"Vi?"

Malcolm shook me awake.

"Wha—?" I sat up too fast and hit him with my forehead.

"Ow." He stood and felt the bridge of his nose. "Good thing we're at the hospital."

"Sorry." I swung my feet to the floor, not fully awake, desperately wishing I were still asleep. I rubbed my eyes, trying to calm my breathing.

He dropped beside me on the couch, and put a bag of chips and a cold soda in my hand. "Who won the game?"

Crap. The one time I want to dream, I have one like I've never had before. I pressed the icy can to my cheek, but the dream's arousal still had my blood pumping.

I yawned to hide my embarrassment. "No idea. Fell asleep."

"I noticed. Must have been a good one. You were making yummy sounds."

Double crap. Yummy sounds? Heat from down below shot up my neck and blossomed on my cheeks. Parts of me that didn't usually throb were throbbing. Painfully. He stared at me until a slow, knowing smile took over his face. Damn it.

"Hope it was about me," he said.

"In your dreams," I shot back without thinking. I really should engage my brain before opening my mouth.

He patted my knee. I started and moved a little farther away from him. It wouldn't do to jump his bones in the hospital waiting area. Maybe there was an empty room nearby.

"And," he continued, "I hope it included some of that whipped cream you're so fond of."

I knew it. I grabbed a magazine off the side table and fanned myself. "That would explain the yummy sounds," I said.

"If you hear me making yummy sounds in my sleep, you can bet I'm not dreaming about whipped cream. Unless…" His eyes locked on mine and darkened, just like they had in my dream.

I stopped fanning. "Unless?" I peered more closely at him. "Good Lord, are you blushing?"

He might have been turning red, but he wasn't shy. He leaned toward me. "Unless I'm licking it off your bare skin," he said in a low voice.

Triple crap. I fanned myself vigorously. "Is it hot in here?"

"I'm not hot," he said.

"Yes you are."

"Glad we got that settled."

"You—" I took my food and moved to a chair across the room.

He picked up a newspaper and began reading while eating his chips. The sound of muffled chuckling came from behind the newsprint, but I ignored him.

It was going to be a long night.

CHAPTER THIRTY-FIVE

"We have Miss Houseman stabilized and are moving her to a room."

A young woman spoke to Malcolm. He was on his feet, rubbing his eyes. He must have dozed off, too. I glanced at my watch. Past midnight. I stifled a jaw-cracking yawn.

"What do you mean, stabilized?" I asked.

She turned to me. Her name tag read, "Dr. Webb."

"Are you family?" she asked.

We both shook our heads. Malcolm explained.

"We'll keep her for observation for a couple of days. You might want to go home and get some rest. It will be hours before she's coherent."

She turned on her heel and disappeared through a door.

Malcolm watched me from near the couch, his arms across his chest.

And image from my most recent dream popped into my head—him silhouetted against the hayloft opening—it reminded me of something. The book, that was it, the one on Sandy's bedside table. Could she be in love with Malcolm?

"You want to go back to the house?" Malcolm asked.

I forgot the fantasy highlander image and sat near the in-the-flesh version. He looked the part—especially rough from sleep, with his hair mussed from running his hands through it, and stubble roughening his cheeks—even in nice slacks and a button-down shirt. Maybe because I knew what was under his shirt.

After seeing him coldcock JJ, and then one-arm the shotgun, I could easily imagine him wielding a sword. He'd studied fencing for the pentathlon. Between that and the swimming, it was no wonder he had such broad shoulders.

Reality, Parker. Let's stay there, okay?

Oh, hell, why start now?

I rested my head on the back of the couch. "We can leave if you need to," I said. "I know you have that client thing tomorrow." But I wanted to stay. Sandy was alone. I knew what that felt like.

"Either way is fine with me. I'll postpone the meeting. I want to make sure she's okay. But you must be tired."

"She should know someone cares enough to wait."

He sat again and put his arm around me, pulled me toward him. "Com'ere."

I resisted, leaning in the other direction.

"Come on. I won't bite, I promise. Not here, anyway. Sit next to me."

"I am next to you. Have you talked to Dex?"

"Yes. Everything's fine. Come on. You're not close enough."

I let him tug me against his side.

"That's better." He ruffled my hair. "You have a good heart, Viola Parker."

I sighed and laid my head on his shoulder. "Guess that makes two of us. Don't tell anyone, okay? I wouldn't want to ruin my reputation."

He lifted me onto his lap and put his other arm around me. "Your secret is safe with me. Are you comfortable?"

I squirmed and shifted my arms and burrowed past his collar to find his neck, sucking a deep breath of his glorious smell right inside me. Instantly, I felt calmer.

"Um-hm. What about you?"

"Don't worry about me."

"That's not fair." I rested my lips against his skin. Not quite a kiss. I wanted to flick my tongue out and taste him.

"What's not fair?"

"You worrying about me but not letting me worry about you." I touched him with just the tip of my tongue. Salty. Nice.

He groaned softly. "You'd better not do that here."

"Are you comfortable, or what?" I asked.

"Not any more." He reached under me and between his legs to make an adjustment.

"Good," I said. No reason why I should be the only one stirred up and damp. "I'm going to sleep, now. And Malcolm?"

He grunted a one-syllable all-purpose response.

"If I start making yummy sounds in my sleep, don't wake me up."

The dream begins in the house with the little white Westie. This time, I sorted through papers on a cluttered roll-top desk. I couldn't find whatever it was I was looking for, and I didn't know what that was supposed to be, either. But I kept looking through the same piles again and again, just like I do when I lose something, muttering, 'it must be here' as if pure belief would make it so.

I knocked pens to the floor and left them. A tape dispenser and stapler followed. I shoved a stack of official-looking documents to one side and uncovered an answering machine. The dog barked.

Wastrel met me in the woods toward the south end of Winterlight. He was tacked up and ready to be lunged. This was something we did a lot when he was alive. I'd stand still holding what amounted to a thirty-foot lead line, and he'd work around me in a circle. Only thing was, we were in dense woods, which made it impossible. Dreamtime—different rules.

Usually, I would walk in a tiny circle myself while lunging a horse, holding my end of the line in one hand and the lunge whip in the other. Instead, I braced my legs and leaned all my weight back, as if we were water skiing. My heels dug into the ground, creating a hole. Leaves and twigs, and then rocks and dirt began to accumulate around me.

Wastrel cantered faster until he galloped around the circle. The sound of his hooves beating the ground filled my ears like gunfire. It was too fast. He could slip and get hurt.

"Whoa," I said.

Bones spewed from under my feet. My arm muscles bulged, began to hurt. I wanted to get away from the bones. I was sinking farther and farther into the ground. Down into the ground with the bones.

"Whoa," I said, louder.

Nothing I did made any difference. He wouldn't slow, and now Nicky was on his back, screaming. A sense of dread seized my belly.

"Whoa. Whoa!"

I couldn't let go. "Hang on to his mane!"

Tears of frustration ran down my cheeks. My arms were being yanked out of the sockets. The rope burned my palms. Stupid. I usually wear gloves.

Something snapped. I jolted awake, shaking, sweating, and crying.

"Vi!" Malcolm shook me.

I sprawled across his chest. Somehow, he'd maneuvered us flat on the couch without waking me, charmed a nurse out of a pillow for his head, and a blanket for me. My hands clutched wads of his shirt in tight fists.

"I'm all right," I said, taking deep breaths and forcing my hands to unclench. "Just a dream."

"More like a nightmare. Do you always dream so vividly?" He stroked my back and snugged the blanket around me. "You're trembling."

I wiped my face on his shirt. He shifted enough to pull out his handkerchief and gave it to me.

Bones, again. What did it mean? Before, they'd been in the house with the little dog. Now, the woods. What was Nicky doing there? And why was Wastrel terrorizing me? This seemed like a very bad turn of events.

As if a dead body in the manure pile weren't bad enough.

Maybe he wasn't terrorizing me, but literally escalating the alert. I need to be slapped upside the head several times before I get it. This could be Wastrel's way of getting my attention. It worked.

"Want to talk about it?" Malcolm asked.

"Did I say anything?"

"You weren't making yummy sounds, that's for sure. Sounded more like 'whoa.' Several times." He rubbed a spot on his side. "And you about tore a couple chunks of meat off my ribs. Must have been some ride."

I was on some ride all right.

I forced myself to relax and focus on the delicious sensation of having so much of our bodies in contact. But it was no good. Well, it *was* good, but I couldn't concentrate.

Was there something I needed to look for in the woods or on a desk? But what woods and what desk? Even if I narrowed my search to the south end of Winterlight, that encompassed a lot of ground. And riding out was currently forbidden. I'd find a way around that, later. I could see if Malcolm had a roll-top desk, but if not, then what? The tape recorder. I flung off the blanket, stood, and rummaged in my purse. The micro cassette was there. I showed it to Malcolm.

"Do you have an answering machine that takes one of these?"

He was still on his back with his arm across his eyes. He lifted his head and squinted at me. "No, why?"

I put it away. I couldn't make sense of the mess in my head and wasn't ready to try and explain. We were just getting comfortable with each other. I'd blow it if I said a dead horse talked to me in my dreams. Root canal without gas sounded more appealing than taking that risk.

No. I had to take the chance and trust. "Do you know anyone with a little white dog?"

He rose, recognition mixed with apprehension in the tense set of his jaw. "My father has a Westie, yes. Charlie. Why?"

Malcolm senior. I looked at my watch. It was five-fifteen a.m. Okay. No need to panic. The jumbled images in my dreams could mean anything. I hadn't seen him, just his dog.

I tried to sound casual. "When was the last time you talked to him?"

"You asked me that Sunday, too. Vi, what's going on?"

"Let's see if we can find out how Sandy is." I started toward the nurse's station. "And coffee would be good," I said over my shoulder.

He had my arm before I made it three strides. I must have looked unhappy.

"Okay," he said. "Coffee, first. Then, you'll explain." He tugged me down the glossy white hallway to the cafeteria.

While we waited, he said, "I talked to Dad a couple of days ago. We're having lunch today." He did a neck roll and scrubbed his hands through his hair. "Or, not. If I'm not going to my client's, then we'll do it another time. I'll call him later."

I took my coffee and blew over the surface to cool it. I needed it in my system, and I needed it now. "Does your father have a roll-top desk?"

He'd been about to take a sip. He went still and stared straight ahead. I could just hear the wheels turning in his head, trying to figure out why I was asking crazy questions.

Finally, he turned to me and said, "Yes."

"Call him now."

Whether it was the urgency in my voice or the intensity of the dream I'd been having literally on top of him, I don't know. He flipped open his phone, pushed one button, and held it to his ear. And waited.

His face grew concerned. He closed the phone. "No answer," he said. "Where would he be at this time of day?"

"I'm going to check on Sandy, then we can go, okay?"

He nodded, distracted. We went to look for a nurse, and ran into the doctor from the emergency room.

"Oh, I was just looking for you," she said. "Miss Houseman is conscious. You can go in, but keep it brief. Come with me."

Sandy looked pale and small surrounded by all the machines. Her eyes were open. Well, one was. The left was swollen shut.

"Hey," I said and took her hand. Malcolm stayed at the foot of the bed.

"The new girl," Sandy mumbled.

"That's me. How're you feeling?"

I wanted to ask her who did this to her, but wasn't sure if this was the time. She looked at Malcolm, started to smile, then her face went blank.

"Must look like shit," she said.

I glanced at him. Nope, didn't need to see the rest of the books on her shelf. She was in love with him. At least a serious crush, just as I suspected. Couldn't blame her. I knew exactly how she felt.

"You look terrific," Malcolm said and patted her foot. "Can we get you anything?"

She closed her eye and went back to sleep.

We stood in the hallway in silence, both of us lost in our own thoughts.

"Look," I said. "Why don't you drive into the city and see your father. Clara or somebody will come get me. I'll call Sandy's boss in a little while. Let him know she won't be in. You go, and don't worry about us."

He nodded and walked away. He got halfway toward the exit before he came back, put his hand behind my neck, and kissed me full on the mouth. I leaned into him and kissed him back, wishing we were anywhere but a sterile hospital corridor. The hayloft would work just fine.

"Thank you," he said. "I'll see you later."

Thank you? For what? For kissing him? For telling him to go?

"Later," I said. But he was already through the sliding doors.

And later, as it turned out, would come much later.

CHAPTER THIRTY-SIX

WHILE WAITING for the gift shop to open, I called Nicky. I was bored, and I knew it would give her a charge. She said hello in a low, unsure voice.

"Miss Nicola Malcolm? Do you know who this is?"

She giggled. "I do now."

In the background, I heard, "Nicky? Who are you talking to? I didn't hear the phone ring."

Crap. She was with Brooke. Her strident voice came through loud and clear. Sounded like they were in the car.

"Just a friend." Nicky said. "I keep it on vibrate so it doesn't ring when I'm in class."

"I thought none of your friends had phones," Brooke said.

Nicky hesitated. I hadn't meant to get her in trouble.

"Um…Jane's sister has a phone, and she lets her use it sometimes."

"Okay. But we're almost at school. Tell Jane you'll talk to her later."

"Jane?" Nicky said to me.

"You're a quick thinker," I said.

She giggled again and whispered, "I have to go. I'll talk to you later. Thanks for calling."

She hung up. Cute kid. Good phone manners. I felt bad for putting her in a position where she had to fib, especially to her mother. Then again, it was Brooke. No need to feel too guilty. From what Malcolm had said, I'd be seeing Nicky a lot over the summer. Maybe once she was away from her mother for a while, she'd open up.

I bought Sandy a bouquet of irises and lilies, started to sign the card, then thought I should make it from me and Malcolm, but that implied a relationship, so I decided to sign it just from him, because I'm sure he would have bought her flowers if he hadn't been so distracted, but then, I didn't want to give her the wrong idea, so I ended up signing it from everyone at Winterlight, especially Fawny-Wawny. I drew a cute little hoof print to make it look like a horse had signed the card.

What little sanity I'd brought with me from the Island was too quickly leaking away.

Sandy was asleep when I took the flowers to her room. I sat with her for a while. She just snored. My time would be better spent sneaking past Dex One's guards to go riding. I tried calling Clara, but my cell phone's battery was dead. I snapped it shut and went in search of a pay phone.

An hour later, I was mucking stalls and glad for the familiarity of it. Clara had filled me in on the comings and goings the rest of the night at Norman's wake. He'd been cremated while I sat with Sandy that morning. She'd be sad she didn't get to say goodbye.

Hank and Clara didn't have an answering machine. My truck was still dead, Malcolm's SUV was in the shop, he had the Jag, his truck was parked out in the field, and I didn't know where the keys were. I couldn't get to the store to buy a tape player. My only option was to go to the south end of the farm and hope I stumbled onto something. But how to get past Dex One's army?

When I'd gone upstairs to connect my phone to its charger, a different guard was camped out, this one an overweight guy in sweatpants and sneakers. With a rifle cradled in his arms, he was no less menacing for the casual clothes and hefty proportions.

A little while later, he lumbered past the stall I was in, and I had a thought. "Hey," I said. "You on a break?" I leaned against the pitchfork in such a way that my T-shirt rode up enough to show an inch of skin.

"Done for the day." His eyes strayed to my belly.

"What's your name?"

"Brian."

I put out my hand. "Nice to meet you, Brian. I'm Vi. Thanks for helping to keep an eye on things."

He shook my hand. I held his longer than necessary.

"All quiet on the western front?" I asked.

"Boring."

"Boring is good, though, right?"

"Yeah. In this case, I guess so."

I let the pitchfork slip from my hand. We both bent to retrieve it, and I made sure my shoulder brushed his and my hair tickled his cheek. "Thanks," I said.

He smiled. "No problem."

"Well, have a nice day."

He hesitated, looked disappointed, said, "Yeah. You too."

I let him get two stalls down. "Hey, Brian?"

He came right on back like a good boy. I hate myself sometimes.

"Have you known Dex a long time?" I asked.

"We went to the academy together."

"So, you're a mounted policeman?"

"Nah, I tried but didn't make it."

"But you ride, right?"

"Don't get much chance."

Five minutes later, I had Brian wedged into a western saddle atop Honey. He'd made a half-hearted protest, but was easily convinced this was a great idea for such a beautiful day. Honey looked bored, which was just how I wanted her, although that was her permanent expression. I hopped on Gaston, and we were off, Noire trotting alongside.

We chatted about the ball game. The Cardinals had won, and it appeared Brian's mission in life was to eat hotdogs, drink beer, and attend games for free. Dex was paying for this gig with first-base-line tickets. Brian and Honey were well matched.

He sat like a sack of potatoes with his feet shoved home in the stirrups and his heels up. Honey plodded along, head low and eyes half-closed, nabbing every blade of grass that tickled her nose.

I took us straight south. About half an hour later I found what looked like a large hay field. A tractor-wide path wound around the perimeter. Grass nearly reached the horse's bellies. Perfect.

I'd let Gaston ease a few lengths ahead of Honey and twisted to look at Brian. "This would be a great place to go a little faster. You up for it?"

"Not too fast," he said. "I haven't done this for a while."

"Just hold the horn. She's real easy. Ready?"

He nodded, and I urged Gaston into trot. Then, canter. Noire streaked ahead. Honey jogged a few steps and Brian bounced hard. She managed two strides of canter before petering out and stopping altogether. The last I saw of them, she had her head buried in a lush stand of orchard grass, ignoring Brian's weak attempts to get her attention.

At the far end of the field, a rusted woven wire fence prevented me from riding into the woods. I rode along until I found a spot where a tree bent the wire to the ground, and Gaston hopped over like a good horse.

Now what, Wastrel? I waited, but my muse was mute, so I forged ahead. I guess it was too much to expect that he might find a way to communicate with me when I was awake.

I gave Gaston his head, and he walked on, deftly stepping over logs and around underbrush as if he had a destination in mind. I ducked low branches and kept my eyes open for anything unusual.

Nothing looked familiar, but the dream had been so frantic, I'd hardly had time to seek out landmarks. I worked in a semi-organized fashion, letting Gaston choose the particulars once I pointed him in a general direction. Where the footing allowed, I pushed him to trot, knowing that Brian would get suspicious if I stayed away too long. In the meantime, I tried to think of a plausible excuse for when I did return. I could blame it on my dog, say she took off after a deer.

After about fifteen minutes, we nearly fell into a disturbed patch of earth. I hopped down and kicked aside leaves and twigs. Leaves and twigs like in the dream. Noire came over and sniffed around, then sat. There must not be anything here, I thought, or she'd show more interest.

I knelt and brushed at the shallow layer of forest debris. Beneath it was loose dirt and rocks. I swept more leaves to the side. The freshly-turned area was a couple of feet wide by several feet long. I pushed my hand as deep as I could and separated the soil, glad to have remembered my gloves. And came up with a handful of bones.

My stomach did a flip and my breathing came hard. They could be finger bones, but it was impossible to know what they came from without a skull. I dug around, found more. I stared for a long moment, trying to decide what this could mean, what I should do. I stared for so long, I began to feel dizzy. Gaston nibbled on the back of my shirt, found my bra strap and snapped it. I elbowed him away. Men.

I grabbed what I thought was a rib bone and stood.

Something rained through the trees. Then, a loud boom shook the air and Noire took off. Gaston nearly jumped over me. I still had the reins, and he dragged me over a stump.

"Whoa!"

He snorted and flicked his ears but stood. I shoved the bone in the back of my breeches and mounted. More debris came out of the sky. I brushed whatever it was off my leg. Pellets. Another boom, this one closer.

Shit. Were we being shot at?

I didn't wait to get my feet in the stirrups. I kicked him and bent all the way down, my head next to his neck, and pointed him at Noire's tail.

He didn't need any encouragement. He wove through the trees at a fast canter without panicking, and I swore that if we made it home, I'd be sure to tell Malcolm what a great field hunter his horse would be.

One more boom chased us, this one muffled, farther behind. Up ahead, I heard Brian calling my name. He'd gotten Honey to the edge of the field. He must have heard the shots.

"I'm coming," I yelled. Whoever was shooting might hear that, too, and realize we weren't alone.

A second later, we burst into the field, and nearly crashed into Brian and Honey. I grabbed her bridle and dragged them with us at trot until we were over a slight rise and out of sight of the woods.

That was close. I checked Gaston for blood, but there wasn't any. I felt along my back to make sure I hadn't lost the rib bone. Still there.

"What the hell were you doing?" Brian asked. "Was that gunfire? You trespass on somebody else's land?"

I thanked the gods or Dex, or whoever was responsible for leaving Brian in the dark.

"Guess so," I said when I caught my breath. "Sorry about that." I laid my hand over my chest. "Goodness. Gaston just took off." I made a zooming gesture with my arm for emphasis. "I don't know what got into him. Took me a while to stop him." Huge, helpless smile.

"Thought you were some kind of big-shot horse-show rider back in New York."

"Yeah, really." I forced out a laugh. "Me, too."

CHAPTER THIRTY-SEVEN

DEX WAS WAITING for us back at the barn, hands on hips, looking, as Renee would say, fit to bust. He took Honey's reins and told Brian to go home, he'd talk to him later. Brian slunk away without a backward glance. If he'd had a tail, it would have been between his chubby legs. Dex pointed to two other guys who hustled forward and took the horses into the barn. Made me wonder what Dex had on them to make them ask "How high?" when he said, "Jump!"

"You," he said to me. "Come."

After a moment's resentful hesitation, I followed him to the main house. He said nothing more, but the rigidity of his neck spoke loudly enough. I was in trouble. The relief I'd felt at escaping the shooter wilted.

"Brian's not at fault here," I said. "I talked him into—"

He made a sharp "stop" motion with his hand. I didn't like the pissed-off version of Dex One, but I should have been prepared. I suppose I deserved a dressing down.

We walked up the front steps and went in the house.

"Sit," he said, pointing at a chair. "I have bad news."

I went cold. "Is Malcolm—?" He glared at me until my rear end found the seat, and the bone jabbed me. I pulled it out and laid it on the table.

"What the hell is that?" he demanded.

"What's the bad news?" I asked.

"You know Malcolm went to see his father, right?"

"Yes." I held my breath.

"He found him. Dead."

I gasped. "Dead?" I tried to take it in, but my brain was on strike against bad news. "How?"

"Hard to say. He had a heart condition. Cardiac arrest, maybe. No obvious signs. No forced entry. But…he had a bruise on his head."

My hand went to my own. The bump was gone, but it was still tender to the touch.

"Yes," Dex said. "Malcolm said it looked like yours."

"And Sandy's."

He nodded and tapped the bone. "You weren't out joy riding this morning. You had a purpose. And Malcolm said you had prior knowledge of the situation with his father."

My heel started bouncing. The rare, nervous habit only showed up when I was very tired or very tense, or, as in this case, both. I'd roll my right foot onto the ball and bounce the heel without touching the floor. It made my whole leg jounce like somebody giving a kid a horsy ride.

"I had a dream," I said. I imagined him mentally rolling his eyes, but outwardly, he was unmoving, listening intently. "Several dreams, actually, that included a white dog with a bone."

His eyebrows went up.

I pressed my knee down. "Dogs always have bones, right?" I said. "I didn't think much of it. Never seen this dog before. But then, I had another dream with bones in the woods at the south end of Winterlight."

He started to speak, and I held up my hand. "Don't ask me how I knew where to look. I just knew. The most recent dream was very vivid."

"Malcolm told me."

"It left me with a bad feeling, and when I asked him if he knew anyone with a white dog…"

"He called his father, got no answer, and decided to check on him."

"Poor Malcolm," I said. I thought I was having a bad week.

Dex shrugged. "They weren't close."

"They couldn't have been if Malcolm senior was more interested in selling the farm for money than finding a way for his son to have it."

So, he was alone. At least I had Penny.

"He found a bone in his father's house. Not unlike this one, by the way he described it."

"Oh." What else could I say? Of course he did.

"Anything else you'd like to tell me?"

I shook my head. I'd convinced myself the gunshots were coincidental. Someone taking target practice. Or…

"Is it a hunting season right now?"

"Turkey, why?"

See? Perfect explanation. "I heard shots when I was in the woods. Just curious." Not that Gaston and I looked like turkeys.

"Why didn't you tell me? Why didn't Brian say anything?"

"You shouldn't have sent him home so quick."

He gave me a disgusted look and picked up the bone. "I'll make sure the medical examiner gets this. Just in case."

He stood and went to the phone. Guess I was dismissed.

I went back to work thinking I'd done what I could. I'd interpreted and responded to Wastrel's messages. If more came to me in the future, I'd take them seriously. But I hoped there would be no more nocturnal visits. I'd be glad to return to dreamless nights.

I hugged Noire and took care of Cali. I couldn't risk her overdoing it, so I hooked her to the lunge line and let her trot in the riding ring, but kept the line short and the pace slow. She wanted more, needed speed, but still favored the injured leg. I took her in, bathed her, and walked her dry in the sun.

She nuzzled my neck and gave me several big, sloppy horse kisses. I looked forward to getting on her again.

It felt good to feel normal for a little while, to be in the routine. All the other horses needed attention, too. I would immerse myself in the work. But no amount of work prevented my thoughts from drifting to Malcolm, imagining him finding his father dead. And the little dog gnawing a strange bone. And Malcolm senior with a bruise on his head like someone with a ring on his hand had hit him before he died.

What would JJ want with Malcolm senior? Perhaps the better question was, what did Malcolm senior have that JJ wanted? The farm. Good lord. The farm would be Malcolm's now. Unless Malcolm senior had a will that said something different. He couldn't have left it to someone else, could he? In my dream, there'd been something important to find on the desk. I tried to remember. Could it have been the will? I needed to talk to Malcolm. Later. He probably had enough on his mind right now. Whether or not they were close, finding his father dead would be a blow.

Within an hour, Dex asked me to come into the tack room. We sat with the beat-up coffee table between us, and he drew a map of the farm. I showed him where I'd found the bones.

"That's very close to the southern edge of the property and the river," he said. "There are lots of smaller pieces of land down there that share that property line. Hunting and fishing shacks all over the place."

"Let's ride down there. I'll show you—"

"Malcolm wants you to stay put, and I'm going to see to it you do."

Oh, so the alpha male had surfaced again. "When will he be back?"

"Don't know at this point. He'll probably stay in town tonight."

"How is he?"

Dex leaned back, clasped his hands behind his head, and scrutinized me with his peat-moss eyes. I crossed my arms and looked away, feigning indifference.

"Dex Two will be there as soon as he can, and Doreen is with him."

My pretended indifference vanished. "Doreen?"

"She's an old friend."

Of course, Malcolm had a life before I came along. A good-looking, nice guy like him was bound to have lots of *old friends*. But Dex was deliberately provoking me. "I'm glad to know he's not alone."

"You're full of shit."

I took my turn assessing him, decided on the truth. "I guess it's no secret I like Malcolm. If Doreen truly is an old friend, then I'm happy she's there for him. That's exactly what he needs right now." The comfort of the familiar. I could relate.

His eyes narrowed. "You're right. Better than Brooke."

"How'd they hook up, anyway?"

"At work. She had an internship, but I'm sure it was an excuse to play hooky from mommy and daddy for the summer."

"Mommy and daddy were mean to little Brooke?"

"Brooke's a spoiled brat. Daddy has deep pockets. Owns a big construction company. Mommy and Brooke spend daddy's money."

"Did you do a background check on her?"

"Not at the time, no. She was young and cute and seemed harmless. She loved the farm and, supposedly, Malcolm."

"You don't believe it."

"She only cared about pissing off her parents."

It was none of my business, but I asked anyway. "Did he love her?"

Dex exhaled noisily. "She got pregnant. She was scared. Her parents would kill her, she said. So, Malcolm married her."

"Did he think she loved him?"

"He tell you about his friend who was killed when he was in college?"

"Yes. It was very hard on him, I could tell."

"It was right after that all this happened with Brooke."

"Oh, I see." Malcolm had been vulnerable, needed someone to take care of, a woman he could save.

"She lost the baby a month into the marriage."

"You think she was ever really pregnant?"

"Nope."

"But they must have been having sex, right, or he wouldn't have thought he had to marry her?"

Dex shifted. The conversation had gone somewhere that made him uncomfortable. "I guess he'd tell you himself if you asked him. He said they did it once before they married. After a party. In the car. She jumped him."

"Oh, and he couldn't fight her off?"

"Sometimes the little head thinks for the big head."

I laughed and wondered that I still could. "That's a good one."

Dex stood and walked to the window. "He thought they'd learn to love each other. She thought they'd live in the city, and she'd be a socialite. She liked being a member of the foxhunting club. They have a white-tie ball once a year. Lots of St. Louis bigwigs are members. But she never took to riding, and she hated the farm."

"Wait, you said she loved it. You think she only said that to snag him? And faked being pregnant to clinch the deal?"

"Exactly. And now I do background checks on anyone who gets within ten feet of him."

"And Nicky?"

"Sweet kid."

He said nothing else. He wasn't going to tell me about Nicky. Which meant there was something to tell, or something he suspected.

"He loves her," he said, and rose. "Now, even if you aren't full of it, you look like shit."

"Gee, you sure know how to make a girl feel better."

"Just go upstairs and get some rest. I'll keep an eye on things."

These guys were fond of telling me what to do, but I had to admit, I didn't mind someone watching out for me a little for a change.

"What about—?" I rolled my eyes toward the ceiling.

"I'm the only one left. Brian's useless. I should've known you'd charm him without breaking a sweat. I didn't realize you were so devious, or I would have put him in the woods and someone savvy in here. The others are either at their posts, on the way into the city with that bone, or down at the south end seeing what they can find. It's just you and me, kid."

Devious? Me? I had nothing on Brooke. Which made me wonder what else she was capable of. But Dex was right. I was beat, and a nap sounded like a good idea. I started for the door, turned back.

"You'd rather be in the city with him, wouldn't you? He could use your keen eye and experience in his father's house, not to mention your friendship. I'll bet you're just itching to get in there and snoop around."

"Don't try to con me, Miss Parker. I don't know what you did to Brian, but it won't fly with Dexter Hamill. However, if you ever want to consider a new career—"

"I'll let you know."

I went upstairs. After a quick call to check on Sandy—condition unchanged—I flopped on the bed looking forward to an undisturbed rest, but didn't fall asleep right away. There were too many unresolved questions. I was making most of them up, true, but they struck me as valid.

What if Brooke had been conspiring with Malcolm senior so she would benefit from the sale of the farm? She was the type to play a father and son against each other. She would use Nicky, too, if she could—threaten Malcolm with taking her away from him—the bitch.

Could she have killed Malcolm senior? And if so, why? Did he renege on their deal? Or did she go there to talk to him and scare him to death by waving an old bone at him? No, she couldn't have been there today, because I'd just talked to Nicky that morning.

Of course, there was no telling when Malcolm senior died. It wasn't necessarily today, or even yesterday.

Whether or not Brooke was part of this, she and JJ were two peas in a pod—lazy, grasping, manipulative, cold.

If Malcolm owned the farm, that changed the equation. As if I knew what the equation was. I'd never been good at solving for the unknown.

My last thought before falling asleep was a selfish one. If Malcolm owned the farm, what did he need me for?

CHAPTER THIRTY-EIGHT

"Vi!"

I swear to God, if a man yelling my name one more time roughly shook me from sleep, I would hit someone. I mumbled something incoherent and resisted consciousness with all my being.

"Vi, wake up."

I tried to roll over and pull the covers over my head, but Dex had me by both shoulders. I was confused because he was calling me Vi instead of Miss Parker. He pulled me to a sitting position and shook so hard my head rolled around.

"Uh-uh," I said.

He tapped my cheek. "Vi, honey, come on."

I opened my eyes and gave him what I hoped was a murderous look.

"What?" I said.

"Christ. You had me scared a minute." He released me and stood abruptly. "Don't do that."

I drooped back to the mattress.

"Don't do what, sleep for a while? Are you kidding?"

"No, sleep for over thirteen hours then not respond when I try to wake you." He pressed his thumbs into his eyes. "I thought—"

"Thirteen hours? I've been sleeping for thirteen hours? That can't be." The clock next to my bed said four o'clock. I looked out the window. Dark. "You rousted me from sleep at four o'clock in the morning to tell me I'd overslept?"

He eased himself to the bed again. I realized he looked whipped, haggard.

It sunk in that he'd been calling me by my first name, and that could only mean something was wrong. Something even worse than Malcolm finding his father dead. My insides squeezed. I touched his hand.

"What's happened?"

He took my hand in both of his. His skin was smooth, his touch gentle, but he was cold, and there was a slight tremor. "It's Nicky."

Jesus. This could not be happening. I didn't trust my voice, so just waited. But I had to blink away hot tears.

"She's been taken. Kidnapped. Brooke called Malcolm a little over an hour ago. JJ showed up at her door. She let him in. He pointed a gun at her and pulled Nicky from her bed. Had her call Malcolm and tell him if he wanted to see his family alive again, to come get them."

I pressed both fists against my mouth until it hurt.

"Half an hour later, JJ changed his mind, hit Brooke with the gun, took Nicky and left. She couldn't get Malcolm because his phone is out. She called me. I'm flying up there and taking my men. When you're done with the morning work, go to Hank and Clara's and wait until you hear from one of us. Do you understand?"

I didn't understand anything, but I nodded.

"They won't be home most of the morning. They went to see Clara's mother. She's ailing. Renee is visiting her sister in Kansas City. But Hank and Clara will be back later. You'll be okay."

"I'll be okay," I repeated without enthusiasm.

"Take this."

He gave me a handgun in a black nylon holster. I pushed it away. His lips thinned into a determined smile.

"He said you'd be stubborn about this. You probably won't need it, but you're taking it whether you like it or not." He took it out and folded my hands around it. "This is a Glock nine millimeter. No safety. The magazine has seventeen bullets."

Oh, good. I could shoot off all my toes and most of my fingers without reloading.

He shifted to get behind me, aligned his arms with mine, and made me point it out the window. Nausea rolled up from my stomach.

"You have to pull the slide back once to chamber the first round." He demonstrated without actually doing it. "Are you right or left handed?"

"Right."

"Okay, hold it like this." He pressed the grip into my right palm. "Don't put your finger near the trigger until you're ready to fire. Left hand here. Lock your right elbow." He pushed that arm straight. "Use the sights to aim if you have time, otherwise, just point, and pull the trigger. Hold it tight. You're strong, but it's got a pretty good kick."

It was smaller and heavier than I expected. The grip was rough and solid and its cold menace felt oddly reassuring. That scared me even more than holding it.

He let go. My arms sagged down. He lifted them again.

"Do you want to go outside and fire it before I leave?"

"No. I'm sure I won't need it."

"It doesn't have a safety."

"I heard you the first time."

He took the gun, put it back in the holster, and laid it in my lap. He tucked a spare magazine into a pouch on the holster. I stared at the rig, trying to fit its dull weight and all the implications that went with it into my life view. There didn't seem to be a place for it.

"Keep it with you," he said.

Willy felt more solid and alive and, well, the bat was bigger than the gun. Willy made me feel safe. "I've got a baseball bat."

"I've heard. But an assailant has to get too close for you to use it. Don't let him get that close. Understand?"

"Who are we talking about?"

He hesitated, then said, "Anyone who threatens you."

I swallowed hard. He stood.

"Here's the deal. Malcolm had to take his dad's Jeep because the radiator blew out in the Jag, and he left his phone charger behind in the rush. He called me after Brooke called him, but the battery went dead while we were talking. He's out of touch until he gets to Chicago. He doesn't know JJ took Nicky. I'll be off line while I'm in flight."

"How long does it take to get to Chicago by car?"

"From St. Louis, about five hours, but at the rate he's driving…"

"And how long until you get there?"

"I'm booked on a six-thirty-five flight. I'll get there at about the same time as him, and I'll turn on my phone the moment I land—at seven thirty-five. Now, I have to go, or I'm going to miss the flight."

I held up the gun. "Are you going unarmed?"

"Not on your life. I have plenty more where that came from."

Figures.

"I have a message for you from Malcolm," he said. "Be careful."

Not what I wanted to hear.

"Wait," I said. I slid out of bed and found my purse, dug through it until I had the tape. "Do you have a recorder that plays one of these?"

He took the tape. "At home, why?"

"I found it under the manure spreader."

He gave me a "so what" look.

"Another dream. Not about the tape, but about looking for something, kind of like with the bones. And that's what I found. I think Norman might have had it on him. It could be what JJ was looking for when he broke in here."

"Why didn't you say something sooner?"

"I don't know. It could be nothing. The dreams are jumbled and confusing. I tried to find something to listen to it with. I'm only just beginning to understand." *Understand* being an overstatement. "I never had any before I came here."

"You never dreamed?"

"If I did, I never remembered them."

"Never?"

"Do we have time for this conversation?"

He shoved the tape in his shirt pocket. "No." He turned.

"Dex?"

"I'll tell him."

"You'll tell him what?"

"What I see in your eyes."

Holy crap. The moment he left, I ran in the bathroom to see, but all that peered back at me was worry. Next stop, the refrigerator for a generous dose of chocolate whipped cream. Only one can left. It wouldn't be enough. I kept it with me.

I tidied the apartment, did a load of wash, took care of the horses. The sun came up, but the sky was gloomy and the air heavy—just like my mood—and it remained dim and uninviting outside. The kind of day that would frizz my hair into a rat's nest. A wind came up with the sun, and it tore at the trees. The horses turned their tails to it.

So, it was all JJ, not Brooke. I had a hard time believing she wasn't involved, but I couldn't imagine what it had been like to have her daughter kidnapped before her eyes. She must be beyond frantic. Malcolm would comfort her.

Stop it, Parker.

But what did JJ want? He wanted to ruin Malcolm. Was there some way for JJ to get the farm? Or did he simply think, in his small, angry brain, there was some way he could get the farm?

No, he didn't want to ruin Malcolm. He wanted him dead. JJ probably cut the brake lines on the SUV. Hank had said he was a fair mechanic.

I went from one task to another, never completing what was in front of me before moving on. Both downstairs and upstairs bathrooms gleamed, and it was barely six-o'clock. Dex called right before he boarded his plane to say he'd heard nothing on the tape so far, but he was only halfway through one side. He'd keep listening and let me know if anything turned up.

To say I was at loose ends didn't begin to touch what I felt. I'd gone numb, just like after we'd found Norman.

I sat, but every time I did, my leg started jouncing. I tried reading, keeping the book firmly pressed against my restless knee, but kept reading the same paragraph without seeing it. I looked at the clock. It never moved more than a minute. I stole a peek at the gun, then darted an apologetic glance to Willy. I'd said I'd go to Hank and Clara's, but it promised to be a long day, and I didn't want to go over there any earlier than necessary. I decided to call Penny. She was an early riser, and it was an hour later there.

My phone was still plugged into the charger. When I turned it on, it beeped and said I had three missed calls and three new messages. I sat at the kitchen table with my whipped cream and pressed the preset for voice mail.

The first was Malcolm from the night before. "Vi?" he said. "Sorry I ran off and left you this morning. I know Dex filled you in on what's happening here. I'll talk to you later." The second was him again at three something that morning. First, there was a moment of silence, like he was trying to decide what to say. "Vi. I…just wanted to hear your voice."

In the first message, he sounded tired. But in the second, the strain and worry in his tone was almost too much to bear.

The number of the third call looked vaguely familiar, but I couldn't place it. I'd just filled my mouth with creamy chocolate when Nicky's voice spilled out of my phone.

CHAPTER THIRTY-NINE

"I'm scared. No one's answering the phone. It's dark. I need help." She sniffed and hung up.

I went to the sink and spit out the whipped cream, then sat and stared at the phone. The time on the call was no more than twenty minutes earlier, but it was still over an hour before I could get Dex. More than that for Malcolm, because he'd have to charge his phone before he could receive a call.

Maybe he'd picked up a charger. Unlikely at that time of night. Less likely he'd take the time. I dialed his number anyway. His phone wasn't available. Dex, same thing.

With the volume on maximum, I forced myself to listen to Nicky's message again. There was no background noise. Nothing to place her in a car or near a busy street. Just quiet.

I figured out how to put on the gun holster, went downstairs, and paced around the tack room for a few minutes, flexing my shoulders against the unfamiliar restraint and weight of the gun. Should I call her? Was someone with her? Did she still have her phone? Would she be able to answer? If I could figure out where she was… She must be so afraid. My head felt like it might explode trying to figure out what to do.

When Dex had wakened me, he'd brought me out of a deep sleep. I'd been so rattled by what he'd said, I'd forgotten my dreams. Wastrel and I had been on Long Island in familiar fields and stables. Malcolm was there, and maybe Dex. Hard to say. The images came and went like a slide show on high speed. JJ's trailer might have been in the mix. But mostly, it was Wastrel and

Malcolm and Long Island. That, I supposed, was the right place for Wastrel, but why would Malcolm be there? Was he supposed to be in New York? That didn't make sense.

Circling the loveseat in the tack room with Noire's eyes following my every move was doing nothing to clarify the situation, so I went to the field, haltered Gaston, brought him in, and began grooming him.

There's nothing like the rhythm of grooming to settle my nerves. He was still shedding his winter coat, so the job was especially satisfying. I started behind one of his ears with the currycomb and made small, firm circles to loosen dirt and sweat, then used the brush in the direction the coat grew to flick away dust and hair and smooth everything down. Three circles, three sweeps of the brush, move to the next section. Curry, curry, curry, brush, brush, brush.

Halfway along his near side, it hit me.

Malcolm was in the wrong place.

It was not quite seven. I tried both Malcolm and Dex, anyway. Neither phones available, couldn't even leave a message.

Had to chance it. I dialed Nicky and held my breath.

I was about to hang up, when, "Hello?" she whispered.

With my voice low, too, I said, "It's Vi. Thank God you're all right. Can you hear me?"

"Yes." She started to cry.

"Nicky. Nicky. Listen. You've got to help me find you. Your father is going to be there soon, I promise. Everything will be all right, but you've got to calm down, sweetie. Okay?"

She sniffed. "Okay."

"Are you alone?"

"There's nobody in this room with me."

"Good. Just hang up if you hear someone coming. We're going to play a little game, okay? It's called Detective." I was completely out of my league and winging it. But I had to get information out of her.

"Detective?"

"Yeah, that's where I ask you a bunch of questions, and you try to answer as many as you can. And you get…whipped cream. A squirt for each right answer. I'll keep track."

"Okay." She sounded a little more cheerful.

"Can you tell me where you are?"

"I can't see anything."

Crap. "Are you blindfolded?"

"No, but it's dark. And it smells."

Jesus. What sort of nasty place had he put her? I paced a short and edgy path back and forth behind Gaston. What could I ask that would help? *Think.* "Nicky, are you in a room?"

"Um-hm. On a bed."

"Okay. Good. That's great. Has anyone hurt you?"

"No. He…"

"Is it JJ?"

"Yes. He gave me some medicine. He said it would help me. We were in a car. I think I slept. I woke up here. My foot is tied to something so I can't get up."

Double crap. She could have been asleep for hours. They could be anywhere. "That's okay. You already have…um…half a can of whipped cream. Is there anyone else there?"

"I don't know. I don't think so."

"You haven't seen anyone or heard JJ talking to anyone?"

"I can't see anything." Her voice rose. "I told you. It's dark."

"Okay, it's okay," I said in the tone I used to soothe upset horses. "I know. You're very brave. Do you think he's nearby now? I don't want him to hear us talk."

"I don't think so. I heard a car. I think he left." She started to cry again.

If she could hear him drive away, but it was otherwise quiet, then she must be in a house, not an apartment in a city.

"It's okay to be scared. But you're going to be okay." I tried to think what made me feel better when I was scared. "Remember the kittens? Imagine they're with you. All purry and soft. They need you to pet them. They miss you. Can you imagine petting them?"

"Yeah." She almost giggled. "They're licking my face."

"Great. That's great. Now, listen. Look around and tell me if you can see even the tiniest bit of light, like a crack under the door or maybe a window. Sit up, if that helps, and put the phone down. Can you do that for me?"

The more information I could give Malcolm and Dex, the better. If all I accomplished was to keep her distracted for a while, that was something.

She said to hold on. My heart forced the blood through my head so hard, it hurt my ears. I could hear the bed squeak as she moved around.

"There's a door and two windows. But the windows have something over them. Like wood, or something."

"Good. Oh, that's really good, Nicky. Now you have a whole can of whipped cream all to yourself. You think you want plain or chocolate?"

"Both."

"We can do that. By any chance, can you reach one of the windows?"

"Maybe. Yeah. I can reach the one over the bed."

"See if you can pull at the wood, okay? Use both hands. Pull the wood away and tell me what you see."

Again, the bed creaked. A bit of scrabbling and a few little-girl grunts, then a loud crack and a startled, "Ow!"

"Nicky? Are you okay?"

She picked up the phone, sounding breathless. "It broke. I scraped my knuckles. I didn't mean to break it."

"That's no problem. The important thing is you're okay. You've just earned a bonus can of whipped cream. You want to keep playing?"

"Yes!"

"Good girl. Can you see through the window?"

"No."

Oh, for cripe's sake. Come on. "Nothing at all?"

"There's something over the window. Like a curtain."

"Can you push it to the side?"

I heard her scraping at something.

"It's stuck. Like somebody glued it. Why would somebody glue up their window? That's stupid."

"Yeah," I said. "Stupid." Maybe it wasn't a curtain. Maybe it was a window decal or tinting. "Is it dark, like a grayish color?"

"Not really. It's more like reddish-purplish with blue stripes."

Stripes? "What else?"

"I can't see the whole thing. There's a red triangle and then blue and maybe stars in the blue part. I'm not sure."

I closed my eyes and tried to fit that into a pattern I knew.

"Vi, I'm thirsty."

"You've been working very hard, but there's still more to do. Nicky, I need you to listen very carefully."

CHAPTER FORTY

SHE BEGGED me not to leave her. Disconnecting was the hardest thing I've ever done. Before we hung up, I told her to work on getting herself untied. I'd be there soon.

She was at JJ's trailer.

If I were wrong, the worst thing that would happen would be I'd have a good gallop. I strapped the biggest western saddle I could find on Gaston and made the stirrups as short as possible, hoping Nicky's legs would reach. I threw his bridle over his halter. Just like the cavalry.

I yanked an old windbreaker I found in the tack room over the holster, shoved a knife in one pocket, phone in the other, and took off, sending Gaston into a frantic gallop the moment my rear end hit the seat.

On the straight stretch along the field, I called Malcolm. I'm not a trick rider, but the fact is, once you get used to the speed, gallop is a smooth gait—easier to sit than trot or canter. On a straightaway over flat ground, there's not much to do but find your balance and enjoy the ride. I hooked the reins over the horn and dialed. Still no service to his phone. I had a decent signal, but the woods were coming up fast, and I'd probably lose it there. Dex's voice mail picked up.

"She's not in Chicago," I yelled, hoping he'd be able to hear with all the wind. "She's at JJ's old trailer. I'm on my way."

Fifty yards from the woods, I tried 911. I had no idea where the trailer was, though, in terms of an address. Dispatch picked up right as we dove under the trees, and I lost the signal. I was on my own.

I used the remaining time to cement my connection with Gaston. He was open and receptive; there wasn't much in his head besides whatever was in front of him. Wastrel had been complicated and asked a lot of questions. Cali could be that way too, but she was learning to trust and focus. Gaston didn't need any convincing of the urgency of our mission. He understood Nicky was in danger.

It would take only a moment to get her out of the trailer. If she were there. Please, be there.

We rounded the turns, blasted through the clearing and over the log. A little beyond that, I stopped. How close could we get without being detected?

What if JJ was there?

He wasn't going to hurt her. He wanted Malcolm. But why had he taken Nicky and left Brooke? Why leave Chicago if Malcolm was on his way? Something about this wasn't right, but I couldn't figure it out.

Maybe he was deranged; years of hatred and wanting something he couldn't have finally made him snap. If that were the case, I couldn't afford to wait. I had to get her out of there.

I slid to the ground and led Gaston forward. Could he tiptoe? He could. Or as close as a horse can get to it. I watched the footing, moving branches out of the way that would snap if he stepped on them. He waited patiently each time I stopped to listen. The wind carried sounds away, though. That was to my advantage in terms of JJ hearing me, but it meant I couldn't hear a thing, either.

The trailer came into view through the dense underbrush. Any further, and the horse would be clearly visible. I tied the lead line to a branch and told him to stay still and be quiet. He wuffled softly against my shoulder. I patted his cheek.

"You're a good horse. A very brave horse. We're not done yet, though. Don't make a sound. There's a bran mash in it for you, I promise." Why was I always promising food?

I left him there and crept forward until I was at the edge of the clearing. I flattened myself beneath a prickly stand of briars. I could see clear under the trailer, and there were no vehicles in front. The back door still gaped.

As we'd planned, I called Nicky and hung up. She's kept her phone on vibrate and had it stuffed deep under the pillow so only she would hear it. If she were alone, I'd get a call back. One ring. I had the volume on my phone off, too. It buzzed a moment later.

I sprinted to the back door and up the steps, knife in hand, stopped for a moment to listen. Nothing. Good. I crouched and scooted down the hallway as quietly as possible. The door at the end was closed. It was possible there was someone else in the trailer, but it didn't feel like it, so I opened the door. Nicky was picking at the rope around her ankle. It was tied to a bedpost. She opened her mouth to speak. I jumped forward and clamped my hand over her face.

She went still. I slipped the knife under the rope and sliced it. She threw herself at me, arms around my neck and legs around my waist. She was heavy. I ran through the trailer, out the door, and fell down the steps. In that moment, I heard a car coming.

I didn't bother trying to see who it was, but scrambled up, faking calm for her sake. "C'mon," I whispered. "We have to run." I grabbed her hand and pulled her to the woods.

The moment she saw Gaston, she froze.

"I can't," she said.

"Like hell," I said. I picked her up and bodily flung her into the saddle.

She yelped.

"Quiet," I hissed. "Close your eyes and hold the horn."

I swung behind her and yanked the lead line loose.

"Yah!" I yelled. Gaston leapt forward.

Nicky screamed. Again, I put my hand over her mouth.

Pellets zinged around us, and a shotgun roared from near the trailer. I recognized the sound. This time, we were not being shot at over our heads. With so many trees and branches, we were safe. He was too far away, and we were moving fast in the opposite direction.

But then, I heard another sound. An engine firing up. A distinct motor noise, like a motorcycle. A four-wheeler.

Shit. Fuck. Piss.

I shoved Nicky's feet into the big, western stirrups, pressed her down and leaned across her, asking Gaston for more. He lowered his head and dug in. We flew over the log. That might slow JJ down, but not for long. A moment later, we were through the meadow.

The four-wheeler followed. Not close, but JJ could see us, and would gain on us soon enough. We had to get off the wide road.

We couldn't go back to the farm. No one was there. I yanked on the right rein, knowing Gaston could pilot through the woods without a trail. We slowed from gallop to canter, and kept moving. But now, I had no idea where we were. And JJ could navigate this land in his sleep.

Our only hope was to lose him long enough to reach a public road or a house where someone was home.

Nicky had grown quiet. I knew she was afraid, but so was I. If a scary horse ride was the worst of it, I hoped I could be forgiven.

We slowed to find our way around a steep ravine. Gaston earned his bran mash more than once by safely finding his way. In the woods, the wind was not as strong, and I heard the four-wheeler to our left. JJ sped along nearly parallel to us, barely twenty yards away. A trail I didn't know. There must be dozens. Damn it. I curved Gaston right. JJ probably planned to get ahead of us, and at this point, I figured he'd just as soon blow my head off as look at me. I had no doubt he had the shotgun with him.

Should I fire at him? No way. I'd as likely shoot myself or Nicky or Gaston as get a round off at JJ. Or drop the stupid thing. And I didn't know how the horse would react.

We came out on another dirt road and accelerated. There was a field ahead. I turned and rode along it. JJ and the four wheeler popped out of the woods not far to our left and came straight at us.

I didn't bother trying to keep an eye on him. I kicked Gaston for more, and he gave me more. Ahead, there was a fence between this and another field. A barbed wire fence that would not be safe to jump. There was a solid-looking metal gate about midway along. It would have to do.

The gate would either save us or kill us.

"Nicky," I shouted. "Stay down. Hold the horn."

I concentrated on Gaston. Jesus. Jumping a horse I'd never jumped before over a four-foot gate in a western saddle without stirrups with a child in front of me. A day ago, I would have called it suicidal. I pushed those thoughts down.

Fifteen strides away. I heard the four-wheeler engine rev.

You can do this, I told Gaston. Piece of cake.

"What are you doing?" Nicky yelled.

"We're jumping that gate."

Ten strides.

"No!" she screamed. "No, I can't. Get me off." She squirmed.

"We have to." I clamped my arm around her.

Five strides.

"No!" She continued screaming.

I ignored her. *We can do this together, I see the take-off spot.*

Gaston's ears were up. He saw the gate. He flicked his ears back. He heard me.

One stride.

Go!

He took off like we were going to Spain. Nicky's scream deafened me.

Never have I felt such a thrill clearing a jump. Too bad I couldn't savor the moment. We landed in another field, this one smaller. Ahead, the cover of dense woods again. Just before we left the open, I looked over my shoulder. The four-wheeler had stopped at the gate. JJ worked on getting it open.

Up ahead, I could see some sort of break. A road, maybe? Hope surged through me. But when we reached it, we were faced with the river—at this point, a narrow and deep-looking channel with steep banks. We stopped. Gaston's sides heaved and his neck and shoulders frothed with sweat. I couldn't hear the four-wheeler, but no amount of distance between us was enough.

I rubbed Nicky's upper arms.

"Hey, we made it over the jump. Thanks for not bailing."

"Don't do that again, okay? Can we go home now?"

"Not right now."

"But, why?"

"Because there's no one at home, and he would follow us there. I have to find a different place for us. You okay?"

She nodded, but said, "I'm tired."

"Me too."

I couldn't risk plunging into the water without knowing how deep it was. I turned Gaston left. We'd keep going until we found a better place to cross.

A hundred yards downstream, the river rounded a bend, widened, and split into two around a narrow island. The banks flattened. We crossed, and Gaston never wavered. I kept him in the knee-deep water for as long as I could, following the gentle current, hoping that would further throw JJ off our trail. We climbed the opposite bank and continued, but soon found ourselves in open fields. Good for moving fast, not good if JJ caught up with us.

As far as I could see was only farmland. No houses. Not a road in sight. That seemed impossible. I kept to the edge of one field for a while, but didn't dare stay in the open for too long. Why weren't there any farmsteads? I couldn't believe the area was this uninhabited.

It was almost seven-thirty. Dex would get my message. But what good would it do? They were hours away.

A few minutes later, a barn came into view. It wasn't very big and sat at the edge of a field planted in corn. But when we reached it, there were no other buildings. No house. No road. No people. We rode up to it, and I dismounted, helping Nicky down. Her legs gave out, and she collapsed at my feet.

"C'mon, sweetie, let's see what's inside."

The big metal door of the building wouldn't budge at first. After kicking away overgrown grass and weeds, it slid open enough for us all to squeeze in, and I shoved it closed behind us. It squealed and complained, a high-pitched sound that would carry, but there was nothing I could do about it.

The main section of the building was tall with a loft above. To one side, a shed might have housed cattle at one time, but now, a few big, round hay bales were piled in it. Next to them sat a bale fork with its spears pointing straight up.

Should we hold up here until we could get help, or keep going? I looked at Nicky. She sagged onto a pile of old burlap sacks and didn't look like she had anything left. Gaston was game, but needed to rest. I decided we'd stay put until I could talk to Dex or Malcolm. They'd probably know exactly where we were and be able to call someone to come get us.

Gaston shook himself. I tied him to a post along the shed wall. A deep, wooden trough ran the length of the room. It contained mildewed hay, bent-together nests of rusted baling wire, pieces of wood siding, a length of rope. The horse had drunk from the river, so I wasn't too worried about him. I should have thought to bring a bottle of water and a granola bar, whipped cream, something for Nicky. I wasn't much of a rescuer.

I shoved the bad hay out of his reach. "Let's go upstairs," I said to Nicky.

I helped her climb the ladder to the loft. We had a better view from up there. She lay down on a scattering of loose straw near a few dusty square bales that formed a pyramid in the middle. There was an opening at each end of the space. I checked both. The one that looked out over the field had a door hanging by one hinge. I pulled it shut and tied it closed with a piece of baling wire. It was missing part of one section, so I could look out without feeling exposed.

Near the peak of the roof, the siding had long ago blown away leaving a large gap. A patch of sky shown through it and several pairs of barn swallows flew in and out, chattering as if annoyed by our intrusion.

At the other end of the loft, trees crowded the opening, and there was no door. I shoved a bale across it. Again, I could still see out, but it would be hard to see in. Hopefully, he wouldn't find us. But I couldn't count on that.

I also stacked a couple of bales over the opening to the loft that led down-stairs, then checked the time. Seven-thirty-four. I called Dex.

"Thank God." I said when he answered. "Did you get my message?"

"Just turned the phone on. Not even off the plane."

"I have Nicky." He listened without comment as I explained.

"You're still in danger," he said. "When you call 911, you'll be routed to a different county. Tell them you're on a cell phone, and you're being stalked by a murdering kidnapper."

"You know he killed Malcolm's father?"

"I'm getting you help as quickly as possible. Feds up here should already be involved. I don't know where you are, but if you describe the route you took, the locals will find you. Malcolm will know, but I have to get to him first. Good work, Miss Parker."

"Thanks," I said. But like Penny says, it ain't over till the fat lady sings. And I didn't think the fat lady was ready for her solo quite yet.

"Sit tight," Dex said. "I'll call you back."

Renee's comment echoed in my ears. Sit tight. Easy for him to say. Whatever else Dex said got lost in static. I think it was something about the tape I'd given him, but the connection went dead.

CHAPTER FORTY-ONE

JUST AS DEX SAID, my call to 911 went to the next county. They couldn't connect me with the local sheriff, so spent a long time relaying messages and questions back and forth. They said they would call the phone company to find the tower I was transmitting from, but I could be anywhere in a twenty-mile radius, so searching for us that way might take more time than we had.

I gave them Winterlight's address and told them we were somewhere southeast of there and across the river. No, I didn't know what river. How many rivers could there be?

The wind came through the sides of the building and made the tin on the roof flap and creak. Downstairs, Gaston fidgeted and jangled the lead rope, probably tossing his head. He liked to play when he was bored. Swallows swooped along the ceiling, building their half-circle mud homes nestled against the rafters.

Nicky put her head on her jacket and fell asleep.

Ten minutes into the conversation with police dispatch, call waiting beeped, and I switched over. Dex said they were on their way and would be in the area in no more than an hour. He hung up without saying how they were going to do that.

I watched the sky. Clouds tore along the horizon, and sunlight shone down like a spotlight hop scotching over the flat terrain. A pair of vultures rode updrafts, never flapping their wings. I leaned against the bale behind me and answered more questions.

Ten more minutes of passing information along to the local guys, and they said a unit would be in the vicinity within the hour. The woman I'd been speaking to was very nice, but it was hard to tell by her professionally patient demeanor if she really believed we were in imminent danger. An hour? She said they'd sound their siren. When I heard it, I'd tell her. Then, she asked me to hold on. I did. They didn't have innocuous on-hold Muzak. Just dead silence. If JJ found us, I'd be dead before they got there.

I probably shouldn't have sat. I definitely shouldn't have leaned back and rested my head. Despite thirteen hours of sleep, I felt as if I were melting into the bale and would leak through the floorboards. If I'd competed ten horses on the winter circuit in Florida, I couldn't have felt more exhausted. *Knackered*, we would have said when I lived in England.

I took out the gun, chambered a round, and holstered it. Just in case.

Some time after that, I dozed off.

I'm not sure whether it was the kick in the behind that woke me, or rolling off the bale onto the wood floor. But I came out of sleep quickly, knowing this was not the time to hit someone.

"Wake up, Slick."

The wrong end of a rifle barrel pressed against my chest.

My insides liquefied, so it's lucky I hadn't eaten dinner the night before and had no more for breakfast than a couple squirts of whipped cream.

I held up my hands. He wanted to kill me, but if there was anything I could do to save Nicky, I would. By some miracle, she was still asleep.

"Surprised?" he asked.

My throat constricted to the size of a thread. I could barely breathe, let alone speak, so I shook my head. Stay calm and think, a voice screamed inside, but all circuits were busy. All I could see was the dull length of metal leading from my chest to JJ's arm.

"Did you really think you could lose me? That you'd win?"

I barely heard him, as if my ears were stuffed with cotton. He shoved the barrel against my throat. If he pulled the trigger, it would be quick. It would be loud, and messy, but I probably wouldn't feel a thing. All I knew was, I had to distract him from Nicky.

I forced sound through my throat, didn't recognize my own voice. "I— I don't know what I was thinking."

"Why'd you have to come here, Slick? You almost ruined everything. But it'll work out. You'll see."

He jerked the gun away and strode to the front opening so he could look out. I launched into a coughing fit and used it as an excuse to crawl away from where Nicky lay.

"What do you think you're doing?" he asked.

His attitude bordered on indifferent. That didn't seem right. I needed to stay cool and keep him talking until help arrived.

"That straw's moldy," I said, waving my hand in front of my nose. I leaned against the wall halfway between him and Nicky, at an angle that made it difficult for him to see both of us at the same time. I took a few deep breaths to settle my rattled nerves. "You waiting for someone?"

"Mac."

"He went to Chicago."

"He'll be back. If that bitch…"

Had I been right? Had something gone wrong between the co-conspirators? "You mean, Brooke?"

"You're all bitches. Useless for anything but fucking."

Okay, so reasoning with him was out.

"Should've done you right when I had the chance," he continued. "You would've liked it in the river. Why'd you run away?"

"Got scared. I don't…you know…not on the first date."

"Cock teaser. You're all the same."

How could I gain a bit of confidence from him? "I didn't mean to. You were different. You made me want to."

His eyes flitted from the window to my face. Good. I'd gotten his attention. Maybe if he thought there'd been a chance of a relationship between us, he'd soften, or at least get confused enough that…what? My elbow rested against the gun beneath the jacket. He didn't know I had it, or the knife in my pocket. But would I use either if I got the chance?

"You're a liar." He turned to the window. "You're all liars."

So much for that idea. There was a hint of hurt little boy whine in his voice. Maybe he'd snapped, as I'd feared. If that were true, we were screwed.

I checked my watch and wondered what had happened to my phone. It'd probably slipped off my shoulder when I fell asleep and was stuck between the bales. It was nearly nine, which meant if Malcolm knew where we were, they might be here soon. Had the police tried to find us? Or given up when there'd been no response from me?

"Malcolm doesn't know where we are," I said. "Why don't we go back to Winterlight?"

"Didn't you call him?"

"No. I talked to Dex and the sheriff. They're on their way."

"They'll never make it," he said, his voice derisive. "But Mac, he'll find us."

He sounded very sure. They knew each other well, Malcolm and JJ. Had grown up together, probably hunted all over the area together.

"Why do you hate him?" I asked.

JJ turned from his lookout post. "Everything he has should be mine."

"You mean the farm?"

"Before Daddy…" He choked up a moment, the little boy in him showing again. "Before he disappeared, he said it would all be mine. Said he'd fixed it so I would have everything we'd ever dreamed of. Then, he went away. And Helen—"

"Helen?"

"My *mother*," he said, giving the word emphasis I didn't understand. "She talked bad about him. Said it was good he'd left. Said he didn't care about us. But she was wrong! And then…"

He untied the little door covering the loft opening, shoved it open, pulled a bale over, and sat. He cocked his head, listening. I did, too, hoping for the sound of a siren, but all I heard was the high-pitched scree of a hawk.

I tried to take in every detail of his appearance. He wore camouflage pants with lots of pockets, lace-up boots, and a brown, knit muscle T-shirt. It showed off his body and reminded me of how strong he was, how there was no way for me to best him. His black hair had been recently trimmed, and his beard, as usual, was neat. On the third finger of his right hand, I saw the bruising ring, a silver signet.

"You ever had a bad day, Slick? I mean, a really bad day?"

I was having one right then, thanks to him, but thought I wouldn't antagonize him further by pointing that out. "A couple," I said.

"Tell me about your worst day ever."

I didn't have to think about it. My worst day was a toss up between the time I realized my parents had never wanted me, and when Wastrel died. No matter what I said, though, his day would be worse, so it didn't really matter.

"There was this horse—"

He snorted. "Figures." He shook out a cigarette and lit it, tossing the match to the ground below. "I suppose you raised him from a baby," JJ mocked. He took a long drag and turned away from the window. Smoke obscured his face for a moment.

"No. He wasn't mine. I was paid to ride him, but I don't think I could have loved him more even if I'd raised him."

"You think people ever really love a baby that ain't theirs?"

That startled me. "I…I don't know." The question had often been on my mind growing up. I knew my aunt and uncle loved me, but there was something different between them and Penny, something more, and I'd always felt left out of their circle.

He took a few more long drags, flicked the spent cigarette over his shoulder and out the window, and lit another. "You probably had a perfect childhood in a big house with real Christmas trees and mommy and daddy always there to take care of things."

"Actually, no, it wasn't like that. It was a small house, and we did have real Christmas trees, but I was raised by my aunt and uncle, not my parents."

"Oh, yeah? They die or something?"

Only in my heart. "No, they just…went away." How the hell had we gotten on this subject? I kept the old anger and hurt locked in a dark closet. I never let it out. But the door had opened; I felt the familiar pain begin to squeeze my chest.

"They left you?" he asked. "How do you know they're not dead?"

"My aunt gets a letter every now and then."

"They don't write you?" He sounded truly surprised.

"No." I shoved the ugly feelings back and slammed the door on them. "They don't write me."

"Dang."

That was one way to react. "You got any more cigarettes?" I asked. I'd tried smoking when I was a teenager. Didn't like it. But it might stop my hands from shaking.

"Thought you didn't smoke in barns?" He smiled and tossed me the pack.

"Moot point right now." I lit up, inhaled, coughed.

JJ laughed, and I could see the dimples in his cheeks. He caught the pack one-handed when I pitched it back to him. "Sounds like maybe you have had some bad days, Slick."

"Just a couple, like I said. How about you? What was your worst day ever?"

He shook his head, perused the landscape for a minute, and double-checked his rifle—a bolt-action Springfield thirty-aught-six. I didn't like guns, but this was a weapon I was familiar with because one just like it was Uncle Vick's prize possession. He kept it in a gun safe and took it out occasionally to stroke its smooth wooden stock. I'd shut myself in the bedroom when he did. He said the action was jammed, it wouldn't shoot, but I didn't trust it. JJ's, in contrast, looked well used and lethal.

"Thought I'd had some bad days before, like when Daddy disappeared," he said, "but last Friday…"

The night he'd attacked me, ransacked the apartment, and stolen my underwear. That day had turned out pretty rotten for me, too. But for once, I could clearly see this wasn't about me. I stubbed out the butt against the floor, making sure there was no life left in it.

"What happened last Friday?"

"I found Daddy."

"Wouldn't that make it a good day?"

His look was answer enough. His face managed to convey grief and anger as well as his contempt for me.

"Found what was left of him, that is, in the woods north of our place. Old Mac ran him down with the hay mower that day we thought he'd run off."

The bones—could it be?

"How do you know?"

"He admitted it, the bastard, and he laughed."

He continued chain smoking, sucking hard and making each one disappear faster than the one before.

"Said how stupid I was all those years to think Daddy'd be back, when he was right by the trailer all that time. But old Mac's dead now, just like Daddy, so he won't be laughing no more. It's going to be okay. Brooke'll see. We'll still be together."

"You and Brooke?"

"Yep. She never wanted Mac, only me." He spit out the window. "At least, once I took her to the river."

He leered at me, and I turned away. Somehow, I didn't picture this story having a "happily ever after." I unzipped my windbreaker a little, as if I might pull the gun, but doubted my own resolve to do it. Something told me to keep him talking even though I knew the more he told me, the more he'd have to kill me.

"Did you tell your mother about finding your daddy?"

He shook his head and muttered, "My mother. What a joke."

"What'd your mother do wrong?"

"I guess I could answer that if I knew her."

His laugh had a brittle, bitter tenor that tugged at my heart for a moment. But I couldn't let him get by my defenses even if we did share a common hurt.

"That woman—Helen—is not my mother. She told me last Friday when I went to tell her about Daddy. She married him right after I was born. My real mother died having me."

I closed my eyes and began to feel thankful for my parents. They might have abandoned me, but they were still alive. There was always a chance of…I don't know what, in the future. I hadn't realized until right then how desperately I clung to that hope.

JJ'd had everything he knew ripped from him, including hope for that chance of his father walking in the door someday. No doubt it had been a lot to absorb. Then, he'd tried to cap off his day by raping me, but Malcolm stopped him, and JJ ended up in jail.

"That was a bad day," I said.

"Yeah," he said and lit another cigarette. "I wanted to kill somebody. So I went to the one place where I'd felt good, where I hooked up with Brooke. But you weren't home."

"Did hurting me make you feel better?"

"You would have come around once you got used to me. Brooke did. I needed to make you mine, take you before Mac did. That's our way."

"Your way, maybe. I doubt it was what Malcolm wanted."

"He wanted you, I could see it in his eyes. That's all that mattered."

What I could see in JJ's eyes scared me. How I'd managed to avoid the crazies lingering at every turn in New York only to find myself in the middle of nowhere with the local wacko was beyond me. The bucolic scenery and quiet had lulled me into a false sense of security. I'd let down my guard.

"You cut the brakes in Malcolm's truck?"

"Did you like your little ride?"

"Was it meant for me?"

"You, Malcolm, same difference."

Not to my mind, but mine was still sane, I think.

"What about Norman? What'd he do wrong?" I asked.

He gave me a little smile of acknowledgement that I'd figured that out. "He saw me and Brooke together. Threatened to tell Mac."

"So, you drugged him and buried him alive?"

"He was takin' that stuff anyway. Sandy got it for him from the vet. I just made sure he had a little extra." JJ stared at me. "Then you had to go and mess everything up with your spring cleaning."

"Yeah, well, the place needed cleaning."

"Yeah, well," he mimicked, "when this is over, you can clean for me."

Not likely.

"And Sandy?" I asked. A strange feeling rose up inside, like I could say whatever I wanted. If I had to be dead, I'd have answers, first. "How'd she get in your way?"

"How do you know she did?"

I touched the sore spot at my hairline. "You have a distinctive style." He liked that, I could tell.

"That there's a cow should go to the sale barn," he said. "She thought she knew what was going on, was going to avenge Norman. I showed her how'd it'd be better if she kept her big mouth shut."

Movement at the other end of the loft caught my eye. Nicky sat up. She was awake? How much had she heard?

"Vi?" She saw JJ, curled into a ball and covered her eyes.

"It's okay honey." I stood, started to move toward her.

JJ pointed the rifle at me. "Where you think you're goin' now? You think I care if she's scared?"

I froze, all the hair standing up on my neck, my breath coming in little puffs. Breathe, I told myself. Slow. "No," I said, "but I do."

He motioned with the gun and turned back to the window. I ran to Nicky, using the moment of gathering her onto my lap to retrieve my phone but couldn't find it. She put her arms around my neck and buried her face against my shoulder.

"Where's your cell phone?" I whispered in her ear, keeping my eyes on JJ. If I could call Dex or Malcolm—

She shrugged. "Don't know. I might have left it at that place."

"Everything's going to be okay," I told her. "Your daddy's coming as fast as he can, I promise. If I tell you to run, you can do it, right?"

She shook her head. "Not without you."

"You have to. There's a tree outside the back window. If I get JJ distracted, you climb down and hide, okay?"

She nodded against my chest. "Where?"

Good question.

"Shut up over there," JJ groused from his post.

"You shut up. I'm just comforting her, okay?"

He swung the rifle up and put a bullet through the roof. I nearly jumped through the roof myself, and squeezed Nicky against me, one hand over her eyes, keeping my own closed tight. The roar made my ears ring, and dust filled the air. Gaston gave a nervous snort below, and Nicky started scream-ing. Maybe I couldn't say whatever I wanted.

"It's not okay," JJ said when Nicky quieted. "Got it?"

I nodded.

After a few more minutes, JJ spoke again. "She has it all figured out. We just needed them out of the way so she gets the ground."

By *them*, I gathered he meant the Malcolms. And then what? JJ and Brooke set up housekeeping at Winterlight? She didn't like the country. She must have figured if they killed Malcolm senior, Malcolm would inherit. Then, if they killed Malcolm—or he died trying to rescue them—before the divorce was final, she would get the land. But live there with JJ? She'd prob-ably ditch him the moment she had the deed in her hot little hands. Or better yet, turn him in for the kidnapping. God, they deserved each other.

It could still work out if Malcolm and JJ both died. The thought of Malcolm dead sent such a shard of pain through my heart, I almost cried out.

"What happened in Chicago?" I asked.

He hesitated just long enough before answering for me to know that whatever came next would be a lie.

"We decided it made more sense to split up."

"I see. Then, why'd you hit her?"

"All you bitches need to be put in your place. Just like Daddy always said. None of you can be trusted."

CHAPTER FORTY-TWO

JJ TOSSED his last cigarette butt out the window and stood. "Show time, Slick. Come 'ere."

I froze. I couldn't make myself go near him.

His lips curled into a snarl. "Have it your way," he said, walking toward us.

I shoved Nicky off my lap and stood.

"That's more like it," he said.

He shifted the rifle to his left hand, put his other arm around my shoulders, and pulled me against his chest. I couldn't stop the shudder that ran through me.

"Now, don't be like that. Look what I have."

He opened his hand. My cell phone gleamed against his palm.

"Call Mac. Say 'Muller's old hay barn. Come alone.' That's it. Don't try to get fancy. Got it?"

"Do it yourself."

He spun me hard into the wall and grabbed Nicky in one smooth movement. She screamed and started crying. JJ didn't say a word, just held the phone out to me. I took it and punched in Malcolm's number.

He picked up on half a ring. "Where are you?"

He was in a car. Hearing his voice sent thoughts of our almost future tumbling through my mind, and all I wanted to do was cry.

"Daddy!" Nicky yelled.

"Nicky—" Malcolm shouted.

"Muller's old hay barn. Come alone," I said. "Nicky's okay."

JJ smacked me. The phone flew from my hand, skidded across the floor and right out the front opening. I sank to my knees. JJ shoved Nicky at me and strode to his post. A new lump began to rise on my head, right next to the old one.

"Don't ever disobey me again," JJ said.

Nicky sat next to me on the floor. I put my arm around her.

"I want my daddy," she sobbed.

"Me, too."

"Shut up!"

We did, and I listened for anything—car-truck-tractor—that might mean someone was coming.

Ten minutes later I heard something—maybe. It was faint and stopped before I could be sure. But it must have been.

"Bring the girl over here," JJ said, returning to his earlier, eerie cool.

My own voice shook when I spoke. "You don't need her," I said. "Let her go. Take me."

"Don't tempt me, Slick." His voice turned hard again, and he aimed the rifle at my head. "Bring her over, then step back."

All I could do when that weapon came my way was freeze like a deer in headlights.

"JJ?" I heard Malcolm call from outside. "I'm here."

"Daddy!" Nicky got up and went to the window willingly. "Daddy!" she said again when she reached it.

JJ grabbed her ponytail and forced her head back. She squirmed and kicked at him.

"Let me go, you meanie."

I started toward them, but he jerked her hair and put the gun barrel to her temple and stayed just inside, where all that could be seen from outside was Nicky with a gun to her head.

She howled, "Ow!" and went at him with her fingernails, scratching his arms.

"Let her go," Malcolm said. He sounded calmer than he should.

"I will," JJ said. "As soon as you give me what I want." He released her hair and clamped his arm around her, pressing her arms against her sides. She kept trying to kick him.

"What do you want?"

"Sign the farm over to me, and you can have her."

Sign the farm over? I hadn't thought of that.

"Is Vi up there?" Malcolm asked.

"Hell yeah," JJ said. "We been goin' at it all morning. She loves it."

"Let me see her."

JJ jerked Nicky back and motioned me forward with his head. Could I shoot him? Not with the Springfield pointing at Nicky's head. I could kick him through the opening, but he'd probably take her with him. It wasn't far to the ground. He'd survive. She'd get hurt.

I went to the window and looked out. Malcolm stood thirty yards away, wearing the same clothes he'd been in the last time I'd seen him. He might sound calm, but the emotions seething just beneath the surface were evident in the tense stance of his body, the set of his jaw.

"I'm fine," I said. "He's lying."

JJ smashed the rifle into my shoulder. I landed flat on my back at the edge of the drop off into the side shed.

Nicky bawled, "Daddy."

"Let them both go," Malcolm yelled. By the tone of his voice, his composure had just shredded. "Then we'll talk."

JJ laughed. "Not a chance, Mac. Bring me the deed. We'll wait."

"I want my daddy."

"Let her go," Brooke's voice screamed from outside. "JJ, please."

"Mommy!"

Malcolm growled something at Brooke that sounded like, "Get back to the truck."

"Go away, Brooke," JJ yelled to be heard over everyone else. "I'll handle this."

"No," she said. "Let her go."

I got to my hands and knees and started toward JJ. He shifted his grip on Nicky—put his arm around her waist and held her out in thin air. She screamed and kicked.

"Bring me the deed."

"Stay calm. We can work this out," Malcolm said.

JJ shook Nicky, and she slipped lower, but I didn't think he would drop her accidentally. He was too strong. Still, I was afraid to move, afraid to startle him.

"No!" Brooke said, clearly near hysteria.

Through a slit between pieces of siding, I could see Brooke and Malcolm. He held her around the waist, just like JJ had Nicky. Brooke was flailing, trying to get away.

"JJ, no," Brooke said, and her voice broke. She went limp. "She's yours. You idiot. Nicky is your daughter."

All went still. Nicky snuffled a little, but the wind, I noticed, had stopped. A couple of swallows peeked over the edges of their nests, but were quiet. JJ dragged Nicky inside and released her. She ran into my arms.

"Let's go," I whispered.

She ran for the back opening. I started to follow, but JJ caught me, twisted my arm behind my back, and propelled me toward the front window. In the moment we were face-to-face, I read what was there. His eyes had gone flat. His plans were unraveling. If he had any feeling about Brooke's news, I couldn't tell, except that he'd released Nicky without a backward glance.

His daughter.

I was his only other bargaining chip, and he wasn't sure I was worth enough.

Neither was I.

I stumbled to my knees and glanced out. Brooke was there, but not Malcolm.

At least Nicky was safe. In that moment, JJ whirled at some sound from the direction she'd gone. He let me go and fired.

I dropped flat, covered my head, and heard a man's anguished curse. JJ started across the loft, the rifle to his shoulder.

I looked up just in time to see a flash of light-colored hair disappear behind the bales. Dex.

"No!" I yelled. I ran at JJ and tackled him from behind.

Running into him was like hitting a wall, but he hadn't been expecting it, and we fell into the straw. The rifle clattered to the floor. He twisted and tossed me off him. I pulled the knife and jabbed blindly, caught his calf.

"You goddamn bitch," he said. He sat and looked at the blood seeping through his pant's leg.

I scurried around the pile of straw to where Dex lay.

"He shot my leg," he said. "I lost my gun. You still have the Glock?"

"Yes." I pulled it out.

JJ came over, kicked Dex in the head, and hauled me to my feet, dragging me over the bales. We ended up sitting on the floor, me between his legs, his free arm with a strangle hold around my neck, and the Glock's barrel rammed against my cheek. Nicky was safe, but had he killed Dex? Fury trounced sense, and I thrashed and kicked, churning the air like a school of piranha on fresh meat. He squeezed my throat. I began to lose air.

Malcolm came through the back loft window.

He spared Dex the briefest of glances and kept coming at us like a steamroller. I didn't like the distant, cold look on his face, and JJ must have understood what it meant even better than I.

He tossed the handgun over the side of the loft, shoved me the other way, and stood, the injured leg barely slowing him.

Malcolm didn't wait. He slammed one fist into JJ's stomach then brought the other up under his chin. JJ reeled and swung blindly. Malcolm ducked and landed one to the kidneys. JJ back kicked Malcolm in the balls. He bent to protect himself. JJ followed with a roundhouse to Malcolm's face, and he went down.

JJ dove. Malcolm rolled out of the way, and JJ hit the floor with a grunt. I grabbed the Springfield with two hands, wary of its power, and returned to Dex's side thinking he could shoot JJ. He was breathing, thank God, but out cold. I couldn't see any blood; it was the fake leg that had been shot. His still booted fake foot lay by the loft opening, and pieces of the prosthesis littered the floor.

Malcolm and JJ looked like they were hugging, but both were landing punches—face, ribs, anywhere they could reach. I didn't know how to use the Springfield and wouldn't risk hitting Malcolm even if I could. They staggered to the edge of the loft. He put one foot over, lost his balance. I stopped breathing. He released JJ to catch himself on a post. JJ swung. Malcolm bent, drove his shoulder into JJ's chest, and flipped him into the shed below.

There was a dull thump and a sharp "Oof," then nothing. Malcolm didn't try to follow. I ran over. He leaned heavily on the post, looking down.

JJ appeared frozen in midair a few feet above the ground, arched into a backbend, his mouth and eyes open, his arms out to the side.

He'd landed on the bale spear.

CHAPTER FORTY-THREE

MALCOLM PUT his hand to my cheek and turned my face toward him. He was breathing hard, trembling a little—or maybe that was me. He leaned back against the stout oak post and rolled away from the scene below, taking me with him, pulling me against him. A primitive sound rumbled out of his chest, a stifled wail of sorrow and relief.

He started kissing and touching me all over and I clung to him and found his lips and need swept through me and I devoured his mouth and his cheeks and his neck and he had his hands in my hair and down my back and he pulled my hips to his and before I realized what I was doing I had his shirt out of his pants and my tongue on his chest and his hands had found my bare skin and they burned and we couldn't stop and I never wanted to stop.

A moan came to us from the other side of the pile of straw, and Dex clearing his throat, and in a raspy voice saying, "A little help over here?"

We stopped. We looked at each other. We both blinked. He'd been lost in the same haze of desire I had. Then, that slow, knowing smile lifted the corners of his mouth. It didn't last, though. With a glance over his shoulder, he set me away from him and went to Dex.

"I've been worse," Dex said. "You'd better find Nicky."

Malcolm nodded, shoved the bales away from the loft ladder and climbed down. Gaston wuffled and Malcolm murmured a few words to his horse, patted his neck. The front door screeched open. In the distance, I heard sirens.

I walked to where Dex was still flat on his back and knelt beside him. He squinted up at me.

"My leg's all busted, isn't it?"

"Yeah. You want to sit up?"

"In a minute. I think I have a concussion. Did that bastard kick me in the head?"

"Yes," I said as I leaned over him and felt around his scalp.

"Where is he? I—"

"Dead." I found a big lump where JJ's steel-toed boot had connected.

"Good." He winced and removed my hand from his head. "Just because I'm momentarily incapacitated, doesn't mean you should wave your lovely breasts so close to my face."

"Your vision is blurred. That's common after a blow to the head."

"My vision is perfect," he said.

We stared at each other. I stroked his cheek and considered unzipping his pants and straddling him. My body still hummed, yearned for release.

"It's normal, what you're feeling. That need."

"Need?"

"Like you could fuck anything with two legs. I'm probably even looking good to you right now. If I didn't have such a wicked headache, I'd take care of it for you myself."

Having him conscious and talking sense was such a relief; I kissed him on the lips.

"Mercy," he said.

"You do look good to me." A small amount of blood from the head wound had oozed onto my fingertips. "I appreciate the offer, but I think what you need is an icepack."

Two hours later, we'd answered questions from the sheriff, state troopers, and the FBI. Yellow police tape criss-crossed the field and the barn. The coroner was still inside with several others. The EMTs had Dex patched up, but he refused to go to the hospital. He said Renee would be along soon to take him home.

The Mullers surveyed the damage to their corn crop from a tractor. Several neighbors had gathered to commiserate. Hank and Clara had brought the horse trailer and taken Gaston home, then returned with iced tea, meat-loaf sandwiches, pie, and whipped cream, and I was feeling as human as I could short of a shower and a long, long nap.

Dex Two had pulled in about half an hour before. He and Malcolm walked off to talk while Brooke hovered nearby, clearly trying to hear their conversation. She stood with an older man I'd never seen before, but kept her back to him and didn't seem interested in having anything to do with him. He'd been talking to the Mullers earlier. Nicky had been playing with Clara, but now headed toward her mother.

I recognized some of the crowd milling about, and most of them knew each other. Fred and Melba, and Melba's sister, Edna with a spare-looking man who I thought must be her paramour, Herbert. Kevie was in the barn. Norman's mother stood with two other women, and each held a can of beer.

One woman stood apart with a purse over her shoulder. That seemed strange—like she'd walked here or maybe thought there'd be a concession stand at this event. She was slim, middle-aged, wearing a dress that fluttered around her knees, and her long, light-brown hair was coming loose from its elastic. She watched intently, her gaze either on Malcolm or the barn, her hands clasped in front, except when she jerked one up to smooth her hair away from her face.

Dex One and I sat on the tailgate of Hank and Clara's truck. His empty pants leg flapped in the breeze.

"You got a spare leg?" I asked.

"At home. That was my good one, though. Better for riding."

Nicky came toward us, hand-in-hand with the man who'd been standing with Brooke. He was tall, square-headed and gray-haired. He didn't appear to have a neck and walked with a stoop like he had a bad back. Just the same, he carried himself with an air of authority. His face had the worn-out look of a horse that'd been rode hard and put away wet too many times. Dex started to slide off the tailgate to greet him, but the man gestured him back.

"Pop-Pop," Nicky said, "this is Viola Parker."

He put out a hand thick with calluses. "Pleased to meet you, Miss Parker. I'm Nicky's grandfather, Kevin Burns. The Captain here's told me a lot about you."

I shook his hand, but I wasn't sure I was pleased to meet Brooke's father. "Mr. Burns."

"The Colonel flew us from Chicago in his jet," Dex said. "That's how we got here so fast. We landed at a nearby private strip."

Colonel? Captain? "Thank you," I said.

"I'm the one doing the thanking today." He bent and kissed Nicky's hand. "Pumpkin, why don't you go find Clara? I think she has some cake."

Nicky skipped off. Burns' eyes followed her until she snuck up behind Clara and startled her. They both laughed. If Nicky was traumatized by the events of the past twenty-four hours, it was hard to tell. But kids can hide their feelings, I should know. Her grandpa was completely entranced with her, that much was obvious. His glance flitted over Brooke, the barn, all the police cars and emergency trucks, and even though I'd never met him before, I recognized the weary look.

"You two know each other?" I asked.

"We've met a couple of times," Dex answered. "We were both US Marines at one time."

"Seems like another life," Burns said.

"Once a Marine always a Marine," Dex said.

Burns nodded. "I've squared up with the Mullers," he said. "They lost a lot of corn with all this vehicle traffic."

"They appreciate that, I'm sure," Dex said.

"I'll take care of your new leg, Captain," he said to Dex.

"Not necessary, sir."

"Yes, it is." He turned to me. "And you, miss, you've suffered from this, too. What do you need?"

Was he serious? Throw money at the problem? Not long ago, I would have given him a list. At the moment, though… "Nothing," I said.

He barked out a laugh, but it wasn't a happy sound. "Everyone needs something."

We held each other's gazes for a long moment. I'd locked wills with his type before. His watery blue eyes had seen a lot. He was used to getting his way, but he was tired. He looked away first and surveyed the surrounding scene again with a shake of his head.

"What a mess," he said. "Don't think I can get her out of this scrape."

Scrape? I'd been swamped by the wake of spoiled brats before. Because someone was willing to get them out of their scrapes, they continued full speed to the next disaster, unaware of what they'd left behind.

"I hardly think kidnapping and murder qualify as a scrape."

Dex put his hand on my leg. "Easy there, cowgirl."

"Leave it, Captain Hamill," Burns said. "She's right. Miss Parker knows what she's about."

Brooke's shrill voice carried to us. "No," she said to Malcolm, "give me another chance. I had nothing to do with it. It was JJ…"

"That's my cue," Dex said. "Your shoulder, please, Vi."

I'd told him I wouldn't answer him any more unless he called me by my first name. I stood and helped him find his balance. With his arm around my shoulders, he hopped to where Malcolm and Brooke stood behind Dex Two's SUV.

Dex Two had the back door open. Inside was a custom-built mini office.

It was all dark glossy wood just like I'd expect in his real office, had drawers with latches like on a boat, and a safe. He wore a white shirt and dark suit, as impeccable as he'd been the night we went out. Despite the contrast with everyone else's disheveled appearance, he looked right at home. I wondered how often he practiced law out of the back of his truck. He acknowledged Dex One and me with a tilt of his head.

"What do you want?" Brooke snapped at us.

Dex One crooked his finger at two men in dark glasses. FBI. Straight out of central casting. They came closer. He fished a micro-cassette player out of his pocket and switched it on.

Brooke's voice purred out of the player's speaker.

JJ, baby, it's your Brookey-poo. Where are you? We
need to get this situation under control, and soon.
The old fart won't make a will, and you-know-who
won't move the date for signing the papers, so…

There was a pause on the tape. I watched Brooke's face and finally knew what it meant to be *peaked*.

Make it go away. Make him go away…forever,
like we talked. Then we'll be together, just like
we planned. Okay? Take care of it. See you next
weekend, baby. Bye.

Dex clicked the tape player off. Brooke's father had come up behind us. She looked at him while one of the FBI agents cuffed her.

"Daddy?"

"I'll go with you," he said, then turned to Malcolm.

Malcolm stood with his arms across his chest, his face set.

"Nicky really should come home, go to school, get back in the routine," Burns said.

"She has a home here. It won't hurt her to miss a couple days of school. We can talk over the weekend."

Burns nodded and offered his hand. Malcolm took it.

"My deepest regrets, Mac. We'll talk later."

Dex ejected the tape and gave it to the other agent. They nodded, put Brooke in the back of a dark sedan and drove off. Burns followed.

Nicky came over a minute later. She looked at Malcolm. I wasn't sure I could stay for whatever was coming next, but Dex was leaning on me, and he didn't seem inclined to leave.

"Where's Mommy going?"

Malcolm looked into her eyes for a long time before answering. Hopefully, Brooke's revelation about Nicky's father went right over her head. Malcolm hid whatever he felt about it, at least from her. I could see pain etched in the fine lines of his face, but it had been a painful day. Perhaps he'd always known, or suspected. Maybe that's what Dex wouldn't tell me.

Malcolm crouched to her level and put his hands on her shoulders. "Mommy made some bad choices, sweet pea. You know what happens when you make bad choices, right?"

"Is she going to lose privileges or have a time out?"

"Both, my girl." He hugged her and rubbed her back. "She's going to lose privileges and have a very long time out."

"Oh," she said. "She must have been very naughty."

Dex One hid a snort in a cough. "That's one way to put it," he said under his breath.

Barely missing a beat, Nicky said to Malcolm, "Don't move. I need to ask you something, but I have to get something—someone—first."

She ran off. Renee's Beetle motored slowly along the edge of the field, and Dex One and I started in that direction. At the same time, that lone woman I'd seen earlier approached Malcolm. She said something, most of which I couldn't hear, but I caught the word "later." She handed him a small, blue envelope. He nodded, tucked it in his back pants pocket, and hugged her. She walked toward the barn.

"Who was that?" I asked Dex.

"That's Helen, JJ's mother," he said.

It was tempting to say, "Not." But it was up to her who knew she wasn't JJ's biological mother, not me.

Malcolm caught up with us. "You sure you shouldn't go to the hospital?" he asked Dex. He took over from me to help him into the car.

"Hell, no," Dex said. "They'll just stick a tube up my dick."

Renee got out and leaned on her door. "Somebody finally kick him in the head?"

"Um hm," I answered.

"He playing hero again?"

"He's pretty good at it."

"He's getting too old for it, if you ask me."

"Nobody asked you," Dex hollered, and he slammed his door shut.

"Have fun," I said.

"Um, um, um." She got in and gave Dex a kiss.

Malcolm put his arm around me and steered me back to Dex Two's SUV. "Dex Two will give us a lift back to Winterlight."

Where the manure was probably knee deep and the horses out of water and screaming to be fed.

"Hank threw the horses hay, but that's about it. We've got work waiting for us."

Us. The word thrilled and panicked me in equal parts. I swallowed hard. "Work would be good," I said.

Dex Two handed Malcolm a thick manila envelope. "Your copies of the divorce decree, and everything of import I could find in your father's apartment. He died intestate. You are the sole heir." He shook Malcolm's hand. "Congratulations. You own Winterlight."

Malcolm looked at the envelope. Surely he realized he would inherit the farm. Holding the official papers, however, appeared to fill him with disbelief. Maybe it was the divorce decree that had him looking doubtful. The day had been so full, he could have simply forgotten.

Nicky dragged Clara over to us.

"Daddy, Clara said I can have a sleepover at her house."

His face cleared, and he looked at Clara. "Tonight?"

"We're going to start a new quilt," Nicky said. "Clara says I can pick out the colors."

"I understand if you want and keep her tonight," Clara said. "Maybe we should do it tomorrow, Nicky."

"No, I want to do it tonight. Please, Daddy?"

He took a deep breath, clearly unsure what was best for the little girl. "Let me think about it, okay? Come with us now, because you'll need clothes and your nightgown, anyway, and we'll talk about it. How does that sound?"

"Ooohhhh," Nicky said in frustration. She crossed her arms and tucked her chin.

"Your daddy's right," Clara said. "You ain't sleepin' nekkid at my house. What if you and Hank both needs to use the toilet at the same time, and you run into each other out in the hall, huh? That would be embarrassin' for ol' Hank. You know how shy he is. He might up an' faint."

Nicky giggled and relaxed. "Okay. See you later."

"Bye, sweetie." Clara hugged her and waddled to where Hank waited at their truck.

Dex Two opened a back door and swept an arm toward the seat. "Your carriage awaits, my little princess."

Nicky climbed in. "Daddy, sit in the back with me?"

"Be right there."

Malcolm still had his arm around my shoulders. He pulled me to him, and kissed me. On the lips. In front of everyone, which included Dex One and Renee, who was just getting her car turned around, and JJ's mother, and, well, most of the damn county. It was an act of possession, a public statement. And I didn't argue whatsoever.

"Let's go home," he said.

CHAPTER FORTY-FOUR

HOME AND WORK. One and the same for me. Dex Two dropped me at the barn and took Malcolm and Nicky to the house. I couldn't wait to get to work, and there was plenty of it. Noire ran up to me, and I knelt to hug her.

"Sorry you missed all the excitement, girl." I smoothed her ears. She licked my face and sniffed my hands and feet, and I remained still until she had her own version of events.

A short time later, I had everyone turned out and water heating for Gaston's bran mash. I hummed, determined to fill the hollow spaces so no thought could settle, no images could intrude, and no questions could be asked.

Downstairs, I heard Nicky's voice.

"I want to see the kittens."

I poured steaming water into a bucket of bran, oats, and carrots, gave it a stir, draped it with a towel, and headed down.

"They're in the loft," I said. "Come on. Let's go see."

The kittens slept in a patch of dusty sunlight, rolled together in a furry vortex. Nicky and I tickled them with pieces of hay and petted their fat bellies. Henrietta slid against me, purring, and I scratched her back. She licked my hand, then the head of one of her tabby offspring when it tumbled against her.

"Good mama cat," I cooed. "You have beautiful babies."

I watched Nicky. She made delighted little-girl sounds, but had shadows around her eyes. I was glad I wasn't the one to explain things to her. I'd have a hard enough time coming up with answers for myself when I got around to thinking, which I didn't intend to do anytime soon.

We went downstairs where Malcolm had started cleaning stalls. Gaston tucked into his mash with enthusiasm. The afternoon wore on until Malcolm announced it was time for Nicky to have a bath and dinner and get to bed. He'd explained earlier she would not be going to Hank and Clara's, and she'd put up a fight. Now, she gave another half-hearted argument about helping Clara with the new quilt.

"You're staying with me tonight, and that's that," he said.

"But *Daddy*," she whined.

"Tomorrow night, I promise." He took her shoulders, about-faced her toward the house, and gave her butt a swat. She marched away with a giggle.

He turned to me. "Come up when you're through?"

I nodded. Everything was done. I just needed to shower. But I wasn't sure the little hot water heater that supplied my apartment held enough to make me feel clean.

Upstairs, I had a message from Penny. I phoned her, but she wasn't home, so I left her a message that I'd try again later, then called the hospital. Sandy's condition had improved. They'd release her tomorrow. I said I'd be there to pick her up and made a mental note to see about getting her place tidied up before returning her there. They put me through to her.

"Well, if it ain't the dream horse detective," she said, her voice scratchy.

I paused to process this comment. "Dex and Renee stopped to see you?"

"Wow, you really are psychic. How'd you know?"

"No special power, just a brilliant piece of deduction."

"Huh?"

"Never mind. How are you?"

"Can't wait to get the hell outta here, take a real bath, and eat some real food, ya know?"

I did know. "How about if I pick you up in the morning, and we go straight to The Brick?"

"You read my mind, new girl. Could you get something for me to put on besides this pukey hospital gown? It ain't my best color."

"You got it."

The line was quiet for a moment. Then, she said, "Hey Vi, thanks for…you know."

"Yeah. You can buy me breakfast."

"Deal. Say hi to Fawny-Wawny for me."

A hot shower and change of clothes later, I felt revived, and let myself into the tiny mudroom off Malcolm's kitchen. Noire padded behind me, sniffing chair legs and doorways, and the floor. The house was quiet. Nicky must have fallen asleep easily and Malcolm still be with her. The almost-set sun sprayed golden-red shadows over the living-room wall. I decided to sit in Malcolm's easy chair to watch them fade, and wait for him. As I snuck past the couch, his arm caught me around the waist, and he pulled me onto his lap.

"Hey," I whispered. "I've had enough scary stuff for one day."

"Sorry. But I've waited long enough to hold you—in private." He adjusted us both deeper into the soft cushions.

We stared at each other a long time. He wore only a pair of shorts and a ratty T-shirt and smelled like soap. I had my hands around his neck and massaged the muscles there with my thumbs. He had one arm around my back, the other resting on my thigh. I kicked off my sandals.

Bruises had started blooming on his face and probably in unseen parts of his body, too. I palpated his slightly swollen nose. He flinched, removed my hand, and kissed my fingers.

"Are you hungry?" he asked.

"I am."

Sitting on the couch in the almost dark was suddenly too intimate for us, I think, and we sprang up. He'd taken out steaks to defrost earlier. I found a bag of broccoli that looked like it'd been in the back of the freezer since the turn of time. But I don't think either of us was concerned with flavor. We just needed to fill our bellies and keep ourselves busy.

We brushed against each other a few times in the kitchen. I opened doors, looking for glasses, and he came up behind me, put one hand on my waist, and pointed to the next cabinet. When he went to the fridge, I found a reason to reach around him. He smiled and moved into me just enough. My body throbbed, a pleasurable thrill of heat bouncing from deep down in my belly up to my chest and back.

I found plates and utensils, and he insisted we eat on the back porch, through a squeaky screen door with the screen bowed out near the handle. Pale pink light, the last of the day, reflected off a pond not far from the house across a yard in bad need of mowing. Frogs sang. An old wooden swing hung by chains, but we sat on the steps and were quiet. Noire settled in the grass at our feet, tail wagging, licking her lips.

He picked at his broccoli, had a few quick bites of steak, and set his plate aside. "Will you stay here with me tonight, Viola Parker? In my bed?"

I hadn't finished either, but tossed the T-bone to Noire, took my plate from where it balanced on my knee and put it next to his. Even in the deepening twilight, he must have been able to see the thousand-million questions on my face.

"I'll just hold you, if that's all you want." He rested his elbows on his thighs and looked at his hands. "I can't really guarantee that's all that will happen if you do come as far as the bed." He half smiled, but he wasn't sure, I could tell.

When I didn't respond, he continued. "It's a new bed. I'm the only one who's used it."

That rising ache in my chest returned. I knew what it was, now. Joy, and fear—my heart trying to feel, my head fighting to contain it. Answers could wait. I told my head to shut up.

"Just tonight," he said. "Tomorrow, we can discuss tomorrow night. And the next day—"

"That's not all I want, Robert Malcolm."

He stopped and looked at me, and the smile started. Then, he grabbed my hand, and we ran up the stairs, quiet like, so as not to wake Nicky. We slid on the polished wood floor in front of his bedroom and skidded through the doorway. The door, an old and solid one, closed too loudly, and we both froze and listened. When all we heard was our own breathing, laughter burbled up and sloshed over. He put his finger to my lips, and I nipped him.

"Is that how it is?" he teased.

I nodded very slowly. "Um-hm."

He leaned in for the kiss, and I closed my eyes, then found myself in his arms, across the room and bounced on the bed. I stifled a shriek.

He climbed over me and said, "Hush," on a breath. After kissing me senseless, he levered himself up, reached into the drawer in his nightstand, and brandished an unopened box of condoms. He looked both sheepish and uncertain.

His concern and forethought sent a pang of tenderness through me. "Good idea," I said.

He looked reassured, then paused, and there it was, the expression he got when his brain's gears were in overdrive. "I haven't done this in a while."

I took the box from him and squinted at it. "They're not expired, are they?"

He snatched it from me, tore it open, and pulled one out. "No, they're new, like the bed."

I laid my palm against his cheek. "I haven't done this in a while either. But I bet we remember how."

And then our clothes were off, and we were between the cool sheets and his skin, all of his smooth, delicious skin was finally against mine, and I lost track of where I ended and he began.

When he entered me, he buried himself deep with one thrust, and we both went still. I rocked my hips to take him farther inside, and a strained groan escaped his throat.

"I can't—"

My mind went blank. "You can't—?"

"If either of us moves, I'll come."

Oh.

I started to laugh. "There'll be a next time, won't there?"

I'd never thought about it before, but it's impossible to laugh without moving.

He swore and dug his fingers into my flesh, and his teeth sank into my shoulder, but he couldn't stop himself.

Fortunately, there was a next time.

And a next. And, well…the man is in good shape, lots of stamina.

I don't remember falling asleep. I do remember not dreaming.

CHAPTER FORTY-FIVE

I AWOKE to darkness and that brief disorientation that goes with waking in a strange room with my head on someone else's pillow. I stretched and felt raw soreness in places that hadn't known soreness for some time, and I smiled and rolled, and…he wasn't there.

I hate that.

I got up, found his discarded T-shirt, pulled it over my head, and tiptoed out. I was almost past Nicky's open door when I heard a sleepy little voice.

"Daddy?"

I thought of continuing, pretending I didn't hear, but I couldn't. I went to her bedside. "It's me, sweetie. You okay? You want me to get your daddy or a glass of water or something?"

She shook her head.

I sat my hip on the edge of the mattress. "Bad dream?"

She shook her head again. "You sleeping in Daddy's room?"

Oh, great. "Yeah. Right next door."

She nodded as if that fit with her expectations. "What happened to JJ?"

Crap. Where the hell was her father? "Well…"

"Is he in heaven?"

Oh, boy. "Something like that."

"My friend Samantha had a turtle that died. Her mommy said he went to heaven, but Sammi said her brother flushed him down the toilet."

Heaven via the sewer. Sounded about right. Malcolm's earlier explanation about Brooke came to mind. "JJ was kind of naughty, though, he made some bad choices."

"Oh," she said. "So, maybe he's in that other place. I'm not allowed to say it."

I nodded and hoped like the-word-she-couldn't-say we were finished. She darted her eyes to the window, then back at me. Nope, her little brain was still clicking. "What did Mommy mean when she said that stuff to JJ?"

Oh, please. "What stuff was that?"

"She said I was his daughter. What does that mean? How could he be my daddy?"

I hoped Malcolm had a healthy savings account. I could just see the therapist bills piling up. For me.

I've never believed in lying to kids. For the first time, I understood the virtue in it. Or, at least the necessity. But I'd no experience with it. I took her hand. "Your daddy…" I started. "Your daddy is—" I stopped and swallowed hard and thought back to a time before I understood that Uncle Vick wasn't my father, to the confusion I felt when they explained. "Who hugs you when you get a boo-boo?"

She gave a little shrug and answered very matter-of-factly. "Daddy."

"Who tucked you into bed tonight, and read you a story, and has always been there for you no matter what?"

"Daddy."

"Who loves you more than anything in the whole world?"

"Daddy."

She could answer so quickly. After they'd explained my situation to me, I'd never been sure again.

"That's because he's your Daddy, sweetheart." I gave her hand a squeeze, hoping I was saying the right thing, considered adding, "and always will be," but thought better of making promises that weren't mine to keep.

"Vi, are you sad?"

"No, of course not."

"But, you're crying." She sat up and hugged me and patted my back. "It's okay. You were very brave today."

I snorted a laugh through my tears. "You'd better get back to sleep, Missy, if you think you're going to help Clara with that quilt tomorrow." I laid her on her pillow, snugged a stuffed purple rabbit next to her cheek, and tucked the sheet around her.

She rolled onto her side and hugged the rabbit. "Okay."

I stood and backed out of the room.

"Vi?" she said before I could clear the doorway.

"Yes?"

"I'm glad you came home with us."

"Me, too." I smiled and went downstairs to locate Malcolm. He was out on the back porch again, sitting in the dark on the swing, not swinging.

"Hey," he said and held his hand out to me.

"Hey," I answered and took his hand and joined him on the swing. He put his arm around my waist and pulled me tight to his side. I had a moment of panic, thinking he was out here regretting what had happened between us, but when I sat, I noticed the letter Helen had given him earlier lying on the cushion beside him.

"Everything okay?" I asked.

He handed me the letter. "Take it inside to read," he said. "I don't want to turn the light on out here. Too many bugs."

I did as he said and went all the way to the kitchen where a florescent under-the-counter light burned. He'd opened the blue envelope carefully—it was neatly slit along a short side—then refolded the pages and slipped them back in about halfway. The two pages of pale-blue stationery showed wear, like the letter had been written long ago, then folded and unfolded and fingered many times before finally being sealed in a matching envelop. Behind the letter were a couple of documents of some kind, but I wanted to read, first.

The handwriting was Catholic-school neat. It was dated thirty-two years before.

My Darling Robert James,

I miss you so much. My body and my heart ache for you. But I'm sure I have done the right thing. Your father insists he will give you a better life, and his wife will love you like her own. I have nothing.

But I want you to know that I will never stop thinking about you. I've met a man who recently lost his wife and has a little son and older daughter to raise. He's asked me to marry him, and I will. Your father is selling him a bit of ground nearby, so I will never be far away.

I hope you will forgive me.

Your loving mother.

The next page was dated ten years later.

Robert,

You are growing into such a fine young man. I am so proud of you. I try to stay away because that is what your father wants, but it is so hard. And now there is trouble between him and my husband— John's been carrying on with your other mother. He does it to punish me because I told him about you. I'm afraid your father will do something if he finds out.

I don't know what to do.

She didn't sign it at that point. There was a break, then a date of a few months later. No salutation.

He's gone. I'm relieved, may the Lord forgive me, but I know your father had something to do with it. I accused him to his face. He didn't deny it, but he said if I told anyone, he would send you away. I would never see you again. I couldn't bear that. He has already sent his wife to stay in the city for a while.

And John Junior—no, no one must know. Please forgive me. I never stopped loving you.

Your mother, Helen James

The first document was Malcolm's birth certificate: Robert James Malcolm. It listed Robert Alfred Malcolm as father and Helen Elizabeth James as mother. She'd given him her last name as his middle, and evidently Malcolm senior had let her. A concession, under the circumstances. The second document was another birth certificate—clearly a copy, not an original. It listed the same father, but Susan Marie Malcolm as mother. I carefully refolded everything and returned to the porch. Malcolm stood out in the yard, looking up at the night sky. It was dense with stars like I'd never seen before.

I wasn't sure if I should say anything. What was there to say? His father had had an affair, and he'd forced his lover—Malcolm's mother—to give up her child. Plus, the daughter Malcolm thought was his wasn't, and the woman who raised him wasn't his real mother, either. She'd had an affair, and his father had murdered her lover. Talk about putting the fun back in dysfunctional—the Malcolms made the Parkers look normal.

"Hell of a day," I said.

He nodded, but when he spoke his voice sounded far away. "Helen said she'd always planned for me to get that letter after she died."

I couldn't imagine what it must have been like for her all those years living nearby and watching her son be raised by someone else while she raised another woman's kids. She hadn't wasted any time changing her mind. I didn't blame her. She could finally have a real relationship with him, if he wanted it.

"So, with everyone else concerned gone, she decided to tell you?"

"It explains so much," he said.

Like all the cookies she baked for him.

He took a deep breath, hooked his arm around my neck. "I'm sorry I was so rude that first morning when we went riding," he said.

Whoa. That was an abrupt change of subject. Okay, I could take a hint. We were done talking about the hard stuff. For now.

"I wasn't exactly a peach, myself. But why were you so unpleasant?"

"I wanted to impress you. But I couldn't because you already had everything done."

"That's funny."

"Funny 'ha ha' or funny 'peculiar'?"

"Both. I had everything done because I wanted to impress you."

He chuckled, that tender sound he'd made on the phone the night I invited him up to see the kittens.

"I was already infatuated with you," he said.

"Even though I can't tell a bull from a…what did you call it?"

"Heifer. A cow that hasn't had her first calf yet."

"As I recall, I didn't say much of anything those first days."

"No, but you were thinking, I could tell. Your face is very expressive. It's what you didn't say that interested me."

"And what didn't I say?"

"This place sucks. I want to go home, right now."

I laughed. "I was thinking that."

"Exactly. I wasn't sure why you restrained yourself, but I liked that you didn't say it out loud. I started to really fall for you the night you showed me the kittens. When you didn't say how scared and alone you felt. But I could see it. No, I could feel it, inside of me. All I wanted to do was to hold you, but I didn't think you'd go for that."

"I wouldn't have. But just having you there made me feel better. And that scared me, too. I started falling for you then, but I was trying really hard not to be infatuated with you. What got me was the next night when we went back to the barn after supper, and you didn't say how much you love this place and how scared you were of losing it."

"You could see that?"

"Felt it. Inside."

He pulled me into a hug and kissed the top of my head, and we stood like that for a while.

A few minutes later, he asked, "Why don't you have your psychic ability on your resume?"

"What psychic ability?"

"What do you call your dreams?"

"Annoying."

"They helped solve a couple of murders, and you saved Nicky."

Yeah, right. And the sooner they stopped, the better. I'd had enough murder and mayhem to last a lifetime.

I pointed at the stars. I could see the Milky Way, and imagined in winter, the sky would be even clearer. "Is that why you named this place Winterlight?"

"Good guess, but no."

He said nothing else, but I sensed him smiling.

"Sooooo?" I prompted.

"Sew buttons, that ought to keep you in stitches."

I hip-checked him. He grabbed my butt.

"Oooh, no underwear. I like that."

Men. Sheesh. I swatted his hand away and pointed at a firefly. "Is that the winter light?"

"We don't have fireflies around here in winter."

Right. "So, why do you call this place Winterlight?"

"Sometimes, in the winter when it's very cold… " he trailed off. Not far away, a cow mooed. "You'll just have to be here this winter to find out."

"I have to stay here for months, mucking your stalls and riding your horses and doing God knows what other kinds of dismal farm-related chores you think up, just to find out what Winterlight's winter light is?"

"Whatever it takes to keep you here."

"Can I smart off to the boss?"

"You are the boss. I told you that your very first day. But I warn you, the weather conditions aren't always right for producing the winter light."

"You mean I might have to stay even longer than a year?"

"If you can take it—and me—for that long."

"I can take it." I locked elbows with him to lead us inside. "And you." I squeezed his arm against me. "But let's ride forward on the buckle, okay?"

We mounted the steps. He opened the old screen door.

"I like the sound of that," he said. "Especially if you ride in front so I can...keep an eye on you."

He made another grab for my rear end, and I let him.

"You'd better be careful, though," he continued. "If you stay too long, this place might grow on you. It could start to feel like home."

The truth is, I was beginning to understand what Penny meant about finding my true home.

"Actually," I said, as we started upstairs. "I like the sound of that."

———

End of *On the Buckle*

CANDACE CARRABUS

RUN

DREAM HORSE MYSTERY #2

OUT

CHAPTER ONE

CERTAIN MEN SHOULD BE REQUIRED to wear a sports bra when riding.

That's what I was thinking as I boosted an overweight guy onto Fawn, a stout quarter horse mare who could carry him without straining anything. Although she did let out a little grunt of protest when he plopped onto the saddle. His parts bounced recklessly. And by parts, I mean man boobs. Moobs.

I'd read a recent study that said riders could throw their horse's balance out of whack if they didn't wear the right undergarments.

I couldn't unsee the moobs, but I could ignore them as I mounted my horse—correct undergarments in place—and set off for the relative cool of the woods. Here it was, late August in Missouri and there was no sign of the heat letting up or rain coming down.

Unfortunately, there was no sign Winterlight Farm would discontinue public riding anytime soon, either.

The girl behind me waved. Lisa was about my age and the most confident of the group. She rode a petite gray mare with black mane and tail named Oreo. I smiled and returned my attention to the trail. Guiding five inexperienced customers is not my favorite way to start the day, but it's not like I have a choice.

Nope. According to the mysterious trust fund set up by my absentee parents, Viola Parker—me—must keep a job for one full year before I turn thirty. *And*, get a glowing letter of recommendation at the end of it. Not only that, I wasn't to know the contents of the trust until the year was up. So, I could be wasting my time out here in God's country. Otherwise, I'd still be back East competing the top jumpers for blue-ribbon crazed owners with more money than sense.

Well, maybe. Truth is, it's unlikely anyone back there would hire me again.

Straightening my spine, I let out a breath and released my frustration, the gentle movement of my horse's stride soothing me. Even though it was still early, sticky heat dampened my skin like a steam bath.

Our path meandered along a ridge for twenty minutes before crossing a valley with a creek running through it. The horse's hooves made only the barest muffled thuds, lifting the scent of warm dirt to my nose. My dog, Noire, riffled underbrush hoping to flush a squirrel.

"Where's Mr. Malcolm today?" Lisa asked.

"Out of town," I answered without turning. I didn't want to discuss Winterlight's owner, who also happened to be my lover.

Lisa didn't take the hint.

"What's it like working for a hottie in a kilt?"

I rolled my shoulders and cracked a couple of kinks out of my neck. Malcolm is a hottie who wears a kilt, and we'd become involved shortly after I'd arrived, despite my rule to not get in bed with the boss.

"He's good to work for," I said. "Fair."

The man was actually a rare and irresistible package of passion, kindness, intelligence, and looks. Too often I wondered what he saw in me, but not enough to break it off.

"Oh, come on, Vi, spill."

Birds swept by, twittering a happy tune, and a rabbit hopped out from under a bush. I half expected Snow White and her seven dwarves to march into view and break into song. If only to make Lisa shut up.

"We've never gone this way before," said the girl riding behind Lisa on Smitty. I think her name was Sue.

"It's cooler," I said, thankful for the change in subject.

"Yeah," piped up Lisa's boyfriend. "Almost makes it bearable to wear this stupid hat."

Deep breath, bite tongue, don't say what I'm thinking. *If you fall off, that stupid hat might save you spending the rest of your life eating through a tube.*

Before I left the east coast, my cousin Penny made me promise I wouldn't smart off. My inability to keep my mouth shut has cost me a couple of jobs in the past. I twisted backwards, giving the complainer a look that was probably lost under the brim of my helmet—the stupid hat he referred to. Yes, I made everyone wear them, whether they rode English or Western, and whether it was their first or thousandth time getting on.

"Liability insurance," I said.

"Yeah," Lisa said. "And if you fall off and crack open your head, I won't be the one spoon-feeding you and weeping."

Nice couple.

I tweaked the reins and Cali halted. "There's a ravine ahead. We're going down, first."

"Going down," the chubster snorted.

Freaking moron. A moron with man boobs. I sucked in another deep breath.

"Your horses know what to do. Sit up straight and keep your heels down. It will feel like you're leaning back. Any questions?"

"When are we going to run?"

Same voice from the back. I tilted to the side so I could see him. "This is what—your second or third time on a horse?"

He shrugged and gave me a *so what?* look from where he straddled Fawn. She ripped a mouthful of dust-encrusted leaves from the side of the trail.

"When you can keep your horse from eating while she has a bit in her mouth, you might be able to handle running." *But please put on a sports bra first.*

Titters from the peanut gallery. I'm glad I can be so freaking entertaining.

He jerked the reins to pull up Fawn's head. I regretted saying anything and made a mental note to put him on a less forgiving horse next time. One who would turn around and bite his leg. We didn't have a horse like that, but I could dream, right?

Just a couple more boarders or horses in training and we'd be able to stop renting to the public. In case I haven't mentioned it, I hate giving trail rides.

I clucked, and Cali moved off, placing her feet carefully on the loose stones and gravel. After a hairpin turn, the trail dropped at a forty-five degree angle before leveling out to cross the creek. The horses would take care of themselves so long as none of the riders did anything stupid, like suddenly yanking one rein and pulling their mount off balance.

Everyone remained calm as we descended. Noire splashed in the creek, which had been reduced to not much more than a trickle by the lack of rain. Her black coat blended in with the dusky shadows of the ravine. We were nearly at the bottom when something large suddenly moved through the woods, and my dog shot off barking and snarling, making a racket snapping branches as she crashed through the underbrush. All the horses jumped. Lisa shrieked. The guys cursed.

Cali spun in the direction Noire had gone. She was still barking, probably chasing some deer. My eyes stayed on the horses, making sure none of them bolted and the riders' butts were still connected to their saddles.

Lisa dropped the reins wrapped both hands around the saddle horn. She'd gone pale.

"Everyone okay?"

"My foot came out of the stirrup," Sue said.

"Just hang on till we get to the bottom and I'll help with that."

Cali's black-tipped ears pricked tight, and she didn't move when I put my leg on her. Her nostrils flared. We heard coyotes howling often enough at night, and neighbors reported seeing bobcats in the area. Those weren't usually predators horses needed to fear.

The woods went quiet, and I waited, listening, but the horses became restless, rustling the crisp leaves underfoot and nipping at desiccated weeds. We walked on, made the level area creekside, I fixed Sue's stirrup, put the reins back in Lisa's hands, and we crossed the shallow stream.

To my relief, Noire came panting back, took a long drink, then laid down in the water to cool off before trotting alongside me and Cali.

"Who was that?" Lisa asked.

"What do you mean, *who*? It was some deer."

"I know what a deer looks like," Lisa said. "Four legs. That was a person."

A person? This deep in the woods? My focus had been the safety of the group. Thick trees and dense brambles made seeing anything almost impossible. Whatever—whoever—it was had been gone in a flash.

What would anyone be doing this deep into the property? It wasn't hunting season. A neighbor wouldn't have run off. I'd tell Malcolm when he got back from his current business trip. He'd know what to do.

Pushing down the churn of anxiety in my gut, I said, "We're going to trot up this hill. Lean forward a little and hold the horn so you don't slip back."

Cali didn't hesitate this time when I urged her forward. But even in trot, her glance and ears kept straying to the right.

People could be predators, I reminded myself. I'd seen it up close and personal. Predators of the worst kind. The kind that horses—and humans— very much needed to fear.

CHAPTER TWO

As we returned from the successful ride—meaning everyone stayed on and there was minimal screaming—Zoe slouched in to work. Her pace and posture conveyed the put-upon sixteen-year-old doing something she resented, but I knew better. Mucking stalls wasn't high on her favorites list, and when she picked up the pitchfork, she was slower than a slug in summer, but she loved being around horses as much as I did. The gleam in her eyes reminded me of me at that age.

She grabbed a halter and lead line and ducked into the pasture, going straight for Honey, the only horse I'd allowed her to ride.

"Hold up there, kiddo," I said from Cali's back.

She froze and gave me a wide-eyed stare. She often got that bunny-being-stalked-by-a-cat look about her, and it made me wonder. Not something I had time or energy for right then, though.

Riders dismounted. I hooked my leg over my saddle's knee roll and loosened Cali's girth. She tossed her head like she always did. "You're late," I said to Zoe. "Again."

"So?"

Insolent little… "So, let Honey go and help with these horses."

Her gaze slid away, and she huffed, then yanked the halter over Honey's ears.

The mare didn't care—she was getting out of work—but I did. I nudged Cali closer, leaned down. "If I catch you taking your frustration out on a horse again, you're done. Got it?"

Man Boobs sniggered, but at a glare from me, he shut it. Maybe Zoe'd be on time tomorrow. Maybe I expect too much? Over the years, a few people have mentioned that I'm very demanding. There's nothing wrong with having high standards, though, or expecting someone to be on time.

Zoe had shown up two months before looking for work, and Malcolm'd insisted help would allow me to spend more time riding. I couldn't argue with that, but we couldn't afford to pay her much, either. All she wanted, she said, was to be around the horses.

She stroked Honey's ears by way of apology, and we all felt better. I did, anyway.

With the riders gone, she and I hosed off the horses and sprayed them with fly repellent before returning them to the pasture. It was the season of horseflies, bot eggs, and cockleburs. Bug spray wouldn't keep the burrs from twisting tails into dreadlocks, but it would prevent itchy stings and those sticky little yellow eggs the bot flies lay.

We set to cleaning stalls before it got any hotter.

After about half an hour, Zoe broke the silence with "Sorry I was late," from the next stall over.

"What happened?"

"Oh, you know. I stayed up to watch some old movie with Mrs. Erdman."

At least she was honest. But Mrs. Erdman was ninety if she was a day. Zoe lived with her for free in exchange for helping out. "Mrs. Erdman stays up late watching movies?"

Zoe snorted in a very teenaged girl kind of way. "No. She falls asleep in her chair and snores with her mouth open while her cat snoozes on her chest."

"At which point, you could go to bed so you can get up in time for work."

She didn't say anything for a while.

Finally she offered, "I guess." She dropped the pitchfork into the wheelbarrow with a clang. "But then, she'd be in that chair all night, and she should go to bed, too, shouldn't she?" Zoe came to lean in the doorway of my stall. "Eventually, I put out the cat and help Mrs. Erdman to her room."

I stopped for a moment, wiped sweat on my shoulder, and stretched my back. "Why doesn't she go to bed in the first place?"

Zoe shrugged. "She says it makes her feel old to go to bed early."

We both laughed.

The girl had been quiet in the beginning but had begun to come out of her shell. She was far from a chatterbox, which suited me fine. I hoped I'd been wrong about the fear, but there was still that occasional startled bunny look.

"Tell Mrs. Erdman it's for her own good."

Zoe considered this for a moment then shook her head. "You ever tried telling someone that old to do something?"

I smiled and went back to work. "I see your point."

After forking the last of the wet straw into our wheelbarrows, we took our loads to the manure spreader.

With the immediate chores completed, I could now exercise the privately owned horses. But it was at least ninety-five degrees already with humidity to match and we didn't have an indoor arena. I went into the tack room to cool off and fortify myself with coffee before dragging a horse and my sweaty self into the sun. Hot coffee. Sounds weird on a hot day, I know. Everyone else I'd met out here preferred iced tea, but I was almost as addicted to coffee as I was to whipped cream straight from the can. Of which I had none.

It's too much to expect a person to give up whipped cream *and* swearing at the same time. But I'd done it on a dare for Malcolm. Proved I could. For a few weeks, anyway.

I sipped my almost-as-strong-as-espresso brew and sank into the tack room's ratty love seat. Some combination of the heat, unrestrained man boobs, and the possible poacher in the woods had my head pounding. What I needed was a couple of painkillers and a quick nap to make me fit for company. That and a run to the store to stock up on whipped cream. Enough was enough.

Keeping a cold can of creamy goodness close to hand was the only way to deal with relentless heat, sniggering customers, potential poachers, and recalcitrant help all while not swearing. Not out loud, anyway.

For a moment, I considered sending Zoe to the store. That would be irresponsible, right? Instead, I sent her to scrub water troughs—easy duty on a sweltering day—and slunk upstairs to the cozy apartment that came with the job.

Falling asleep was easy. It always is. Resting, though...

The dream begins with fog. Out of it trots Wastrel, smelling of heaven like always. Much as I loved that horse, I'm not happy to have his ghost vividly appear behind my eyes again. I've slept dreamlessly since JJ died, as I had all my life before coming to Winterlight.

Then, Wastrel started galloping through my nights, digging into things I didn't want to know about, forcing me to piece together obscure clues and solve a crime that had nothing to do with me.

I'd thought we were done.

Hoped we were done.

I was wrong.

I am determined to ignore him. My dream self turns my back, but I can't keep it up. He's so sweet, and we play for a few minutes. First, he won't let me near him, our usual game, but soon he's at my side crunching a carrot I produce from the pocket of my pants.

Then, he's tacked up, I'm aboard, and I can feel the constriction of a show coat around my shoulders, the tall collar of the ratcatcher at my throat. My heels are deep in my sleek black boots, and we've picked up canter. We circle and gain speed, clearly preparing to jump a course. Just like the old days. It feels so good to be on his back again, I smile.

The fog clears and the competition arena comes into focus, the striped rails and panels, the flowers and grass. I can hear the crowd and smell Wastrel's sweat. It's the jump off. His head is up, ears forward. I've memorized the course. The first fence is a blue vertical, then we have a sharp right to the combination…

No. This is the last time I rode Wastrel, the last time I rode a grand prix.

We are *not* going through this again. I don't care if it's just a dream. I yank one rein, but he's galloping, ignoring me. I lean back, shove my legs forward, and pull with all my might just as it all explodes.

"No!"

I thrashed awake and landed on the floor with a thump, breath whistling in my throat, heart hammering my ribs, Noire licking my face. Blearily, I sat up and leaned against the bed, forcing the dream fear down. But shaking it, shutting out the memories, was impossible. I pressed the heels of my hands against my eyes, hearing the splintering wooden jump, the shattering of my heart, and tearing flesh—Wastrel's and mine.

The day of that accident, I awoke in intensive care, hooked to every machine the hospital had. They told me Wastrel had been put down. Later, when my body had healed, I'd abused alcohol beyond all limits, but nothing had dulled the pain.

The first time Wastrel appeared to me in a dream was a few days after I arrived at Winterlight. Somehow, he told me the accident wasn't my fault. He'd wanted to end it. I'd always known he didn't like competition, but his owner forced it, and we'd gotten through it together.

That's why I had to pay attention. I hadn't heeded Wastrel the first time he visited, but he'd truly been bringing me helpful messages, even if they were hard to decipher.

Why that horse show? Why the course where we crashed, he died, and I got carried off on a stretcher? What mystery might be brewing now? I didn't want to find another dead body or rescue anyone.

For the time being, I put it out of my mind. If last time was any indication, Wastrel would return when next I closed my eyes, and I'd try to make sense of what he showed me. A trip to the store for whipped cream was essential now. I grabbed a peach and went downstairs.

Zoe came in, soaked but smiling. "Do we have any more customers today?"

"No." I took down a bridle and decided that staying inside to clean tack made the most sense. "But Ciquala, Miss Bong, Barbie, and Gaston all need exercising. We'll ride later after it cools off."

"We?" she squeaked. She went pale.

"Yes. You'll ride Ciq while I ride Miss Bong, and then you'll ride Barbie while I ride Gaston. They're good horses. You'll be fine."

"Don't you usually gallop them?"

By her wide eyes and thin lips, I'd say she had a fear of galloping. But I felt the need for speed. Malcolm and two of our boarders liked to fox hunt in the winter. Part of my job was keeping their horses fit for that.

With a frustrated sigh, I said, "I galloped them all a couple of days ago. Today, we'll mostly trot."

She nodded, unhooked a bridle and sat. I got out the saddle soap.

It should have been soothing. I like cleaning tack. But the dream…dread had my gut churning on anxious anticipation of whatever was coming down the pike.

Noire scratched on the door to go out, then raced to the front of the barn, barking at a bright yellow car that pulled in and stopped.

Zoe and I followed my dog. "Is that a taxi?" I asked.

"Looks like it." She zipped out the back door saying, "I'm going to check on Fawn."

Had the taxi spooked her? Fawn didn't need checking. We had to talk. I wanted no surprises for the rest of my time at Winterlight.

All four of the taxi doors opened, and the trunk lid popped up, but only the driver got out. He went to the back and produced several large suitcases. What the hell? My stomach did a scared flip. I almost cut through the back door just like Zoe had. Changing the subject and running away were my two favorite modes of defense.

Curiosity and the weight of responsibility kept me rooted in place. With Malcolm away, I was in charge. But why hadn't the passengers gotten out?

I walked toward the front of the barn. Some sort of discussion or argument was going on inside the vehicle.

A hand grasped the taxi's door frame and an elderly man emerged from the front seat, pulling himself tall. He had thick gray hair sweeping back from his temples and forehead, and a full beard and mustache. He cradled several potted plants against his chest as if they were his only and most prized possessions. I'd never seen him before.

A younger man got out of the back seat. Also tall, thinner than the first, his hair sporting glints of silver.

The air, already still and shimmery with heat, grew stifling, backing my breath up into my chest. I recognized the unmistakable profile first, the nose with the slight slope, well-defined lips, strong chin.

Images from the dream kicked my gut and made me sway with the same disorientation I'd felt as Wastrel and I began the course.

From the other side of the cab came a woman in large sunglasses and a simple sleeveless black sheath, her dark hair slicked back into a signature chignon.

I put one hand against the wall. The other covered my chest, willing my heart to continue beating. Where had they come from?

The elder man's eyes drank in the scenery like a prisoner released from solitary. He put down the plants, slammed the taxi door, picked a handkerchief from his pants pocket, mopped his face.

Zoe came up behind me. "Is that weed?"

Leave it to the sixteen-year-old to jump to the most optimistic conclusion.

"Tomatoes."

"How can you tell from here?"

"My Aunt Trudy has tomato plants she defends militantly—as that guy likely does," I said with a short nod in his direction. "I can tell by the way he holds them."

"Like a bomb?"

"Like a baby."

CHAPTER THREE

THE WOMAN SPOKE FIRST. "Is that you, Viola?"

"One-hundred-thirty-seven dollars and fifty cents," the driver said.

Without glancing away from me, she said, "Make yourself useful, Adrian. Pay the man."

The words came out clipped, cultured, the accent well practiced.

Zoe moved her hand back and forth in front of my face. "You there?"

I shook my head.

The scene had gone all razor-edged black-and-white contrasts except for two colors that stood out: the shiny red of the woman's dangling earrings and the yellow cab.

Adrian handed over a stack of bills and the cab left, raising a cloud of dust to blow through the barn.

The woman coughed delicately. The two men, both tall and fit looking, made no comment. I remained where I stood, clammy and queasy.

Keeping my voice low, I told Zoe, "Stay here."

"Who are they?" she whispered back.

I gazed at them a moment longer, trying to make the two in front a different pair of people. But their lean figures and elegant features refused to become anyone other than who they were.

"My parents."

CHAPTER FOUR

Zoe, like the good teenager she was, or maybe more like the friend she was becoming, ignored my directive and followed when I took a couple of jerky steps toward the front of the barn. Forward, when every cell screamed *back*. Compelled in the direction of pain instead of away from it, my feet betraying my heart.

My insides were frozen, my brain locked up, and the rest of my body rigid. I stopped. Zoe stood beside me.

"Aren't you going to say something?" my mother asked.

She and Adrian had taken a tentative step closer, too, and stood silhouetted in the square opening of the building. The older man wiped his face again and watched. My mother turned to my father.

"Why won't she say anything?"

He'd finally pulled his gaze away from me to take in his surroundings, a view which must have been so alien, them having spent nearly their entire lives in urban European locales.

"This…must be…a surprise," he said, as if the thought had just occurred. Whether this comment was meant for me, his wife, the as yet unidentified man, or himself, it was hard to tell.

Shock was more like it, but my brain had begun to function enough for me to clear my throat and ask, "What are you doing here?"

"A fine welcome," my mother said.

"You weren't expecting them?" Prickly awareness laced Zoe's tone…but I couldn't gnaw that bone just then.

"Not. At. All." I paused to drag in a shallow breath.

"Are you going to leave us standing out here in this heat?" Again, she turned to my father. "I told you we should get a hotel."

"What are you doing here?" I repeated, more loudly. "How did you find me?"

Zoe's body jerked as if she'd been slapped. "You hiding out here?"

My eyes cut sideways. What the *hell* made this kid so finely tuned?

"Not exactly. I'll explain later."

Clearly, my parents and their traveling companion intended to stay.

Needed to stay? The thought came as a surprise.

Why, on a day when I had no whipped cream and Malcolm wasn't home? His steady strength beside me would bolster my ability to cope, to maintain my sanity. Without him near, I felt even less hospitable than usual, so much so I could begin to dislike myself.

What did they want? I gestured at he of the many plants.

"Who is this?"

Adrian and the elder looked at each other while my mother lifted her chin and longingly studied the cab's dust cloud. Color leached back into the scene, their faces pale against the pasture and trees behind them. For a sec, they were all etched in stark profile, like a pre-Raphaelite painting.

Again, my breath hitched. Even with age, the older man's face was my father's.

My father, who'd always claimed to be an orphan, shrugged, shoved his long fingers in his pockets, and turned his gaze to the ground. Guilty, guilty, guilty.

My *grandfather*—Jesus, who else could he be?—who until that moment had never existed, lifted his shoulders in a resigned version of the same shrug and added a heavenward roll of his eyes for good measure. Then, he flicked a glance over his shoulder so quick, I almost missed it. He smiled and shifted the pots he held from one side to the other. They were all—plants and people alike—beginning to wilt.

My mother crossed her arms and looked like she wanted to tap her foot. "That's Giacomo."

Giacomo straightened his spine and nodded at me. "Giacomo Russo," he said in a voice raspy with stories waiting to be told. Something in my chest— my heart I suppose—did a big thump.

With a fatalistic sigh, I walked through the barn, past my parents, and up to Giacomo, taking one of the plants. He hesitated, just for a blink, then handed it over with a grateful smile. His eyes skittered to my parents, subtly rolled again, then met mine with a gleeful gleam.

He and I were going to get along just fine. I picked up another of the plastic pots.

"Come inside."

I led the way to the house, a distance of about three hundred feet up a dirt and gravel driveway that would ruin my mother's high heels.

I could have grabbed one of their suitcases. I didn't want to. I could have hugged them. That was out of the question. I could have dredged up an iota of welcome. If they were…welcome.

As I trudged toward the house, I came to grips with my main feeling.

Fury.

I was absolutely, completely, totally enraged they had invaded Winterlight. Despite all the craziness since I'd arrived, I realized right then I'd come to think of the farm as *my* place, too. Not just Malcolm's. I'd been embraced here, respected. Looked up to, even. I belonged in a way I never had before.

I could not share this place with them. *Would* not.

At the same time, curiosity sprinted to catch up. Although they'd abandoned me as an infant, they'd also created the trust fund that had driven me here. The mysterious trust fund—amount undisclosed—that could be my ticket to freedom, or might be next to nothing.

How did Giacomo fit? What had Wastrel been trying to tell me? Is this what the churning and the dream were about? I really needed a fresh batch of whipped cream.

By the time I reached the porch, my need to understand what the hell they were doing here had almost shouldered aside my anger. Almost.

From behind me came the sound of wheeled luggage bumping and scraping up the drive, but no conversation, no questions, no demands.

Noire trotted to my right, and Zoe stuck to my left.

"What do you want me to do?"

Her concern, and her unexpected loyalty, touched me.

"Keep an eye on things in the barn. Clean more tack."

"Clean tack. Got it."

I set the tomato plants on the porch. My parents caught up. I thanked Zoe and held the door. They dragged their bags over the threshold into the front room. Giacomo came up the steps slowly, his restless eyes taking in the sturdy lines of the old farmhouse, and as near as I could tell, counting the windows. He set the plants he carried next to the others.

My father had hauled up two large way-beyond-their-prime Louis Vuitton soft-sided suitcases. My mother managed to bring in one small carry-on which she dropped the moment they entered. Three or four more frayed pieces leaned against each other in front of the barn.

They could stay there all night for all I cared.

My parents could, too.

Zoe caught my eye before turning toward her chores. *Yell if you need me* she telegraphed. The kid knew something about difficult parent-child relationships. I just wasn't sure what it was.

I let the screen door slam and stifled a satisfied smirk when my mother jumped.

"I suppose you'd like something to drink." I headed down the hallway to the kitchen.

There, I leaned against the counter and hyperventilated. *Why* hadn't I gone out for whipped cream when I had the chance? I got an ice cube and held it to my forehead, then slid it down my neck. The sense that the top of my head might blow off passed, and I fixed four glasses of iced tea, adding sugar to one for my dad and lemon to mine. My spidey sense told me Giacomo would be content with whatever I gave him. But I couldn't remember how my mother took hers or if she even deigned to drink ordinary tea. After all, she was no ordinary woman. At least, not in her estimation.

When I returned, she perched on the edge of a flat, backless bench, her strong dancer's legs neatly crossed at the ankle and her hands in her lap, pulled tightly into herself as if too much contact with the real world might dull her shine. My father struck a forced pose of nonchalance by the fireplace, his arm resting along the white mantle.

God help me.

Giacomo settled back into the sofa like a stone sinking into mud. His white button-down shirt had dark stains beneath the arms. The ancient striped tie hanging loosely down his front had a couple of spots on it.

I passed out the drinks. Dad thanked me and tipped it back. Mom looked doubtful—or was that disdain in those downturned lips?—and didn't take the glass. I plonked it on the table next to her atop the latest issue of *Horse Illustrated* and dropped myself onto the end of the couch opposite Giacomo.

My grandfather—did I really have an extended family?—and I sipped tea.

I'd asked what they were doing here—twice—and had yet to receive an answer. As we stared at each other, I did a little calculating and came up with the number five.

Five months.

The sum total of time these two had ever spent with me since I was born. Small wonder I felt no connection but plenty of resentment. The chance they'd developed a sudden flash of parental love didn't exist. Which meant only one thing...

They needed me.

God help them.

I glanced at the clock above the fireplace. My mother's sharp gaze followed.

"Are we keeping you from something?"

"There's always work to do," I said as evenly as I could.

"Honestly, Viola, you never change," she said. "You look well, by the way. The country agrees with you. Aren't you glad to see us? It's been a long time."

Sixteen years. *Not nearly long enough.*

"Since we're being honest, no. I'm not glad to see you. Why should I be?"

"Vi—" my father started, but not unkindly.

"*Viola,*" my mother cut him off. "What an awful thing to say."

Dad put his hand on her shoulder and murmured a soothing, "Not now, *Gem Gem.*"

His pet name for my darling mother, Gemma Marie.

She tossed his hand away and rose, smoothing her dress. Dad pushed her back to the seat. She sat with a huff, thinking better of whatever scolding she'd been about to hurl.

Exactly how I'd issued from these two defied logic, but there it was. How Adrian might have issued from Giacomo was clearly another story altogether.

My mother produced a wadded-up tissue from some hidden pocket and dabbed her forehead. "Viola, can you please turn up the air-conditioning? It's positively sweltering in here. I don't know how you stand it."

"I'm usually outside," I answered, leaning forward, drinking more tea, and refusing to blot the sweat on my upper lip. "We don't keep the AC on when no one's in the house, except in the bedrooms upstairs. Perhaps you should go to a hotel. The nearest one is thirty minutes down the highway. I'd be happy to give you a lift. You won't be able to hail a cab out here."

Oh, the satisfaction I'd get from flinging their luggage into the back of my pickup and making them cram into the cab with me, my mother straddling the shifter. I almost smiled.

Giacomo grunted, but exactly what aspect of the conversation he was punctuating, I don't know. My parents glanced at each other, communicating silently like they must have done on the dance floor for years. A hunted look flickered over my mother's face. There and gone in a flash, quickly replaced by her renowned haughtiness. This time, it was her profile that caught me off-guard, as if I'd suddenly seen my reflection off a storefront window out of the corner of my eye.

Spooky.

My father's face gave less away. You wouldn't think I could read them so well, but he reassured her with his eyes. *Follow my lead.*

"Vi," my father said. "We'd like to stay here with you."

His usually smooth tenor caught briefly on the words *with you.* He sipped the last of his tea and added, "for a little while."

"A little while?"

The phone rang. Grateful for an excuse to get away and desperate to hear Malcolm's voice, I dashed to the kitchen and grabbed the receiver.

"Malcolm?" I nearly shouted. "You won't believe—"

"It's Clara. Why are you yelling?" she asked. "Did I see a taxi over there?"

God bless our neighbor, Clara.

"Yes. Yes, you did."

"Ever'thing all right?"

After a deep inhalation, I exhaled noisily through my nose.

"Guess not," she said. "You need pie? Just pulled a rhubarb custard out the fridge. I might could bring it over on the Gator." She sniffed, then sneezed. "Woo. Think I got cinnamon up my nose."

Relief made my knees turn to water. Clara was as far as you could get from my mother, and tough, too, didn't take crap from anybody. She had a sixth sense about when I needed a piece of straight-from-the-oven—or fridge —pie, a commodity that flowed endlessly and magically from her kitchen. The Gator was her favorite new thing—a six-wheeled utility vehicle with a dump bed she used any excuse to take out for a drive.

"My parents are here."

"Why, I didn't know they was comin' to visit. Why didn't you tell me? I woulda baked a cake."

Company was always cause for celebration in Clara's book.

"They just showed up. Pie works fine."

"Oh, I forgot. Your parents done you wrong and you don't exactly like them."

I hate them, I almost blurted. Truth? I didn't know them well enough to expend the energy it took to hate.

Which was easier to say than do. Or not do.

What I felt was confused. Beneath the anger, and entwined with years of frustration and unanswered questions that had produced an ill-adjusted and equally ill-tempered adult, lay a child.

A child still longing to be loved.

Aunt Trudy and uncle Victor—the people who raised me—loved me, of that I was sure, even if they tended to keep their emotions close. But sometimes, they tried too hard. They knew I had a giant, gasping wound. Their attention didn't make up for knowing my real parents had abandoned me. By choice. Not by necessity. The little girl inside still howled with the pain. But I'd always thought this hurt was one my father understood, a thread that connected us despite almost never being together. After all, he'd been left on the steps of an orphanage still slick with afterbirth.

Or so I'd always been told.

Now, it appeared, the story—our connection—had unraveled.

Clara's voice brought me back to the present. "Vi?"

Much as I wanted someone else in the house, anything to buffer the fire that had leapt to life in my chest, dragging Clara into it wasn't kind.

"Now probably isn't the best time. I'll call you later if we need the pie."

"I got Cool Whip."

My insides went all squiggly. It wasn't as good as the canned stuff but worked a treat in a pinch.

"Bring it over."

CHAPTER FIVE

ZOE WOULD SURELY WANT PIE, too, I thought as I slowly returned to the front room. I'd call her in, and we'd make inane small talk. The inevitable confrontation—the one I felt pressing against my insides—would be avoided, or at least, postponed.

When I got there, Adrian and Gemma turned their heads to look at me. Dad wore a hopeful half smile. Mom tried to hide behind her cultivated disdain, but fear lurked in unexpected shadows around her eyes and tightness at the corners of her mouth.

Giacomo's head lolled on the couch cushion. He snored, his open mouth revealing a decent set of teeth.

Prickly heat rushed my neck and scalp. The air in the room, already heavy with damp, congealed at my temples and tripped down my spine.

I needed to get out. Now.

My parents sharing the air I breathed didn't help. Adrenaline propelled me forward.

"Have to do something outside."

The screen door slammed against the wall then squeaked back into its frame behind me.

"Stay here," I ordered over my shoulder.

As if they'd set so much as one of their highly esteemed and insured toes inside the barn. As if they'd lower themselves to learn anything about me or what I cared about.

My heart clogged my throat. Despite the unrelenting sun burning my head—or maybe because of it—I ran.

Noire bounded up as if this were a game, shaking water off her pelt, smelling of the pond.

A gazzilion thoughts and questions collided in my brain.

Needed to call my cousin, Penny. Did she know my parents were stateside?

What would Malcolm say? If he was smart, he'd fire my ass.

No, we had a contract.

I jogged past the luggage, into the barn, and stopped, breathing hard. I stood there a moment with my eyes closed. The scents of fresh straw and hay and sweat and horses and leather all mingled together like distinctive perfume in my nose.

It grounded me.

Malcolm needed me. My job was safe.

I was a selfish bitch.

That was nothing new. I'd had only me to look out for me for so long, it was hard to shake the habit.

I went to the tack room and called Penny. She answered on the first ring.

"Hey," I said, "that was fast. You sitting on the phone?"

A slight hesitation. "No." A note of distress, quickly covered. "I'm waiting for the doctor to call."

I gave myself a mental head slap. Penny was due to have a baby in a couple of weeks.

"Is everything all right?"

"Probably nothing serious."

Too fast an answer. Crap. All my worries flew out the window. Well, most of them, anyway. "What aren't you telling me?"

"Nothing, really. It's fine."

"You've never been a good liar."

She sighed. "Remember how I was a little short of breath?"

"That was weeks ago. You're just getting it checked out now? *Penny*." I said her name like I say Noire's when she rolls in something dead.

"*Not* helping," she scolded.

"Sorry."

Penny and I were like sisters, seeing as how we'd been raised together. Almost twins. Her parents took me in while her mother—Aunt Trudy—was pregnant. I was just six months older than my sweet cousin. But she often took the role of the more mature older sister.

"It could be a couple of things," she said. "I might have to spend the rest of the pregnancy in bed."

She could use the rest. But this wasn't the way she'd want to get it. And her husband wasn't exactly the nursemaid type.

"But then everything will be all right?"

"Yeah, yeah. Everything's going to be fine."

I'm not sure who she was trying to convince, me or herself.

"How's everything there?"

Something in her voice, a forced lightness, a reluctance to hear the answer to a question she felt compelled to ask.

I tried to keep it down, but couldn't stop new anger from bubbling up.

"You knew!"

"I'm sorry. It's not my fault, I swear. It was Mom. She said she wanted to send you a birthday card. She must have given your address to them. It wasn't me, I swear!"

I closed my eyes and shook my head. My birthday had been back in May, right after I'd gotten here. I'd never gotten the bogus card.

"I believe you."

Did it really matter how my parents found me? So long as it wasn't Penny—the one person in the world I could depend on.

Noire barked, and I heard Clara's Gator coming down the road, reminding me she had pie.

And Cool Whip.

"I'm going to call you later," I told Penny sternly, taking my turn as bossy older sister. "And you're going to tell me what the doctor said, okay?"

"Okay." I heard her shift. The big belly must be hard to situate comfortably.

I should be there to help her, not halfway across the country in the middle of nowhere.

"Thanks, Vi," she said.

"What are you thanking me for?"

"For believing me. For not being mad."

I never could stay mad at her. "You should have warned me," I said, but not with malice.

"I tried. Your phone isn't accepting messages. Forget to charge it again?"

"I guess." The wonder was I hadn't broken or lost the thing. The temptation to throw the electronic gadget against the wall was overwhelming at times. I sighed.

After a pause, this time to sip her coffee—I know her better then myself—Penny asked, "Is it awful, them being there?"

"How awful it is remains to be seen. It was a shock, that's for sure. But they just arrived a little while ago along with someone named Giacomo. Do you know *why* they're here or who he is?"

"No. And I'm pretty sure Mom and Dad don't know, either. Mom said, 'you know how they like to be mysterious.'"

She imitated Aunt Trudy's smoky voice so perfectly, I laughed, but quickly sobered.

I sighed again, rolling my shoulders to release a mote of tension. "They're a mystery, that's for sure."

"What does Malcolm think of all this?"

All the muscles in my back seized up.

"He's away on business right now so he doesn't know yet."

"You can fill me in when you call later. I'll be here. Frank's bringing home Chinese."

That, at least, was something.

As I stepped out of the tack room, I saw the Gator slow. Clara peered down the darkness of the barn aisle, trying to determine if I was inside or up at the house. Noire sniffed her, checking for doggie treats, and Clara probably figured if my dog was here, I was, too.

I waved. "We're coming," I yelled.

Zoe looked up from the noseband in her lap. "We are?".

"Yes. Clara brought pie."

"Sounds great."

We joined Clara on the Gator, me taking the passenger seat. Zoe climbed onto the back.

We started up the drive, but Noire turned around, barking.

"What now?" I asked no one in particular.

Sandy's crappy little car sputtered up to the barn. She got out with a wave.

"Hey, ya'll, what's up?"

She was stuffed into a hot pink leopard print sports bra. No T-shirt, as usual. A lavish roll of fat bulged between the bra and the top of her three-sizes-too-small-super-stretch jeggings. Her bleached hair hung stiffly around her shoulders, and the skinny—we use that term loosely—jeans were stuck into unlaced black Army boots.

A smile lifted one side of my mouth.

"My parents are here. We're going up to the house to see them." Couldn't wait to see their faces when they got a load of Sandy. "Clara brought pie."

"And Cool Whip," Zoe added, holding up the plastic tub.

"Sounds like my kinda party," Sandy said. She opened her car door again. "But before we do, I brought you somethin', Vi."

She produced a grocery bag, but I couldn't make out what was in it. Sandy wasn't exactly the gift-giving type, but it fit that if she was going to buy me something, it would come from Walmart.

"Catch," she yelled as she tossed it my way.

I grabbed the bag before its contents conked Clara on the shoulder. Whatever was inside was long, hard, and cold.

Salvation.

I pulled out the can, tore off the lid, and squirted a giant dollop of cream into my mouth.

Chocolate, no less. I usually use plain and reserve chocolate for extreme stress.

"Feel better?" Clara asked.

I nodded, my eyes closed, and passed the can to her.

"How'd you know?" I asked Sandy.

She'd gone back to her car and pulled out two more bags. These, I could see, were full. Perhaps a dozen cans of delicious serenity. She pointed her chin at Clara.

"A little birdie told me."

Clara declined to share. "You need it worse than me."

A happy warmth welled up inside, pushing aside the crazy welter of resentment and old anger as I realized that Penny wasn't the only one I could depend on.

The strain to Sandy's pants as she joined Zoe spoke of imminent outbreak, but she made it without busting loose and dropped the other two bags with a clunk.

Clara shoved the Gator into gear and started forward, neatly steering around the lonely luggage.

I passed my can to Zoe and asked Sandy, "How much did you buy?"

"All of it. But they only had the one chocolate."

Instead of waiting for Zoe to pass it back, I cracked open a can of plain, took a hit, and savored the sweet, creamy goodness. "That's what I call an on-demand anti-depressant."

"Well," Sandy said, opening one for herself, "If'n your parents are here, we're gonna need it."

CHAPTER SIX

WE MANAGED to enter the house spaced out so the screen door skreeked open and slammed shut four times in quick succession.

My family stood and sat right where I'd left them, as if my admonishment to stay put had frozen them in place.

When the door banged closed behind Sandy, Giacomo brought his head up with a snort, and my mother grimaced like her last nerve snapped. Her face glistened with a sheen of sweat, and mascara smudged her lower lids.

Or had she been crying?

This thought threw me for a loop until I reminded myself I had no way of knowing what my mother would look like if she'd been crying.

Or laughing.

Or if she were bored or excited or…

This line of thinking did me no good.

"Back in a sec," I told them and took my hoard of whipped cream to the fridge. Wouldn't Malcolm be pleased to see us so well stocked?

Before returning to the front room, I took one more squirt of chocolate for insurance.

Clara met me at the kitchen door.

"Let's cut this pie before it melts."

Pie might not fix everything, but it was a good start. She jerked open the cutlery drawer to find a sharp knife—her favorite tool.

Sandy came in right behind her. "I'll get plates and forks," she announced. "And napkins."

Zoe followed with, "We all want iced tea right? I'll make more."

Had the stoney glares of Adrian and Gem Gem caused my troop to retreat?

"They scare you?" I asked.

No eye contact. Not a peep.

"Oh, brother," I muttered.

Armed with two cans of plain, I marched back to the front room. I set them down on the coffee table and switched on the giant old air conditioner that had been installed through the wall near the ceiling in one corner. It lumbered to noisy life but quickly began circulating cooler air.

"Our neighbor, Clara, brought over a pie."

Clara carried the jiggly custard dotted with bits of pink from the rhubarb, still clutching the knife between her fat fingers.

This should be good. And I wasn't thinking about the sweet-tart combo now resting on the coffee table. Although that would be wonderful, I was sure.

The first time Clara offered me pie, I refused it. She went still and looked at me as if I'd sprouted a second head, that knife poised to slice off the offending appendage if I didn't come to my senses. I did and never again thought to say *no thank you*.

"And," I added, brandishing my weapons, "we have whipped cream."

My father's eyes lit, but my mother's went glassy as if the sight of so much sugar and fat in one place would put her in a coma.

I should be so lucky.

Sandy brought in a stack of paper plates topped with sheets of paper towels and a handful of mismatched forks. No doubt, my parents were used to gold-trimmed china, expertly folded linen, polished silver, and liveried footmen.

Maybe not the footmen.

Zoe brought in the sweating pitcher of tea and set it on a paper plate next to the pie.

"There," I said. "Mom, Dad, Giacomo, I'd like you to meet our neighbor Clara Davis, my friend, Sandy Houseman, and Zoe Frost. She works for us."

Zoe shot me a mildly annoyed look at not being included in the roll of neighbor or friend, I suppose. I rolled my eyes and swept my arm toward my parents.

"Adrian and Gemma Marie York. And Giacomo Russo."

"My father-in-law," Mom supplied.

I beamed at my friends like a loopy monkey. "My grandfather!"

My last name, Parker, I'd taken from my aunt and uncle. York was the name given to Adrian at the orphanage.

Or so I'd been told.

Was anything what it seemed?

My father pushed away from the mantle and extended his hand to Clara, every move fluid and exact. She took his and he kissed the back of hers, staring intently into her eyes all the while. She shivered and made a little dip like a half-baked curtsey.

Oh, for cripe's sake.

"Thank you for bringing the pie," he said, his voice deeper than when he'd spoken to me. "*Very* thoughtful."

She giggled.

Shoot me now.

"Very nice to make your acquaintances," my mother said. I noticed her tea still sat at her elbow, untouched, the ice melted. She'd faint from dehydration at this rate.

Sandy lifted her arm in my father's direction as if in a trance. He took her hand and kissed the back of it as sincerely as he had Clara's. Sandy sighed so deeply I thought she might swoon. Romance novel addict that she was, she'd probably never wash that hand again.

I shot a speaking glance at Zoe. Clearly, I'd hurt her feelings by introducing her as our employee rather than as my friend. Would she succumb to his charm, too?

Zoe arched her back and tucked her chin. She stuck out her hand, grabbed my father's, gave it a hard shake and me a decisive nod.

Someone was loyal. Someone had as good a bullshit meter as I did. I'd find a way to repay her for that.

I knelt next to the coffee table, picked up a fork, aimed it toward the center of the pie, and said, "Dig in!"

My mother twitched.

"Just kidding, *Mom*," I said, nearly choking on the word. "You haven't landed in the Wild West."

She sniffed. "I never—"

"Ever had rhubarb custard pie?" Clara interrupted. She inched the knife beneath the first piece, slid it on a plate, and offered it to my mother.

The air in the room froze, and not from the chugging air conditioner. My mother kept her hands tightly clasped in her lap, whether because she was unsure about the delectation or the paper plate, I didn't know.

Then, she flattened them on her thighs.

"Wait, wait," I said. "It's not ready."

My mother's hands spasmed, and she and Clara turned to me. Everyone turned to me. I picked up the nearest can of whipped cream, buried the slice of pie in it, and laid a fork alongside.

I decided to try for that same sexy, sophisticated smile of my dad's. Hey, I have his genes, right? I should be able to pull it off. I'm afraid what was probably on my face was a sly and satisfied grin.

"*Now*, it's ready."

Maybe the beginnings of a smile cracked the careful veneer of my mother's face.

Maybe not.

She passed the whipped cream smothered piece to my father. "About half that size, if you please." She directed this to Clara.

Clara obliged, and I put a little squirt of cream on top.

There, definitely an uptick at one corner of Gemma's mouth, quickly squelched. Was it possible that beneath the haughty exterior lay a real person?

Unlikely.

Giacomo took his without comment and eyed it uncertainly. He took a bite, chewed, smiled, held up his fork, and said, "delizioso," before cleaning his plate.

By the time I'd gotten my piece, my father was hawking for seconds. Clara snagged his gaze and pointed the knife tip at the half of a half left by my mother, then at a full slice. He winked, and she loaded his plate with the larger piece.

My mother ate slowly and dabbed her lips with a paper towel corner.

"That *was* delicious," she said.

It occurred to me I'd have to make dinner for them.

Find a place for them to sleep.

Move myself back to the apartment above the barn.

Tell Malcolm.

Find out what the hell they were doing here. More importantly, how long they intended to stay. This, I decided, could wait until morning.

At which point, I'd need to make them yet another meal.

To hell with that. Surely they could make their own breakfasts?

And even though we'd just had pie, it was about lunchtime. If they'd flown in this morning, they probably needed a decent meal right about now. Not that there was anything wrong with pie and whipped cream.

I might be pissed they'd shown up without warning, furious they were here at all, and freaked to be dealing with them without Malcolm, but I could be hospitable. Just because they'd abandoned me as an infant didn't mean I had to turn my back on them now, no matter how much I wanted to do just that.

Anyway, Giacomo came with tomatoes. And that was a good thing.

"Well," I said, standing and brushing my hands on my jeans. "I'll show you where you'll be sleeping."

My father took my mother's hand and helped her up.

At that moment, the room darkened and all our gazes flew to the window. Heavy clouds had swallowed the sun. A roll of thunder shook the windows, making us all jump. A few drops of moisture patted the porch steps.

"Finally," Sandy said. "Guess you won't need to be watering this after-noon, Clara."

Clara grinned, showing the gap where a couple of molars were missing. She usually wore a bridge. "And a good thing, too," she said. "Pump's about wore out."

Zoe crossed to the door. The rain started to get more serious about its intentions. "So much for working the horses."

"Maybe it'll cool things off a little, and we can ride later," I said.

Zoe nodded, staring through the screen. "Did you want all that luggage to get washed?"

For a moment, I couldn't figure out what she meant.

"Oh, crap." I bolted through the door and down the steps.

"Take the Gator," Clara yelled.

I jumped into the seat and cranked the engine. Sandy slid in beside me, and Zoe ran ahead. She was already swinging the largest piece through the air by the time we reached her. It thumped into the bed. Sandy and I each nabbed a suitcase and flung them on top of the other. Zoe picked up an old-fashioned square cosmetics bag and started running back to the house.

I made a circle as fast as the Gator was able—which was kinda slow. Clara's husband, Hank, grumbled you needed a forty-acre field to turn the thing around. With six wheels, quick maneuvering wasn't what it was made for.

"Hell of a kid," Sandy observed as we rumbled up the drive.

"Lot's of energy," I said.

The kid in question had already deposited the bag inside and was coming back for more.

My parents and Clara stood on the porch watching. Through the curtain of rain, my father had a funny look on his face—a kind of self-deprecating or apologetic frown. My mother looked as if she'd like to worry her lip but couldn't allow her lipstick to get smudged.

We pulled up, and I killed the engine. Clara grabbed a smallish bag and hauled it in. Sandy and I took the rest.

"This one here's on the light side," Clara said when we were standing in the front room again.

Me and Sandy and Zoe dribbled water into little pools around our feet.

"Now that you mention it," I said. "They were all lighter than I expected."

My mother's eyes had a strange glint to them. My father heaved a deep breath.

"That," he said, "is because they're all empty."

CHAPTER SEVEN

I STAYED in the apartment above the barn after getting my parents settled in Malcolm's room and Giacomo ensconced in the guest room. If he had any thoughts about the pink comforter and stuffed animals on the bed, he kept them to himself. The room was reserved for Malcolm's eight-year-old daughter, Nicky. But she'd visited in July and wouldn't be back until Thanksgiving.

Surely, they'd be gone by then.

Even though I changed the sheets in the master, dumped my stuff into a pillowcase, and grabbed my toothpaste and shampoo from the bathroom, I knew my mother knew that the master bedroom had, of late, also been mine.

This made me feel darkly guilty. That made me angry. Angrier than I already was.

What the *hell* were they doing here?

With empty suitcases, no less?

On top of that, there was a polite but frosty tension between them that I'd never seen before. Plenty between them and me, but not between the two of them. It wasn't just Giacomo, although I was curious why he had suddenly joined the family after nearly fifty years of nonexistence. I had a feeling the strain was at least partly because of him, but something else was going on, too.

Needless to say, I didn't ask them more questions that night. I simply couldn't be in the same building with them any longer.

So, I sat alone on the couch in the apartment, vegging out in front of the television, avoiding both thought and sleep. With half the whipped cream in the apartment's fridge, and half my new cache at the house, all contingencies were covered. Neither of my parents would use it, of that I was sure, despite my father's enjoyment of it on his pie. They would never risk their figures that way. Giacomo was an unknown. On all levels.

Of course, I wasn't really alone. Noire sat next to me, her glossy black head on my thigh, breathing quietly. Occasionally, she licked her lips, made a soft sound, or moved her legs, and I wondered if she dreamed of her own version of canned whipped cream. She favored hot dogs, and I could depend on them for sneaking pills into her when necessary.

Henrietta, the barn cat, curled against my other leg, then stretched and rolled to her back, showing me her shaved belly. Her stitches were due to come out tomorrow. Sandy, who worked at the vet's office, had promised to come over and do it. I'd removed both stitches and staples from horses, but cats didn't tend to sit still for that sort of thing.

Four kittens had been born in the apartment closet right after I moved in —right in my basket of dirty clothes. Night, all black like his mom, sprawled next to Henrietta. Snowball fell asleep on my shoulder after sucking on my earlobe and kneading my neck, and Tiger and Tigress opted to snuggle into Noire's warmth. Outside, it was hot, but the apartment's AC worked extremely well. It was almost cold.

And peaceful.

I could depend on my critters for comfort and companionship. Except for my old friend Wastrel. He had other matters on his equine mind.

Before long, I'd polished off the last of the can of chocolate whipped cream by way of dinner and fell into a sugar-induced coma.

In the first dream, we'd returned to the horse show. *That* horse show. Jesus. Wasn't it bad enough he'd nearly killed me once? And himself in the process?

Apparently not.

Again, we cantered our circle to start the course, with something feeling off—something I couldn't put my finger on—then right out of the ring and away.

From there, he was standing on cross ties at Winterlight. Right downstairs with all the other horses. His silky coat felt dense beneath my fingers, as if the first cool nights of fall had hit and his pelt had begun to thicken in preparation for winter.

I put him in the pasture with the others and all hell broke loose. My real horse, Cali, immediately paired up with him, which made Captain, her best friend since coming to Winterlight, jealous, and he attacked Wastrel.

Fortunately, you can't hurt a dream horse, and he couldn't damage anyone, either.

Honey got into the fight because she was best friends with Captain before Cali got there, and that made Smitty mad because he had a crush on Honey. But Smitty, being a timid horse, didn't try to defend his turf. Instead, he ran behind a stand of blackberry bushes and hid.

Next, I'm on Wastrel's back again, and we dive off a platform like the circus riders of old. Only we're plunging straight toward a large swath of solid concrete.

I jolted awake with my heart clobbering my ribs, my neck kinked from sleeping sitting up, and stinking from my own sweat.

The cats and dog hadn't moved. Someone blared at me from the TV about the latest, greatest appliance that would make me live forever.

At the moment, that was the last thing I wanted to do.

It was early morning, earlier than I usually started, but sleep was pointless, so I eased the critters away, got up, and stretched.

First thing, I'd check on Smitty. I knew he wouldn't have a scratch on him, but I had to make sure. When I say these Wastrel-hosted dreams are vivid, I'm not kidding. I smell his heavenly scent and feel heat coming off him. Sometimes, I could swear my body ached from the beating it takes during these nocturnal visits.

This time, however, I could thank sleeping on the couch.

I got in the shower wishing it was Saturday. Saturday we had rides scheduled from morning until evening. Exhausting myself with work was exactly the distraction I needed. Plus, Malcolm would be back by then. Sometimes, he checked in when working at a client site, but I wouldn't call him unless it was urgent. If my parents showing up wasn't a level-one emergency, I don't know what was.

Yet, something kept me from making the call. Something like fear. Fear that he'd kick us all out. Fear that I'd use the situation as an excuse to run away—my typical modus operandi when the going gets tough.

Downstairs, I got started as day chased away night. Smitty was fine. The short thunderstorm had tamped down the dust, but not much more, and it wasn't cooler. Gaston worked well. He'd been stiff and resistant to the left when I first started riding him and didn't always pick up that lead, but now he carried himself with balance in both directions. I couldn't wait for Malcolm to ride him so he could feel the difference.

Zoe arrived on time. My day was looking up.

"How're your parents?" she asked.

Miss Bong—also known as Bongo—stood on the cross ties. I didn't pause my grooming rhythm.

"No idea."

I hadn't checked on them. Nor had they condescended to come to the barn.

Fine.

What the *hell* was I supposed to do with them?

Zoe stared at me for a moment, but whatever she saw in my face forestalled further questions. "We have a ride?"

"Yes. In half an hour. Honey, Fawn, and Captain need to be groomed and tacked up. You can ride Smitty."

"Really?"

Smitty was a much nicer ride than Fawn. "Yeah, you're more than ready."

"Thanks!"

She ran to get the horses.

This group of four riders were rank beginners, but the horses were relaxed and ready to take it easy because it was already hot and the rain had made it even more humid than the day before. I let Zoe take the lead, and I brought up the rear, letting Miss Bong's long stride flow into my back to ease some of the tension from my shoulders.

We skirted the fields and Noire happily flushed rabbits. My mind gladly wandered. But I couldn't keep it off the present for long. If the previous series of Wastrel dreams were any indication, these latest ones contained clues. Did these clues point to my parents, or Giacomo, or a different set of people or events entirely?

And what about the unlikely poacher down in the ravine? As soon as I had a chance, I would return with Noire and look for tracks or anything that might indicate someone doing something they shouldn't. Not that there'd be much left to see after the rain.

After a meager lunch of cheese and crackers scrounged from upstairs, Zoe and I sat in the tack room cleaning bridles.

Adrian and Gemma still hadn't made an appearance, and guilt began to erode my indifference. I pulled a rein through a towel soaked in leather conditioner, put it down, and stood.

"I'm going to the house."

Zoe glanced up from polishing a snaffle bit. "Want me to come with you?"

I did.

Wiping my hands on my jeans and sighing, I said, "No. It's time I put on my big-girl panties and face them."

"Hey, they invaded your space. They should be worried about facing you, not the other way around."

I smiled. "You're pretty smart, you know?"

"I know."

"Don't let it go to your head."

She smirked and bent to her task—moving on to the sweaty cheek pieces of Gaston's bridle. I ran upstairs for some creamy reinforcement, then called Noire. I wasn't going to enter the lion's den completely alone.

It was when I stepped down into the aisle that a loud boom ricocheted through the barn. Horses in the field jumped, lifted their heads and looked toward the house. Zoe came through the tack room door.

"Was that—"

"I think—"

The sound had been both familiar and foreign. But my brain was catching up fast.

Again, a crack bent the air, sending a tremor through me. A couple of the horses bucked and took off.

"Shit," I said, starting to run. "Those are gun shots."

CHAPTER EIGHT

I RAN. Ran like the devil himself had a bead on me.

Which someone had, once, not long ago, someone evil. But that time, I'd been on a horse. A very fast horse.

Oh god oh god oh god.

Again, I found myself running straight at my fear instead of disappearing in my preferred direction—away.

Wishing I had four legs, I forced more power into the two, sprinted up the driveway, pounded across the porch, and tore the screen door off one hinge getting inside.

Needed to breathe. *Not* picture the images rushing my brain.

No one in the front room.

Sliding down the slick old hardwood of the hallway on the soles of my riding boots, I careened into the kitchen.

There, my parents sat at the table, each reading a section of the days-old local weekly paper. My father wore glasses.

No blood.

Had they killed Giacomo and stashed the body? If so, they were mighty quick.

They brought a gun? Knives? My eyes went to the wooden knife block near the stove, my thoughts more scattered than the shots that got me here.

"Where's Giacomo?"

My parents glanced up and stared at me. Too calm, too studied.

My mother shrugged and went back to reading.

They were cold-blooded freaking murderers.

"In the garden, I think," my father said. He peered over his reading glasses, then angled his head toward the mudroom and side yard.

We don't have a garden.

With a hand to my diaphragm, I tried quieting my breathing. It whistled like hell's own banshee. "I heard shooting."

The corner of my mother's mouth twitched. She had no makeup on. I'd never seen her without. "So did we," she said without taking her eyes off whatever interesting tidbit of county news had caught her attention.

At this rate, I'd be a cold-blooded killer myself by sunset. Resisting the urge to wrap my hands around the slim column of her elegant neck, I strode past them to the mudroom and peeked through the side door.

Giacomo was out there all right. He'd planted his tomatoes in a neat row, the freshly turned earth looking like a new grave. Planting a garden made a statement about intent. Like, they intended to be here for more than a little while. I pushed the door open and calmly stepped out, that calm being only on the surface. Beneath, my mind caromed like pool balls after the break. I'd been awful quick to jump to the worst possible conclusion about my parents.

The tomato plants' sturdy stems emerged from the freshly turned dirt in a neat row, and the old man hammered a crooked metal post into the ground on one side of it.

I began to breathe.

The shotgun, one of Malcolm's, lay at Giacomo's feet.

"What are you doing?" I yelled to make sure he heard over the clanging. My tone came out more harsh than intended. Hey, I'd just nearly had a heart attack imagining every horrible possibility with regard to people and guns, and I have a vivid imagination. I could be forgiven.

He stopped hammering, looked at me, and took the moment to wipe his high forehead across his shoulder, a hank of his thick gray hair falling into his eyes, then gestured at the plants as if that explained. What was he, a mime?

"I mean, what are you doing with that gun?"

"Crows," he said with a generic sweep of one arm.

I scanned the surrounding trees. "There aren't any."

"Because I let them know. They not welcome."

"By shooting at them?" Whatever happened to good old fashioned scarecrows?

"How else?"

Jesus. I was going to have a *lot* of 'splaining to do when Malcolm got back. I should just call him.

What would I say? *Hey, babe, the parents I haven't seen nor heard from in years dropped by for an extended visit, brought my demented grandfather with them, and he borrowed your gun to plant his tomatoes.*

Yeah. No.

Oh, and by the way, they're sleeping in your room.

This was a conversation better had in person. But I should at least give him a heads-up. I'd leave him a message, that's what I'd do, not with any specifics, but strongly encouraging him to call me before coming home. I could only hope he didn't turn us all out when he got back. He was a very understanding guy, but this invasion might just push him over the edge. I'd seen him mad, seen him handle that shotgun. We didn't want to go there.

He'd also tried to get me to handle that weapon. For my protection when he was away, he said. But I don't like guns. I prefer Willy, the baseball bat I keep next to the bed.

Speaking of, I'd left Willy upstairs when I'd made room for my parents. I needed to get that bat and take it to the apartment.

I didn't know what to say to Giacomo. I didn't think Malcolm would appreciate someone borrowing one of his guns, not to mention the ammunition needed. That probably cost money. Money, I had a bad feeling, neither my parents, nor my grandfather, had.

Gah. *What* was I supposed to do with them?

"You should probably put that gun away."

I should pick it up and put it where it belonged myself. I would, if I could stand to touch it. Which I couldn't.

Giacomo grunted as he tied a string to the metal post and stretched it to a matching one on the other side of the tomatoes. Then, he gently, carefully, draped the vines over the string. Nearby, he had a watering can. Where had he found this stuff?

I really didn't know these people, and I'd entrusted Malcolm's house to them. This is how they repaid me? And his hospitality? By rifling through his belongings?

Noire bounded around the corner of the house, then, gayly carrying a six-foot long branch in her mouth.

I yelled, "No!" but she plowed right through the tomatoes.

The look of horror on Giacomo's face would have been comical if he hadn't simultaneously reached for the gun.

I dove between him and my dog, pushed her away from the plants with one arm, and knocked him to the ground with my shoulder. The gun bounced out of his hand. I snatched it up and stood, panting.

One tomato plant was bent over, but the rest were upright. Giacomo sat, wiping his hands together. He looked at his plants then glared at me.

"What's-a wrong with you?" he asked. Growled, more like, his accent thickening.

A tired old question that would probably never be answered in my lifetime. In this case, though, even I had to admit he had a legit reason for asking. I'd shoved my own grandfather face first into the dirt.

Well. There was me in a nutshell. When it came to choosing between people and animals, people didn't stand a chance. I'd even picked up the shotgun because it threatened my dog. I held it loosely, butt on the ground, the barrel encircled by my finger and thumb. Instinct had made me grab it, but I wouldn't touch it more than necessary.

"Sorry," I said, even though I wasn't.

I extended a hand to help him, but he shook his head and crawled on hands and knees to the injured tomato, tenderly straightening it.

Seeing as how I wasn't getting anywhere with him, I left him to his plants, and went back to the kitchen. There, I grabbed a can of whipped cream from the fridge and went upstairs without saying word one to my parents. They'd made themselves breakfast, it looked like, or lunch. There were plates on the table with crumbs on them. At least they could do that much for themselves.

In the bedroom, I grabbed Willy, the hefty familiarity of the smooth wood calming me. So different from the cold weight of the metal barrel in my other hand. I remember Malcolm telling me it was a Browning. I would call it Browny. Naming it lessened its menace. I could hold something with a name. I didn't have to like it, but I could do it.

The bed had been made. No clothes draped the chair or hung on the back of the door. My parents had traveled much of their lives, so I'm sure they knew how to keep themselves contained.

What about those empty suitcases? They were traveling light. I would have to ask questions at some point. Confront them about what they were doing here and why they had a tomato-crazed old man in tow. But not until I talked to Malcolm. He would know how to approach this. A non-hysterical way to approach this.

Back downstairs, I went to his study. There, in the corner, stood the gun safe, a heavy iron box about five feet tall.

Malcolm was strict about keeping his guns locked up when he wasn't using them. This locker required two keys to open the main door and then another to access a smaller cupboard inside that held a couple of handguns and all the ammo. One of the main keys was locked in Malcolm's desk. He kept the other with him when he was home. When away, he locked that in a filing cabinet. The keys to the desk and filing cabinet were hidden behind books on the other side of the room. The key to the small cupboard he left in the lock.

I leaned Willy and Browny against the desk, relieved to release the cold metal of the gun, and went to the bookcase. The books hadn't been moved, but I pulled them out anyway. The keys were there. I checked the desk. Drawer, locked. Same for the filing cabinet.

Malcolm's precautions notwithstanding, a half-empty box of shells sat on the corner of the desk, and the safe's door gaped, a space like a broken tooth revealing where Browny should be.

Careful not to jar the lethal weapon—for all I knew it was still loaded—I put it where it belonged.

Somebody had a lot of 'splaining to do, and it wasn't only me.

CHAPTER NINE

"You've always told everyone you were left at an orphanage as an infant," I said to my father, trying, and failing, to sound reasonable.

I'd locked the gun safe—for all the good it would do—and gone back to the kitchen.

Adrian tucked one temple of his reading glasses into the neck of his T-shirt and pressed his hands against his thighs.

"I *was* left at an orphanage as an infant."

Gemma rolled the newspaper and held it on her lap with both hands. The movements of her slim fingers mesmerized me. But I quickly brought my attention back to Adrian.

"How is it you suddenly have a father?"

Of the million other questions battling for my attention, the mystery of Giacomo won.

"I've always had a father."

"Not interested in word games, Dad." I lifted my ponytail—frizzy with the humidity—off my neck and leaned against the counter. "I've always had a father, too, but I used to pretend you were dead because that hurt less than the truth."

He had the grace to wince. He exchanged a look with my mother, or tried to. Her gaze fixed on nothing in particular, unfocused. A stab of alarm tightened my chest.

"To be honest," Adrian said, "we don't yet know the entire story ourselves.

Suffice it to say that Giacomo had his reasons—good reasons—for leaving me like he did."

My heart sped up. If he was building some elaborate new justification for why they ditched me, I would scream. I took a squirt of fortitude from the can I still held.

"Somehow," he continued, "he always kept track of me."

This was beginning to sound like a familial pattern. Thank God I'd had the sense to remain childless. Unless you counted horses. And dogs. If that were the case, I had offspring. Offspring I *didn't* abandon.

My mother's knuckles turned white from gripping the paper like a lifeline. "He was living in Florida," she added, as if that helped.

Dad rubbed his hands down his lean thighs. He wore the same gray slacks as yesterday. They were a little frayed at the hems.

"He needed our help," he said.

"So you dropped your dancing shoes, left Europe, went and got him in Florida, and came here?" I slammed the can of whipped cream on the counter and gestured with both hands to either side of my head. "Now it all makes sense."

Still staring into nothingness, my mother opened her mouth to speak, but the sound of a car creeping up the drive drew my attention to the hall where I could see the front of the house.

The first thing I noticed was the screen door angled across the doorway where it hung by the bottom hinge. I made a mental note to fix that before Malcolm got home. The second was the familiar but unwelcome markings of a sheriff's vehicle pulling up to the walkway.

Deputy Joe stepped out but stayed behind the car door, his hand hovering near his weapon, eyes darting from side to side.

"It's okay," I yelled and hurried out so he would see who it was and that I was unarmed. "Hey, Joe, what brings you here?"

Yes, I was on a first-name basis with local law enforcement, and, as far as I knew, good terms.

"911 call reported shots fired."

"Who called 911?"

He consulted a small pad of paper. "Doesn't say. Caller ID indicated Mr. Robert Malcolm."

That would be because this was his place so of course the landlines were in his name. My parents joined me. Without looking at them, I asked out of the side of my mouth, "Did you call the police?"

"No," they said in unison, their voices strained. They went back inside.

Must have been Zoe. I needed to wring someone's neck, and it might as well be hers. Joe's eyes continued to scamper around the yard, pasture, and finally, the porch. Sweat beaded on his forehead. Two giant sweet gum trees made it cooler in the yard than inside, but Joe stood in direct sun.

"My parents and grandfather are visiting, and my grandfather borrowed a gun to scare the crows away from his tomatoes."

Sometimes, truth is best, even if it sounds crazy. Evidently, it didn't sound crazy to Joe. He nodded and relaxed, leaning his forearms on the window frame of the cruiser door.

"They helping you with your new business?"

I closed my eyes, wondering what new level of hell I might be entering now. "What new business?"

"Something to do with being a detective using a dream horse?"

He managed to say this without smirking or laughing, but the corner of his mouth quivered.

All breath left my body. *Sandy*. Damn her. The Dream Horse Detective Agency was her idea, not mine, and not one I was on board with. The dream horse in question, however, Wastrel, well, he was mine, despite all efforts to oust him from my previously uninterrupted sleepy time. I hadn't shared him and his cryptic clues with anyone other than Malcolm, Dex, and Sandy. The guys wouldn't have said anything to Joe.

I added Sandy to my those-who-must-be-strangled list. This was not the sort of thing I wanted people to know about me.

"Uh...yeah." I forced a chuckle that sounded fake even to my ears. "That was just a silly idea we came up with one night. Too much to drink, probably."

I bit my lip. Way to throw Sandy under the stampede. But she had no business blabbing that I was starting a detective agency. Especially when I wasn't.

He leveled a *yeah, I've got your number* look at me before putting on his sunglasses. "Too bad," he said. "Things got interesting here for a while after you moved to town."

"Interesting. Right."

He slapped the car roof. "Well...cows to catch and high-speed tractors to ticket."

I laughed for real. "Good one, Joe."

"Keep it clean, Parker." He smoothed his short dark hair with one hand. "Don't waste our time and resources with nuisance calls."

I backed up a couple of steps. "You got it. Have fun protecting and serving."

He eased into the car seat, gave me two thumbs up, and grinned before backing around to head out.

When I turned, my father had a screwdriver and was fixing the broken screen door hinge.

"I would have done that," I said when I got back to the porch.

"Happy to help."

I stood there for a minute, feeling confused and useless and unsure how to proceed.

"Thanks," I said when he looked at me.

He nodded, and I went inside knowing I should continue the conversation with my parents, wanting to see why Zoe felt the need to call 911, but suddenly, achingly, so tired I could barely move.

I heard the squeaky fourth tread of the stairway and knew my mother had gone up. I'd like to go lie down in an air-conditioned room, too, but that luxury had to wait. Giacomo helped himself to a glass of iced tea from the fridge.

"Cops?" He held the cool glass to his cheek, letting the condensation drip through his beard and onto the front of his collared shirt. No tie today.

"I think my barn worker must have called them when we heard the shooting." I put the whipped cream away. "Let's try to keep that to a minimum from now on."

"I make a scarecrow tomorrow." He shrugged. "It don't work so good as the scattergun."

"I understand."

It's not like it was rare for people to shoot off guns around here, even if it wasn't hunting season. People shot them for fun, for target practice, and what have you. Made no sense to me. Malcolm had competed in the pentathlon when he was younger, which included pistol shooting in addition to riding, fencing, swimming, and cross country running. Which explained his amazing body *and* why he had hand guns. But I didn't know if he hunted. In any case, he had a safe full of both long and short firearms that I didn't like.

"I'm sorry about before," I said to Giacomo. "Are you all right?"

He pulled himself taller. "Eh," he said with a dismissive hand gesture. "Takes more than a shove from a little girl to hurt Giacomo Russo."

At five foot six and a hundred and thirty pounds of muscle, I wasn't exactly a little girl, but I was glad he was all right.

"I'll try to keep my dog out of the garden, and you stay away from the guns. Okay? They belong to Mr. Malcolm."

He poured himself more tea, his back turned for a moment. I didn't like his lack of response.

Going for casual, I asked, "How did you get the gun out, anyway? How did you open the safe?"

Giacomo shut the refrigerator door too hard and everything inside jiggled and clanked.

"How you think?"

"I don't know," I bit out, then took a calming breath before continuing. "That's why I'm asking."

He drank his tea, smiled, his eyes twinkling as they had when we first met, and I had the first hint that when younger, Giacomo Russo had been a charming rogue.

"Easy," he said with a wink. "I pick the lock."

CHAPTER TEN

I PICK THE LOCK. I pick the lock.

Giacomo's statement, baldly matter-of-fact and unapologetic, whispered through my brain as I put my truck in gear. I didn't need Wastrel to confirm what I felt in my gut. Something wasn't right about this situation.

Dex One could do a background check on the old man. What if he was a clever con artist taking advantage of my parents? He might be, but he was my grandfather, all right. He and dad shared the same profile and endearing lopsided smile.

I put it all out of my mind and headed to the farm implement store to buy a new bale spear. Two days ago, I'd managed to snap the old one after getting stuck in the ditch while harrowing the pasture. Apparently, levering two tons of tractor with a two-inch thick length of steel isn't recommended. Replacing it before Malcolm got back seemed like a good idea. No reason to give him something else to be annoyed about. My parents would be enough.

I'd left Zoe in charge after dressing her down about calling the police.

"Someone was shooting," she'd said. "Guns are dangerous."

"People shoot all the time out here."

Not that it still didn't make my heart leap from my chest every time.

"But I thought—"

"I know what you thought. Just don't be so quick next time."

"Next time?"

"There won't be a next time. You know what I mean."

She frowned, clearly not clear on what I meant. But there wouldn't be a next time, so I let it go.

I also left a message for Malcolm. Nothing hysterical, just a calm note urging him to call me as soon as he could.

Sandy pulled in, hopped out of her car, yanked open the passenger door of my truck, and slid onto the seat before I could say *no*. She slung her arm around my dog. Noire licked her sweaty face. The air conditioning didn't work in Sandy's car. It was feeble at best in my truck but enough that we could keep the windows closed.

"Where're we going?"

Her grin kept me from kicking her out, but I really wanted some alone time.

"Town," I said. "I broke Malcolm's spear."

"His…" Her eyebrows shot up. "Wow. That didn't take long." Her grin widened as I focused on pulling out onto the blacktop. "They don't sell them at the tractor store, you know."

I looked at her.

She snapped her fingers at me. "Earth to Vi. Not enough whipped cream this morning?"

"That thing on the front of the tractor for picking up big round bales? Where else would I get one?"

"Ooohhh…." She rolled her eyes. "You mean the *bale* spear. I got it."

"What else—oh." I snorted. "Very funny. No, I didn't break Malcolm's *spear*. You read too many romance novels."

She shrugged, the movement lifting her generous chest nearly to her chin. A purple tie-dyed sports bra already had the girls hoisted high.

"I didn't think you could read too much," she said in a small voice.

Her hurt tone sliced through my self-absorbed haze. I knew she had confidence issues and looked up to me. Why, I have no idea. I guess it's enough I'm from New York and different. In a Monty Python *and now for something completely different* kind of way. I also knew she had a crush on Malcolm, or used to. Maybe still did. It would be hard *not* to crush on a super-hero handsome guy with a fabulous body who worked around the farm in a kilt. Sometimes without a shirt. God, I hoped he didn't freak when he found out about my parents.

"No," I said. "You can't read too much."

We continued in silence for a half mile of winding road, the fields to either side striped with rows of drying corn and soy beans. Another pickup came from the other direction. Sandy waved.

"Who was that?" I asked.

"I don't know."

"Then why'd you wave?"

"You're supposed to wave to ever'body."

"*Supposed* to? Why?" Waving to the wrong person where I came from could get a girl in trouble.

"It's friendly-like. Anyway, even if I don't know 'em, they prob'ly know somebody I know. Get it?"

I didn't. "So, you wave just in case?"

"No, I wave 'cause it's friendly."

"Nobody around here would recognize me."

"Look, Vi, you got to understand. They. Know." She emphasized her point by poking me in the shoulder. "They know when somebody's new, they know your truck, they know Malcolm, and they know you work for him." Poke. "They also know Clara and Hank. Hell, you're on a first-name basis with the sheriff's deputy." Poke. "Half the county prob'ly already knows your family's here."

"Not a happy thought."

I rubbed my shoulder, and she jabbed her finger into my forearm. "And, you know me. So, if you thinks you're invisible or somethin', you got another think comin'."

I sighed. Invisible was good. "I don't stick my nose in anyone's business, and I don't want them sniffing around mine."

"It ain't so bad." She rubbed her hand over her mouth. "I might of died if you hadn't come lookin' for me that time."

"I—" She'd been drugged, raped, beaten, and left to die, but she could still joke about a man's *spear*. Her spirit inspired me to be better.

"So don't act like you don't care, neither." She crossed her arms under her breasts, nodded, and stared through the windshield. Point made.

Point taken.

A car approached from the other direction. I felt Sandy watching me out of the corner of her eye. I lifted one hand from the steering wheel and wagged it at the other vehicle at the last moment.

Sandy did an extravagant eye roll, the kind that made me wonder if she could see her brain.

"What? I waved. Did I do it wrong?"

"It was too late. And you don't have to use your whole hand. Save that for when it's someone you do know. Just use a couple of fingers."

Waving at strangers. An art form.

"She didn't wave at me."

"Don't matter. You still gotta do it."

I breathed a sigh of relief after we reached the highway without meeting any other traffic.

"Do I wave to people out here?"

"'Course not."

No, of course not.

"Let's go to the drive-thru at McDonald's when we get there," she said. "I ain't had no lunch."

Mine had been craptastic, so while I usually avoided junk food, this sounded appealing for a change. Anyway, they had salads, right?

Sandy squeezed my dog and turned on the baby talk she used when speaking to animals. "Would you like that Noiry-Poiry?"

I ground my teeth, but Noire's tail thumped and her ears perked up.

"Huh, pwitty girly-whirly? Who'd like a nice juicy burger-wurger from Mickey-Ds?"

My dog had more patience than I did. I turned on the radio and tuned her out, mentally making a shopping list for the grocery store. At the top? More whipped cream.

Twenty minutes later we idled in the drive-up line of the fast food restaurant. Noire put her front feet on my thigh so she could pant out the window in anticipation of her burger-wurger.

My truck sounded like it might die at any moment. Malcolm had cleaned and recharged the battery shortly after I arrived in Missouri, but the '99 Chevy had nearly two-hundred thousand miles on it, and I wasn't sure how much longer it would last. With being able to use Malcolm's vehicles occasionally, I hoped to nurse it through the winter until next spring when I found out how much the trust fund was worth. If it wasn't even enough to buy a new truck…

"Think happy thoughts," Sandy said.

"What?"

"You're face is gettin' all tight like it does when you've got somethin' worryin' you."

"It is not." Though it didn't really surprise me. I've never been good at hiding how I feel.

"Hell yeah, it is."

I forced a smile, and we ordered. I joined the junk food frenzy. Nothing like a little salt and grease to turn your mind to happy thoughts.

As we waited for our turn to pay, Sandy said, "Manroot."

"Huh?"

"It's one of them words from romance novels that they use in place of…you know."

"Penis?"

"Yeah, that."

The car in front of us moved up, and we followed.

"Throbbing manroot," I said after a moment.

Sandy hooted. "I knew you read them."

"Some." I didn't have much time to read.

"Molten rod," she said.

I almost choked. The car in front of us edged forward again, and we got a little closer to the window. Noire's hot breath hit my face. I elbowed her back, rolled up the window, and turned the fan to high.

"Turgid member," I said, revealing that I'd read more than I let on.

Sandy buried her face in Noire's neck to stifle herself.

We reached the first window, and I rolled down mine enough to hand over the money to a cute teenaged boy.

"Swollen shaft!" Sandy yelled just as he gave me my change. I dropped the coins on the ground.

"Holy shit."

She howled with laughter.

"Shut up!" The car in front of us sat there, and I couldn't get my window to work.

The boy leaned down so he could see Sandy, then looked at me and winked. I smiled at him, and we inched forward just enough to get away.

"Are you insane?" Tears leaked from the corners of my eyes as I tried to keep from laughing.

"Oh. My. Gawd. You shoulda seen your face."

I wiped my cheeks, glared at her, and bided my time until we had our food and were once again on the road. When I saw her shove a quarter of her Big Mac in her mouth, I shouted, "Pulsing shaft!"

Meat, cheese, lettuce, tomato, pickle, onion, and special sauce shot forward to hit my windshield. I snorted soda all over my steering wheel. Noire lunged for the hurled bite and swallowed it before we even knew what she was doing.

Half an hour later, the guy at the implement store shook his head as we left. We couldn't stop giggling the entire time we were there. Because, well, *implement* and *spear*.

I'd needed the laugh and felt much lighter while attaching the shiny new bale spear to the tractor. I took groceries to the house, thinking I should have asked my parents and Giacomo if they wanted anything before I went. They had no way of going on their own. And perhaps no money, either. I really should ask whether they did, but had decided I'd wait until Malcolm came home. He'd get the needed intel in a calm and reasonable way. I'd go all demanding and accusatory on them before they said two words, and that wouldn't help. Plus, they'd have to answer him. After all, it was his kindness they were relying on.

My mother watched me put everything away. She wore a short yellow linen dress. With her hair pulled into a pony tail, she looked cool and elegant even with crappy air conditioning.

"I'll make a salad for supper," she said. "Perhaps you'll join us tonight."

We were not ready to sit down and pretend we were a happy family. Something else to delay until Malcolm returned.

"I still have a lot to do down at the barn." I rubbed sweat off the back of my neck and tried to look apologetic. "By the time I take a shower—"

"I know you work hard, Viola."

My jaw locked up. "You know nothing about me." There. It was out of my mouth, out of my mind, my heart. And it came out nice and steady, without heat rushing my throat.

She paused, one hand on the fridge door handle, her back to me. The tendons in her slim forearm pressed against her skin. It didn't make me feel better that she was tense too. I used the moment to stretch my neck and breathe deep before saying, "And I go by *Vi*."

Opening the fridge, she said, "Yes, but I named you Viola."

"Why?" So many questions, but this one had always bugged me.

"I was very young when I had you."

"Barely seventeen, I know," I said to her back, wondering if all important conversations must take place in the kitchen.

"The last thing I studied in English class was Shakespeare's *Twelfth Night*."

Had she even finished high school? The few times we'd been together, I'd been too angry to wonder.

"*Twelfth Night?*"

She put an armload of salad fixings on the counter. "Do you know the play?"

I like Shakespeare but haven't exactly had time to read his entire body of work. "Not that one."

"You should. It's very romantic and funny."

"I'll put it on my to-do list." A long list with little chance of ever being completed.

The effervescent mood brought on by my time with Sandy began to flatten.

My mother slipped an apron over her head—where the hell had that come from?—and began washing a head of romaine. "Viola was an orphan, too, you know. Shipwrecked. A very resourceful and intelligent character." She took out the cutting board and a knife and got a bowl down from the cabinet, thoroughly at home in someone else's kitchen. "Shakespeare's Viola disguised herself as a man for protection but was always forthright and honest in her dealings with others."

I leaned on the counter and watched her fingers work. "Even while deceiving them as to her true nature?" I asked. Was there a hidden message in what she was telling me? I wasn't good with deciphering code. Let alone discussing literature with my mother.

"Yes. She had secrets." She sent a tentative smile over her shoulder. "Don't we all?"

"Some more than others. Me? I'm an open book." I glanced at the clock. It was already five, and I did have chores waiting.

My mother hid whatever non-verbal response she might have to my comment by keeping her back to me and chopping carrots.

She used the knife blade to slide them into the bowl on top of the lettuce and said, "I won't spoil the end of the story." She turned toward me and pushed a stray hair off her forehead.

I sidled to the kitchen doorway and set my shoulder against the frame with my arms crossed. It was a little closer to the exit, and I was desperate to escape this awkward veiled conversation. "Feel free to share spoilers," I said. "I doubt I'll read it anytime soon."

"All right. Well, along with talk of madness, there is a great deal of deception and mistaken identity."

"Sounds like real life."

"Yes, well. Viola doesn't only impersonate a man, she also takes the role of someone of a lower class than herself."

"You gotta do what you gotta do." I pushed away from the doorframe. "You're sleeping in Malcolm's room, and he'll be home tomorrow, so I'm not sure what we'll be able to arrange after that."

She nodded and followed me down the hall. An itchy feeling between my shoulder blades told me she still carried the knife.

"The story seems to be about love," my mother said to my back. "All kinds of love."

She was definitely trying to drive home a message, here, but it was a little late for her to go maternal on me. I hoped she didn't intend to make her point with the knife. Given how dense I can be, I understand why someone might feel like that was the only way to get my attention. On the other hand, Sandy's poking had been enough for one day.

At the porch, I turned to my mother and took the bait. "So, what is the play really about?"

"I think it's the secondary title that has more meaning. It's also called *What you will.*"

I've taken my share of literature classes where the teachers make you deconstruct stories to death. In lieu of knowing what an author intended, they make it up. My mother appeared to have rambled into water over her head with this one.

"I'm a little tired for a Lit 101 quiz, Mom."

"I know, Viola—Vi. I guess what matters is that even after all the confusion, in the end, Viola finds love and happiness."

Sounded like the sappily-happily ever after of all romance books.

Too bad it was all fiction.

CHAPTER ELEVEN

Sleep is my favorite. Well, second favorite. Riding is my number one most loved activity.

But sleep…I know a little Shakespeare, too. Sleep used to be like death to me, the temporary end to *the heartache and thousand natural shocks that flesh is heir to*, as Hamlet said. Like floating on clouds of whipped cream, sleep was sanctuary, or used to be, before I came to Winterlight, before Wastrel started visiting. Now, I felt more like Henry IV when he wondered *O gentle sleep, nature's soft nurse, how have I frightened thee?*

Not that I couldn't go to asleep. That was easy. And staying there worked as well. But it wasn't a sanctuary. It wasn't gentle.

And falling asleep with the words *what dreams may come…*drifting through…not my best idea.

Wastrel takes me down a tight city street. For a change, I ride him bareback. No show clothes, no competition ring. No jumps. The clip-clop of his hooves on cobblestones comforts me. Diesel fumes, garbage stench, and the reek of day-old frying oil assault us. But it is quiet. Early, by the slant of light glancing off the brownstones making a canyon of the narrow lane. The cars parked to either side are older, putting the era at around the sixties, maybe. We've never time traveled before.

Up ahead, a man wearing a hat and suit walks away from us down the middle of the road as if he owns it, his step jaunty. He carries a bouquet of white flowers with dark greenery. Not roses. The blooms are too flat and have too few petals. I want to get a sniff, if only to rid my nose of the stink, but Wastrel refuses to go closer.

We follow the man when he cuts between two cars and onto the sidewalk, then goes through a door into a narrow entry to slap his gray fedora onto a hook. A horse wouldn't have fit in the entry, but I'd resigned myself to the unnatural physics of dreams.

The man goes up an equally skinny flight of stairs taking the steps two at a time. I'm not even sure I'm still on horseback at this point, but I can't change my direction or control anything that happens. I must wait and watch what Wastrel shows me.

A shaft of sun coming through a tall window brightens a tiny square landing and lights up the man's wavy dark hair as he goes through a door without knocking. A flash of profile before he ducks in, too fast for me to tell if he's someone I know.

The scene shifts to nighttime. The change jolts me, and I grab for Wastrel's mane. We're floating above a car creeping along a narrow country lane, headlights off.

We're back on the brownstone landing, and I feel menace, something dangerous coming behind us, but I can't turn away from the man in the suit and the woman who greets him with open arms and a bright smile.

We veer back to the country scene and another man, out of the car now, also carrying white flowers. These I can smell because the air in this place isn't clogged with car exhaust and cooking food. Gardenia. Love them.

He goes up a couple of steps, his gait tired but eager, unlocks a door and closes it quietly. Like the other scene, I'm behind him, can't see his face, and in this locale, nothing of the surroundings is clear, as if the edges of a painting got smudged before it dried.

I'm jerked back to daylight, to the man and woman hugging. Dizziness rocks me for a moment. She exclaims at the flowers. I feel the love they have for each other but also the stealthy darkness coming up the stairs. It's going to swallow us. I try to yell. I'm not sure who I'm warning or what the risk is, but no sound comes out of my mouth.

The woman looks right at me—through me—and her eyes go wide with horror. She puts her hand out. *No* she screams.

There's a loud boom.

The noise pulled me right out of bed to my feet where I swayed and caught myself on the bedside lamp. It tipped over and broke. I groped for the wall switch and flicked on the overhead light.

Noire stood on the bed, startled awake by the sound of glass breaking, then pricked her ears toward the window and let out a low woof.

The clock said it was two in the morning. I scrubbed my face, still half in the dream, wondering if the shotgun blast had been real.

A shotgun. A man driving on a country lane. Shit.

I bolted through the small living space, down the stairs, and out into the barn sprinting through it on the balls of my bare feet. Vaguely, I knew the chunky gravel of the drive dug into my soles but ignored it.

The house was dark, but with many of the windows open, shouting came through. A shriek cut the air, and a light went on upstairs.

As I slammed up onto the porch, I noticed Malcolm's SUV parked over on the side.

What the hell was he doing here?

The front door didn't give when I rattled the knob.

"Malcolm!"

As I ran around to the mud room, I couldn't be sure I'd made any sound, just like in the dream. The side door was locked, too. I punched through the glass pane, flipped the deadbolt from the inside, and jumped across the threshold, hoping to clear the shards.

I skidded down the hallway like I had earlier and made for the stairs, grabbing the round newel post and using it to fling myself halfway up.

Light and anger spilled from the main bedroom.

My breath came in short gasps as I took in the bizarre scene. Malcolm stood in the doorway holding his shotgun in one hand, the barrel pointed straight up. His other hand gripped a hunk of my father's nightshirt and held him at a stiff arm's length. Dust and plaster floated in the air along with the smell of gunpowder. I didn't bother looking for the hole that must be gaping in the ceiling seeing as how everyone appeared to be alive.

The sound of the toilet flushing told me where Giacomo was. My mother sat on the edge of the bed, leaning forward. Her sleek, dark hair hid her face, and she held her head. The strap of her peach nightgown had slipped off one shoulder.

Malcolm's features were set and hard. I'd seen that look when someone had kidnapped his daughter and tried to kill me. I didn't like having it directed at anyone I knew.

Dad's eyes flashed hot and angry. The set of mom's shoulders made me think she was in pain. When Giacomo joined us, still zipping his fly, ill-contained amusement danced at the corners of his mouth. He had the gall to wink at me. Whether that was meant to be conspiratorial or reassuring, I have no idea.

This was my family.

And I was in a shit-ton of trouble.

CHAPTER TWELVE

FOR A LONG MOMENT, no one spoke. We stood frozen in a whacked-out tableau that made me imagine I'd fallen into a Shakespearean scene. No telling whether the play was tragedy or comedy.

"Somebody start talking," Malcolm said, his voice equal parts taut, tired, and tough.

Robert Harvey Malcolm, laird of Winterlight, had returned to his keep and was not happy about its condition.

He had that sweet rumpled look he always had when he came home from a business trip. A bit of beard, his wavy surfer hair mussed from running his hands through it, tie loose, and sleeves rolled up to expose his freckled forearms.

They all stared at me, and if ever I wanted a hole to open beneath my feet, it was then. Was I the one who had to start?

"Mom," I said, "are you all right?"

"Mom?" Malcolm said loudly enough that Hank and Clara, a mile away, likely heard.

"Yes." I kept my tone even. "And you can let go of my dad."

He looked at me like I'd grown a second head. "They're. In. My. Bedroom."

"He hit me with the gun," my mother said, her voice faint. She moved her hand to expose a red welt blooming on her forehead.

Shock rooted me in place. My father said something in another language, a bad word, by his inflection. Malcolm released him at the same time dad slapped his hand away and joined my mother on the bed, putting his arm around her shoulder. She flinched, and he started to pull away, then drew her against him and rubbed her arm.

"Are you dizzy?" I asked. She shook her head. I turned to Giacomo. "Get some ice."

He nodded and went down the stairs. My fingernails dug into my palms. My right hand throbbed. I'd forgotten I'd punched out a window. I held it behind my back. Unlike my mother, I've had a lot of practice ignoring pain.

"Queasy?" I asked her. I've never been hit with a gun, and I always wear my helmet when riding, but I've still managed to concuss myself, and I know the fuzzy headache it brings.

"No," she said, and I hoped it wasn't that bad. Without looking away from her, I said to Malcolm, "I called you earlier."

"I've been traveling all afternoon, Vi. Forgive me for having the courtesy to not return your call after midnight."

My father stood and drew my mother up with him. "Come, Gem Gem." He scowled at me as if this was all my fault. Malcolm and I moved aside to let them by.

When they reached the squeaky stair tread, Malcolm slammed the bedroom door so hard the windows rattled. A chunk of plaster hit me in the head.

"I didn't know what to do," I said. "They showed up yesterday, along with Giacomo—my father's father—"

Malcolm held up his hand to stop me. He set the gun against the wall and took my mother's place on the edge of the bed.

"Did it occur to you to call me *yesterday?*"

It had. I'd dithered, too afraid to risk it, sure I could handle everything on my own. That would be true if all the actors in this drama were horses instead of people. Or dogs. Them, I could deal with. People, not so much.

"Yes and no."

Looking at the weariness on his face, knowing that it was more than jet lag, I realized that once again, I'd blithely rushed into a relationship, and yet again, I'd royally screwed it up. With Malcolm, I'd actually paused to consider the ramifications of getting involved with him. For about a minute.

This would have happened sooner or later. I'm a freaking mess magnet. My parents' arrival just moved up the inevitable.

He scooped both hands through his hair, and when he spoke, his voice had softened. "I finished up early. Wanted to surprise you." He rested his elbows on his knees, his thick thigh muscles straining the fabric of his khaki slacks.

"Instead," he continued, and I realized his tone had gone too soft, "I walk into my house and get attacked by a stranger wielding one of my own guns. Can you imagine?" He squinted at me. "Mind telling me why the hell the old man had my shotgun?"

Still soft, but with an inflexible edge. Damn Giacomo. Hadn't he agreed to stay out of the safe? The shock had worn off. Murky exasperation took its place.

"Mind telling me why the hell you clocked my mother with that gun?"

He stood and came toward me, close enough for me to feel the heat of his anger. I flattened myself against the door.

"The old man snuck up behind me when I came in the bedroom." His voice rose, but still, his tone remained reasonable. "It was dark—because I wanted to surprise you. It all happened so fast…"

I'd seen this deadly calm side of Malcolm once before. I'd hoped to never see it again. He paced to the other side of the bed, and I held my breath.

"Didn't take much to get the gun away from him, but by then your father was yelling in French and your mother was up and moving. Did I mention it was dark?"

I nodded.

"And that I was expecting you?"

He hadn't, but that was a given.

"She shoved me."

"My mother?" That seemed so out of character as to be made up. She was pushy, yes, but not physically.

"Maybe she thought I was the old man?"

I shrugged. "Maybe." More likely she stumbled into him.

"Reflex," he said.

"Reflex?"

"I thought I was being attacked, Vi. That something horrible had happened to you. You can't imagine what went through my mind in those moments. I defended myself."

Against my mother, who, for all her haughty superiority, was incapable of attacking anyone. I pictured the terrifying moments in the dark when no one knew what was happening.

He paced back toward me, jerking on the knot of his tie, yanking it off, and slinging it toward the back of a chair. It slithered to the floor. Kind of like my heart.

I'd done this to him, brought this scare under his roof. I supposed that made us even. After all, it'd been his ex-wife and her lover who'd kidnapped Nicky and tried to kill me. They'd wanted to kill Malcolm, too. Anything to get their hands on the farm. The lover impaled himself on a bale spear during a brawl with Malcolm, and the ex was cooling her pedicure in jail, awaiting trial. Their scheme had failed, in large part because of me and Wastrel.

He came over to the tall dresser by the door and put his wallet and phone on top, just like he always did. I'd caught my breath from the mad dash to reach them, and now it left my body in a whoosh. I knew him. Knew his habits, his likes and dislikes. We'd immersed ourselves in each other for weeks working side by side during the day when he could manage it, riding, putting up hay, fixing fence. At night, our bodies learned each other's contours. Our fingers knew the touch that made our pulses race, our lips and teeth, where and how much pressure to make our breathing hitch.

And our hearts, well, I could speak only for mine. I'd been ignoring it, but in noticing that simple, everyday gesture, I knew it was gone. I would miss him. Miss this place.

When I first came to Winterlight, Malcolm had mentioned creating a partnership of some kind. I wanted to wait until I learned the trust fund's value. Then, all the craziness happened, and the partnership idea hadn't come up again. Even though he said he was worried something awful had befallen me, I knew what had to happen next. What always happened next. Enough was enough. Expecting him to take this latest incursion on his sanity with equanimity was too much.

I put my good hand on the doorknob. "I'll go pack. We'll be out of here by tomorrow."

He stopped in the act of kicking off his shoes and fixed me with a stunned glare. Then his gaze dropped to my right hand. Dang it. I moved it behind me again. It really hurt. I needed an icepack.

"I'll work until you find someone else."

We had a one-year contract but only had to both agree to break it. I'd never get the trust fund, but my parents needed it worse than me.

Once again, the look on his face indicated I'd grown a second head, or maybe antennae. He started unbuttoning his shirt and put his back to me, his shoulders stiff.

"Run away when things get tough. Is that all you know how to do?"

In that moment, I hated him. Because it was true.

"That's not fair," I blurted. "I'm doing this for you."

He whipped his button-down shirt across the room and spun on me. "Bullshit. You're doing it for you because it's easier than staying put and working through things."

In that moment, I also hated Dex One. He'd done a very thorough background check before Malcolm hired me, and there was no denying my history.

"I *have* tried. It's not working." Lame. So lame.

Malcolm crossed his arms and leaned down so his face was right next to mine. I tried not to inhale his enticing scent—soap and starch and sweat.

A long breath wreathed my shoulder. Some of the tension left him. All of it settled on me.

"No," he said.

I turned my head away. He was still the boss of me, though he never asserted that authority. If he didn't agree…I'd leave anyway. It wouldn't be the first time I'd quit an untenable situation, consequences be damned. But for once, I wanted to stay, and not only because of the trust fund. This was my parents' fault.

I hated them, too.

He grabbed my wrist. "You're bleeding."

"Don't change the subject. That's my tactic. It's better this way."

His head snapped up, but I wouldn't look at him.

"Better than what?" he asked sharply, then continued to breathe over my ear and neck.

I shivered. "I'm having dreams again," I whispered. "I think it has to do with my parents. I don't know what's coming, but after last time…"

My voice stumbled over the images I tried to keep locked in a closet. A dead body in the manure spreader, galloping from a madman with Nicky struggling in front of me, being held at gunpoint, Malcolm and the bad guy grappling at the edge of a hay loft.

Squeezing my eyes tight, I shoved the thoughts back into the dark where they belonged.

Malcolm's hand lifted toward my face, and I recoiled, but he would never hit me, so I tried to cover it. Too late. I could feel his incredulous stare willing me to look at him. I gritted my teeth against the urge to turn into the warmth of his palm poised an inch from my cheek.

"Better than what?" he asked again, gently this time. He cradled my damaged hand, brought it up where he could see it, kissed my bruised and bleeding knuckles, then lowered it again.

"Better than putting you through this craziness that follows me wherever I go. You don't deserve any of this."

"Vi. Life isn't fair, and it isn't about who deserves what. What do you truly want?"

I wanted to sink into him so far that I'd never have to come up again. It hurt to breathe, and my neck felt like a noose had tightened around it. I wanted to stay.

"I don't want you to leave," he said.

I squeezed my eyes tight and forced air past the constriction in my throat.

He touched his forehead to mine. "I heard you," he said. "When you screamed my name outside." The pads of his fingers stroked my jaw. His thumb caught the tear I didn't even know had spilled. "Admit it. Some of the same thoughts that went through my mind went through yours."

I nodded and risked a glance at him, his beautiful face fractured by the moisture in my eyes. The quiet fury had fled. His finger hooked the deep armhole of my ratty tank top and traced the edge of it until his knuckle grazed the side of my breast. My heart and body arched, reaching for him.

"This is a good look for you," he said.

A silent, relieved, and happy laugh huffed out of me. "Are you sure?"

He had one hand on my ribcage now and the other slid behind my head. He pulled me into him, to the place that felt like home. The rapid beat of his heart matched mine.

"Sure I like this look on you? Oh, yeah." He emphasized his point by sliding his hand down to fondle my butt.

"No, about…" I angled my head toward the hallway, the stairs, and all the rest. "Them." After a pause, I added, "me."

"You're not getting away that easily but, oh, let us never, never doubt what nobody is sure about."

I slumped in his arms. "Please, no more Shakespeare."

"What? That was Joseph Belloc, poet." He took my shoulders and moved back so he could look at me. "You need ice on that hand."

He tugged a fresh T-shirt over his head and gave me one as well. His was soft from wear and hung down to the middle of my thighs. I hadn't exactly been thinking about my lack of clothes when I tore down here. Being wrapped in his shirt was like being cocooned with his kindness. I'm a sucker for kindness.

We went into the hallway, me leaning on him because my knees were weak from relief. The stifling heat outside his air-conditioned bedroom hit me like a wet broom.

"What do you have against Shakespeare?" he asked.

"Nothing." I sniffled. Weak, that's what I was. And more grateful to him than I could express. "My mother was trying to tell me something earlier using the characters and plot of *Twelfth Night*."

He paused at the top of the stairs. Muffled voices drifted up from the kitchen, the sound of ice clinking, a soft laugh from my mother.

"Ah," Malcolm said. "Viola disguised as Cesario. Interesting."

The breadth of the man's knowledge. A trip to the library to brush up on all this was in my future. "I…I think she was trying to say she named me for her."

His gaze dipped into mine and skimmed right down to my soul. I honestly didn't know what he saw in me. But the fact that he saw *something*, something that made him say *no* when I tried to run, gave me hope. Hope for me, hope for us.

"Well, Viola-not-disguised-as-anyone-but-herself. No one's sleeping. Why don't we go downstairs and ask?"

CHAPTER THIRTEEN

DOWNSTAIRS, Giacomo stood under the porch light's glow sipping a tumbler of red wine. Moths circled his head like planes backed up at LaGuardia. My mother sat at the kitchen table, eyes closed, holding a package of frozen corn to her head. Next to her were the fragrant gardenias in a glass vase. My father paced between his wife and father as if unsure whether either could be trusted on their own recognizance.

The moment we hit the hallway, he stopped and came toward us. Thinking to head him off, I moved in front of Malcolm.

"Dad—"

He didn't even look at me. "We're very sorry Mr. Malcolm—"

Malcolm held up his hand. "We'll sort it out in the morning. Is your wife all right?"

"I'm fine," she said from the kitchen. "If you knew how many times Adrian's clocked me in the head with his elbow during practice, you wouldn't be worried."

Not exactly. I'd be *more* worried. If only because my mother used the term *clocked*.

My father winced. He stared at my mother, but she didn't open her eyes. He glanced over his shoulder to where Giacomo still stood just outside the screen door, his back to us, the half-empty tumbler dangling from his fingertips.

Dad's voice hushed. "It's just that Giacomo needed our help. We were ready to come home anyway, and we hadn't seen Vi in so long…"

Malcolm sucked in a deep breath, but before he could say anything to stop this sudden torrent of information, I pinched his butt. We might not find out why I was named Viola tonight, but Dad looked desperate to spill, and I wanted to hear what he had to say. Even if it *was* nearly three in the morning.

Malcolm's free hand grazed his scalp again, and a memory flashed in my brain of Aunt Trudy threatening to snatch me or Penny bald if we didn't do what she wanted. This triggered a brief pang of homesickness at odds with my desire to stay at Winterlight. If I were a sailboat, I'd be rudderless in high seas. Then, Malcolm gave my hip a squeeze to let me know he understood. That anchored me.

He pivoted and walked toward the living room at the back of the house, and, most likely, his stash of single malt Scotch. I grabbed my father's wrist and dragged him after us. We passed the wide office doorway, a room that originally was for dining. The gun safe hung open, again. What compelled Giacomo to lie to me and pick the lock—twice—to keep a weapon close?

Dad started to lower himself into Malcolm's leather recliner but I shook my head and pointed to the matching couch. He sat slowly, as if second guessing his decision to follow me, and I plopped next to him. Meanwhile, Malcolm poured about an inch of amber liquid into his favorite cut crystal glass. After a moment, he added another half inch and got down a second glass to pour an equal amount in it. He handed one to me, and I passed it to my dad. My head needed to remain clear.

"Let's start with Giacomo," Malcolm said after sitting on the edge of his recliner. It tipped forward with a squeak. "Why did he need your help?"

My father studied his hands where they rested on his thighs. "He wasn't completely clear on that. He only said he needed to get out of Florida right away."

"Wait," I said. "How did he even know how to find you if you were given up for adoption as a baby?"

He reached over and took my hand. His was cool and smooth against my calluses "That's a good question, Vi, and I still have a lot of my own." He sighed. "When he first called, I didn't believe him. I wanted to, but I never trust anything that sounds too good to be true. He knew details about the orphanage and the exact date I was left that no one else could know." He lifted his eyes to mine. "I admit I was thrilled by the prospect of being reunited with my father."

"So you just believed him?" I wasn't sure the details Giacomo knew couldn't be had for the right price. "He could be anyone. He knows how to pick locks." Could my parents really be this gullible?

He chuckled. "You have your mother's skepticism. Gemma insisted on a paternity test. It was positive."

"You do look like him," I said.

Malcolm took a fortifying swallow of Scotch, and I longed for a shot of whipped cream. But getting it would require leaving, and I didn't want to miss a word.

"So," Malcolm said, "you dropped what by all accounts was a very successful dancing career and rushed to Giacomo's rescue. Even though you don't really know what kind of trouble he's in? And you brought him here?"

Uh oh. Maybe we should have left this till the morning.

Dad sipped his drink and looked across the room to Malcolm. The two men assessed each other over the fumes of their liquor. I would have pegged my father for a wine drinker, but the strong peaty flavor didn't appear to faze him.

"We're broke," he said with a shrug. "The career hasn't been all that successful for a while. It was time for a change. In case Viola didn't mention it, most of the luggage we arrived with was empty."

"I hadn't gotten that far," I said.

"We needed a place to regroup," he continued. "Frankly, we had nowhere else to go. Giacomo was adamant about not returning to New York, so here we are."

"You could have called first," I said.

"We could have—"

I fixed him with a glare to deflect my guilt at not calling Malcolm when they arrived. Having this trait in common wasn't something to celebrate.

"We should have, you're right. It was your mother's idea. She thought it best to not give you warning."

He put the crystal glass to his lips, tipped back an unhealthy swig, coughed, and wiped his mouth.

"I find it best not to argue with her," he said.

I exhaled forcefully and gave Malcolm a helpless look.

Dad brought my attention back to him. "What would you have said if we had called?"

I answered that without hesitation. "No."

"Exactly. She was right."

"Can you parse the particulars later?" Malcolm asked. "I'm more concerned with whatever kind of trouble Giacomo's in."

On cue, Giacomo appeared in the living room doorway.

"Someone's after me," he said with no trace of accent. "And he wants me dead."

CHAPTER FOURTEEN

Giacomo claimed there had been an accident long ago, someone had been hurt, but it was all an old misunderstanding, and the man who was after him wouldn't track him here. He clammed up after that. Deep creases of fatigue dragged his eyelids down, as if he'd been carrying a burden for a long time. We were all tired, and Mom was making noises about getting back to bed. Malcolm gave in and said we would talk more in the morning. He grabbed a few things from upstairs and we went to the apartment.

If Wastrel came knocking, I didn't hear, and it was good to rest dreamlessly, even if only for a few hours, even if I felt like I could sleep for a week. But only if there were no dreams.

In the morning, Malcolm helped feed the horses, and we decided to go for a ride before it got hot. I wanted to show him where we thought we'd seen the trespasser. I left a note for Zoe, and we got Gaston and Cali ready.

"Whoever it was," he said after mounting, "they're long gone by now."

He settled himself with a happy sigh and patted the big chestnut's neck. Malcolm usually rode in boots and breeches, but he hadn't thought to get a pair the night before. Neither of us wanted to disturb anyone at the house at the crack of dawn, so he wore jeans and used a western saddle. Gaston tossed his head as Cali edged over to him. I tweaked the rein to keep her from getting too close. She was as likely to nip his neck as nuzzle it.

"I'll call our conservation agent and let him know someone might be poaching." He led us up the driveway past the house.

"Okay." I rode up next to him, and Noire caught up with us, too. "But I still want to go down there and look around."

"Lead the way," he said with a smile had nothing to do with riding or poachers.

I knew he wanted me in front of him so he could watch my butt. Men. Sheesh. One track mind. My parents and Giacomo were here under dubious circumstances, we might have a poacher, Wastrel had roared back into my nights, and all Malcolm cared about was the view.

Fine.

I urged Cali to the front. She swished her tail in Gaston's face, and he let out a horsey grunt of annoyance. I arched my back and stood in my stirrups for a moment so I could wriggle my hips, all under the guise of stretching my heels down and finding my balance. An appreciative groan came from behind. I flashed a grin over my shoulder.

Cali jogged a few steps thinking this all meant it was time to go faster. As an off-the-track thoroughbred, she was always up for speed. I let her move out. She picked up a good working trot, tucked her chin, and rocked her back up under my seat. Coiled within her rippling muscles were a couple of playful bucks waiting for the right moment. Said bucks didn't usually unseat me, but I stretched my heels deeper just in case.

At the edge of the alfalfa field, we had a nice straight path with springy footing. A gallop would do us good.

Five minutes and several in-stride bucks later, Malcolm and I were side by side in the cool of the woods, laughing like kids as the horses walked on the buckle, catching their breath.

"We'll move your parents into the apartment," he said.

"What? No." The apartment was mine, part of our contract, my pay. So what if I'd been ready to walk the night before? "Why should I give up my space?"

"You sleep at the house. With me."

"I know, but—"

"Why should I give up *my* space?" he countered in an unusual show of possessiveness.

I chewed my lip. "What about Giacomo?"

"The couch in the apartment pulls out. It's a little tight, but the entire place is air conditioned. They'll be more comfortable."

I grumbled something along the lines of not caring about their comfort.

"Giacomo will be farther from the gun safe, as well."

That would be a good thing. He'd be farther from his plants, too.

"He planted a garden."

"That was fast."

"He brought tomato plants with him."

"From Florida?"

"I guess. I haven't really talked to them."

"You have to."

"I was hoping you would."

I'm such a freaking coward.

He reached across the space between us and took my hand. His was warm and strong, his touch comforting and soothing, the way it must feel to a horse when you stroke their neck.

"They're still your parents. And your grandfather. You've never had one of those before, have you?"

I hadn't. My maternal grandparents died before I was three. Penny's paternal grandmother was still alive, but she lived upstate and we rarely saw her.

He squeezed my hand. "We'll do it together, a little at a time. It'll be all right, you'll see."

"What about my dreams? I can't make any sense out of them, but what if—"

His cell phone chirped. Goddamn thing. I never bring mine riding. Call me a purist, but when I'm on my horse, I want to concentrate on that. No distractions. It was an ongoing disagreement between us.

He reined Gaston to halt, pulled out the device, consulted the screen. "I have to go back."

I huffed. "Okay." I started to turn Cali around.

"You don't have to. Take your time. I'll let your parents and Giacomo know they need to move down to the apartment."

We hadn't exactly agreed to that, but what could I say? At least he wasn't kicking them—or me—out.

Deep down, I knew he was right. Not just about the apartment, but about my having to deal with them. It was going to be a while before I'd admit it, though. God, I wished he was kicking them out.

That wasn't the kind of guy he was, and, of course, that was just one of a long list of reasons why I liked him. More than liked him.

Yeah, it would be a while before I admitted that, too.

I rode close, took his arm, pulled him to me, and kissed him deeply, trying to infuse that with some of the appreciation and gratitude I felt.

He made a yummy sound and ended it. "If we don't quit, I won't make it back to work."

Pointing my chin at the ground, I said, "We have privacy here."

"Tempting," he said. He held up his phone. "But this client has a problem only I can fix."

A lock of his hair had escaped his helmet and stuck to his skin. I stroked it back from his temple. "Okay, Superman. Go rescue them."

He picked up his reins.

Words wriggled around inside me trying to escape. I couldn't seem to put them in a sensible order. "Just…"

His eyes searched mine. "Just what?"

I blew out my breath. "Just thanks."

"For what?"

Geez. Couldn't the guy accept my freaking gratefulness and let it go?

"For being you," I blurted, which was both more and less than I'd intended to say.

He smiled in a way that might have revealed more than he'd intended as well, gave me a salute, and eased Gaston into a slow canter back toward the house. Noire followed, but when she saw that I was staying, she came back. Cali pawed and tugged at my hands, wanting to catch up and pass the other horse. She couldn't help herself.

I turned toward the ravine. Noire loped ahead, stopping to sniff at the base of a tree, then continuing. A red squirrel scampered away, and she sprinted after it, but it streaked up a trunk to a high branch before she could reach it. It sat there chittering at us until we were farther up the trail.

Early morning sunlight slanted through the trees flecking us in splotches of yellow. Birds sang. I'd learned some of their calls and recognized the staccato *ki-ki-ki-ki-ki* of a pileated woodpecker even though I couldn't see it in the dense green canopy.

We started down the steep hill. The sun wasn't high enough to dispel shadows from the ravine yet, and my eyes took a moment to adjust. The scent of damp earth rose up. Cali tensed, remembering the fright from last time. Noire stayed near. No deer or poachers to chase this morning. Cali sloshed through the creek, a little higher thanks to the too brief rain, and I dismounted on the other side. Off the trail, the underbrush was thick and heavy with dried wildflowers, seed pods, and burrs. I reminded myself I'd need a shower as soon as I got back to check for ticks and wash away the chiggers.

Thorns caught in my T-shirt and scratched my arms. I walked slowly, leading Cali with one hand, holding branches aside with the other. I scuffed my feet in the leaves and twigs on the ground, the swish and crunch reminding me of fall. Despite the heat, it was only a few weeks away.

What was I looking for? No idea. Nothing in my dreams so far led me to suspect there was anything or anyone here. And I still wasn't convinced we'd seen a person at all.

Noire lent her superior sense of smell to the search, and a little farther ahead, she stopped and started digging, snuffling and pushing dirt with her nose.

The area around her had been disturbed. Not disturbed exactly, but cleared. As if… I grabbed Noire's collar.

"Quit." She jerked forward. "Leave it." She looked at me, not understanding why I'd keep her from doing her job. "Sit." She sat.

Something or someone had been here. Had cleared a small area as if for a tent or a sleeping bag. The leaves were pushed aside and the dirt beneath smoothed. No sign of a fire. We would have seen smoke from the house, and with everything as dry as it'd been, a fire wouldn't have been safe. Another clear area led to the creek edge. I kicked around some more, wishing I had brought my phone for a change. It wasn't very smart, but it had a camera.

I continued in the direction our trespasser had run, believing now that a person had been here. A strip of reddish-brown fabric hung on the four-inch thorn of a honey locust. The spikes grew in star-shaped clumps right out of the trunk like sea urchins attached to dock posts. The tree was a menace to human and animal alike. I pocketed the material and gave the tree a wide berth. Ahead, the ground rose steeply and the creek tucked under a rock outcropping to the right.

The sun chose that moment to crest the ridge behind us. It sparked on a shiny object halfway up the hill, and I tugged Cali toward it. Our shadows blocked my sightline, and I lost track of it for a moment, chiding myself for dragging my horse through the woods after what was probably a worthless piece of quartz. We moved to the side.

There.

A pale aquamarine marble glinted at me. It sat atop a handful of dull limestone rocks like a diamond set in lead, looking as absurd and out of place as a pair of shiny international ballroom dancers did on a dusty horse farm in Missouri.

CHAPTER FIFTEEN

WE MEANDERED through the woods for another half hour, the marble a heavy lump in my pocket. Having gotten her silliness out on that first gallop, Cali maintained a loose-jointed walk. She'd taken to trail riding well despite the competitive streak inherited from racing. Noire trotted in our wake, occasionally stopping to sniff or dig. All of us were enjoying the relative coolness of early morning. None of us were in a hurry to get back. But I could stall for only so long, would have to deal with my parents and face whatever mystery Wastrel had dreamed up this time.

If only it were all truly a dream.

By the time I rode into the barnyard, heat waves shimmered over the barn's tin roof. I stopped for a moment looking from the house to the apartment, wondering if Malcolm had already talked to Adrian and Gem Gem. The idea of having them upstairs from where I spent my day sounded as appealing as getting in a sauna. Noire made a beeline for the water bowl. Oh, right, we were already in a sauna.

I took Cali into the barn, untacked, hosed her off, and left her in a stall with some hay. Then, I made my own beeline to the air-conditioned tack room. I stood for a moment, listening. No sound came from the apartment. I went up, got some whipped cream and a glass of ice water and plopped down at the kitchen table, staring out the window.

Noire curled at my feet. Having my dog near always made me feel better, even if she panted hot air on my leg. But no matter how many times I told myself everything would be all right, nothing changed the feeling I'd swallowed a cup of eels.

Footsteps climbing the stairs heralded Zoe, and I tried to pull myself together, but it was a man's voice that came from the hall.

"Did someone kill the cat and forget to tell me?"

"Dex?"

"The same." He strode into the kitchen and dragged me up into a hug.

As if all the attention from Malcolm wasn't enough, Dex One was no slouch in the affection department, either. Dex One was Dexter Hamill, retired mounted cop and sometime PI. His horse, Ciqala, lived at Winterlight.

He smiled, and the corners of his coffee-colored eyes crinkled. His usual military buzz cut had grown out since the last time I'd seen him, and he'd grown a mustache. Wisps of graying blond hair brushed the collar of his polo shirt. He must have needed a different look for the last job.

"Got more of that water?"

"Of course." I started to get a glass for him, but he motioned me back to my chair.

"It's hot," he said, as if I hadn't noticed.

"Thanks for letting me know."

He got a glass, filled it, then settled his lean hips against the counter. Moisture clouded his snowy polo shirt, making it cling to his muscled torso.

"Nice 'stache," I said, hoping he wouldn't notice when my nervous knee started up, bouncing erratically beneath the table. Dex One didn't miss much. I might be diverting my anxiety by admiring his pecs, but he could tell I was worried.

"Something you want to tell me, Miss Parker?"

I stood to get more water and force my jumpy knee to quiet. "What do you mean? Is there something you want to tell me?" I kept my gaze on the ice cube tray but could feel his eyes on the back of my neck.

"Something's bothering you."

I laughed a little as I sat again and swirled the ice in my glass. "You a mind reader, now?" But what was there to say? Wastrel was back and there was nothing I could do about it. Anyone in the vicinity could be in mortal danger. Aside from that, my parents were in mortal danger from me.

"Don't forget, I did your background check. I know how your mind works." He waggled his eyebrows.

I began to feel better. Dex had that way. But even though he flirted, he'd once said he loved Malcolm like a brother. His allegiance was, and always would be, to Robert Harvey Malcolm.

"I'm fine," I said. "Just a little tired."

He reached under the table and steadied my jittery leg. "That's my girl."

I wasn't his girl, I was Malcolm's. But Malcolm was also my boss and would be for another eight months. I had to stay at Winterlight that long if I wanted to receive the trust fund. Even though the amount was a mystery, it represented independence.

At least, I hoped it did.

If I'd been smart, I never would have let my relationship with Malcolm be anything more than that of employer-employee.

I'm not always smart.

Dex One leaned closer. Unlike me, he smelled good, like he'd just stepped out of the shower. Provocative, the scent of freshly scrubbed man when I was all sweaty and stinky. My overheated skin prickled with awareness.

Maybe I should have responded to his advances instead of falling for Malcolm. Dex One was more my speed—a no-expectations kind of guy. Not that Malcolm had put any pressure on our relationship. But he was definitely a long-term kind of guy. Me, not so much. Even at the ripe old age of twenty-nine, I still wasn't sure if I was ready for commitment.

My friend Harry had called me cold backed not too long ago. When that term was applied to a horse it meant she had a sore back and didn't want a saddle or person on her. I'd resented it at the time, but the truth was, I didn't want anyone on my back, either, then or now.

I forced myself to rally. "You're right about the heat. I don't think I'm going to ride anymore today. Hey," I said to change the subject, "Have you talked to Renee lately?"

Renee was Dex One's sometimes girl friend. When I first arrived at Winterlight, she was there often, but her sister had become ill, and she'd moved in to care for her shortly after. That was in Kansas City, so we hadn't seen her for a while.

Dex pushed himself away from the counter, giving me his sideways suspicious PI look.

"She's fine. She'll be here for Dex Two's gala next week."

"I look forward to seeing her," I said, wishing he and his skeptical look would move along. "Malcolm's up at the house."

"Let's go up together."

"I have work to do."

"You just said you aren't going to ride. What are you not telling me?"

I put my hands out. "Okay. Okay. My parents are here and Wastrel is back."

He jerked like I'd cuffed him on the chin. "Good God, woman."

"Right? It's hard to imagine one person being so lucky."

"I'm not sure which to be more concerned about."

"Me neither."

"Do they know?"

"About Wastrel?"

He nodded.

I shook my head.

"Which came first—the dreams or the parents?"

"Dreams."

"Were they in them?"

"No. I mean, I don't think so. It's hard to tell sometimes. I have no idea if there's any connection."

He went to the window, sighed, and scratched the back of his neck. "Anything else I should know about?"

I hated to get him all worked up about what might be nothing. But he'd been really mad last time when I hadn't told him all there was to tell. Problem was, I didn't know what was significant.

He faced me, eyes narrowed again like he could see under my skin. Dang. I'd hesitated too long.

"Tell me."

It was my turn to pull back. I wouldn't want to be a criminal he wanted something out of.

"Wednesday morning, one of the riders thought she saw a person running through the woods."

"And?"

I crossed my arms. "And what?"

"Don't play games with me, Miss Parker. I know you."

"You're a real pain, you know that?"

Leaning down so he got close to my face, he said, "I can be a bigger pain, if you like."

"No thanks. I went back today. It looked like someone might have been camping there. All I found was this." I showed him the marble.

He took it and held it up to the light. It sparkled and reflected the sun just as I imagined the Mediterranean would on a day like today. He frowned and gave it back.

"Anything like this in your dreams?"

"Nope."

"Maybe you should ask that horse a few questions."

"Yeah, I'll make a list and submit it to his assistant."

"You're his assistant."

"Not funny."

With a glance at his chunky black-ops watch, he said, "Well'p, too many bad guys, not enough time." He dumped his glass in the sink, gave my shoulder a playful punch, and turned to leave.

"Wait, that's it?"

Without turning around, he said, "You'll tell me if there's anything I need to know."

Not a question. Again, I hesitated too long.

He gave me a look. "Right?"

My turn to sigh. "Yes."

"Okay then. I'll stop at the house to see Malcolm and meet your parents."

"There is one thing. My parents brought my grandfather with them. My father's father. Maybe you could check him out?" I hated to put Dex on Giacomo's tail, but something about the old guy didn't add up.

"Why? Wait…grandfather? Isn't your father an orphan?"

"That's what I'd always been told."

"I'm on it." He turned again.

Zoe met him at the top of the stairs.

Her eyes skittered over Dex One then slid away. "Oh, sorry." She turned to go.

That stupefied bunny look had darkened her features again. I didn't like it. Maybe I should have Dex check up on her, too.

Dex flipped on the charm. "How do, miss?" He swept his arm toward me. "No need to run away. Friend of Miss Parker's?"

"It's okay, Zoe. Dex was just leaving."

He winked, gave me a *we'll-talk-later* nod, and strode out.

"Who was that?" she asked after the screen door slammed downstairs.

"Dexter Hamill, private investigator. Ciqala belongs to him."

"I thought Miss Bong belonged to him."

"She belongs to Dex Two." I canted my head toward the stairs. "That was Dex One."

"That's confusing."

"Once you see the Dexes together, you won't confuse them. They're as different from each other as their horses are."

Zoe got a glass of water. She still had her back to me when she said, "He's pretty *hawt*."

"*Haught?*"

"Yeah, you know. Good looking. Great body."

"Oh, you mean *hot*."

Through the back window, I could see the subject of this observation standing by the fence petting his horse, the muscle definition in his arms evident even at a distance. I couldn't fault her taste, but...

"He's too old for you by at least twenty years."

"You've already taken Mr. Malcolm." She guzzled her drink. "You can't hog all the hot guys."

I didn't want to have this conversation with Zoe or any other sixteen-year-old. "They are few and far between, I agree. But they're both too old for you."

She gave me a *whatever* shrug. "I can look, right? Why the limp?"

"Half his leg is missing. A horse fell on it. He wears a prosthesis."

Confusion scrunched her features for a long moment. Or maybe it was deep thought. I imagined Dex One's hotness level plummeting.

In a throaty whisper, she said, "That's über-hawt."

CHAPTER SIXTEEN

IT'S NOT like the men of Winterlight can't take care of themselves. Quite the contrary. Both Malcolm and Dex One are smart, fit, and crack shots. Both can spot bullshit a mile away. And it's not like I'm the jealous type. Who has time for that? I had no proprietary ownership of said men. Part of me wanted to claim Malcolm for my very own, a part buried deep. But I wasn't ready. Anyway, I couldn't, not with the craziness of my parents and my friendly neighborhood dream horse.

Just the same, possessiveness surged through me, biting and dark. Who did Zoe think she was, calling Dex and Malcolm *hawt*?

I rose and refilled my water glass. "Up for a little riding lesson this morning?"

Zoe's hazel eyes flashed wide, and she beamed around a big bite of pretzels she'd found in the cabinet. With a vigorous nod, she mumbled, "I'b lub thad."

"You can ride Smitty again. It isn't getting any cooler, so hurry up."

She ran downstairs to get him ready. I chased my water with another hit of whipped cream before following.

By the time we got to the riding arena, I'd cooled. My temper, that is. My intention had been to teach her a lesson, but not about riding. Getting back at her for proclaiming Winterlight's men *hawt* was the truth. I decided she hadn't really meant anything by it, the men could defend themselves, and it was too damned hot to give a shit.

Plus, she's a good kid, if a bit too easily spooked. I still wondered about that, but did I have the brain space to work another mystery? Nope. I sent her into a working trot.

My agreement with Malcolm stipulated I didn't have to teach lessons even though it would bring much needed income to his bottom line. Working with Zoe didn't count. It was a way to pay her for the hard work I forced her to do.

Halfway around the ring, Smitty stuck his nose out and his trot started to fall apart. Zoe leaned forward and her posting gained too much air.

Whoa now, I whispered. "Shorten your reins," I said to Zoe. "Sit up straight. Steady him." *Steady yourself.*

It was groups of little kids bouncing around on—and falling off of— ponies I couldn't handle. Private lessons for adults, though? Maybe I should consider it. Surely it would be better than the trail rides.

Or not. I can talk myself into or out of anything. But if it would help Malcolm…

I brought myself back to Zoe and Smitty. "At C, ride a twenty-meter circle."

She looked around in a panic.

"You're coming up to it. It's at the middle of the other end of the arena."

I'd added the dressage markers after coming to Winterlight. I didn't expect her to be familiar with them, but she made an effort to bend Smitty and ride a roundish shape. More like an egg. She'd pulled him together but now her reins were too short, her hands were posting along with the rest of her, and Smitty's head was getting higher and higher. At X, an invisible maker dead center of the ring, he began to drift sideways toward the gate, his eye rolling to me in a plea for help.

"Halt," I said as they sidestepped past me.

Zoe yanked the reins, Smitty tossed his head, and they stumbled to a stop. After a moment, they both huffed out a breath.

"I'm sorry—"

I held up my hand. "Don't apologize. You're doing fine."

"I am?"

"Well, yeah, if what you were asking for was an oval with your horse bent to the outside and a discombobulated leg yield at X."

"That's not what I asked for."

I put my hands on the reins and gently tugged them through her fingers to give the horse some slack. He wiped slobber on my side in thanks. "Are you sure?"

"What do you mean?" Confusion scrunched her cheeks.

"Horses almost always give you exactly what you ask for," I said.

"But I—"

"But you have to be very sure, very clear of what you're asking."

She looked toward the woods for a moment. "I was steering him with my right rein to turn on the circle."

"Yes you were."

"So, why was he going the other way?"

"What was your body doing? Your legs? Seat? Weight?"

Her shoulders slumped. "I don't know."

"Your body communicates with your horse as much as your hands. More, actually. What about your mind? Were you thinking about where you going?"

She rolled her eyes. "No. I was wondering how Mrs. Erdman is doing."

This took me by surprise. Nice of the kid to worry, but how much could a ninety-year-old lady be doing in this heat? "Mrs. Erdman? Wait, she has AC, doesn't she?"

Zoe nodded. "Yeah, but she borrowed my car to go see a friend."

"She has a driver's license?"

Her lips curled in, then she frowned. "I didn't ask."

Christ. "I hope you have good insurance."

"I—"

A horrible shriek came from the barn. Smitty whipped around, nearly dumping Zoe. She gasped and grabbed mane. His front hoof came down hard on my foot. I almost made the same sound that had startled us.

We both spoke.

"What the hell?"

"What was that?"

Howls followed. Garbled yelling. Then a man, I think, keening. *Keening.*

I took a fortifying breath and started running, ignoring my throbbing toes.

It took only moments to get inside. Henrietta the cat sprawled on the tack room steps. Otherwise, the barn was empty. Yelling came from the apartment.

For a second I hesitated, my hand on the doorknob thinking I'd have to start keeping whipped cream down in the tack room. Then, up I went, yet again right toward what I'd be better off running away from. All I could think was, *what now?*

And there they were. My father and Giacomo on the couch, my mother in the bathroom running water.

Adrian patted his father's back, clearly unsure what to do. Giacomo leaned forward with his face in his fisted hands, muttering, and I figured the shriek had come from him. Had he stubbed his toe? Barked his shin? Had my dog laid waste to his garden? What? Gemma came out with a wet wash cloth and shoved it at the old man.

"Can't make sense of what he's saying." She retreated to the kitchen.

I looked to Adrian. One brow lifted, and he cut a sideways glance at his father, conveying more with that simple expression than any words could. The familiarity of it forced me back half a step. I could have been viewing myself in the mirror.

Giacomo lifted his head. I barely recognized him. His face before had been weathered but often wore a charming smile, and he always had a spark of mischief in his eyes. Now, he looked years older, haggard, with a dull sheen of dread clouding his gaze.

His fingers uncurled. In his palm rested the marble I'd found earlier.

"Where you get this?" he asked.

What the hell? Clearly, Malcolm had talked to them and they were moving to the apartment as he wanted. A little heads-up would have been nice. I'd left the marble in a tray on my bedside table thinking it would be pretty in the morning light. In Giacomo's big hand, its opalescence was dimmed, its depths hidden.

Images from recent dreams flashed through my brain. None contained a marble. Cold sweat popped out of my pores.

"The woods," I said. "Why?"

He opened his mouth and that bitter moan I'd heard a few minutes before filled the room again. Tears dribbled over his wrinkles to gather in his beard.

The *hell*.

He made to stand but couldn't free himself from the deep couch cushions. Adrian took his arm and helped. Giacomo slowly straightened, looking like his whole body hurt.

My mother stood in the doorway to the kitchen, looking like her whole body defined disdain. But that was normal for her. Whatever was going on with Giacomo was just the latest in a lifelong catalog of people and things she scorned.

"This," Giacomo said, making it sound like *these*. He cradled the marble to his chest. "This belong to Josephine." His voice broke on the name.

"Apparently, she's been dead for forty-seven years," my mother said.

My face, if not my entire body, surely showed disbelief. "Not possible. Who's Josephine?"

"*Sì*." He nodded slowly, eyes on the marble. "Josephine," he whispered. "She was my wife."

CHAPTER SEVENTEEN

INSANITY. That's what this was. Maybe it ran in the family. Not a comforting thought, but then, it would explain so much.

It was a freaking marble. There must be millions. True, this one was large and very pretty, but—

"Look," Giacomo said.

He beckoned me to follow as he held the glass ball up to the window, turning it between his thumb and forefinger. Light shimmied inside it like dawn through the crest of a wave.

"Hand blown." He glanced at me to make sure I was listening. "One of a kind." He turned it a little more. "I no see for over forty years." He rubbed his free hand over his mouth pushing his mustache up and away, and his eyes lost focus as he drifted inward, no doubt remembering something from long ago, but he snapped back. "See these bubbles here?"

Bubbles. Yup. We'd roared into crazy town. To humor him, I peered into the orb. For a nano-second, Wastrel galloped there, just as I see him in my dreams, his mane and tail flying up and out—

"'E's Pegasus. See? Like the stars."

I pulled back like I'd gotten too close to a cliff edge, lost my balance, hooked my heel on the edge of a chair, and fell into it. Grabbing the armrests, I bounced back to my feet just as quickly and, without a word, left.

My head pounded in time to my steps as I walked fast through the barn. Zoe had Smitty on the cross ties, running a cold hose over him.

"Hey—" She started.

I gave her the talk-to-the-hand hand and continued up to the house. I needed to get away from them. From this place. If I wasn't already insane, I would be soon.

I flung open the screen door. It slammed the wall and came unhinged again. So much for my father's repairman capabilities.

Malcolm sat in his office working at the computer. Some classical symphony played softly from hidden speakers. He glanced up with a smile, but when he saw me, the smile vanished.

"I found a marble in the woods," I blurted, my breathing too fast.

His brows drew together but he waited, knowing more was coming.

"Giacomo says he recognizes it. He hasn't seen it in over forty years, mind you, but still, he knows this marble because it was hand blown and it's one of a kind and it has bubbles—*bubbles*—that look like the constellation of Pegasus, and that's how he knows the marble belonged to his wife, Josephine."

I put my hands on my hips and paced toward the window. "Bubbles," I muttered. "He was wailing, Malcolm. Crying. It was very convincing."

"You don't believe him?"

I whirled on him. "Do you?"

He leaned back in his chair and switched off the music. "A few months ago I would have said it was preposterous." He rose and came over, putting his hands on my shoulders. "But since knowing you and Wastrel, I'm more... let's say open to possibility."

My body relaxed a fraction the moment he touched me. "I haven't dreamed about a marble for Christ's sake."

"Maybe you will."

I shoved his hands away. "I don't want to have these dreams at all. I certainly don't want my parents here. Or Giacomo, whoever he is and whoever's after him." I pictured the deep sadness in the old man's eyes for a moment. Sure, I felt sorry for him. But... "And I sure as hell don't want to dream about them. Any of them."

"You don't believe he's your grandfather?"

"Oh, I know he is. The resemblance to Adrian is too strong to deny. But what do we know about him? He's been missing—by choice as far as we know—for forty-seven years. Where has he been all this time?"

"Dex is working on it."

"That's good. But will it tell us how my grandmother's marble ended up in your woods?"

My grandmother. I tried to imagine her, to fill in another hole in the family tree. My mother's parents had been gone before I was three, but because they were also Aunt Trudy's parents, they'd been around. I'd met them, and there were pictures in the house I'd been raised in. What had Adrian's mother looked like? Did Giacomo have a picture?

Malcolm took a deep breath. "Dex will find out everything he can." He took my hand and tugged me to his leather office chair, sitting and pulling me down onto his lap. "Whether that solves the mystery of the marble…"

I sat stiffly, not wanting to let go of my anger, not wanting to give in to his embrace.

He stroked my back and gently forced my head against his shoulder. "Let Dex do his job, and try to relax until we have something definitive."

I huffed and tried to put it all out of my mind. But I kept seeing Giacomo's sagging face, his tears, and through them, his certainty.

Malcolm put his hand on my leg, his thumb tracing the seam of my jeans up the inside of my thigh. My breathing slowed as my heart sped up.

He kissed the top of my head. "I changed the sheets," he said.

Such a good man. And I was…not in his league. Silently, I let him soothe and arouse me.

"And patched the ceiling. We're not air conditioning the attic anymore."

I smiled into his chest, tilting my head enough to brush my nose against his jaw.

"You're not alone, you know," he said. "You don't have to face the world by yourself all the time. It's okay to lean on someone else."

His hand crept up my thigh, his thumb making circles all the way.

I'd always been alone. Had never relied on anyone else, never asked for help. People had a tendency to let you down.

I snuggled more deeply into his shoulder and rested my hand at his waist, knowing for the time being at least, I could rely on him. Would it last? Doubtful. But then, if the shootout in the bedroom hadn't scared him off, maybe there was hope.

He wasn't wearing his kilt today, but it was still obvious how he was feeling. Images of dreams, thoughts of long lost marbles, even my anger became slippery, harder to hold onto.

"Have someone in mind I could lean on?"

He shifted me to the side, reached into his pants, and arranged himself. "I have something in mind, that's for sure."

I slid my hand to his crotch and stroked his hard length through the fabric of his jeans. "So I noticed."

"Why don't we—" he started.

"Let's go crease those fresh sheets," I said at the same time.

He laughed and stood, carrying me upstairs. So romantic.

Our clothes flew through the air the moment we crossed the threshold and he slammed the door behind us. The air conditioning felt divine on my bare skin. I didn't look at the patched ceiling, pushing him down on the bed and climbing on top. I nabbed a condom from the bedside table, briefly wondering if my mother had poked through the drawers.

I shoved thoughts of my parents aside. Quickly, I had Malcolm deep inside me. He closed his eyes and let out a throaty moan. He needed this. We both did.

And hour or so later, I snorted awake from a light doze. I didn't want to sleep. Wouldn't, if that's what it took to keep Wastrel away.

Malcolm had his arm around me, his front to my back. I could tell by his breathing that he'd fallen asleep, too. I stretched and purred. His arm tightened, causing a wave of gauzy contentment to spiral through me. An unfamiliar feeling, that. One I could too easily get used to.

I opened my eyes and looked at the clock.

"Crap." I pulled away from him. Hours had ticked by, and I'd more than dozed off. But as was often the case, being skin-to-skin with Malcolm had kept Wastrel away.

He scrambled after me. "Where do you think you're going?"

"I left Zoe alone in the barn with my parents." I already had my jeans on. "Look at the time."

It was nearly four. The whole day gone. But for those hours, I'd been without worry, anger, or dreams.

Bliss.

He rolled to his feet without comment, heading down the hallway to the bathroom, giving me a wonderful view of his superbly muscled backside. Glorious, glorious man. Was it any wonder I drooled when he wore that kilt?

A moment later, I had my T-shirt pulled over my head and hopped on one foot as I pulled my boots up so I could peek between the slats of the blinds to see if anyone had come to visit.

As I watched, Zoe's dirty blue sedan came over the hill to the front of the barn, dragging a great cloud of dust behind it, Mrs. Erdman at the wheel. I don't know where she'd gone to visit her friend but was glad to see both she and the car returned in one piece.

She rolled down the window as Zoe emerged from the barn with a wave, said something, and went back inside. Mrs. Erdman kept the car running if the cloud of smoke around it was any indication.

Wait. Smoke? It billowed from underneath, poring between the wheels. "What the hell?"

Malcolm came back in and leaned down beside me to see what I was what-the-helling about.

"Who's that?"

"It's ninety-year-old Mrs. Erdman in Zoe's car."

His eyebrows shot up. "Well, good for her. But it looks like…" He jerked the string to open the blinds fully even though he was still naked.

He grabbed his jeans and yanked them up his legs.

"Looks like what?"

"Hurry," he yelled as he pounded down the stairs. "That car's on fire."

CHAPTER EIGHTEEN

SMOKE NEARLY ENGULFED the big sedan. Somehow, Mrs. Erdman had hooked a mattress on the bottom and dragged it for who knows how far. As we reached the scene, flames licked the front tires and shot from under the hood.

Zoe stood frozen in the barn doorway with her hands on top of her head. "Ohmygod-ohmygod-ohmygod," is what I think was coming out of her mouth.

"Get the fire extinguisher," Malcolm yelled. He grabbed the hose by the fence, yanked the hydrant handle up, and started spraying the car.

The extinguisher? "Get Mrs. Erdman," I screamed back.

I could hardly see her through the smoke. She scrabbled at the door handle and her seat belt, eyes wide with terror. Smoke slinked to the interior. She coughed.

Cold fear tangled my brain.

Malcolm lunged for the door handle but snatched his hand back. He sprayed it with water, covering his mouth and nose as he did.

"That door doesn't open," Zoe shouted. "Get her out!"

My parents and Giacomo came running.

I pushed Zoe toward the tack room, wanting her away from this. "Call 911."

She turned frightened eyes to me. "Are you sure?"

Jesus. "Do it!"

The fire spread to the back of the car and clawed both sides, grasping at the windows.

My father brought the fire extinguisher and started squirting white foam over everything.

I ran inside to get the other hose.

When I came out, Giacomo had used his tie to open the passenger door. He tugged Mrs. Erdman over the console and seat by one arm. She screamed and fought him, panicked and crazy.

My mother ran to that side and got hold of the older woman's other arm. Together, they pulled her out. I sprayed more water. Nothing helped. Noxious black smoke choked us.

"Get her away," Malcolm ordered Giacomo and Gemma.

They half carried, half dragged her inside the barn. Zoe joined them, a glass of water in her hand. Whether that was for Mrs. Erdman or to help put out the fire, I didn't know.

"Vi, hurry up and move your truck."

I hadn't even noticed how close Zoe's car was parked to my truck.

Shit.

That truck might be falling apart, but it was all I had. I sprinted upstairs for my keys. Before I could get back, an explosion rocked the building. Windows rattled and dust shook loose.

My throat threatened to close. They'd gotten Mrs. Erdman clear, but had Malcolm and my father gotten far enough away?

I rushed back down the barn aisle. All of them—Malcolm and my father included—stood just inside, out of the sun and away from what was now a huge fire.

The trunk lid had blown open and the hood had detached entirely. It sat smoking in the cow pasture. The air reeked of burning rubber as tires melted into the dirt.

Malcolm handed me the hose and took the keys. I kept water flowing while he moved my truck. The paint had been scorched right off the passenger side, but it started and moved so I wasn't wheelless yet.

More importantly, Mrs. Erdman sat up, sipping water. Zoe helped her while Giacomo held her hand.

"Wow, you guys," I said to my parents. "Thank you."

The fire extinguisher—now empty, I assumed—hung from my father's hand. My mother smoothed her hair and blotted her neck with a damp cloth. No one spoke.

I cleared some of the smoke out of my lungs with a hearty cough. "How'd you know what to do?"

Adrian's gray eyes calmly skipped over me, looking me up and down as if we'd just met.

"We might know nothing about you"—he paused to set down the extinguisher—"but you know even less about us."

CHAPTER NINETEEN

As if the fire weren't enough, hot shame now threatened to strangle me entirely. Sweat pricked my scalp. My legs shook, but I recognized that as dissipating adrenaline.

Two things I knew.

One, contrary to my suspicion, my parents were speaking to each other. Otherwise, Adrian wouldn't have been able to fling back at me what I'd said to Gemma the day before.

Two, I hated them. They'd ruined my life once, and now, when I'd finally found a place, maybe even a future, they threatened to do it again.

I needed to get away. From them. From everyone. The apartment was no longer mine. We were already in my main refuge—the barn. Anyone could follow me to the house.

I pivoted, ducked through the fence to the horse pasture, and walked.

Behind me, the squeak of the hydrant handle told me someone had turned off the water. A vehicle came up the driveway. Probably the first of the local volunteer fire department.

I didn't turn. I didn't care.

Toward the middle of the field, a thorny snarl of blackberry bushes shot higher than my head. There'd been precious little fruit in July when the berries started to ripen. Lack of rain had seen to that. Horses gathered in the shade of the oaks and hickories growing on the far side of the dense wall of bushes. That's where I went. No one could see me there.

Clara had domestic blackberry plants in her garden that she watered, and they yielded enough fruit to make blackberry cobbler. I'd eaten it hot with melting vanilla ice cream. The sweet-tart clash of flavors made my eyes burn, but I ate it until my stomach hurt. That had been during my whipped cream abstaining days. I should have detoured to the house to get some before coming out here. The comfort of dusty horses would have to do.

They were drowsy, lower lips hanging, eyes half closed, tails swishing idly. Captain stamped a foot as I ran my hand over his back. Ciquala snorted. Fawn and Smitty stood nose to tail. Cali's head bobbed as I approached. I pressed the flat of my palm between her eyes. She leaned into me, nudging my hip.

I rested my cheek on her neck, my fingers clenched in her short mane.

The pressure of unshed tears crowded my chest and crept into the back of my mouth, the pain worse than the choking smoke, and pushed at the backs of my eyes. I squeezed my eyelids tight, leaned harder into my horse's calm solace, but it didn't help.

An angry sob broke free. Cali shook her head, my grip on her mane too tight. But she didn't move, didn't complain, didn't judge.

Miss Bong moved closer to us. Honey squeezed between Gaston and old Fergus, Oreo on her flank. Even Barbie, who wasn't a bad horse despite having belonged to Malcolm's ex wife, edged near. The mares, always the bosses of the herd, made a protective circle around me even while they nibbled at what was left of the grass at our feet and pretended they were doing nothing. Nothing at all.

And everything.

My legs gave out. I sank to the ground, my face in my hands. Stopped trying to choke back the anger and fear and disappointment and hurt. I didn't try to sort out the feelings. For while I hated my parents, self-loathing always crouched in my belly like a cornered wild animal.

I sat there for a long time. The horses stayed near, their bodies warm, but air moved between them. Eddies created by their tails caressed my skin. The horses took my distress and passed it on to the wind. Slowly, I felt lighter, cooler.

With a sigh, I told myself I had to face my parents. Find out what the heck was going on. Take them shopping. There must be things they needed, especially if their luggage truly was empty. I'd been selfish to ignore them. It's not as if we'd ever been on good terms. Worse, now. Truthfully, we weren't on any terms. I'd decided to hate them long ago based on years of anger at being dumped. Who wouldn't be pissed about being rejected by their parents?

Sitting there with my thoughts circling like vultures did me no good.

I got up and started across the field, thankful Malcolm hadn't felt the need to find me, to console or fix me. The remains of Zoe's car smoldered in the driveway. Inside the barn, it was quiet. I turned on the hose, got a drink, turned it off, and stood there, thinking.

Were they upstairs or at the house? Instead of putting one foot in front of the other to find out, I made sure all the stall-cleaning implements were straight. They hung in a neat row—pitchforks, two brooms, and a large plastic shovel—on the wall to my right. All clean. I always put them away clean. Keeping order in my surroundings brought me a measure of peace. I nudged the broom handle a little to bring it parallel with the pitchfork next to it.

"Perfect," said a voice behind me.

"Shit." I jumped and spun.

My father sidestepped the thin stream of water moving toward the drain. Light on his feet. But a lifetime of dance would do that.

"You startled me." I sounded angry, feelings still bunched between my shoulder blades.

"I see that. Sorry."

Sorry for making me jump or for what he said earlier or for being here or for leaving me? So much to be sorry for and I was sick of it. His gray eyes bore into me for a moment and I nearly flinched, but then they softened, the corners crinkling in good humor.

"I see you inherited my love of order."

He had a love of order? God help me. In my peripheral vision, I saw his gaze roam the wall of faultlessly straight tools, but it was as though he saw beyond to something else.

"Your mother says I have OCD."

My cheeks relaxed. Not quite a smile, but an acknowledgement. "Heard that a few times myself."

Is this how it would be? The slow revelation of small details eroding my carefully fortified walls? Were we alike? Had Gem Gem sent him out to test the water?

Did I have to be so suspicious?

For now, yes. Until I knew more about what brought them here, I had to guard the walls. It's not that I didn't believe what he'd told us about being broke and needing a change. There simply had to be more to it than that.

"As if liking order is a bad thing," he added.

Laughter started, but my cell phone buzzed in my pocket. I hadn't realized I'd picked it up when running out of the house. It reminded me I'd never called Penny back. Checking caller ID, it wasn't her or any number I recognized. Hardly anyone called my cell phone.

Frowning, I glanced at my father. He smiled and gave a nod. Not that I needed his permission. I was torn between not wanting to talk to him at all and grabbing tight to the tenuous connection our exchange had started to create.

I took the phone into the tack room. There was a beat of silence after I answered, then a voice I hadn't heard in a while said, "How you be, V?"

For half a breath, a cold finger stroked the back of my neck, though I couldn't say why. "Holy crap. Harry?"

"How're you doing, gorgeous? It's Michael, now, by the way."

"Michael? When did that happen?" Harry'd always said Michael sounded too serious, so he'd used his middle name, Henry, or the nickname, Harry. Plus, his mother always called him Michael, and he hated that.

"Even perpetual partiers grow up."

"If they don't die from the fun, first," I said. Which I'd often worried he would. "It's good to hear your voice."

"I've missed you."

"That's going too far, and you know it."

"I'm wounded, V. How could you say that? We were always so good together."

"If by good you mean drunk."

"Oh, come now. You can't steer twelve-hundred pounds of horseflesh around a jump course if you can't see straight."

"Not that you didn't try."

"And went completely off course and got disqualified. You were always the better rider, anyway. Not sure why I bothered."

We were silent for a moment, both of us probably remembering the not-so-good old days, and me wondering at how easily we'd fallen into our old banter.

Harry—Michael—was good-looking enough to grace a Ralph Lauren ad. I used to have a huge crush on him and the lifestyle his parents' wealth afforded—the horses his parents afforded. But the partying was too much. First, it was the cocaine paraphernalia I found in the tack room. He admitted to using but swore he was getting help. Stupidly, blindly, I believed him. But when I walked in on him with a man, I walked out and never looked back.

Let's just say he and the other guy weren't having a business meeting.

"Allie and Baba say hello," he said.

That's what he called his parents, Alcott and Babette. They were also charming, and their East Hampton *cottage* had been on the cover of Architectural Digest. As had their Fifth Avenue digs.

Allie and Baba had embraced me and made me feel like I belonged with them despite my origins. Being part of their circle made me feel safe, almost content.

"How are they?"

"Always doing their bit for the economy. They're in Barcelona."

Longing swept through me. I sank into the tack room's ratty lounger, its frayed armrests reminding me of just how low I'd come. "What about you? How are you?"

He'd disappeared the year before and no one knew to where. Or, if they knew, they weren't telling.

I sprang up and paced to the door, determined to push away this dissatisfaction. I'd been content at Winterlight before my parents showed. A deeper, more satisfying contentment than what I'd felt with Harry's parents. Mine wouldn't stay forever. This would get sorted out, and I'd be happy again. Out of the corner of my eye, I watched my father wandering down the barn aisle, glancing up the loft ladder, peeking over stall doors. Was he waiting for me?

"I'm better than ever, Vi. Clean and sober."

Something in Harry's voice made me believe him. "Michael, huh? Finally getting serious?"

He chuckled, his old smugness tucked into the sound like a cherry nestled inside a chocolate. "I'll never be as serious as dear old Alcott, but yeah, I'm getting there."

"Glad to hear it." My responsibilities, not to mention my parents, tugged at me, but I wanted to catch up with him. Talking like this with an old friend, so easy, was a balm to my battered senses.

Though Harry—Michael—wasn't really a friend, not in the best sense. Because of his addiction, he couldn't be trusted. Or maybe it was me that couldn't be trusted around him. We might have been good together in a certain way, but we weren't good for each other.

"I'm sure you're busy," he said. "When are you returning to civilization?"

"Ha ha. Believe it or not, things are civilized here. I do need to go right now—"

"That's my V, always keeping her nose to the grindstone."

He sounded a little sad. I wanted to cheer him up. To cheer myself by talking to him. "Can I call you at this number?"

"That'd be great. Don't work too hard, okay?"

"Okay."

"Oh, wait, one more thing, before I forget. Remember High-Class Acres?"

Was he kidding? Ed Todd's place had been my dream. Elegant old Colonial, miles of four-board fencing surrounding manicured pastures, a twenty-stall barn with a lounge overlooking the indoor arena. I'd worked for Ed off and on over the years and always entertained fantasies of what it would be like to have a spread like that.

"Of course." I lowered myself back to the easy chair and held my breath. Ed had been like a grandfather to me. And not one who picked locks and stole shotguns.

"There was a fire."

My stomach clenched. Fire? Again?

"I heard it started in the loft. The fire department got there pretty quick, but the west end of the barn is gone. And Ed…"

I gripped the phone. "Ed?"

"He got the horses out, and then he collapsed. He's in the hospital, but it doesn't look good."

"No, no, no." My throat closed up again. I pictured Ed, mostly blind, frantic to save the horses, unheedful of his own safety.

"Right. Well. The point is, the place will be for sale in the next few months."

That was Harry. Skip over the sad part about the lonely old guy no one cared for and move on to the part where someone benefitted.

But I cared. I went to the desk and grabbed a phone book to find an airline that could get me to the Island.

Steeling myself against my worry for Ed, forcing the waver out of my voice, I said, "Been saving your pennies?"

"Never. What a thing to say."

Michael Henry Brown really was a trust fund kid. He'd had a big one, but I suspect he blew through it long ago and now sponged off his parents.

"What are you suggesting then?"

"Rumor has it you're going to inherit a big wad of cash within the year. You can buy it yourself."

CHAPTER TWENTY

HANDS ON HIPS, I gazed out the tack room window seeing not the riding ring, but Ed Todd's kind face, hearing his blustery, curmudgeonly voice. I knew he was old, but a world without him? Unfathomable. I wanted to see him. *Had* to see him. Before…before. I wouldn't think the thought.

A glance out the door told me Dad still milled around the barn, obviously waiting for me. Mom probably had dinner going.

How did Harry or anyone else hear about the trust fund? There were *rumors*? Penny and Ed Todd were the only ones who knew why I was in Missouri for a year.

I found the number for an airline and reached for the phone. It rang, making me jump.

"Winterlight F—"

"If you're done pouting, come to the house."

Pouting?

Pain forced its way into my throat again. Was he serious? I tried to glean from Malcolm's tone whether he was. He sounded serious. I didn't need this.

"I have to take a couple of days off."

A slight pause. Maybe he was reconsidering his approach. He should.

"Now?"

"I know it sucks with my family here, but there was a fire and Ed Todd was hurt and…" My voice broke.

"Easy now."

I pictured Malcolm standing in his office staring in my direction. I could almost feel his eyes on me, questing, probing. I turned to look toward the house, even though the barn was between us. Maybe he'd feel some of what I was feeling.

"Ed Todd," he said as if to himself. "That the old guy you used to work for?"

I took a deep breath. "I need to go see him. Just the weekend," I said.

"But you will come back."

He'd softened, his voice soothing as a down pillow. In spite of everything, he wanted me back. There was something else in his tone, an unspoken worry, but I couldn't dissect that right now.

"Yes."

"Cancel tomorrow's rides and give Zoe the weekend off."

"Where is Zoe, anyway?"

"I took her and Mrs. Erdman home."

"Thanks."

"Right now, I want you to come to the house and face your parents. Explain what's going on."

I huffed by way of answer.

"In the meantime, I'll see if I can get you on a flight."

We hung up. My father sat on the steps outside the tack room. I dropped beside him.

"I've been summoned to the house."

He slowly shook his head. "Man, I know that feeling."

Were we supposed to bond now over what a bitch my mother was? Was I more like him or her? I wouldn't have thought either, but a lot of what I'd thought had turned out to be wrong.

He put his hand on my knee.

"Nothing for it but to face it."

He started to rise, but I covered his hand with mine. "Wait." I cleared my throat, forced out a question. "I thought you were mad?"

He put his arm around my shoulder. "Vi, my dear, we can spend our lives being mad over what's been, or we can go forward. Try to be better." He took a deep breath. "I guess we've all done and said things we regret, that we'd change if we could."

I nodded. "It is what it is." Cringe-worthy for sure, but the best I could muster at the moment. I hoped we were discussing ourselves and not just dropping platitudes.

"It was what it *was*," he corrected gently. "But it can *be* different. Better. If we want." He patted my knee. "And we do. That's partly why we're here."

"But not the only reason."

His eyebrows shrugged and a resigned puff of breath escaped, much like the huff I'd just given Malcolm.

I *knew* it, knew there was something going on with them that they'd been hiding. Not that I'd asked, I admit. But the knowing gave my spirit a slight lift.

He stood, pulling me up with him. "We'd better go before Malcolm mounts a search party."

"He is the superhero type."

"Seems like a good man."

"Yes."

We started down the barn aisle. I couldn't believe we were holding hands. What was I, a toddler, for Pete's sake? But it felt so damned good, my hand in his, both of them strong, mine calloused, his not. I tugged him to a halt. He turned to me, saw the questions in my eyes, nodded.

"The other reasons we're here will take a little more explaining."

"I have to go to the Island for a couple of days." Tears threatened, and he squeezed my hand. Reassurance? Understanding? "But I'll be back on Sunday."

He pulled me toward him, neatly twirled me under his arm and right against his side. For a moment, I felt nearly as safe as I did when Malcolm folded me into his arms. My breath hitched on a painful squeeze in my chest. If Adrian had carved me open with a hoof knife I couldn't feel more raw and exposed.

"That's a date," he said, and he danced me out of the barn.

Forward. To something different. Maybe to something better.

CHAPTER TWENTY-ONE

Turned out, the soonest I could get on a flight was early Saturday morning. We stood to the side of a long line waiting to go through security, Malcolm's hands on my shoulders, his thumbs pressing firm circles against my collar bones. I'm not sure he realized he was doing it.

Sometimes his calm presence was overbearing. Part of me wanted to shove him away, do something stupid to rile him. Another part of me craved his touch, wanted to melt into him, never come out.

"I'm fine, really," I said, lifting my shoulders. Not enough to shove him off but enough that he stopped circling and stroked his big hands down my arms.

He nodded. We both knew I was far from fine.

Dinner the night before had been subdued. Since my father and I had agreed to talk on Sunday, the dramatics were postponed. Instead, some silent communication between him and my mother assured a bland conversation about the hot, dry weather, the comforting quiet of the farm, the price of pork bellies.

Their silent communication thing irritated me. Even if they currently were at odds with each other, they were connected. Their link hummed with exclusion, intimacy, a special rapport, and the simple warmth of a long, affectionate relationship that eluded me.

Or, that I avoided. I get it. I don't need an analyst to tell me I was abandoned so I leave relationships and situations before they can leave me.

And here I was leaving a good job, a potential future, and Malcolm.

Running out like a green horse overfaced with a four-six vertical. I had no ground line. No way to measure the height to jump, no way to see what was on the other side.

"The horses will miss you," he said.

I focused on his throat, the glimpse of luscious chest hair peeking out above the collar of his shirt.

When I first pulled into the drive at Winterlight, I told myself I didn't have to take the job, didn't have to stay, didn't have to get the trust fund—amount undisclosed.

I still didn't.

But Malcolm had no way of knowing the thoughts swirling around my brain since the phone call.

He'd made me a round-trip reservation, extracted a promise of return.

But…

The temptation to leave and not come back pulled harder than a runaway.

"The horses will be glad to have attention from you for a change," I countered.

He lifted his chin and squeezed my arms. Like a good rider on a green horse, he calmed and steadied me, gave me space to breathe, kept turning me toward the thing I feared.

We'll do it together, he'd said of facing my parents. Together like my parents? Was that really possible? True, there was tension between them now, but that surely had to do with present circumstances. Malcolm trusted we could figure things out together. I had my doubts. He saw me more clearly than I saw myself. And still, he wanted me to return. His patience and strength made me skittish.

"The cats will miss you."

Being skittish—an almost constant state with me—made me edgy and snappy. "Cats don't miss people. People miss cats."

"Noire will miss you."

"She likes you more than me."

"Only because I sneak her treats."

Another retort waited on my tongue. I was so tired of being snappy. All. The. Time. Harry's call reminded me it used to be a full-time occupation. One that kept me from decent jobs, decent friends. It's why Penny made me promise not to smart off before I left for Winterlight. I hadn't been doing a very good job of it. She'd also made me promise to not drink or sleep with the boss.

Fail. Fail. Fail.

I needed a couple of days away, dreaded the reason I had to go. Out of the corner of my eye, the security line grew, even this early. It made me anxious to get going, to get to Ed Todd.

"I'll miss you," he said finally.

His Adam's apple bobbed. He didn't usually fear speaking his mind, his feelings, but he was worried, probably suspected the thoughts circling my head.

When I didn't respond, he said, "The horses need you even if they won't miss you."

This was closer to truth.

"Remember what Nicky said before she went back to Chicago?" he asked.

Nicky, his daughter-not-daughter. He'd had his share of pain and loss. "I think so." The security line was beginning to distract me.

He repeated what Nicky had told him. "The horses are much nicer now that Vi is here."

Now, I understood why he'd wanted to leave so early. He wanted to tell me things. Things he could have said in the car. But there, I could tune him out. Face-to-face, not so much. God, he knew me. It was annoying. Made me want to lash out.

"Be careful," I said, diverting the flow of whatever he was planning to say.

He stiffened. "Vi, I—"

"Something's not right with Giacomo." Malcolm probably thought I'd meant for him to be careful about whatever else he was planning to say. I rushed on. "I don't understand the dreams I've had. He said someone is after him. Someone was in the woods, I'm sure of it. And there's that marble that was his wife's."

"That's impossible, and you know it."

"You said you could believe it after everything else that's happened. He's been awfully quiet since I found it."

His brows drew together in a suspicious frown. "I don't think he's the chatty type to begin with."

"Just watch your back. And him." After another glance at security, I added, "Don't forget to feed everyone. Fergus had some swelling around his front left ankle. Wouldn't hurt to put a cold hose on it."

He gripped my arms, reminding me how big and strong he is. But he would never use force. Not with me. Instead, his gentle strength could be my undoing. I tensed against him.

"I know you're tough, Vi. But it's okay to feel…" He followed my gaze for a moment and somehow pulled my eyes back to his. "You've been hurt. Deeply. I understand that. You have a right to be angry."

There was a 'but' coming. I could feel it. Old pain fought with the new hope. Goddamn his tenderness.

"Please stop." I struggled to pull out of his grasp. "I have to go." My voice sounded choked.

"No. You need to hear this. You can lean on someone. It's okay to ask for help. You don't have to tough it out alone." He pulled me against him, stroked his hand into my hair and pressed my head to his shoulder. "Don't be afraid. Let me help you."

His other arm wrapped around my back, crushing the air out of me. I loved the way our bodies fit together. Loved everything about us. And that scared the crap out of me. I bit down on the gasp of desperation that arose thinking about a future with him.

I squirmed. He held tight.

He spoke quickly into my ear, his voice a strip of leather encased in satin. "You're more than your anger and fear, Vi. You are smart and kind, loyal and warm hearted and…"

I was beginning to like the list even if I didn't believe it. I let out a long breath, and his hold on me relaxed. "And?" I prompted

His chest jumped with a bark of laughter. "Fun and interesting. I'm never bored around you."

He pushed me back enough to look into my eyes. His were blue like a sunny day at the beach.

"You just want me back to take care of the horses."

"And your parents."

"You had to bring them up."

"It's more than the horses, Vi, you know that."

I pulled my arms from where they'd landed around his neck, hanging on like a bucked off cowboy held a rescue clown. I'd almost forgotten where we were. The airport sounds were suddenly too loud.

Rubbing my eyes, I said, "I don't know what I know except that I'll see you on Sunday."

"You keep your word, too," he said. "That's another thing I like about you, and a very admirable quality."

I nodded. "You're not so bad yourself. And… and…" I forced it out. "I'll miss you, too."

A rueful grin climbed one side of his face. He knew it was the best I could do at the moment. He grasped my shoulders again, kissed my forehead —light as a whisper, strong as a promise—turned me toward security, and swatted my butt. My carry-on, a backpack, slipped off my shoulder. By the time I slid it up and turned to wave, he was gone.

CHAPTER TWENTY-TWO

PENNY PICKED me up and we went straight to the hospital. Ed Todd wasn't there. A nurse told us he'd been moved to a hospice on the north shore not far from where Penny lived.

My heart dropped into my stomach on hearing *hospice*. Penny and I exchanged a look. She put her hand on my arm.

"It's not always for…palliative care," she said. "Some people go for rehab."

We looked at the nurse. She blinked. "That's true," she said.

Which didn't exactly answer the question we'd obviously been asking.

With the hospice close to Penny's house, I could take her home before visiting Ed. Seeing him felt even more urgent than it had the night before. After picking me up at the airport, Penny gratefully let me slide into the driver's seat since her huge belly barely fit under the steering wheel.

"Why didn't you send Frank?" Her husband was a busy plumber, but he rarely worked on Saturdays. "Aren't you due any moment?"

"End of the month. And you know Frank doesn't get off the couch on Saturday unless the pope himself springs a leak."

I nodded, focused on merging onto the expressway.

"Everyone's in an awful hurry for a Saturday morning," I said.

"Aren't you in a hurry?"

"Yeah, but…" Once I'd gotten the sluggish sedan settled in the center lane, I shot her a quick glance. "What?"

"Who are you and what have you done with my sis-co?"

I smiled. We'd started referring to each other as *sis-co* when we were about eight years old. "You haven't called me that in a long time."

"You'll always be my sister-cousin." She circled her palm around her ginormous belly. "With this little guy swimming around, I can't help but think of kids…us."

"But everything's okay with the pregnancy? You?"

"Oh, yeah. Just normal preggy stuff. I can't eat anything without getting heartburn, I have to pee every twenty minutes, sleeping is a long-lost dream, can't sit or stand for too long. It's great." She pressed her side and winced. "I think he's going to be a soccer player the way he kicks."

"You know it's a boy? I thought you were waiting?" Traffic lightened as we got farther east, and I was glad for baby talk distraction. I'd had a few squirts of whipped cream before leaving for the airport and nothing but coffee since. I'd like to say I slept on the plane, but my stomach cramped and my heart beat too fast every time I thought of Ed.

She shook her head. "No. I switch between 'he' and 'she.' Can't very well call her *it*."

"No, you can't."

She reached across the seat and squeezed my hand. "Ed's a tough old guy. He'll be all right."

I sighed. "I've missed you."

"Me too."

We drove in silence until reaching the exit to head north. There, someone cut in front of me to make the light.

"Freaking moron," I said.

Penny took a breath. The kind she took before saying or asking something difficult. But I couldn't take any more bad news. I was about to say something but had to slam the brakes again because of another idiot driver.

Penny braced against the dash. The jolt popped the words right out of her. "Do you still hate it?"

The question startled me. "What? Hate what?"

"The job. Right after you got there, you said I'd sent you to hell."

"No—"

"And now your parents—"

I reached for her but couldn't take my eyes off the busy road and stupid drivers. She grabbed my hand midair and held it tight.

"No," I repeated, more softly this time, gripping her fingers in what I hoped was reassurance. "I did hate it, but I don't, not anymore."

"Because of Malcolm."

I thought about this for a moment. "Not only because of him."

"So, you like it?"

"I love it."

This came out faster than expected, surprising us both. I snorted a disbelieving laugh, would have to examine this thought more later.

"Really? I mean, it must be so different. And you, you're different."

"Am I?"

"You have to turn here," she said, sounding astonished.

"What?" Focused on getting to Ed, I'd almost missed the road to our house. *Her* house. Hers and Frank's. It wasn't where I lived anymore.

"Yeah. I don't know how to explain it exactly," she continued, and I'd forgotten what we were talking about. "But you used to yell at people to get out of your way because they were going too slow for you."

I'd done that a lot all right. But I'd been gone only three months. No one changes that much in so short a time. Do they? I pictured Winterlight, the grassy pastures and horses, rows of corn gilded with soft light at sunset, the stillness of the woods at dawn, felt the quiet, a quiet I'd thought unrelentingly tedious at first.

After another deep breath, I said, "I guess driving a tractor will do that to a person." I stopped the car in front of their white split-level ranch. "Thanks for lending me your wheels. Not sure when I'll be back."

"In time for dinner, I hope."

"Unlikely." I glanced at the clock on the dash. "It's almost time for that now."

"What are you talking about? It's barely midday."

I put the car in park and pressed my eyes. "Right. Sorry. You meant supper. Yes. I'll probably be back in time for that, but don't wait. I'll call when I know more."

She gave me a look I'd seen on other people's faces but never hers. The one that made me wonder if I'd sprouted a second head. Her eyebrows lowered. "Is your mobile charged?"

I dug the ancient flip phone out of the side pocket of my carry on. The battery showed one quarter power. "Yup. I'm good."

Penny undid her seat belt, leaned over to kiss my cheek, and climbed out, one hand on her lower back. If I needed a reminder about birth control, seeing her discomfort would do it.

Ten minutes later, I shoved an oily bag redolent with the scrumptious scent of fast-food fries into my carry on, slung that over my shoulder, found the hospice center information desk, and was pointed to Ed's room.

He looked asleep and shrunken. Why did people shrink when they were in the hospital? Was the air pressure different? In my case, I'd recoiled from the hiss and bump of the machines I'd been hooked up to, from the rhythmic reminders of what had happened to me and Wastrel.

I stood in the doorway a long moment. If there were machines here, they were well disguised. The room was not huge, but homey. Lights were off, curtains drawn, but a soft nimbus from the sun leaked around the edges, giving the space a muted glow. It smelled of flowers, not disinfectant.

A few steps in and I found a chair, put my bag on the floor, set the food on the bedside table.

Ed Todd's skin had a gray tint, as if the smoke had permanently changed his complexion. His breathing was shallow, with too long of a break between exhalation and inhalation.

I caught my own breath, swallowed hard against a swift and devastating punch of awareness of my youth and strength and pure aliveness.

Ed wasn't here for rehab.

One weathered arm lay outside the covers, bruises splotched beneath the crepey skin from elbow to finger. I covered his hand with mine, not pressing or squeezing, not wanting to wake him, desperately wishing he'd speak.

"You saved the horses, Ed," I whispered. Harry hadn't mentioned whether Milly, the skinny white barn cat had gotten out. Harry wasn't much for details.

Ed took a stuttering breath and I swear his nose twitched.

"Been waiting for you," he croaked slowly without opening his eyes.

"Me or the angel of death? You look like shit."

"If death brought fries, I'd invite him into bed."

"Well, don't expect me to climb in there with you."

"You never were any fun." His voice crackled like crumpled newspaper. "Never mind. Your gift always was—"

He began coughing. I put my hand on his shoulder. He waved me away. The fit subsided. "—with animals. Your gift. Stay with that. They need you."

My eyes began to sting.

"Jesus, Ed. Why'd you have to do this to yourself?"

"You said it. Had to save the horses."

"When you getting out?"

The corners of his mouth turned down a little, but quickly bounced back. His eyes opened a crack. "Doesn't look like I am this time."

"Bull. They can't keep you. Come on, sit up." I looked for the bed control, couldn't find it. "I'll feed you some fries. You want a glass of water?"

He sighed, closed his eyes again, licked his lips. "Don't want anything. Hurts to swallow."

My nervous knee bounced, and my stomach went all queasy again.

"Smells good. You eat."

I couldn't.

His fingers fluttered against mine. "Closer," he whispered.

I scooted the chair forward and leaned in, rested my head next to his.

"De...lib...erate," he whispered.

I lifted my head and looked at him, stroked his forehead. "What are you saying?"

His breathing became labored, sawing in and out like a horse galloping a cross-country course.

"I'm calling a nurse."

With surprising strength, he held me in place, gave a shake of his head. "The fire," he rasped.

I tried to see out into the hallway and catch the eye of a passing nurse, but no one was there.

"What about the fire?"

"No...accident."

CHAPTER TWENTY-THREE

I'm TRYING to jump a hurdle riding a toy stick horse instead of Wastrel. It's my second try. The jump is positioned at the top of a wide but very steep ramp, and the approach is a sharp angle. A jump judge stands nearby. He's telling me I can't make it, I will be disqualified, I might as well quit.

Even I don't think I can make it. The course has already been long and tiring and my legs feel like lead. Wastrel is somewhere nearby, out of my line of sight.

Gripping tight to the toy's wooden handles, I miss the second try and nearly fall off the ramp. I can't see over the top, can't see what's coming if I clear this jump, but I'm determined to do it.

Circling back to give myself as much of a running start as possible, I take huge canter-like strides trying to pump strength and energy into my legs, but it just isn't there.

The jump judge shakes my shoulder, says something. I turn sharply to look at him, my momentum broken.

It's a woman, vaguely familiar.

"Vi Parker?"

I blink and shake off the dream. My hand still covered Ed's, but the light in the room had changed, darkened. The air smelled different, stale.

"It's Susan," she said, "Ed's sister. Do you remember?"

We'd met a few times over the years. I'd been to dinner at her house. "Yes." My fingers twitched. Ed's hand was cold.

Gently, with too much care, she took my elbow, pulled me up, and my stomach dropped.

"He's gone, honey. Thank you for being here with him. He'd been asking for you."

"What?" I thought he'd looked near dead before, but the change was obvious in his sunken cheeks and slack mouth. "No."

My face grew hot. I rose and stumbled back. My chest convulsed and an ugly sob escaped. Susan steadied me, then pulled me into a hug.

"I know, honey. It's hard." She patted my back. "He was a good man. You brought a lot of joy to his life. He talked about you all the time."

Susan is a nurturer. She'd always watched out for her brother, even while raising five kids of her own and being plenty busy with grandchildren. Crying into her shoulder felt as natural as riding a horse.

She rubbed my back some more. "We'll all miss him."

They took Ed away. I watched his bed roll down the hall until it turned a corner. I'd never see him again, never work horses with him, never joke with him. The shock had worn off but not the disbelief. My chest began to feel tight but I breathed through it, didn't start crying all over. Susan said he'd be cremated and there'd be no service, not right away at least. She might do something at his farm later, she said. I gave her my cell phone number and current address and left.

When I got to the car, I stopped trying to hold back the tears. It was past midnight. I didn't even know what time he'd died.

Back at Penny's, she'd waited up, sleeping in the recliner. She knew what had happened the moment she saw my face, and I got another round of hugs —awkward around her big belly—and back rubbing. She made me eat pasta and drink a glass of wine and drew me a bath with lavender oil.

Before falling into bed, I checked my messages. One was from Malcolm letting me know everything was fine there, to call if I needed anything or just to talk, everyone missed me, my parents were behaving. This sucked a watery laugh out of me. The other was from Harry telling me to let him know when I was on the Island so we could get together. My return flight wasn't until later on Sunday, but I didn't call him back. Instead, I got on Penny's computer and booked an earlier flight.

I needed to get home.

CHAPTER TWENTY-FOUR

IT WASN'T LOST on me that I'd been startled by everyone on the Island being in too much of a hurry, that I'd chosen to fly back early instead of getting together with Harry, that when thinking of returning to Winterlight, I'd called it *home*.

What I didn't understand was how this shift had occurred in little more than one hundred days without my even realizing. I'd been working under the assumption that once I completed my year and got the trust fund, I'd return to New York. After all, things wouldn't work out with Malcolm. That kind of goodness wasn't available to people like me. Not long-term. As usual, I'd get out before he could reject me. My heart would be safe. It would be for the best.

This is what I'd been telling myself all along.

I sat in a window seat, leaning against the airplane wall, eyes closed, disinviting contact with the outside world. Losing Ed left me feeling like my insides were scratched raw. The scared creature that lived in me seemed to have dug her way out or died trying. Now there was only a wind-torn hole so big a horse could jump through.

How a person could feel such exquisite numbness and scorching pain all at once defied reason. Actually, that's not entirely true. I'd briefly glimpsed this exhausting stew of wrenching sorrow and howling emptiness when Wastrel died, but I'd been in the hospital and gladly pumped full of drugs that kept me from feeling or thinking. When the prescriptions expired, I'd self-medicated with alcohol.

Which led to my inability to keep a job and eventually landed me at Winterlight. My thoughts skipped around this, though, never staying put long enough to really consider all the connections and implications.

And then there was Ed's near-death revelation that the fire at his place hadn't been an accident. I'd forgotten about it in the confusion after I woke up next to him, dead. Him, not me.

How did he know? He must have discovered something. Had he told anyone else? I had a feeling telling the cops back on the Island wouldn't do much good with only the whispered words of a dying man for proof. And it would only upset his sister, Susan. Maybe I could turn this one over to Dex One to investigate.

Malcolm met me at the airport with a kiss and a hug, took my bag, and didn't try to force conversation. That made for a blissfully quiet ride from the airport to the farm. I couldn't wait to do some hard physical labor. Too bad we'd already baled hay. A few hours of bucking bales under an unforgiving sun would ensure I fell into bed too exhausted to do anything but sleep. Hopefully, without dreaming.

I'd dozed on the plane but hadn't drifted deep enough for Wastrel to visit.

At the house, we walked past Giacomo's small but lovingly tended garden to get to the mud room. For a change, the old man wasn't keeping watch from a chair just inside the shade cast by the big oak out back.

"He's taken to going for walks in the morning," Malcolm said. "For his constitution."

"When did this start?" I'd only been gone overnight.

Malcolm smiled. "Yesterday."

I paused, looking over the plants. They'd already had decent sized green tomatoes on them when Giacomo stuck them in the dirt. Some were beginning to ripen, and I looked forward to my first tomato and mayo sandwich on toast.

Something caught my eye. Dropping my purse on the steps, I went to take a closer look.

"What the hell?"

Tied to one of the stakes as a support for the plant Noire had bent over was my favorite bra, one cup perfectly embracing a single large tomato. "Are you kidding me?"

Malcolm came over. He grinned when he saw what I pointed at, then snorted.

"Don't," I said. "Don't say a word." I knew what he was thinking about. Shortly after I'd arrived at Winterlight, a pair of my panties had gone on quite a journey.

He burst out laughing.

I narrowed my eyes at him. "Not funny."

"But it is."

He was right. Part of me wanted to be indignant, and part of me *was* annoyed, but I couldn't help giggling at another piece of my underwear being used in a way it wasn't intended. Thanks to the last twenty-four hours, even I could see that in the big scheme of things, this was insignificant. Plus, laughing felt good. Ed Todd always appreciated a good joke, and I could hear his voice making a crack about the cup size and number of tomatoes it would hold. As Malcolm put his arm around me, the tattered hole inside began to feel less ragged.

"It's a good excuse to talk to your grandfather," he said.

"Oh, I will. You can be sure of that."

The man himself chose that moment to round the corner of the house at a jog, his face ashen and dripping, Noire on his heels. Giacomo ran up to us and held out his hand. Nestled in his thick palm sat another marble. Unlike the sparkling translucence of the blue one I'd found, this one was densely black and dull as if it absorbed light rather than reflecting it.

We looked at Giacomo.

"The *bastardo* found me," he said. "'E's a gonna kill me."

CHAPTER TWENTY-FIVE

MALCOLM LED Giacomo inside to get something cool to drink, and I went to the barn to find my parents. Noire followed, bouncing against my leg with joy and slobbering my hand. I bent to pet her.

"Who's a good girl?" Her tail wagged her whole body. "Will we ever find out?" She cocked her head. Her tail slowed. "Just kidding. You're the good girl." I ruffled her ears, and she stood on her hind legs and licked my face. I hugged her. "Come on, you goof."

The horses grazed peacefully, feet stamping and tails swishing. They probably all needed a good dose of fly spray.

Inside the barn, the aisle was swept clean although the tools weren't hanging as straight as I'd like, and a piece of straw threaded the tines of the pitchfork. I'd fix that later.

My father sat in the worn chair in the tack room, wearing his reading glasses, reading one of the horse magazines piled on the coffee table.

"Where's mom?" I asked.

"You're back," he said at the same time.

"Yes, and Giacomo found another marble."

He stared at me as if I'd spoken Chinese. "Gemma's upstairs."

My hand still grasped the doorknob. I wanted to go back to Giacomo. "Can you get her and come to the house?"

He began folding the newspaper with admirable but slow precision and made no effort to get up.

Shaking my head, I took the steps two at a time. My mother sat on the couch, reading a book. I'd concluded they were speaking but clearly things were still strained between them. Otherwise, why would she be up here and him down there? It was time to get to the bottom of all their nonsense.

She glanced up and smiled when I bounded in.

"Giacomo found another marble. He's very upset."

"Another...oh." She stood. "Is he at the house?"

"Yes."

"I'll be there in a few minutes."

I started to say something about Adrian.

"I'll make sure you father comes, too," she said.

I nodded, pivoted, and went back down, wondering whether to be annoyed she'd known what I wanted. Inhaling the healing fragrance of the barn, I committed to not being aggravated by anything or anyone today. I would listen to Giacomo's story without interrupting.

Maybe.

And then, *maybe*, I would take a nap and see if Wastrel had anything to say. The sooner we got this situation—or situations—resolved, the better. Then, we could all get on with our lives.

Separately, if I had anything to say about it.

Giacomo sat at the kitchen table with a cool rag on his head. He had a tumbler of wine in his hand despite it being barely lunch time. An untouched glass of iced tea sat on the counter. Evidently, it hadn't done the job of soothing the old man's nerves.

Malcolm leaned against the counter, arms crossed, patient as the devil. He wore shorts that showed off his muscular legs. I still had on the jeans I'd worn on the plane—I always wear long pants when traveling—and they'd begun to stick to me, but I wouldn't run upstairs to change and risk missing anything. Out the front window, I watched my mother come up the drive at a brisk walk. She looked cool as usual in a white skirt and top. Dad came along behind her at a more sedate pace, hands in the pockets of his slim gray trousers. If reluctance to talk to his father slowed his steps, I could relate.

Once they came inside, we shifted to the living room where we could all sit comfortably. I grabbed a can of whipped cream out of the fridge and took a generous shot as I followed the rest of them down the hall.

In a saucer on the coffee table were the two marbles, one large and bright as a cloudless day, the other smaller and menacing as a storm front.

Malcolm and I exchanged a look. Did he expect me to conduct the interrogation? I frowned and shook my head.

"All right," Malcolm said, settling into his chair and leaning toward

Giacomo with his elbows on his knees. "Where did you find the black marble?"

Giacomo swept the wet rag off his head and swung his arm through the air in the general direction of nowhere. "In a nest. In the barn."

"The barn?" I asked. There were a few swallow nests in the loft but you'd need a ladder to see inside them. They were way up in the rafters.

Giacomo pointed, this time more specifically. "The old barn. On the threshold." He wiped his face, took a drink, and looked at Malcolm. "'E's watching me," he whispered. "The *bastardo*."

Malcolm studied the backs of his hands for a moment. "Who is this bastard who wants to kill you?"

Adrian jerked as if he'd been kicked and moved from where he'd been standing beside Gemma's chair. He sat next to his father and patted his shoulder. Giacomo's lips moved but no sound came out.

"Take your time," Adrian said. "We're here to help."

Geez. What psychology Cliffs Notes had he been reading?

"Benito," Giacomo sputtered.

A portentous name if I ever heard one.

He lifted moist eyes to his son. "It's why I wrote you. Why I had to leave Florida. He tracked me there." He shook his head and muttered *Dio santo* along with what I took to be a few curses in Italian.

Malcolm took a deep breath. "Why does Benito want to kill you so badly that he would follow you halfway across the country?"

And invade our lives went unspoken.

"Have you been on the run your entire life?" my mother asked.

My father's head came up. He stared at his wife, then turned to his father. "Is it why you left me at the orphanage?"

Malcolm held up his hand. "One question at a time."

"*Sí, Sí,*" Giacomo said.

Honestly, the man had lived in this country for at least seventy years, and I'm pretty sure he'd been born here. For the life of me, I couldn't figure out why he insisted on clinging to this fresh-off-the-boat persona.

But I'd promised not to get annoyed.

"Benito was in love with my Josephine. And her father, he was the boss, you know? You understand what this means, to be the boss?"

"Like the godfather?" I asked.

He nodded. "Just like that. The boss, he groomed Benny to take over his whole life." A sad smile creased his cheeks. "But she loved *me*." He jabbed his thumb at his chest with pride then spread his hands wide. "Ah. My Josephine. She was so beautiful."

Considering Giacomo's reaction to the blue marble, I sensed this story didn't have a happy ending. "What happened to her?"

Giacomo knuckled his eyes, then grabbed Adrian's hand. "She got pregnant. Her father, he would kill me. We went to Las Vegas to be married. The boss, he was very, very angry, but Josephine, she was strong. She stood up to him. Told him it was what she wanted and that was that."

Adrian looked uncomfortable but whether it was because his father was squeezing his hand too tightly or because it was the first he was hearing his history, I couldn't tell. I sat on the edge of my seat. This was my story, too.

"We had a little apartment. I worked three jobs. She was soon to have the baby." He lightly beat his and Adrian's joined hands on his knee, took another swig of wine.

I stood and went to the window. Something stirred inside me, an uncomfortable oily sensation swirling in my gut. I shot more whipped cream at it.

"One morning," Giacomo continued, his voice tight, "I'm coming home from my job at the toll booth. I know she will have breakfast waiting. It's later than usual, light already because I stopped to buy her favorite flowers—white camellias."

I turned to stare at him, the scene from my Wastrel dream coming back full force, stealing my breath. The city, the narrow stair leading to an apartment, the woman waiting within. The dark malevolence stalking up the stairs.

Giacomo took a long sniffling breath. My mother produced tissues from somewhere, gave them to him, walked over to stand beside me.

"They followed you," I said. "Benito and another man."

Giacomo's eyes found mine. "How you know this?"

I shook my head. "Good guess."

His eyes narrowed in suspicion, but he went on. "Yes. They follow me. Benny and his younger brother Eduardo."

I dug my fingers through my hair. My stomach seethed with anticipation. I wanted to shout about the shooting, to end it, but I bit my tongue and let him tell it.

"They came to kill me. To take Josephine to her father, force her to marry Benito. But she sees them when she opens the door. They are right behind me. I can see it in her face."

His eyes were wide, remembering, his lips trembling. The pain was sharp and fresh for him, and I felt it in my chest. My mother pressed her fingertips to her temples, and my father stared at my grandfather, helpless to stop or change the story, needing to hear all of it.

On a choking sob, Giacomo said, "I turn. He fires."

His shoulders shook as he stopped trying to hold back. I barely understood him as he told the rest.

"He missed me. He hit Josephine. My Josephine."

My father's face, usually such a study in cool confidence, crumpled like a heartbroken child's. I took a hit of whipped cream and offered the can to my mother. She declined, covered her mouth with her hand, but didn't go to her husband. I didn't know who to try to comfort, and I'm not very good at it, anyway, so I just stood there trying not to throw up.

Giacomo took a moment to steady himself. "I grabbed the gun. We struggled. I didn't want to kill anyone. I just wanted to get to Josephine. But it went off again. And again. I didn't know who was hit. They ran away."

This hadn't been part of my dream. I'd woken with the first shot.

"Later, I found out Eduardo died. Benny, he lost his eye."

"My God," Adrian whispered. "What about Josephine…what about my mother?"

"She went into labor," Giacomo said. "Right there at the top of the stairs, with her life bleeding out. She had the baby. And then…and then…"

My mother murmured, "Jesus, Mary, and Joseph," under her breath and knelt in front of Giacomo, taking his head to her shoulder.

"She died in my arms," he sobbed. "She died, and I ran away. I took you to the orphanage and I ran away. She told me, with her last breath, she told me to keep the baby safe, keep him away from her father. To love him enough for both of us." He leveled a long look at his son that was so filled with longing and anguish, my stomach twisted.

"What do I know about taking care of a baby?" he asked. "I did what I thought was best. But I never forgot. I stayed in touch with the sisters at the orphanage. They kept our secret. I called when I could. They told me about you as you grew up."

"Where did you go?" Malcolm asked.

"To the cargo ships. Took a job as a seaman and sailed the next day."

"For how long?" I asked.

"Until a couple of years ago."

That was nearly fifty years of running.

"And then you checked yourself into a nursing home in Miami and started growing tomatoes?" Adrian barely disguised the misgivings in his voice.

Giacomo shrugged. "I couldn't do the work on the ships no more. My back. The nurses, they treat you good at those places. I thought I was safe from Benito after all these years. But the tomatoes, no, I had them all along.

Josephine gave them to me when we married. The seeds were from her grand-mother's garden in Italy."

"Surely not the same tomato plants that are outside," I said.

He nodded. "I save the seeds and plant them every year. I will make you the best sauce you have ever tasted."

That was something to look forward to. If he survived whatever Benito had planned for him.

"What about the marbles?" Malcolm asked.

Giacomo stretched one hand toward the saucer, couldn't quite reach. My mother picked them up and held them out. He took the blue one.

"This was Josephine's. Her father gave it to her. I was in a hurry when I left or I would have taken it. I took the baby and the seeds and the clothes on my back. Benito, he must have found it later."

"He *was* camping in the woods." I looked at Malcolm. "He must have dropped it when Noire went after him."

"Maybe," he said. "Probably."

"And this one?" My mother pointed at the black marble in her palm.

Giacomo pulled back, didn't pick it up. "That," he said, crossing himself, "is the sign of the eye thief."

CHAPTER TWENTY-SIX

GIACOMO STARED at the black marble in blank terror. Gemma looked at him as if he were a large, infuriating insect. Adrian gaped into the middle distance, probably trying to wrap his mind around this horror story that was his.

And mine. Geez. My grandmother. His mother. My mother was many things I didn't like, but at least she was alive. And that meant the possibility existed to fix things between us.

Malcolm scooped both hands through his hair and looked at me with exasperation. If he was going to pin the blame for this on me...I stopped myself. He is a reasonable man. If he hadn't blamed me when Giacomo blew a hole in the bedroom ceiling, he probably wouldn't blame me for this, either. Maybe he saw the momentary doubt in my eyes, because his softened. He came over and wrapped his arms around me.

By God his strength was reassuring.

"I need to call Dex," he said quietly. "Stay with them. Find out what *the sign of the eye thief* means. Can you do that?"

I nodded.

He squeezed me tighter. "It will be all right."

"How do you know?"

"Because I said so."

"Oh." I smiled. "Okay, Superman."

He patted my butt and turned to the others. "What is Benito's last name?"

Giacomo snapped out of his daze, ran a hand over his face, took a breath. "Columbo. Benito Antonio Colombo."

Malcolm went to the office.

Mom saved my having to inquire about *the sign*.

"What does it mean?" she asked. "The eye thief?"

"Because I shot out his eye," Giacomo said. "When he kills—he killed many times for the boss. Always, I see it in the paper. Always, it is a sign for me. 'E comes in the night and cuts out your left eye and replaces it with a black marble like that." He covered the left side of his face with his meaty hand. "'E's coming."

My mother turned to me. "We should leave." Her eyes stayed on me for a long moment then dropped to the floor. "It isn't right to do this to you and Malcolm."

"Where would we go?" my father asked.

"Yes, where would you go?" I echoed. Honestly, at the moment, I wasn't sure whether I wanted them to stay or leave. But if they had somewhere else to go, maybe they should.

My mother's shoulders drooped. That was all the answer I needed.

"Dex will know what to do," I said. "In the meantime, how about some lunch?" Food always made everything better.

I squirted whipped cream into my mouth and headed to the kitchen. There, a quick inventory told me we needed to go to the store. Especially if we were in for a siege.

I made grilled cheese sandwiches and we ate in silence. After a little while, Malcolm joined us.

"Everyone sleeps in the house," he said. "I have an air mattress. Giacomo will sleep on that in our room. Gemma and Adrian will take Nicky's room. Dex will be here later with a few of his men. Someone will always be keeping watch."

Giacomo looked up. "I get the scattergun?"

A line appeared between Malcolm's brows even though I could tell he was trying not to scowl. I could just imagine what he was thinking.

"Yes," he said, then he directed his attention to my parents. "Do either of you know how to use a gun? I mean really use one, not just hold it."

They shook their heads. He already knew how I felt about them. He'd tried to get me to learn how to handle the shotgun back in May and I'd refused. When push came to shove, I'd let Dex One give me some quick instructions with a pistol, but when the time came to use it, I'd been disarmed in a blink.

"I'll keep Willy close by."

Malcolm gave me a reproachful look. "I don't want Benito getting close enough that you could use a baseball bat."

"You are right, Mr. Malcolm," Giacomo said. "But he is cunning, Benny is. He prides himself in getting close to his target. He don't use a gun if he can help it. He cripples the victim with a knife, first. "

My father had been quiet, but now he spoke up, his voice thinned by revulsion. "Do you mean to say that he sneaks up on a person and takes out their eye before he kills them?"

Giacomo had refilled his wine glass, emptying one bottle and helping himself to another. He thumped his chest and belched. "*Sì*. Exactly that."

"Fucking hell," my mother whispered.

Everyone turned to her, shocked. My feelings about her flip-flopped. Suddenly, she was someone I could like. A couple of swear words shouldn't matter, but to me, they revealed more about her than she probably intended. I smiled.

"Yes. Fucking hell," I said. "And we're going to need more wine."

"We'll give Dex a shopping list," Malcolm said. "For the time being, no one leaves the farm. And no one goes anywhere alone."

"Put whipped cream on the list," my father said, taking a generous hit from one of my cans.

We all turned to him, just as surprised by that as by mother swearing.

He shrugged. "What? It helps."

"It will make you fat," my mother said.

"I should live so long."

Gemma's lips stretched into a thin line, but she dropped it.

Giacomo took another slug of wine. Malcolm rolled his eyes heavenward. I suppressed an exhausted and giddy laugh.

Who would have thought the threat of an eye-stealing murderer could bring out everyone's best?

CHAPTER TWENTY-SEVEN

WE WORKED in pairs to get my family moved from the apartment back to the house and settled. Despite Malcolm's concern, I kept Willy to hand. He strapped a pistol to his belt, handed Giacomo the scattergun, and loaded the rest of his arsenal, hiding weapons strategically around the house and barn, making sure everyone knew where they were, just in case.

As the day progressed, clouds heavy with the potential of much-needed rain gathered in the west, the first promise of a good soaking we'd seen in weeks. I had no reason to feel happy, yet thoughts of cool moist air, less dust, and greening grass made my steps lighter.

Dex One arrived with four of his men including Brian who'd helped out when JJ threatened us last May. Brian had slimmed down some and looked serious, dressed in black and sporting a matte watch just like Dex's. I was glad Dex hadn't fired the guy. Last May, I'd tricked him into letting me take a horse out to do some reconnaissance. He'd ridden Honey. We'd been shot at.

Can you say *Deja-vu all over again*? Although the idea of a silent knife scared me more than gunfire.

After consulting with Malcolm, Dex told his men where to patrol. I snapped a lead line on Noire to keep her from following them. She doesn't like being leashed, and keeping her by my side while also holding Willy was awkward at best. I tried shutting her in the tack room, but all the excitement and comings and goings had her agitated, and she barked nonstop until I let her out.

The preparations kept everyone busy and distracted. I called to check on Mrs. Erdman—she was fine—and to tell Zoe to stay away for now.

"Can you come pick me up for work in the morning?" she asked before I could explain.

"Erm…no. We have a situation here. No rides for a couple of days. Everyone gets vacation." I hoped our *situation* would be resolved within a day, that Dex would find Benito, that life would get back to normal.

When had I become such an optimist?

I heard a door close and assumed Zoe had gone into a different room for privacy. "I don't want a vacation. I don't have a car. I'll go crazy if I have to spend another day playing cards with Mrs. Erdman."

Sounded like she was already on the edge. I felt sorry for the kid but couldn't risk bringing her into our crazy world.

"No," I said. "Malcolm's orders." Not exactly true, but I knew if he knew I was talking to her, that's what he'd say.

I pictured Zoe's face, the frustration in her eyes as she tried to think of something to convince me.

"Don't you have any friends you can call?" I asked. "Go swimming or something?"

"I'm not from around here."

That wasn't really a huge revelation. I'd suspected she had secrets. "Look, Zoe, whatever *your* situation is, I can't deal with it at the same time I'm dealing with *our* situation. Okay?"

"No. What is your situation?"

"I'm not at liberty to say."

A long huffy breath came down the line.

"If I bring you my truck," I offered, "will you stay away until I say it's safe to come back?"

She hesitated, but said, "Yeah. Okay. I guess."

"Swear."

"I swear to stay away."

I promised to be there in a little while, hoping to convince Malcolm to let someone follow me over. I saw him conferring with Dex and decided it made more sense to not bother him with this little matter while they were in the middle of planning our siege defense. Instead, I snagged Brian from where he sat in the barn.

He held up a hand to ward me off before I could say anything. "Don't talk to me, Miss Parker. I'm working."

Well. Dex must have given him a *very* stern lecture after our last encounter.

"You look great," I said. "Been working out?"

He smiled. "Yes. And no."

"No?"

"Whatever you're going to ask, the answer is no."

"Not very neighborly today, are we?"

"C'mon. You know the deal. If I mess up again, Dex will can me."

"I just need you to follow me to a friend's house. It's five minutes away. Dex already okayed it."

He eyed me with distrust, as well he should.

"We'll be together," I added. "You'll be doing your job by keeping an eye on me. Nothing's going to happen here in broad daylight."

He snorted at that. We both knew it was a crock.

He stood. "I'll double check with Dex."

I leaned backwards out of the barn door to see if Dex was still talking to Malcolm. They were walking around the side of the house. "You sure you should interrupt him right now? He's talking to Malcolm."

Brian frowned and put his hands on his hips. Or as close as one of those bandolier thingies strung with weapons, tools, and communications devices would allow. I couldn't tell whether it was helping to hold his pants up or contributing to their gravity induced slide toward the ground. He tugged on his waistband.

"Okay. Let's make it quick."

Oh, how I love the smell of victory. Even small ones. I ran for my keys and we were off.

My truck complained the whole way, but at least it started, and if it kept Zoe out of our hair until this was over, it was worth it.

Ten minutes later, we pulled into Mrs. Erdman's long drive. Brian stopped near the road. Zoe came outside when I pulled up to the house.

"That was quick."

"And we're in a hurry." I threw the keys at her. She grabbed them out of the air.

"Who's that?" she asked with a tilt of her head toward the black SUV by the road.

"A friend. Sorry about this, but we have to go."

"I wish you'd tell me what's going on. I really could help."

"No can do." I slammed the truck door and a piece of rust popped off the wheel well. "Take good care of it."

"I seriously doubt I could do any more damage to it than you already have."

Smart ass.

"Just don't loan it to Mrs. Erdman, okay?"

"Ha ha." She peeked into the front seat. "Is this a manual?"

I stopped and turned. "Please tell me you know how to drive a stick."

She shook her head. "I'm sure I can figure it out."

"Oh, hell no. I can't afford a new transmission." I waved to Brian. "Slight delay. Need to give a quick lesson here." To Zoe, I said. "Get in the driver's seat." A glance over my shoulder showed me the door to the SUV opening. I shoved Zoe. "Hurry up."

"All right, all right," she grumbled as she climbed in.

I pointed at the floor. "See that pedal on the left? That's the clutch. You have to use that to shift gears. Got it?"

"I guess." She jammed the keys in the ignition.

"Press the clutch to the floor and keep it there before you start the engine."

She did as told.

"You're going to have to make a tight three-way turn to get out."

She looked keen, eager. "Okay."

"Look at the shifter. The knob shows you the gears. See? First, second, third, fourth, reverse, and neutral. You want reverse, so push it to the side and down."

She fiddled with the thing. Out of the corner of my eye, I saw Brian with one hand to the side of his head, talking into what I assumed was a spy-like ear thing. I put my hand over Zoe's and shoved the truck into reverse.

"Feel it?"

She nodded, put both hands on the wheel.

Keeping my eyes on Brian, I said, "Crank the steering wheel all the way left, give it a little gas and slowly ease out the clutch. Slowly. Then, push the clutch in again."

"Where do you think you're going?" Brian yelled.

By some miracle, we didn't stall as the truck swung around into the bushes along Mrs. Erdman's drive. Zoe let out a surprised little squeak. She looked from me to Brian and back.

I jammed it into first. "Turn the wheels right, give it gas, and let out the clutch again. You press the clutch when I tell you, and I'll shift. Got it?"

"Got it."

"Try not to hit that man."

She giggled, having entirely too much fun. "I'll try."

We jumped forward, jolted up on the front lawn around Brian, then bounced back to the driveway.

"Clutch!"

We rounded the SUV in second and screeched onto the pavement in third.

"Nice work," I said.

"Told you I could figure it out."

"You are smarter than the average bear."

"Huh?"

"Never mind. You should probably put a little gas in the tank."

"I can do that. Thanks, Vi. I appreciate this. Sure I can't come see the horses?"

"Nope." I pointed ahead. "When you get up there where the road straightens, shift it into fourth."

She did. The truck jerked us against the seat belts, then smoothed out. We drove a little farther and found a place to turn around just as Brian caught up and pulled behind us. I couldn't see his face through the tinted windows, and really, I didn't have to. But I waved.

It's the friendly thing to do.

Brian and I returned to Winterlight. The clouds passed over without dropping any rain on us, leaving the air sultry and still and hotter than ever. Late in the afternoon, when the sun turned the horse's shadows into elongated dinosaurs drifting around the pasture, my parents retired to the kitchen to start dinner. Malcolm and Dex took the front porch. Yes, I'd gotten a thorough dressing down from both of them. But all's well that ends well, right? Okay, it wasn't over yet. I'd displayed the appropriate remorse, and we'd let it go.

Giacomo and I sat by his garden. We seemed alone, but I knew one of Dex's men was in the garage, another in the old barn. Close, unobtrusive, deadly.

Willy leaned against the house, and the scattergun rested across Giacomo's lap.

"So, these are heirloom tomatoes?"

"Heirloom, *Sí*." He pointed at two plants on one end of the row that had longish fruits. "These are San Marzano. Good for canning. But this one," he indicated the one that needed my bra to hold it up. "Italian. Like me. Good for salad or sauce." He scooped one hand under the red cup of my bra, weighed it. "They will get bigger. A pound or more. " He put two fingers and his thumb to his lips, kissed them. "*Delizioso*."

I pointed at the spandex support. "That's one of only two non-sports bras I own, and it's my favorite."

He shrugged and leaned forward. "I no find the pantyhose. You leave it in apartment. I think you no need." He added a suggestive ogle of my chest.

My grandfather's a dirty old man. Great. I shot him a look to match his turn of thoughts.

He chuckled. "I find something else."

"Yes, you will."

We sat in silence for a while.

I love long summer evenings. Even though it was August, and the days were shorter than they'd been in late June, the light turned everything that warm red-gold color, and the air softened.

When I'd first arrived from the East coast, I'd never thought to get used to the open and sparsely populated countryside. I'd come to like the way the quiet isolation cocooned us. Obviously, given my sudden aversion to the traffic and pace back on the Island, I'd adapted.

Tonight, though, the coming dark hummed with menace, and despite the comparative safety of where I now lived versus where I used to live, I could wish for a little less sparseness, a little more population. There were miles of uninhabited woods out there where a cunning killer could hide. How long had Benito been spying on us? Despite the heat, I shivered.

Malcolm had called Clara and Hank and informed them of the heightened terror alert. We were all to join them for dinner tomorrow night.

That was, of course, assuming there were no attacks tomorrow.

Dex had brought night-vision goggles and planned to *go hunting* after dark. I didn't like the sound of that, but he promised to take his second in command. Malcolm, I could tell, itched to go with them, but he would stay, he said, guard his home, his family.

My family.

Still raw from losing Ed Todd, the thought of losing anyone else ate at me, stirring that greasy stew that curdled in my gut. I kept thinking of Giacomo's story about my grandmother, Josephine, about how much time and energy I'd wasted being angry at my parents. I would get to know them. Let them know me.

The mud room screen door squeaked open, and my father stuck his head out. "Time to eat."

We went in. Malcolm had taped up the window I'd broken. Someone had swept up the glass. That seemed so long ago, when I'd punched out the pane in my panic to get to him, but it was only the other night. My knuckles hurt and still wore bandaids. My toes were a little sore from when Smitty had stomped on them. My mother had a bruise on her forehead where Malcolm had grazed her with the butt of the shotgun. We were wounded, but determined.

Dinner was a roast and potatoes and broccoli and salad and good. The situation hadn't dulled anyone's appetite. And there was wine. Lots of wine, especially for Giacomo. He was glassy-eyed before the peach cobbler Clara made for us came to the table. Maybe we'd sleep.

Maybe not.

My father told a couple of stories about him and mom at dance competitions. Early on, in the states. Later, all over Europe and other parts of the world. They always won, he said.

"For a long time, that's how it was," my mother added. "We *were* the competition."

They were both extra quiet after that. We all were. We could keep thoughts of the bogeyman at bay for only so long, after all. But I knew, *knew* their quietude meant something. It was a clue to why they'd quit Europe and come back to the states when Giacomo contacted them. Had they stopped winning?

That mystery would have to wait.

We went to bed. Giacomo said he would help keep watch. But he slept. I know because he snored with the ferocity of a drunk elephant.

Malcolm wrapped himself around me, his front to my back. Needless to say, we didn't sleep naked like usual. Just the same, his erection—his *spear*—pressed against me, demanding attention. If the last couple of days didn't call for some good hard sex, I didn't know what did. And what the heck was it about being surrounded by people, by the possibility of discovery, that made me want him even more?

Carefully, I slid out of the bed, pulling him behind me. We padded down the hallway to the bathroom, turned on the shower and got in. It was an old house, and the walls weren't exactly well insulated, but there was a room between us and my parents. Hot water, slippery soap, a hotter man powerful enough to support me with one arm and still touch me the way I liked. Not that I needed that extra stimulation. I sank my teeth into the meat of his shoulder to keep from screaming my hallelujahs out loud.

Afterwards, back in bed, he held me until he thought I'd slipped into dream time, then quietly went into the hall to relieve Brian, who tiptoed downstairs to nap on the couch.

Some time after midnight, the weather broke. Rain and wind scourged the house, thunder rattled the windows, lightning lit the walls. Usually, I enjoy lying in bed listening to a good storm, but that night each thunder thump made my whole body jerk.

Eventually, I slept.

We start the course with a large circle, Wastrel feeling a little unbalanced. It's that same jump course again, but I'm determined to ride it out, to see where Wastrel is taking me. Two strides from the first jump, he rotates hard to the right and we leave the ring. We're cantering through a marsh, yet the footing is good, not boggy at all. More like a shallow creek with a sandy bottom. With each stride, water splashes up to cool us. We jump into a large box floating above the water, halt. While standing there, Wastrel bobs his head and paws the hard floor. I know I'm supposed to pay attention, that there is meaning in his actions, but as usual, I don't get it.

He swishes his tail. I smell smoke and think of Ed Todd, imagine I can feel the heat of the fire and hear the screaming and kicking of the horses even though there is nothing inside the box with us. I force myself to sit and listen, to feel. I remember what Ed said about my gift, about his fire not being an accident.

We jump down, back to the marsh or river. It is dark, but the moon is out, glowing pale crystalline blue like a faceted gem and casting a long reflection on the water's surface. Wastrel stops and paws again causing the moon's light to scatter away from his hooves like mice leaving a flooded nest. We canter along the reflection, following it all the way to the moon, which we jump. As we come down on the other side, Wastrel kicks out, sending the orb bouncing along the water like a skipped rock to shatter into a thousand new moons to light our way.

Dawn brought fog, and we all groggily bounced off each other in the kitchen fixing our coffees. Giacomo took his black, complaining it was too weak. He usually drank espresso, he said, but I seriously doubted they served that at the nursing home. My mother added a pinch of artificial sweetener— which I didn't even know we had—no milk, and took hers at the kitchen table. My father, a tablespoon of real sugar, extra milk. He'd prefer one of those syrupy creamers, he said, then mumbled the old adage about beggars not being choosers as he took his cup down the hall to the living room.

Dex came in looking bedraggled and defeated. He'd seen several deer, every raccoon, possum, skunk, fox, coyote, bobcat, and owl in the county as well as a muskrat, but no Benito. Nor had he found any sign or tracks, but they could have been washed away by the rain. I handed him our largest mug fixed the way he liked with a little milk, no sugar.

Into the second largest mug we had, I added a generous serving of whipped cream to my coffee and did the same for Malcolm when he extended his cup. He gave me a lusty wink by way of thanks. I hid my smile behind my cup, but I think my mother picked up on the vibe.

"Sleep well, Vi?"

I sat at the table with her. "I did. How about you? Did the storm wake you?"

"A storm woke me, yes." *She* winked at me.

My face heated. I'll be damned. I'd have to remember there were no secrets in this house.

I'd just begun to relax when a scream rent the air.

"Shit!" Dex yelled and took off through the mud room.

"Who's missing?" Malcolm asked as he went after him.

Cups were set down too hard and coffee splashed over the table and counter when we all followed.

"Giacomo," I said. "Where's Giacomo?"

"*Merde*," I heard the old man shout from outside. "In the garden."

Dex skidded to a halt by the row of tomato plants. One-by-one we all ran into each other trying to pull up. The rain had made the grass slick and the ground soft.

Giacomo knelt in the mud peering into a hole.

The tomato plant with my bra entwined in its branches had been dug up and removed. Shoved where its roots had been, one of the plastic pots the plants had arrived in.

In the bottom of that sat another black marble.

CHAPTER TWENTY-EIGHT

DEX GOT ON HIS TWO-WAY, ordered his men in, and stormed up the driveway, his jaw so tight I feared he might crack a molar. That left the rest of us standing around a wet hole staring at a marble. My mother and I were both barefoot. Her toes were perfectly manicured with light pink polish. Mine, not so much. When was the last time I'd pampered myself? No idea. Maybe never. My feet were usually in boots.

My father picked the plastic pot out of the hole. "How do you think he did this without waking anyone?"

Giacomo's skin looked like bleached parchment. "'E's a ghost."

"The real question," Malcolm said, "is how he got past Dex's men."

I glanced to the team assembled in front of the barn. "By the body language and raised voices, I'd say that's exactly what Dex is wondering."

Dex jabbed his finger in one direction, then another, then a third. Three men took off. Dex came toward us. Malcolm went to intercept him. They consulted, then Dex took off after the others. Poor guy hadn't had a chance to change into dry clothes or drink his coffee.

Malcolm came back, but his gaze followed Dex. "Brian hasn't checked in."

"Enough," Giacomo muttered. "I go." He dumped out the dregs of his coffee, tipped the shot gun over his shoulder, and started walking along the dirt road that led past the soy beans to the woods.

"Whoa, whoa." I chased after him, sticking to the grassy verge. I wanted to go, too. To get on a horse and gallop out. That wasn't going to happen.

"Hang on there, old man," Dad said.

"Oh, for pity's sake," Mom said.

Malcolm jogged by me, snatched the long gun off Giacomo's shoulder, and got in front of him, halting him in his tracks. The old man was tall, and I suspected in better shape than he let on, but Malcolm had six inches of height on him, not to mention being around forty years younger and in prime physical condition.

Still, Giacomo tried to duck around. "He wants me. Nobody else gets hurt."

Malcolm took Giacomo's arm. "Not how we do things here."

I caught up to them. "Maybe he's right. Maybe we should go."

Malcolm gave me that look, the one that said he did occasionally wonder why he kept me around but this wasn't open to discussion.

"Not to the woods," I explained, thinking he might have misunderstood my intent. "But away from here. To a hotel or something."

Dad came up. He wore flip-flops, and while his feet weren't as pretty as Mom's, they were well cared for. I guess ballroom dancers had to take good care of their tootsies.

"Agreed," he said. "Coming here wasn't a good idea. We're sorry for all the trouble."

Malcolm glared at us. "You'd be sitting ducks at a hotel. Benito found Giacomo after fifty years of being on the run." He looked at each of us in turn, waiting, no doubt, for someone to argue. No one did. "No," he said. "You stay."

My mother still stood by the tomatoes. "That's settled. I'll make breakfast." She went inside.

I watched her, wondering at how she'd changed in a couple of days. When they arrived, she'd been quiet and withdrawn, but this crisis had sparked a response in her. If I hadn't just experienced my personal revelation about how quickly someone could change, I wouldn't believe it.

I started for the barn. "I'm going to do the morning chores."

"No, you aren't," Malcolm said. "Not alone."

"I'll go with her," my father offered.

"Stop being so bossy," I said to Malcolm.

"I *am* the boss. And until Dex or one of his men is here, we stay together. We have only an inkling of what this guy is capable of or if he's working alone. In the house, now."

Adrian and Giacomo didn't disagree and headed for the side door.

I put my hands on my hips and glowered at him.

"Don't fight me on this, Vi. And don't try to sneak around me, either."

He knows me too well.

"Giacomo assumes he's Benito's only target," he continued, "but we don't know that for sure." He came over and pried one hand away from my body, pulled it to his lips and kissed my palm, smiling the whole time.

I fought every inch of the way. I'm strong but there's no denying he's way stronger. He almost never played the boss card, rarely lorded his superior strength over me, and only occasionally laughed at me. There was no way to win against that triple threat.

We both knew he was right. I wouldn't concede the point aloud, but I did let him take me inside.

Mom had made a rasher of bacon and fluffy veggie omelet for each of us. The eggs were courtesy of Clara and Hank's hens, the bacon from one of their hogs, the veggies from their garden. The omelets were very good, seasoned with dill. We refilled or reheated our discarded coffees, pulled in extra chairs, got cozy around the small kitchen table, and dug in.

I liked it. We didn't talk about dancing or horses or the eye thief or the fact that Brian was missing. We rubbed elbows and passed the salt, stole bacon from each other's plates, and laughed.

Halfway through, I realized Noire wasn't patrolling for dropped pieces of food. Out of habit, I'd let her out when I first got up and hadn't seen her since. I went to the side door and called. She didn't come. Prickly cold crept up my scalp.

"Giacomo, do we need to worry about any Godfather type action with regard to the animals?" I'd started thinking about Gemma and Adrian as Mom and Dad but still hadn't reconciled to referring to him as *Grandpa*.

He paused his chewing, leaned back from the table. "What you mean?"

"I mean, you know, the horse." I drew my fingers across my throat. "In the bed?"

He blinked at me a few times, then waved his knife. "Eh, no. Benny loves the animals. When we were kids, he had a dog he adored. Followed us everywhere. He fed the strays, too."

Forks and coffee cups froze in place. Every head swiveled to him.

"You grew up together?" my father asked.

"*Sí*. We are *cugini*—cousins through our mothers."

My dad looked at me, his eyes wide. I connected the dots.

"That means he's our cousin, too." I sat down again, feeling weak in the knees.

Giacomo had already shoved another bite of omelet into his mouth. "Of course," he said around it. "We have a big family."

Slowly, everyone resumed eating, needing to digest this news along with the food. I'm sure I wasn't the only one wondering why this hadn't been mentioned before. Maybe forty some years at sea scrambles a man's brain as surely as the eggs on our plates.

Before conversation could resume, I heard Noire barking out near the barn. Relieved, I went to the front door to call her inside. Another taxi rolled up the drive, this one a white minivan instead of a yellow car.

The chances of one public transportation vehicle coming to Winterlight were slim to none. The odds of a second one coming so soon after were zero. Yet, there it was. It couldn't be good.

When I didn't return to the kitchen right away, Malcolm joined me on the front porch.

"What now?" he asked.

"My thought exactly."

The taxi stopped outside the gate, the back window opened, and a young man with shoulder-length blonde hair stuck his head out. The top and sides were pulled up into a man bun. In heavily accented English, he asked, "Is this the ranch of Miss Viola Parker?"

He had bright blue eyes, high cheekbones, a straight nose, and full mouth. He reminded me of Harry. In other words, he was impossibly good looking.

I felt Malcolm tense beside me. He crossed his arms over his chest. "Who are you?"

"Oh, so sorry. I am Mr. Milanko Stanislaw."

The screen door squeaked behind us.

"Miko?" my mother said. "What—"

"Ah, my belle Gemma Maria. Thanks to the gods I found you."

"You know this guy?" I asked.

Miko hopped out and slung a backpack over his shoulder. He handed a wad of bills to the driver.

"Hang on," Malcolm said. "What do you think you're doing here?"

The screen door skreaked again.

"What the hell?" my father asked. "What is he doing here?"

Oh boy.

"Don't make a scene," my mother hissed.

"Don't make a scene?" My father's look was incredulous. "He's the one who made a scene. *You* made a scene with him."

"It wasn't like that. If you would just let me explain."

Malcolm and I took a step back.

"Don't bother," Dad said. "Get in the taxi and go with him if that's what you want." He stomped back into the house, slamming the inside door. The screen jumped off its top hinge again. I caught the edge and set the corner on the porch floor.

A bright pink spot bloomed on each of my mother's cheeks. Her eyes glittered.

"Miko," she wailed. "Why are you here? How did you find us? I told you to stay away."

The taxi began to back up.

"I cannot, my belle, my love. I miss you so much, I cry to sleep every night. My heart is paining and my eyes are too tired. I must find you. We must be together or I will be dead."

"Stick around," I muttered. "You can join the club."

Malcolm gave me a sharp *shut up* look.

"This cannot be, Miko. *We* cannot be. You shouldn't have come, and you can't stay here. Viola, stop that taxi and make sure he gets in it."

She went back inside, slamming the door again. The bottom hinge popped off the screen. Malcolm caught it before it landed on us and leaned it against the wall. "Not sure the old house can handle this much drama."

I stared at the space where my mother had been, then looked at Malcolm, then at Miko's sad face, then down the driveway. The taxi disappeared over the hill. I wasn't about to run it down.

Noire pranced onto the porch. The fog had lifted but the sky was still heavily overcast, and it started to drizzle, then quickly turned serious. Miko's backpack slipped to the ground as the downpour flattened his pretty hair. He looked at the door his love had gone through, and I believed his heart was paining him. My heart pained watching him.

"Jesus Christ," Malcolm said. He gestured to Miko. "There's some breakfast left. Get in out of the rain."

Miko smiled, grabbed his backpack, and came up the steps. Noire sniffed him, wagging her tail the whole time, so whatever had happened between him and my parents, he wasn't a bad guy. A tad misguided if he'd followed them here from Europe. The lovesick puppy couldn't be more than twenty years old.

He reached for the doorknob. Malcolm stopped him. At this point, I think Malcolm's patience must have been worn paper thin. Mine was long gone.

"Hang on," he said. "Before you go in, explain why you're here and what you intend to do?"

"What you mean?" Miko's face was all innocence. "I come for my woman, Gemma Maria."

CHAPTER TWENTY-NINE

MALCOLM RAN his hands through his hair. It was shorter than Miko's, darker —more golden—but wavy and plenty long enough to get my fingers into. When he was tired or frustrated or angry, he often scraped his hands over his scalp. Maybe it helped him think. More likely it kept him from punching someone.

"I don't think the lady is interested," he said to Miko. "And I don't want you bothering her or upsetting her and her *husband*."

His emphasis on the last word left no doubt as to whether Miko had a place in the family. Miko's hand dropped away from the door knob.

"I will convince her. We belong together."

At that moment, Dex came around the corner with his men. They supported Brian between them. He had one arm around Dex's shoulders and the other covered his face. There was blood—on his arm, on his shirt. He hopped on one leg, the other hung limp and dragged a trail through the wet ground behind him, and there was more blood on his pants.

"Sit. There." Malcolm pointed Miko to one of the chairs on the porch. "Don't move."

Heedless of the downpour, we ran out to meet Dex while one of his men brought around an SUV. They got Brian into it. He grunted and groaned and hissed as they slid him across the back seat.

It was a good sign that he was walking, or hopping, but the blood…that cold sweat that had started when I realized Noire was missing flared again. "Shouldn't we call an ambulance?" I asked.

Dex shook his head. "This is faster." He slapped the roof and the car took off. "He's going to be all right."

I couldn't tell whether he believed that, said it to reassure himself, or us.

Malcolm squeezed Dex's shoulder. "What happened?"

Dex pressed his thumb and forefinger to his eyes for a moment, breathed deeply. "Benito got the jump on him after the storm started. He sliced his hamstring, tied him to a tree, gagged him. Cut an X across his left eye socket." He crossed his index fingers over his eye. "Didn't take the eye, though."

Without realizing , I stepped back, my hand to my throat. "Oh my God."

Malcolm put his free arm around me, pulled me against his side.

"But then, he put a tourniquet on his leg," Dex went on. "I think he wanted him to live. At least, long enough to tell us what happened."

"Did he say something?" Malcolm asked. "Benito?"

"Yes. He said, 'I will not take your eye. You tell him. Tell Giacomo. I will take his, and everything he cares about. An eye for an eye.'" Dex stamped his foot. "Shit. I'm getting too old for this."

I was too old for this. Or too young. Not sure. Either way, I needed to go to the house and make more coffee before I said or did something I shouldn't. Unfamiliar feelings battered me. Impotent rage because of what Benito did to Brian. Confusion about my parents and Giacomo and their place in my life, mine in theirs. Grief over Ed Todd kept sneaking up and wrapping cold hands around my throat. Fear, too, was like an icy finger tracing my spine. Helplessness. A desire to run so strong my feet itched.

I wanted to punch something, needed to go riding. A drink or two or six would help. Curling up into a ball held appeal. What had I been thinking taking my truck to Zoe? If I could get away for a while, I could track down a nice, dark bar, maybe with a mechanical bull. That way, I could drink, ride, and probably find someone to punch all in one spot. I could pass out in a corner and be at peace, if only for a while. No one would know where I was.

I sighed. It wouldn't last. Dex would find me. He was spooky that way.

Alternately, I could take a horse into the woods, find Benito and take him out. Even if he was my cousin once or twice removed. He had no right to terrorize us like this, to hurt people who were in no way involved with his vendetta. To hurt any of us. I stoked the flames of my anger to keep the welter of other emotions in the dark.

Raised voices came from inside, rising over the drumming of the rain like a Greek chorus run amok. Miko no longer sat on the porch where we'd left him. Few people dared disobey Malcolm when he used *that tone*. That Miko had ignored the Laird's directive spoke of either his determination or youthful stupidity. I stood there with my hand hovering over the doorknob, uncertain I wanted to step into whatever pile of steaming excrement had materialized now. As if we weren't already knee deep. Noire sat beside me wagging her tail, spinning water in an arc across the porch floor. She loved having so many new people around. For her it meant more treats and attention.

A smacking sound came from inside followed by a grunt and a screech. Had someone just been punched? The door opened, sucking me toward it. My mother reached out, grabbed my wrist, and yanked me in.

My father and Miko grappled with each other in the living room. They were well matched in height and build but it was obvious neither of them knew how to fight. Noire ran in and started barking, circling them. Whether she wanted in on the action or was trying to break it up is hard to say.

I covered my mouth and pretended the crazed yelp of laughter that wanted to escape was a cough. Miko hooked one foot behind my father's legs, they toppled to the couch, then the floor. I watched in horrified fascination as a lamp whirled off a side table and crashed against the wall.

My mother pinched my upper arm. "Do something!"

"What do you want me to do?" I yelled at her. The whole place had gone insane.

"Stop them."

I took a deep, calming breath, put Brian and Benito out of my mind. "Sometimes it's good to let men work things out like this." I pointed at them. "It appeals to their baser instincts."

What psychology Cliffs Notes had I been reading?

Miko and Adrian rolled to the other side of the room, knocking into another table. I grabbed the lamp on that one before it could meet the floor and set it up on the mantle. Noire bounced over them and barked some more. The men were yelling insults at each other in another language. French, I think.

"Don't we have enough to worry about?" my mother asked.

Although I'm pretty sure my dad wanted to kill Miko, and Miko was only trying to defend himself, I didn't think they were really going to hurt each other. I raised my voice to be heard over the din. "Dad's been very tense with all this stuff with Giacomo. Maybe it's good to let them burn off some energy."

"Are you serious?" She kicked Miko in the ass. "Stop it this instant."

They both ignored her, rolled back to the other side of the room, pushing the couch against the wall. Dad had Miko's bun now, and he jerked it hard. I think Miko was trying to bite him. Apparently dancers fight like adolescent girls. I'd concluded Miko was also a dancer, something in the way he held himself, his gait, but had yet to confirm that. My mother's eyes blazed at me.

"Okay, okay." I went to the kitchen, filled a pitcher with water, came back, and dumped it on them. They fell apart like coupling cats, sputtering and howling. Noire commenced to licking their faces. So helpful, my dog.

My father seized the moment to slap Miko on the ear. Geez. Boys. He got up, touching his lip, which was bleeding, and shot daggers at my mother, who didn't move toward either of them. Miko stayed on the floor, staring at my father like he hadn't expected the older man to put up such a fight. He touched his eyebrow, red with rug burn and beginning to swell.

"Who started it?" I asked.

"He did!" they both said.

Sorting this out would be like getting the truth out of a couple of toddler girls caught squabbling over Barbies. In other words, a waste of time.

My father would expect me to side with him. I wasn't the one to arbitrate this. But something had to be done, and Miko needed to leave. Whether that would be alone or with my mother in tow remained to be seen.

I turned to her. "Can you go get Malcolm and Dex and ask them to come in here?" I walked her toward the front door but didn't want to leave the boys unsupervised for long. "And then maybe you should go upstairs for a while, okay?"

"I'd like that."

"I'll come up in a bit. You want an iced tea or something?"

"What I want is a stiff drink."

"That makes two of us but maybe iced tea for now?" We hardly needed to add alcohol to the mix.

She lifted her slender arm and pushed a few stray hairs off her forehead. "Some cool water will do. But I can get it."

I patted her shoulder. "Okay. Good."

A few minutes later, I had Dad on the couch with a bag of frozen corn on his lip, and Miko in a chair across the room with our only ice pack on his brow. Each of them looked anywhere but at the other. The similarity to the lull between rounds of a boxing match should have made me smile, but I wasn't exactly in a jokey mood, even if their spat was comic relief from the truly serious business of Benito and Giacomo.

And Brian. Jesus. I wanted to ask Dex how badly he was hurt but was afraid. I didn't think he'd be as sanguine as Malcolm about my responsibility for this mess.

The phone rang as my mother returned, Malcolm and Dex following. I answered with "Hold on a minute," as Mom got herself a glass of water and went upstairs. I covered the receiver and quickly explained to the men what they would find in the living room.

Dex grunted, Malcolm rolled his eyes, and they went down the hall. I returned to the call.

"Hello?"

"Miss Parker, how good it is to hear your voice. How is my Little Miss Bong?"

"Humphrey J. Dexter the Third," I said, forcing cheeriness into my tone. "It's good to hear your voice, too."

Dex Two didn't like the name Humphrey, which is why he went by Dex. But since we also had Dexter Hamill, retired mounted cop and sometime PI, we kept them sorted by referring to them as Dex One and Dex Two. When together, they always argued about who was really number one. The gray mare known as Little Miss Bong belonged to Dex Two. Which reminded me that I needed to get out to the barn and feed the horses and cats.

"Bongo is fat and sassy," I said, filling a glass of water for myself. "How are you?"

"Very well, thank you. And you?"

Dex Two is kind of old school in the manners department, which I find refreshing.

"I'm well," I lied, hoping he didn't want to come riding. There was no need to bring anyone else into our situation. At the same time, the interruption was welcome, gave me a few minutes to catch my breath. Not to mention an excuse to not be in the living room.

"I'm calling to let you know you should be receiving in the mail today your formal invitation to my annual Labor Day get together."

"Oh, right." I flipped the calendar from August to September. We had the event written in on the Saturday evening of the holiday weekend. Dex Two's *get together* was a formal affair for three hundred downtown. I still needed a dress.

"You haven't forgotten, have you? I'm looking forward to seeing you there. Both of you."

"No, of course not. Only…"

"Never say something has come up to prevent your attendance?"

"No," I squeaked, and took a drink to clear my throat. "No, of course not. We'll be there."

"Is everything all right, Miss Parker?"

"Yes." The low murmur of male voices hummed down the hallway from the living room but I couldn't make out what they were saying. "It's just that my parents have come to visit. And my grandfather."

"Wonderful. Give me their full names. I will have Daphne issue invitations."

Daphne was Dex Two's secretary. He's an attorney with a swanky office in a high-rise in the city. More to the point, he's Malcolm's attorney.

"Pardon me a moment, Miss Parker." I heard papers shuffling. Dex Two is a meticulous notetaker. "Do I remember correctly that you and your parents were…estranged?"

"You remember correctly. Their visit wasn't planned—"

Giacomo came into the kitchen scratching his head. "*Idiota*," he said with a sharp hand gesture.

Who was the idiot? Adrian, Miko, himself?

"Miss Parker?" Dex Two prompted.

"I'm here. Their visit wasn't planned, but it's going surprisingly well. I'm not sure how long they're staying, but I'm certain they'd be delighted to attend your get together."

"You remember it's formal?"

"That won't be a problem."

Most of their luggage was empty, but surely they still had a couple of dressy outfits? Giacomo, on the other hand, we'd have to take shopping. I doubted he'd had much use for a tux on the cargo ships or at the nursing home. All depending on whether he was alive in another week, of course. Focusing on what we'd be doing when we got on the other side of this situation helped it feel temporary, surmountable.

The volume of the voices in the next room elevated. "I don't mean to be rude, Dex, but I need to go."

"Of course, Miss Parker. I know how busy you are. Always a pleasure. I'm not sure I'll be able to fit in a ride between now and the party—so many last-minute details, you know—but I will call if so."

More like he'd have Daphne call, but whatever.

"Sounds good. Thanks."

We hung up. I let out a long breath, hoping none of us would be needing Dex Two's services in the near future, and returned to the living room with Dex One's refilled coffee mug.

Dex had his back to the room and stared out one of the long windows. Malcolm stood like an angry referee, legs apart and arms across his chest. Dad and Miko had lapsed into French again.

I touched Dex's arm. He flinched. He's not easy to sneak up on, so I knew he was deep in thought. Certainly, he wasn't paying attention to the drama behind him.

"Have you heard anything?"

He rolled his shoulders. "They got him to the hospital. He's in the emergency room. That's all I know right now."

I handed him his mug. He took it with a grateful tip of his head and went back to staring out the window. He smelled of sweat and wet dirt. The knees of his khaki pants were dark with mud and had bits of soggy leaves stuck to them. Dried blood smeared his arms.

"I'm sorr—"

"Don't say it, Vi. This isn't your fault. I should have fired him after his last ill-advised encounter with you, but *this* isn't your fault." He jabbed his chin toward the out of doors.

Okay then. I shut my mouth, tired of trying to take the blame.

"Enough," Malcolm said to the other two. "I can't keep up. English or not at all."

Malcolm spoke both French and Spanish, but it's hard to stay fluent if you don't have others to use it with. I might have to finish my college degree if there was any chance of us staying together. Although when I'd started thinking there might be a future for us—hoping?—I don't know.

Giacomo wandered in, a tumbler of red wine in his hand, his fingertips stained brown. He'd been digging in the garden, probably removing any trace of Benito's visit. He leaned one shoulder against the doorway, his eyes twinkling with amusement. I wasn't the only one getting a kick out of this distraction from our other situation.

"It comes down to this," Dad said. "She tangoed with him." He nearly flung the bag of corn at Miko. "This whelp."

He returned the frozen vegetables to his lip and used his other hand to make a sharp dismissive motion that I'm pretty sure meant something crude in Italian. I glanced at Giacomo whose shaggy eyebrows had shot up.

Shaking his head, my father next spoke as if to himself. "After all we've been through together." He turned his head to the stairs, and yelled, "You tangoed with another man."

CHAPTER THIRTY

EVIDENTLY, tangoing with another man is tantamount to cheating. At least as far as my father was concerned. Had they done more than tango? We needed my mother's version of the tale. Though, I'm a big believer that there are three sides to every story. Hers, his, and the side you never hear.

But first, I really needed to get the horses taken care of.

"Come with me to the barn?" I asked Dex.

"Gladly."

"I'm going to take care of the horses," I said to Malcolm. "Dex is coming with me."

"Good. I'll keep on eye on these two." He swung his gaze around to Giacomo. "Three."

"Take this sorry excuse for a dancer with you," my father said. "Get him out of my sight."

"That's a good idea," Malcolm said. "Miko, go with Vi and Dex. Do as they say."

Miko rose and pulled himself tall without even a glance toward my father. He shook his hair out of his face. "I would be pleasured to go with you, daughter of my love."

Oh, brother.

"Just don't get in our way."

Dex took hold of Miko's arm. "Stick close to me, whelp."

Outside the barn, I opened a gate to let ten of the horses into stalls. Each of them knew where to go. Dex shut stall doors as the horses went in. The other five I fed outside. Everyone got an amount of grain according to their size, weight, and work level.

We were closed on Mondays, didn't have any rides. That was a blessing, but I figured we'd cancel Tuesday's as well. It was income we needed, but it couldn't be helped.

Or maybe we'd find Benito today.

Or he'd find us.

Either way, this situation would be resolved. The one with my parents I was less confident could be cleared up quickly.

"What can we do to help?" Dex asked.

"Throw three bales down from the loft, if you don't mind."

Cali finished eating, so I brought her out and put her on cross ties, got a hoof pick and brushes. It felt good to work, to focus on what I could do without thinking but always put my all into, the activity I loved more than anything.

By the time I had the mud cleaned out of Cali's feet, Dex and Miko were coming back down from the loft, and three bales sat in the middle of the aisle. I took the box knife we kept handy for this purpose and cut the twine holding the bales together.

"See how it comes off in sections?" I pointed this out for Miko's benefit, not Dex's.

He nodded. "I come from farm. I know hay."

"Great. Each horse gets two of these sections. Put some in each stall and six piles out in the field." I always put one extra because they often chased each from pile to pile like a horsey game of musical chairs.

Technically, two flakes of hay per horse wasn't accurate. If I were doing it myself, I would be more precise, adding a little or removing some according to the horse's size, but for today's purposes, nothing would be hurt by keeping it simple.

"Except Mikey," I said. "Pony in stall seven. He gets one."

Like most ponies, Mikey was an air fern constantly under explosion watch.

Dex and I watched Miko heft several flakes of hay and distribute them according to my orders. He looked like he'd done it before.

"Could be handy to have around," Dex said.

"I don't think it will be good for his health to hang around for too long."

Dex gave me a wry smile, got his gelding, Ciqala, put him on a second set of cross ties and started brushing him. I brought out Honey, known for falling asleep when being groomed, and clipped her to the third set of cross ties, figuring I'd see just how much Miko really knew.

When he'd finished putting hay out in the field, I handed him a set of tools.

"Did the farm you come from have horses?"

He nodded. "Yes. You know the Ukrainian Riding Horse?"

"No," I said. "I haven't heard of them. Is it a warmblood breed?"

"Yes, yes. From Hanoverian and Thoroughbred stock."

"That's a good cross. So, you have experience with them?"

"My uncle raised them. Before I become dancer, I want to be jumper rider. Like you, Viola Parker."

Small world. "Fantastic." I put my hand on Honey's neck. "This mare is an American quarter horse." She wasn't registered, but she had the right conformation. "They are also considered warmbloods because many of the breed's foundation sires were Thoroughbreds."

He stroked her back. "She is very beautiful. Like Russian doll."

"Clean her up and don't forget to pick out her feet."

Starting behind her ears, he flipped her mane to the opposite side of her neck and started brushing her with long, powerful strokes.

Honey's eyes rolled back in her head.

I fed the cats and went back to grooming Cali.

The rain had taken the edge off the scorching air, but it was humid. Before long, we were dripping, yet one by one, we put each horse on the cross ties and got them thoroughly groomed, something that didn't usually happen on a daily basis. Even Mikey, who Miko volunteered to take because he reminded him of his childhood, got polished up and his long mane and tail detangled. With the dust removed from his coat, his black patches shone, and his white parts gleamed.

I didn't want to like Miko but couldn't help it. Despite his fixation on my mother, he was good people. He had a gentle hand with the horses, worked tirelessly, and Noire approved of him, too. Considering the guy had probably been traveling for the past twenty-four hours, hadn't had breakfast, received a cool reception, been in a fight, and grilled by Malcolm, he was cheerful and uncomplaining.

It didn't hurt that he was easy on the eyes—a young, unsnarky, unsullied by drugs and alcohol version of Harry.

I was finishing up Fergus, Malcolm's old thoroughbred, when I heard Clara's Gator coming up the road.

I walked out to meet her. "Hey, Clara, you know we're on lockdown here."

"I know it. That's why I figured you could use some pie."

"I can always use some pie."

"Is that Dexter Hamill I see in there?"

Clara had once told me *that man can park his boots under my bed anytime.*

Dex came out and gave Clara a hug.

"How're you keeping, woman? You look younger every time I see you."

Seventy-some years old and she blushed.

"Fair to middlin, Dex. Yourself?"

"Truth be told, I've been better. But you shouldn't be out hot rodding on this thing alone."

"Now, Dexter Hamill, I appreciate your concern for these bones, but it's just a hop, skip and a jump from our place to here. Ain't nobody's gonna bother old Clara."

"I wouldn't be too sure about that. You stay alert, now, you hear?"

"I hear."

"I don't suppose you have any fresh-baked pie on you?"

Clara smiled coyly and pointed to a foil wrapped bundle on the passenger seat.

"I tried a new recipe—August pie. Because it's August. It's got peaches and raspberries in it."

The corners of Dex's coffee-colored eyes crinkled, and I was glad to see him smile.

"Sounds delicious," he said, injecting his tone with a sexy drawl.

Clara leaned around us to peer into the barn. "Got someone new working? Where's Zoe?"

"Erm...well, Zoe's off until we get our situation situated," I said.

Miko joined us. "I put Mikey to the field?"

"Yes," I answered. To Clara, I said, "This is Miko. He's..." How the hell did I explain this?

He wiped his hand on his jeans and stuck it out. "A friend of Miss Viola Parker's parents come to visit from Ukraine," he said. "Very cheerful to meet you I am."

"Oh." Clara fluttered her eyelashes. "The feeling's mutual, young man. Do you like pie?"

Miko's stomach rumbled by way of answer. "Yes, yes. Very much."

If he also liked whipped cream, that would seal the deal. I was keeping him.

"Well, it will be at the house when y'all are ready," Clara said. "I need to get back to the garden. Them tomatoes won't can themselves."

She motored off. We went back to work. A few minutes later, I heard her go by again.

We filled the water trough, picked up poop, put the last of the horses out, swept the aisle, and hung up the tools. I glanced at the clock in the tack room. Only ten a.m. It promised to be a long day. But pie would help. We went to the house.

There, my father and Malcolm sat in the living room, reading the paper. It was a week old, and I know Malcolm they'd both already read it. Giacomo snored in the recliner. My mother, apparently, was still upstairs. Leaving Dex and Miko in the kitchen, I went up, hoping there would still be August pie left when I returned.

She was not in their bedroom.

She was not in our bedroom.

Or the bathroom or the storeroom.

I went downstairs, double-checked the living room and sitting room and even the office before returning to Malcolm.

"Where's my mother?"

He glanced up, brows scrunched. "Still upstairs."

"No. She isn't."

My father sat forward. "What do you mean she isn't? She hasn't come down."

"I checked every room. She isn't up there."

"The attic?" Malcolm suggested.

I hadn't thought of that. All three of us trooped to the second floor, then up the narrow and steep stair that led to a sauna-like cobwebby space filled with boxes.

Unless she'd floated, thereby leaving no marks on the dusty floor, then folded herself inside one of the larger packing boxes, she wasn't there, either.

The phone rang.

We hurried back down, but Dex answered it before we got there.

"Oh, hey Hank," he said as we reached the kitchen. "Nope. Clara left about twenty minutes ago." He shared an alarmed look with Malcolm. "Yes, I'm sure. We were in the barn and heard the Gator go by."

Hank's panicked voice boomed from the other end of the line. "Well, she ain't here neither."

"We're on it." He hung up and was already to the front door when he yelled, "Clara didn't make it back to the house."

"Wait," I shouted. "My mother's missing, too."

CHAPTER THIRTY-ONE

WE BOLTED OUT of the house and ran down the driveway. After that, it was a hard right past the barn onto the gravel road that led to Hank and Clara's, a little less than a mile away. Malcolm, the ex-pentathlon guy, outstripped us. Dex was a close second, even with a prosthetic leg, but Adrian, in loafers, swore as he fell behind Miko who sprinted by in his running shoes. I ran as hard as I could, but it's not my thing, unless a horse is doing it beneath me.

As I went by the barn, I cut into the storage shed along the side. There, I hopped on the ATV and fired it up. I roared up behind my dad, skidded to a stop, and motioned him behind me.

He threw his leg over the seat.

"Hang on!" I yelled.

He grabbed my hips, and I gunned it. The road curved away from Winterlight and down into a densely forested ravine. It followed a creek for an eighth of a mile before ascending to level ground again where open fields spread to either side. Beyond that, it finally ended at Hank and Clara's. We caught up with the other three at the bottom of the hill. They bent over something on the road.

"Shit," I said.

"What? What is it?" my dad yelled, his voice strangled with fear. Either that or he'd swallowed a bug. "I can't see." His heart pounded my back.

I try not to panic until there's something to panic about. But Jesus God. My mother. Clara. I could barely breathe, didn't answer because I didn't know what was what.

I killed the engine and we joined them. Clara rolled on the ground, eyes wild, struggling against Dex and clearly screaming, "Get off me, get off me," even though she was gagged.

Malcolm always carried a multi-tool on his belt. He used it to cut the zip ties holding Clara's hands. She came up swinging.

"Clara!" Dex took her by the shoulders and shook her. "It's me, Dex. Calm down."

She blinked, took a breath, stilled, then went limp just as Hank came up the road from the opposite direction on their ATV. Dex and Malcolm eased Clara to a sitting position and untied the black bandana used to gag her.

"Oh my God," she wheezed, one hand covering her heart. "Oh my God."

Hank shuffle-ran to kneel at her side and touched her cheek. "Clara, it's me, Hank, your husband. Are you all right? Do you know me?"

She looked at him like he was a giant flopping fish that'd materialized out of thin air. "Of course I know you, you old fool. I got tied up, not bonked on the head."

Malcolm and Dex both let out a breath.

Dex crouched beside her, his good leg folded beneath him, the other straight out to the side. "Was Gemma with you?"

"'Course she was. She wanted to help with the tomatoes."

"What happened to the Gator?" I asked.

Clara looked around and then at each of our faces. "I don't know. It all happened so fast. He took Gemma…" She put her face in her hands. "Oh, no. It's all my fault."

"No," Hank soothed. "No it ain't."

"But she said you knew." She sent a pleading look at Dex. "Said you said it was okay for her to come with me back to our house." Her gaze landed on Adrian. "I'm so sorry." She started to cry.

Miko said, "I cannot understand what is happened. Where is my Gemma? Does she go to tango with another man?"

Too late, I saw a white-hot rage boil over in my father. He swung around and punched Miko in the jaw. Miko spun and face planted in the dirt. He flipped himself over only to find my father straddling him, flexing his fingers like he'd take any excuse to hit the boy again.

Malcolm and Dex grabbed Dad's arms, pulled him back.

"Let's be clear on what happened before anyone throws any more punches or accusations," Malcolm said. "Clara, the man who did this, did he say his name? Can you describe him?"

Clara put her hand over her heart. She still hadn't caught her breath. "He stopped us with a gun and made us get out and lie on the ground. Tied us up and gagged us. I mean, I guess he gagged Gemma. I couldn't really see."

"There, there, now," Hank said. "You couldn't have done nothin.'" He put his arm around her. "Can't you see she can hardly breathe? Give her a minute."

Frustrated with how long this was taking, I said, "I'm sorry, but I don't think we have a minute."

"You saw him, right?" Malcolm prompted gently. "Before he tied you up?"

She put one hand on Hank's shoulder to keep him calm. "Yeah. I seen him. Ugly old thing. One side of his face was scarred up bad." She touched her fingertips to her eyebrow as if to make sure it was still the same as it had been that morning. "He put that gun barrel right against my neck. Cold as death." She shivered.

"Did he say where he was taking her?" my father asked.

Clara shook her head. "He just said, 'You tell Giacomo I take everything he loves. He must come alone.'"

"Come where?" I asked.

"He didn't say. He just shoved me with that gun." She rubbed her neck. "I'll never forget how that felt." She got to her feet. "He was wearing a black eye patch. Does that help?"

I hadn't doubted it was Benito, but that confirmed it.

"Thanks, Clara, very helpful," Dex said. "If you remember anything else, let me know right away, okay?"

"There is one other thing," she said, brushing her hands together.

We all looked at her, hoping for the one piece of information that would lead us to my mother.

"He took my Gator."

CHAPTER THIRTY-TWO

MIKO SPRANG TO HIS FEET. "This is bad. Who is this man who took her? Why he take her?" He'd been cradling his jaw, but he put his hands to either side of his head and turned in a circle. "Gemma," he yelled. Then louder, "Gemma!"

"I doubt she'd hear you," Clara said, "even if they was in range. That Gator's so loud it drowns out the cicadas."

Miko's arms dropped to his sides. My father shook out his hand. I imagined his knuckles stung. I flexed my fingers, still sore from punching in a window. The glass probably had more give than Miko's face.

"My father's cousin, Benito, is out for revenge over a long-ago killing," my father explained to Miko. "It's a long story."

Dex kicked at the underbrush along the edge of the shoulder. Shortly past Winterlight, the county maintenance ended and it became a private road. That meant it was more dirt than gravel. And that meant tracks would be a lot easier to see.

"Clara, that Gator has eight-inch heavy-duty field tires on it, right?

"I don't know." Clara looked at Hank.

"Yep. Just put new ones on." He went over to Dex and Malcolm. "Six of 'em set me back five hundred dollars."

They all studied the road surface. I held my breath.

"He didn't turn around," Malcolm said.

Adrian and Miko joined the party, so I figured I would as well.

"He went this way." Dex pointed toward Hank and Clara's place.

"He couldn't have gone far," my father said, "or he would have ended up there, right?"

Hank rubbed his chin. "I would have seen the Gator on my way here."

Malcolm's eyes narrowed. "There's a path off this road that runs along the creek and eventually hooks up with our trails." He traced a line in the air that must have followed the path through the woods. "It's rough in spots. We almost never use it, but the Gator could make it part of the way. After that, they'd have to be on foot."

I was already headed to the ATV. "I know the trail you mean. A horse could make it." We didn't have a moment to lose.

"Don't go off half cocked, Miss Parker," Dex yelled.

"She's right," Malcolm said. He followed me.

"Take our ATV," Hank said. "Clara, you can walk from here, right?"

Clara lifted her chin. "Of course."

"Benito probably has a car parked somewhere," my father said.

Malcolm jogged ahead of me and got the ATV started. "Hank, are you sure you two are all right?"

Hank nodded.

"Get that bastard," Clara said.

"Vi and Miko with me. Dex, bring Adrian."

We sped back to Winterlight.

At the barn, I took charge, grabbing tack for each horse and giving it to who needed it. I took Miko's arm as I handed him Miss Bong's bridle. She was great for bulldozing through the woods, and I knew Dex Two would want us to use her.

"You really can ride, right? Not just ring stuff, but real riding?"

He grinned and pulled himself taller. "Yes, Viola Parker. I am like American cowboy."

Not really an answer. "We'll leave you if you can't keep up." I gave him a spare helmet.

He took the bridle and helmet from me. "I have boots in backpack. I can get?"

"Hurry up."

He sprinted out of the barn. Dex always wore boots, as did I, and Malcolm had a spare pair in the tack room. Each of us took our own horse. My father watched us, looking helpless. I realized we'd left Giacomo alone in the house. What a bunch of freaking *idiotas*.

"Dad, can you go check on Giacomo, make sure he hasn't gotten himself into trouble or wandered off?"

Malcolm came up. "Adrian, we need you at the house to man the phone. You good with that?"

Adrian nodded to both of us and turned to go to the house.

Noire stood on her toes and pirouetted around me, excited we were all going riding.

"You're the good girl," I said to her. "But you can't come with us today. Dad?" He stopped and looked at me. "Can you take Noire with you?" I attached a lead line to her collar to make it easier.

He took the leash, then jerked me against his chest. "Be careful and bring her back."

I blinked and nodded.

Dex had gone to his truck and returned carrying a duffle bag. He stopped my father on his way out and gave him a walkie-talkie, then brought one to each of us. He was limping more than usual, which meant the fake leg was bothering him. The run probably hadn't helped. I frowned at him, and he gave me a look, so I let it go and clipped the radio onto the back of my waist-band. He'd communicated our plans with his second who'd been out patrolling. Unfortunately, not in the area where Benito had been. The guy was slippery.

"Miss Parker," Dex said. "You and Miko follow the trail they took. Let me know when you find the Gator."

I knew what Dex was thinking. This put me and Miko the farthest behind Benito. He and Malcolm would take point and hopefully catch up with them, rescue Gemma, and take down Benito without our involvement.

I guess I didn't answer fast enough, because he added, "This is important, Vi."

He almost never used my first name. "I got it. What do we do after that?"

"Keep going. We'll come around from the other direction."

Miko returned wearing a pair of highly polished oxblood paddock boots. "We close Benito in vise," he said.

Dex nodded to him. "Any chance you know how to handle a weapon?"

Miko shook his head. "I throw knife okay."

"Works for me," Dex said. He handed Miko a walkie-talkie, showed him how to use it, then produced a sheathed knife and gave that to him.

Dex looked at me. I lifted my hands. "I'll hold the horses."

"You'll also hold this." He crouched, strapped a small handgun to my ankle, and pulled my pants leg over it. "In case I lose mine."

"Right. In case you lose yours."

He cracked a half smile. "It's the same one you had last time. You remember how to use it?"

"I remember it has no nail." I said this on purpose to annoy him.

"No hammer," he said with a shake of his head.

Our radios sputtered and Dad's voice came through.

"Um, ten-four? The package is secure."

Oh brother. Someone had been watching too much television.

We mounted up. Malcolm brought Gaston alongside Cali, put his hand on my arm. "You have your phone, too?"

I patted myself down. "Nope. Don't know where it is."

"And if you did, it probably has no battery power."

"Too right."

"When this is over—"

"Are you going to spank me?"

He gave me a look. Neither of us were into that, but I liked to tease him.

"You're getting a new phone, and you're going to keep track of it."

I saluted. He dragged me close enough to kiss. With our helmets on, we had to tilt our heads to reach. Warmth washed through me at how he'd taken on my parents and this whole thing with Giacomo and Benito without a second thought. If he had second thoughts, he kept them to himself. I still couldn't believe he hadn't kicked us all out. With a final encouraging squeeze to my arm, he turned Gaston to catch up with Dex and Ciqala. I watched until they trotted past the house and disappeared around the bend.

I double checked Cali's girth and noticed Miko doing the same. So far, so good. I squeezed her straight into a solid working trot. Miko came alongside, moderating Miss Bong's huge stride to match Cali's. He posted in rhythm with me. His heels were down, his hands close together, but not too close, and he kept a light contact with Bongo's mouth. Good. She didn't need or like heavy hands.

Cali protested my inattention with a toss of her head. She sensed our edginess, curled her neck and champed the bit in anticipation of speed. I relaxed my fingers a hair. Miss Bong, older and half draft, would stay steady. She was very close in type to the horses Miko was used to riding. I nodded at him. He gave me a grim smile in return.

We stayed on the grassy shoulder until the gravel ran out and the footing became more forgiving, then picked up canter. At the top of the hill, I slowed to trot again for the descent, watching Miko out of the corner of my eye the whole way. He was fine.

We picked up canter at the bottom, found the trail, trotted the turn into the woods, then went back to canter. Soon, the path narrowed, so Miko pulled behind, and I gave Cali her head.

We galloped. Under normal circumstances, I love to ride after it rains and would give myself over to the sensory pleasure of my horse's stride, the sound of her hoofbeats thudding the ground, the scent of the forest. Today, I concentrated on the trees, the footing, the turns, and what lay ahead.

During one straight stretch, I spared a glance behind me. Both Miko and Miss Bong had clods of dirt on their faces and chest kicked up by Cali's hooves. Miko gave me a jaunty wave. I'm not sure he truly understood the seriousness of the situation. Maybe that was just as well.

The Gator tracks were easy to see in the low, muddy spots. Any grass and brush obscuring the ground had been squashed flat by the heavy vehicle. Clearly, Benito wasn't worried about being followed.

Maybe he wanted to be followed? If so, it changed nothing.

I slowed a little. Something on the ground at the side caught my eye.

"Hold up," I said so my sudden stop wouldn't cause a collision. I pulled Cali down to walk, circled back, and hopped to the ground.

"What is?"

"Hang on."

The horses snorted and shook themselves out, rattling the saddle flaps and stirrup leathers.

I leaned down. There, in a clump of tall yellow flowers, a cigarette, unsmoked. I plucked it out.

Miko dismounted, took it from me, and turned it between his fingers, pointing at the brand name printed on the side. "This belong to Gemma. She tries to quit but still smoke on the bad day."

"The bad day?"

He shrugged. What were the bad days like, I wondered? It didn't matter right now. We already knew they came this way. Now we knew my mother was all right at least at this point.

We kept going.

Not much farther along we came upon the empty Gator parked where a large tree had fallen, blocking the path.

We stood there for a few minutes, listening, but the woods were quiet except for bird song. We dismounted again and walked around the vehicle. I radioed Dex and Malcolm our location. They were twenty minutes from the expected rendezvous point. Dex said to wait for further instructions.

I was examining the passenger side for any trace or clue when I heard Miko gasp. I looked over to him. He pointed at a red handprint on the driver's seat.

Blood.

CHAPTER THIRTY-THREE

ALL COLOR SEEPED out of Miko's face like it'd been siphoned off by a hose. His eyelids fluttered.

"Oh, crap. Don't faint, don't—"

His fingers opened on Miss Bong's reins. He began to crumple to one side. With my reins looped around my shoulder, I hopped across the seat and shoved my hands into his armpits as he slid to the ground. But Cali didn't like being on one side of the Gator and me on the other. She shifted into reverse, taking me with her. I lost my grip on Miko as she wrenched me back. I let go of him to keep hold of Cali. Miss Bong wandered off in search of grass to nibble, her reins dragging on the ground. I wasn't confident she would stick around when she realized no one was paying attention, and I didn't need two horses to chase.

"Shit, shit, shit."

I scrambled off my side of the Gator and dragged Cali over to Miss Bong. The big mare let me catch her, thank goodness. I hate tying horses by the reins, but there was no choice. I found a sturdy tree and attached them to it as best I good, then went to Miko.

He lay on his side next to the Gator, out, and still very pale. I rolled him to his back, tapped his cheek. He felt cold.

"C'mon, Miko. Wake up." I unsnapped his helmet and slid it off, doing the same with mine.

The Gator had cup holders and one held a grubby half bottle of water. I opened it and splashed a little over his face.

Nothing.

I wriggled my arm under his shoulders, lifted him, and dribbled water into his mouth. Most of it ran over his chin.

No response.

Had he fainted because of the blood, or the thought it might be Gemma's —which I refused to consider—or simply because he was exhausted and hadn't eaten? We should have left him at the house, made him eat and rest. So stupid.

I reached for the walkie-talkie, but it wasn't attached to my waistband. Thinking I must have dropped it when Cali yanked me through the Gator, I climbed over the seats and looked, but it wasn't there. On the other side, I got on all fours and searched the ground.

A shadow fell across me at the same time something cold touched the back of my neck. For a moment, I thought the horses had gotten loose and Cali was nibbling on me.

But then my brain caught up and registered that sensation, one I'd felt before.

A gun barrel.

"Don't move and don't make a sound."

The voice was low and very close to my ear. It wasn't familiar, but I knew who it was. I'd like to say I whirled around and disarmed him, shot him in the knee and saved the day, but I'd stopped breathing when the cold metal touched my skin, and I could only do exactly what he said.

"Lie flat and put your hands behind you."

He pressed his foot to the small of my back to underscore his order. I dropped to my belly and crossed my wrists. The zip ties were tight and cut into my skin. I gritted my teeth as he tugged me to my knees, forced my mouth open, and tied a bandana around my face as a gag.

I still hadn't seen him. Didn't want to.

The whole time, I imagined Miko waking up and conking my assailant on the head.

He didn't.

Jabbing the pistol's muzzle between my shoulder blades, Benito shoved me forward, off the trail, and into the woods.

CHAPTER THIRTY-FOUR

BENITO FROGMARCHED me away from the trail at a steep angle and down into a ravine. We were quickly well out of sight of everyone and everything. Thick underbrush snagged at my jeans, and branches scraped my face. I turned my head into them, hoping some of my hair would get caught and leave a clue as to what direction we'd gone. I also scuffed the ground hard when I could.

Which reminded me I still had Dex's gun strapped to my ankle. I couldn't reach it and would probably shoot myself in the foot before I'd make good use of it.

Ed Todd hadn't liked guns, either. I don't know why I thought of him at that moment. But he hadn't been far from my thoughts since the call from Harry. Ed, though, he'd fought in Viet Nam, so he knew how to use all kinds of weapons and had been a good shot. He'd admitted it was a handy skill to have.

He often said it was better to have and not need than to need and not have.

If I got out of this alive, I'd let Malcolm and Dex teach me to shoot. I'd overcome my fear and revulsion of guns, get good at using them, and hope I never needed one again.

Ever.

Because once I did know how to use one, then I wouldn't need it, right? That's how it works.

Now, I tried to remember everything Dex had showed me last May. We'd practiced a stance and how to hold the weapon with two hands. To keep my finger off the trigger until I was ready to fire. Not to point it at anything I didn't intend to kill.

I'd wait. Maybe a chance would come when I could reach it and use it. I'd catch Benito off guard. As if. I had a bad feeling that Benito, like Dex, would be almost impossible to sneak up on.

Within a couple of minutes, we reached my mother. Profound relief dropped me to my knees in front of her where she sat tied to a tree. Like me, she wore a gag and her hands were zip tied behind her. The guy had come prepared. But then, he'd had about fifty years to plan.

I looked her over quick and didn't see any obvious injury. Nothing to account for the bloody handprint on the driver's seat. With my eyes, I tried to ask if she was all right. She nodded to confirm.

Benito had a bandana tied around his bicep. Blood had seeped through it. More ran down his arm. The print on the seat had been his. Had my mother done that to him? God, I hoped so. Or maybe it was Clara. She almost always had a knife on her. You never knew when you might have to slice up a pie. Or a murderer.

Benito untied Mom from the tree and lifted her to her feet. For a moment, he was distracted. I could have run. He probably wouldn't have shot me for fear of the sound drawing others to us.

More likely I'd trip and knock myself out.

Finally, I got a look at him. He was shorter than both of us and nearly as slim. Surely we could take him? We were at a disadvantage with our hands bound, but maybe. I forced myself to be hopeful.

Malcolm and Dex would find us.

Benito would make a mistake.

Mom and I would sit on him until help arrived.

He wore a patch over his left eye, just as Clara had said. His forehead, cheek, and temple were scarred and lumpy, his nose one sided, his cheek caved in. Even his hairline was uneven. Apparently, plastic surgery hadn't been an option. Giacomo had never said what kind of gun they'd had that terrible morning. I'd assumed a pistol but wondered now if it'd been a shotgun.

My thoughts swung to Josephine dying at the hands of the man who supposedly loved her while delivering new life.

Adrian. My father.

I shook it off, needed to stay focused, but then my thoughts swung to Clara and what he'd done to her. Then to Miko, lying alone and unconscious in an unfamiliar forest. The horses might or might not still be there when he awoke. If he awoke.

Benito didn't speak. He ran a narrow blue nylon rope through my arms and my mother's so we were connected to each other, pointed in the direction he wanted us to go, and drove us from behind.

My mother's pretty pleated white skirt had a scalloped edge at the hem. It was torn and dirty. Her bare arms and legs were scratched and bleeding, but it all looked superficial. The yellow espadrilles she wore weren't practical for traipsing through the woods, but they were better than sandals. They were soaked and dirty, though, so she'd been through the creek. Her small cross-body purse still hung at her hip. That must have been where the cigarette had come from. Much good it would do us.

I tried to talk around the bandana. It was stiff with newness, so at least I knew it was clean, but it didn't exactly taste good.

"Where are you taking us?" That's what I heard in my head, but to anyone listening, I'm sure it was unintelligible.

Apparently no one was listening, because I got no answer. My mother slid me a look with a slight shake of her head. She must have already tried talking to him. Benito was a cool customer. My guess was he was going to use us as bait to lure Giacomo to whatever he had planned for him.

Taking his eye, for starters.

Would he take ours?

Sweat broke out on my forehead and stung my eyes, making me keenly aware that I had two. Benito had only one. He wanted everyone to be like him. Half blind and disfigured.

None of this was insight. It was all supposition, all to keep myself from thinking about what might happen. I tried to pay attention to our direction but was lost once we were off the path. It was around midday, so the angle of the sun was no help.

I lost track of time, too. Neither my mother nor I wore a watch, and we couldn't have seen it if we were. But I'd guess we walked for at least an hour. We stopped once and crouched while Benito listened, but it wasn't anyone coming to save us, and we moved on.

My mother began to trip every few steps, and I did what I could to keep her from falling. I was hot and thirsty and beginning to feel light-headed. Where was a can of whipped cream when you needed it?

Eventually, we stepped out onto a trail I knew. It was far to the east end of the property and ended at Helen's house.

Helen was Malcolm's mother. He had his own weird and convoluted family history, and hadn't known until recently who his biological mother was. When Helen revealed the truth, he'd gifted her a few acres of land, and she'd installed a pre-manufactured home. We visited with her weekly. They'd become friends.

What did it mean that we were headed in that direction now? Perhaps that once we reached her house, we'd be at a paved road. Where Benito probably had a car, just as my father had said.

Once we were off the land, we'd be much harder to find. There had to be a way to keep that from happening or at least delay it.

We reached Helen's house, walked across the yard, and entered the back door. Benito wasn't worried about us seeing where we were, and there was no one nearby to see that there was a strange man going in and out of Helen's house.

Was she even still alive?

Bile rose in my throat. I stumbled over the threshold and fell on the hard floor of the kitchen, pulling my mother down beside me.

All looked in order.

Benito hauled us to our feet, dragged us into the living room and sat us on the couch. If he'd hurt Helen…

Where was she? If she'd been going out of town, she'd have told us. Her tabby cat, Sylvester, jumped up on the couch, purring.

Benito patted the cat's head, and the cat let him. I was seriously confused, even though Giacomo had said Benito liked animals.

Banging came from down the hall. Muffled cries. It could be Helen. Did he have her gagged and tied in the bathroom?

Benito disappeared around the corner and came back with her, trussed up just like us. He slit her zip ties with a wicked looking curved blade that had a very pointy tip. He removed her bandana as well.

"You bastard," she spat. "I've been in that room for days. I'm starving and I need clean underwear." She rubbed her wrists.

"Get them drinks." He waved his gun at her.

What the hell was going on?

He removed our bandanas.

"What the hell is going on?" I said. "Helen, are you all right?"

Helen scurried to the kitchen. Her ankles were hobbled so she could take only small steps, but she returned with a glass of water for each of us. "I'm all right. What the hell is going on?"

The question of the day.

She put a glass to my lips. I shook my head. "My mother, first."

Mom drank, then I did. "Has he told you anything?" I asked.

Helen shook her head.

"Why are you doing what he wants?" my mother asked her.

"He said he'd kill Robert if I didn't."

Sharp pain shot through my chest. Robert is Malcolm's first name. Her son. I've always used his last name, because most people do. When he asked me to call him by his first name, I tried. For about a day. It felt too intimate. Since he's still my boss, I needed the appearance of keeping my distance, even if it's only pretend.

I blew out a noisy breath. "Helen, this is my mother, Gemma." They nodded to each other. "And that's Benito, the eye thief."

Benito smiled with only one side of his mouth. "Benito Antonio Colombo," he said with a tip of his chin.

"Benito and my grandfather, Giacomo—"

"Wait," Helen said, "I thought you and your parents..."

"We were. They came to visit. It's a long story. What matters now is Benito and Giacomo were in love with the same woman, Josephine."

"Ah, Josephine," Benito said in much the same tone Giacomo had. She must have been quite a woman. "I have never loved another."

"Right," I said with a sarcastic frown at him. "But she loved and married Giacomo. And this dick, here, he killed her."

Benito sprung to his feet. "No!" He pointed both the gun and the knife at me. "It was Edwardo, the stupid *coglione*," he hissed. "He missed Giacomo and hit my Josephine."

"She wasn't your Josephine." The words crossed my lips that fast. I really needed to fix the broken connection between my brain and mouth.

One swift stride and he had the knife pressed to my left cheek.

"You're just like her. Beautiful and bold. If not for that, I would take your eye right now." He tucked the pistol under his arm, dug in his pocket, brought out a black marble, and held it in front of my face. "You want one of your own?" He pushed it closer. "Do you?"

Afraid to move, breathe, or blink, I whispered, "No."

He pocketed the marble and removed the knife. "Good. Then shut it."

I nodded, let out my breath. My mother exhaled, too.

Before he could make it back to the loveseat, I quietly said, "Still, she died because of you."

He whirled on me. "Because of Eduardo! And I shot him. My own brother. I killed him because he killed her."

Geez. Meanwhile, Giacomo had spent the rest of his life feeling guilty about the little brother.

"But Giacomo," he continued, "he did this." He tapped his eye patch. "He took Josephine from me, and he took my eye. Now, he will pay in kind."

I didn't like the sound of that, but I didn't like any of this.

After a few moments, my mother asked, "Now what?"

Benito sat on the love seat. He rested the pistol on one thigh and the long, curved knife on the other. "Contrary to what my cousin might have told you, I am not a barbarian." The good side of his face smiled. The bad side, the left, seemed frozen. "Now," he continued, "we take refreshment before moving on to the next leg of my journey." He paused to press his fist to his mouth. "The final stop. The end."

CHAPTER THIRTY-FIVE

OBEDIENT AS A PET DOG, Helen made peanut butter and jelly sandwiches and fed them to us. If I were her, I'd do the same, especially if someone I loved was threatened. There was nothing about Benito that suggested he wouldn't follow up on his threat. Benito, thankfully, fed himself, his chewing awkward and messy. When we finished, he untied one of us at a time, and we got a potty break. I tried to find something in there to hit him over the head with, but the room had been stripped bare as a truck-stop toilet.

He zip tied Helen's hands again, gagged her and secured her in the bathroom. Our bandanas were stuffed in our mouths and tightened. He took us out the front, and shoved us through the back door of a windowless cargo van, slamming and locking it behind us. The van was old and rusty and had a business's name painted on the outside—nothing I could make sense of—nothing that connected it with the images in my dreams. Inside, it was dark and smelled of dirt, but once my eyes adjusted, a quick glance told me a sturdy plywood wall separated the front seats and the rear. The ceiling and sides were unfinished.

And there by the door, lying on its side, Giacomo's tomato plant, one bra strap still tangled in its branches. It looked like the rest of my bra had been shut in the door. The plant needed more dirt and a good watering. Next to it, a plastic sandwich bag of black marbles. I shuddered.

Benito didn't get in the van right away. Was he going back to the house?

My mother mumbled something.

"Shhh," I forced through the bandana.

The front door of the house opened and a moment later, a *pop pop* came from inside.

A wail escaped me. "Nooo."

My mother's face scrunched into a question.

"I think he just killed Helen," I cried. "Oh my God, no."

Mom got the gist of what I said, and her eyes squeezed shut. A tear slipped out, then another. My cheeks were wet as well.

Benito really was a *bastardo* no matter his civilized pretense.

The driver's door of the van opened and the vehicle dipped as Benito got in. Bad shocks. A moment later, we were moving. We took a left out of the driveway. That direction led to the highway.

Shoving my desperation and horror aside, I communicated to my mother to lie down on her side with her back to me. I did the same so that my fingers were level with the back of her head. After nearly fifteen minutes of frustrated picking and accidental hair pulling, I got the knot in her bandana loosened enough for her to spit it out. She moved her jaw around to stretch it, then undid my bandana, getting it done more quickly then I had hers, probably because she had longer fingernails.

We were on the highway now, traveling fast. It was hot, but there was a vent in the partition, so a little cooler air leaked in.

It also meant Benito might be able to hear us, even over the sound of the engine, the air-conditioning fan on high, the radio blasting oldies, and the rusty vehicle's squeaks and rattles. There was no need for him to know we'd freed our voices.

Mom started to say something, but I shushed her and motioned her to my side of the van so we could sit next to each other.

She leaned close and asked, "What's going to happen?"

Who could guess what was in the mind of someone like Benito? Keeping my voice low, I said, "I think he wants to lure Giacomo somewhere so he can kill him. Where and when, no idea."

He'd probably kill us, too, maybe as a way to torture Giacomo, but I saw no reason to say that out loud. Instead, I wriggled around to check every crevice and opening, looking for a way to cut through our restraints. To the side of the sliding door, there were a series of openings with a rough inside edge. Getting my wrists in there to saw through the plastic ties would be awkward, but I had to try.

I tilted my head to motion Mom close again, and whispered, "Are you all right? Did he hurt you?"

She shook her head. "I'm glad he didn't tie my ankles." She crossed them and stared at her feet.

She was probably imagining she'd dance again. With Miko? With Dad? Did it matter? I doubted Benito's future vision for us included gliding across the ballroom floor. Looking at my mother's feet, I couldn't help but picture Helen's bound ankles. Oh God, poor Helen.

"I'm sorry I ran away," my mother muttered. "I had to get out of the house. Adrian and Miko…" She frowned and shook her head again, sighed.

Too well, I knew that urge to run, to escape conflict, especially if I'd caused it. The muscles in my arms already hurt, so I stopped sawing for a minute.

"I have a gun," I whispered.

"You…what? Why haven't you used it?"

I gave her a look. "It's strapped to my ankle, so I can't reach it. Plus, I don't like guns, plus I'm not sure how to use it."

"Why do you have it if you don't like it?"

"Dex made me take it when we went looking for you."

Leaning on the hump made by the wheel well, she tilted her head back and looked at the ceiling, clearly feeling badly about her ill-conceived escape.

"How did you get out of the house?"

"Climbed out the window onto the back porch roof. Used that big bush next to it to get down."

More resourceful than I would have given her credit for.

"Is Clara all right?" she asked.

"She is. Miko I'm not so sure about."

"What do you mean?" Her voice rose. "Did Adrian—"

"Shhh. Not Dad. Miko and I were riding—"

"You went riding?"

"Not like that. Geez. Give me a minute to explain."

She pursed her lips but stayed quiet while I explained how we found Clara, then went out searching, leaving Dad and Giacomo at the house. When I told her Miko had passed out, she frowned.

"I keep telling him he has to eat. He's worried about gaining weight. It's ridiculous."

I started back to cut through the ties. "Mom, what, exactly, is your relationship with Miko? And why is Dad so upset?"

"*He's* upset?" She started getting loud again, I widened my eyes and she sputtered, "What about me? If it weren't for him—"

"Start at the beginning."

The van leaned hard as if careening around a curve, maybe getting off at an exit. The bag of marbles shifted and several rolled out, pinging around the interior and dropping into whatever pocket they came to like pin balls. We braced ourselves until the van leveled, following the course of the marbles with morbid fascination. Benito must have gone from one highway to another. I wasn't familiar enough with the road system to guess where we were or might be headed.

"Earlier," I said, trying again to cut the zip ties, "you told Dad not to eat whipped cream because it would make him fat. Don't you think you're sending mixed messages?"

"Miko is still growing. He doesn't have to worry about gaining weight. Your father is nearly fifty and starting to go soft around the middle."

"Oh my God, are you serious?" Now my volume rose. I took a breath to calm myself before continuing on a hush. "The man is lean as a sapling."

Mom rolled her eyes. "I see him naked."

"Too much information."

She also inhaled deeply through her nose, let it out slowly. I could tell not having her hands free was driving her crazy. She needed to clasp them, or drum her fingers. Maybe even chew her nails.

"Miko was your father's idea."

"What's that supposed to mean?"

"He hurt himself, your father. It's been several months ago now. He twisted his knee and tore his ACL. He had to rest and do physical therapy. But I needed to keep practicing."

I knew a thing or two about the stress of competition—how it wore on you both mentally and physically. "So, you've been competing all these years?"

"Yes, but not as much as in the past. We decided to open a studio in Paris and teach."

I rested my arms, couldn't tell if I was making progress other than chafing my wrists raw. "Sounds very romantic," I said, fighting my sarcastic tone, but losing. "I suppose your studio was upstairs from a bakery and had high ceilings and tall windows that opened onto charming Juliet balconies." Bitterness leaked out, even at a whisper, but I couldn't seem to stop myself. "And you ate fresh baguettes for breakfast topped with artisan cheese, and drank *chocolat*." I spat out the last with as close to a French accent as I could muster.

Her neck lengthened and her eyes narrowed slightly. There was the haughty woman I knew. But I can't say I was proud of my childish display or my winning ability to bring out her worst.

"There *was* a bakery on the corner. That's not uncommon in Paris. We were struggling, but getting more clients all the time. Investors helped us get started. After all, we'd made quite a name for ourselves over the years."

Did any of this really matter given our situation? It did. I needed to know, even if learning the details hurt. "*So* happy for you." I renewed my sawing with extra energy. Sweat soaked my T-shirt and stung my eyes.

"Why are you so angry?" she hissed.

My arms stilled. My whole body went stiff, and the hurt child inside me roared awake. "Oh, I don't know, Mom, maybe it has to do with the way you left me to be raised by someone else and never—" My voice cracked. I cleared my throat. "You never made any effort to see me or know me." I despised how shaky I sounded.

Her breathing accelerated. I could practically hear her heart pounding inside her chest. "I tried. I wanted to. But Trudy…"

"Now you're going to blame it on Aunt Trudy? Like she didn't have enough to deal with caring for your infant when she was already pregnant with Penny and then having her own baby so it was like raising twins?"

"Is that what she told you?"

The radio up front suddenly cut out. I froze and bit down on what I'd been about to say while my mother and I held our breath. A tense minute later, the radio volume went back up, but not as loud as it had been before.

Keeping my voice down, I said, "Aunt Trudy didn't have to tell me. That's the way it was."

My mother shook her head slowly. She chewed her lip. She was always so tightly restrained. What I'd said rattled her. Her mind was racing. I saw it in her eyes.

Haltingly, she said, "That's not actually the way it was."

I let out a frustrated breath. "Okay. Tell me how it really was." I couldn't wait to hear her side of it.

Her mouth close to my ear, as if we were teenagers sharing a secret, she said, "Trudy is eight years older than me. She and Vic were about to celebrate their fifth anniversary, childless *again*. They wanted babies so badly. Then I got pregnant. Your father and I barely passed each other in the hallway—"

I pulled away from her. "You had to do a little more than that to get pregnant, Mom, come on."

"Of course we did. But I mean I got pregnant the first time. Trudy was so angry. Not just because I hadn't finished high school, but because she wanted to have a baby and couldn't, and I—"

"Didn't want a baby but got pregnant without trying. I get it."

"No."

Too loud, too loud.

Benito banged on the partition and yelled, "You'd better not be talking back there!"

He seemed to listen for a few minutes, but then forget about us as soon as

Frank Sinatra's "New York, New York" came on, and he launched into a spirited singalong.

My mother and I relaxed a hair.

"No," she repeated. "You *don't* get it. It's not that I didn't want to have children, Vi, I did. But not that young."

"Fair enough. I can understand that. But if Aunt Trudy was already pregnant with Penny, what was the big deal?"

"That's just it. She wasn't."

"But…" Now I was the one baffled. "Our birthdays. Penny and I are only six months apart."

My mother gave a small shake of her head almost like she was trying to loosen something stuck in her ear, then put her lips near mine again. "She wasn't pregnant, or if she was, it was very early, and she didn't know yet. She insisted I give you to her to raise. Ordered it."

Aunt Trudy was very…*demanding* about what she wanted, so this didn't surprise me.

Mom continued. "Her pregnancy wasn't easy—whereas mine was—and she had Penny prematurely. That's why your birthdays are only six months apart."

Penny had been premature? How could I not know that? We both fell silent. The van had made another turn and began to slow. It stopped, then started again, stopped, started, bouncing every time Benito jammed the brakes. He honked his horn and cursed. We were stuck in traffic. Did that mean we were in the city?

"And then," my mother went on quickly, "Trudy said it would be best if I didn't contact you. It was too upsetting and confusing. You have to understand. I looked up to her. She's my big sister. And she was so happy to have children."

"And you were so young," I murmured, as much to myself as to her.

Adrift in a swirl of thoughts and feelings, I wondered why I couldn't have heard this story when I had Malcolm to hold on to.

Geez. Malcolm. Where was he? They'd surely found the Gator, horses, and Miko by now. Had they been able to follow us? Found Helen? What would Malcolm do when he found his mother dead? My throat got tight, and the pain in my chest made it hard to breathe. I pushed those thoughts away again, tried to concentrate on keeping our day from ending the same way.

Mom nodded. "It seemed to make sense at the time. Your father and I were free to pursue our dream. But…" She rose to her knees, sat on one hip, leaned.

The van jerked to the left as if Benito had abruptly changed lanes. She fell against me. I couldn't catch her, had made no progress freeing myself. All I could do was stick my shoulder out to keep her from falling flat.

She looked at me. In the dim interior of the van, her eyes were wide, glittering, her brow pinched.

My eyes, *my* brows.

She leaned her forehead against mine. "Vi, my sweet girl, my entire body ached for you, to hold you, to smell you, to feel your soft skin against mine. Your father, he didn't say much, but he was so sad." She wiped her face on my shoulder. "We were a sorry pair."

My heart constricted so hard I thought it would stop. My mother had missed me? "I…um…" Coherent thought fled. "It's going to take me a while to process this, Mom. It's so different from what I've thought my whole life."

"Trudy told me she had told you the truth."

It was my turn to look away, to turn from the pain within what she said. "No, she never told me."

My aunt, who had raised me and who I'd looked to as my mother for so long, had lied to me. For what? To punish her little sister? She'd kept that anger close, nurtured it, just as I had mine. Aunt Trudy had never exactly disparaged my parents, not in so many words, but she'd made it clear they didn't want me. That she had. That she was my true mother.

Was it possible the one person I'd thought responsible for my sanity was actually the one responsible for my insanity?

My hatred of my parents had made me who I was. Strong but resentful with a defensive attitude that kept people at more than arm's length. Unfailingly committed to my horses but trusting of critters more than people. So fearful of abandonment that I desert others before they can reject me, just as I'd been cast aside as a baby.

Or thought I'd been.

We hurtled toward God only knows what Benito had planned for us, I had yet to learn where Miko fit in, I'd probably never see Malcolm again—the one person I'd allowed inside my thick walls—and none of it really mattered because my entire freaking life was a lie.

CHAPTER THIRTY-SIX

A SHORT TIME LATER, we must have gotten off the highway because we made turns and frequent stops, as though we were in an urban area. At one point, we stopped and someone else got in. Benito had an accomplice, someone who hadn't been at the farm. They talked but I couldn't make out what they were saying. My mother and I helped each other get the bandanas back in our mouths, even if they were hanging loose in the back.

Finally, we parked and the engine was turned off. Benito and his passenger got out but no one came to get us.

I tried to calm my heart, to keep my composure for my mother's sake, whose rapid blinking and fidgety legs made me think she was about to fly to pieces. My mind considered and rejected ideas for getting away. I might be able to get to my gun at some point, but he had one, too, not to mention that blade that could scoop out an eye with a flick of the wrist. The man was a cold-hearted killer and wouldn't hesitate to use either weapon. Or both.

If there was any chance of escape, it had to include getting my mother to safety as well, and that might prove challenging. She was in good shape from dancing, and properly motivated, but could I depend on her to keep it together?

The back door opened and Benito stuck the gun in before showing his face. Smart man. Stupid me. I should have been ready. I could have kicked him. But how far would we get with our hands tied? I had no idea where we were, if we could get help, or if we'd end up in worse trouble.

Benito motioned to us with the pistol.

Okay, maybe not worse trouble.

We slid out and landed in the weedy backyard of an abandoned brick two story with equally run-down buildings to either side, all flat-roofed and overgrown with vegetation. A short chain-link fence separated the parking area from the yard.

The wooden back porch sagged to one side. There were two doors, one with a boarded-up window to its left. The other was open, and I could see a stairway inside leading up.

The posts of the porch had once supported a second-level deck, but the left half of it had fallen down, kind of like Benito's face. Two upstairs windows, one with a few pieces of wood nailed over it, the other half glass, half open. A torn curtain fluttered over the sill.

Nothing about the place was familiar. I couldn't see to the front where there had to be a street. We could be anywhere. There was a certain similarity to Malcolm's father's old house in Soulard, but St. Louis was full of street upon street of two-story brick homes.

Benito herded us through a squeaky gate toward the open door. My mother whimpered as she stumbled forward. Her wrists were bleeding. Mine probably were as bad or worse, but they'd gone numb about a half hour before.

Even though it was hot, for a few moments, the temperature outside the van was a relief compared to the stuffy interior, and a light breeze sent a chill through me as we crossed the yard. Then, we were inside the narrow stairwell, where no air moved.

Shreds of oriental carpeting remained at the edges of the stairs. Every step groaned and threatened to crack beneath our feet, and I was reminded of the one at home that creaked.

Home. Winterlight. I would kill to see it again.

I didn't like killing, hated to see anything suffer, but if it came to it, I would.

That realization made me surprisingly light and focused. I kept observing details, for all the good it would do. The interior walls of the stairwell were brick. There were no lights. The place reeked of decay and dust, mildew and rotten garbage.

Straight ahead at the top of the stairs, a hall continued into a dark unknown. To the right, a doorway opened onto what used to be a kitchen. A few scraps of gold-flecked linoleum stuck to the floor. The non-boarded window with the curtain let in light and provided a good view of the alley. Two wooden chairs sat in the middle of the room, back to back.

Benito tied us to these. Before he sat me down, I caught the tail end of a pickup rumbling down the alley, then the window was out of my line of sight.

Our captor dragged another chair over to face me, just out of my reach. Not that any of my limbs were free, but this man was careful. Calculating. As Giacomo had said, cunning.

He took out a flip phone, jerked the bandana out of my mouth.

"What is the number of the house where Giacomo is?"

I lifted my chin and stared at him, had no intention of making this easy. "It's in the book. Look it up."

"Stubborn, I see. Like your grandmother, God rest her soul." He brought out the curved knife. "That is not a problem."

"Is that how you were going to convince her to marry you? At knife-point?"

With the swiftness of a striking snake, his hand flicked forward, ice slid across my shoulder, and blood soaked into the sleeve of my white T-shirt.

My body jerked, and I hissed, "Shit."

"For God's sake, Vi," my mother cried around her bandana, "give him what he wants."

I gave him the number. Benito pushed keys and put the phone on speaker. "If Giacomo doesn't answer, say you need to speak to him. Nothing more, understand?"

I nodded. A thin dribble of blood reached my elbow.

It rang only once before my father picked up. "Gemma?"

Benito chuckled darkly, motioned at me with the knife.

"I need to speak to Giacomo."

"Vi? Thank Christ. Are you all right? Is Gemma with you?"

"Yes, Dad, and she's fine. Put Giacomo on now."

I wanted to ask if Malcolm was there, but if he had been, he'd have answered. Were they still out looking for us?

"Where are you?" he asked.

"In an abandoned house—"

Again, the cut was instant and precise. Blood trickled down both my arms.

"Adrian, get Giacomo now," my mother said with a hint of her normal commanding self.

He must have understood her because a moment later, "*Ciao*," came through the airwaves.

"*Ciao, cugino.* I have your lovely granddaughter with me. And her mother. Viola, she is like Josephine, no?"

A stream of angry Italian words spewed from the phone.

"Yes, yes, yes, always the same from you, cousin. Now, if you want to see them again alive, you must come. Alone. We will finally finish this. *Da uomo a uomo, Sì?* Man to man."

CHAPTER THIRTY-SEVEN

"I NO HAVE THE DRIVING LICENSE," Giacomo said.

"That has never stopped you before," Benito replied, serene, *civilized*.

Giacomo muttered in Italian. "I no have the car, Benito. How'm I supposed to get there?"

"Oh, cousin, you disappoint me. You used to be so ingenious. If you like, I can send you an eye. Will that help you find a way? Should it be your daughter-in-law's or your granddaughter's?" He took an exaggeratedly patient breath as if this conversation was too tiresome and pedestrian. "You choose."

My mother moaned.

Something like a growl came through the phone. "Address."

Benito told Giacomo where we were. "No police, Giacomo. Only you. Understand?"

"*Sì.*"

"It will take you almost two hours to get here. I will be waiting for you. It will be a reunion." He tapped his temple with his forefinger as if something had just occurred to him. "On second thought, bring Josephine's son. The whole family should be together one last time." He touched a button on the phone's face to disconnect and tucked it into his breast pocket.

I stared at him, afraid to take my eyes away. He stared back. "So much like her," he said.

The blood on my arms had already dried. The cuts were remarkably shallow considering the blade. The man probably considered himself an artist with that knife. I wondered if he disinfected it after taking an eye. The thought made me gag.

Benito rose and moved the chair to the window, checked his watch, then walked past us and down the stairs. A few minutes later, he returned with the tomato plant, bag of marbles, and an old suitcase. He put the drooping plant and the remaining marbles on the kitchen counter. My bra finally came loose and dropped to the floor.

"Why did you take the tomato plant?" I asked him.

He let his head fall to one side as he considered the Big Italian plant. "Only to torment my cousin. I know how important they are to him. Something of Josephine's. Like that blue marble you found." He looked at me without smiling. "You are clever, like him. Maybe too much so."

Maybe. "You should give it some water."

Without taking his eyes from me, he put it in the sink and opened the tap. Nothing came out. He put his hands up in a mocking helpless gesture.

"Okay," I said. "Then why don't you do something useful with that knife and let me loose so I can strangle you?"

"Oh, Vi," my mother grumbled, making it obvious her bandana was loose. "Can't you just be quiet?"

Benito leaned against the counter, took out the knife and turned it as if considering it for the first time. He lifted it to his face and held it beneath his good eye. "Do not tempt me to use it on you."

I curled my lip at him. He chuckled.

"I could learn to like you, Viola *York*."

If he meant to rattle me by using my parents' name, it wouldn't work. I'd deliberately taken my uncle's last name of Parker when given the choice.

"You know where that name comes from?"

"Shakespeare," I said.

"Not Viola, but York?"

"No idea, but I have a feeling you're going to tell me."

"Nowhere," he said with a dark laugh. "Giacomo made it up to throw me off the trail. It worked, for a while. But it means nothing, has no…history."

He probably wanted me to ask him about his name's history, but I had no interest in that so decided to take my mother's advice and keep my mouth shut for a while.

Benito consulted his watch again and disappeared through a door into another room of the apartment, taking the suitcase with him. I let my head drop back until it rested on my mother's shoulder. She leaned her cheek against mine.

"Are we going to die today?" she asked with remarkable dignity.

"Will Dad contact Malcolm and Dex before coming here?"

"I think so."

"Then there's hope. Other than that, no idea."

"I'm sor—"

"Don't," I said, cutting her off like Dex had done with me earlier. "You can't be held responsible for the actions of one madman."

"Do you think he's crazy?"

"Don't you? Wouldn't you have a few screws loose if half your face had been blown away?"

She nodded. Between our backs, I brushed her hand with mine. She responded and we hooked our fingers together.

"Let's try to rest a little," I said, feeling drowsy.

"Okay," she said.

I let my eyes drift closed, wanting to escape this nightmare if only for a little while.

The only way I can describe what happened next is to say my entire body shifted left about an inch. Like when a big shudder goes through you, but somehow, my body paused mid-shud. The room brightened, and Wastrel stood before me, his breath warming my cheek. I darted my eyes hard to the side to see if my mother was aware that a horse now stood over us, but her eyes were closed, her breathing regular. At least one of us was getting a break.

I was not asleep, of that I'm sure. I lifted my head and put my nose to Wastrel's nostril, breathing with him. His whiskers tickled my lips.

The room transformed before me. Sunlight splashed against the shiny floor, filtered by new sheer curtains at the window. A woman stood at the sink, washing a head of iceberg lettuce. The tomato plant and marbles had been replaced by a green pepper, a cucumber, and a couple of carrots. She shook water off the lettuce, put it on a cutting board. Holding it with one hand, she used the other to open the lower cabinet to the left. There, on the inside wall was one of those magnetic bars that hold kitchen knives. She pulled a chef's knife off the strip and sliced the lettuce into neat ribbons.

Wastrel hadn't moved, but he made a whuffling noise as if to make sure I was paying attention. As in the dream—had that been just last night?—I smelled smoke.

The woman scraped the lettuce into a bowl, reminding me of my mother standing at the sink in the kitchen at Winterlight. Before slicing the other vegetables she had laid out, the woman reached for the stub of a cigarette hanging off the edge of the counter and took a long pull then blew smoke up toward the ceiling. As she flicked ash into the sink, she turned and blinked.

Could she see Wastrel? She looked startled, then the room darkened, she faded, and so did Wastrel.

I didn't want him to go. "No—"

"Wha?" my mother murmured.

"Nothing," I said. "Rest."

My body shifted again, as if completing the earlier shudder. What the hell had just happened? It wasn't a dream. More like a vision. I stared at the lower cabinet to the left of the sink, wishing the door had fallen off like it had from a couple of the others. Was it possible? Had Wastrel just manifested in real time to tell me there was a knife in the cabinet? Or was it a symbol to do with Benito's blade? Either way, how was I supposed to get my hands on it?

And what about the smoke? I wished we were next to the cabinets just so I could bang my head against something.

I. Did. Not. Understand.

But if Wastrel was trying to communicate, surely there must be a way out of this situation. Surely, there was hope.

I thought through everything he'd showed me so far from the very first dream following Giacomo to the apartment he shared with Josephine, to the diving horse, to the toy stick horse, to riding over water and jumping the moon. And now this…vision of a knife and cigarette. What connected these ideas? What could be interpreted literally and what was a symbol?

I let my head fall back to my mother's shoulder, clenching my jaw to keep from groaning out loud in frustration.

Knowing Wastrel meant well, knowing there were important hints in his messages—hints that might save our lives—and deciphering the meaning of his visits were two very different things.

Focusing on my breathing, I tried to relax without falling asleep, to empty my mind and be in a meditative state of centered calm, the place I am in before entering the competition arena.

Soon enough, Benito returned. Perhaps he'd been meditating in the next room, preparing himself for what was to come next.

He'd changed into a black suit. The starched white shirt wasn't buttoned all the way up, exposing a vee of his chest and a milky oval stone hanging on a gold chain. He carried a bundle of cloth. This he shook out to reveal an old red shirtdress.

"You will put this on."

I narrowed my eyes. Was it a maternity dress? "No, I won't."

He carefully hung the dress over his arm, tipped my chair forward, jerked me up by the arms, and moved us in front of my mother. Her eyes were wide, blinking. She'd dozed off. She inhaled quickly through her nose, brought herself awake.

He lay the flat edge of the curved knife against her cheek. He didn't speak, didn't have to.

"Okay," I said. "But you'll have to untie me."

He backed us into the other room. I tried to give Mom a reassuring smile, but I'm pretty sure it was just an ugly grimace that had nothing encouraging in it.

Benito sliced the ties holding my hands and quickly stepped away from me. Grateful, I eased my arms to the front, my shoulders complaining the whole way, and rubbed my raw wrists.

He slid the knife into a leather sheath and took the pistol from his waistband.

I started to pull the dress over my head while assessing this new space. Two windows looked out on the next building's wall. Scarred wood floors, peeling wallpaper, a wire hanging from the middle of the ceiling. Two doors in the wall opposite the kitchen. A closet, maybe? And...

"No." He waggled the gun at me. "Take off your clothes. And your shoes and socks."

A chill went through me. What was this about, and what would he do to me when he saw Dex's gun? I couldn't risk it.

"Can I have some privacy?"

He kept the gun on me as he went to one of the doors on the other side of the room. "In here. Don't close the door all the way."

Perhaps there was something civilized left in him after all. I eased through the opening into what had been a small bathroom. A few pieces of blue tile clung to the wall above what was left of the vanity. The sink was gone. The toilet as well. Only a hole in the floor to mark where it once had been. A tiny window above the tub let in enough light for me to see my reflection in a cracked mirror—the kind you buy to put in your locker at school. It leaned on a piece of two-by-four cross bracing where a medicine cabinet had once been.

Despite my tan, I looked pale in the room's gray light, my eyes bloodshot. Most of my hair had escaped its tie, but not in any organized way. It clung to my damp cheeks and forehead.

Worried Benito would open the door at any moment, I first undid the gun and hid it behind the mirror. Somehow, I'd get my hands on it later. Then, I unlaced my boots and removed my socks. I stood on them, as if it mattered what the soles of my feet came in contact with at this point. With exaggerated care, I folded my jeans and T-shirt and stacked them on my boots in the corner.

Other than my arms, the rest of my body was even more pale than my face, not that I could see much of it in the tiny mirror. The fresh cuts on my shoulders gleamed like neon lights. I summoned enough spit to rub the dried blood off my arms.

I picked up the red dress and held it by the sleeves, looking at the back of it. It would be a tight fit.

I remembered the strip of fabric I'd found in the woods right before finding the blue marble. What had happened to it? I'd pocketed it and forgotten. Pulling one long sleeve straight, I examined it more closely. The dress was old, a pattern and style from the sixties. Hand made by the way the seams were finished. There, a recent tear in one elbow. I put it down and searched the pockets of my jeans. The last couple of days had gone by so fast, I hadn't had a chance to do laundry, had pulled on whatever pants were handy.

From my left back pocket, I pulled out the strip of fabric. It was a match. What the hell was Benito doing carrying around a dress everywhere he went? I picked it up again, held it at arm's length, turned it around.

The upper right front of the dress around the shoulder had a good-sized hole in it, surrounded by several smaller ones. I slipped my hand through the neck and stuck my fingers out the frayed openings, felt the stiffness of stained material.

Icy terror stole my breath, froze my bones, stopped my blood.

This was my grandmother's dress. The one she'd been wearing the day she died.

CHAPTER THIRTY-EIGHT

No, was my first thought.

I can't put this on, my second.

I forced air into my lungs, little sips, then a big gulp. My heart started beating again, wild, erratic. Blood rushed through my veins, warmed me, got my mind in gear.

What did this sick fuck have planned? Did he want to reenact that morning's events with me playing the part of Josephine?

"Come along, my sweet," Benito said.

His voice sounded different, cajoling, almost seductive, and that sent a new tendril of dread coiling through my gut.

I snatched the gun from where I'd hidden it and tried to strap it to my thigh. The holster was stretchy but too small.

"Hang on," I said. "I'm almost ready."

I pulled the gun. I could shoot him through the door. What caliber had Dex said this thing was? I turned it, trying to see some indication of its power, not that it would mean anything to me. I guess people who own guns know that kind of thing and don't need it stamped on the grip. With my luck, this was a pea-shooter and the bullet would barely dent the thick wood of the solid old door. Worse, it would ricochet and I'd shoot myself. Benito would get pissed and cut out my eye.

Or my mother's.

If I were alone, I'd chance it.

I put the weapon back behind the mirror, took a deep breath, and stepped out of the bathroom.

Benito looked me up and down, a strange smile curling the good side of his face. He canted his head, then circled his hand, indicating I should turn around. The thought of putting my back to him sent a shiver through my whole body, but I did as told.

Gently, he tugged out my hair tie and smoothed my hair down my back. I tried not to tremble at his touch on my scalp, forced myself to keep breathing, to stay still.

"Better," he said, taking my shoulders and turning me to face him once more.

I swallowed. He looked me over again, and his smile faded. He touched the hole above my right breast, put the backs of his fingers on my skin. His eye gleamed as he stared at the spot, but I'm not sure he was seeing it, or me, or this place.

"Don't touch me."

He didn't react.

"*Il mio cuore*, do you remember what you said when you gave me this?" He tapped the stone at his throat.

"No," I said, not willing to play into his fantasy.

"Ah," he sighed, then laughed softly. He chucked me under the chin. "Always the coy one."

I jerked away from him, but again, he didn't appear to notice. He took my hand and guided me to the kitchen. There, he dragged my chair over to his by the window. We sat side by side. His fingers were surprisingly soft.

My mother speared a question at me with her eyes. I flicked my free hand to let her know it was all right, to just be quiet for now.

Benito picked up where he'd left off. "We were in your father's garden, do you remember?"

I started to argue, realized a response wasn't really required.

"You said the rainbow moonstone would help to clear my mind and enable me to rest. You knew I had trouble sleeping. You liked to say that I kept forgetting who I really was on the inside. The moonstone, you said, would help me remember."

"And have you remembered?" I asked. "Who you are on the inside?"

"For a time, it did help, but I strayed, Josephine, after you went away. I took the moonstone off because it hurt too much to think of you. I almost never slept, and I forgot for a long time."

He flattened my hand on his thigh, stroked my fingers with his. It was all

I could do not to jerk away. But it felt right to let him go on. Maybe I would learn something I could use against him. And it's not like I had a choice.

"Now, I know the moonstone connects us. What will bring us together again."

What the what?

Benito's phone chirped. He extracted it from the inside pocket of his jacket. I imagined he must be boiling inside his black suit. The polyester dress I wore was hot enough. I'd been keeping my eyes forward, searching the backyard and alley for any sign of help arriving, but it was quiet, not even a dumpster-diving stray dog. I took a quick sideways glance at Benito. His skin glistened with sweat, but he didn't seem to notice, or didn't care.

"Yes?" he said to his phone, his voice back to its normal clipped style. "Good." He listened for a moment. "No, no. All is prepared. Just do your part as we planned."

He rose.

"Was that your friend you picked up on the way here?" I asked.

Benito glanced around the room. "An associate," he said.

He yanked the tomato plant out of the pot, scooped my bra off the floor, and took both out to the balcony. I was surprised the heavy fruit still clung to the stem. He used the bra to strap the plant to the railing so that it hung over the edge. That seemed exceptionally callous.

I took the moment to sidle over to the counter. Keeping my eyes on Benito and my hands behind me, I groped for the lower cabinet next to the sink and pulled on the knob. The door resisted, then made a loud pop as it came unstuck. Benito turned. He tilted his head to one side, a habit. Was he seeing me or Josephine at this point?

"Sit," he said.

I went back to the chair but got my mother's attention and tried to make her look in the cabinet. Was there a knife? I made a cutting motion with the edge of one hand against the other. She peered at me, concentrating hard, her elegant brows drawn tight. I pointed at the cabinet. She looked, looked back at me, shook her head.

Did she not understand? Couldn't see? Or was there no knife? What the hell, Wastrel? What was the point of that vision?

As Benito came back into the room, I realized I was free and could have shoved him off the balcony. What the hell, Vi?

But where was his associate and what was his part in this?

What did I have to lose? "So, where is this associate of yours?"

Benito dragged my mother's chair over to the counter so that she faced the door that led to the hallway. He removed his jacket and hung on the back of his chair. "In a strategic location," he said in answer to my question.

"I see. And what is his job?"

"Insurance."

Not helpful. "Why don't you let my mother go? You don't need her."

"Insurance."

Damn it. Had he thought of everything?

He adjusted the moonstone then stood next to my mother and pointed the gun at her head.

"Wait," I yelled, then realized something was off. Was he posing for some twisted selfie? I followed his line of vision to the top of the stairs. A full-length mirror had been placed there, angled in such a way that the reflection of my mother and Benito could probably be seen from down the stairs.

"Perfect," Benito said.

He went to the mirror and moved it into the kitchen, then came over to me and grabbed my hands. With the swiftness and precision of a cowboy roping a calf, he had my wrists zip tied together again. He led me to the top of the stairs. A little ways back in the dark hall, a rope hung from a rafter with a carabiner attached to the end. He snapped the carabiner to the zip ties, then yanked the other end of the rope to pull my hands over my head until I hung by them. He tied off the rope somewhere behind me.

"No," I said again, finally understanding his plan. Ignoring the pain in my wrists, I lifted myself by my hands and kicked at him. He wasn't very big, and I'm pretty strong. I tried to kick him down the stairs, but all he had to do was whip out that knife, nick my cheek, and I backed off. He pointed the gun at my mother for good measure.

She and I maintained eye contact while he gagged me once more, tied my ankles together, and caressed my hair one last time. If I could, I would have spit at him. He put the mirror in front of me, which left me helpless and in near total darkness.

Giacomo would spot his precious tomato plant hanging from the balcony. Enraged, he'd barrel up the stairs, notice Benito's reflection, and fire at him. Except he wouldn't hit Benito.

He'd hit the mirror and kill me.

CHAPTER THIRTY-NINE

I TRIED to swing my legs toward the mirror. But he'd attached them to something behind me to prevent that. He *had* thought of everything.

"It's almost time," Benito said.

I shouted every swear word I could through the bandana. Where was Giacomo? Where were Malcolm and Dex?

"You can be quiet," Benito said, using his bored voice, "or I can take your mother's eye. Your choice."

I shut it. There was a chance my mother would get out of this alive and intact. Me, not so much. That pissed me off. Everything I'd thought I'd known had turned out to be a lie. The truth was better, and the potential existed to build a new relationship with my parents. Like my dad had said, it was what it was, but it could be different. *We* could be different. Better. Combine that with Malcolm and the trust fund, and the future was worth looking forward to.

I wouldn't let Benito take it away.

But I couldn't think of way to stop this, either.

A few minutes later, I heard a car pull up out back. A door opened and closed, then another. Hushed voices. My father and grandfather fighting about how to approach, probably Giacomo insisting Adrian stay back, and Adrian wanting to rush in and rescue Gemma.

Were they alone or were Dex and Malcolm nearby? I needed to scream. Didn't dare. Surely, they could hear my breathing. It echoed all around me off the old brick walls. Sweat stung my eyes. Blood thrummed my ears so hard it hurt.

I knew the moment Giacomo saw his tomato plant.

"I'm going to kill you, you son of a bitch," he yelled, all trace of accent and off-the-boat syntax gone.

"Why don't you come up and try," Benito said.

"Come down here and face me. *Da uomo a uomo*, like you said."

"Oh now, cousin. Don't be so hasty. You must come up the stairs, just like that day so long ago."

"Where are Vi and Gemma?"

"Come up and see old man."

Silence.

I jerked my legs. What the hell had he tied me to? I took a deep breath, tensed my whole body, jerked again. A crunching noise came from behind me. Had my legs moved closer to the mirror? Maybe. Had Benito heard the sound, too? Maybe not. The gate down below squeaked open and shut.

I had to kick that mirror down before Giacomo came in.

He mounted the porch steps. Again, I put everything into jerking whatever held me. Still not close enough.

The door at the bottom of the stairs slowly opened. From behind me came a scraping. I hadn't moved so what had caused it? I twisted, tried to fling myself around, thought I saw a shadow shift.

From down the stairs came the distinctive slide and click of a racking shotgun. I couldn't help it. I screamed.

My mother screamed.

The blast in the narrow brick stairwell was like having my eardrums pummeled with boxing gloves. A heavy thud banged me sideways against the wall, knocked the wind out of me. Glass shattered. Heat scorched my face. And just before everything went black, I heard Benito laughing.

CHAPTER FORTY

I came to, confused and in the middle of chaos. A heavy weight pinned me against the wall but I was no longer hanging from the ceiling. My hands were still tied, but I was sitting on the floor. Broken glass glittered everywhere. With my hearing muffled, I scanned the kitchen, but couldn't see my mother or Benito. I might have called out, but couldn't tell for sure, like in a bad dream. Distantly, it seemed, people were yelling and grunting. There might have been bodies getting punched or thrown, or both, in the next room.

Either I was in hell or still alive. The latter seemed unlikely, but as I was right where I last remembered being, it must be the case.

I tried to move. I'd thought the heavy object lying across me was a piece of the wall, but it was soft and warm. With my bound hands, I pushed against it. It rolled over.

I stared at the colorless face in shock.

"Zoe?" I shoved her shoulder.

Nothing.

"No, no, no. Zoe!"

What was she doing here? Her skin had flecks of blood on it but I couldn't tell where it was coming from. I tried to shift, to get above her. Her chest felt hard. I shouted her name again and again.

Finally, she moaned.

"Zoe, Zoe, please be all right. What are you doing here? How did you get here? Are you hurt? Come on."

"Oh, shit," she slurred. "That hurt."

"Oh my God. What the hell are you doing here?"

I realized she must have been the heavy object that shoved me into the wall. I thought I'd been shot. But the shotgun had fired, the mirror had shattered…With my fingers, I picked at her shirt, encountering something heavy and stiff.

"Vest," she breathed.

"A bulletproof vest?"

She nodded, coughed, tried to sit up. I helped as best I could, hearing better, but very confused. I had to see where everyone else was, what was happening in the next room.

"I need a knife to get out of these." I held up my hands.

"No you don't."

"What?"

She slid the ties around until the connection was right between the tops of my wrists. "Just do this." Her breath came in short gasps, but she demonstrated putting her hands above her head then bringing her arms down sharply against her abdomen. "Hard as you can."

I scooted my butt around until I sat at the top of the stairs so my elbows wouldn't crash into the brick wall behind me and did what she'd shown. The zip ties snapped and I was free.

"Where were you a few hours ago?"

"Following you."

"You'll have to explain all this later. I need to get my feet free."

She pulled a multi-tool out of her pocket and sliced through the rope holding my feet. Which she could have done with the zip ties, too, danged show off.

"Who are you and what have you done with my Zoe?"

She fell back, holding her hands to her chest. "Later. I need to catch my breath."

"Are you sure you're all right? Let's get this thing off you and make sure." I unzipped the heavy vest—the kind cross-country riders wear—the sides came apart, and a large cast iron pan slipped out.

"What the—"

"Had to improvise." She felt around herself. "I'm okay. It worked like it was supposed to."

"*Supposed to?*" We'd be having a long talk. Later. I touched her face.

Zoe winced. "A few pellets must have hit me." She opened her eyes. "You too."

Or glass. I wasn't feeling any pain, though.

"Go," she said. "Make sure everyone else is okay."

I scrambled over her into the kitchen. It was empty. The shotgun lay on the floor.

In the next room, Benito lay across Giacomo's legs, half on his side, half on his back, wheezing as he tried to reach his nasty curved knife—a few inches from his fingertips. Blood glistened on his hands. His crisp white shirt was dotted with red. I couldn't see his pistol.

My mother stood over Benito, staring at him, her hands clutching her throat. Two eyes. No blood.

Giacomo sat against the wall, both hands covering his left eye, screaming and swearing. Lots of blood.

I sagged against the doorway, my legs buckling.

My mother saw me.

"Vi?" she sobbed. "I thought you were dead." She rushed over and put her arms around me.

I tried to hug her back but couldn't make my arms work. I began to think I'd been shot after all and just didn't realize. I felt so weak. "What happened? We need to call an ambulance." I squinted at my mother. Her features were fuzzy and dark spots floated in front of my eyes. "Do you have a phone?"

"Yes. Vi? Talk to me. Tell me what's wrong baby."

I took a deep breath. It didn't hurt. Maybe dying didn't hurt. "Giacomo...need to get help."

"Yes." She fumbled for her purse.

"Josephine?" Benito sounded feeble.

I breathed in again, certain I wasn't dying. On all fours, I crawled to him and Giacomo, flicking the knife away from Benito's fingers as I went.

With a watery hiss, he tried to collapse onto his back, but something prevented it. He gave up on reaching his curved blade and grasped the moonstone instead.

"Josephine, I'm coming."

Giacomo had gone quiet, his mouth drawn into a tight grimace, breathing heavy, right eye fixed on Benito. I forced myself up and to the bathroom, brought Giacomo my T-shirt. He pressed it against his eye socket. I couldn't tell whether he still had his eye or not. Either way, he had to get to an emergency room soon.

I leaned over to see why Benito couldn't lie flat. The handle and half the blade of a kitchen knife stuck out from his lower back. A growing pool of blood soaked into Giacomo's jeans and the scuffed wood floor. I looked at my mother. She held her cell phone but stared at us. The corners of her lips turned down. Had she done this to Benito? She stayed in the doorway, dipped her chin.

My mother had stabbed Benito in the back. The knife had been in the cabinet after all?

Benito reached a trembling hand toward my face. I slapped it away.

"Josephine isn't waiting for you," Giacomo gritted out. "The moonstone won't take you to her." He clenched his jaw, eased his legs from beneath Benito, and dragged himself closer. "I gave her that necklace." His thigh was also bleeding.

Benito blinked at Giacomo. He tried to speak, couldn't.

"Josephine said you needed it more than she did," Giacomo continued, his voice strained. "She asked to give it to you, and I let her." He sank to an awkward sitting position on the floor.

I got my socks and pressed them against the wound in Giacomo's leg.

"Josephine said you were *pazzo*," he said. "That we had to be careful. She was right. You *were* crazy. Crazy stupid. To come at me in my own home. You killed her. Took her from me. From all of us."

Benito's eye opened wide. He shook his head.

"He told me it was Eduardo," I said. "And he shot his brother because of it. You didn't kill Eduardo, he did."

"I loved her," Benito rasped. His grip on the moonstone loosened, his breathing grew faint.

Giacomo jerked the necklace off Benito's neck. "It doesn't matter who pulled the trigger. Your obsession killed her. You put my granddaughter in her dress and tried to make *me* kill *her*." His voice broke and his eye squeezed shut. "There is only one place for you." He pushed Benito down until the tip of the kitchen knife punctured the white shirt. "Go to hell."

Benito's eye closed forever

I stumbled back and away, retching.

Tires squealed outside, and in the distance, I heard sirens. My mother came out of the kitchen, took my arm, and got my butt into a chair next to Zoe. Some color had returned to the girl's cheeks. She really was okay. I hoped she hadn't looked into the next room.

"How are you so chill?" she asked in a feverish whisper.

I shook my head. "I'm not." My breath whistled in my tight throat.

Mom pushed my head down between my knees, and I slowly let air out. Then, inhaled, deeply, slowly.

"Benito?" a man yelled from the stairwell. "I've got him, Benito. What's next? You done up there?"

What the—?

Shit. The associate.

I lifted my head in time to see my father appear at the top of the stairs. Another man's arm wrapped around his neck. A gun pointed at his temple.

CHAPTER FORTY-ONE

"ADRIAN!" my mother shrieked.

"Nobody move or he gets it," the accomplice said, his voice high and nasal. "Where's Benito?"

I pointed toward the other room.

He cocked his head at my mother. "Get him."

I swallowed hard, tore my eyes from my father to my mother. "But—"

"Hurry up." He squeezed his arm tighter around Dad's neck for emphasis.

The guy was taller and broader than Dad, and even with his hair hanging in his face, I could see Dad's eyes bugging out of his head. His toes barely touched the floor.

The shotgun wasn't far from my feet, but I couldn't get to it and fire before Benito's accomplice pulled the trigger. Anyway, I'd kill my father at the same time.

"I..." my mother started. "He's..."

Sounding weak, Giacomo said, "Come and get him, Little Tony."

Little Tony? I wanted to return to Giacomo, feared he would bleed to death before help arrived.

Tony looked as baffled as I felt. "Giacomo?"

"Who else?" Giacomo answered.

"What'd you do to Benito?"

"Nothing he didn't deserve."

I hoped the sirens coming closer included an ambulance. And that we wouldn't need it for my father. Or me or my mother. Neither of us dared breathe.

"Why you still hanging around him after all these years?" Giacomo asked.

Little Tony relaxed a hair. Dad's feet touched down.

"Everything was a mess after you left, Giacomo. I didn't know what to do."

"If you have my son in a headlock, you need to let him go."

The gun barrel eased away from Dad's head. A smile creased Tony's face. He was younger than Benito and Giacomo. Another cousin? My lungs began to work again.

"Don't move!" Dex ordered from down below.

Tony jumped and released Dad. He fell hard onto his hands and knees.

"Don't shoot!" I yelled.

A gun went off.

Tony hit the floor screaming, "Jesus fucking Christ!" and grabbed his foot.

Dex came into view, arms out stiff, revolver pointed at Tony, then into the kitchen. He didn't give screaming Tony a second look as he kicked the accomplice's gun across the floor.

Dex's sweeping gaze took us in—me and Zoe on our rickety chairs. Mom and Dad standing next to each other after exchanging a brief hug—then he gave a curt nod and proceeded into the next room. I noticed Zoe's eyes following his every move like she was memorizing them.

Dex's second came up the stairs, stepped over Tony, and disappeared down the dark hall.

Dex crossed to the bathroom, kicked open the door, inspected that space, yelled, "Clear!"

His second echoed that from somewhere deeper in the building. I bolted into the next room, Dad right behind me. Giacomo lay flat and no longer held my T-shirt to his eye. What I could see of his skin had gone gray, like Ed Todd's. "No," I said.

Dex knelt beside me. With brisk, efficient movements, he took my bloody T-shirt, tore it apart and made a tourniquet for Giacomo's leg. He pressed another piece of it to the side of my grandfather's face and tied it around his head.

By the sound of pounding steps, Malcolm took the stairs two at a time. He must have hopped right over Tony.

Tony'd stopped screaming but still whimpered. "Hey, I'm bleeding here," he groused.

Malcolm came in, grabbed my arms, and pulled me against his chest where his heart beat madly. Mine hadn't exactly settled down, but it was good to know he was scared for me. For all of us. He didn't speak, but a great tremor went through him. He pressed my head against his shoulder and squeezed me like he'd never let go. I didn't want him to. Wasn't sure my legs could hold me any longer. He picked me up and carried me to the kitchen, set me on my feet but kept a protective arm around me. I turned my face into the safety of his chest.

Dex took Tony's arms and dragged him to one side. "Paramedics are coming up. Need to make room."

"Hey," Tony whined again. "I'm bleeding here."

"Shut up," Dex ordered. "You shot off your own toe. You'll live."

Dex assessed each of us until his eyes came to rest on Zoe. "What the hell are you doing here, young lady?"

I pulled my face away from Malcolm. "She saved my life."

Zoe blinked at Dex but held his gaze without flinching, unintimidated, and—smiling? I think the shotgun blast had addled her mind.

Dex's eyes snapped to me then back to Zoe. He was still hepped up on adrenaline, I could tell, needed to release it, to vent on someone. But it wasn't going to be Zoe. He turned to Tony.

"Who the hell are you?"

Miko had come in but stayed to one side, clearly unsure who he should be standing with at this point. Miko. He was okay! Dex and Malcolm must have found him. Didn't matter now. He had good color in his cheeks and looked fully recovered. Taking the seat I'd vacated, he introduced himself to Zoe. She offered a dazzling smile and they shook hands. I'd never seen her beam like that.

The paramedics came in. Dex led them to the next room. I kept hold of Malcolm's hand and followed them to Giacomo.

We crowded around him, ignoring the paramedics' efforts to shoo us away. They found a pulse, started oxygen, taped a bandage over his eye, put a collar around his neck, and were already relaying his condition over a radio as they lifted him onto a stretcher. They secured him and started moving out of the room. My father held his father's left hand. I held his right.

As we went through the kitchen, I leaned down and said, "You owe me a pot of sauce, old man. Don't forget."

I thought I felt him squeeze my fingers before they took him down the stairs.

CHAPTER FORTY-TWO

"ALL RIGHT," Dex said after the paramedics packed up and left. "This is a mess. Cops will be here any second. We need a simple, consistent story for what went down. I'll talk to them first, and hopefully, we can all go home before midnight."

In a calm voice, my mother asked, "Am I going to jail?"

"Why would you?" Dex asked.

She sniffed. "I stabbed Benito."

"Really?" Dex said. "It's harder to shove a knife into a person than most people realize." He stuck his bottom lip out and nodded. "Nicely done."

"She's stronger than she looks," I said.

"But—" my mother started.

"Was he attacking you?"

"No, he was attacking Giacomo, trying to cut out his eye." She reached for the back of a chair. Miko stood so she could sit. "And...and..." She swallowed, collecting herself. Her voice firmed with anger. "I thought he'd made Giacomo shoot my daughter."

I grabbed her hand and held it with both of mine. She'd kept it together and saved Giacomo. She hadn't flown to pieces. My grandmother survived a shooting long enough to deliver my father, and my mother, furious that I'd been shot, killed a man. The women in my family were kick ass powerful and resilient. I'd remember that the next time I thought of running away from my troubles.

"You're getting ahead of the story," Dex said, "but that's good to know. It's okay to use lethal force to defend an innocent party from lethal force. This falls within that description."

Everyone nodded in agreement. My mother took a big breath and let it out. Dad put his hand on her shoulder.

"Except—" I started, thinking about how Giacomo had forced Benito's body down onto that knife. The men in my family were tough, too.

Dex held up one finger to stop me. "Would it have changed the outcome?"

"Nope."

"Then I don't need to know. And neither do the police. Understand?"

I nodded.

I described what happened when we arrived at this abandoned house. My mother told us that after Giacomo fired, Benito met him at the top of the stairs, where Giacomo slammed the gun butt into Benito's face. He staggered into the other room, and they continued fighting. She was able to get hold of the knife in the cabinet, free herself, and stab Benito.

I whispered an apology to Wastrel for not believing him.

The police arrived, followed by a second set of paramedics. They started swabbing wounds. In addition to the neat slices Benito had given me, Zoe and I both had superficial cuts from the glass.

"I don't understand how we weren't shot," I said to Dex.

Hands on hips, he examined the hallway. "He aimed high," he said. "Shot through the rope holding you."

Zoe's improvised vest hadn't deflected the pellets, but a near perfect circular welt ringed her chest, ribs, and abdomen. Probably from the impact with me. The medic was stumped until Zoe produced Mrs. Erdman's iron skillet.

They got Tony's sneaker off and bandaged his foot. His right little toe was gone. My mother allowed them to disinfect the scratches on her legs and arms.

By silent agreement, we all declined a ride to the hospital.

I started explaining what had happened in the woods and at Helen's.

"Oh, God, Helen." I took Malcolm's hand. "I'm so sorry."

Malcolm and Dex exchanged a look. "Why?"

"You didn't find her?"

"What do you mean?" Malcolm asked. "What does my mother have to do with this?"

I sank to the floor. Just couldn't stand up anymore. My mother took over with how Benito had taken us through the woods. Malcolm crouched beside me, rubbed my back, and I broke the terrible news about Helen.

He stood and whipped out his cell phone, pressing the shortcut for her number. I heard her voicemail pick up. He left a curt message for her to call him immediately. Next, he called Hank, confirmed Clara was fine, then asked him to get to Helen's immediately, and call back as soon as he did. Third, he called the county sheriff and informed them there may have been foul play at Helen's address. He slid his phone into his pocket and stood by the window, staring at the wall of the house next door.

I put my head in my hands, and tried, unsuccessfully to keep the tears in. Now that the threat was gone, I felt shaky, exhausted, and like crying for days.

Tony corroborated everything we said about Benito and his intentions. For his part, he didn't seem to be guilty of anything much other than being stupid enough to follow Benito around, though I couldn't speak for what he might have done in years past. He *had* threatened my father. I had a feeling if Giacomo were here, he'd not want fingers pointed at Little Tony. Benito bore the guilt and responsibility for all this terror and mayhem.

I returned to the bathroom and pulled on my jeans. Dex had a spare polo shirt in his SUV, and I put that on, couldn't wait to get out of that dress. I needed to go outside. Even with broken windows, the tiny kitchen had grown stifling as the afternoon wore on and more people came in. I made for the stairs.

Malcolm's phone buzzed, and he answered before it was halfway through the first ring. He turned to me, eyes shining and face jubilant as he said, "Mom?"

I smiled my first real smile of the day and started down the stairs, then heard Malcolm say, "Sorry, sorry. I know. Okay. Just tell them it was a mistake."

Apparently, Helen wasn't too happy about having the sheriff at her door. That was a problem we could live with.

I sat on the bottom porch step, the only one I thought safe. The sun had moved around so that the back of the house was in shade. A light breeze ruffled the tall grass and weeds of the abandoned yard, taking with it the smells of decay, blood, and death.

Police cars jammed the alley, and two television news vans pulled in behind them. Oh, joy. Despite Dex's best efforts, we all had to answer questions, tell our part of the story. Yellow tape surrounded the house and yard. The coroner took Benito away.

Little Tony took the high road, candidly admitting his involvement in Benito's scheme for revenge. He said cooperating was best, sounding like he'd been in this predicament before. He shrugged and said maybe they'd cut him a deal. For sure he'd get a meal in an air-conditioned cell. He smiled cheerfully and waved at the reporters as the police cuffed him and put him in the back of a squad car. We promised to call Dex Two and do what we could for him. He said there was no rush.

After what seemed like hours, during which I went back inside to avoid having a reporter's microphone in my face, Dad asked if we could leave. He wanted to get to the hospital to check on Giacomo. We all did.

I wanted to know if we could take down the dehydrated tomato plant. I doubted my bra could be salvaged, but it was worth a try. And maybe Giacomo's prized plant could be revived with some tender loving care. Also doubtful.

Nope. Both were bagged as evidence along with Mrs. Erdman's frying pan. The black marbles were also tagged and taken. No one had tried to claim them. And Josephine's handmade maternity dress. They took that, too.

It was near dark by the time Gemma, Adrian, and Dex got in Malcolm's truck. Dex's second—whose name I'd never gotten—drove Dex's SUV with Zoe and Miko. Malcolm took the wheel of my truck, pulling me across the torn bench seat to sit next to him. I had to straddle the shifter.

I didn't care.

We found the nearest Chinese buffet and stuffed ourselves before continuing to the hospital. On the way, I spotted an Italian restaurant. We pulled over, and I ran in and ordered an espresso to go.

The hospital was a gigantic complex on the edge of a park. Giacomo had already had surgery to clean up his socket. Although Benito hadn't managed to completely steal the eye, he'd damaged it beyond saving. In the future, my grandfather could opt for an ocular implant and a prosthetic eye, or he could wear an eye patch.

He'd been shot in the thigh, but it was only muscle damage, no tendons, ligaments, or bones were hit. He'd have a scar but full use of the leg. He must have been prepared to avoid the hamstring slice, but somehow, Benito had still gotten to his eye.

A doctor no older than me told us all this before we went into the room.

Giacomo was sedated and sleeping. Machines beeped, noting his pulse and respirations, and a bag dripped fluids and meds through a needle into his arm. We sat with him for a while, me and Dad on either side of the bed, while the others wandered in and out, went to the cafeteria to buy coffee, chatted. Malcolm spent most of the time on the phone with Dex Two.

Mom made herself scarce, whether out of deference to Dad or because they were still mad at each other, I didn't know. I was too tired to care at that point.

The television was on, sound off. I flipped through the stations. Something caught my eye, I went back.

And there it was. The tomato plant and my bra. Headlining the news.

I sighed. Then snorted. Then laughed. My father lifted his head. I pointed at the screen, and he smiled, chuckled. Life just didn't get any better than that.

Giacomo's color had improved, but sitting by him reminded me too much of the vigil I'd kept with Ed Todd. Except Giacomo was going to live. When my Dad's eyes started to droop, I decided we should go home and try to get some sleep. I left the espresso on Giacomo's over-bed table, and we left.

Zoe and Miko had opted to sit in the waiting room. They were talking animatedly and laughing when I picked them up for the ride home. The resilience of the young. I had only ten years on them but felt ancient. Miko hadn't tried to talk to Gemma. Perhaps he finally realized that ship had sailed. Or maybe a younger sloop had caught his attention.

If that were the case, I'd call him fickle and have to warn Zoe not to let her affections get involved too soon. As I watched them mooning at each other, I feared it might already be too late.

Meanwhile, Zoe had a lot of 'splainin' to do, and the long ride home was the perfect opportunity to quiz her. I made her ride with me and Malcolm. Miko waved and made a sad face when he got in the front seat with Dex's second—Trevor, I'd learned over sweet-and-sour chicken. Once we were on the highway, I feared I'd be asleep against Malcolm's side before long, so I started quickly. "So, Zoe—"

"I know. But what was I supposed to do? First, you introduced me to Dex, then, after Mrs. Erdman burned down my car, I—"

"Wait. First of all, how did you find us? Did you say you were following us?"

"Right. You said I couldn't come to the farm, but I knew something was wrong, so I was driving around the area. I saw that van pull out from that house on the far side of Winterlight, and something didn't seem right."

Good instincts.

"What gave it away? Was my bra hanging out the side door?"

"That, and it was a pool service van. Same company my parents use. I know that house doesn't have a pool, and what would someone from that company be doing way out there, anyway? Plus, most of their workers are pool boys, if you know what mean."

I did. Benito didn't exactly fit the profile. I shook my head, marveling at how she'd put all that together. "Okay, so you followed us. Did you think to call the police or Malcolm?"

She hadn't hesitated to dial 911 when Giacomo fired the shotgun that first time.

"I didn't know you were in there. Don't have the house number on my phone. I tried the barn, but nobody answered."

At least she had a phone, one she probably kept charged.

"And what, exactly," Malcolm asked in his dad voice, "were you planning to do when you got to the house?"

"Did you have the vest and frying pan with you in my truck?" I asked.

"Yes, and I don't know. I saw the van parked behind the house, but I guess you guys were already inside, so I still wasn't sure it was you. That's why I went around the front and snuck in that way."

Malcolm took his arm from around my shoulders to run his hand through his hair, then held it on the back of his neck. I could tell it was all he could do not to reach across me to smack the kid in the head.

"So," Malcolm said, his tone terse, "you snuck into what should be a condemned building, and then what?"

"Then I heard them talking, so I knew it was Vi and her mother."

"Do you have a weapon?" I asked.

She shook her head. Malcolm slid me a sideways look that said I shouldn't encourage her in whatever fantasy world she was living in.

"I got to the back of that hallway from the front apartment, and I saw what he had planned. At least, I was pretty sure what was going on. It all happened kind of fast after that."

No shit.

Malcolm grunted but somehow didn't comment.

"And what does Dex have to do with it?"

"You introduced me to him."

Why did I feel like she was blaming me for something? "I know, but—"

"Let me finish. I had a lot of time on my hands. Mrs. Erdman doesn't have cable, but she does have a good internet connection, so I started doing some research."

"Into bulletproof vests?"

"No. Well, yes. Did you know you can't just go to the store and buy them?"

I'd file that under information good to have and not need, like learning to use a gun. I waved my hand to get her to continue.

"Mostly, I researched what it takes to be a private investigator." She crossed her arms and nodded decisively. "Just like Dexter Hamill."

CHAPTER FORTY-THREE

IF ZOE WANTED to be a PI, that was fine. I was so drained, anything would have been fine. I suggested she discuss it with Dex. He would be straight about whether it was a good fit and what she could expect from that career.

All I wanted was a long, hot shower. As did everyone. We took turns taking short ones so we wouldn't run out of hot water.

I sent Miko to the apartment and told him to stay put until morning. Him on a one-way flight back to Paris was best for all concerned. My parents went to their room, but I heard their door open and close shortly after we were in bed, and someone went down the stairs.

We weren't sleeping, simply holding each other, grateful to be home and safe. Noire sighed at the foot of the bed.

After a minute, Malcolm said, "You should go see who that is and if he or she needs something."

A few days ago, I would have begged him to go with me. After what we'd just been through, everything else seemed easy.

My mother sat in the living room in the dark. I switched on a lamp and joined her. "How are you doing?"

One delicate shoulder lifted. She'd stabbed a man. A bad man, but still. Whatever she'd imagined when they left Paris, it wasn't that. In her lap, she gripped an object I couldn't see.

"I'm worried about you and Dad."

"That makes two of us."

"Want a drink? Water? Something stronger?"

She nodded. I poured her a short Scotch and set it in front of her, got myself a glass of water.

"He was really scared for you," I said after sitting across from her again.

"Yes. But he won't bend on this Miko thing."

"Did something happen between you?"

"Nothing but dancing."

"The tango."

"Not just the tango, the Argentine tango."

"Oh." I began to understand.

"Adrian thought he saw something."

"Apparently Miko thought so, too."

"It's impossible to dance without becoming close. I put my all into it as always. Miko misinterpreted that as something more than it was."

She sipped her drink, wrinkled her nose. "I'm not as young as I used to be. I enjoyed his attention. There's nothing wrong with that."

It wasn't news that she was vain. "Mom. The man followed you here from Paris."

"Youthful exuberance. Plus, his parents indulge his every whim."

"He mentioned he wanted to be a jumper rider before he discovered dance."

"See? Your father just won't listen."

Dad found it best to not argue with her. She said he didn't listen. Pride and stubbornness went along with my family's strength.

I drank my water and went for a refill. Back in the living room, I asked, "Has Dad danced since he got hurt?"

"A few steps to demonstrate nuances to Miko."

"I think I know what part of the problem is."

"Do you? Please explain, because I've wracked my mind trying to figure out what to say."

"Dad was young like Miko when you two first met, right? Young and handsome and talented?"

A soft smile played at the corners of her mouth, almost painful in its private remembrance. The sparks must have really flown when they were first together. She didn't have to answer.

"You two were magical together, unstoppable."

"We were."

"Maybe he's feeling his age, too. He sees himself in Miko, but Dad was a poor kid from an orphanage sweeping up the dance studio at night. It's not much of a stretch to imagine him thinking Miko could steal you away."

She made a scoffing sound.

"Mom, no matter what you think, you're still gorgeous. Dad's never loved anyone but you. Have you ever worried about him straying?"

She picked up her drink, stared at it, put it down. In a small voice, she said, "No."

After a few silent minutes, I said, "I'm going to try to get some sleep."

We stood, she reached for me. We hugged, awkward, but getting more natural each time. She handed me a stuffed animal.

"What's this?" I could see it was a palm-sized teddy bear, but...

"One of our first big competitions was in Stuttgart. It's not far from Giengen where the Stief bears come from." She ran her fingertip over the bear's ear. "You were about two years old."

"I...you..." Tears clogged my throat. "But..."

"Trudy said not to send it. That you had plenty."

"Oh, Mom." I pulled her back into a hug. "I'm so sorry she did that to you."

"To us," she said. "She did it to us."

I guided us back to the couch. We sat and held each other.

"Could you talk to him?" she asked.

"To the bear? What's his name?"

She swatted my shoulder. "No. Your father."

I understood her fear, but thinking back to how Malcolm had encouraged me to talk to them, I said, "This is something you have to do yourself."

"But how?"

"Maybe you have to show him."

"I don't know what that means."

She'd never had to work for his affection.

"I don't know, Mom, but I'm sure an opportunity will come."

I hoped an opportunity would come. Soon.

Another storm came through, leaving the morning air refreshing and cool. The horses snorted, flicked their tails, and shook rain out of their manes when we brought them in to have their breakfast. Noire ran down to the creek and came back sparkling with water droplets and carrying a giant stick. Miko threw it for her for as long as she wanted, which was a long time.

I hadn't slept much. I don't know if anyone did. But after I went back upstairs, Malcolm put his arms around me, I didn't dream, and that made it okay.

Clara cooked a huge breakfast of egg casseroles, sausage, and fresh-baked bread. Helen joined us, sharing the details of how Benito had ordered her to crouch in the tub, then shot two holes in her ceiling. It'd scared her nearly to death, she said, but he hadn't killed her. That shred of civilization in him had manifested at the right time.

And even though it appeared that one look at Zoe had gotten Miko over his moonstruck devotion to Mom, my parents were still stiff and standoffish with each other. I'm sure it hadn't helped that Mom slept on the couch. For all Dad knew, she'd rendezvoused with Miko.

We took our time with chores. No one had to be anywhere. We napped. Dad went for a walk after calling Giacomo. He told us not to drive all that way to visit. He was resting, too.

Malcolm disappeared into his office to work but surfaced every hour or so to check on each of us, trying to be unobtrusive, I'm sure, but I knew what he was up to.

Clara insisted on making supper as well. Dessert was a fresh August pie. I never had gotten a piece of the first one. I'd forgotten to bring whipped cream. It was delicious without any.

That night, I slept.

As soon as I had the work done on Wednesday, made lighter with Miko's help, me and my parents left to visit Giacomo. We would leave Dad at the hospital, then Mom and I were going dress shopping for Dex Two's gala.

Such a mother-daughter thing to do. When I was young, Aunt Trudy would drop me off at the mall by myself. This new experience had my stomach acting foolish, doing a girlish dance of excited anticipation. We would have lunch, too. Heck, maybe we'd get pedicures. I wouldn't mind having pretty feet for a change.

I also felt guilty. Sandy and Zoe were both attending the party, and we'd talked about going shopping. We would still need shoes. Maybe we could do that. Mom had plenty of them, she said.

As it turned out, Zoe didn't care. She and Miko were going riding, and she could wear one of her prom dresses. Sandy called to apologize because someone at work had lent her a dress. By the time we left, I felt better.

Malcolm gave us his SUV to drive, the one I'd flipped back in May avoiding a doe and fawn. The brake lines had been cut, too, but that's another story. The body shop had had it for weeks, and now it was all smooth and shiny. The brakes were fixed. The inside even smelled new.

We got on the road, my mother sitting up front with me, Dad in the back. I needed to get them talking and jumped to the topic that'd had me burning with curiosity since they'd arrived.

"So, guys, the empty suitcases? Don't you have mountains of clothes from years of competition?"

"Simple," Dad said. "We sold all of it to buy our tickets."

"It's true, Vi," Mom said. "We'd invested a lot getting the Paris studio set up."

"I thought you said you had backers."

"They backed out when your mother took up with Mr. Milanko Stanislaw."

My mother's lips tightened into a white line. My father's tone about frosted the windows.

"Why don't you use the trust fund?" The words came out without much forethought, as usual, but upon testing the idea, I didn't regret making the offer. If it would make things better, they could have it. It probably wasn't enough to make much of a difference to any of us.

"It's. Not. About. The. Money."

I fired up the defroster, thinking that maybe my mother was right, that I needed to talk to Dad. Underneath that glacial exterior, I guessed his heart was deeply wounded. And he was afraid.

"It's an irrevocable trust," my mother explained. Her long fingers pleated her black skirt. "We set it up a few years ago when we had quite a bit saved. We can't touch it. You're the sole beneficiary."

"Then I'll sign it over to you. Whatever."

What did she mean by *quite a bit*? At this point, knowing they'd wanted me and had thought to create the trust was more than enough.

"The rules governing these things are strict. You can't get the money until you're thirty."

That was only nine months away. "But then I can do whatever I want with it, right?"

My mother stared out her window. "I suppose."

"It's for you, Vi," my father said from the back, his tone warmer. "For you to set yourself up. You're ready for that now."

"Originally, it was a revocable trust," Mom said.

"But then Victor…" Dad's voice trailed off.

Uncle Vic. He'd never approved of my obsession with horses. I could imagine what he'd told them. Probably the truth, but he had a way of spinning honesty that made it something else entirely. It explained the provisions of the trust.

"It's okay. At first, I *was* upset by the whole *keep a job for one year and earn a glowing letter of recommendation* thing. Not to mention the *amount undisclosed* part. It made me really mad. But coming to Winterlight has been good."

"Until we showed up," Dad said.

I tilted my head from side to side as if considering. "Even that."

Especially that. I'd shut out the events of Monday. I think everyone was avoiding thinking about Benito. We could make a therapist rich. We drove in silence for a time, me mulling all they'd said, them lost to their own thoughts.

We were in the city when my mother spoke again. "Last I inquired, the value was around one hundred thousand." She turned toward me and smiled. "American dollars. But I haven't checked the balance in months."

I stared at her. A car honked its horn. I jerked the wheel to bring us back into our lane.

I'd been operating under the safest assumption—the one that kept me from being disappointed—that the trust was crap.

A hundred thousand dollars is *not* crap.

I focused on breathing in and out before I blacked out. "That's…more than I expected."

More then I'd ever dared imagine. I couldn't wrap my mind around that many zeroes. Like the truth of my parents' feelings for me, it would take a while for this to sink in.

Dad squeezed my shoulder. "We never forgot about you, kid."

I patted his hand, grinned at him in the rear-view mirror. He winked.

"What's it like," I asked, "suddenly having a father after all this time? Giacomo's complicated."

He gave my shoulder a playful pat. "That he is. Life will never be dull with him around. But I bet you have an inkling of how I feel."

I did. "Speaking of," I said. "Who's paying his hospital bill?"

"He is," Mom said. "*He* won't be a burden."

The emphasis she put on the word *he* made me think she worried they would be. Or she would be. Their relationship had to be fixable. They'd always been so connected. Not that I'd spent much time around them, but there had been a few months during the summer I was thirteen that they'd been stateside. They'd rented a space, were giving lessons. I went every day after riding and worked hard to master several ballroom dances. *Master* is too strong a word, but I grew competent. Not that I have much use for the waltz.

I thought back to how against it Aunt Trudy had been. I'd thought she was trying to protect me. She'd been right because they'd returned to the international circuit and never looked back.

Or so I'd thought.

I'd thought so many wrong things. Been led to believe so many falsehoods. Now, I understood that Aunt Trudy was only protecting herself, or once again, punishing her little sister.

Before that, though, I'd believed they were home, that we'd finally live together as a family. It'd crushed me when they left. I'd screamed and cried and begged them to take me with them. Been physically ill and unable to eat or sleep.

How that must have infuriated Aunt Trudy. She'd never treated me the same after that.

But watching them, how they looked at each other, still so in love. *So* romantic. The dance moves were sensuous and seductive. They moved as one, like me and a horse, only better. Alone at night, I'd practiced the precise tilt of her head, the provocative swing of her hips, the sultry, smoldering look in her eyes when he spun and dipped her. I'd wanted to be her. Wanted someone to look at me the way Dad looked at her.

After they left, I'd wanted to be the exact opposite. *I'd* never looked back.

I shook myself. We were at the hospital.

Giacomo sat up in bed chatting with a nurse.

She laughed and patted his arm. "You old charmer. Well, you have visitors, and I should get back to work." She smiled at us, her eyes darting around as if she were embarrassed, and went out.

He opened his arms wide. "*La famiglia.* Come."

He hugged me and Dad. Mom kissed his cheek.

"Wow," I said. "You look great."

"A couple of good nights' sleep is all I needed, but they want to keep me *for observation.*" He made an extravagant dismissive gesture with one hand.

"A friend is having a party this weekend," I told him. "You have to be well rested."

He narrowed his eye. "What kind of party?"

"A fancy one," Dad said. "I have a spare tux that will fit you perfectly."

"Will there be wine?"

"If I know Dex," I said, "only the best and plenty of it."

"*Bene,*" Giacomo said. "The same man who was at the farm? I knew I liked him."

"A different Dex. I'll explain later. Have the police been here, yet?"

His face grew serious. "No. Why? Is there more trouble? Hey, what happened to our cousin Little Tony? I didn't get to see him."

"Tony confessed to being Benito's accomplice. I think he's being sent back to New York."

"Oh. That's too bad. He was a good kid."

Debatable, but whatever. "So, someone will probably be here to question you." I was surprised they hadn't come already. "Dex One said to remember that Gemma stabbed Benito."

"I know she did." He reached for her hand, raised it to his lips, kissed it. "You saved my life."

My father came by his suave charisma naturally. My mother paled a little, though, and I was sorry to remind her of what she'd done.

"Mom, they have a Starbuck's here. Could you get Giacomo an espresso?" I gave her my wallet. "On me."

"*Grazie*. The one you brought me Monday, it was cold by the time I found it."

"How did you know it was from me?"

He lifted his shoulders. "Who else?"

I took a fortifying breath. "Do you remember talking to Benito before he died?"

"The snake blamed Eduardo."

"Okay. Do you remember *how* Benito died?"

His eye lit with cold satisfaction. "*Sì*. I pushed him down on the knife. Sent him to hell."

I was so hoping he'd blacked out and forgotten.

"He was done for, anyway, wasn't he?" my father asked.

"Unfortunately, that's not the point," I explained. "Giacomo, could you leave out that detail when the police question you?"

"Why? It's the truth." He smiled and patted my arm. "Why don't you call me *nonno*?"

I closed the door. "Okay, *grandpa*. It seems you can use lethal force to defend an innocent party from lethal force." I tried to remember exactly how Dex had put it. "But once the bad guy's quietly bleeding out, if you strike at that point—"

There was a knock at the door, it opened, and two uniformed police officers came in. Crap.

"Don't worry," Giacomo said. "I love you."

Dad and I went out into the hallway. "What the hell was that about?" I asked.

"He's not the bumbling gardener character he portrayed. Trust him."

"Like you trust Mom?"

"I don't want to talk about that."

Exasperated with them, I said, "You're going to have to," my tone more caustic then intended.

I'm not sure what gave me the courage to speak to him sharply or why I thought I had the right to intervene, but now that I had them, I wanted to keep them. Together.

Mom came down the hallway with the espresso. I almost drank it myself. Tempting as that was, I entered the room and put it by Giacomo's bed.

"Dad will be outside if you need anything." I kissed his cheek, whispered, "*Nonno.*"

He winked at me.

We left Dad sitting in the hallway.

Mom and I hit the swankiest mall in town. I might not have had the trust fund yet, but I felt flush and could afford to splurge. Malcolm paid me a decent wage, and I'd spent very little of it since arriving at Winterlight.

After trying on almost everything in our size, we both ended up with jewel tones. Hers was a brilliant sapphire blue column, one shouldered, crepe, with a high slit to show off her amazing legs. Simple and elegant with a touch of crystal trim to give it a little glitz. For me, a dark emerald green with a square neckline, cutouts on the sides, and a chiffon skirt of tiny pleats. It would be easy to walk in, my main criteria. Plus, it would blend well with Malcolm's kilt, which I knew he'd be wearing Saturday night, the darling man.

We had lunch and didn't talk about anything in particular. I wanted to tell her about Wastrel's part in all this, but I'd exceeded my stress limit, at least for a few days. She had too, if her reaction in the hospital was any indication. Plus, I don't think I could handle one of her withering looks when I told her of my dreams and visions. We'd come a long way in a short amount of time, but that might be pushing our fragile rapport too far.

Purchases stashed in the back of the SUV, we returned to the hospital to collect Dad. There, we found Giacomo watching a soccer game on TV and Dad asleep in the chair by the bed. The events of the past few days were fast catching up with me as well, and I grabbed a coffee before we got back on the road to home.

Mom and Dad both slept, both snored. I listened to the radio, quietly humming along with a few songs so as not to wake them.

Near dark, when I pulled into Winterlight, my truck was parked in its usual spot, which meant Zoe was still here. Dex's truck sat next to the house. A strange car had pulled right up to the barn doorway—an expensive-looking sedan—and right behind it, a sheriff's SUV.

Assuming it had to do with Benito and maybe Helen, I got out but heard angry voices inside, men and women talking over each other.

An unfamiliar female shouted, "Calm down," over and over in a strident tone.

Above them, Zoe screamed, "No, I won't go back. You can't make me!"

CHAPTER FORTY-FOUR

WITHOUT WAKING MY PARENTS, I rushed toward our newest drama. Deputy Joe stood to one side of the barn aisle looking bemused. A woman had Zoe by the arm. A man had the woman by the arm. Miko stood beside Zoe, a look of fierce concentration on his face, trying, and failing, to keep up with the argument, whatever it was.

"What's going on?" I asked Joe.

"They saw her on the news and came to collect her."

"What? Who are they?"

"Her parents. She was supposed to be spending the summer with a friend in Chicago."

That explained why she was so skittish and hyper aware.

"And your job here?"

He shrugged. "Her parents want her to go with them, but I can't make her. She's eighteen."

What? "She told me she was sixteen."

"Lied about her name, too. It's Emily. Emily Frobisher."

The name she'd put on the job application was Zoe Frost. What the hell?

"Where's Malcolm?"

Joe shrugged again.

"Vi, tell them they can't take me."

I waded in with my hand out. "Hi there, I'm Vi Parker, manager of Winterlight. Zoe works for us." The mother had to unhand her daughter to shake with me. "Is there a problem?"

"Her name is Emily. Not Zoe," her mother said. "And she is supposed to start medical school tomorrow."

"I'm sorry, I didn't catch your names," I said, trying to diffuse some of the tension.

"Dr. Leon Frobisher." Emily's dad shook my hand. "This is my wife, Dr. Crystal Frobisher."

Oh brother, double MDs. This might be challenging. Good manners were a good start, though.

"Why don't we go inside where we can sit?" I showed them toward the tack room.

As I went by Miko, I told him to get Malcolm. He sprinted off.

Crystal wore capri length running pants with a silky blouse, looking like she'd run out of the house mid costume change. Leon wore stretchy khakis and a polo shirt with a country club logo above the breast pocket, looking like he'd just come off the golf course. They both viewed the tack room's questionable furniture with distaste, but sat. It almost made me laugh because they reminded me of my parents.

I looked at Zoe. *Emily.* "Medical school?"

"Pre-med. But I don't want to go to medical school. Never have." She sat in the lounger, arms crossed, a mutinous expression on her face. "It's what *they* want."

"You were accepted to Wash U, honey," her dad said. "That's not an easy school to get into."

"You only want me to go there because that's where you went. None of this has to do with me." Tears laced her voice.

Tears of frustration, I'd guess. They'd probably had this conversation several times before.

"Young lady, you are not going to waste your life playing with horses."

This from the mother.

"It was good enough when you could brag to your friends about my expensive horse and all the ribbons I brought home, all the shows my students went to."

Wait, she had her own horse? Students? Was anyone around me what they seemed? Sometimes, I longed for my old life where Ed Todd made crude jokes and Harry drank too much. I knew what to expect. Life was simpler.

"That's a hobby," her mother said, "not a way to make a living."

I felt one eyebrow creep up toward my hairline. Crystal breezed on, not realizing she'd insulted me. I doubted she would have cared if she did.

"You agreed to go to Wash U."

Miko came in with Malcolm and Dex, and I instantly relaxed.

"Everything all right here?" Malcolm asked. He and Dex took up positions on either side of Zoe...*Emily*. Miko stood behind her. If the Frobisher's thought they had the upper hand by bringing the sheriff, they appeared less sure now. Especially because Joe stayed outside. I smiled.

"Apparently, Doctor and Doctor Frobisher were surprised to see their daughter, Zoe—whose real name is Emily by the way—on the news because they thought she was spending the summer in Chicago."

On the news at the scene of a stabbing and shooting in an abandoned house in a crappy part of the city, to be precise. They must have been horrified. Shocked. I would have been. No wonder they'd rushed out without changing their clothes. The only surprise was they didn't have their lawyer in tow.

"They've come to take her home where she's supposed to be attending medical school at Wash U. Do I have that right?"

"Medical school," Dex said. "That's big stuff, Miss Emily."

"And you are?" Mr. Doctor Frobisher asked.

I watched Dex ooze into his southern gentleman persona as he stuck out his hand and drawled, "Dexter Hamill, Private Investigator. I'm considering taking Miss Emily as an apprentice. While she goes to school, of course."

I glanced at Emily. She looked as surprised as I did. But eager and excited, too.

"That's ridiculous," Mrs. Doctor Frobisher said.

Her father looked perplexed. Of the two, I sensed he was the softer one, possibly more open to other directions for his daughter.

"And dangerous," he said. "Is that what this is about?"

"The danger?" Emily asked. "No. It's interesting. And I'm good at it."

"How could you possibly know?" her mother asked.

"Excuse me," Malcolm said. "Let me introduce myself. I'm Robert Malcolm, and this is my estate."

Oh for pity's sake. He never referred to Winterlight as his *estate*. Between him and Dex, I'm not sure who was more crafty when it came to playing a part.

"I think we'd be more comfortable at the house." He opened the door to the tack room, leaving them little choice, good manners and all, but to go through it.

They trouped out. Malcolm and Dex followed, but Malcolm gave me a roll of the eyes over his shoulder before he did. Zoe—Emily—and I followed a little ways back, which gave me a chance to talk to her before we got to the house.

"Okay, pretty little liar, what's this all about?"

"I'm sorry I didn't tell you the truth. I just had to get away from them for a while to think."

"Let me make sure I understand. You have a horse. You've competed extensively, you give lessons, and take students to shows? What the hell, girl?"

"I needed to relax and figure out who I really am, not try to live up to anyone's expectations."

"Except your own."

"Except my own, right. At least someone understands me."

"Better than you know. On that, you didn't discuss this apprenticeship thing with Dex?"

"No. I told him what I'm interested in, and he gave me advice about what to study, but I was as shocked by that as you."

My mind whirred, happy to churn on something other than blades, blood, and tango.

"Just go with the flow in here, okay?" We mounted the porch steps. "This could turn out all right."

My parents were nowhere in sight. They hadn't been in the car, and they weren't downstairs. Maybe they were talking. I could hope.

Deputy Joe had also snuck away. Smart man.

Malcolm had the Frobishers all comfy in the living room with a glass of iced tea in front of each of them.

"I don't understand this apprenticeship," Crystal said.

"It's simple," Dex explained. "Miss Emily will work for me part time—in the office only—while she attends school for a criminal justice degree."

As far as I knew, Dex didn't have an office. I'm not sure what he was up to.

The Frobishers looked like they'd been hit with a bat, but otherwise, they were taking it well.

"You can move your horse here," I said. "If you want."

Zoe couldn't stop smiling. "I do. And I can still live with Mrs. Erdman. She needs me."

"We don't know any of you," Mr. Doctor Frobisher said.

"It doesn't matter," Mrs. Doctor Frobisher said. "This conversation is over. Emma, get your things. You're coming home right now."

Oh. Apparently she wasn't taking it as well as I thought.

"No, Mom. I already called them and dropped out. I don't want to go home, and you can't make me." She looked at Dex, adulation and gratitude shining in her eyes. "This is what I want. This is what I'm going to do."

All things considered, her voice was even, reasonable.

The doctors sat side by side on the couch. Mr. Doctor Frobisher's eyes rested on his daughter for a long time, then he looked at Dex, then Malcolm, then me. He put his hand on his wife's.

Miko must have stayed at the barn, realizing he didn't have a place in this convo, that his presence might only complicate things. Smart boy.

"I believe that Emily is fine here, dear," Mr. Doctor said. "She has been for months. These people obviously care about her. One more day won't make a difference. Why don't we get some dinner. We can talk more tomorrow."

Crystal pulled in her lips but surprised me by not arguing.

Mr. Doctor turned to Malcolm. "You can understand what a shock it was for us to see her on the news, I'm sure." He turned to me. "I understand she saved your life?"

"She did."

He looked at his daughter. "We're very proud of you, Emily. You gave us quite a scare. Please don't do that again." He rose and pulled Mrs. Doctor up with him. "Thank you for your hospitality, Mr. Malcolm. We can see ourselves out."

"Before you go," Dex said with a reassuring smile, "take my card. Feel free to do a background check on me."

Mr. Doctor took the card with a smile that said he'd get his attorney on that first thing.

Emily went after them. "Does this mean—?"

"We'll talk tomorrow," her father said firmly.

They left.

"I don't know whether that was acquiescence or a strategic retreat to regroup," Dex said. "He might be back with his lawyer."

"That's what I'm afraid of," I said with a yawn. I had sat in one of the side chairs and felt unable to get out of it.

Zoe—Emily, came back down the hall. "Thank you so much Mr. Hamill. You won't regret it." She picked up her purse. "I'm going home—to Mrs. Erdman's—see you tomorrow."

I forced myself up to walk her to my truck.

"I have a car, by the way," she said as we walked down the driveway. "It's in my name, so they can't take it away. I had to leave it home because I took the train to Chicago."

"Did you ever really go to Chicago? Wait, you mean another car besides the one that burned?"

"Yeah, that was my brother's old car."

"Listen, I'm exhausted but have one question. Would you consider giving lessons here?"

"Sure," she said.

At my truck, she gave me a quick hug.

"Thanks for everything, Vi. You're the best. Well, Dex is the best."

"He is. Have a good night."

I watched her drive away, then went out to the blacktop to see if anyone had picked up the mail. By the size of the stack, no one had been to the mailbox in a couple of days. I brought it to the house, passing Dex on his way out. He waved. I found Malcolm in his recliner, a Scotch at his elbow. I slid over the armrest onto his lap. He put his arms around me and picked through the mail.

"There's something for you."

I took it from him, peered at the return address. It was from Ed Todd's sister.

"It's probably a thankyou for being there when Ed…died." My heart still stuttered when I said the words. "She didn't have to do that."

I opened it. It was a letter. She did thank me. But that wasn't all. The words on the page blurred as my eyes filled with tears.

"Vi, what is it? What's wrong?"

I handed it to him. He read it, then looked at me, and what I saw in his eyes made my heart melt.

It was fear. After that came a flash of uncertainty and something else, something that made me want to run out once again. It looked a lot like selfish possessiveness. I suppose, under the circumstances, I could understand that.

Ed Todd had left his farm to me.

CHAPTER FORTY-FIVE

SATURDAY ARRIVED and you'd think one of us was getting married with the amount of nervous energy and fluttering tummies we all shared. Me, Mom, Sandy, and Emily—I still had to mentally shift from Zoe to Emily each time I thought of her—went and got pedicures in the morning.

The previous two days had been busy. Emily and her parents had reached an agreement. She would work part time for Dex One and part time for us, and continue to live with Mrs. Erdman. She'd already started the fall semester at a college in Hannibal, taking classes toward a degree in criminal justice. She had her car, and her horse was due to arrive on Sunday. At the end of the first semester, they would reassess.

I'd be going back to the Island in the next week to sign papers to transfer ownership of Ed's farm into my name. I was still in shock about this turn of events and walked around in a denial daze, unsure what it meant for my future. Every time I thought about it, I saw that fear in Malcolm's eyes. Of course, I'd finish my year's contract at Winterlight. But I understood his fear. I'd felt something similar every time I'd thought he was going to fire me.

Miko would go to the Island with me. He would stay at Ed's and keep an eye on things until I figured out what the next steps were. He had a six-month tourist visa, so we'd have to decide something before then. There had been discussion of his applying for a green card. Or possibly a student visa.

A shiny new smart phone arrived addressed to me. I'd assumed Malcolm ordered it, but he hadn't. It came from Harry with a note that he was tired of not being able to reach me. He hoped this new phone would inspire me to keep in closer touch. Or at least motivate me to keep it charged so it could receive a message. I wasn't entirely sure how I felt about this gift. I'd pay him back, but it made me uneasy.

I guess I did need a communication device. My old phone had disappeared, or I'd left it somewhere and forgotten, or dropped it. The last time I remembered having it was the week before at Penny's.

Speaking of, she'd had her baby! A girl. They'd named her Isabella. I received beautiful pictures and videos of Isabella on my new phone, and that made me feel better about the device.

I talked to my beloved sis-co, but didn't share everything that had happened. Anything that had happened. Not even how Aunt Trudy had lied to me. Especially that. I saw no reason to darken the joy of Penny's first days as a mother.

Brian had been released from the hospital. He got to keep his eye but would have a heck of scar to tell stories about. He'd have to do physical therapy after his leg healed.

Giacomo had also been released. He had a bandage over his eye socket and a rakish patch over that. It suited him.

Everyone couldn't fit in Malcolm's SUV for the drive to St. Louis, so we split up. Dex took one of his SUVs with Emily, Miko, Sandy, and Renee. I'd been so delighted to see her again, had missed her wisdom. We hugged and promised to catch up later. Malcolm's mother, Helen, had been invited to the gala, but she politely declined, saying fancy parties weren't her thing.

My parents and Giacomo—my *nonno*—rode with me and Malcolm. Dad and his dad were resplendent in their tuxes. Dad's was basic black with satin lapels but Giacomo's was a deep damson plum color. The old guy wore it well, appeared comfortable in the snug formal attire, and it made me think there was even more to him than I suspected. He hadn't wanted to take the prescription pain killers they'd given him at the hospital, but we insisted—the eye socket obviously hurt—and he acquiesced. I had a feeling Dex Two's female guests would be swooning over him.

Malcolm wore his dress kilt and Prince Charlie jacket, matching waistcoat, tuxedo shirt, and black bow tie. Along with that, his dress sporran hung in front. My breath caught when he came down the stairs, casually shooting his French cuffs, and my tummy did several aroused backflips.

When he saw me, he froze, one foot on the last step, the other in midair. His right hand clutched the banister as if he needed support. My mother had tamed and pinned my hair into a one-sided chignon, and decorated it with a sparkly comb. I wore makeup. Not much, but I rarely wore any, so I knew I looked different. She'd lent me a diamond and emerald choker—a good fake, she'd clarified, a copy of one by Faberge—and matching dangly earrings. I felt like a princess.

He'd never seen me dressed up. Cleaned up, but not like this. His eyes flicked to my mother, who looked magnificent in her blue dress. She'd piled her hair high and wore dramatic makeup. Not as much as she would for competition, but more than me.

After clearing his throat, he said, "Gemma, you look stunning."

She thanked him with a regal nod, taking his compliment as her due. But she needed it, I could tell, because Dad hadn't said a thing.

Malcolm came down the last step nodding to Dad and Giacomo, and they acknowledged him—man speak for *don't we look swell?*—then reached for me.

"Come here, gorgeous."

"Okay, my scorching hot highlander. Since you put it that way." I grinned and put my hand in his.

Dex Two had valet parking so all we had to do when we arrived was alight and walk up the stone steps between a pair of chubby bears who guarded the entrance to the Peabody. The flat stone face of the building had a balcony carved into the second story with eight tall columns across the front.

Dex One drove in shortly after us. Miko helped both Emily and Sandy out. Sandy stared at the building and the people and the cars for a long time until Renee leaned close and whispered something in her ear. Sandy pulled up her jaw, lifted her skirt, and came up the stairs in a simple black dress with a low neckline and snug waist that showed off her curves.

Thanks to Harry's family, I'd attended events like this before. Though far from jaded, I wasn't agog either. I waved to them and waited while they caught up.

Emily's prom dress had a flowing purple skirt and intricately beaded high-necked top. Sleeveless. Renee glowed in a gray, strapless mermaid gown. Dex sported a silver bow tie to go with it.

Altogether, we looked like royalty. Not bad for a bunch of barn rats.

Malcolm pulled our invitations from his sporran to show the door man. We crossed the ticket area to a sweeping staircase that took us to the grand lobby, a two-story high art deco space with marble floor and gold accents. A balcony circled the entire second floor. Very elegant. Cocktail hour was in full swing.

Tables were set up on both levels. Bars were placed around the edges. At the opposite end, a live band played. Our table was on the first level near the dance floor. Each accommodated ten, so our group fit perfectly.

I watched my parents. Dad did all the right things. Escorted Mom, pulled out her chair, asked if she wanted something to drink, but I could tell by the pinched look around her eyes and the set of his jaw, things were tense. I suppose we could have requested to have Miko seated elsewhere, but that wasn't fair to Dex Two, or more likely, Daphne. It was enough that he'd accommodated all of us on such short notice.

Giacomo put himself at Sandy's disposal, getting both of them a glass of wine. Red for him, white for her. She blushed at his attention, and fluttered her eyelashes, although I think it was nerves rather than artifice. If he weren't my grandfather, I'd be half in love with him myself. I smiled my thanks. He shifted his eye to leer at Sandy's cleavage, then winked at me, the devil.

Dex Two swung by. I introduced him to my family, including Emily and Miko. He kissed the back of my mother's hand.

"I am so pleased to finally meet you," he said. "I do hope you will save a dance for me. A waltz perhaps? The band can play anything, anything at all."

"Of course," she said, though her eyes skated nervously to Adrian for a brief moment before she smiled at Dex Two.

Thankfully, he hadn't requested the tango.

He opened his arms to include the entire table. "Let me know if you need something. Most importantly, relax and enjoy the evening."

Dinner consisted of our choice of a filet mignon, salmon, or chicken piccata. Most of us had the salmon, Giacomo grumbling that he doubted the piccata would meet the standards of his palate. Malcolm went for the steak, then complained at the petite serving size. The high-ceilinged room rang with the clink of table, flat and glassware, the rise and fall of voices, and an undertone of soft jazz from the ensemble.

For dessert, four ice cream sundae bars were set up. My mother declined. Dad indulged in a bowl of strawberries buried in whipped cream, and I feared I'd created a monster. Mom wouldn't even look his way while he ate. Sandy and Zoe—dang it—*Emily Emily Emily* went full bore with three flavors of ice cream, fruit, nuts, whipped cream, chocolate sauce, walnuts, and M&Ms.

The concept was new to Miko. He kept it simple with vanilla ice cream, a few crumpled Oreos, hot fudge, and sprinkles. Malcolm and I both skipped, but there were plates of cookies out, and I thought I might snag one of them later. Giacomo had plain chocolate ice cream. A simple choice for a not-so-simple man.

Dinner wound down, and the service staff cleared tables as the musicians launched into a big-band era swing piece that encouraged a lot of people to get up and dance. It had me tapping my feet.

"You will dance with me?" Miko asked Emily.

"Oh…I don't know how. Not like that." Her eyes flitted over the dance floor.

Miko looked over the twirling couples. "Look," he said, "No one can dance. I show you."

I could tell she wanted to. "Go on," I said. "How often do you get the chance to look gorgeous, attend a gala at a beautiful place, and have such a cute guy offer to teach you to dance? Go for it, girl."

She jumped up. "Okay. Let's do it."

Miko led them out. I could tell he'd prefer to have more room, but he began leading her through the steps, and she picked it up pretty quickly, giggling the whole time. They were cute.

Dex One and Renee danced slowly because of his leg. Sandy had gone to the lady's room, Giacomo to refill his coffee cup. The infectious beat drummed through my parents, I could tell, even though they tried to ignore it. I thought it must be like the sound of hoofbeats to me, a primordial force that makes the heart thump, blood course more quickly. It was impossible not to heed its call.

Leaning close to Malcolm so I could whisper in his ear, I asked, "Can you cha cha?"

"It's been a while, why? I'm rusty, but I can."

"Perfect." I hid my mouth behind my hand. "It's my parents' favorite," I said. "Can you do me a favor?"

He gave me a conspiratorial smile. "What do you have in mind?"

I explained. He nodded. "Don't go away. I'll be back in a few minutes. Be ready."

No wonder I loved him. Wait. Love?

Maybe.

The feeling rushing through my body, centering in my chest. Unfamiliar yet recognized. My feet itched some, but not to run.

I tried to keep track of his progress as he wended through the crowd, stopping to talk to people here and there, but he was on a mission and never stayed long. Eventually, I lost track of him.

A few minutes later, I saw him in close conversation with the band leader. The band leader nodded. Malcolm said something else. The other guy smiled and nodded again. As Malcolm made his way back to the table, the swing song ended. There was pause. Several couples left the floor. He stopped to talk to Miko, who took Emily's hand and led her…somewhere. Not to our table.

Then, the unmistakable opening rhythm of Santana's Oye Como Va started up, a classic slow cha cha song. Malcolm's eyes were already dancing as he shook out of his jacket and took my hand.

"How's your cha cha?" he asked.

A quick glance at my mother showed her drawn forward, as if the music had the power to bring her to her feet. It probably did.

"Rusty," I said. It was one of the dances I'd learned, but it'd been a long time.

He twirled me out to the floor just as the melody began.

My hips picked up the beat as he pulled me into hold, bringing his hips close to mine, closer than they should be in cha cha, but I wasn't complaining.

We started with some basic walk steps forward and backward. I fell into time with him. Side steps, rock steps, hip twists, chasse. Dang. I remembered, and I loved it. Why hadn't we done this before now?

"Very nice, Miss Parker," he said as we did some cross steps.

He held my gaze with his, very intense, not unlike the way my parents used to look at each other. My tummy did more gymnastics. If he kept it up, I'd lose the rhythm.

"Is there anything you can't do, Robert Malcolm?"

His kilt flipped around his thighs as he worked his hips. "Live without you," he said without smiling.

Shit. I blundered an underarm turn, brushing the top of my head on his arm, my heart pounding harder than the dance could account for, then tripped through the alemana. That's when I saw my mother's hand slap the tabletop. She shot to her feet, looked down at her husband, and began to back toward the dance floor, arms out, hands beckoning, keeping her eyes on him the whole time.

Had the opportunity come?

Unable to resist the call of the dance, my father rose. He took his wife's hand.

They walked out to the middle of the floor as if the music hadn't started yet, as if they were entering a competition.

Or a battle.

They faced each other, not touching. And then, by some unseen signal, they began dancing.

Which made what we were doing look like a freaking demolition derby.

They danced around each other, and side by side, then Dad spun Mom into hold and led her around the floor, legs flashing hips bumping. Back and forth, together, apart, they showed everyone how it's supposed to be done. Malcolm turned me into his chest and led me off the floor.

"You did it," he said. " You got them up on the dance floor," he said.

"Let's hope it works."

Giacomo came to my side, his coffee cup cradled in one hand. He lifted it toward the couple on the floor. "Well done."

"We're not finished yet," I said.

I watched and waited, breathless, as I think many were. The floor was clear now except for my parents, and they didn't seem to notice, or were simply used to it.

The final beats signaled the end of the song, and they finished with Mom in a lunge. They were magnificent. Everyone watching clapped and cheered. That didn't include every person in the place, but as those who were sitting farther back realized something was going on, they came closer. People upstairs lined the railing.

As my parents straightened out of their final position, a single violin began a haunting melody. Then, a concertina started. What contemporary band has a concertina? One that can play tango music, that's what. Dex Two hadn't been kidding when he said they could play anything.

Dismay briefly tightened the corners of my mother's mouth but she recovered quickly. She didn't glance at my father, just waited, waited for him to make the first move. He began to walk away. Where the hell was he going? My mother hung her head and walked in the opposite direction. What the…no!

The lights dimmed. When my father reached the far side of the dance floor, he turned to stare at my mother's back. She lifted her eyes, found mine. I smiled, hoping it was something like that secret smile she had shown me a few days before when talking about my father. I gave an encouraging nod. Returning her eyes to the floor, she pivoted on the ball of one foot, so graceful, kicking her dress behind her. Slowly, almost dragging her feet but in time with the music, she made her way back to center, where my father now stood.

She lifted her arms as if she might embrace him, but then put her back to him and gradually moved one leg out to the side, bending the other as she slid her body down his front, her face rapt. He gazed into the distance as if he didn't care, but as she rose and took one step forward, he grabbed her wrist, pulled her around and dipped her, all in perfectly controlled slow motion.

Sandy came up beside me. "What's going on?" she asked.

"Just watch," I said.

Dad viewed her exposed throat as if he wanted to bite her. The music swelled and sped up, he drew her into him, and they floated across the floor, chest to chest, legs flicking up and down, hers between his, his between hers.

That summer I was thirteen, I'd wanted to learn to tango. My mother said no. Adamantly. I was too young, she said, to understand the nuances of the dance.

Watching them now, I understood. They made walking look like seduction, the quick-quick, slow-slow steps building toward a climax, staring into each other's eyes as if they were the only two in the room, in the world. Then my mother would lower her gaze again, yielding to him, her hand around his neck as if he were her only hope of survival. His hand would be high on her back, possessive, then down at his side as if unsure he could contain her spirit. This was soul-searing intimacy laid bare for everyone to see.

It wasn't only her reluctance to teach me tango that I understood. Life and relationships were nuanced as well, too complicated for a child to comprehend. Yet, I'd been going through adulthood letting a child's anger and hurt guide me.

No more.

They had come home, come for me, not turned away when I lashed out. They'd gifted me with love and forgiveness. I could do the same for them.

Dex One and Renee came to stand on the other side of Malcolm. Renee reached behind the men and touched my arm.

"Hey, New York, now I know where your fire comes from." She watched my parents for a moment, turned back to me. "They're fantastic."

"Yeah," I said, "they kind of are."

My parents' lips came near to touching, then he twirled her away, and anguish filled her eyes. I could feel it. Everyone did. The entire place leaned toward them, pulled by their passion, as if they were the center, the sun, and all else revolved around them. Dad held her tight, her leg rode up to his hip, and he caressed her calf before she extended her foot out to the side and around, and then dropped into another lunge, bent backwards nearly double.

They came together, and it looked like they would finally kiss, but again she put her back to him, slid down his front, her hands stroking his thighs. His face showed a mix of agony and arousal.

"Jesus Christ," Sandy said in a hoarse whisper. "I think I just wet my panties."

"Don't be gross," I hissed. "You're watching a spiritual experience."

She snorted. "If you say so. But I know foreplay when I see it."

"Hey, these are my parents we're talking about."

"Whatever. They made you, didn't they?"

Indeed they had.

Mom collapsed into Dad's arms. He dragged her across the floor, her legs looking like she could no longer support herself. But it was all part of the dance, the give and take of life, the push of the past, the pull of the future. Malcolm's arm slid around my waist, his fingers warm on my hip.

"What do you think?" he asked. "Mission accomplished?"

They danced across the floor quickly again, spinning around each other, their legs kicking with nearly every step, the hem of Mom's dress snapping as Dad led them round and round. They rode the music like I ride a horse, one with it, as though it gave them life or sprung from them fully formed. Quick-quick, slow-slow. He lifted her onto his hip, she slid down, swiveled. The music built to a crescendo, and then it ended. They were in each other's arms, chest to chest, their lips so, so close.

The room was hushed, the anticipation palpable. The wait staff stilled, entranced. Not even the tinkle of crystal stemware broke the spell. My mouth had gone dry. I could smell Giacomo's coffee and the whiskey on Malcolm's breath.

My parents breathed hard. Dad closed his eyes and leaned his forehead into Mom's, whispered words only she could hear. She nodded as a sob convulsed her body. Her hands skimmed up the back of his head. She drew him to her. They kissed.

A thrill rushed through me to squeeze my heart with euphoria. The silence broke, the applause so wild it almost hurt.

The truth is, my parents are alive.

I used to pretend they were dead to make their absence in my life tolerable. But they are very much alive, present. Welcome.

Dabbing at sudden tears, I leaned close to Malcolm. In a choked whisper, I answered his question—and many others.

"Mission accomplished."

End of *Run Out*

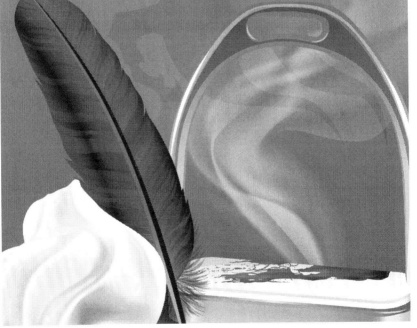

CANDACE CARRABUS

WRONG

DREAM HORSE MYSTERY #3

LEAD

CHAPTER ONE

A VULTURE PECKED at a lump of road kill a short distance ahead. Some might take finding a dead body in the morning as a bad sign. Not me. Not anymore. I've learned to look on the bright side, to be grateful.

A few minutes before, my ancient pickup began to chug, the temperature gauge screamed *overheating imminent* and the oil pressure flicked to zero.

Not exactly what I needed five days before a life-changing deadline.

I had guided the truck to the narrow slice of gravel between the crumbling edge of blacktop and grassy drainage ditch. That's when I spied the vulture.

Leaning on the steering wheel, I shifted my gaze to my dog, Noire, who sat on the seat beside me, her ears pricked to the winter wheat outside, her nose at the gap above the window.

"Stay," I said.

She snapped her big black head to me, brown eyes questioning.

"I'm sure there are rabbits and other critters out there, but I need you to stay."

She sighed and turned back to pondering the fields.

I rummaged around until I found a couple of used napkins, popped the hood, and got out. The liquid clinging to the dipstick resembled milky tea rather than black coffee. I'm no motor head, but even I could guess this did not bode well for my engine's state of health.

I shouldered my purse, strung a piece of baling twine through Noire's collar by way of a leash, and locked up the vehicle. With my dog at my heels,

I started walking, knowing the bags of horse feed in the bed would be safe out here in God's country, also known as rural Missouri.

I could call my boss, Robert Malcolm. He'd come get me. But it was a soft spring morning, would be barely seventy degrees at midday. Birds sang to each other, and only a few cotton ball clouds hung in the sky.

Anyway, Malcolm was super stressed lately, working more than ever. Sometimes I thought he was hiding from me, from us, afraid of what would happen in less than a week.

To be fair, I hadn't given him any indication of what I planned to do when our one-year contract concluded. That's because I wasn't sure, and I'd taken to falling asleep in the tack room or on the couch in his living room, rather than climbing into bed with him as I had for nearly a year.

Avoiding each other. He probably thought he was giving me space. I probably thought I needed space. He hadn't exactly begged me to stay.

I needed to decide. Should I stay with him at Winterlight, or return to my farm back on Long Island? Ed Todd's farm, that is. I'd never get used to thinking of it as mine, even though I'd fantasized for years about owning it.

He'd died the previous summer. A couple of weeks later, I'd gotten a shock when I found out he'd left the valuable piece of real estate to me. Unfortunately, he hadn't left any money to pay for upkeep or taxes, let alone feed the retired horses who lived there. Insurance covered some of the damage left by the fire, but I really didn't know what to do. No matter how many lists of the pros and cons of each option I made, I was no closer to knowing than I had been six months ago.

Except, except...I might want to stay in Missouri. Part of me thought I should want to return to my roots, but whenever I imagined going to the East coast, a squirmy sensation invaded the pit of my stomach. Sometimes it felt like excited anticipation, others, more like worried apprehension.

The vulture abandoned his breakfast at our approach. He sat on a fence post, patiently waiting for us to move along. Taking a deep breath and exhaling noisily, I tugged Noire away from the dead possum before she could roll in it, and steered us onto the road to get over a culvert.

A warning tingle zipped up my neck like the feeling right before a horse spooks. I heard it the same moment it was on us. A speeding car coming from behind, the engine roaring at the top of its gear.

Jerking Noire's rope, I hopped over the ditch, turned my ankle, and fell. My purse slingshotted over the wire fence into a cow pasture.

A sports car zoomed by, the whoosh of wind kicking up leaves and sucking the breath out of me.

I looked in time to see it was black, foreign, and had New York plates.

CHAPTER TWO

NOT LONG AGO, I would have jumped to my feet and screamed a string of expletives at the long-gone driver. That would make me feel better but do little else. Whoever was behind the wheel was either an idiot or suicidal maniac. He or she was one sharp turn, a patch of gravel, or a slow-moving combine from vulture pickings.

Natural selection at its best.

They weren't from around here. That would be obvious even without the out-of-state plates. What they were doing speeding around the area was anybody's guess. Probably lost.

I stood and tested my ankle, brushed myself off.

It was when I turned to retrieve my purse that I felt the weird shift, went cold at what it meant.

Shit. Slamming my eyes closed, I sent up a quick prayer that when I opened them, I wouldn't see a horse in the cow pasture or anywhere else nearby. Not because equines don't sometimes share fields with bovines. It was one horse in particular I didn't want to see. The one who used to haunt my dreams. Last time I'd seen Wastrel, he'd manifested right in front of me while I was fully awake. Despite having been my favorite ride when alive, as a dead messenger, he never brought glad tidings.

I cracked one eyelid. A shimmer surrounded us. Noire whimpered and leaned against my leg. He snorted. Wastrel, that is. Even without looking, I'd know his scent, that mix of a chocolate milkshake, lilacs, bacon frying, freshly-turned earth, new-mown grass, a just-washed baby, and the air on top of a mountain or at the sea that somehow combined into something delicious and peaceful and uplifting unlike anything you'd ever smell on Earth.

I sighed and stroked his cheek. Each time he showed himself, I hoped it was the last. Maybe for a change he was bringing good news, or an answer to the questions swirling in my mind like the tornado that'd hit west of us the week before. He stood right in—through—the wire fence separating me from my purse, which, I noticed, had landed just a scooch shy of a wet cow patty.

"What do you want?" I asked, but not with anger. I could never be mad at Wastrel.

Noire licked my hand.

"Not you, sweetie," I said, resting my knuckles against her muzzle. "This guy. Can you see him?"

She thumped her tail but gave no indication one way or the other about the big bay. Perhaps she simply accepted the appearance of a ghost horse as normal. Perhaps I should begin to think that way, too. Wanting him to go away hadn't done me any good.

Wastrel tossed his head. The shimmery light coalesced into a dense fog, muffling light and sound as surely as a padded cell. I stepped closer, put my arms around his neck, leaned into his warmth, closed my eyes again.

And saw what he'd showed me in dreams several times a few months back. Us riding a jump course at a horse show—*that* jump course—the one where he crashed and died. Crashed and died *on purpose*, nearly taking me with him to oblivion.

As in the dreams of last summer, something feels off, like he's lame, or the footing is bad, and he can't find his balance. But I wouldn't ride him if he were hurt or the ground was too hard or slippery. His owner would have tried to force us to compete no matter what, but I would have refused. Small wonder I was fired as often as I was hired back then. If only there had been a reason to say no that day.

What did it mean? What was the point of taking me back to that course over and over again? A horn blared. Disoriented, lost in memory, I worried we'd drifted into the road, or that the speed demon was back. I opened my eyes. Wastrel and the fog were gone. A pair of cows sniffed my purse. One slid out her tongue and licked it.

A familiar truck sat behind mine. Our neighbor, Hank, hobbled alongside, his hand grazing the top edge of the bed.

"You lose somethin' or run out of gas, or what?"

Of all the things I've lost, I miss my mind the most…

The hood was still up on my truck. I limped back and gestured toward the engine. "I think it's broken."

He grunted. "Surprised it ain't died before now. Looks like it'd crack in half if you put it on a lift."

Not funny. But true.

He peered into the engine compartment, pulled the dipstick, shook his head.

"What?"

"Prob'ly a cracked block." Hank lifted his cap and scratched his ear. "Mehbe the head gasket. More likely the block."

"Is that bad?"

"It ain't good."

After being nearly run over by a speeding car, having my purse eaten by cows, and Wastrel bringing visions of who knows what, a dead truck was the least of my problems.

CHAPTER THREE

A PAIR of shapely legs brought her to us with two strides.

"Martina?" Malcolm asked in a surprised tone. "What—" He made a choking sound like he'd swallowed an engorged tick.

I could wish.

Throwing her arms around his neck, she stood on her toes, pushed her breasts against his chest, and kissed him hard on the mouth.

My eyebrows nearly touched in a frown. *Wrinkles*, I imagined my mother saying.

Too slowly for my liking, Malcolm detached Martina's arms—and lips—and set her away from him. She dropped her gaze to the hem of his kilt and lingered there, then fluttered her eyelashes and smiled.

Coyly.

Not a word I like, and one I hope is never applied to any action, facial expression, or words of mine.

"What a surprise," Malcolm said. He looked past her to the rig. "You have a horse?"

She twirled and clapped her hands. "Two, actually. You know I've always wanted them."

He *knew*? Just how well did he know?

The trailer bounced as one of the horses shifted.

"I thought you were in San Francisco," Malcolm said.

"San Jose, but who's counting?" She emitted a throaty laugh.

My fingers curled, and not in a good way. In a way that would become a fist if I didn't move out of their vicinity.

I pivoted and walked down the barn aisle wishing I could stomp, but my ankle wouldn't have tolerated it.

I had no right to question him, nor to be possessive or jealous. *Of course* he had a history. We'd known each other almost a year, but he'd had thirty-one before that. Years when he undoubtedly had plenty of other relationships. We were really only friends with benefits. Well, employer-employee with benefits, but *who's counting*?

In the tack room, I threw my fist against the door that led to the upstairs apartment and yelled for my grandfather, Giacomo, who currently lived there.

I should have stayed in the apartment, never gotten involved with the boss. I broke my own rules and this is what it got me. Heartache and regret.

An annoying little voice reminded me that I hadn't committed to staying at Winterlight, let alone committed to a long-term relationship with Malcolm, so…I told my conscience to fuck off.

Giacomo didn't answer. He must have already been working in his garden. I took the stairs two at a time, filled the bathroom sink with cold water, stuck my face in—I wouldn't have been shocked to see steam rising—and didn't come up for air until I heard Malcolm yelling from the barn.

Pushing wet fingers through my hair, I picked out a few mud clumps, chucked my stinky T-shirt, pulled a clean one from the drawer still reserved for me, and headed downstairs. In the tack room, I snagged a ball cap and jammed it on my head before going into the barn.

There, each new horse hung his head over a stall door. A chestnut and a bay. Pretty. Tall. Well-bred. Probably thoroughbreds. The bay looked like he might have some warmblood in him.

The chestnut stood in Cali's stall. I clamped my teeth on a growl and breathed deeply. We *needed* boarders. Getting two in one day was amazing. If that was, indeed, what was happening.

Malcolm wrapped his fingers around my bicep. It must have felt unusually tight because he cast me a curious sideways glance before saying, "Vi, meet Martina Zenger. We went to college together."

I stretched my fingers before putting my hand in hers. She had a cool, limp grip. I squeezed and shook. Her knuckles popped.

Oops.

Martina smiled. Okay, grimaced. Whatever.

"Vi is the manager of Winterlight," Malcolm said, his voice filled with pride that soothed my ruffled pelt. "You need anything, let her know."

"Oh, Robert," Martina said, "don't be silly. I'm sure I won't need anything, but if I do, I'll call you. Is your mobile number still the same?"

He coughed. I resisted the urge to wallop him on the back.

"Mr. Malcolm is often away on business," I said. "He can't be interrupted when he's at a client site."

"I know all about client sites," Martina purred. *Purred.* "Robert and I are in the same business."

"Oh, really?" The words escaped too quickly. Shut it, Vi, just shut it. Who cares?

"I've been working in online game programming for the last couple of years." She swept her blonde locks over one shoulder and continued. "But I got tired of it, tired of the pace. I thought Missouri would be the perfect location to catch my breath. And what could be better for that than horses and a farm?"

"There are plenty of other farms in Missouri," I said.

What the hell was wrong with me? She might be a perfectly nice person. Why did I feel so threatened? She obviously had money, or an enormous credit limit, based on her vehicle, trailer, and clothes. But I'd have money soon, as well. In less than a week, once the trust fund paperwork was completed, I'd have a couple of hundred thousand dollars in my pocket. I planned to buy a new rig, too. Especially since my truck was now officially dead. My trailer was okay, but who wouldn't want a matched set?

"Yes," she said with a dismissive wave as if I hadn't spoken at all. "Computer programming. The inner workings behind the windows and apps, you know. Very complex."

Had this woman just *mansplained* computers to me? Even if she had, her attention, her entire being, remained focused on Malcolm.

Okay, maybe not perfectly nice.

Giacomo strolled into the barn wiping his hands on a rag. He'd gained weight in the past eight months. In August, he'd been whip thin and fit, especially for a man of seventy-two. After a winter of regular meals, though far from pudgy, I doubted I'd be able to count his ribs if he took off his shirt. His face had softened, but that could be the result of no longer being on the run. Fifty years of staying one step in front of his murderous cousin had taken its toll.

With his thick gray hair, full beard, and the black patch over his left eye, he could have walked straight off the deck of a pirate ship, circa 1700.

He paused, cleaning dirt from his fingers. His sharp eye danced from me to Malcolm to Martina and back, sensing, no doubt, the tension.

"Got the beans planted already?" I asked, glad for the interruption.

He nodded. "I need a fence to keep the rabbits out. Especially before I put in the tomatoes."

"Clara can recommend what's best," Malcolm said.

Clara had been gardening her whole life. If she didn't know how to keep rabbits out of the vegetable patch, nobody did.

Giacomo straightened. "I know what I need."

Maybe feeling threatened by another person ran in the family.

"Ooohhh, fresh-picked tomatoes," Martina murmured. "I can't wait." A clear statement about her intended length of stay if I ever heard one. She offered her droopy hand to Giacomo.

He shook with her, but glanced at their clasped hands like she'd given him a dead fish, pulled away with a nod, and said to me, "You come with me to the store."

"Love to."

"Wait," Malcolm said. "Martina needs to fill out the paperwork, and...so on."

And *so on* being the third degree I always gave new boarders about their horse, riding habits and schedule, training needs, previous feeding regimen, tack and storage needs, vaccination record, veterinarian, farrier, and more.

"The form is on the clipboard in the right-hand drawer of my desk." A desk I never used. But there's a desk, and I'm the manager, so that makes it mine. "I'm sure you can fill in the blanks and...so on."

I tossed a saccharine smile at Malcolm. He gave me a squinty look but said nothing.

Giacomo and I hot-footed it out of the barn, jumped in his new Smart car, and sped down the drive.

The vehicle wasn't all that smart for country living, but Giacomo divided his time between the farm and my parents' place in St. Louis. The city house had belonged to Malcolm's father. He'd passed away the year before. Malcolm had no time to clean out the brick two-story let alone prepare it for sale, so it had sat empty for a few months. My parents needed a cheap place to live and wanted to be in an urban area, so a deal was struck. They were cleaning and fixing it up in exchange for next-to-nothing rent.

Malcolm was generous that way. In all ways, and I chided myself for immediately assuming the worst regarding Martina. What can I say? Old habits die hard.

My parents, Adrian and Gemma, had opened a dance studio in Soulard and begun giving lessons, settling in well after spending their adult lives traveling the world for ballroom dance competitions. All indications were for them remaining in Missouri. Yet another point in favor of my staying. Not to mention the large plot of unused land next to the barn Malcolm had given Giacomo for his garden. The summer before, my grandfather had arrived with a few tomato plants and not much else. The small garden he'd planted by the house flourished under his care. He had much more ambitious plans this year.

How would they feel if I left?

We turned onto the highway and headed for town, for the nearest farm supply store where Giacomo could buy the fencing he wanted for his garden.

"Who was the girl with the sloppy handshake?" he asked.

"Some old friend of Malcolm's." I kept my face turned away, my eyes on the passing fields and trees.

Giacomo grunted, a world of opinion expressed in one sound. "I've seen her type before. You don't have to worry—"

"Who said I'm worried?"

He sucked his teeth, gave me the side eye. "He's smarter than that, Malcolm. That's all I'm saying."

I still found it disconcerting to have my immediate family around after growing up without them. They were so…involved in my personal life. Invested, even.

Nosy.

I told myself that they loved me, that's all. But I didn't have to like their awareness of my feelings. I could get away with telling friends to mind their own business. Family, not so much. I should be grateful to have them. And I was. Even though they could be irritating.

I returned my attention to the window without comment. The weather continued clear, the trees glowing with spring green straight from the crayon box. Emily, who helped out around Winterlight and gave riding lessons, and I had ridden out the day before and found the forest floor dense with wildflowers. I'd learned the names of some. Bluebells and Dutchman's Breeches. They reminded me of the first birthday I'd celebrated at Winterlight, nearly a year ago, when Malcolm had surprised me with a posey he'd picked in the woods behind the house.

Truth? I loved Winterlight—never mind how much I cared for Malcolm —and I knew my heart was strongly leaning toward staying. But that annoying voice, it nagged at me. What if Malcolm decided he didn't want me? What would be the point of staying then?

Meanwhile, I couldn't ignore the appearance of Wastrel. That dead horse never brought good news, and the fact that Martina showed up on the same day foreshadowed danger for all of us.

My purse vibrated and I pulled out my phone. The screen indicated it was Miko calling from Long Island. Milanko Stanislaw, the cutie-patootie Ukranian dancer who'd shown up on the heels of my parents thinking he was in love with my mother. Thankfully, he'd gotten over her quickly, transferring his affection to Emily, a woman his age. Miko's background included working on his uncle's horse farm outside Kiev. I'd sent him to New York to keep an eye on Ed Todd's place for me—and reduce the potential distraction for Emily while she attended college.

Ed Todd's. *My* place.

Miko and I talked weekly, and it was a relief knowing I had someone trustworthy who took good care of the horses and loved the cat.

"Hey Miko," I answered.

"Hey Miss Viola Parker."

His usual line but not his typical jaunty tone. My chest tightened. "What's wrong?"

He paused and cleared his throat. "I have situation here."

Never a good conversation opener. I held my breath.

"Is my parents. They need me at home."

Relief swept through me, the pain in my chest easing. None of the horses were hurt or sick. But apprehension sailed in with my next breath. "Home as in…" I had to pause to clear my throat. "Kiev?"

Please let the answer be *no*.

"Yes, yes. Kiev."

"When?"

"Today."

CHAPTER FOUR

"TODAY?" I glanced at the clock on the dash. Nearly lunch time. An hour later on the East coast. I could probably catch a flight to the Island in the afternoon and be there by midnight after a layover in Baltimore. Not a pleasant thought, but… "Do you already have a ticket?"

"Yes. So sorry, but my father is in hospital. My mother is insisting."

"Of course you have to go. What time is your flight?"

"Six. I am already packing, and must leave soon for airport. My mother make reservation before calling. I am very sorry."

"Stop saying that. It's fine." It wasn't, but I'd figure it out. "Anything I need to know?"

"No, no. The blacksmith, he was here yesterday. All the feet are trimmed. Feed, there is enough for two weeks. I put them up before leaving."

Meaning he'd put the horses in their stalls. There were only two left—the paint-thoroughbred gelding, Beau, and the gray Hanoverian mare, Sasha. Both of whom I'd ridden and showed when I first started out. And, of course, there was Millie, the white barn cat. Though ancient, she pretty well took care of herself.

"Everything will be okay. Thank you for all you've done these past months, Miko. I can't tell you how much it means to me."

"It has been my honor to assist you in this, Viola Parker. You will give the message to Emily?"

"Of course. But you can text or call her. I'm sure she'd love to hear from you."

He hesitated enough for me to suspect something had happened between them. Long-distance relationships were hard at best.

"Yes," he said. "But…"

Plus, he was distracted and worried about his father at the moment.

"Don't worry. I'll tell her."

"Thank you. I…"

"You'd better get going." He had barely enough time to get to JFK for his flight.

He thanked me and clicked off as Giacomo parked. I sighed, switching mental gears. It occurred to me we weren't going to get much fencing in this tiny car.

"Trouble?" Giacomo asked.

"Miko's father is in the hospital. He's flying back to Kiev today."

My grandfather stared at me for a long breath, mentally calculating what this meant. "You have a friend there you can call to step in?"

"Back on the Island?"

That hadn't occurred to me. Probably because there really wasn't anyone I could ask, not anyone I'd trust. I'd burned too many bridges. Harry maybe. We hadn't talked in a while, and I didn't know what he was doing with his time these days. Considering him made my intestines twist. Could he be trusted? He said he was clean—drug and alcohol free—but his history…he'd claimed to be sober before.

"*Sì*," Giacomo said. "If you leave your job now…"

He left the rest of the thought dangling—if I left Winterlight now, I wouldn't complete the year required by the trust fund, wouldn't get the money. Money that represented independence, freedom.

I'd still have Ed Todd's place, and that prime bit of acreage was worth way more than the trust fund. If I sold it. Which I wasn't sure I wanted to do.

Where was a crystal ball when I needed one? That thought naturally led me to Renee. She'd returned from Kansas City where she'd been caring for her sister, was back to riding Smitty on a regular basis. She'd once told me my aura had dark patches, and that I needed to find my herd. That people, like horses, were herd animals—needed others to rub up against to be truly happy. Anytime anything weird happened at the farm, she walked around with what looked like a giant smoking joint but was actually what she called a smudge stick—white sage. Supposedly the smoke cleared out or absorbed the bad energy.

After everything had happened the year before with Giacomo's cousin, Benito, she'd *cleansed* his moonstone necklace by leaving it out overnight during a full moon, then *charged* it with positive affirmations. Thus, supposedly, wiping away all of Benito's negativity and making it safe for Giacomo to wear.

All that to say, Renee was as close to a crystal ball as I could get. As Giacomo and I walked into the farm store, I texted her to see if she could talk. For good measure, I sent a message to Harry, too. Not explaining my dilemma, just to say hi and see what he was up to. Harry, who now went by his first name, Michael, as part of his stated intention of buckling down and getting serious about life. He'd gifted me the smart phone in my hand. The least I could do was occasionally use it to communicate with him.

Giacomo bought a solar charger, roll of wire, and the step-in posts needed to run a couple of strands of electric around his garden, and it all fit in the cargo area of his car just fine.

We pulled out of the parking lot but turned in the opposite direction we needed to go if we were returning to Winterlight. Which I thought we were. I lifted my eyebrows at Giacomo.

"Coffee shop," he said.

"What coffee shop?"

"The Roasted Bean. Main Street."

I'd never been there. "What's wrong with the coffee at home?"

"You no make the espresso and the latte."

"Sorry to disappoint. Barista isn't part of my job description."

"That's why we're going to the Roasted Bean." He reached over and patted my arm. "You'll like it."

Giacomo swerved into a space right in front of the brick storefront. No need for mad parallel parking skills with the Smart Car.

Inside were exposed brick walls, a tin ceiling, polished concrete floor, a few tables, and a fireplace with two comfy-looking leather couches in front of it. Very inviting. I did like it.

"Good morning, Giacomo," said the lady behind the counter. "The usual?"

He had a usual? I needed to hang out with gramps more often. He held up two fingers.

"Two dirty chai tea lattes coming right up," she said.

"What, exactly, is a dirty chai tea latte?"

Giacomo pulled out his wallet. "You'll like it. Trust me. Go sit and relax a few minutes."

I sunk down into the leather sofa. Big mistake. Super comfortable So comfortable I might not get up. Unfortunately, I didn't have the leisure time to just hang out at a coffee shop, no matter how nice it was. I had to figure out what to do with myself. In both the short and long term.

I looked around at the artwork on the walls. There was a book shelf and another that held games. A young couple played Scrabble at one of the tables near the front. A guy sat at a long counter against the wall with his laptop open in front of him. The fireplace was on and added to the ambience. I would be coming back to the Roasted Bean.

If I stayed in Missouri.

Giacomo brought me my fancy drink. I waited until we were back in the car to taste it. It was sweet, but that sweetness was balanced by a strong coffee undertone. My grandfather had been right. I liked the place, and I liked the drink.

"You approve?"

I nodded.

"Chai tea latte with a shot of espresso." He lifted his. "Dirty chai tea latte."

I held mine up. "To dirty chai tea lattes."

Renee sent me an answering text as we drove back to the barn saying she'd just gotten there. It was all I could do to keep from asking if Martina was still around. After all, it's not like I cared.

Okay, maybe I cared a little.

At Winterlight, Giacomo backed as close to his garden as he could and unloaded his supplies while I walked down the barn aisle. Martina's horses still stood in the first two stalls on the left. The bay lounged under the window dozing. The chestnut munched hay. The other eight stalls were empty. While we enjoyed perfect weather, the horses stayed in the pasture as much as possible. They had a run-in shed at the far end, a thicket of trees toward the center, and the barn overhang up here if they needed shelter.

Renee had Smitty on the cross ties and was bent over picking out his back left hoof.

I walked up and put my hand on the gray's nose. "Hey, good boy, how are you today?"

"Oh, I'm fine," Renee said. "How are you?"

"So funny."

She stood and stretched her back, her dark eyes sparkling. "It's just like you to greet the horse before the person."

"What can I say? They're my true herd."

She snorted. "Right. What do you need to talk about, white woman?"

I stroked Smitty's neck, then slid my hand down and scratched his chest. He closed his eyes and stuck out his nose in appreciation. I knew all their favorite spots.

With a glance over my shoulder to where Martina's rig sat parked in the drive, I answered Renee's question. "Stuff."

"Um-hmmm. I saw some stuff go up to the house with Malcolm."

Renee patted Smitty's butt and gestured for me to follow her into the tack room. I got her a cup of water while she pulled a large deck of cards from her canvas messenger bag. "I've been waiting for you to ask," she said as she began shuffling.

"Ask what?" I hadn't told her about Miko's phone call, but the woman definitely had some spooky intuition.

"You have a big decision in front of you." She sat on the edge of the rocker-recliner. It tipped forward with a squeak. "At least, you think it's a big decision."

Taking a seat on the bench opposite I said, "I suppose you believe it's a no-brainer."

She lifted one shoulder. "Not for me to say."

I watched the oversized cards lift apart and sift together, mesmerized by the flashing colors. Each one had a painting of an angel on it with an accompanying message. I'd never asked for a reading, hadn't asked today, but I'd take any guidance at this point, whatever the source.

"You're right," I admitted. "That looming decision feels like an impossible choice to me, but I have something even more immediate on my mind." I explained today's problem.

She nodded without speaking, going within. "Remember," she said as if we'd done this before, "the angels don't always answer the question you ask, but rather, the question that needs to be answered."

Not helpful.

After a moment, she stopped mixing the cards and laid one face down on the low table between us. I leaned forward, resting my elbows on my knees. Renee repeated the process two more times, then put the rest of the deck aside.

"The first," she said, turning it over, "is considered the origination of the current situation."

The card depicted a bearded angel in a golden cloak with his wings spread. The message written below him said *Take Back Your Power!*

"The second card," Renee continued, flipping the next, "speaks to the current situation."

The middle card had a portrait of a long-haired angel, his wings only a suggestion behind his shoulders. The message was *Take Your Time Making This Decision.*

She paused, hand hovering over the third card. My heart sped up. It didn't seem possible that what amounted to artwork on scraps of paperboard could really apply to anything specific, let alone me, but…

"Do you feel like you've relinquished any of your power in the past months?" Renee asked. "Another way to think about that would be if you've handed off authority to someone else?"

I closed my eyes and breathed slowly through my nose, centering myself as I often did when riding, especially before competition. A place where visualization held sway over reality. Had I given away my power? What power were we talking about, anyway? Who would I give it to?

"Perhaps," Renee prompted, "it's more a matter of self trust?"

My eyes flashed open. That was it. I didn't trust myself to make this decision. But why not?

Renee nodded as if she read the realization in my face. She pointed at the middle card. "This one is obvious. Take your time making this decision. But then, you've already had months to think about this."

"And I have only five more days."

"Do you?"

"That's when the deadline is."

"It's only a deadline in your head, New York."

Her nickname for me. When she wasn't calling me white woman. Her skin might be darker than mine, but I was far from pale. Not that it mattered.

"What do you mean?"

"There's no rush. The trust stipulates you must keep a job for *at least* one year by the time you're thirty. It doesn't say you have to leave that job. Maybe waiting for a while after the pressure of the deadline passes will allow all to become clear." She sipped her water. "It's not like Malcolm's going to kick you out on day three hundred and sixty-six."

I frowned. Hadn't thought of that. "Maybe."

She still didn't turn the third card, and my nervous knee started up, my right heel bouncing up and down off the floor.

"Vi, what do you want to do?"

"I don't know," I snapped. "That's the problem."

"I don't mean about staying here or going back to Long Island. I mean, what do you want to accomplish with your life? What will your legacy be? What is the good you will provide?"

"I…what?"

"Haven't you ever thought about it?"

I admit, I don't tend to take the long view. I've never really had the chance. Surviving the short term has always taken all my attention.

Closing my eyes again, I tried to picture what my ideal life might look like. The boundaries of my body softened, and I felt myself in a saddle, my legs wrapped around the barrel of a horse. Could be Wastrel or any of the horses I've ridden in the past or will ride in the future. What matters is the mysterious connection I have with each, a link that enables me to team with them in a way few riders can.

I've never understood nor questioned it. When young, I'd thought it was like that for everyone, but after I began working with Ed Todd and competing on a regular basis, I learned that was not the case. Before he died, he reminded me that my gift had always been with the animals. That I should stay with that. What if this skill, if that's what it was, could be taught to others? The world would surely be a better place for horses of every stripe. And that was a world I could live with, a powerful legacy to leave behind.

Was it possible?

I opened my eyes. Renee had revealed the final card. The artwork: an angel cradling a globe with love and light radiating from its center.

The message: *This is Your Life's Purpose.*

CHAPTER FIVE

I STARED at the card until my eyes watered and the image blurred. When I blinked and lifted my gaze to Renee, she wore a cat-like smile, both smug and kind, if such a thing were possible. She might as well have a neon sign on her forehead proclaiming *I told you so.*

"That's…. How?" Too many feelings battled for attention. "It's…" I gathered my galloping thoughts. "You already pulled that card before you asked about my legacy. Before I…"

Renee nodded, offered a helpless shrug. "I can't explain it. I'm merely the medium."

"In other words, *there are more things in heaven and earth, Horatio, than are dreamt of in your philosophy.*"

"You said it, white woman."

Resting my elbows on my knees again, I combed my fingernails over my scalp, as if that might bring order to the twenty high-speed ping-pong matches going on inside my head.

"The third card," Renee explained, "is the outcome. But only if everything stays the same. It represents potential. You can change the outcome with a thought."

"Riiigght."

"What were you thinking before you opened your eyes?"

"Um…" I hadn't tried to explain it to anyone in a long time. Ed Todd understood, but once I started talking about a mystical link between me and a horse, people gave me that look that said I'd sprouted a second head. Yet, if anyone could understand, it would be Renee.

"You don't have to tell me," she said. "What matters is you are being guided in the direction you were born to go. This path brings you joy and excitement, perhaps the opportunity to help, yes?"

"That's the long-term goal. It's great to have this…angelic support of that idea, but it doesn't help me know what to do right now with Miko leaving in a few hours."

"Let's do another reading."

In for a penny… "Okay."

She inserted the three cards into the deck and shuffled again. "Focus on your question. Based on the first cards, you have a strong connection to your higher self. You simply have to trust you can access it when needed."

I seriously doubted I had a higher self, but I dove back into that peaceful place I entered whenever I wanted to concentrate. Maybe it *was* my higher self. I always felt steady and calm when there, and that helped produce a steady and calm horse. I'd never thought to apply the same technique to myself on a regular basis.

Soon, the first card was down. A moment later, a card flipped out of the deck. Renee grabbed it and put it next to the first. A few more shuffles, and the third card was in place.

I reached for them. Renee slapped my hand.

"Don't touch my cards."

"I thought these were my cards."

"It's your *reading*, but the cards are imbued with my energy, and no one else touches them. Got it?"

I nodded. She turned the first one over. It said *Prioritize*.

Again, a little too obvious. Or maybe I was making things more complicated than they had to be. Ed Todd's animals needed to be taken care of. There wasn't anything I could do about that. If they were here, it wouldn't be an issue. I stared out the window for a few moments, mulling over that thought and how I might present it to Malcolm. Maybe there was something to this whole medium reading business, because I was feeling more clarity by the moment.

The second card repeated *Take Your Time Making This Decision*. Again. Same as in the first reading. But I didn't have time with this decision, that was the problem.

"One of the possible meanings of this one," Renee said, "is to investigate your options and alternatives."

"Giacomo suggested I call someone there." Maybe Ed Todd's sister could swing by and feed the horses. That would give me a little breathing space.

Renee nodded and flipped the last card. It depicted a pink-robed angel. He held up a torch with one hand and an open book with the other. The message: *Teaching and Learning.*

"I know you don't give riding lessons," Renee said, "so this isn't about that."

"No," I said, thinking about how I communicated with horses—the channel I tuned in to. Could it be reproduced? "I'm not sure what it's about," I said, my thoughts not yet coherent enough to share, "but this *has* been helpful. It's given me a lot to think about. Thank you."

"The answers you seek are within you, Vi. You have only to ask." She scooped the cards off the table and tucked them away. "But I'm happy to give you a reading anytime."

"I'm going to see about someone else feeding and turning out Ed Todd's horses in the morning, then talk to Malcolm." I stood. "I still have to go back there, but I might be able to wait until tomorrow. When I return, I want to start with you."

"Start what with me?"

I tilted my head to the side. "Working on my life purpose, silly. What else?"

She smiled and went out to the barn as Malcolm came in.

"Hey," he said when the door closed behind him. "Are you okay? You ran out of here in a hurry."

I stiffened. "Giacomo needed me."

"Did he?"

Change the subject. Change the subject. Change the subject.

"Something has come up back home."

"Home?"

I winced. Was Long Island my home or Missouri? Maybe a trip back was exactly what I needed. Getting away from Malcolm in all his glory would help. He still wore his kilt, damn him. And he looked concerned. A little annoyed, but mostly worried. Because that's how he was, always giving me the benefit of the doubt. I should cut myself some slack, and him, too. Trust myself more, like the cards suggested. But it wasn't my nature.

Or it was all bullshit.

"Miko has to fly back to Kiev today because his dad's in the hospital."

"Oh. That's too bad. What are you doing?"

"What do you mean what am I doing?"

"About your horses back there."

My horses. Even after eight months, I still had a hard time convincing myself that beautiful place and Beau and Sasha were mine. I'd wanted it for so long, giving it up now that I finally owned it felt impossible, like a betrayal. Ed had tried to give me the gelding and mare years ago, but I wouldn't take them. I rode other people's horses, couldn't afford my own. Then Harry had acquired Cali for me. Within a few months, I'd been forced to come to Winterlight.

Which had been nothing but good.

There *had* been some bad, but that wasn't the fault of Malcolm or this place or this job, or me for that matter. This life purpose idea was too fresh for me to wonder about trying to achieve it at Winterlight instead of back East. I'd dreamed of riding the best horses for so long, of competing—and winning—at the top shows. Switching gears after all this time didn't come easily. I'd done the competition thing before it all came crashing down thanks to Wastrel and his need to escape what was obviously not *his* life's purpose.

Maybe Renee could do a reading on Wastrel and what the heck he wanted from me.

Malcolm leaned against the tack room door. He would wait until I gave him an answer no matter how long that took. The pressure of his patience made my head feel like a too-full balloon.

"I need to go back."

"Do you?"

"Why does everyone think they know better than me?"

"What are you being so touchy about? It doesn't hurt to get someone else's opinion once in a while, Vi. You simply have to ask."

Maybe I'd stick to asking my higher self her opinion. At least someone would agree with me. "There are two horses and a cat who need feed and water in less than twenty-four hours and no one to do it. It's my responsibility." I put my hands on my hips and went to the window, turning my back on him.

I heard him let out a long breath. "Penny?"

"My cousin? You've got to be kidding. She has an eight-month-old daughter. Plus, she doesn't know one end of a horse from another."

"You could talk her through it for one or two feedings."

"Can't leave the horses in their stalls for that long."

"It wouldn't hurt them as long as they had plenty of water."

He had enough experience to not take my statements at face value. He was right, but I didn't have to like it. "I can't ask her."

"How about your uncle?"

"Uncle Vic? He'd as soon eat them as feed them."

"There must be someone."

"If you know so much about it, why don't you do it?" Gah, why was I picking a fight with him? I had just been in my peaceful place and pondering a life purpose for Pete's sake.

"Okay."

"What?"

"Tell me what needs to be done, how to get there, and I'll go. I've heard so much about it. I'd love to see the place. See where you grew up."

I *hated* how reasonable he was. He was impossible to argue with. Yet the thought of his leaving—not being around Martina—that was appealing. He had work, clients, so…the whole thing left me breathless. It was simpler when I had no options.

"I can't ask you to do that."

"You don't have to. I offered. You can't ask Penny, you won't ask your uncle, you can't ask me. How about Giacomo? Can you send him? He's proven himself handy with the horses. Anything you throw at him, really. The guy's remarkably capable."

"Kind of like you," I said to the window.

"A lot like you, too." He walked over to stand beside me and put his arm around my waist. "We make a good team."

I huffed.

"Don't make this harder than it is," he said. "I'd rather you stay here with these two new horses. Martina knows computers and that's it. She's going to need help."

Two horses who needed me back East. Two who needed me here. "You can help her."

"I have to work, and you know it. She needs your expertise."

Which belied his statement about going back East in my place. Unless he had an ulterior motive for leaving. "Emily can give her lessons," I said.

"True, but you need to ride the horses, make sure they're ready before she gets on them. I have a feeling they're more than she can handle. Especially the thoroughbred. He only came off the track recently. Martina means well, but…"

I let my head drop back, blew out a breath, and asked the question. "Old girlfriend?"

He pulled away from me. "What? No."

A little too strong of a protest. "Could have fooled me."

"Me, too."

I looked at him. He wore a bemused frown.

"She was a few years behind me in school. An undergrad I taught when I was working on my graduate degree."

I snorted. "Obviously something was going on between you."

"Are you pissed about this?"

"What do you think?"

"I think you're mistaken."

"I doubt it." I moved to where my phone sat on the desk. "I'll see if Ed Todd's sister can feed and turn out the horses in the morning, but I'm going tomorrow afternoon at the latest." I picked up my phone, started scrolling for Susan's contact info. "I need to sort things out."

He didn't speak for a long moment, and I could feel his eyes on me, willing me to look at him. I kept my head down.

"Yes. You do," he said, his tone bitter and hurt.

I was an idiot. Why was I doing this to him? To us? "I'm sorry—"

All I saw was a swish of plaid as the door closed quietly behind him.

CHAPTER SIX

THAT WENT WELL.

Renee poked her head in. "You okay?"

"Why shouldn't I be?"

"I saw that man leave. Something's not right."

I clamped my lips together to keep from telling her to butt out.

Ten minutes later, I was on Cali's back. She doesn't like being hurried. There had been a lot of tail swishing and head bobbing to let me know what she thought of my hasty movements as I gave her a quick brushing and tacked her up.

If I had a tail, I'd swish it in annoyance too.

I crossed my stirrups. With my ankle sore from being twisted, it was less painful to ride without them. I encouraged her forward into a working trot around the outside track, feeling good that I'd made the footing perfect for her. I could ride around the bale-spear-stealing lagoon and pretend it wasn't there.

After a thorough warmup that included collected and extended canter as well as lateral work, I loosened the reins and let her stretch. My thigh muscles screamed, but in a good way.

Some of the tension had left my shoulders. My phone sat on the top of a post by the gate, and I checked it for messages. Susan had answered me.

Love to feed and turn out the horses. Got cleaning and packing to do in the house anyway, if you don't mind—it's your house. <smiley face>

I let out a long breath, feeling more stress easing out of my back.

<smiley face><heart> THANK YOU! I'll let you know when I'm getting in.

Secretly, I sneered at the smiley face and heart. Until Harry sent me this smart phone, such nonsense hadn't been an option for me, nor did I care that I couldn't receive such inanity from others. But everyone else seemed to like them.

Renee parked Smitty next to Cali. "Good news?"

The small gray was one of the few horses Cali tolerated to be that close. They touched noses.

"Yes. Susan can cover until I get there. I don't have to rush out there like I thought."

She nodded. "Malcolm will be relieved."

I glanced toward the house. "I guess."

"Vi, I say this with all the love I can, so please take it in the spirit intended."

I put my phone back on the post and lifted an eyebrow at her. "What?"

"You're an idiot."

She tapped Smitty with her heels and rode away.

CHAPTER SEVEN

THE GOOD NEWS FROM SUSAN, plus riding, put me in a much better frame of mind than I'd been in an hour before. Otherwise, I would have argued with Renee.

But the truth was, she was right.

What to do about it was another matter. I put Cali back in the field after hosing her off, noting I needed a good washing down as well. There were other horses to ride, and in my not-too-distant past, that's what I would have done. Kept riding and working and ignoring the argument Malcolm and I had, hoping that later we'd just pretend it hadn't happened.

But he'd shown me how to be better in a relationship. How to apologize and not get angry. To forgive. All things I'd always been capable of in my primary relationships—the ones I had with horses—but had totally sucked at with people. The fact that he and I were still together after nearly a year…it was the longest I'd lasted with a human male.

Twenty minutes later, Renee had headed out, I'd nipped into the shower and now walked up the driveway. I found Malcolm in his office, staring at his computer screen. He looked up when I walked in.

I stood there for what seemed like minutes but was probably only a couple of breaths before blurting, "I'm sorry."

He leaned back in his chair, stacked his hands behind his head, and kept his face neutral. His eyes were narrowed. In the monitor's glare, they looked flat. I couldn't tell whether they held his usual warm fondness or a cool edge of displeasure.

A tremor of fear coiled in my gut. Had I gone too far this time? What more could I say? *Think*, Vi.

"And also…" I started, dropping my gaze and picking at the seam of my jeans.

He slowly stood. "Also?"

"Erm…also…"

He came and stood in front of me, leaned down to put his face next to my neck, and inhaled. I forgot what I'd been about to say. Would it always be like this? This swift incendiary ardor that sprang up whenever he came near? Was it good or bad? I didn't like feeling out of control.

"Also?" he asked again, his warm breath lifting my hair.

And yet…he never let me fall. No matter the intensity of our attraction, the depth of our emotions, he always made me feel safe. "I…um." Spit it out, Vi. "You were right."

He pulled back and blinked. "I was? About what?"

I'd surprised us both. It wasn't something I admitted often. If he was right, that meant I was wrong, though I'd never say that out loud. I leaned my head back, baring my throat like a she-wolf submitting to her mate. If that wasn't trust, I don't know what was. "Oh, you know, about everything."

That was easier than enumerating all the things he was right about.

I yelped as he scooped me into his arms, carried me up the stairs, and into the bedroom.

He'd taught me about makeup sex, too.

Delicious, delicious, delicious.

We took our time, and I told him again—this time with my body—that I was sorry. He took me with slow but unyielding possession, letting me know that it was okay, we were okay.

A couple of hours of delicious, and we fell asleep in each other's arms. I'd completely forgotten about my sore ankle.

I smell smoke. It's like the dreams from last summer. Then, it had been cigarette smoke. This smells like a wood fire. I hear crackling. It's comforting, like winter nights snuggling with Malcolm. But Wastrel stands near. This isn't a warm and fuzzy kind of dream.

Wastrel dreams never are.

He leads me toward the fire. A building is burning, black smoke billowing up in clouds to blot out the sun. The place is familiar, but I can't see much of it.

A convenient wind blows the smoke away for a moment, and I glimpse the cupola on the roof.

It's Ed Todd's place, the morning of the fire, the day Ed did fatal damage to his throat and lungs saving the horses.

Beau and Sasha are whinnying, kicking. I hear Ed's voice soothing them around his blistering coughs. The man is near blind. In these conditions, I know he's feeling his way to the halters, the stalls, the horses.

The hose is within reach, but all I can do is watch. I'm a frozen witness. As is Wastrel. He stands beside me. My hand is on his shoulder. He's trembling. I'm crying. It's not just the smoke.

Smoke covers everything again, and just before I think it's over, that there's no more to see, no more I can stand to see, a figure runs out of the far end of the barn.

Not a horse.

Not Ed.

I crane my neck, but it's a shadow, maybe only an eddy of smoke. But then, I hear running footsteps, see the shape again. A man wearing a cap, running with a hand cupped over his nose and mouth.

The scene shifts, making me dizzy. I am sitting at Ed's bedside, holding his hand. Not the hospital, but hospice.

I hear his words, words I'd forgotten, or submerged deep into my subconscious immediately after he died.

"The fire," he murmurs. "No accident."

I surged up with a gasp, dragging air into my lungs and coughing as if I'd been inside that smoking barn.

Malcolm came awake and sat next to me in the same moment. "What is it?" He put his arm around me.

"Ed Todd," I said, my throat thick with a sob trying to escape. I scrubbed my face with my hands, pushed my hair back, looked at Malcolm.

"What?" he asked.

"He was murdered."

CHAPTER EIGHT

DINNER WAS QUIET. Just the two of us. Often we ate next door with Clara and Hank, or someone else was here, like Giacomo, or one of the boarders. Not, thankfully, Martina. My grandfather went into the city to see my parents. Renee's garden was calling her, Sandy had overnight duty at the vet's office, and Emily had finals to study for.

This was my human family—a collection of blood and non-blood relations spanning a couple of generations. I also counted the horses, cats, and my dog, Noire, who sat at the bottom of the porch steps eagerly waiting for one of us to drop a piece of steak.

I iced my ankle. We didn't talk about the dream, my going to Long Island, the looming end of our contract, or Martina.

Especially not Martina.

I couldn't get her out of my head.

We watched the sun lower itself behind the western tree line sending finger-like shadows across the pasture. The horses had no interest in it. At this time of year, they rarely paused cropping the rich new grass.

Large black birds also pecked at the grass in the pasture. They made an odd squawking noise, like a squeaky gate. Smaller than crows and ravens, they had slender bodies, long tails, yellow eyes and an ever-so-slightly sinister aspect. The setting sun picked iridescent blues and purples from their feathers.

Except for our breathing, no sound of human habitation reached us.

I set my plate on the table and leaned into Malcolm with a sigh.

This could be my life. Peaceful. Contented. How had that happened? I'd been the exact opposite for as long as I could remember.

The life I'd left behind, the one discontented Viola Parker was in charge of, was chaotic.

In the years before coming to Winterlight, I'd changed bosses nearly as often as boyfriends. My mounts had been the best horses available at the top of their game. If they weren't, I took them there. The wins piled up, became expected. It had been exciting, but messy, with the only modicum of stability coming from my home base at my cousin Penny's house, and the stints helping Ed Todd in between *real* jobs. I liked the tranquility and steady pace at his place but fought against it.

But what if that was the real job? What if all the mess and chaos weren't necessary? Was it possible to do things *and* be content?

"Grackles," Malcolm said, pulling me from my thoughts. "Those noisy black birds in the field."

"What about them?"

"They eat a lot of corn."

The man's breadth of knowledge never ceased to amaze me. He loved his world and was relentlessly curious about the life around him.

He switched gears. "We have that horse show in a couple of weeks. Who are you taking?"

I knew what he was doing—forcing my mind past the deadline. It would be the third of three schooling shows we'd competed at starting in February. Well, that I'd competed in. Malcolm had come along as groom, which he was very good at. I'd shown his horse, Gaston, in the baby green hunter division, and Cali in beginner jumper. They'd both performed well, although Gaston threatened an equine meltdown in the warm-up ring at the first show. The enclosed space of the indoor arena with so many horses going in different directions had been overwhelming. We'd had to go outside to cool off, then watch from the sidelines before I got on to make him concentrate on his own work. After that he'd been fine and pretended his silliness had all been an act. I let him think I believed that.

Riding Cali through the same situation felt like straddling a bottle rocket with the fuse lit, but she never exploded. She'd seen enough on the track to not be rattled, but she liked to keep me on my toes. I liked to let her think she had me scared.

We all had our illusions to maintain.

"Renee wants to take Smitty," I said. "And Emily was thinking of taking her horse, but it depends on where she is with finals. We can always load him last minute if she can make it."

He nodded, and I felt his shoulders relax, as if he'd been anticipating I'd say something else—like I wouldn't be here then. Renee was right. Nothing said I had to leave Winterlight right after my year was up. I needed to go East for a couple of days, but then I'd be back. I'd been training the horses, and Malcolm and I had decided together to take them to this series of shows—including the one that fell after the end of our contract.

"Once the semester is over," I added, "Emily will have a couple of students who want to show. That would be good for business."

"If they do well."

"They will."

He bumped my shoulder with his. "I've always admired your confidence."

"Likewise," I said. After a minute, I added, "The first time I went to a show with Ed, I asked him what the competition would be like—what caliber of rider would be there. He gave me a funny look."

"I know that look."

"How could you? You've never even seen a picture of Ed."

"I know how I look at you when you say something absurd."

"I was seven years old. It was a reasonable question."

"I just have a feeling I know what he said."

I huffed. "You're so smart, you finish the story."

He put his arm around my shoulders. "Oh, come on. It's better if you tell it. I'll act surprised."

I gave him some side eye and a smirk. I'd tried staying mad at him. It never lasted.

"Okay." I pitched my voice as low and gravelly as it would go, and that still didn't match Ed's croaky baritone. "He said, 'Kid, you *are* the competition.'"

Malcolm barked a laugh. "Nothing's changed."

"Actually, everything's changed."

"If you say so."

I pulled away from him enough to let a little air flow between us and wrapped my arms around my knees. He leaned back and rested his elbows on the top step, his gaze drifting over the pasture. The sun had dropped below the horizon, and while the last of its golden light bathed us in a warm glow, the temperature rapidly dropped and it began to feel chilly.

"You've made a huge difference here, Vi. I hope you know that. The horses are happier, business is brisk."

"I'm glad," I said. "That's what you hired me for. At least you don't have to rent horses to the public anymore."

"That alone would have been worth the trouble."

"What trouble?"

It was his turn to throw some side eye my way. "Let's just say you're not the easiest person to have around all the time."

What the actual hell? I knew it was true, but to have him say it out loud…. I looked at him then quickly away, feeling my throat get tight.

He put his big hand on my thigh. "It's no secret you demand the highest standards from everyone when it comes to the horses. Standards that others sometimes struggle with."

"But—"

He squeezed my leg. "Yet you ask nothing for yourself."

"I don't—"

"Need anything. I know. That's what you think. But that's just a defense against getting hurt."

He'd brought this up before, that I could ask for help, that I didn't have to brave the world alone. I spread my hands, and he grabbed one before I could argue.

"You've been hurt. A lot. I get that."

He understood hurt. His ex wife was a piece of work who first faked a pregnancy to trick him into marriage, then had an affair and passed off the child she had as Malcolm's. I think he knew all along, but he accepted Nicky as if she were his own and couldn't love her more than he did.

"I'm trying," was all I could think to say.

But it wasn't all that true. It was hard to shake a lifetime of doubt and mistrust. Of depending on me and only me. For that matter, I hadn't always been the most reliable, either. Especially not after Wastrel killed himself, and then a girl named Heidi taking a lesson from me had a horrible accident and died. Me leaving life had seemed like a good option, too.

What I did was curl up at the bottom of a bottle for months. It was Ed who poured me out, dried me up, got me back in the saddle. Nothing had been the same after that, though. Colors were less vivid. Me and everything around me felt flat as a popped balloon. It had been my cousin Penny who'd insisted I take this job at Winterlight, where the world had brightened considerably.

When I imagined returning to my old life, it was the one before Wastrel and Heidi died, before it became easier to dull the pain with alcohol. Before I learned how my aunt had betrayed me, and I reconciled with my parents. When anger fueled me, when chaos lent purpose, when the mess of my own making provided something to rail against.

The truth was, other than the physical reality of Ed Todd's place, I had absolutely nothing to go back to.

CHAPTER NINE

THERE WAS nothing to go back to.

Nothing.

Nothing I *wanted* to go back to.

I didn't miss the chaos, the mess.

Which meant what? I could sell Ed's place. But was that a betrayal? He'd saved me in so many ways. Made me who I was. The good parts. What had he wanted me to do with the farm? He knew I wouldn't be able to afford the upkeep. Plus, building a new business takes a long time. Especially when one's reputation is shattered. The barn, house, and fencing all needed work or outright replacement, and the one thing it had always lacked—an indoor arena—cost tens of thousands to build. Did I want to spend all of my trust fund on that?

These thoughts swirled around my tired brain the next morning as I reveled in the physical release of work. My ankle felt fine, and I decided to distract myself by getting to know Martina's horses, so brought the bay out and put him on cross ties. He led and stood quietly, with minimal curiosity about me or his surroundings. He had some winter coat left, but the new hair coming in had that rich burnished umber color, and his black mane had been trimmed short. He was put together well—short coupled with a broad back and perfect angles at the hip and shoulder. Good, solid cannon bones.

With my hand resting on his neck, it occurred to me that I'd be better off investing my money in Winterlight. Or even starting from scratch in

Missouri, where my reputation, if lacking, at least wasn't in the red. Where the cost of living was lower. I'd be able to do more with less.

Winterlight needed an indoor arena, too. Malcolm and I had discussed it many times. He'd been planning to use the money from the sale of his father's house, but my parents needed a place to live, and...geez, he'd sacrificed one of his own dreams for me, or my family.

Could I do less?

I reviewed the form on the bay. His name was Elijah, and he went by Eli. Six years old, unregistered thoroughbred-trakehner cross, formerly in training for dressage at a farm in Colorado. I flipped the page forward. The chestnut, Jockey Club Registry name of Qouji's Secret, came from the same farm. He was barely four. Looked like he'd been started on the track but hadn't shown promise, so they sold him as a show prospect. He went by Wheezy. I hoped that was only an attempt to keep his barn name close to the sound of his registered name, and not a clue as to his respiratory health.

Both were up to date on vaccinations and blood work. They'd had their shoes reset within the past couple of weeks.

In the tack room, I inspected the new saddle and two bridles hanging on the spare racks. And by new, I mean never used, never oiled. One of the bridles was simple, with a loose ring French training snaffle. The other was a full, meant for the highest levels of dressage riding. A level I kind of doubted Martina had achieved. I lifted the saddle to look closer, and let out a low whistle. Passier. Worth about four-thousand dollars.

"Morning," said a voice from the door.

Martina stood there in a pair of spotless white full-seat breeches with the brand name stamped on the thigh. Again, one of the most expensive available. Retail, at least three hundred. I sure as hell couldn't afford to wear them, but it doesn't cost to peruse a catalog and dream.

It also doesn't cost to ride well. Spending money on tack and clothes can't fix a lack of balance, rubbery legs, or harsh hands. You *should* invest in training. From that perspective, it costs.

She held a Starbucks travel mug in one hand, her cell phone in the other, and a new riding helmet hung by its strap from her elbow. "Nice, right?" She pointed her chin at the saddle.

I let it drop back to the rack.

"Um-hmm." I slid by her.

"Why is Eli out?"

I grabbed a curry comb and brush. "Just getting to know him."

She followed, the tall columns of her black boots reflecting a slash of light from the window. Probably custom. Add another thousand-plus dollars to her receipt.

"I'd think you'd want to ride him."

"I'd think you'd want to spend time with a horse on the ground, first."

She hesitated, and I felt her glance drop to the floor as I bent to scrub a clump of mud from Eli's hock.

"Oh. Of course." I pictured her flipping her hair over her shoulder before she added, "That's what I do, too."

I smiled but didn't look at her. "Of course."

She slurped her coffee. If she was a slurper, I'd have to kill her. It would be one of many reasons, but the one that would put me over the top.

"But you are going to ride him, right?"

"Eventually." I straightened and used the curry comb to scrape dust and hair from the brush. If some of it floated over to dull the shine on her boots or landed in her coffee…hey, I can't help which way the wind blows.

I put the brushes where they belonged, grabbed the hoofpick, and lifted Eli's left front. So far, he'd been a perfect gentleman, but I knew better than to assume that would translate into how he might behave under saddle.

"What's he like?" I asked.

"Like? Who?"

"Eli."

"He seems…nice."

Oh…oh. No.

I paused between Eli's left front and left hind to look over his back to where she sat on the tack room steps—on a folded towel she'd taken from the shelf. God forbid she get a spot on her breeches. I had to bite the inside of my cheek to keep the smirk off my face. "I mean to ride."

She slurped. Nervous quirk? That would be a problem because I had a habit of making those who were nervous even more nervous. Still, I doubted anyone would blame me for whacking her with a shovel if the slurping happened one too many times.

It took her a moment to meet my gaze, and I gave her points for holding it.

"I haven't ridden him."

My eyebrow shot up, and I ducked behind the horse to cover it. "I see. What about Wheezy?"

"No."

In the silence that followed, the metal of the hoofpick against Eli's shoe was loud as a farrier's hammer on an anvil. I moved around to his right hind, deftly flicking out the manure packed around his frog. Martina gasped. A piece had landed in her lap, and she stared at it as if an alien had just erupted from her chest.

With my bare fingers, I snatched it up and held it in front of her face. "Grass and water," I said. "But you might as well know that dirt and dust and shit and horses go together." I tossed it, wiped my hand on my jeans, picked up Eli's front right.

"I know that," she snapped.

"Of course you do." I finished and straightened, putting my hand on the bay's shoulder. "Why did you buy two horses without riding them first?"

"First," she said. "I intend to learn. That's why I'm here."

Lucky me.

"Second," she said with a smile that told me she'd rallied, that she didn't intend to be intimidated by me, "because I could."

CHAPTER TEN

ONE OF MY MOTTOS IS, just because you can, doesn't mean you should.

There was nothing left to say. I prepared Eli to take him to the ring and longe him, grabbing one of our well-loved bridles with a simple, eggbutt snaffle. I didn't bother with a training surcingle or side reins. This was just going to be a quick let's-see-what-you're-made-of session.

I clipped the longe line to the bit attachment, gathered up twenty-five feet of what was essentially a webbed leash, grabbed a whip and tugged on my gloves. Martina chased after us.

"Why aren't you using this?" She shoved one of her new bridles at me.

"It isn't ready."

As if her bold statement about buying the horses had knocked all the stuffing out of her, she blinked at the bridle, her pretty forehead scrunched into a frown, and her lip trembled.

If she was a slurper *and* a crier, we were done. I took a deep breath, dug around my heart for some compassion—mostly for Malcolm's sake—pursed my lips, let out the breath, and said, "It needs to be oiled before it can be used. Okay? Softened up. I can show you."

She nodded.

I pointed at the French snaffle attached to her bridle. "Is that the kind of bit Eli was being ridden in?"

"I think so."

"It's perfectly good, but the one I'm using is, too." I held up the reins in my hand. "This is fine for now."

She nodded again and followed me to the ring, her boots squeaking with each step. They weren't broken in, either.

The list of reasons to kill her grew with each moment. For Malcolm, I would cut her some slack. Clearly, she had more money than sense, and someone back in California or Colorado had spotted her coming a mile away.

I couldn't fault her enthusiasm for throwing all she had at this new endeavor, and she said she intended to learn. I'd take her word for it, for now. I told her to stay by the gate, and she did.

I stopped Eli at the middle of the ring and patted his neck. His ears flicked back, then forward as I put the reins into the throat latch. With the line looped through my left hand the way I liked, I lifted the whip. He walked forward.

"Good boy," I murmured.

I continued to push him forward and out, until most of the line was taut between us. He'd done this before. That would make things easier.

"Trot."

He shook his head. Okay. Not all horses are trained to voice commands, or the same ones.

"T-ROT," I said with more energy. At the same time, I lifted the whip toward his rear end.

His stride lengthened, but he stayed in walk. This could be a good thing. Martina needed a horse with more whoa than go, and I'd been hoping that the even-tempered and kind traits of his Trakehner side were the parts in charge of his brain.

I clucked and flipped the whip at him, not snapping it enough for it to crack. He shuffled into trot.

"Good boy," I said.

He lapsed into walk.

"Good boy doesn't mean whoa," I said and clucked and flipped the whip at him again. He jogged around me with as little effort as possible. At that gait, he looked more like a western pleasure prospect than a dressage candidate.

Martina stood watching with rapt attention, her hands pressed together in front of her mouth as if she were praying. That gave me pause, but I returned my attention to Eli.

I stepped toward him, said, "Trot ON," and flicked the whip close to his haunch.

He pushed forward into what was nearly a working trot, collecting himself some, seeming to remember what he was about.

"Good boy." I kept the whip up so he'd know I meant for him to keep going.

Martina clapped her hands just as he went by her.

Eli tucked his nose and crow-hopped into canter. He didn't exactly take off, but he did a couple of rolling in-stride bucks, then fell back to trot, as if the effort had exhausted him.

I halted him, adjusted the longe line, and sent him in the other direction, which was a repeat of going to the left, as if he'd forgotten what *trot* meant and needed the whip nearly touching his hocks to keep moving forward.

That is, until Malcolm came out of the house. Although it was across the pasture, on a still morning, sound carried well, and the squeak and slam of the screen door could have been as close as the fence.

Again, Eli stiffened his back and legs and hopped on all fours, looking like a demented bunny off his meds. He jerked the line.

I followed with him to keep slack between us, said "Easy, easy," but he'd got up a head of steam and launched into a zig-zaggy gait that included bucking, steps of passage, counter canter, flying changes, and finally a pirouette that got the longe wrapped around his head. All of this in weirdly calm slow motion.

"Whoa, now. Whoa." I tucked the whip under my arm so it was pointing away from him and walked forward, carefully coiling the line so there would be no stray loops to tangle a foot in.

He stood, breathing a little heavily, ears swiveling from front to side, eyeing me like I might be a demon, or perhaps a slamming screen door. He remained still, if watchful, let me touch him, get the longe off his head.

"Everything all right?" Malcolm asked.

He was at the gate next to Martina, in his kilt. I loved it when he wore the kilt. I didn't love seeing him standing next to Martina in it. Her body had gone all oozy soft and…coy. She had herself angled toward him as if he were the sun and she a flower. He stood with his forearms on the top rail, attention directed my way, not noticing or maybe ignoring her. Not noticing was good. Ignoring was better.

"Fine," I said. "He's probably confused about being in a new place with new people."

Or he had a major screw loose. Time would tell.

"Are you going to ride him now?" Martina asked.

"No." I rubbed Eli's forehead. "He's had enough for one day after a long trip."

"I want to do it."

"Do what?"

"What you did. With the leash."

I took a moment to examine the line in my hand, counting to keep myself from saying something I shouldn't. Seemed like I spent a lot of energy trying not to say the wrong thing.

"You mean you want to longe him?" Malcolm asked.

"Yes, that. Can you show me?"

Through slitted eyes, I saw that she was speaking to Malcolm. I might as well have sunk into the swamp that still mocked me and my cleanup efforts from the far end of the arena.

"Vi, do you think Martina could longe Eli for a few minutes?" He spoke evenly, giving nothing away—telling me I could do it or not—whatever I thought was best.

"Sure. So long as no one slams any doors."

Malcolm glanced over his shoulder to the house. "Is that what set him off?"

I shrugged as Martina walked to me. I showed her how to hold the line and the whip, but told her to keep that pointed down and dragging on the ground.

"Just walk," I said.

I backed away while she pulled herself tall, arched her back, and lifted her chin. She clucked, and Eli moved off with a relaxed stride.

I positioned myself next to Malcolm but stayed on the inside of the fence. "She shouldn't get on him for a while, I don't think."

"That bad?"

"Too soon to tell."

Martina stood on her toes as Eli walked a circle around her. She flashed a grin at us—at Malcolm—and shook her hair back, every inch the confident horsewoman, as if she'd done this a million times, as if she weren't clueless. Clearly, she'd studied the art of *fake it til you make it.*

Or maybe this small act made her feel as if she'd accomplished something. Baby steps.

Eli walked around her a few times, keeping to the end of the line as he should. She watched him intently, and I sensed a coiling inside her, as if she struggled to fetter a dark force within—like Eli—pretty on the surface, but muddled within by conflicting desires and goals.

I thought she'd quit after this mild success, but instead, she lifted the whip, clucked, and shouted, "Trot."

"What the hell?" It really irritated me when people ignored my instructions.

"Didn't you tell her to keep him to walk?" Malcolm asked.

Eli charged into a ground-eating trot. Martina tucked the loops of line under her arm, clapped, and shrieked "Good boy." Then, inexplicably, she somehow cracked the whip.

Eli's tail went up, his muscles bunched, and he leaped into the air with all four feet, performing a spectacular capriole before landing and taking off, bucking like a bronc straight out of the gate.

"Shit."

I started running. Malcolm vaulted the gate right behind me.

Gone was the gelding's meandering zig-zag. Gone was the barely jogging Western pleasure gait. He shot toward the far end of the ring. I'd shown Martina how to hold the line, how *not* to put her hand through the handle, but not when to let go. The line snapped taut. She jerked into the air and landed with a thud and a yelp. I wouldn't have been surprised if her shoulder was dislocated. She hung on as Eli dragged her straight toward…Oh. My. God.

"Let go," I yelled.

My thoughts spun to Eli hurting his legs as he bolted right into the swamp hole. Desperate to avoid disaster, I telegraphed a message to him, a warning of the danger, an internal shout to *stop,* but he couldn't, or wouldn't, hear me.

At the last moment, he jumped. With one giant effort, he cleared all twenty feet of the obstacle with room to spare.

Martina let go, but not before her entire body splushed face first into the stinking wet mud and rotting hay.

We stopped, stunned. Eli strained against the fence in the far corner. Martina shrieked and sputtered. Malcolm waded in and pulled her up by her armpits.

I went to Eli. Of course I did. Poor guy was scared to death.

Unclipping the line, I released the reins from the throat latch and pulled them over his head.

Malcolm dragged Martina to dry ground where she sat with her legs splayed, rubbing her shoulder and spitting mud.

"I'm all right," she said in a tremulous voice.

But. Her breeches were toast. No longer white, a thick slab of dirt and wet hay caked the waist band and had probably slithered inside. Her boots were scratched, her palm—where she'd clung to the line—burned raw. Sludge smeared her entire front from chin to toes. Sticky clay—how well I knew it— clumped in her hair. Malcolm wiped it from her eyes, but she pushed his hand away and struggled to stand. Ever the gentleman, he helped her.

I walked Eli over, but he stopped several feet away, nostrils flaring, not wanting to get closer to the smelly, whip-cracking banshee.

Who could blame him?

"It isn't too soon to tell after all," I said.

Malcolm glared at me with a combination of exasperation and irritation. "And?"

"It is that bad."

CHAPTER ELEVEN

MALCOLM AND I HAD A FIGHT.

Not about Martina.

It was after he insisted she be allowed to shower upstairs in the apartment, after he told me to give her a change of clothes to wear. After I dug out my baggiest, saddest sweats and matching T-shirt along with a worn-out pair of flip-flops and told her not to worry about returning them.

If the fire in her eyes was any indication, she'd probably burn my stuff first chance she got. She stomped to her car. Hard to stomp in flip-flops, but she managed, carrying a plastic grocery bag stuffed with her muddy clothes out to one side, her boots to the other.

All of those things made me mad, but what got my simmering pot to boil over was Malcolm informing me he'd made flight reservations to New York the next morning.

For *us*.

Without consulting me.

"What do you mean, you're coming?" I needed to get away. Alone.

"You can't say Ed Todd was murdered and expect me to let you go by yourself."

Very little infuriated me as much as a presumptive, overprotective male. I'd been teetering on the edge of self-restraint for weeks. With the deadline looming, my truck dead, and Martina strutting around, I went over. "Oh, you're going to *let* me? *Allow* me? Since when do I need your permission to do anything?"

We squared off in the tack room where I'd gone to wipe down the bridle Eli used.

He shoved one hand through his hair. "That's not what I meant, and you know it."

"Sure sounded like it." I whipped the crown piece through a folded sponge so fast it stung my fingertips.

"You know, you really are difficult sometimes."

"Oh, that's just great. Yesterday I wasn't the easiest person to have around. Today I'm difficult. Anything else you want to add to the list?" I took the bit to the sink to rinse it off. "Impossible, perhaps? How about hard working and dedicated? They on your list anywhere?" The argument triggered my neatness OCD, and I scraped at a smudge on the bit so hard my fingernail snapped.

He exhaled noisily. "Difficult covers it. But I'm not changing the reservation no matter how much you try to twist this into something it's not."

"I'll be fine. It's not like I don't know how to take care of myself." I slammed the bit into a towel and dried it, knowing full well he was right but unable to halt my bolting thoughts. "You'll just be in the way."

Silence.

Shit. I hadn't meant to say that out loud.

"If by *in the way*, you mean I'll have your back, then yes." His voice had a bite to it now. One I knew too well. "You're damned right I'll be in the way. And I don't give a rat's ass whether you like it or not."

I whirled on him. "You really have a hero complex, you know that?"

He covered the distance between us in two strides, got right in my face, jerked the now-dry-and-close-to-combusting-bit-and-towel out of my hands, and tossed them on the counter.

"If you didn't need saving so much, I wouldn't have to be a fucking hero."

I tried to push him away, a futile objective at the best of times, but with him this wound up, I might as well have been pushing a team of mules uphill. He grabbed my wrists before I could put my hands on his chest. I opened my mouth to protest, but he yanked me against him and shut me up with a searing kiss.

For about a second, I fought him, but that was pointless because I didn't want to. My body curved into his. I wrested my hands free to push them into his hair, taking tight hold to pull him even closer.

I needed him. Wanted him. Had to possess him. Especially after seeing Martina fishing for his attention. That should have had me cheering that he wanted to come with me rather than stay here with her.

He lifted me onto the counter, spread my legs, and pulled me against his erection.

That kilt, now, it's very convenient at times. Wished I wore one myself because it took entirely too long to shimmy out of my jeans to give him access. I let them puddle at my ankles, not even bothering with my boots.

He stepped into the circle of my legs, and with one thrust nearly sent me flying, but we held on to each other. I rocked my hips to match his rhythm, burying my face in his neck and sinking my teeth into his shoulder.

Mine, said every fiber of my being.

His strong hands grasped my hips, holding me firm to his onslaught.

Mine, his body said.

There would be bruises.

It wouldn't be the first time.

My breathing hitched as I got closer to climaxing, and I dug my fingernails into his back. His hands slid to my bottom to keep me close, each plunge going deeper, harder. With a growl, he groped between us to touch my most sensitive spot. I cried out, my entire body going rigid. He came at almost the same moment I did, propelling me up and against the wall with the power of it.

We didn't move for several moments, then he slowly lowered me back to the countertop, the husky beat of our shallow breaths the only sound. That is, until the door scraped open.

A roughly muttered, "Shit," and the door clicked closed.

I didn't have to open my eyes to know it had been Dex One. A new heat flooded my body. He couldn't have seen anything. Malcolm's back was to the door and his kilt covered most of us. Other than my bare legs wrapped around his waist, that is.

Yeah, shit.

Malcolm wiped his sweaty forehead against my shoulder, let his cheek rest on my collar bone.

"God, Vi."

I huffed a short exhale, took a deeper pull of air into my lungs. "That's goddess to you."

His snort of laughter made him fall out, and we organized ourselves.

"I need to go talk to Dex." He headed for the door.

I followed, zipping my pants as I went. "Hey, I'm sorry about before."

"Yeah, me too." He grinned, and there was a wicked glint in his eye. "But not after." He put his hand on the doorknob. "Also…"

"Also?"

"As difficult as you can be, you're worth it. You make me better."

I smiled, admitting to myself that sometimes I chose to be difficult for the sake of being difficult, and having him along on the trip might be great.

Not only because of how much I enjoyed being with him physically. "Maybe," I said. "It's not such a bad idea that you come with me to Long Island."

He laughed. "So all it takes to get you to agree is some smoking hot sex? I'll remember that."

"That's not—"

He squeezed my shoulder. "I know."

We went out. Dex One stood silhouetted against the far opening of the barn, hands on his hips, looking out. Malcolm went that way. I grabbed a halter and lead and headed to the pasture, unsure which horse I would work next. Certainly not Martina's other mount.

Just as I stepped into the sunlight, a sound stopped me. The smack of flesh on flesh followed by a pained grunt.

"What the hell is wrong with you?" Malcolm gasped.

Geez. Had Dex punched him?

"What the hell is wrong with *you*?" I'd never heard Dex use that tone with anyone, let alone with Malcolm.

I despise eavesdropping, but my feet were rooted to the spot.

"What are you talking about?" Malcolm asked.

"Think back a few minutes. You'll figure it out."

They'd been best friends for years. Malcolm had saved Dex's life once when a horse fell over backwards and pinned him underneath it. One of the first things Dex ever told me—by way of warning—was that he loved Malcolm like a brother.

"That's none of your business," Malcolm said.

"You know better."

"It's none. Of. Your. Business."

If there'd been a bite in Malcolm's voice earlier, it was now sharper than honed steel.

"Maybe you should lose the kilt and start wearing pants again. That way, you'd have a better chance of keeping your dick where it belongs."

Another punch. I assume Malcolm put one on Dex's chin this time. What the heck was this really about? I doubted they usually got into each other's personal business like this.

Scuffling. Hissed words I didn't catch. Someone slammed into a stall door. My heart slammed into my throat. Eli or Weezy kicked the wall. Horses are sensitive. This much aggression right in front of them would be upsetting. For me, too. Give me snarling dogs or belligerent horses any day. But people fighting? Couldn't deal with it. So, I stood there, too scared to run away, unable to help.

Dex's voice sounded strangled when he said, "You don't hump a woman against the wall where anyone could walk in."

Heavy breathing from both men.

"That's what this is about?" Malcolm's tone had turned incredulous. "I'll say it again. When and where I put my dick is none of your business."

"It is when it involves Miss Parker."

"Since when? You have a hard on for her yourself?"

Another punch, this one probably to the gut. I flinched as their bodies banged against the stall doors again. A water bucket sloshed. One of the horses whinnied.

I might not know how to deal with grown men acting like children, but I couldn't let them upset the horses. Forcing false ease into my steps, I strolled around the corner like I hadn't been there the whole time and started to say something inane, like, "Hey Dex," but they had their hands around each other's throats. Dex's face had turned crimson. Malcolm's was contorted into an ugly grimace.

I shouted, "What the hell, you two?" and ran for the hose. Yanking the hydrant handle up, I squeezed the nozzle and squirted them.

They fell apart. Dex put one hand to his neck, gave Malcolm a narrow-eyed look clearly meant to put him on notice, stormed to his truck, and gunned it down the driveway, spitting gravel in his wake.

Malcolm went out as well. He didn't explain. He didn't look at me. I started after him, called his name, but he silently stalked up the drive to the house.

This time, it was me who jumped when the screen door slammed.

CHAPTER TWELVE

I slept in the tack room recliner. I might as well have worked through the night for all the rest I got. Especially since to catch our flight, we needed to leave by four a.m.

After splashing water on my face, I went to the house. It was empty. A slip of paper on the kitchen table said Sandy and Emily were on tap to care for the horses and Giacomo to take me to the airport. Something had come up at a client's, and Malcolm would be there for the next couple of days.

He didn't specify where *there* was. He didn't sign the note.

Queasiness twisted my gut. A text message would have been better. He didn't even wish me a safe trip.

Two hours later, I plopped next to a window seat in an empty airplane row and stuffed my backpack under the seat in front of me, hoping the flight wasn't full, that no one would try to talk to me, and that the rumble and noise of the engines would quickly lull me to dreamless sleep.

The sick feeling hadn't abated.

I pulled the window screen down, wadded my quilted vest into a pillow, and closed my eyes, tuning out the slamming of overhead bins as the flight attendants prepared for takeoff.

Even when someone sat next to me—honestly, couldn't they have taken the aisle seat?—I didn't budge.

It was the scent of him that made hope surge, made me look.

And shock that thrusted aside the nausea when I opened my eyes to see Dex One clicking his seat belt into place.

CHAPTER THIRTEEN

WITH HIS MIRRORED sunglasses on and his chin pointed ever-so-slightly away, Dex's profile could have been etched on oak for all it yielded. The moment I opened my mouth to ask what was going on, his hand came up in a sharp stopping motion.

Which meant he was watching me even though he acted like he wasn't.

My teeth clacked together in annoyance. With a huff, I repositioned myself, determined to ignore him more forcefully than he was ignoring me.

I'd be willing to chalk up whatever this was to testosterone overload and let it go if I weren't squarely in the middle of it.

Men.

We didn't speak the entire flight. I stole a peek at him a couple of times. He drank coffee. I feigned sleep, since the real thing eluded me, and the flight attendants left me alone.

As we taxied for the terminal, I asked, "You going to tell me what this is about?"

"I have people to see in New York. Seemed like as good a time as any to do it. Seat was available."

Neither the sunglasses nor the set of his jaw changed. I'd have called bullshit, but there was no point with Dex. He'd tell me if and when he was ready. No amount of wheedling would get it out of him.

At least he wouldn't be tagging along with me. No one would. I chewed my lip to ease a surprising pang of disappointment at that. I hated feeling confused and unsure. Thanks to Renee, I kinda sorta had a purpose. One I could pursue anywhere. On the one hand, that was good, but on the other, it didn't help me decide the best course of action. I hoped this trip would, and I didn't need Dex's presence muddying the waters.

My phone dinged several times as soon as I turned it on.

Ciao Bella. 'Rent rant on the way. Scusa!

"Crap," I muttered.

"What?" Dex asked.

We were walking together to the car rental desks.

"Message from Giacomo. He must have gone to see my parents after dropping me at the airport. Now, they're pissed I left town without telling them first."

"Why didn't you tell them?"

I slid him a look. "I forgot, okay?"

"You've had eight months to get used to having them around."

"Don't lecture me about how to deal with my parents."

He shrugged.

How could you fly to NY without telling me first? A text takes two seconds. A call would have been better. <Angry red face><angry red face><angry red face>

At least my mother hadn't asked how I *dared* to get on a plane without first consulting her. That would have been her style not so long ago.

Your mom's unhappy. If mommy's unhappy, daddy's unhappy. <Winky face>

At least my father still had a sense of humor. My mother continued.

How long will you be gone? What are you doing back there anyway?

Since settling in Missouri, my mother had become anti-Long Island. That might have something to do with learning how her sister had lied to both of us years ago. I answered her.

Not sure. A couple of days.

I turned off my phone and dropped it in my backpack.

Dex and I each rented a car and went our separate ways. I followed him until he got on the Expressway going west. I headed east.

Even though it was after the morning rush, traffic filled all the lanes, but the farther I went, the lighter it got. I donned my sunglasses against a bright day, set the cruise control, and called Penny to let her know I was in town. Talking to her grounded me, and I could use her perspective on my situation. Plus, she knew all about my parents. Hers, Uncle Vic and Aunt Trudy, had raised me right alongside her when my parents left the states. They had their own idiosyncrasies, but at least they'd stuck around. For most of my life, I'd hated my parents for dumping me. But the truth, as is often the case, was much more complicated than I'd ever thought.

Voicemail. I left a brief message saying I hoped we could get together, but I didn't know how long I'd be in town.

I focused on the road, remembering how it used to be. How whenever I approached Ed Todd's, my spirit lightened. I loved seeing him and the old farm, renewing my connection with what I'd always felt was my true home. Without him there—and my life on the brink of I wasn't sure what—a somber sense of apprehension tightened my gut. I wanted to turn tail.

And run where? Winterlight? Malcolm? That seemed too obvious, too easy. As if I wasn't seeing the whole picture.

By the time I pulled into the tree-lined drive leading to *my* farm, alight with all the cheer and optimism of spring, I'd talked myself into a serious funk. When I saw a car parked by the house, I wasn't sure whether to be glad, resentful, or suspicious.

Sasha, the gray mare, nearly white with age, and Beau, the paint gelding, with more sway in his back than I remembered, grazed side by side in the pasture to the right. You never could get a piece of paper between them. Back in the day, even if I was only showing one of them, we'd take the other along as well. Seeing them like that, like they'd always been, brought a hint of brightness to my heart.

I pulled up to the house. The front door hung open. Good omen or evil? No bad vibes assaulted me, the horses were peaceful, not watchful, and birds sang their spring mating calls. I exited the car.

"Hello?" I called as I approached the portico.

"Vi? Is that you?" Susan came out wiping her hands on a dish towel.

I hadn't expected her, but relaxed into her motherly embrace when she held out her arms with a wistful smile. Ed had never married. His sister had always watched over him. That meant she watched over me, too. He connected us.

"It's good to see you." She patted my back and sighed. "But your cutie-patootie Rusky was a slob."

Miko was Ukrainian, but I didn't correct her. "It's not like your brother was much of a housekeeper."

"True enough. Now that you're here, we'll whip the place into shape."

I hadn't been planning to use my time to clean, and I didn't appreciate her assuming that's what I was here for. But then, I didn't have any plan. I liked things tidy, so I might as well mop instead of mope. I could think while I scrubbed.

"Let me get my stuff."

After depositing my backpack on the couch, we got to work. I wasn't convinced Miko had been a slob. More like he left in a hurry. Susan assured me the room he'd been sleeping in was fairly straight, but the kitchen and living room had been tossed.

As if someone had been searching them.

This thought briefly froze my insides. Had someone broken in? And if so, what were they looking for?

I checked the door to Ed's office. Locked, as I'd left it. Even in the dim hallway, I could make out scrapes around the latch like someone had tried to force it. Ed didn't have many possessions, or even care about anything, besides the horses. I shook off a shiver. My imagination gets ahead of me sometimes.

Yet, I couldn't let it go. I found Susan wiping out the sink in the bathroom. "Has anyone else been here since Miko left?" I asked her.

She answered without looking away from what she was doing. "As a matter of fact, I saw that old boyfriend of yours...what was his name? Glen?"

"Glen Deutsch?" Years ago, he'd been my boss, not a boyfriend. But there had been benefits, and they weren't only the great horses in his barn. Last I'd heard, he'd fallen on hard times, moved to South Carolina, and was charming the rich ladies down there into buying expensive mounts for him to train.

"Black hair, rakish grin?" she asked.

"That's him." The boyish lopsided smile and dimple had gotten him in plenty of panties and trouble. "He always was too handsome for his own good."

"Well, his hairline's receding and he's gotten paunchy, but he's still a looker."

"Was he asking about me?"

She finally turned around, leaned her hip on the vanity. "Not exactly. He was pulling out when I got here this morning."

"Did you stop him?"

"Of course. He said he'd been off the Island for a few years and was looking up some of his old friends."

"What did you tell him?"

"Nothing."

Susan appeared the quintessential grandmother with her permed gray hair, ready smile, and soft roundness. But after raising five children, helping with at least twelve grandchildren, and keeping tabs on her brother Ed, she had a core of steel.

"That's probably just as well."

"And why's that?" she asked in a tone that told me she already knew.

"No reason. It's just strange that he'd come out of the woodwork now."

She flicked her dust rag at me. "Exactly what I thought. I told him I was looking after the horses for a couple of days but could pass on a message if he liked. He said that wasn't necessary, wished me good day, and that was it."

Chances were, he knew Ed was gone and the land belonged to me. But I wasn't the kind of woman he targeted. Those ladies were older, rich, and loved horses who won blue ribbons. Like Harry's mother, Babette, though she'd never fallen for Glen's charms. Not that he hadn't tried.

"Have you been in the house since Miko left?" I asked. "Before this morning, I mean."

"No. And I sure do apologize for the mess. I wanted to get it cleaned before you got here."

"Oh, that's no problem. Totally not necessary." I'd probably sleep in the tack room anyway. I stared into the middle distance for a few moments.

"Vi?" Susan waved her hand in front of my face. "Earth to Vi."

I blinked. "Hmmm? Oh, sorry. Just thinking."

Remembering how generous Ed used to be with spare keys to this house. Just about anybody could have let themselves in over the past couple of days.

Somebody who needed to find something.

Somebody who might have set a fire.

Somebody who could be a murderer.

CHAPTER FOURTEEN

AFTER SUSAN LEFT, I called a locksmith.

They couldn't come until Wednesday. I tried another and another, going down the list in the dusty yellow pages until I had contacted every one within a fifty-mile radius. I got no answer, number disconnected, or no available appointments until the following week. None would come out over the weekend.

I dropped the inches-thick phone book onto the counter with a heavy thump and realized it was several years old, the pages curled and brittle. Half the places I'd called were probably no longer in existence. Ed might have been the only person who still used a real phone book. Which he couldn't see unless he used a bright light and magnifying glass.

I left the now clean house and went to the barn. While working with Susan, I'd calmed my imagination and concluded Miko had probably misplaced his mobile device and tore the place apart finding it before he left for the airport.

I can talk myself into anything.

My phone dinged three times, and my heart leapt as I looked forward to an apology or explanation from Malcolm. I'd be happy with a *hello*. Then my heart settled right back in place. More likely, I was in for a longer tirade from my mother. But the messages weren't from either of them.

This is Martina
I groomed Eli, he is a good boy. <Smiley face>

Wheezy wouldn't stand still. He stepped on my foot. <Frowny face> How do I make him stop?

I didn't even try to squelch the churlish mix of anger and disappointment that swept through me. The only way she could have gotten my number was via Malcolm.

My grip tightened but I resisted the urge to slam my phone to the concrete barn aisle and grind it under my boot. Instead, I called the pizza place on the corner and ordered. Then, I texted a one-word response to Martina.

Patience.

That word could have been a note to myself. I shut down the device. With a large cheese, green pepper, and mushroom pizza on the way, I brought in the horses to groom them, planning to inventory and tidy the tack room-lounge after that. An exciting Friday night.

If I were home—if Winterlight was, indeed, home—Malcolm and I would be discussing what to have for dinner. We had attended all the fish fries during Lent. With Easter in the past, and the weather fine, he'd most likely fire up the grill while I put together a salad. My cooking skills weren't exactly legendary but I could rip romaine and chop carrots with the best. Sometimes, we'd jump in the car and meet my parents somewhere toward the city.

I pushed these thoughts away. I wasn't here to reminisce, but to figure out my future.

Ed's—*my*—twenty-five acres were tucked away from main thoroughfares not far from the north shore and the beach. Even so, the steady hum of traffic resonated in the distance. It wasn't a welcome sound. I'd prefer the drone of a tractor. Birds sang, but they competed with pop music from a radio in the neighborhood. The school bus had gone down the road a little while before, and I'd heard shrieks of laughter as children were cut loose for the weekend.

When I was a teenager, the area had been the country—or as close as one could get on Long Island. Now, subdivisions encroached on all sides, likely making this oasis more valuable than I'd thought. There were business cards from realtors in the kitchen and office attesting to interest.

I'd hate to see the place flattened, the majestic trees toppled, and a hundred houses built where I'd spent so much time at peace. But that alone wasn't a reason to keep it.

Other than the sounds of nearby civilization, the farm was quiet, but not in a tranquil Winterlight way. It was as if the land were holding its breath, waiting.

New lumber inside the barn marked repairs, but the old parts of the ceiling were smoke stained, a grim reminder that a blaze had been set and Ed murdered. I'd considered the possibility of him being an accidental casualty of vandalism. But if the fire had been started on purpose as he said…

I sighed. Once again, I'd worked myself into a funk.

With a pat to Sasha's neck, I returned her to the pasture, folding my arms on the top fence rail and resting my chin on them. She trotted to Beau, who lifted his head and wuffled at her, then they both lowered their noses to the lush spring grass.

A breeze picked up a few of last fall's leaves and sent them skittering over the asphalt drive. Cooler air caressed my sweaty neck sending a shiver through my body. I started for the barn, but a shadow passed through my peripheral vision. I spun quick. Three horses stood in the pasture.

Wastrel.

Beau and Sasha's heads shot up and their ears pricked toward the barn. I heard a crackling. Uneasily, I swiveled, smelling smoke.

The middle of the building was engulfed.

I rushed for the hose but my feet wouldn't contact earth. It was like swimming through Jell-O. By the time I had water flowing, the blaze and black billows of smoke had disappeared.

My hand found the hydrant handle and pushed it down. I breathed deeply to slow the painful thumping in my chest. My skin felt hot, as if I'd faced intense heat. I rubbed grit from my eyes. When had I last slept? Clearly avoiding it didn't prevent Wastrel from showing me whatever he thought I needed to see.

I didn't want to go on this ride with him. I wanted this to be over. I had to sleep. I couldn't live with waking nightmares.

But I had to find Ed's killer, and I was sure now that's why Wastrel was back. If only Ed had left me a clue. I glanced to the field. Two horses again, as it should be.

Rolling my head in a vain attempt to crack a few kinks out of my neck, I went inside the barn to sniff around, making sure it had been…what? Vision? Hallucination?

No evidence of a new fire. Exhaustion pounced onto my shoulders like a barn cat descending from the rafters. It was not the kind of fatigue that induced rest.

"Ed, talk to me, buddy. What happened here that day?"

Nothing. I could no more summon Ed's spirit than get Wastrel to provide clear messages. I grabbed the broom to sweep up shedded hair and dirt, working it into a neat pile I scooped into the wheelbarrow with a broad shovel. I hung up the utensils, straightening the handles as I always did, put my hands on my hips, and surveyed the space. For a brief moment, I imagined gleaming horses stood on cross ties having their manes braided while Ed barked orders. The mingled aromas of liniment, hair detangler, and fly spray filled my nostrils. I closed my eyes and inhaled deeply.

When I opened them, the barn was empty again, bereft of activity, of life.

Desperate for diversion, I retrieved my phone and texted Harry. Maybe he'd like to share a pizza. I could count on him to set me straight, or at least, distract me.

Two new texts. One from Emily.

I might have to kill her. Where's the whipped cream?! <Winky face>

She didn't have to explain who she meant. I smiled. The other was from Sandy.

Em says you went to NY. New boarder makes her want to do shots of whipped cream. I take a day off and the whole place goes to shit. <Smiling poop face>

That made me laugh out loud. Sandy added,

Let me know if you need anything.

Which brought an unexpected tear to my eye. I really needed to get ahold of myself. My phone rang moments later.

"How you be, V?" Harry's voice boomed.

I yanked the phone away to protect my eardrum from his traditional greeting.

"Harry—Michael—that was quick."

"Oh, V, you can call me Shirley for all I care. I'm sorry I made you feel like we had to get all formal. But what the hell? You're here? That's fantastic. Let's get drunk and cry about the good old days."

"Let's skip the drinking and crying. I don't remember the good old days being so great."

"That's because you were self-medicating most of the time."

"I was not. Not even part of the time. At least, not until after Wastrel. And I never rode under the influence."

"Oh right, that was me." He laughed. "Remember the time—"

"I just got a pizza," I cut in before he cruised down memory lane into teary town. He really would start to cry. "Where are you?"

"I was heading east to see Allie-Baba, but I'd much rather detour to you."

Allie-Baba, his parents, Alcott and Babette Brown.

"They're such old bores these days," he continued. "All Allie ever does is crossword puzzles, and Baba is redoing the kitchen for the hundredth time. She keeps muttering, *it is what it is*."

We didn't call her *Our Lady of the Platitudes* for nothing.

"Are you at the farm?" he asked. "I'm on my way. Seeing as how you're probably already gorging yourself on the best pizza in the world, you'd better order another."

I could easily survive on New York pizza until I had to go back to Missouri. Which had to be by Monday or I'd lose the trust fund. "You know me too well."

"Preach, baby. Look for me in twenty." He clicked off.

He arrived at the same time as the second pizza—loaded with pepperoni the way he liked—carrying a six-pack of my favorite beer in one hand, and in the other, two bottles—one of vodka and one of vermouth.

Martinis.

He'd sworn he was clean and sober, that the party boy had grown up. Maybe that applied only to his cocaine habit?

If I didn't want to get sentimental about my life at Winterlight, I sure as hell didn't want to wax nostalgic on the old days with Harry—drunk or sober. Calling him had been a mistake.

I paid for the second pizza, and we took it into the lounge where I had a pot of coffee brewed, hoping I could direct his attention there. But Harry opened the liquor bottles, found a glass and made himself a drink. I crossed my arms and prepared to launch into a scolding lecture as he opened me a beer. But then he put it all on a shelf and stepped back.

"There," he said. "A shrine if you will." He smirked at me. "But not to be worshiped." He helped himself to coffee and lifted his cup to the makeshift alter. "To what was but no longer is."

My relieved breath extracted a few slivers of anxiety with it. I joined him, raising my mug in salute. "To what no longer is."

We sat on the couch, me heavily, he with languid grace. Harry wasn't wearing one of his signature stock ties, but he still exuded crisp sophistication, even if he had just come from working horses. Or maybe because of it. A Kelly green polo shirt and black breeches highlighted his long frame, though he'd swapped out his tall boots for a pair of suede barn clogs, the kind Malcolm favored.

A sharp pang of longing tightened my throat. I stood to refill my mug while Harry dug into the pizza as if he hadn't eaten in days. He was thinner than I remembered, and I wondered if some new addiction had taken him. Or maybe his body had finally cleared out all the toxins. He looked fit.

An odd sense of remoteness overtook me, as if we'd just met and didn't know each other at all. I sat again and asked, "Have you been riding a lot?"

He finished chewing a massive bite of pizza, washed it down with a swallow of coffee. "Yes. In fact, I'm competing two hunters on Sunday at Cold Field. I just finished working them when you called. You should come to the show."

Cold Field Farm. Just the mention of the place was enough to make my insides seize up. It was where I'd been competing Wastrel when he crashed.

"Maybe I will," I said, knowing I wouldn't.

Millie the barn cat slinked in, rubbed my legs, and jumped in my lap. She sniffed my pizza.

"What are you doing here?" Harry asked. "Checking on the help?"

"No. Miko had an emergency at home. I'm currently helpless and—"

"V, for fuck's sake, I'm thrilled to see you, but you could have called. I would have been happy to feed these nags for you."

I tore a piece of cheese off my slice and fed it to Millie who had long ago proved she could digest anything. "I thought of that."

"But…what? Didn't think you could trust your old friend?"

That was exactly it, and his self-awareness disconcerted me. "I—"

"Forget it." He wiped his hands on a napkin and closed his pizza box. "You were right to be concerned. I haven't always been what you'd call dependable."

"I just figured you were busy with your own stuff," I lied. "You do seem…better."

Harry leaned into the worn couch making it creak, rousing thoughts of Ed Todd and the hours we'd spent talking in this room. Harry crossed his ankles and brought his coffee to his lips with a wink and self-satisfied smile. "Never better. Especially now that you're here." He regarded me with fierce attention. "God almighty, I've missed you."

This was the old Harry. The one I first met and had a crush on. Confident, passionate, seductive. A lock of dark hair fell over his forehead. His eyes, blue-green like pale jade, were clear, no bags beneath. Feathery wrinkles fanned out from the corners of his eyes, but a healthy swatch of pink tinted his high cheek bones as if he'd just come in from a gallop.

His phone buzzed where it sat face down on the old trunk that served as a coffee table. He picked it up, glanced at the screen, and his face scrunched into concern. "Oh dear," he muttered.

"Is everything all right? Is it your parents?"

"No, it's Joshua, the guy I'm riding hunters for on Sunday. His jumper rider came down with mono. She can't go."

"Mono? Is she…?"

"A teenager? Yes. Feeling old, old friend? I feel ya, believe me. Luckily,

Joshua appreciates experience." He patted his chest. "Unfortunately for me, his jumper is all he really cares about, so if he's riderless, Joshua won't go to the show at all. The hunters are more of an afterthought."

Harry's eyes snagged mine with an avid gleam. I knew exactly what he was thinking.

"Nope. Not doing it."

"What's the matter? Lost your mojo?"

I closed my pizza box, reserving the last pieces for breakfast. Millie moved from my lap to the trunk and began grooming her paws. She could feign indifference, but if I didn't put the box away, she'd paw it open and lick all the cheese off of what was left.

"Not at all," I answered Harry. "It's just not what I'm here for."

"There's a speed class."

My favorite, and he knew it.

"Plus..." He let the thought trail off as if he'd lost interest.

"What?"

"You'd be doing me a huge favor, V," he said in a rush. "I'm trying to rebuild my street cred. Joshua is the only one who's given me a chance. It will be our first show together, and I'm hoping for a long and profitable relationship. I can demonstrate the hunters are worth his time."

It's not like Harry had to work. He'd burned through his trust fund years before, but Allie-Baba supported him no matter what. If he wanted to buy this farm, they would do it. I stood and filled my mug with water. More coffee was not what I needed. Like it or not, I had to sleep.

He continued, "If I bring you to Joshua, he'll be ever so grateful."

Harry's best interests were never far from his thoughts.

"Only if his jumper wins," I said.

"Which he will, with you on him."

I stared out the window over the sink. The view was of the riding ring where standards and rails were still set up in a simple course. When had it last been used? Paint had peeled off the rails, and part of the coup had rotted making it lower on one side than the other, but I'd told Miko not to touch any of it. Leaving all that wood out in the weather wasn't good, but Ed had put it up. Near blind, he'd still been able to set the right distances. I couldn't bear to take it down.

Squelching a twinge of regret, I returned to the present and asked, "Is he any good—the jumper?"

Harry came to stand beside me. "Let me put it this way, if the teeny bopper can navigate a course on him and pick up a ribbon here and there..."

"A push-button ride?" I asked. Not that he had to be for me to figure him out.

Harry shrugged. "He likes what he does."

"Why don't you ride him?

"Vi, come on. You know jumpers aren't my thing. That's your world."

We stared at each other while a smile began on Harry's handsome face.

It was one more day, and there were bound to be people I knew at the show. Maybe someone would be willing to sit the farm until I could come for the horses. Or maybe even rent it until I figured out what to do. I'd return to Winterlight on Monday in time to complete my year.

But still, did I want to ride a strange horse at the same show grounds where Wastrel crashed? He kept taking me there in the dreams. Was that what he was trying to tell me? That I had to return to where my downward spiral began? Maybe it was just what I needed to finally expel him from my nights.

Have I mentioned I can talk myself into anything?

I said, "I don't have anything to wear."

His smile widened. For a moment, I felt bedazzled, just as when I first fell under his spell. I shook myself.

"We can fix that," he said.

He led me into the next room, one used mostly for storage, but it had some old lockers for the boarders, when there had been boarders. Dust and soot coated every surface. The fire had been in the main part of the barn, started in the ancient fuse box due to mouse-chewed wiring, according to the investigation, but smoke had gone everywhere. I'd taken the curtains down in the lounge last fall because they stank of it. Miko had obviously been in and out of there, but it didn't look like anyone had been in this room for months. I sneezed.

Harry went down the line of lockers, lifting the latch and opening each door. The familiar clack and squeak reminded me of unhappy high-school days. The first one was empty. The second had a hair brush, mirror, and bobby pins on the shelf. A bucket of leg wraps sat at the bottom. A large ragged hoodie of indeterminate color hung on one hook. The contents of the next included an old but decent pair of black paddock boots, too small for me, with matching half chaps folded on the shelf above.

I began to feel like Goldilocks, anticipating the item that would be just right even though the reek of smoke had no doubt permeated this area as well.

The fourth locker held matching garment and boot bags. The initials KAS were monogrammed onto the blue plaid of each. My eyebrow lifted in curiosity. "Who would leave all this here?"

"Remember the three Ks?" Harry asked.

The three boarders—teenaged girls—had kept their horses at Ed's a few years ago. They were all blonde and sickeningly adorable, with names like Kayla, Kaitlyn, and Kaylee, or maybe one of them was Kylie or Kelsey.

"Grounded, Flighty, and Spacey?" That's what I had called them. They'd paid their board on time, been kind to Ed, and were good to their horses. Which meant I'd tolerated them when I had to be at the farm at the same time they were. "One of them left this here?"

"You know teenaged girls."

"I guess, but how did you know about it?"

"I used to visit Ed occasionally."

Other than the time Harry supposedly came looking for his lost stock pin, this was news to me. After that visit, the heavy trunk in the tack room had been shifted out of place causing Ed to trip over it, konk his head, and knock himself out. I'd found him barely coherent, lying in a puddle of spilled tea with a big knot on his forehead.

"Since I went to Missouri? Really?"

"Maybe it was only once or twice. Anyway, one of those times he mentioned they'd all moved on to college. Their parents sold their horses and tack, but they all left some stuff here for him to do with as he pleased. He never could be bothered to do anything."

I reached for the garment bag. It was made of waterproof material which gave me hope whatever was inside might have been protected. Two of the girls were petite, but Kayla, the one I remembered best and called Grounded, she'd been about my size.

Harry unzipped both bags with a flourish worthy of Vanna White. On the hanger were tan breeches, a white show shirt, and hunter green jacket. The boots were black Spanish tops, barely worn. I held one up to the bottom of my foot. A half size too big, but they might do for a single day.

Harry's limpid eyes were sparkling, doing stupid things to my tummy.

"Say yes, V. It will be like the *really* good old days." He put his hand on my shoulder and squeezed. "Before."

He meant when the future had promised nothing but glittering success. Before Wastrel killed himself and sent me to intensive care. Before Heidi got tangled in her pony's legs because of a prank and died in my arms.

Before depression, self-medication, zero prospects.

Despite all that had happened since the really good old days, our shared history made Harry's company reassuring, restful. Other than Ed, he was the only person who truly understood what I'd been through.

I rubbed the jacket's lapel, the high-tech material slick between my thumb and fingers. I could already feel the reins in my hands, smell the sweat of the horse beneath me, hear the beat of his hooves, see the distance to the first jump.

It was only one more day. It would be good for me.

"Okay," I heard myself say. "I'll do it."

CHAPTER FIFTEEN

A PRICKLY STAB brought me out of the dream with a jerk. Millie snuggled at my side where I slept on the couch, purring and kneading the underside of my arm.

With. Her. Claws.

Gently, I repositioned her and she curled in on herself, sliding one paw over her eyes. The venerable gal had kept the barn mouse-free for years and provided company to Ed toward his lonely end. Would she mind being relocated to Winterlight?

After Harry left, I'd stayed up late cleaning and oiling the saddle I used to ride in and wiping down a helmet, thinking that the first thing I'd do with my new truck and trailer would be to take Beau, Sasha and Millie to Missouri.

But if I didn't return by Monday, I wouldn't get the trust fund. I'd be stuck at Ed Todd's with no source of income. Hard as I tried, I still couldn't think of the place as mine. I loved it, but not all the memories were good, and as I looked around with a critical eye, all I saw was work. The house, barn, and fencing all needed repairs or rebuilding.

And I'd be doing it alone.

I'd been flying solo for a long time before moving to Winterlight so that didn't scare me. Yet, it was a shock to realize how much I'd come to enjoy being around others. How I'd learned to depend on them.

On Malcolm.

If the note he'd left me was true, he was at a client site and therefore unreachable except for extreme emergency. Hope that he'd call or send a message anyway had quickly withered.

The first gray light of dawn shimmered through the tack room window. In the barn, one of the horses shifted with a sigh, old bones creaking. Beneath the blanket I'd brought from the house, I stretched. Millie rolled to her back.

Miko had said he rarely saw the cat. She'd never been much for people, other than Ed and sometimes me, so she hadn't had someone to sleep with in a while. Her presence, and through her, my connection to Ed, eased what I realized was loneliness, or maybe homesickness. Perhaps I provided the same for her—a link to her beloved old friend.

I sat up. I'd talk myself right into the dumps again if I kept at it, and I had work to do. Harry would arrive at eight. Joshua had been ecstatic—Harry's word—when he heard I would show his jumper.

In an act of heroic self-discipline, I didn't check my phone for messages until after I made a pot of coffee.

Nothing from Malcolm, but a short one from Dex.

Caught a break. Dinner tonight?

Dex didn't punctuate with any emoticons. No unmanly emotional demonstrations from him. Maybe that was why I liked him so much.

I frowned at the screen. Okay, we were both away from home and more or less in the same geographic area, so I guess this made sense. But it was more likely he was checking up on me. On Malcolm's behalf? In the past, that would unquestionably have been his motivation, but after the way the two of them went at it the day before I came here, probably not.

So…what did he want with me? I was uncomfortable with the strength of his reaction to walking in on me and Malcolm. Was I being neurotic? Probably.

And just like that, the night's dream hit me with such a jolt, I grabbed the nearest saddle rack to steady myself.

I was riding Wastrel in the show where we crashed. Instead of my usual competition attire, I had on borrowed clothes—the ones from the locker. As we cantered our warm-up circle past the bleachers, I saw a shirtless man standing with his back to us. His stance—the indolent tilt of his hip—was familiar. His hand rested just above the belt of his jeans. He let his arm drop to reveal a tattoo of an iridescent black bird on his back. As I watched, the bird began to move, to flap its wings, catching sunlight with feathers that could have been made of oil and silk. It emerged from the man's skin and flew away. Straight at us. I ducked. It grazed the top of my helmet and disappeared.

I twisted to see the man. He glanced over his shoulder and bared his teeth in a smile. I recognized the face but everything else about him was wrong.

It was Dex.

CHAPTER SIXTEEN

Harry picked me up precisely at eight in an older red BMW sedan. The Browns always drove Beemers. I put the saddle in the back, he handed me a trenta Starbucks—black with a generous shot of whipped cream—and we were off.

I didn't tell him I'd prefer a dirty chai tea latte from Roasted Bean. Preferably with my grandfather. It would only hurt his feelings if I said anything, and then he'd sulk. Six-foot-four of pouty Harry was more than I could take of a morning.

Other than that, it did feel like the good old days as we cruised the Expressway talking of nothing in particular, laughing. I needed a laugh. The dream had shaken me. It wasn't the bizarre image of a bird flying out of Dex's back. I'd come to accept the weirdness of my dreams. It was the faintly menacing smile he'd flashed that made my gut twist each time I thought about it. Thankfully, the morning chores of caring for the horses and cleaning stalls had calmed my jitters, as physical work always did. I needed a clear head when riding a new horse.

I hadn't responded to Dex's text.

When we got out of the car, a shaggy dog bounded up to us and put his paws on my shoulders. I was always happy to greet the barn critters, but this guy just made me miss Noire. "Good morning, big fella."

"That's Scooby Doo." Harry said. "Get down, Scooby."

"He's okay." Pushing white hair out of his eyes, I said, "You don't look like Scooby Doo."

"Joshua rescued him, and that's the name he came with."

That made me approve of Joshua without even meeting him. A minute later, we were introduced. He led a striking bay stallion around the indoor arena. Vagrant stood 16.3 hands, had good bone and the typical deep chest and long body of a thoroughbred. Just how I liked them.

Joshua was a compact and intent man of middle age with graying dark hair and brown eyes set against pale skin. He wore breeches and boots but didn't ride his horses, he explained, because as a surgeon, he couldn't risk his hands. His firm shake combined with the rescue dog made me warm up to him right away. Even if thinking about that hand holding a scalpel and cutting into people made me want to wipe mine on my breeches.

Someone's breeches. The fit of them was loose and short. I wore two pairs of socks to fill the boots, and they were too big in the calf, but they'd do for one ride. We weren't far from a tack shop, and I decided we'd stop there afterwards for a better fitting ensemble. I could always use spare breeches and boots.

He had Vagrant tacked up and ready, but I wanted to see the horse work freely first. Joshua accommodated my request without comment and turned the bay loose. We were at the man's private residence, but he had a setup to rival the best professional outfits. With a decent-sized indoor arena in addition to a large outdoor one with good footing and enough jump equipment to set up any course he wanted, it was considerably nicer than Winterlight. I understood why Harry hoped for a long working relationship with the guy.

Or perhaps more than a working relationship. Harry's body language as he stood next to Joshua reminded me of Martina with Malcolm. That memory stung. I pushed it away. Harry and I hadn't talked about his penchant for swinging both ways in a long time, and I'd kind of forgotten about it. I'd assumed—perhaps hoped—it was a phase he'd grown out of.

In the past year, I'd learned my assumptions were not to be trusted. Especially when it came to people.

Vagrant trotted like a plow horse, each hoof fall shaking the ground. Heavy on the forehand didn't cover it, but a plan of how to approach him began in my mind. After watching him move on his own for a few minutes, we stood together. I let him smell me and ran my hands over his body, talking—whispering words of his strength, beauty, and intelligence—and sending him mental pictures of what we would accomplish together.

I rode Vagrant outside. Harry gave me a leg up before he mounted one of the hunters he would compete the next day. The sense of rightness I'd felt while we were driving hit me again. Harry and I worked well together. We always had.

I put Vagrant through some basic warmup movements, focusing on lateral work to improve his suppleness and lots of transitions to lighten his front end, all the while breathing through my center, using my mind more than my body to communicate. He'd been surprised at first, as most horses were, to find me knocking at his mental door. By the time we started schooling over fences, we'd reached an accord. He understood that by carrying himself differently—in balance—he wouldn't have to work so hard. He didn't have to run headlong at every jump and throw himself at it.

No doubt the teeny-bopper had pushed him to rush his fences thinking that was the fastest way to the other side. It was also the fastest route to disaster. It was only Vagrant's innate athleticism that had kept him and the girl safe so far.

The two geldings Harry rode went well also. I began looking forward to the show. We agreed with Joshua on the time for the morning and went to lunch.

As soon as we got in the car, Harry put his hand up for a high-five. "That was fantastic, V. I've never seen that hack go so well."

I gave him some side eye. "You said he liked his job."

"Did I lie?"

"No, but you could have informed me he's a stallion, that he was heavy on the forehand and rushed his fences."

"I didn't want to color your opinion of him before you had a chance to judge for yourself. Anyway, you already fixed that with just one ride. Same old V."

I huffed and settled back in the seat. Harry always managed to temper his lies of omission with a compliment to deflect my annoyance. The day had turned gray, and the weather report called for rain overnight. We had pizza for lunch—what else?—and swung by the tack shop. On the sale rack, I found a pair of breeches that fit, then paid too much for paddock boots and half chaps.

"Where to now?" Harry asked. "We have a few hours before dinner."

"Dinner?"

"Yes. I made reservations for us at your favorite Italian place. I know how you like to load up on yummy pasta carbs before a show."

"Oh, crap."

"Hey, we can eat anywhere you want."

"No, it's not that." I'd never answered Dex. Plus, Penny had called and wanted me to come over. "I can't."

Harry accelerated onto the Expressway. "We can do it another night. Allie-Baba want you to visit as well. They invited you tonight, but I wanted you to myself. How long are you going to be here? Say it's for good, sugar. Wasn't today great?"

"Yes, today was great. But I have a job, Harry. People and animals who depend on me."

As I said those words, they felt true. As right as the day had been, I couldn't stay. I just needed to figure out what to do with Ed Todd's. Putting it up for sale seemed like the logical thing. I needed to talk to Susan, see how she felt about it, see if she had any idea what Ed had been thinking. Maybe someone in the family wanted it.

"There are people here who depend on you, too, you know." Harry kept his eyes on the road and continued when I didn't comment. "Joshua would drop the teeny bopper in a hot New York second if you wanted to ride Vagrant."

"It's tempting, but I don't think so."

"Say you'll think about it."

"I'll think about it."

But I didn't have to. I pulled out my phone to call Penny. Three new messages.

Martina again.

Wheezy keeps stepping on my feet. He doesn't like me. <Disappointed face>. You will fix him, right?

I would fix something, that was for sure.

Got to fly. Robert and I are having dinner downtown.

If I were an emoticon, I'd be that angry red face my mother had sent. And the grimacing one. Or the green nauseated one. Dark thoughts came to me about what I'd like to do to Martina's face. Still nothing from Malcolm. If they were having dinner, he wasn't at a client site, and that meant he was deliberately not communicating with me.

I answered Martina that I would work on Wheezy's ground manners next week.

The only fix is time and patience.

I hoped she would get the message about patience.

I called Penny, said I'd be there soon, then texted Dex.

"Home, Jeeves," I said to Harry.

He let out an annoyed breath.

"What is it?"

"Nothing. It's better this way. We have an early start. It's fine."

It didn't sound fine, but I let it go. Harry always had been moody. Should I ask him to watch over Beau and Sasha until I could come for them? If I had them and Millie situated, I could return to Winterlight without worry, finish my year, get the trust fund. Surely all would become clear at that point.

Yet, something kept me from asking the favor even though he'd offered. For that matter, I could probably move them to Allie-Baba's. Babette had always been happy to let me use her barn when I needed it. She'd treated me like the daughter she never had, often better than she treated Harry—her only child—and I felt badly for putting off dinner. Especially if I was going to ask for her help.

Dex texted back that he'd pick me up at Penny's at seven. Of course, he already knew the address. He'd done a thorough background check on me before he'd let Malcolm hire me, and Penny's house had been my home at the time.

Thinking about Dex's protectiveness of Malcolm made their fight all the more mystifying. They were like brothers, with Dex, the older one, always having Malcolm's back.

At Ed's, I entered the house through the back. He might have been free with keys, but not to the rear entrance. I'd made sure all the windows were locked and had braced a chair under the front door knob until I could get the locks changed. If someone wanted in badly enough, they could break a window. But the rooms were as they'd been left.

Tidy. Quiet. Vacant.

Before melancholy could get hold of me, I made short work of showering, changing, and getting back on the road to visit Penny and my eight-month old niece, Isabella.

Isabella, it turned out, wasn't fit for human consumption. She was teething and colicky, and only her mother's breast would soothe her. Penny looked tired, and her husband, Frank, was in the basement watching television away from the annoying cries of his child.

I cleaned up a sink full of dishes and put a load of towels in the wash while Penny gave Issa a bath. Then I walked the baby for an hour so Penny could take a shower and a quick nap. My niece drooled on my shoulder and regarded me with serious eyes. She was content so long as I kept her moving. If I tried to sit, she started to cry.

"Frank helps with Issa," Penny said in his defense after she woke up. "He does. He's a good father. But work has been slow, and he's stressed, so I sent him downstairs. It's better than listening to him grouse about it."

It was no secret I thought Penny could do better than Frank. That was the real reason she hid him when I was around.

I refrained from muttering, *whatever*, sat next to her on the couch where she nursed her daughter, and stroked Issa's forehead. Her eyelids began to droop.

"It's time for her to go down for the night, thank goodness. Poor thing is worn thin between the drooling and not feeling good. She's started pulling herself up on everything."

I was pretty sure Penny was the one who was worn thin. "Are you getting enough sleep?"

Penny jiggled Issa and avoided eye contact. "Of course. Never mind about me. What about you? Have you decided what you're going to do?"

I let my head drop back to the cushion with a sigh. "It's good to be here, but I honestly don't know if it's home anymore."

"Home is where you make it, Vi. When you talk about Missouri and Winterlight and Malcolm, you always sound happy."

"Do I?"

"Well, not at first. If I remember correctly, you accused me of sending you to hell."

"I thought you had."

"You would have been miserable here, too."

I elbowed her arm. "Are you saying I'm just a miserable person so get over it?"

She giggled. "You know what I mean."

I did. I hadn't realized just how unhappy I was until I'd been at Winterlight for a few months.

"I doubt you'd find anyone like Malcolm around here."

"I think there's only one six-foot two, eyes of blue, smart, kind, funny, kilt-wearing, pentathlete-super-hero-horse-farm-owner."

"Who'll put up with you," she added without missing a beat.

There was only one Robert Malcolm. Of that I was certain. "That's the thing I wonder about."

Penny put Issa to her shoulder and patted her back. "You mean you wonder what such a dreamy guy is doing with a belligerent, defensive horse girl who never finished college?"

"Gee. Way to make me feel good about myself, Sis-co."

"If you can't get the truth from your sister-cousin, you can't get it anywhere. But seriously, have you told him how you feel?"

"Of course not."

"Why of course not?"

"Because I work for him. He needs to give me an objective evaluation so I can get the trust fund."

"Objective went out the window months ago, Vi. I warned you not to get involved with the boss, but did you listen?"

"I did pretty good with the other two rules."

Penny rolled her eyes at me. "I'm going to put her to bed." She went down the hall.

I followed her. "You have a T-shirt I can borrow?" I pulled the damp fabric of the one I wore away from my shoulder.

"Oh, sure. Sorry about that. I should have given you a spit rag." She rummaged through a drawer. "Seriously, Vi, you should finish college. But otherwise, I know beneath that confrontational persona—which, by the way, you use because you're scared of getting hurt—you are smart and funny and kind, too. That's why Malcolm puts up with you."

"Okay, Miss Psychology Major. I get it."

"Thanks for your help this afternoon," she said. "It's nice to get a break."

So much for all the support Frank was supposedly giving her. She pulled out a long-sleeved red shirt and handed it to me with a funny look.

"What? Do I have baby drool in my hair?"

"No." She gave a soft laugh. "You didn't take the chance to say something nasty about Frank."

I changed shirts real quick, and as I pulled the red one over my head, I crossed my eyes and stuck out my tongue. "The Midwest has rewired my brain. Meet the kinder, gentler Viola Parker."

With a glance to the crib, she put a finger to her lips and led me to the hallway. "More like kilt guy has made you feel safe."

We went to the kitchen. I hadn't considered that angle. "I even speak to my parents," I said. "Who would have thought?"

She started a pot of coffee. "Not me."

"Save me a cup of that brew. I'm going to the bathroom."

"I don't have any whipped cream," she called after me.

"I'll live," I said.

I wanted to spend the whole night drinking coffee and laughing like we used to. I regretted agreeing to go to dinner with Dex. At the same time, Penny needed to rest if she could. Or to grab some quality time with her useless husband.

As I finished and opened the bathroom door, I felt the change—a rich fullness saturated the air, and not from the blubbing percolator.

On sock feet, I padded the hall in silence, afraid something had happened with the baby. But Penny wasn't in the bedroom. I heard a masculine throat getting cleared toward the front of the house and reversed.

And there, in the living room, taking up more space than he had a right to, stood Dex. In a navy suit, white button-down shirt, maroon striped tie and matching pocket silk. I'd seen him in a tux once, but never a suit. Dex was of medium build and at first glance, not especially handsome, not in the heart-stopping, life-guard way Malcolm is. Nor was he just-stepped-out-of-a-Ralph-Lauren-ad beautiful like Harry. That is, until you noticed his eyes. The intensity there changed everything. In the tux, he'd been man candy on a stick. The suit did not diminish his yumminess. Which Penny's slack-jawed stare attested to. I glanced over my T-shirt and jeans.

"You didn't tell me we were dressing up."

Dex's eyes were all warm molasses as he drawled, "It's Saturday night in New York, Miss Parker. I didn't think I needed to."

A snore drifted up from the basement. Penny didn't appear to notice. A twitch of Dex's eyebrows was the only indication he heard. I swept by my cousin and whispered, "Close your mouth, Sis-co." Louder, I said, "Penny, meet Dexter Hamill, retired mounted cop and sometime PI. You can call him Dex."

Dex's thick, white-blonde hair was swept back from his forehead. When I first met him, he sported a military-severe crew cut. Since then, he'd let it grow long enough to brush his collar. A short beard only added to his allure. He took Penny's hand. "At your service, ma'am. Rumors of Miss Parker's cousin's beauty were not exaggerated."

Penny continued to stare, and if I didn't do something soon, she'd start drooling worse than Isabella. Maybe motherhood had short-circuited her brain. I'd heard that could happen. I'd never seen her struck dumb by a man before. Although I had to admit, if Dex had sauntered into the barn like this the first time I met him, I might have been a little tongue-tied, too. Clearly, Penny wasn't getting out enough.

"Dex, would you excuse us a minute? There's coffee in the kitchen. Help yourself."

I pinched Penny's arm and dragged her to the bedroom.

Once there, she put her hands to her head. "Oh my God, Vi, you didn't tell me there were more gorgeous men out there."

"They grow like weeds."

"Does he wear a kilt, too?"

"Not that I know of."

"Those eyes. Did he call me beautiful? He did, didn't he?"

"He did."

I took in her flat hair and sweats. Despite looking tired, her skin glowed. "You are beautiful. Don't ever doubt it."

"I'm moving to Missouri."

"I'd love that. But right now I need to borrow a dress." I stuck out one foot. "And shoes."

Penny and I had always been able to share clothes. Unfortunately for Penny, my wardrobe allowance went to breeches. Fortunately for me, she spent hers on nice things, and we shortly had me looking presentable in a cobalt blue cocktail dress, black heels, and a pretty silk wrap to keep my shoulders warm. I pinned my hair into a French twist and swiped on mascara and lipstick.

"Put these on." Penny handed me a pair of dangly earrings.

I hooked them into place. "I'll mail all this back to you."

"Keep it. I never wear the earrings, and it will be a while before I fit into that dress again. Or have any desire to put on high heels."

Making a mental note to touch base with her more often, I put my arms around her and pressed a kiss to her cheek. "Thanks." I checked my reflection and tugged at the dress's deep neckline.

"Stop it," Penny said. "You look ravishing."

Getting ravished was not on my agenda. "You have more cleavage than I do. Especially lately."

"Yeah, well, breastfeeding will do that for a girl. You have plenty. Now, go have a good time. I'll be letting my imagination get the best of me."

"There's nothing between me and Dex." I gathered my clothes and threw them in a bag to put in the rental car. "We're friends."

"That's what you think."

I whipped my head to her. "What do you mean?"

"I mean it might be Saturday night in New York, but guys don't dress like that—or smell like that—to take a *friend* to dinner."

"Your imagination already has the better of you."

"Whatever."

Back in the living room, I caught the almost imperceptible widening of Dex's eyes when he saw me, and then the quickly hidden smirk from Penny. Surely she wasn't right about this.

Dex turned to her as he opened the door. "A pleasure, ma'am. Thank you for the coffee. Best I've ever had."

"Oh brother," I muttered. "Let's get out of here before the crap gets too deep."

Dex guided me down the front steps with a hand at the small of my back. *This is not a date*, I repeated to myself as I walked to my rental. I'd take my own vehicle and leave when I wanted.

"I'll bring you back to your car," Dex said.

I stopped. Saying *no* to Dex is very hard. "Um. Okay."

Dex opened the passenger door of a white Mustang. I got in and fastened my seat belt. "I have a horse show tomorrow, so I need to get back at a reasonable time to sleep. You look very handsome by the way," I added when he was in the driver's seat.

"And you, Miss Parker, are exquisite."

Heat crept up my neck as he put the car in gear and peeled away from the curb.

"No promises on what time we'll return, Cinderella," he said.

What had I gotten myself into?

He shifted to second, the engine vroomed, and he pointed the car toward the setting sun. Giving me a wink, Dex said, "We can sleep when we're dead."

CHAPTER SEVENTEEN

MY BODY PRESSED into the seat as the car accelerated onto the highway. "You planning on that being soon?"

"Why, Miss Parker, do I detect a derisive note of distrust?"

"Careful, you're starting to sound like Dex Two." Humphrey J. Dexter the third, Malcolm's attorney—known around the barn as Dex Two—spoke with vivid eloquence.

"Never will I ever speak like that bombastic ambulance chaser."

His statement had the desired effect. I laughed and relaxed. The two Dexes liked to trade barbs, but they were fond of each other. Plus, Dex Two was as far as a lawyer could get from being an ambulance chaser.

"Didn't I see you leave the airport in a gray SUV?"

"How observant. Maybe you should join Emily at her criminal justice studies."

"No thanks."

He touched the knot of his tie, and I wondered if it was too tight or if he simply wasn't used to wearing one. Why he'd gotten so dressed up eluded me. The suit fit him like it was custom made. I doubted he'd wandered into a department store and picked one off the rack on a whim.

"The SUV was for business."

"Ah." I gestured at the dashboard. "So this is pleasure."

"Of course, Miss Parker. What else could it be?"

What else indeed?

Half an hour later, we turned onto a quiet side street in a south shore village and pulled up next to an unimpressive entrance. A simple wooden door and arched awning were all that distinguished it from the side of the building. Maybe Dex had a meeting before dinner he neglected to tell me about?

A valet opened my door, startling my purse right out of my hands. Dex came to my side of the car quickly and shouldered the boy aside to take my elbow. As if I needed help getting out of a car.

It reminded me of when Dex Two had taken me to dinner and the symphony when I first moved to Winterlight. But then, I knew he had no interest in me other than friendship, and he was doing it as a favor to Malcolm because I was new to the area. This time, my footing felt less sure.

An odd impression of the past year appeared in my mind, events and adventures aligned like books on a shelf with Dex One and Dex Two the bookends propping it all up.

I had relaxed for a moment, but it hadn't lasted. Still, I refrained from wiping my sweaty palm on Penny's dress before putting my hand in Dex's. Nothing escaped his keen scrutiny, so he already knew he was making me nervous.

Inside the door an elegant and expensive looking restaurant opened before us. People were waiting to be seated. Dex kept hold of my hand and tugged me with him to the hostess station.

"Oh, yes, Mr. Hamill. Party of two. Right this way."

She took us into the main dining room, up a narrow flight of stairs, then to the back of the building where a table was situated in front of a tall window overlooking a garden. There were other diners up here, but this room was much quieter than downstairs, candlelit, intimate. Strategically placed potted plants made each table a secluded island. Dark walls, matching draperies, a couple of languid ceiling fans, and the scent of exotic spices and garlic gave me the sense of having stepped into another world.

Dex pulled out my chair. A waiter brought water. Dex ordered wine. A red. Baba ganoush for an appetizer. My head was full of questions, but I sipped the wine and let him take the lead, the very picture of cool restraint.

But honestly, if he didn't look up from his oversized menu and start talking soon, I'd kick him. Or possibly stab his hand with a fork.

The waiter delivered the appetizer, and we ordered dinner. A mixed grill for him, chicken kebobs for me. Despite what Harry'd said about carb loading, I didn't like to overdo it the night before a show. Though the jumper classes were later in the day, and my stomach would no doubt be settled by then if I did over-indulge.

"Tell me about the horse show," he said. "You just got here yesterday. That was fast work."

"Oh, I wasn't looking for it," I explained. "A guy Harry knows needed a rider for his jumper. Good timing, I guess. Or good luck for the horse owner."

"Yes. Good timing."

"Why does it sound like you don't believe that?"

"I don't believe in coincidences or luck."

I tore my gaze from his. "This is a nice place. How did you know about it?"

"Don't change the subject, Miss Parker."

"Okay, Dex." I took a bigger drink of wine. It was good. "What, exactly, is the subject?"

"Good question." His smile seemed genuine, yet I felt like I sat across from a crocodile.

"Keep your inscrutable detective games to yourself."

"You always did have a good bullshit meter."

"Yeah, and the reading is getting in the red. You might as well explain yourself sooner rather than later."

His eyebrows scrunched together. "Explain myself?"

"Don't play dumb," I said. "It's insulting to both of us."

His fingers drummed the table. A gold signet ring I'd never seen before flashed on his pinky. I didn't know how to behave with this version of Dex.

"Ah, yes," he said. "Playing dumb and insults. Two things you know a lot about."

I plunged a triangle of toasted pita into the baba ganoush. "My sucky attitude isn't news."

"No, it isn't. But it should be."

I glanced around, hoping the waiter or someone was nearby who could get me out of this conversation. I knew I should have driven my own car.

"Why?" I sat back in my chair. "How about your sucky attitude? How about the way you attacked Malcolm? Would you like to talk about that?"

His eyes narrowed and his voice contained an undertone of warning. "That's between me and Mac."

"With me sandwiched right in the middle?" I gulped more wine. Why, exactly, did I have to insert the image of a threesome into my brain?

"Yes," he said. Then after a pause, "And no."

The waiter brought our meals. We both picked at our plates, using the distraction of hot food to cool off. At least, I needed to cool off. It was hard to tell with Dex. After all, crocodiles are cold blooded.

A few minutes later, he drank his water, wiped his mouth, and leaned back, his demeanor softening.

"The thing is, Vi, you are very smart. Very talented. Despite your damaging history, and the scornful persona you project, on the inside you are generous and kind. Funny and compassionate. Honest, loyal, disciplined, hard working."

I laid down my fork and knife. He'd called me by my first name. He only did that when he really wanted to get my attention. He had it. "Enough already."

All this gushing right after Penny had said almost the same thing, it made me uncomfortable.

He touched the back of my hand, and I sucked in a breath, then sucked down more wine.

"On the outside, you're sexy as hell." He waggled his eyebrows at me.

I smiled, shook my head, and pulled my hand out from under his warm fingers.

"You don't take crap from anyone," he continued quietly. "But you treat yourself with contempt and disrespect."

I looked out the window to avoid his dark-chocolate gaze. A hunk of chicken had lodged in my gullet. I swallowed against it, but there was nothing there. Only unshed tears trying to escape. Damn him. The sun had set, and the garden below was at most a murky suggestion of stems and blossoms. Soon, the glass would reflect only our shadows and secrets, made wobbly by the uncertain candlelight and our unsettled breaths.

I cleared my throat, folded my napkin on the table, and pushed my plate away, making room for my elbows. "Pretty speech." I twined my fingers together and rested my chin on them. "What do you want from me?"

"I want you to make a commitment," he said. "To yourself."

All that had been on my mind the past few weeks was whether to stay in Missouri or return to New York. That was plenty for me to work on without adding more commitments.

The waiter cleared the table. Dex filled my wine glass. I'd had enough to loosen my tongue, to not care if I sounded confused. "I don't know what you mean."

He leaned forward and rested his elbows on the table. The cedar wood scent of his beard oil filled my nose. My grandfather must use the same brand because it reminded me of him, and homesickness waylaid my heart. Homesickness for Winterlight and my family there.

Dex took my hands and leaned even closer, pulling me toward him. "I mean that you deserve more than what you've allowed yourself."

"More than what?"

"More than dropping out of college, mucking stalls for someone else, and letting him screw you on a countertop."

Ah. So. Now we'd reached the crux of the matter. The countertop sex had been quite pleasurable, but that was none of his business. None of that was anyone's business but my own.

Yet, I took his meaning. According to his code, that wasn't how a man treated a woman. And for that reason, I shouldn't have allowed it. Malcolm shouldn't have initiated it.

"You deserve dinners like this," he went on, his wine-scented breath mingling with mine. "You should have people working for you so you can make the best use of your time."

"Which is?"

"Right now, it's riding, but it could be anything you want."

"I like mucking stalls. I like the physical activity."

"Riding is physical activity."

I tipped my head to one side. "So is sex," I purred by way of taunting him. Ah, me and wine. Such a good pairing.

He released my hands like they'd turned into hot pokers and sat back. Interesting.

With a signal to the waiter, he had the check paid. I didn't bother offering to cough up my half knowing it was futile. Then we were down the steps and waiting for the valet to bring his car.

After a few uncomfortable minutes of silence spent standing on the sidewalk, I said, "Thanks for dinner. It was very good."

"Promise you'll think about what I said."

I nodded. Harry had extracted the same promise from me just a few hours before. Unlike what Harry wanted from me, though, I would think about what Dex had said. Later.

The Mustang came screeching around the corner, the valet having entirely too much fun with it. But it wasn't a white car zooming straight at us. I blinked, wondering why someone would drive so fast down such a quiet street.

The next thing I knew, there was a pop pop, and I was thrown hard to the sidewalk with Dex on top of me.

The wind was knocked clean out of my lungs. I recognized the feeling from falling off horses, and quickly scanned my body out of habit to check for injuries. No sharp pain. Pretty sure my French twist saved me from a concussion. How had I gotten flat on my back?

When I could breathe, I asked, "What the heck?" and shoved Dex's shoulders.

He didn't respond. Or move.

There were no shouts for help. We were alone. I heard the squeal of tires again as the car sped around the corner at the end of the block. And then my voice, screaming his name.

CHAPTER EIGHTEEN

DEX'S HAND covered my mouth. "Enough," he ordered.

I bit him and hissed, "Jesus. I thought you were dead."

"Well, you screamed to wake the dead. So here I am."

I shoved him again, and he pulled himself up, hopping a little on his fake leg to find his balance. He helped me to my feet as the Mustang glided to a stop beside us.

"Everything all right?" the valet asked.

"Turned my ankle," I said, sensing Dex wanted a quick exit.

Dex shoved a tip into the boy's hand and firmly guided me to the car. "Are you all right?" he asked after we were moving.

He was in hyper-vigilant mode, eyes darting every which way. I could smell the adrenaline. Or maybe that was me.

I pulled pins out of my hair with shaky fingers and fluffed it out, rubbing my scalp. "I might have a little bump." I breathed deep, but my legs were so wobbly, I'm not sure I could have walked if I needed to.

"Mind telling me why someone is shooting at you?" he asked.

"Me? I thought they were shooting at you." I tried to make light of it, but my voice shook.

He floored it onto the highway, moved into the fast lane, and whipped past Penny's exit without so much as a blink, keeping his eyes on the rearview mirror as much as the road ahead.

"Um…" I pointed out the window.

"Not going back there."

My heart had already lodged in my throat. It nearly jumped out of my mouth. "You think she's in danger?"

"Doubtful. But if someone is after you, they know the car you've been driving."

I texted Penny that I wouldn't be back for the car tonight. That would send her imagination into overdrive. "Shouldn't we have called the police? Made a report or something?"

Dex turned on the radio and tuned it to an easy listening station. He must have thought I needed soothing. He was right.

"Did anyone but you and me see what happened?" he asked.

"I don't know. I don't think so."

"Then it didn't happen."

"Someone will find the bullets. What if they went inside and hurt someone?"

"Too small a caliber for that."

I took another deep breath, listened to the music, and made a run at convincing my racing heart we hadn't just been shot at. Nope. Despite what Dex said, it happened.

"This car isn't exactly inconspicuous," I said. "You sure it wasn't someone shooting at you?"

"I do have friends in low places, but none that are after me for anything at the moment."

"No one's after me."

"You don't know that. Didn't you say Ed Todd was murdered?"

"I said that to Malcolm."

"And he told me."

"Did he send you here to keep an eye on me?"

"No. But you need someone—"

"To babysit me?"

"To watch out for you, Vi. For cripe's sake. Don't make everything so hard."

I huffed. The comment didn't sting quite as much coming from him as it had when Malcolm had said almost the same thing. And really, was it so bad to have people around who cared? Ed had, though he'd never shown it in any obvious way.

"Ed was murdered," I said. "I'm sure of it. I have no idea why, but it has nothing to do with me."

"Is it possible someone wanted him out of the way—so you would get the farm sooner rather than later?"

I lifted my shoulders. "How would I know?"

"Maybe he had dirt on someone and was threatening to reveal it. That can be a powerful motive for murder."

"Right. Motive. I remember you telling me that before. But none of that makes sense. If we're throwing out wacky ideas, maybe there was a dispute over a horse. Maybe he had an affair, dumped her, and she got mad."

"Now you're thinking like a detective."

"It was a joke."

"How long did you know Ed?"

I thought back. "About twenty five years."

"And how old was he when died?"

"I don't know. Late sixties? Seventy maybe." How was it that I didn't know how old he was?

"Which puts him in his mid forties when you met him. You don't think he had a whole life before you came along? You don't think there's history there you know nothing about? You think he told you everything? You think he told a five-year-old kid anything?"

The questions came as hard and fast as the bullets. "Okay, okay. Of course not." I rubbed my forehead, feeling a headache coming on. "I guess I never thought of Ed like that."

"Like what? A man?"

"Yes, okay? He was…"

"Look, Vi, you were a kid. You idolized him, right? He was like the father you never had?"

I nodded, feeling tears clog my throat. I still missed Ed so much it hurt.

"We never think of our parents like that. Like they had a life before we came along, like there was something for them besides us."

It was the most personal thing Dex had ever divulged, and I'm not sure he meant it to be revealing. It made me wonder about his past. Something I knew nothing about. Something to probe him on at another time.

"No one knew Ed was leaving the farm to me."

"You sure about that? Just because you didn't know doesn't mean he didn't tell someone else."

I hadn't thought of that.

Dex grunted and kept his attention on the road ahead and behind, driving fast. We kept our thoughts to ourselves, but I imagined his synapses were gridlocked like mine. A little while later, we zipped past the exit for Ed's place without slowing.

"Where are we going?"

"To a hotel as soon as I'm sure no one's tailing us."

"No, we have to go to the farm. I have to check on the horses. What if…."

Oh my God." All air left my body, and I swear my blood stopped pumping for a few moments.

"What?"

I swallowed hard. "If someone *is* after me, then they know I've been staying there. What's to keep them from hurting the horses? Or Millie?"

"Millie?"

"Barn cat."

We continued east until the traffic thinned. The promised rain started, a soft patter on the windshield and roof. Between that, the wine and excitement, and the stress hormones draining from my system, I couldn't keep my eyes open. Next I knew, we were pulling into Ed's, creeping up the drive with the headlights off. The rain had stopped, but steamy tendrils of mist rose from the blacktop drive to envelop the car. Once we were near the house, Dex sped up and drove around the back, tucking the Mustang behind a large spruce tree.

"I thought—"

"I'll make sure the coast is clear, you quick check the critters, and we're out. Got it?"

I nodded.

He sat for a moment, staring through the windshield into the woods behind the house. He probably imagined assailants hiding in the dark. I saw only the trails that wound through the trees bordering the farm, trails I'd bumbled along on Sasha and Beau when we were all younger. Probably overgrown now.

"You need to rest," he said.

"Yeah." Since he didn't appear to want to move, I pushed my door open. In the harsh glare of the overhead light, he looked like he could use a good night's sleep, too. I'd been so taken by the urbane version of himself he'd presented, I hadn't noticed how weary he looked. Which might have been his intention. He was a master of prevarication and diversion. Even knowing he'd want to stand guard and I had little chance of convincing him otherwise, I asked, "You too?"

"When you're safe." He opened his door, stepped out, and collapsed.

"Oh, my God." I ran to his side, my heels sinking into the soft earth. I kicked out of them and knelt next to Dex. "What happened? Are you okay?" I slid one hand under the back of his head. He was lying partly in a puddle. His tie had flipped up into his face. I smoothed it down, loosened the knot, and undid his top button.

His eyelids fluttered. He lifted his head and looked at his hand where it rested along the outside of his left thigh. Slowly, he peeled it away from his soaked pants leg. Even in shadow, there was no mistaking the blood covering his fingers. He let his head drop back into my palm.

"Guess one of them rounds grazed me."

"Holy shit." I yanked Penny's scarf from my neck and tied it around the wound. Good thing she didn't want her stuff back. "Why are you only telling me this now?"

"No reason to worry you."

Dex winced and hissed, but somehow, I got him up, through the back door, and onto the couch, grabbing a knife from the block on the counter as we went. If someone was waiting, I'd get a piece of them. I untied the makeshift bandage and gently inspected the wound.

"Just cut it off."

"Your leg? I really don't think it's that bad. Just a graze, like you said."

He snorted. "My pants."

"You sure? This is an awfully nice suit. Looks expensive."

He tried to shrug out of his wet jacket. "It was."

I helped him peel off the suit coat. Beneath, he wore a leather shoulder holster and pistol. That gave me pause, but not for long. He was usually armed. I unbuckled it and set it on the table. He jerked his tie all the way loose and threw it aside, the male equivalent of a woman getting out of her bra at the end of the day.

"Take this." His hand shook as he shoved the holster at me. "Make sure no one's here."

I hesitated, but did as told. The tremor in his hand scared me more than the specter of any potential attacker. I could handle carrying the gun for the short time it would take me to clear the rest of the house. I'd spent time over the winter getting more comfortable with weapons. I used to hate them, but I'd learned to respect and tolerate them as the tools they were.

Removing the pistol, I held it straight down at my side and went to the hallway. It wasn't a big house, and we'd already been through the kitchen and living room. That left the office, bathroom, and the two bedrooms in the back, an area I hadn't ventured to for many years.

On the way, I noticed the office door ajar. Had I locked it? I couldn't remember. I'd been in a hurry when I left. With one finger, I pushed the door open and brought the gun up in front of me just as I'd been taught. I stood and listened for a moment, then switched on the overhead light with my shoulder.

The room was trashed. Desk drawers hung open and books and papers were strewn across the floor. I muttered several swear words. It wasn't a large room and lacked a closet so there was nowhere to hide. I backed out and pulled the door shut. One crisis at a time.

I checked the bathroom across the hall. The shower curtain was already pushed to one side where I'd left it. Empty. Ed's bedroom was next. Like the office, it had been searched. At that point, I was sure there was no one in the house. Maybe the basement, but the entrance to that was outside. I'd wait until Dex could stand before I even mentioned it. Just the same, I checked the closet and under the bed, carefully stepping over the piles of clothes and personal items.

That left the guest bedroom, the one Miko had been using. I hesitated before switching on the light. It was still tidy, the bed made, the dresser drawers in place. The closet stood open and empty. I let out my breath and returned to the bathroom for supplies.

Dex demanded a scotch before I started cleaning him up. "Bourbon will do. Even a blended whiskey."

"What do you think this is, The Ritz?" I rose to search the liquor cabinet, knowing Ed hadn't been much of a drinker, but thinking I needed fortification for myself as well. Where's a can of chocolate whipped cream when you need it?

What I found was a half-empty fifth of cheap gin. I grabbed it and a glass.

"Just give me the bottle," Dex growled.

I propped a few pillows behind him so he could drink without dousing himself. He guzzled it down.

The gash went straight across Dex's thigh, dark and angry against his pale skin. It had carved a half-inch deep groove, shallower at the front and back. The couch cushion beneath his leg was toast. I dabbed at the still bleeding wound with a clean cloth.

"You need stitches."

He took another swig of gin but his gaze was steady when he looked at me without smiling. "Just use butterfly bandages and wrap it up good and tight."

Such a man.

I did as he asked. He watched me the whole time. "You're good with your hands," he said when I finished.

"Years of bandaging horses." I stood. "Speaking of, I need to change and get Beau and Sasha in."

"They can stay out for one night."

He was right. But Ed always liked to bring them in. Until it got hot and buggy. Then, he kept them in during the day and put them in the pasture at night.

"I still need to check on them and feed them. And Millie."

He grabbed my hand before I could get away. "I'll go with you."

"You shouldn't move for a while."

He swung his legs down and sat up. "I'll be fine." He shook his head and rubbed his eyes. "You do need to change."

"What? Why?"

"That dress. The view. It's making me dizzy."

"Oh, for cripe's sake."

His laughter kept me company as I returned to the bathroom and changed into the clothes I'd been wearing earlier. When I got back to the living room, he was trying to stand. I put my hands on his shoulders and pushed him down to the couch.

"I'll take the gun," I said.

He bent to pull a second handgun from an ankle holster and laid it on the couch next to him.

"Get a flashlight." He nodded. "Leave the front door open."

I tucked the gun into the back waistband of my borrowed breeches, found a flashlight in a drawer in the kitchen, and stepped out onto the front stoop.

The air was moist and warm. I stood still for a moment, absorbing the quiet, imagining I could smell salt water from the Sound not far north of us, a scent that should have been like a healing balm to my soul. But the thought that someone could still be on the property had me on edge. What if someone were hiding in the barn?

I snapped on the flashlight, but the beam refracted through the moist air, illuminating not much of anything but gray fog. The pale glow from the dusk-to-dawn light also did little to penetrate the dense cloud that had settled. I could barely see the horses but knew they stood eagerly at the gate. Beau whinnied. Despite the rich spring grass, they wanted their grain.

I kept the light on them and walked closer. They were keen to be let in, but not upset or worried as they would be if there were strangers about. I knew if I opened the gate, they'd go straight to their stalls. I turned off the flashlight, undid the latch, and let them through, trotting in between their bodies, using them as a barrier between me and whatever—whomever— might be waiting in ambush.

I ducked into Sasha's stall with her, my hand on her shoulder. Her skin twitched beneath my hand, but she was warm and solid. I listened, but it was quiet.

Something brushed my leg, and I jumped, banging up against Sasha. My thumb found the switch and the flashlight revealed Millie winding around my ankles.

"Geez. Way to give me a heart attack, cat."

I went out of the stall and switched on the barn lights. To the left were the two rows of stalls facing a center aisle. To the right, a short hallway where the tack room, feed room, and storage areas were. Straight ahead, the wash stall. The stall cleaning equipment hung on the wall inside the door, and this is where my attention went, thinking any of the implements could be a weapon, and I wanted to make sure they were all accounted for.

The pitchforks, brooms, and shovels, which I always left hanging straight and clean, were crooked, out of alignment, askew, and the pitchfork had hay and manure clogging the tines.

Knowing Ed had been murdered should have scared me. Knowing someone had broken into the house—twice—and was looking for something should have made me anxious. Getting shot at had unnerved me for a short time. But those things hadn't worried me, not really. Because I was sure they had nothing to do with me.

Seeing those tools like that, though, like they'd been too many times in recent months at Winterlight? Cold prickles prowled up my neck and over my scalp. I stopped breathing. I started sweating.

This was personal.

And I was terrified.

CHAPTER NINETEEN

I TOLD DEX EVERYTHING.

I threw a scoop of grain at each horse, grabbed Millie, and ran back to the house, slamming the door so hard it rattled the windows. Dex jerked awake and pointed his gun in my direction, then quickly lowered it when he saw it was me. He blinked and his eyes cleared.

"What?"

Millie jumped down and strolled into the kitchen. I followed, opening the fridge and cabinets and drawers, looking for something, anything to quiet my shaking hands.

I tried the bathroom. There, I came face-to-face with myself in the mirror. Mascara smudged my lower lids, my hair looked like it had been styled by Medusa, and I could have been living underground for the past year given the pallor of my skin.

The cabinet held multiple bottles of prescription drugs, all labeled for Ed. I had no idea what any of them were, so I slammed that door and returned to the living room, feeling calmer for having tried.

Dex had waited patiently but now turned his laser focus on me. I had no choice but to spill. Out came the latest dreams and visions, the months of crooked tools being brushed off as the wind, an animal, coincidence. I included the break-ins and the odd visit by Glen Deutsch. I even told him about the black car with New York plates that nearly ran me off the road a few days earlier in Missouri.

"You had a dream about me?" he asked when I finished.

"Really? That's your takeaway?"

He gave me a tired smile. "No, but I'm surprised your takeaway is still that this has nothing to do with you."

I sank deeper into the old sofa. Dex's body took up most of it, but there was enough room for me at his feet, so long as I didn't want to lie down. Millie hopped up to my lap. I petted her more forcefully than needed, but she tolerated it and began to purr.

"You haven't left anything out this time?"

"How would I know?"

He seemed to think about this for a few moments, then said. "We need to sleep. I'm fine here."

"Sleep? I can't sleep."

"You have to."

"Oh, you mean…"

"Perchance to dream?"

"Don't quote Shakespeare to me, thou weedy weather-bitten moldwarp."

"Ouch. I think. Just call in Wastrel or whatever it is you do to get a clue."

"I don't *do* anything."

"You sleep." He glanced toward the hallway. "Is there a bedroom you can use? I'm not moving."

"I'll stay here if it's all the same to you." I stroked Millie's back, hooked the hassock with my foot, and pulled it over so I could put my legs on it.

"Oh, so *now* you want to sleep with me."

I didn't look at him because the temptation to stretch out next to his length and put my head on his shoulder was strong. "I think you drank too much pain killer."

"I drank all of it, and it wasn't enough." He'd shut his eyes, but he snapped his lids up again, very alert. "There a reason you don't want to use one of the bedrooms? One you'd like to share?"

I pulled a soft quilt over myself and Millie, let my head rest back, and closed my eyes.

He prodded me with his toe. "A reason that might have a bearing on this case?" When I didn't answer, he poked me again. "The more I know, the better I can help."

I nodded.

"Can you spare some of that blanket?" he asked.

The quilt was huge, so there was plenty of it. It smelled faintly of Ed's cigar smoke. I arranged it over Dex's feet and legs. He pulled it up to his chest. I should have offered him some covers before now.

"Are you going to be okay?" I asked him.

"Nothing a little rest won't fix. Now, tell me why you won't use the bedroom so we can get some sleep."

"You're a damned nuisance when you want to be, you know that?"

"So I've heard."

I'd told him so myself once or twice in the past. With a resigned sigh, I said, "It was a long time ago." The only person who knew what happened that day was Ed. And he hadn't been a talker.

"How old were you?"

Why did I have the feeling he knew where this was going? Dex was too sharp sometimes, and he possessed uncanny intuition. It made him good at his job, but annoying as a friend. He knew a lot about me, my history. The fact that he didn't already know about this incident meant Ed took our secret to his grave. Of course, there was the perpetrator, but I couldn't imagine why he would have blabbed about it.

Unless he blabbed an altogether different version of the story. A lie. One that put him in a good light and me in a bad one. I grew hot just thinking about it, my stomach tightened, and my breath shortened.

Softly, he asked again, "How old were you, Vi?"

"It was about a year after I first started here, so six or seven."

"Started what, taking lessons? Your uncle paid for that?"

"No. I mucked stalls—did whatever was needed that I could physically handle—in exchange for any chance to ride and the occasional lesson."

"Got it." He tucked his hands behind his head and stared at the ceiling, listening but giving me a break from the heat of his peat-colored eyes. "Go on."

"Ed had a thriving business. Lessons, boarders, people going to shows every weekend. Horses for sale. A lot of people came in and out."

"Of the house?"

"Yeah. Ed was very easy going. He gave a key to almost anyone."

"You should have mentioned that sooner."

"Right. Sorry." I picked at the edge of one of the quilt's squares. "I tried to get a locksmith yesterday, but no one could come until next week."

"So, lots of people could still have access to this house." He blew out a frustrated breath. "It's easy to install new locksets. I'll go to the hardware store first thing and take care of it." When I didn't speak for a few moments, he said, "Go on."

"Yeah, so long story short, there was some guy here to look at a horse, and I was in the kitchen having lunch and listening to the radio. He—the guy—came in looking for Ed and went down the hall like he was going to the office."

"Was Ed in his office?"

"No. He was outside."

"Was anyone else in the house?"

I shook my head. "A minute or two goes by and I hear him calling from the back asking me to help him with something. He was very polite and called me *young lady*. I remember I liked that."

Dex pushed up onto his elbows and gave me his full attention. I flicked my eyes to him and away, keeping them soft-focused on the middle distance, not really wanting to recall that day. I hadn't thought about it in a long time, but I remembered every detail like it was yesterday.

"So, you went."

"I went. He was in the spare bedroom with his back to the door. He told me to close and lock it because this was private. I couldn't see what he needed help with, and I thought maybe it was some sort of surprise for Ed."

Dex whispered, "Oh, Vi."

"He asked me if I wanted to ride more, to ride really nice horses. He said he'd been watching me and had some special horses I could ride. I said yes, of course. I'd like that. He spoke very quietly. I had to go closer to him. And then he said, 'I like dirty barn girls.'"

I stole a glance at Dex. Healthy color had returned to his cheeks, but now he was getting very red. Angry. I rushed through the rest. "He turned around, and his pants were unzipped, and he grabbed me and forced me to my knees in front of him."

Dex's voice was tight with emotion when he said, "You don't have to tell me the rest."

"Actually, it's not what you think. Ed busted through the door before anything could happen and threw the guy out. Told him to never come back. To take his filthy money elsewhere. Ed said if he ever found out the guy had tried this again, he'd kill him."

By the look on Dex's face, he would be happy to kill the guy himself. "Do you know his name? Would you recognize him if you saw him again?"

"No. But as he went down the hallway, he said something like, you're ruined. You'll be sorry. And a bunch of threats that Ed ignored or didn't hear, because Ed was too busy berating me for being so stupid."

"Ed cared about you, and you scared him. I know the feeling. You were only six. Not stupid."

"That's nice of you to say." I felt a little light-headed. As if finally telling someone had sucked the oxygen out of the room right along with that guy's ghost.

"Is it possible Ed made good on that threat?"

"Doubtful." Millie came out from under the quilt and resettled herself on my legs, stretching then curling up and wrapping her tail over her nose.

"Was he in the habit of making idle threats?"

I shrugged. "No idea, really. That's the only time I heard him say something like that."

Dex nodded, and I could just about hear the gears clicking in his head as he began to work on this. "What about the tools? Who knows you are totally OCD about them?"

"Anyone I've ever worked with."

"I'm trying to narrow this down."

"I know. But I really have no idea."

"Sleep," he said. "Make that horse talk to you."

"I don't have any control over his comings and goings or what he shows me when. And I don't know what his clues mean, anyway."

"Just try. We'll figure it out together."

Togetherness. The thing I resisted most strongly. I didn't want to involve anyone else, though, didn't want anyone to get hurt. Ideally, I'd resolve whatever this situation was on my own. Dex's eyes were closed, and his chest rose and fell evenly. Already asleep. Already involved. Too late to go the lone wolf route on this one.

I considered texting Harry to let him know I wasn't coming to the show. But my phone was on the other side of the room or maybe in the bathroom where I'd changed clothes. Millie's comforting weight on my lap made me loathe to rise and get it.

I couldn't cancel this late on Joshua anyway. He'd already lost one rider, and Vagrant deserved the chance to shine. Which he would. Not ego. Fact.

I tried not to think about what Dex had said. That this was all about me. And the implication that what I'd thought a random event from long ago could have anything to do with what was happening now.

But the thing with the tools. I hadn't been totally honest. Sure, anyone I'd ever worked with knew I liked them a certain way. Over time, making them crooked had become more of a joke than anything else, a way to annoy me. But there were a couple of people who knew how much it really bugged me. Ed was one. I doubted he would haunt me like that. Harry was another. What possible motivation could he have for gaslighting me?

These thoughts, I knew, were not the best to fall asleep on, but I couldn't stop my mind from circling the wagons, so to speak, and eventually, I drifted off.

It's the horse show. We're in the ring, cantering a circle. I'm anxious, looking at the spectators, looking for the man who wore Dex's face. We circle again, which technically means we're off course and should be eliminated from the class. Wastrel feels worse than usual, so wrong I think I'm riding a different horse, but I'm too busy looking at the crowd to check. I keep catching a glimpse of a man I think I recognize, but he is always turned away too much for me to be sure.

Then, we're out, and I'm walking beside Wastrel. We are weaving through a maze of horse trailers, trucks, and horses being groomed and tacked up for the ring. There is yelling a few trailers down, a fight. A familiar voice screaming *No, please*, and *I need more time*. It's Harry. I try to go toward him, but there are too many trailers to get around and horses walking in front of us.

The scene shifts again, and we're in what feels and smells like a funeral parlor. Norman's visitation. Wastrel didn't attend it originally, but here we are. People I know are lined up to the side of the casket. Malcolm, Sandy, Renee, my parents, Hank and Clara. They appear solemn, but not sad, until they see me. Then, they begin to weep.

I approach. It isn't Norman reposing in the box. It's Harry.

He sits up, his face distorts into a hideous clown-like smile, and he begins to laugh. As he does, one by one, his teeth fall out. He tries to catch them, but they bounce off his upturned palms, turn into mice, and run away. I try to follow but can't move. My legs are rooted, as good teeth should be.

The room fills with smoke. I am on Wastrel's back. The tack is gone as is my show attire. We gallop out of the room, the building. Once outside, Wastrel turns into a black bird, and we fly away from death and teeth and mice. We soar above the dark smoke, circle once, and then the bird folds his wings, and we dive straight for the blackness.

CHAPTER TWENTY

I woke Dex at six thirty. The hardware store opened at eight, but the show started at the same time. I needed to get there earlier to walk the course and school Vagrant. We were only about twenty minutes away. Dex could take me down there, go buy the new locks, install them, and be back in time for my jumper classes.

If he could get around at all. I was half inclined to secure him to a water pipe with his own handcuffs. But he'd probably hurt himself worse trying to get free.

I considered driving off in the Mustang without waking him. But Dex was resourceful. He'd take a cab to every stable he could find just so he could tell me how pissed off he was at getting left behind.

And the truth was, even though his behavior the night before had been out of character, I wanted to keep him near. To keep an eye on him and for him to watch over me. The crooked tools had me totally freaked out.

We reached a compromise. I drove us to the show, and he stayed with me. But only after I called Penny's husband, Frank, and made him promise to go to Ed's and change the locks. He wasn't happy about getting rousted from bed so early on a Sunday morning, let alone leaving his house. No surprise there. I hated that Penny would have to listen to him complain. Even so, I begged, Frank grumbled, Penny insisted, and he grudgingly agreed.

Penny tried pumping me for information about dinner the night before, but I didn't have time and wasn't about to discuss it with Dex listening. Even if I were able to talk, I would never tell her we'd been shot at. *I'd* been shot at.

I threw an aluminum lawn chair in the back seat along with the saddle, helmet, and a few other things. Dex laughed when I produced an old cane of Ed's from when he'd had an operation on his foot.

"Do I look like an invalid?"

"If I thought that, I would have brought the wheelchair."

He insisted he was far from needing assistance, yet he limped more than usual and used it as an excuse to drape his arm around my shoulders.

The sun had been up for an hour and the fog had begun to burn off when we lumbered up to Joshua's rig at the far end of the field, me laden down like a pack mule. I unfolded the chair and pointed at it. Dex sat.

Harry stood near the pickup truck with his hand on his hip. The stance reminded me of something but I couldn't think what.

"Good morning," he said with a grin.

I felt his curiosity about Dex as if it were my own yet forced myself to return the smile. All I could think about was his teeth falling out and that maniacal laugh. Not a sound I'd ever heard him emit. And I'd seen Harry in all sorts of giddy states. It echoed through my brain and sent a shiver down my spine.

Joshua poked his head around the end of the trailer where he combed Vagrant's tail. "Hey Vi, good to see you."

I walked to them and scratched Vagrant's neck as much to soothe myself as anything else. "Could you have parked any farther from the rings?"

Joshua patted Vagrant's butt. "He does better farther away from the other horses."

"Stallions," Dex drawled. "Unpredictable."

Harry's need to know got the better of him. "And you are?"

"Oh, sorry." I made the introductions. "Dex is a friend from Missouri."

"All the way from Missouri?" Joshua asked. "That's a heck of a trip to watch a horse show."

"Combining business and pleasure," Dex said with a wink.

I rolled my eyes. Harry narrowed his, and if he had laser vision, Dex would have had a big hole burned in his chest.

"I'm going to walk the course and find some coffee. Not necessarily in that order. Takers?"

Dex said, "I'll have one with a little—"

"I know how you like it," I told him and immediately regretted my choice of words.

Harry's eyebrows shot up.

Dex chuckled. "That you do, darlin'."

"And I know how *you* like it," Harry said, "and I've known for far longer. But I'll come along and get my own."

I ignored them. "Joshua?" I asked. "Anything from the concession?"

He held up a large travel mug by way of an answer, and Harry and I set off for the show rings. I felt nervous and stiff about being alone with him, similar to the sense of remoteness I'd had on Friday of not knowing him at all. I hated being suspicious of everyone around me.

My phone buzzed against my back. I forgot I'd shoved it in my waistband when I went to see Vagrant. I wouldn't normally carry it around but still hoped for a message from Malcolm.

Hope thunked hard into my belly when I saw the message was from Renee.

Hey New York, how's New York? <Laughing face> You better keep your promise to teach me your horse whisperer stuff. <horse head><running horse> It's in the cards… <Winky face><praying hands><heart>

I wouldn't have expected her to punctuate with so many emojis. I didn't even know there *were* so many.

Tomorrow. I texted back. *Be ready.*

<Thumbs up>

I'd just slid my phone back in place when it vibrated again.

My mother. The first message since Friday's short rant. Evidently, it took her two days to calm down.

You know tomorrow is your birthday, right? Are you at least going to be home for that?

Seeing as how my trust fund stipulated I keep a job for one full year by the time I was thirty, I could hardly forget.

Geez. I was going to be thirty years old.

I planned dinner. At Winterlight.

I hoped that wasn't mom-speak for party. I did *not* want a party. But I did want to get back. If only to give Malcolm a piece of my mind. He might have a rule about not being interrupted when he was at a client site, but he always texted me to say good night. Three days of radio silence was the longest we'd gone without speaking, even if it was only a conversation about the horses. At this point, I had to conclude that whatever feelings he'd had for me had changed. Did he want me to stay or go? I felt our connection fraying. Dinner at the farm would be awkward. I was quick to tell myself a clean break was just as well. Gave me freedom to start fresh.

If it was just as well, why did I feel like I had a boulder in my belly and a pair of hoof nippers clenching my heart?

Tomorrow, I texted back. *Let's eat out instead.*

Harry craned his neck to see my screen. I shut the phone off and returned it to my waistband.

"Tell me you're not leaving before your birthday," he said. "It's a big one. I was planning on us celebrating it together."

Why did everyone but me have plans for me? "I don't want to make a big deal about it. Maybe we can have breakfast before I leave."

"Breakfast in bed?"

"Harry, what the heck?"

"Don't play dumb." He took my arm and pulled me to a stop. "You know I've always loved you."

I tried to shrug away from him but he held on. "Not like that."

"Exactly like that." His fingers dug into my upper arm. "And you love me. Don't deny it."

God help me. Where was this coming from? I extracted my arm from his grasp. His eyes glittered with tears, but they didn't move me. My dreams had me thinking he could be involved in what had been happening, and this sudden declaration of love was just the latest move in his plan. Although I couldn't understand what his play was any more than I could believe he'd set fire to Ed's.

"Let's talk about this later. We have horses to ride."

He let me walk away but his long legs brought him quickly alongside. "You're right," he said with a smile. He always had been changeable as a chameleon. "But I'm holding you to that. Dinner tonight."

I let out an annoyed breath. Dinner with Harry was not on my agenda. Then again, maybe it would help me get to the bottom of Ed's death. Especially if I included Dex. That would make Harry very cross, but that wasn't my concern right then. "Okay."

Harry snaked his arm around my waist. "Great. Just like old times. You know, you and me, petal, we could make that place of yours a going concern again."

Is that what this was about? "Yep," I said, using the need to walk around a pile of manure as an excuse to move away from him.

"This is so great. You being here. Us together again at a show. It's perfect."

"Perfect."

But it wasn't perfect, and as we got closer to the main part of the show grounds, memories rushed ahead, pulling me along like a dark undertow. Me riding Wastrel, the approach to that last jump, the crack of splintering wood beneath us, his bellows of pain. I shook myself. I could do this. I could ride Vagrant in that same ring.

The fog might be gone, but the grass was wet and the damp air smelled green. My feet were soon soaked. Had I been home, I'd be in muck boots. There it was. *Home.* I didn't have to think about it. It wasn't here anymore.

"You didn't tell me you had company," Harry said as we got in line for coffee. "Is that Dex guy why you couldn't have dinner with me last night?"

I kept my gaze on the concession menu. "Jealous much?"

"I'm not proud. Absolutely."

"We're. Friends. That's. All. Just like you and me."

He forced a laugh, but there was a strange set to his jaw that made me think he found me the exact opposite of amusing. "Of course we're friends. For a *very* long time."

Again the emphasis on how long we'd known each other. What was he up to?

The other line moved forward, and Harry stepped over to it, getting a little ahead of me. As I looked at his back, it hit me—the reason his stance had looked familiar when we first arrived. The man in the bleachers from my dream. The one wearing Dex's face. The body had been all Harry.

Half a tense hour later, I'd walked and memorized the course and begun to warm up Vagrant in the open field between where Joshua had parked and the rest of the trucks and trailers. When we went to the schooling area to pop over a few practice jumps, Harry rode beside me on one of the hunters while Joshua led the other.

I forced air through my nose to calm myself. I didn't want Vagrant picking up on my scattered thoughts and fears.

Dex walked next to Joshua carrying the chair. Joshua was an orthopedic surgeon, and they were in a deep discussion about Dex's old riding injury and prosthetic leg. Or so it appeared. I could feel Dex watching me out of the corner of his eye the whole time, and for once, I didn't mind.

Harry was quiet. He fussed with his stock tie and concentrated on keeping his gelding's nose away from Vagrant's. Dex had been right. Stallions can be unpredictable, and I appreciated Harry's effort to not let his mount mess with mine.

As soon as we entered the schooling ring, another horse cantered by, the rider intently listening to his trainer who was yelling from the sidelines. The horse bumped us. Vagrant squealed. The guy didn't even notice let alone apologize. I trotted the stallion forward, giving him something else to think about and circled to a cross rail, calling it as I did. Despite the polite heads-up, another horse cut in front of us, the rider clearly struggling with control.

"Sorry!" she yelled without looking our way.

Vagrant got distracted and rushed the fence. I sank deeper into my heels and breathed through my arms, down the reins to his mouth, and from there to his mind, reminding him of what we'd worked on the day before, of what we were going to do today. He could ignore the other horses running every which way, the yelling people. He twitched one ear to me and settled, waiting for me to let him know when it was time for the next jump. After a couple of good results, we left. I didn't want to over school him. He was the type to bore quickly and get lazy. The sooner we got our first round behind us, the better.

Joshua and Dex followed. Dex seemed okay, but I worried about that wound opening up. At least he kept the chair handy and used it.

On course in the jumper ring, a pretty chestnut mare turned toward the triple combination on the far side of the arena—three jumps one right after the other. It took two strides to get from the first jump to the second, and then it was one stride to the third element. The rider guided the mare with confidence, but the mare added a stride and got too close to the second element. She lost her momentum as she landed and appeared frozen with the rider looking down as if she couldn't understand what had happened. I tried to send them good vibes. She was either going to have to add a stride again—which would make clearing the spread almost impossible—or jump very long from a near standstill. I hadn't watched them enough to know if the rider had the experience to get this horse safely to the other side or if the horse had the scope to handle it.

All this flashed through my mind in an instant. I held my breath. Then the rider lifted her head and looked beyond the third jump. Her entire body said, *up*, and yet she didn't jerk the reins or kick. The mare gathered herself onto her haunches and made a gigantic effort. Her front legs reached forward.

It wasn't pretty, but they made it. They had a rail down on the final jump of the course, but if I were the rider, I wouldn't care. That mare had a lot of potential, especially with such a tactful person aboard.

To my shock, when they trotted to the gate, I saw the person aboard was Rebecca Brannon, otherwise known to me as Becca Scissorhands.

She pulled her horse up short when she saw me. Her light gray eyes went wide. "Vi Parker? What are you doing here?"

I pressed one leg to Vagrant's side to make room for Becca's horse, keeping a close watch on the stallion's ears. If the mare were in season, things could get interesting. His nostrils flared. The mare swished her tail. Vagrant arched his neck. I made him walk forward along the fence to give him something else to think about.

"Sure," Becca called, "ignore me."

I circled back. "I'm not. But this is a stallion, and—"

"I understand."

That brought me up short. Becca and I went way back. Not in a good way. In the past, she would have sneered and made an obnoxious remark about my inability to handle a hot horse. She also would have found a way to loudly call me *Vi the Valkyrie*, the nickname she'd coined after Wastrel died. According to mythology, the Valkyries chose who lived and died in battle.

We'd never liked each other. Me because she was a horrible rider with harsh hands that tortured a horse's mouth and weak legs she supplemented with a too-eager whip. Her because I was a better rider who got to compete the best horses.

Becca wasn't carrying a whip today. But that didn't surprise me as much as how she'd ridden the course. And I always give credit where credit is due.

"That was quick thinking back there. Well done. You have a nice horse."

"Thank you." Her shoulders lowered as if she'd been holding her breath. "She's not mine yet. Still testing her out."

We sat side by side on our mounts and watched a competitor take a couple of jumps. The mare curled her lip when Vagrant tried to sniff her. I tweaked the rein to bring his attention to me. Becca stroked her mare's shoulder but otherwise didn't fuss. The Becca I knew would have jerked the reins and smacked the horse hard. I eyed her profile out of the corner of my eye. She had a ski slope nose, pale lips, and a pointy chin. Her short blonde hair was dark with sweat where it showed around the edges of her helmet. She sat quietly, her petite frame relaxed.

In a moment, the conversational pause would become uncomfortable, and I thought about making an excuse to keep the stallion moving.

"I'm trying to be more like you," Becca blurted.

I turned and blinked at her. She might have been speaking Chinese for all I understood of what had just come out of her mouth.

"To ride more like you," she amended into the silence. "After what happened with that mare."

She meant Cali. My horse. Cali had put Becca in the hospital right before Harry bought the mare for me. It had been Becca's fault. And it sounded like she was admitting it.

Four-five-nine on deck, yelled the gate keeper, *eight-two-one follows*. Dex caught my eye from where he sat along the rail.

"I'm eight twenty one," I said.

Becca nodded, clearly relieved at having made her astonishing statement. "You up at that old guy's place where the fire was?"

Bad news always travels fast. "Ed Todd's place, yes." I saw no reason to elaborate.

"Too bad about him and the fire, but I was glad to hear no horses were hurt."

"Yes." I tuned out Becca and watched the horse and rider in the ring. The rider turned too sharply into one of the jumps and the horse ran out. If it happened three times, they'd be eliminated.

"He was funny," Becca said, "always talking into that old tape recorder."

I snapped my head to her. "What did you say?"

"Ed Todd. He was always making notes or something. I don't know why he didn't just get a smart phone."

Four-five-nine on course, eight-two-one on deck.

"Right," I said, remembering Ed had been obsessive about writing his daily diary. When his vision got bad, he started using the voice recorder. What had happened to it? And the notebooks? Maybe Susan knew.

Eight-two-one to the gate.

"I have to go," I said.

"I'll catch up with you later. Watch the footing in the far corner. It's a little soft."

Becca turned the mare away, sunlight glinting off her gold stirrups. I'd seen and drooled over them in catalogs. It didn't surprise me Becca had a pair. She'd always gone for flash over substance. But her comments made me wonder if there might be some grit under her veneer after all. She'd sounded sincere.

I shook my head and focused on riding. Joshua looked anxious where he still held one of the hunters and stood near Dex. I gave him a thumbs up. Harry must have the other gelding in a class. I tried to see over to the hunter ring but had to take Vagrant into ours.

As I rode the stallion forward, someone yelled, "Go get 'em, Vi."

Dex glanced toward the sound at the same time I did. A man waved. It was Glen Deutsch. Susan had said he'd been at the farm Friday morning. What had he wanted? Was he one of the many people who had a key to Ed's house? Had he been inside searching? For what?

I shook my head again in an attempt to empty it. I couldn't allow myself to be sidetracked by untimely thoughts. The last time I'd been here, I was carried out on a stretcher. That wasn't going to happen again.

I urged Vagrant into trot as we passed the bleachers. The ones where the shirtless Harry-Dex man had been in the dream. On the top fence rail sat a black bird just like the one that flew out of his back. It watched me ride by, its gaze direct and unsettling. Then it took off and flew next to us until we reached the corner.

Vagrant bucked when I asked for canter, excited and anticipating the jumps, and again, I brought my focus to him. For a few strides he felt off, out of balance, just like Wastrel in the dreams. I quickly slipped into that meditative space I always go to in competition. The people and other horses, the bird and the past all slipped away. There was nothing but Vagrant and me and the jumps.

We straightened out of the turn and approached the first element, a vertical of red-and-white striped rails with flowers at the base. Vagrant's head lifted when he saw it. I shifted my weight back to keep him steady. As I did, a shudder went through me and sweat dripped in my eyes. I blinked to clear them. Three strides out and the jump had become a blue-paneled oxer. What the hell? Vagrant's gait transformed to collected, smooth, and cadenced.

Wastrel.

Wonder, fear, and joy speared through me all at once. I had no time to pull up safely so held on and hoped.

He cleared jump one easily. Wastrel had always taken care of me.

Until he hadn't.

Upon landing, he stuck out his nose and tugged on the reins. Vagrant again. My vision hadn't fully cleared, and a bank of fog enveloped the ring. I could see nothing beyond the next element which wavered between the yellow wall it was supposed to be and the green rails and brush from my last ride on Wastrel. I heard only my mount's and my breathing. I'd entered the ring certain I could pilot Vagrant around the course well. Now I didn't know whether to keep riding or stop. Was this even real?

Wastrel seized Vagrant's body and mind again and carried me forward, effortlessly jumping each element, just as he had that day.

Until he hadn't.

I would not let fear get hold of me. I exhaled tautness out of my shoulders and loosened my grip on the reins as we turned right for the triple combination where Becca had run into trouble. I tried to connect with Vagrant's mind, but it was Wastrel who answered. Wastrel in all his glorious complexity and power let me know that this time, all would be well. I simply had to listen. Yet, as we cantered the corner, the one Becca had warned me about, time decelerated. In slow motion, his gait turned choppy and stiff, just the way it always felt in the dream. I forced myself to take my eyes off the coming jump, to look down, to try to understand.

He was on the wrong lead.

I blinked.

We were on the wrong lead.

That never happened with Wastrel. Is this what he'd been trying to make me see since last summer? But what did it mean?

Time sped up again. I shortened his stride with a couple of half halts, waited for the moment of suspension, swung my left calf back, and the next stride was on the right lead. We were over the first element of the combination and had two strides to the next. But as we landed, the next jump became the trunk in Ed's tack room. Again, time slowed, and I watched as it opened and old magazines flew out and winged away just like the blackbird.

We had to keep going. This was a vision, not real. I trusted Wastrel. I squeezed my eyes shut, grabbed mane, and jumped blind, right through the flying magazines.

We went clean and finished in good time. The fog blew away. Wastrel disappeared. Shouting and applause rang in my ears.

Joshua beamed as we left the ring at walk. I rubbed Vagrant's neck, the sharp tang of his sweat filling my nostrils.

"Good boy," I said, though I honestly wasn't sure how much had been him and how much Wastrel.

"I've never seen him so calm and relaxed," Joshua said. "That was amazing."

If only he knew.

"It was," I said, excited and stunned and relieved and more than a little light-headed. Something astonishing and significant had just happened, and I wasn't quite sure what it meant.

I didn't have a clue let alone a lead with regard to Ed's murder. What could I be on the wrong lead about?

We stayed near the ring until the class was over. I went through the ride again and again in my mind, wanting to remember, trying to figure it out.

After everyone finished, we ended up in second with a time just over the first-place ride. I could shave off a couple of seconds in the next class.

Becca got sixth. I had a feeling if she rode the mare a little more boldly, she wouldn't have to worry about extra strides or getting too close to the jumps. As we walked back to the trailer to take a short break before the next class, I looked for her and the mare but couldn't see them in the rows of trailers.

"I need to find Harry so he can change horses for the next class," Joshua said. "If you see him, tell him I'm looking for him." He clucked to the bay gelding and jogged in the direction of his rig.

I hopped down, ran up my stirrups, and loosened the girth. Dex came up beside me.

"What happened out there?"

"What did it look like?"

"Like that horse sprouted wings."

Maybe Wastrel wasn't a demon haunting me as I often thought, but an angel guarding me. "I'll explain later." Maybe Dex would be able to shed some light on Wastrel's clues.

"Okay," he said slowly. "Then who was that guy who yelled to you right before you went in?"

"Remember I told you someone I knew from years ago had been at the farm Friday morning before I got there? That was Glen."

"He's not the guy who liked dirty barn girls, is he?"

"No. Too young."

"Let's find him and ask what he wants."

I didn't like the gleam in Dex's dark eyes. "If by ask, you mean interrogate," I said, "then let's not."

"You're no fun."

"I'm not here for fun," I said.

"Then what the hell's going on?"

Fatigue made me nearly stumble over an uneven spot on the ground, and Dex's hand came up to catch me. "It started as a favor to Harry."

"You have a feeling there's more to it?"

"I don't know. No one seems to be who they were." Including Dex, but I kept that thought to myself. After a moment, I added, "Or what I thought they were. Everyone and everything's different."

"Maybe it's not everyone and everything else that's changed, Miss Parker."

At least Dex was back to calling me by my last name. I heard the implication in what he suggested, but that was deeper than I had the time or energy for at the moment. Anyway, Penny had already told me the previous summer that I'd changed. And that was after only three months at Winterlight. I didn't believe it then. Now I knew she had been right. The place had crawled inside me, become part of me. Or I'd become part of it. While I accepted that I might be seeing the world differently, that didn't explain why everyone else had gone off their rocker.

I needed more time with Wastrel. I needed to sleep and dream, figure this out, and go home.

Joshua wasn't at the trailer. He must have found Harry, swapped horses, and returned to the competition area. Two blue ribbons fluttered in the truck window. Harry had done well, but now I understood what he meant about the hunters being an afterthought for Joshua. None of us had seen his rounds.

I started to hand the reins to Dex but noticed blood seeping through his pants leg. I took the chair from him, opened it, and made him sit. "You're bleeding again."

"Am I?" He looked at his thigh with disinterest. "Just a little."

"Only a flesh wound?"

"Exactly."

Shaking my head, I put a halter on Vagrant, tied him to the trailer, and went to the dressing room to search for a clean towel. I also wanted to congratulate Harry. To act as I normally would.

"Harry?" I called. He must be nearby. Both geldings were on the other side of the trailer munching hay, still sweaty where the saddle had been.

"Sorry I missed your rides." Nothing.

"Congrats!" He didn't answer.

I found a neat stack of folded towels in a drawer and took a couple to Dex. He pressed one to his leg. Vagrant stood quietly, his nose nearly resting on Dex's shoulder. Being possessed by another horse had him all tuckered out.

I checked the cab of the truck to see if Harry might be grabbing a quick nap in the back seat. Not there. I walked to the other side of the rig where I nearly stepped on his phone. Unlike me, Harry was never without his mobile device. When I picked it up, my thumb brushed the home key bringing the screen to life. On it was a text notification from his mother.

Time's up!

I couldn't imagine what it meant, and last I'd heard, Babette only used landlines. In any case, it was unusually short and direct for Babette. I stuck the phone in my waistband.

The trailer's ramp was up and I had to stand on the fender to look in. At first I thought someone had thrown one of the horse's fly sheets in there. My eyes took a moment to adjust to the darkness within.

It was Harry, sprawled out, his head pillowed on a pile of manure. He wasn't napping.

CHAPTER TWENTY-ONE

"OH NO." I undid the latches, dropped the ramp, and ran to him.

He was alive but unconscious and bleeding. A swollen cut over his eyebrow. Another oozing gash over his ear. His nose had a gouge out of the bridge and wasn't as straight as the last time I'd seen it.

"Vi?" called Dex from outside. "What's wrong?"

Next to Harry sat a stirrup iron with the leather still attached. A gold stirrup like Becca's. It had blood on it. Harry's blood.

Dex limped to the ramp still holding the towel to his leg. I pointed at the stirrup.

"Don't touch it," he said. "That's evidence."

He started to make a call. Harry groaned and put his hands in front of his face.

"No...need more time...please..."

I froze. That was exactly like my dream. Dex lowered his phone and stared at us.

"Harry?" I pulled his hands away and tapped his cheek then stopped because he probably already had the mother of all headaches.

"Vi?" His eyelids fluttered. "Vi? Is that...you?" he whispered theatrically.

I swear to God, if this was an act, I'd beat him with a stirrup iron myself.

"You stay here," I told Dex. "I'll get help."

"No!" Harry screeched. He pushed himself up with a grunt, eyes wide in a pallid face. "Don't call anyone."

"What the hell is going on?" I asked. "Did Joshua do this?"

"Of course not. I'll explain, but…" His eyes pleaded with me. He lowered his voice. "You have to hide me."

I exchanged a look with Dex. His expression gave nothing away as he shrugged. "I'll get the car."

Sympathy warred with skepticism inside me. Fear tried to rise to the surface, but exasperation with Harry's drama beat it down. While I was sorry he'd been beaten up, clearly he wasn't as damaged as I'd first thought. And I couldn't help thinking he'd brought this on himself. Now he wanted me to hide him? I handed him his phone and watched his face when he saw the message from his mother. His Adam's apple bobbed up and down and what little color remained in his face drained away.

"You tell Joshua why we're leaving," I said.

Running out on the guy was wrong, and I didn't understand what was happening, but I felt that undertow pulling at me again, an unstoppable force I couldn't fight.

Harry tapped out a message and let me help him to his feet. Outside, I set him against the trailer. His gazed bounced every which way. He could be looking for someone or severely concussed. I ran for a bottle of water and more towels.

"We can't just leave the horses." I unbuckled the girth and removed the saddle from Vagrant after poring half a bottle of water over Harry's head and making him drink the rest.

"Joshua said he'd be right back." He held one arm close to his ribs and dabbed at his eyebrow with the towel. "Just get me out of here. Now."

"He's okay with us all leaving? What about your car?"

"I can't drive. I can't even see straight."

Dex pulled up in the Mustang and popped the trunk. I threw our stuff in there including the gold stirrup. When I shut the lid, I saw Joshua coming toward us.

"Let's go," Harry said. "I don't want him to see me like this."

Even a beating couldn't put a damper on Harry's vanity. I squeezed him into the back seat and made Dex move to the passenger side. He wasn't in any shape to drive either.

I shifted into first gear and lowered the window as we met Joshua. "I'm really sorry about this."

"No problem. It was amazing to see Vagrant go like that, even once. It shows how much potential he has." He gave me his card. "Please call if you change your mind about riding for me. I hope everything turns out okay."

He started to peer into the back seat. Harry sank lower. "Gotta go," I said as we drove away.

Each bump in the field made Harry moan, and it was slow going getting through the packed parking area.

"I told him one of your horses had colic," Harry said.

"How does that explain why you had to leave?"

"Moral support."

I closed my eyes for a moment and shook my head.

"You brought the stirrup?" Dex asked.

"Of course. What would Joshua have thought if he'd found it?" Out of the corner of my eye, I could see Dex fighting a smile. "Are you still bleeding?" I asked. The rental car place wasn't going to be happy with the condition of their car.

"Just a little."

Nerves had me tapping the steering wheel with the fingers of one hand while I searched for my phone with the other. Harry should just get on a plane and lay low somewhere for a while. His behavior might be suspicious, but he was still my friend until proven guilty. Otherwise, I would never run out on a client like this.

"Watch it," Dex yelled.

I gasped and slammed the brakes. I'd nearly run into Becca's mare. Harry slid into the back of my seat. Much swearing and whining followed. My niggling distrust about his motives had me feeling somewhat indifferent about his condition.

"Leaving so soon?" Becca called.

I lowered the window again noting the gold stirrups were missing from her saddle. Dark thoughts swirled inside me.

"Something came up," I said. "What happened to your gold stirrups?"

"Oh, you noticed them, did you?" She gave an exaggerated eye roll almost as if...was she making fun of herself? "Sadly, I have only one pair," she continued, "and I decided to switch saddles for the next round." She patted the mare's neck. "Still figuring out what works best for this girl."

Something inside me relaxed a hair. "Try riding her forward more boldly. You'll get better takeoff spots and have a faster time."

Becca smiled. I couldn't recall ever seeing her teeth before. They were straight and white.

"Thanks for the tip. Now that you've pulled out, I might have a chance." She waved and rode off.

I couldn't imagine why she might have beaten Harry with a stirrup—

other then general principles—but she didn't act like she'd just walloped anyone. I glanced at Dex. He looked deep in thought.

"Can't you go any faster?" Harry hissed.

"Not unless you want me to plow through a few horses," I said. "Do you need a doctor?"

"No. I'll be fine."

He didn't look fine, and by the way he held his arm, it was badly bruised or broken, or maybe protecting cracked ribs.

We were nearly to the main entrance when Glen Deutsch jogged into view, waving at us to stop. Harry ducked down as low as he could.

Gritting my teeth, I lowered the window.

"Hey Vi, remember me?" He thrust his hand through the window. "Glen Deutsch."

"Of course I remember. Thought you'd moved down south."

"I did, but now I'm back, and I'm…hang on." He checked his pockets, pulled out a card, handed it to me. "I'm in real estate now. I'd love to talk to you about Todd's. If you're thinking of selling, that is. I know horse people."

I took the card and tucked it next to Joshua's in the console. Selling the place to horse people would be ideal. "Thanks—"

"I know the house needs work, but someone will want it."

"Okay. Gotta run, but I'll be in touch."

How did he know the house needed work unless he'd been inside?

I waved. He waved. If one more person stopped us, I would plow somebody down, but a minute later we were finally on the road.

I glanced in the review mirror at Harry. "Did you see who did this to you?"

"No, no. I thought…for a minute. But no."

"Are you sure you don't need a doctor?"

He shook his head.

"Then you'd better start 'splaining, old friend. What happened?"

"Some guys wanted to send a message."

Anger and disbelief boiled up from the stew of emotions roiling in my gut. "Some random guys came to the show to beat you up?"

"No, of course not. I owe them money." He dabbed at his forehead. "Not them, but their boss."

This was starting to sound like a bad cops and robbers movie. "Let me guess. For drugs."

Silence. Damning silence.

"We can't all be perfect like you, petal," he said in a small voice.

I tried to get a read on this from Dex, but he'd donned his mirrored sunglasses.

"I'll take you to the airport," I told Harry. "You can get on a flight to wherever you want. You have your wallet?"

"Yes, but…what about…us?"

I clamped my jaw against shouting that there was no *us*, but didn't think that would help. "I need to find someone who can care for Beau and Sasha. I can't leave right now."

"What if we drive?"

"To where?"

"Missouri, of course."

I glanced into the back seat. His eye was almost swollen shut beneath the cut brow. His stock tie hung loose round his neck and had soaked up most of the blood. Some still trickled from his nose. He looked young and vulnerable.

"You want to come to Missouri?"

"I want to go wherever you're going, V."

This revelation shut me up. Whatever delusions he was operating under, the blows to his head had worsened them. But he had me thinking.

"I don't have a way to transport the horses to Missouri, and finding someone to do it could take days. Not exactly a speedy getaway, if that's what you need."

"I do. And, I do."

"You really do need a speedy getaway?"

"If I don't want to get my legs broken."

I didn't even want to know how much he owed.

"We can use my trailer," he said.

The thought made me uneasy, driving all the way out east—assuming his trailer was at Allie-Baba's place—then back to Ed Todd's, loading the horses and Millie, heading west. It would be the middle of the night by the time we got on the other side of Manhattan.

But that thought—getting off the Island and going home—eased some of the anxiety coiling inside me.

"What do you think?" I asked Dex.

His chin came up. He'd dozed off. "Sounds like a plan."

I got out my phone to call Susan, and it rang. Caller ID indicated Penny. I forced cheeriness into my voice.

"Hey Sis-co, I was just going to call you. How did Frank make out with the locks?"

Her voice shook when she said, "You haven't heard from him?"

"I…no."

"Then…I hoped…." She sobbed.

"What? What's wrong?"

"He's gone."

"What do you mean, he's gone?" My voice sounded strained, and I swallowed to loosen my throat, wishing I'd grabbed a couple more bottles of water.

"He took his tools, Vi. He left us."

CHAPTER TWENTY-TWO

IT WAS MY FAULT. If I hadn't showed up, if I hadn't asked—insisted—he go change the locks, Frank would still be home with Penny. If I hadn't come back to the Island, Dex wouldn't have been shot. For all I knew, I was to blame for Harry getting beaten up, too.

Guilt, thick and heavy, swept everything else out of my mind. I said the only thing I could think of. "Are you sure?"

More crying. The baby started whimpering. I pictured Penny sitting on the edge of her bed holding Isabella close, trying to soothe her infant while her world fell apart.

"I told you, he took his tools."

Frank was a plumber, and a good one, but it was no secret I'd only tolerated him for Penny's sake. He took his tools? All my scattered feelings of worry, fear, and confusion coalesced into hatred.

"Where do you think he went?" I'd personally hunt him down and make him pay. I had a lot of pent-up frustration that needed venting.

"I don't know. Probably his brother's."

Frank's brother was Frank times two. My trusty baseball bat was back in Missouri, but I was sure I could lay hands on another.

"Vi?"

"Yeah?"

"Don't do anything. Don't tell Mom. I'll call you back." She hung up.

Dex put his hand on my thigh. "Penny's dirtbag husband ran out on her?"

"How did you know he was a dirtbag?"

He peered at me over the top of his sunglasses. "If he left your charming cousin and his child, he's a dirtbag."

Plain and simple. Dex's black-and-white rules for how a man should treat a woman. I was beginning to appreciate his outlook.

Putting Penny's domestic situation aside for the moment, I glanced in the rearview mirror at Harry. "We need a plan."

"We have one," he said. "We go out east, get my truck and trailer, pick up your horses and that nasty old cat, and drive off into the sunset."

"Running away never solved anything," Dex said.

This time, if Harry had laser vision, Dex would have a hole in the back of his head.

"True," I said, "but this is a temporary fix, right Harry? You need breathing space to get the funds together to pay back your dealer. Then, you're going to find a nice rehab center and get better. For good."

Harry hesitated a second too long before answering. "Right. But I've already been to rehab."

"Is that where you disappeared to a couple of years ago?"

"Yes. It worked. I swear I haven't relapsed."

"Then why do you owe this guy money?" Dex asked. "They don't threaten to break legs for nothing."

"Vi," Harry said, "can we stop and get something to eat? Talk privately?"

"We can go to a drive through, and we'll talk right now. Dex is a private investigator, and you can trust him."

"Wait," Dex said. "I have a better idea. Take me to Penny's house. We'll pick up your rental car. You two can go get the trailer while I go to the farm and keep watch. Just in case."

I felt my brows draw together as I narrowed my eyes at Dex. He gave a slight dip of his head, assuring me he knew what he was doing. He must have decided that Harry wasn't a danger to me or he'd never suggest leaving me alone with him.

I took the next exit so we could go back the way we'd come. "Are you able to drive?" If the Mustang hadn't been a stick, I wouldn't have worried. But the gunshot wound was to Dex's left leg, and he'd need it to work the clutch. I hadn't known you could rent a car with a manual transmission.

"If it makes you feel better, I'll take your car," he said.

I wasn't sure what to make of such an agreeable Dex, but I trusted him and would do as he asked.

At Penny's house, I left Harry in the car. She met us at the door dry eyed, but started to cry when I pulled her and Issa into a hug.

"It's all right," she said, wiping her face on my shoulder. "We're fine. Everything will work out."

I didn't argue even though I knew she was lying. "Harry's going to help me drive Sasha and Beau to Missouri," I said. "Dex will take my rental car to the farm."

"But I'd love a cup of your delicious coffee, first, if it's not too much trouble," he said with a smile.

Penny blinked, then smiled back. "Of course." She headed to the kitchen.

Dex turned to me and winked. I'd never loved him more than I did in that moment.

Knowing my sis-co was in good hands, I returned to the Mustang. Harry moved to the front seat and pushed it all the way back to make room for his long legs.

With a curl of his lip, he said, "He's charming."

I laughed. "Dex grows on you."

"Doubtful."

I got us back on the highway going east. "Tell me the truth, Harry. You don't really think there could ever be anything between us, do you?"

"A man can hope."

"Come on. First you want to start a business together at Ed Todd's, then you want to run away to Missouri. It doesn't make sense."

"Run away *together*. Wherever you want to be is fine with me, V. You're the only one who makes me whole."

For cripe's sake. "We're not running away together. Get that through your head. It would never work. You have to know that. What is this really about?"

He lifted his shoulders, then dropped them with an exaggerated sigh. "All right. It's Baba."

I shook my head at the abrupt change. "Your mother?" I thought of that odd text message she'd sent him. *Time's up!*

"You know she's bi-polar, right?"

"No, I didn't know that."

"She's fine so long as she takes her medication. But something happened with her and Allie, and he cut her off."

"Why?"

"They won't tell me. He says she's insane. She insists he's sick. I heard him tell her, 'Let's see who the sick one is when you don't have any money for your games.' And she said something like she's not playing, and how would he like it if his secrets got out?"

I frowned. That wasn't the Allie-Baba I knew, but then, if this trip had taught me anything, very few people ever showed who they really were.

We drove in silence for some time.

"A change would do me good, V. I can tell the Midwest has had a profound effect on you. If you let me come, I promise to stay out of your hair. I'll find a place to live in the city. I'll even get a job."

Harry would say anything at this point to get out of his predicament. "Doing what?"

"Doesn't matter. Unlike some people I know, I finished college. A business degree from NYU is nothing to sneeze at."

I steered him back to the matter at hand. "You said this is about Baba."

"Right. Apparently Allie did do something because she came to me when she needed one of her prescriptions filled and couldn't get it."

"So you went to your old dealer."

"And I asked him a favor." He paused as if remembering. "It was just going to be the one time."

I sighed. "It always is. Can't Baba give you the money? I mean, if the drugs really were for her?"

"V, I'm hurt. You have to believe me. It was for her, I swear. She doesn't have access to the accounts and is on a tiny allowance."

"Your father won't give you the money?"

Harry shook his head. "I asked him. He said a very odd thing."

"What was that?"

"Alcott said, 'I suppose...' and he paused there like he does." Harry paused very much like his father would. "I remember thinking he looked kind of sad. Then he said, 'A real father would do that.' He was drinking a cocktail, not his first of the night. I chalked it up to a combination of him being shitfaced and a reference to some insult Baba had flung at him."

"That's it? No explanation?"

"He dismissed me as if I were an unruly two-year-old. Told me to run back to my drug-addled mother. After all, the two of us belonged together."

In my mind, Harry's parents had always been so superior to mine. I touched his arm. He flinched. I gave him a look.

"I lied earlier, okay? I probably should have seen a doctor."

I got off at the next exit, found a drug store and bought Ace bandages, a sling, pain killers, bandaids, alcohol wipes, bottles of water, a couple of cheese sticks, trail mix, cookies, ice, and a can of whipped cream. I took a healthy shot of that before I even got back in the car.

As I ripped open the bandage package, I said, "There's an urgent care nearby. You want to go?"

He shook his head, and I didn't insist. That undertow still pulled me along. I felt the need to ride it forward, even if that was out to sea. Harry and

I had patched each other up plenty of times in the past after falling off horses. While getting him cleaned and wrapped, I was amazed he didn't complain more. The arm probably wasn't broken, but it was hella bruised.

He knocked back several painkillers and held ice to his head. I turned on the radio and drove.

Half an hour later, my phone dinged. Dex.

All is well at the farm. What do you want to take from here?

I hadn't thought beyond getting the horses and Millie. Then I remembered Becca's offhand comment about Ed and his notes. I called Dex and told him to look for the voice recorder and handwritten diaries.

"ETA?" he asked.

"Got another hour of driving depending on traffic." I looked at Harry. "Is the trailer already hitched up?" He nodded, and I returned to Dex. "Should be up there in two-and-a half, maybe three hours."

I thought of telling Dex where to find the shipping boots for Sasha and Beau, but I was afraid he was already overdoing it. I certainly didn't want him hauling out hay bales or anything heavy. We hung up, and I called Susan to let her know what I was doing, that she wouldn't have to worry about the horses and Millie any more.

"I'll sure miss those critters," she said, "but I'm glad you're taking them. I guess this means you're selling the place?"

"I guess."

"You don't sound sure."

"It makes me sad to think about it, but it's for the best. Remember that guy who stopped by Friday? Glen's in real estate now, so I'll probably have him list it. He says he knows horse people who would be interested. I'd like that a lot better than some developer building houses on it. Is that okay with you?"

"I'd love to see the place busy with horses and kids again, even if it's not you running it."

I was glad to hear that, and I had a feeling Glen was okay, that he happened to be in the wrong place at the wrong time the other morning, that he hadn't broken in. It was obvious from the outside that the house needed work. "Listen, I wanted to get the locks changed but didn't get a chance. Do you think you could get that taken care of as soon as possible?"

She said she would and we hung up. My phone dinged again.

I took Wheezy out on the lead line to eat some grass. I thought that would make him happy, but he still steps on my feet every chance he gets. Why does he hate me? <Crying emoji>

I called Emily's cell phone. She picked up immediately, and I could hear laughter in her voice when she said hello. The sound lifted my heart. She hadn't laughed a whole lot since she'd heard Miko returned to Kiev. I felt like a bad friend for not checking in with her and couldn't wait to get back to Missouri. Even if Malcolm didn't want me. My body and heart ached for him, but I'd survive.

"Holy smokes, Vi," Emily said. "That Martina woman is a piece of work. I hope you're going to be back soon to deal with her."

"I'll be on my way shortly. Is her horse really trying to kill her?"

"I would if I were him, but no, he's just clumsy, and she's no ballerina. Half the time, his front end doesn't know what his back end's doing. The rest of the time, I don't think he cares."

"Why aren't you helping her?"

"I would if she'd let me."

I hung up with Emily and used Siri to send a message to Martina.

If Emily's around, ask her to help you. I'll be home in a couple of days.

I realized I'd told Renee and my mother that I'd be home on Monday, but if we were driving, that was unlikely, especially because right now, all that was keeping me from falling into an exhausted sleep were periodic jolts of adrenaline. I needed to send them update messages but decided to postpone until I wasn't behind the wheel. Driving instead of flying also meant I'd miss the contract deadline. I would have to text Malcolm whether he liked it or not. But that would also have to wait. We were off the highway and negotiating local traffic. I needed to pay attention.

A new message from Martina popped up on my screen.

<Thumbs up> Thanks.

Maybe she wasn't all bad. Maybe I'd be out of a job in a couple of days and it wouldn't matter. I set that worry aside along with Penny's troubles as we pulled into Allie-Baba's.

Tall, dense hedges growing along the road hid the place from curious passersby. A few turns down the curving drive, and we, too, were invisible from the rest of the world, cocooned in the lap of Brown luxury. And dysfunction. After what Harry had revealed, I sincerely hoped neither Allie nor Baba were around.

"Are your parents home?"

"What is this? Sunday? Doubtful. Allie's probably at the club, and Baba's most likely at the city apartment."

"Are you going to be able to drive your truck? I don't want to leave the Mustang out here."

"Sure. It's an automatic. I'll be fine, thanks to you."

We pulled around to the barn where I assumed Harry's dually and goose-neck were.

"Where's your rig?"

Even with his face swollen and starting to purple, I could tell Harry was confused. "I don't know. It should be here." He started to open his door. "Take me to the house. I need to grab a few things."

I circled the Mustang to the back door by the three-car garage, and we went inside. The house was immaculate as usual, straight out of *Better Homes and Gardens*. As if no one lived there at all. The kitchen reno Harry mentioned must have been completed. It all looked the same to me.

Harry went down the hall to his room. I wandered from the kitchen through the sunken living room to the dining room. There, I paused, brushing my hand over the glossy mahogany table. I'd spent many an evening here eating delicious food and enjoying Allie-Baba's company. Well, mostly enjoying Harry's snide remarks and sideways glances at his parents. We'd shared so many private jokes about them over the years. I'd never realized what he'd been hiding. Or maybe the current weirdness he'd described was something new.

The table had a powdery coating of dust on the surface. Unusual. The next room contained Allie's enormous carved cherrywood desk—it had belonged to his grandfather—floor to ceiling bookshelves, a plush oriental carpet. He'd been an attorney, but like Harry, didn't need to work. Their wealth went back several generations.

A handwritten note drew me to the desk. When I saw what it said, disappointment twisted my gut. I took it to Harry.

He had a leather Gucci duffle bag open on his bed and was stuffing it with clothes. He'd changed his shirt but otherwise, we both still wore our boots and breeches from the show.

"You should read this." I handed him the note.

He read it, swore, and crumpled it into a ball. It was from his father. It said that if Harry was looking for his rig, it had been repossessed because the loan hadn't been paid in months. It was dated the day before.

"Fine," he said. "That's just fine. Isn't it?" He tossed the wad of paper in the trash. "We'll take Baba's truck and trailer. It's only an old two-horse bumper pull, but that'll work. She never uses it anymore."

"Are you sure? Should you call her first? Is it all up to date?" The last thing we needed was to get going only to learn the truck's plates were expired or the trailer's spare tire had dry rotted. I knew all about old rigs and what could go wrong.

"Are you kidding? She keeps the trailer in tip-top shape and just got a new Range Rover to pull it. It's in the garage. If the keys aren't in it, they're in one of the other cars. Can you get the Rover out while I finish up here? I'll meet you at the barn."

The Rover sat in the first bay. It didn't have any keys in it. The next bay was empty, and I assumed Allie had a car with him at the club. In the far bay sat a sleek black BMW M4. I halted in my tracks. It looked just like the car that had nearly run me and Noire off the road on Wednesday. That seemed ages ago rather than only four days, and thinking about it brought a new pang of homesickness. I'd have loved nothing better than to bury my face in my dog's fur right then.

I squeezed between the car's back bumper and the garage door. Of course it had New York plates, but I hadn't seen the number when it whizzed by us. I shook myself. Why would either of Harry's parents have been in Missouri?

Thoughts pinged from one side of my brain to the other. Every item in the garage came into sharp focus. My eyes sprang from a pair of black trash cans to a green hose coiled and hanging from a rafter to the bright red Rover to the white door leading to the house. Panic lodged in my chest like an inflated rock.

Neither of Harry's parents would have any reason to be in Missouri.

But Harry might.

I thought of my perfectly straight pitchfork, broom, and shovel handles that kept getting inexplicably out of alignment. And how Harry knew better than anyone how it drove me crazy. Alarm exploded from my chest to prickle along my skin to my fingertips.

I could make a run for the Mustang. I should get the Beemer's keys so Harry couldn't follow. I didn't move, unsure what to think or do. Is this what Wastrel meant? Was I on the wrong lead thinking Harry had nothing to do with all this?

I opened the M4's driver-side door. A rank smell hit me, sickeningly sweet and rotten. I could barely put my head inside. I started to reach for the keys, but stopped. Lying in the passenger seat was a to-go cup from the Roasted Bean Coffee Shop. It wasn't a chain. There was only one. The very same one I'd been to with Giacomo.

This car *had* been in Missouri. The question was, who'd been driving it?

But even a coffee left for a few days in a hot garage couldn't account for that smell, one that was familiar and foreign at the same time. The fine hairs stood up on my neck. Holding my breath, I slowly turned my eyes to the back.

Alcott Brown slumped in the seat.

I jumped back with a screech hitting my head on the door frame.

"Holy shit."

I paced in a circle with my arm over my nose and mouth, breathing hard, trying to gather my wits, trying not to throw up. Did Harry know? Did he do it? No, that was crazy.

I looked around for something to fish out the keys, anything that would allow me to get them without putting my head back in the car, but that was a waste of time. I leaned in and couldn't help glancing at poor Alcott again. His skin was gray, face puffy. Blood had dried around his nose and mouth and on a gold stirrup iron in his lap. The stirrup leather had been draped across his thigh.

Around his neck hung a piece of paper tied to a string. On it were written the words, *He liked dirty barn girls.*

CHAPTER TWENTY-THREE

I DIDN'T CARE whether or not Harry did it. I ran into the house yelling for him. He met me in the kitchen, his Gucci duffle in his good hand, his other secure in the sling. He dropped the bag to catch me with a loud *oof*.

"I'm sorry," I blubbered. "It's Alcott. He's in the garage—"

"Good. He and I need to talk."

I pushed away from him. "No. You don't understand. He's...he's...."

"What? Drunk again?"

I put both hands over my face for a moment, then lowered them. "Dead, Harry. Someone killed him."

Harry let out a choked sob, his eyes rolled back in his head, and he staggered into the counter against his bad arm. I tried to catch him, but he was too heavy. His legs gave out, and we slid to the floor.

Had I known he would react like that, I would have made him sit down first. He'd gone pale again. I got up to run cold water on a dish towel, then patted it over his face and neck. This time, as he came around, I knew he wasn't faking. Tears leaked from the corners of his eyes as he blinked up at me.

"We need to call the police," I said.

"I need to see him." He tried to rise.

I pushed him down. "Not a good idea."

The note around Alcott's neck. The meaning began to sink in. Had someone left it for me? But no one knew what had happened that day except me and Ed.

And the man who did it.

Who would have known I would find Alcott? No one.

Except Harry.

I sat back on my heels. My cell was in the Mustang. I stood and went to the kitchen phone.

"Please," Harry said. He pulled himself up and got between me and the phone, still clearly shaky. "No police."

"We have to. This wasn't an accident. And if someone's after you, you'll be safer in custody."

He rubbed his hand over his eyes, flinched when his fingers brushed his swollen brow. "Why would someone do this?"

"I don't know, but whoever it was had something to do with your beating. There's a gold stirrup with him just like the one you were hit with."

"A gold…" His eyes cleared. "We have to go."

"Why? Do you know who did this? Was it the same guys who attacked you?"

Harry took my arm and pushed me out the door. "Get in the car and go. I'll be right behind you with the trailer."

"I'll help you hook it up."

"No time for your stubborn routine, Vi. I will call the police, but right now, we have to go."

"Tell me what's going on."

He glanced toward the garage and tears welled up again. He sniffed and wiped at his nose. "Don't worry about me, okay? I need you to remember something."

"What?"

"You were never here."

CHAPTER TWENTY-FOUR

THE MUSTANG FISHTAILED as I floored it out the gravel driveway. Once clear of the property, I downed a shot of whipped cream and tried to calm my breathing. As soon as I reached the highway, I called Dex and told him what had happened.

He swore with color and vehemence. "You're on your way?"

"Yes."

"Don't speed. Getting pulled over won't help. Where's Harry?"

"He said he'd be right behind me. He also said he'd call the police, but before that, he begged me not to."

"Was he in shock?"

"I think so." I squirted more whipped cream in my mouth.

"You've stocked up on your favorite de-stressor."

"Wouldn't you?"

He chuckled. "Listen, I know someone I can call. Just in case Harry forgets to contact the authorities. Get here safe, and we'll talk then. You okay?"

I put the whipped cream can in a cup holder and held out my hand, fingers spread. They trembled. Sweat trickled down my back despite the air-conditioning being on high. "Not really."

"Understandable, but you've dealt with worse. Remember to breathe in between whipped cream shots. I'll call you back in a few minutes."

I didn't want to hang up. "Have you found Ed's voice recorder or diaries?"

Dex sighed. "No luck. It could be exactly what the person who broke in was looking for."

Goddammit. There must be incriminating information in them. I tried to keep the note's accusation at bay. Had Ed made an entry about what happened? If the perpetrator knew Ed, he knew his name might be written down.

Why go after Ed all these years later? Unless there was a chance the secret would be revealed? That would ruin someone like Alcott Brown, someone who had so much to lose. But why would Ed threaten to tell?

Too many missing pieces, and I could still be on the wrong lead. We had to find Ed's notes.

By the time I arrived at the farm, it was late afternoon. Golden sunlight slanted through the trees enclosing the horses in a subtle halo where they stood in the pasture. My rental car sat in front of the house. I parked the Mustang next to it and remained there for a few moments. I hadn't gotten that sense of relief when I pulled in. This wasn't my safe haven any more.

Proof of that met me at the door. Dex greeted me with, "Can't find the cat."

"She doesn't like people, especially strangers. If Harry doesn't show up, though, it won't matter."

"Call him to see where he is. Police are on their way to the Brown residence, and some are coming here, too."

"Here? Why?"

"Because Harry's probably on his way here. And you found a dead body."

Deja vu all over again. Almost a year ago, it had been Norman in the manure spreader.

"Harry told me to remember that I was never there—at his parents' place. What did he mean?"

"He's protecting you. Maybe he's a true friend after all."

"Of course he is."

I fished my phone out and started to call, but a sound stopped me. I slid past Dex into the house. Penny sat in the easy chair with Isabella in a baby carrier on the floor next to her. She gently rocked Issa with her foot.

I was glad to see them, of course, but startled and confused. "What are you doing here?"

"We're going to Missouri with you."

"You're going…"

I looked to Dex. He'd come in and closed the door. His gaze rested firmly on my cousin and her daughter. He was usually a master of the poker face, but there was a softness around his eyes I'd never seen before. I turned back to Penny. She gave me a look just shy of an eye roll. I gave her a narrow-eyed stare that had her on her feet and following me to Ed's office.

"What the heck happened in here?" she asked after I shut the door. "Looks like a bomb went off."

"Never mind that. What's going on?"

She dropped into Ed's creaky desk chair and drummed her fingertips on the desktop. "I didn't want to worry you," she started, then her eyes cut away. A moment later, she went on in a rush. "Things haven't been great for a while. Frank never wanted children. Once I got pregnant, our relationship went from bad to worse. And now that Issa's here..." She ducked her chin.

"Oh, Penny. I'm so sorry." I went over and put my arms around her shoulders.

"Thanks. Honestly, I never thought he'd leave us. But now that he has, it's a relief."

I crouched next to the chair, wiped a tear from her cheek, and took her hands. "You sure it's for good? I mean, I know he took his tools and all."

"Yeah. After you and I talked, I called him. He said it's over. He can't do fatherhood. I can have the house."

"So why leave?"

She shrugged. "A change of scene will clear my head. If it's not too much trouble."

Harry had said almost the same thing. But instead of the trepidation I'd felt at the idea of Harry in Missouri, the thought of having Penny near made pleasure expand in my chest. I breathed easier than I had all day. "Of course it's no trouble. We'll figure it out when we get there."

Isabella began to whimper. We returned to the living room to find Dex had picked her up. He cradled her against his shoulder and rubbed her back. She quieted. Oh brother. My surprise at Dex's behavior the night before was nothing. This was a side of him I never imagined.

Penny took Issa and disappeared with her down the hall, probably to nurse. I sank to the couch and tried Harry's number, but he didn't answer. Letting my head drop onto the cushion, I thought to rest my eyes for a few minutes.

Wastrel and I stand outside Ed's barn. As before, flames and smoke pour through the windows and door. I hear Ed talking between coughs, probably trying to calm the horses as he leads them out. But Beau and Sasha run through the smoke to the pasture, eyes wild and tails high. I look for the person who set the fire, ready to identify Alcott Brown, but the figure is too shadowed, visible through the smoke for only a moment. Ed collapses just outside the doorway.

I can't move to help him. I look at Wastrel. He bobs his head up and down. There is nothing new here.

"Show me what I need to know," I say.

Wastrel paws the ground with one hoof then walks away. We are in the tack room. The fire is gone. Millie sits on the trunk, her tail twitching. She jumps to the floor. I follow her out to the barn aisle where her travel crate sits just inside the door.

"What?" I ask.

"Vi, wake up."

Someone shakes my shoulder.

"Vi, the police are here."

I recognize Penny's voice. What's she doing in my dream?

My lids were heavy, but I managed to lift one a crack. A lamp was on next to me, too bright. Where was I? Penny wrapped my fingers around a hot cup, held it there. I blinked. The smell of coffee filled my nose.

"Okay," I said, my voice sounding far away. "Okay," I repeated and forced my eyelids up.

Ed's living room came into focus. Penny sat next to me, still pressing the coffee mug against my hand. A uniformed female officer stood near the door with Dex. A male officer escorted Harry out.

In handcuffs.

"Wait."

I spilled coffee on both me and Penny getting up too fast, swaying on my feet. She jumped up with me, pulling the mug to safety with one hand and steadying me with the other.

The officers exchanged a look. The guy with Harry paused. In deference to his injured arm, his hands were secured in front of him. He looked like shit with his hair hanging over his forehead, his good eye glassy.

I put my palm to his cheek, barely touching. "Are you okay? What happened?"

"Miss Parker," Dex said, his voice filled with warning. "They've already read him his rights."

"And he confessed," the officer said.

"To what?" I asked.

"V?" Harry asked through cracked lips.

"I'm here." I looked at Dex. "He's under arrest?"

Dex nodded.

Harry blinked slowly like I had a moment before, as if he were coming out of a deep sleep. "I didn't do it, V. You have to believe me."

I squinted at him, trying to discern whether he was still in shock, acting, or having a psychotic break. All I knew right then was it was senseless to argue or try to delay the police.

"Do you want me to call someone? A lawyer?" He must have one. He had a banker, chiropractor, broker, masseuse, accountant, and who knew what else.

"Alcott Brown," Harry said. "Call my father. He'll take care of everything."

CHAPTER TWENTY-FIVE

IF HARRY WAS SHOOTING for an innocent-by-reason-of-insanity plea, he had me convinced. Whether his vacant expression and befuddled statement were real was anybody's guess. He could have snapped. If I found my father like that, I might become unhinged.

I answered questions about my background and history with the family. I didn't tell them I'd been at the house, mention the coffee cup from the Roasted Bean, or that the car had been in Missouri just a few days ago. I didn't know Harry's reason for insisting I was never there. They didn't ask about the note around Allie's neck. Maybe Harry removed it before anyone else saw it. The police wrote down my contact details, advised me to remain available should they need a follow-up interview, and left. They took the gold stirrup I'd collected at the horse show.

I watched through the window until they were out the driveway. "Is he being charged with murder?"

Dex came to stand beside me and put his arm around my shoulders. "Yes."

I sighed and leaned into him, but it was Malcolm I wanted. Malcolm's strength shoring me up, comforting me. I'd had a hollow ache inside me for days, and I didn't expect it to go away anytime soon. "At least he brought Baba's rig. I wasn't sure he would."

"Can't use it without him. Could be construed as theft."

"What if they find out I was there?"

"Unless Harry mentions it—which I doubt—you don't have to worry."

Dex shifted his weight from one leg to the other. He'd changed out of his bloody pants and must have taken a shower because he smelled good. The stink of death still clung to me, and I couldn't wait to get under a hot and forceful spray of water. I might never emerge.

"We're back to square one for taking the horses to Missouri, though I guess it doesn't matter so much now that I'm not rescuing Harry."

"You're very loyal," Dex said.

I exhaled noisily. "Maybe to a fault."

"Remains to be seen."

"You don't believe he did it?" What Dex thought mattered to me.

"Doubtful. But you know him best. Do you think he did it?"

"No."

Harry was as smart and sophisticated as he was weak and manipulative. But a murderer? Unlikely.

Wastrel, my friend, why couldn't you simply show me the face of the person responsible for all this?

If *all this* was even connected.

I dragged myself out to the barn for my backpack and caught my breath when I walked into the tack room. Millie sat on the trunk twitching her tail just like she had in my dream. I ran my hand down her back. She stood and purred.

"Hey, old girl. Were you hiding from Dex?"

I'd recently read that people who talk to their animals are smarter and more creative than those who don't. I must be freaking brilliant. I felt anything but at the moment. Dumbfounded and saddened by the day's events, I was no closer to figuring out who killed Ed or what was going on. The snug fit of my breeches was all that kept me on my feet, and I kind of wished I still had my helmet on to keep my marbles from falling out.

Millie jumped down, ran to the corner, returned with a dead mouse, dropped it at my feet, then hopped back up on the trunk.

"Thank you so much. So thoughtful." I scratched her head, fighting back frustrated tears. She pushed against my hand, still purring. "I hope you don't mind moving to a new barn. There are other cats." I sniffed. "They're kind of lazy, though."

I sat on the couch for a moment, tired to my bones but desperate for a shower. Millie came over to my lap and curled up. I sighed. I supposed a shower could wait. A bit of time away from other people, even those I loved, was just what I needed.

I'm back on course with Wastrel. Like earlier today, we turn for the triple combination and time slows. Wastrel is on the wrong lead again. I correct it, we ride forward. Again, a jump turns into the trunk with magazines flying out.

Horses neigh. Someone is stabbing my thighs with needles.

Millie launched off my lap to hide, using all eighteen of her claws and snagging several pulls in the fabric of my new breeches. No doubt, I had eighteen slices in my skin, nine on each thigh.

Outside, a diesel powered something rumbled up the drive. I went to investigate, noting on the way that Millie's travel crate was sitting on the floor inside the door, just as in my earlier dream. I made a mental note. I'd need to get her in it before we got on the road. She'd never liked it, and I'd likely be bleeding from more slices by the time we were done.

A red, one-ton pickup with a camper shell towed in a white and silver four-horse trailer and cruised to a stop in front of me. When the door opened, Becca stepped down. She wore shorts, a T-shirt, and sneakers. Her pixie haircut had been gelled into spikes. I'd never seen her outside of a show or barn or wearing anything other than boots and breeches.

This day got weirder by the minute. A horse whinnied from inside. Beau answered from the field. Sasha eyed the trailer like it might have a cougar inside.

Before I could ask what was going on, Becca spread her arms and said, "I bought her. We won the next two classes thanks to you."

She hugged me, enveloping me in the scent of watermelon. I stood there like a tree trunk, shocked into silence.

"Something just clicked, you know what I mean?" Becca released me. "Of course you know what I mean. It must be like that for you all the time. Is that what it's like?"

I tried to keep my face from contorting into all the ugly disconcerted and confused frowns that it felt like. "Is that what *what's* like?"

"When you ride?" She took a few steps away, then came back. "I've watched you for years sitting up there like you're doing nothing and winning and winning and winning no matter what horse you rode. Making it look like it was all the horse, and you were just along for the ride. Like your horses could fly. While the rest of us struggled to steer our earthbound beasts around without taking down any rails."

I really didn't know what to say. But I didn't need to say anything because Becca went on, pacing back and forth and speed talking well enough to give a Missouri auctioneer a run for his money. She might as well have been talking to herself for all the response she needed from me.

"It was like you were a witch or something. Not that I didn't think you were. I did."

Likewise, but I kept that thought to myself.

"But not because of your riding."

"I get your point."

"Then today, after I watched your round, and after what you told me when you were leaving, I decided to ride her differently. To—I don't know what exactly because I don't know what it is you do—but to stay out of her way a little more. To encourage her to do what I knew she could do. To do less, I guess. Does that make sense?"

I nodded.

"And it worked. It was amazing."

She had an attractive flush to her cheeks and a sparkle in her eye. I knew that feeling well.

"That's great," I said. "Congratulations. But what are you doing here?"

"Are you kidding? I want more. I bought the mare. Did I already say that? And I want to train with you. You're setting up shop here, right?"

I stood there for a moment, blinking at her, wondering if maybe I was having another dream. Wondering if…if…what if Wastrel meant I was on the wrong lead about my life? Should I set up shop at Ed Todd's?

Gah, I was so confused.

No, Wastrel's clues were always about the bad guy, the mystery. I still needed to solve the crime of who murdered Ed. Not to mention Allie. Not to mention who shot at me. And also maybe figure out who beat up Harry. Poor Harry. I couldn't imagine him in jail. But he really might be better off there for the time being.

"Actually," I said to Becca, "I'm taking the horses to Missouri. I'm going to set up shop there."

I'd said it out loud. It sounded right. It felt right.

"Fine," Becca said. "I'm up for a road trip. You lead. I'll follow." She looked me up and down as if she'd just noticed me standing there. "Why are you still dressed like that? You smell like doo doo. Seriously."

"I was just going in to take a shower." Not that I owed Becca any explanations.

"How are you getting the horses to Missouri? That old two-horse?" She gestured at Baba's rig.

"Um, no. It's…parked there temporarily for a friend."

"That's okay. They'll fit in here." She jabbed her thumb over her shoulder at her trailer. "This is a four-horse slant. We'll have room to spare for whatever else you need to take. When are we leaving?"

"I…wow. This is all such a surprise." My brain had whiplash. We didn't have a way to transport the horses, then we did because Harry offered his rig, then we didn't because his rig was repossessed, then we did because we could use Baba's trailer, then we didn't because Harry got hauled away in cuffs, and now we did because Becca wanted to train with me. What were the chances? Did I want Becca Scissorhands in Missouri? She'd be doing me a huge favor taking us there, and I needed to get back. Sooner rather than later. I couldn't process all this on so little sleep.

"Soon," I said in answer to her question. "There are a couple of other people who'll be along for the ride. Let's go inside." I needed that cup of coffee Penny had tried to give me. "Do you want to unload the mare? You can put her in one of the stalls. There's an open hay bale in the aisle and buckets for water."

"Sure," Becca said.

I went to retrieve my backpack. No sign of Millie. Still, I stared at the trunk for a moment, wondering what the point of it being in the dreams was. A couple of years back, I'd come here after a horse show to find Ed knocked out on the floor. He'd tripped over the trunk because it had been shifted several inches away from its usual place. I always made sure everything was in the same position for Ed because he could barely see. So long as nothing moved, he got around fine. I sat and rested my elbows on my knees, put my face in my hands. I often thought that if I'd never gone to Missouri, he might still be alive.

Months after Ed's fall, Harry confessed he'd been here looking for a tie pin the night before. He'd moved the trunk, but swore he'd put it back. I'd always wondered, though. Had he really positioned it exactly where it belonged? He knew how I was about everything being in its place. *Could* I trust Harry? He'd lied about killing Allie, I was sure of it. He was a good liar. But why confess? Was he protecting someone?

I ran my hands over the trunk's worn leather top. Becca's mare clip-clopped into the barn, then swished into the deep pine shavings of a stall. I heard her sigh.

The hinges creaked as I lifted the lid. I waved away the dusty scent of aging paper. Old magazines filled it to the brim. The thing weighed a ton. The issues on top were from the early nineties. Ed had probably stopped getting them about then because he couldn't enjoy them anymore. I wondered how far they went back.

From the barn came the squeak of the water being turned on, then a bucket filling. Becca hummed and spoke in soothing tones to her new horse. The mare made a tired wuffling sound.

Sticking the fingers of both hands down as far as they'd reach to either side of a stack of magazines, I pulled them out and set them on the floor. A few more, and I was to the eighties, then the seventies. There was Rodney Jenkins aboard the great jumper Idle Dice on the cover of *Practical Horseman*. I remembered Ed talking about them as well as Harry DeLeyer and Snowman.

The water squeaked off followed by the rustle of hay, the stall door sliding open. Becca murmured, "There's a good girl."

I set aside the issue with Idle Dice on it—that was a keeper—and pulled out a few more. I wasn't even sure why I was doing this.

And then, I reached the end. No more periodicals. But it was far from the bottom of the trunk.

Beneath all those years of magazines were piles and piles of spiral note-books. I picked one up and smiled. Written on the front in Ed's commanding hand was *June-December 1988*. Now, I understood what Wastrel had been trying to show me.

"Ed, you sly old coot."

I'd found his diaries.

CHAPTER TWENTY-SIX

WE DECIDED to leave that night after dinner and at least get on the other side of the city before bedding down for the night. Becca and I would take the horses and Millie. Penny and Dex would return the rental cars, take a cab to pick up hers, and catch up with us when they could.

When I went inside, Becca in tow, Penny had a full-blown pasta dinner in progress. The enticing scents of sautéing garlic and onions combined with simmering tomato sauce and fresh-baked bread made my mouth water. I'd missed eating Sunday dinner at Penny's.

I introduced Becca, explained she'd be taking me and the horses to Missouri, and joined my cousin in the kitchen, giving my hands a good wash in the sink.

"Yum. You whipped this all up while I was outside?"

Penny set aside a salad, sidled close, and whispered, "Becca as in Scissorhands?"

Penny had listened to me rant about the girl and her horrible riding for years. "Yes." I dipped my pinky in the sauce and licked it.

"After the way you always talked about her, I expected her to have a long nose and warts."

I glanced over at Becca. She sat at the table between the kitchen and living room doing something on her phone. "I think she's changed," I whispered. "Her riding has, anyway." Maybe she never was that bad. I'd never given her a chance.

"I keep telling you, Vi," Penny said in a normal voice, "you're the one who's changed."

"I second that," Dex called from the living room. He sat on the couch watching TV with his feet on the hassock.

Becca didn't look up but chimed in with, "Abstain."

What was this? The freaking senate?

"That's enough from the peanut gallery," I said.

Penny gestured at the stove. "I had all this at home. I brought it with me. Dex lent a hand." She cut her eyes to the living room and back to me, lowered her voice again. "He's very nice. Helpful with Issa."

"Penny," I hissed. "You can't latch on to the first guy who isn't like Frank."

"I'm not *latching on*. Just stating a couple of facts. Go take a shower. You stink."

"Second that," Becca said.

I huffed, shouldered my backpack, and headed to the bathroom. Right before I got in the shower, my phone dinged.

Ciao Bella. What time you getting in? I'll pick you up.

My grandfather. Before my parents showed up at Winterlight with him the summer before, no one had known who he was. My father had maintained he'd been adopted and knew nothing about his parents. But Giacomo had kept track of his family, and now we were reunited. He'd turned out to be a smart, funny guy who knew a little bit about everything and was content simply to have a patch of soil to plant his garden.

I loved that he started each text message to me with *Hello Beautiful.*

We're driving. Back late Tuesday. See you then.

The thought of the drive made me even more tired than I already was, but it would be good to get back. With one foot in the tub, I added,

Can you tell my parents for me? Mom is expecting me tomorrow.

A moment later, he answered simply,

Sí.

I'd been standing under the hot water for all of a minute when the door opened and closed. Penny and I'd lived together for so long before I moved to Winterlight that a shut bathroom door meant nothing.

"I need to stand here for a while," I said. "Start dinner without me."

"Okay," Dex said.

This togetherness was going to kill me—if a random shooter or stirrup-wielding attacker didn't get to me, first. I almost looked forward to spending a couple of days in a truck with Becca. "Can't you wait or go outside?"

"Nope. We need to decide whether to read in those two."

"Read them in on what?"

"The situation."

I was sick of there always being a *situation*. "Which situation is that, Dex? The one where someone set fire to the barn on purpose and killed Ed? Or the situation where someone—maybe the same someone, maybe not—has been messing with my head by moving the tools? Or is it the one where someone shoots at me from a speeding car?" I heard the rising hysteria in my voice but couldn't stop. "Or is the situation where someone else, or maybe *not* someone else, beats up Harry with one gold stirrup and kills his father with another? And let's not forget about the situation where someone has broken in here looking for who knows what. Which situation are we reading them in on?"

Dex sighed. "We can't set out on this journey with them completely in the dark about everything. Especially with an infant in the mix."

"Yeah, you want to explain that to me? I mean, I'm all for Penny coming to Missouri for a while, but the timing isn't great."

"When was the last time you tried talking your cousin out of something she'd made up her mind to do?"

I poured shampoo into my hand and lathered my hair, thankful for the opaque shower curtain. Not that it would stop my laser vision from blowing a hole through Dex. If I had laser vision. "You had nothing to do with it?"

"No ma'am."

I doubted it. Dex could persuade without a word. "And you tried to talk her out of it?"

"If you don't believe me, ask her."

"I will." But the truth was, if Penny had already made up her mind, nothing would stop her. Like when she decided to marry Frank. Nothing I'd said would budge her.

"What do you think we should tell them?" I asked.

"That you suspect the fire here was set intentionally. Ed told you as much. And you've been trying to find out who did it."

"That's it?"

"That's enough."

I pressed the heels of my hands into my eye sockets until it hurt. "Is it? We don't know if the fire has anything to do with the shooting or if that has anything to do with Harry's attack or if that has anything to do with Allie's murder. Let alone who's been moving my tools."

Dex let out a long breath and then was quiet for so long, I thought he'd left. I should have been so lucky.

"I expect," he said in a soft but steady voice, "there's a connection between what happened to you here when you were a child, and Mr. Brown's murder."

He liked dirty barn girls.

I'd been trying not to think about it, but that was impossible. I'd wracked my memory for the the sound of the man's voice, unsure whether I wanted confirmation it was Alcott or to know it wasn't. Could two different men say those exact words? I tried to remember if he'd ever treated me oddly after I started hanging around with Harry. Had he looked at me funny or said something that could have been taken differently if I'd been paying attention? Nothing came to mind. He was always in the background, aloof, but not unkind. Harry had never intimated his father had odd predilections.

Who was I kidding? The man who said that to me, who tried to put his penis in my mouth, was a pedophile.

"What's the point," I asked, "of telling Penny and Becca anything? Do you think we're in danger? That someone might follow us?"

"Until we connect the dots and know for sure who's responsible, then we don't know what could happen, or what this person or these people are capable of."

"Maybe with Allie dead and Harry in jail, it's over. Could the fire have been meant for him?"

"Is there any reason Mr. Brown would have been here the day of the fire?"

"I have no idea." I began rinsing my hair. "If I could talk to Harry, I could ask him. Should we leave with him in jail? Maybe I should stay, bail him out or go to his hearing, whatever the next step is."

"The hearing might not be for a couple of days, and I expect the dollar amount of his bail will be out of your reach."

"What about a lawyer? Do you know someone? Obviously, it's not going to be his father. I should at least call Baba."

"I think you should stay clear of it."

"But—"

"He's your friend. I know." Dex flipped on the exhaust fan. "It will be interesting to see if the tools get moved anymore with him locked up."

"But why would Harry do that? What possible motive could he have for making me think I'm crazy?"

"Didn't you tell me that Harry has always gotten what he wanted?"

"Yes."

"Everything? Always?"

I thought back over the years. I was about to answer *yes* when it hit me what Dex was getting at. He must have taken my silence as the answer he wanted.

"I'm hungry," he said. "And your sister-cousin's cooking smells amazing. Hurry up."

The door clicked shut behind him. I added conditioner to my hair and slowly worked it through. I had no intention of rushing this shower unless the hot water ran out.

The door opened again. It had to be Penny this time.

"Start without me," I said, trying not to sound annoyed. "I won't be much longer."

"Okay," Penny said.

I knew by her tone that it wasn't. That she wasn't in here to make quick use of the toilet any more than Dex had been.

I moved the shower curtain and looked at her. "You okay?"

"Sure. I'm fine. Or, I will be. What about you?"

I put my face back into the spray. "I'm not the one whose husband left."

Even if she hadn't been happy, it was still a shock, still a huge change. If it were me, I'd be upset. When we got some extended alone time, I'd get it out of her, and I'd tell her more about what was going on than Dex's brief *reading in*. Until I did, she had no reason to suspect anything was wrong with me.

"Have you talked to Malcolm?" she asked.

I inhaled water, coughed and sputtered. "No," I said when I could.

She ignored my near drowning. "Why not?"

I turned my back to the spray and stood there with the water pulsating on my shoulders, hoping she'd go away. I didn't have a good answer. And by all that's holy, she *is* a stubborn one. She'd let dinner be ruined if I didn't come up with something. I could stay in the shower until the water ran out, and she wouldn't care. Sometimes I thought she had ice in her veins.

"Vi?"

"Yeah?"

"I made a mistake with Frank. I know that now. I went for what I thought was practical, but there was never any passion between us. I've never felt like you do for horses or even for friends. Not until Isabelle came along."

"And what is that feeling, exactly?"

Without hesitation, she answered, "Like you'd die for them."

That about summed it up. The water was beginning to cool, and I was hungry, just like Dex. "Is this going somewhere?"

"Remember what I said to you last night about how you light up whenever you talk about Malcolm? I've never seen or heard you like that with a guy."

It was true. "And?"

"Oh my God, you're obstinate sometimes."

"Takes one to know one."

She snorted at that. "My point is, if you love him, don't let him go just because you're afraid to say how you feel or that he won't love you back or you might get hurt or your relationship is only about work. You've never let fear keep you off a horse. Even after Wastrel."

"I'm not afraid of horses. But this is my heart we're talking about. Not my body. It's different."

I shut off the water, grabbed a towel, wrapped it around me, and sat on the edge of the tub, knee-to-knee with her. She took my hands.

"Not really," she said. "Either way, it's a risk. One you might never recover from. It always scared the crap out of me to see you jumping a half-ton animal over a five-foot jump."

She paused to gather herself, looking up at the ceiling for several moments. She grabbed a tissue and blotted her eyes. I'd always wondered why she stopped coming to shows.

Penny squeezed my fingers. "But you loved it *so* much that you never considered it might not work out, you might get hurt. Or even..." A tear escaped. She swiped it away.

"Die?" I said.

She nodded and shook her head, then whispered, "The risk was worth it, right?"

I sniffed. "Always."

"Gamble, Vi. On love. On yourself. You're a good bet." She pulled my phone out of her pocket. "At least send him a text message before you come out of here. Okay? Isn't he worth taking a chance for?" She put the phone in my hand, closed my fingers around it. "Lay it all on the line like you do on a jump course."

She didn't wait for an answer, but left, a cloud of steam escaping into the hallway with her.

I took my phone and stared at the screen for a long moment, then brought up my last text convo with Malcolm. It had been about towing my dead truck back to the farm. He'd said I'd have a new one soon and punctuated it, not with silly faces, but with a truck symbol followed by dollar signs, exclamation marks, and a dog animoji because Noire would have a new ride.

The feeling I usually ignored surged, rolling inside my chest like rising dough. Was this what love felt like? Fear and joy in equal amounts so painful it might suffocate me?

I thought back a few months to the beginning of the year. It had been cold for weeks. No snow, but the ground froze. Not much riding. Lots of tack cleaning, organizing the feed room, grooming horses. In previous winters, Malcolm and both Dex One and Dex Two had fox hunted with the local club as often as they could. One of the tasks I'd been hired for was to keep their horses fit for the long hours of trekking cross-country after the hounds.

Dex One had taken on a case out of town, Dex Two's environmental concerns kept him busy and convinced him fox hunting was bad. Malcolm's clients requested extra work, and he rarely turned down extra work. There had been no hunting. Instead, there had been snuggling with Malcolm by the fire when he was home. When he wasn't, I spent many days in the city helping my parents with the renovations on the house they rented from Malcolm.

One January night, on the way from the barn to the house, Malcolm said we should cut through the pasture instead of walking up the drive like we usually did. He tugged me through the gate, and I followed. The temperature had been below zero. It hurt my nose to breathe, but we wore our Gumby suits—thick insulated coveralls—and fur hats. No air moved. I could hear the horses chewing their hay. A thin slice of moon like a handleless sickle hovered above the trees.

We stopped in the middle of the field. When I looked up, the Milky Way spread above us from one side of the sky to the other like a sparkling cloud bank. For the span of a heartbeat, I was outside my body, part of the cosmos, a being of spirit with no physical limits.

The sensation was similar to the pressure I felt in my chest as I stared at my phone. Hollow as if my heart had escaped, and at the same time, swollen as if unable to contain so much feeling at one time.

"Look," Malcolm had said that night. He pointed at the ground.

At first, I didn't understand. I didn't want to come back to Earth. Then, I saw it. Tiny pinpricks of light in the dry grass brilliant as a million diamonds.

"Is that it? Is that the winterlight?"

"That's it." He'd put his arm around my shoulders and pulled me into a hug. "I'm glad you stayed here long enough to see it."

I held tight to the memory and the good feels that went with it. Taking a few deep breaths, I moved my thumbs over the screen.

I'm coming home. Can't wait to see you.

I pressed send. The pain in my chest threatened to overwhelm me. Before it could, I added,

I want to stay at Winterlight. Do you want me to?

My finger hovered over the send arrow. I mustered that all-out energy I harnessed on a jump course, just like Penny advised, and let my fingertip drop to the screen.

Five minutes later, my damp hair hanging down my back, I dug into a mound of Penny's delectable meat sauce and ziti. We slathered butter on bread still warm from the oven and washed it down with sparkling water. Penny bounced Isabella on her knee while she ate. Issa played with a few unsauced noodles, sliding them onto her fingers before putting them in her mouth.

I sat there acting normal but feeling shattered, raw, exposed, elated. Shaky.

No one noticed. Maybe Penny did, but she avoided looking at me too hard.

"So, Becca," I said, "how can you leave town so easily? Don't you have to pack? Give notice at an apartment or something?" I knew nothing about her.

"I live in my truck. It's the only way I can afford it let alone save enough to buy a horse like that." She shrugged. "My dad is gone, and my mom moved to Arizona a couple of years ago. I might actually get to see her once I'm in Missouri. It's a heck of a lot closer than New York. She's excited."

And just like that, not only did I know more about Becca, but I felt a kinship with her.

"Do you think there's a clue about the fire in the diaries?" she asked after we told them what we suspected.

"Maybe," I said. "Hopefully."

"More likely in the recordings he made in recent years, don't you think?" Penny asked.

"Possibly, but we haven't found them. His computer was stolen, but if anything else was taken from his office, I can't tell. I don't know where he kept the voice recorder." I speared two ziti with my fork, ate and swallowed them before continuing. "On him, would be my guess, but I asked his sister, and she said that if he'd been carrying it, by the time he got to the hospital, it was lost."

We might be at a dead end, but I would start reading his notebooks in the morning. If I could find an entry about Alcott Brown assaulting me, we could at least put that part of the mystery to bed. Though it would make me sad to know for sure.

We cleaned up dinner. Me, Dex, and Becca went to the barn to ready the horses. Penny stayed with the baby and to make enough coffee to keep us all alert for a few hours. She'd probably pack snacks as well. I tried to imagine what her drive with Dex and Isabella would be like. Interesting, at the least. I hoped she'd let him take the wheel and grab some rest for herself. I chuckled. Dex would insist. She'd resist. I'd like to be there for that argument. No doubt, he'd melt her with his twinkling eyes and sexy drawl.

I paused on the front porch while Dex and Becca went ahead, each grabbing one of the horses from the field. The sun had set but the hazy glow of twilight lingered. Above the western tree line, feathery clouds glowed orange and pink on the bottom, dusky purple on top.

In the barn, Becca's mare dozed with one hind leg cocked. We loaded hay and extra bags of shavings in Becca's trailer. I left Dex filling the trailer's water tank. He multi-tasked by texting someone on his phone. A little while later, I walked out with a fifty-pound bag of grain over my shoulder, and he was still at it, the texting, that is, not anything useful.

"What's so important it can't wait until we get going?"

I didn't mean to be cross with him, but I really did want to get on the road. Now that the decision had been made, the heavy current of that undertow tugged at me once more, urging me to move.

"Needy client," Dex said. He pocketed his phone. "What else do we have to do?"

Becca came up next to him. "You're not leaving the tack, are you?"

I supposed we should take as much as we could. If I were going to be starting over on my own, I'd need equipment and supplies. "No, let's take everything useful we can fit."

Soon, we were packed and ready. All except for Millie. I walked around the other side of the barn, using calling her as an excuse to see the place. To walk the familiar paths I'd trod so many times. Maybe for the last time. That thought didn't make me as melancholy as it had a few days before.

Malcolm hadn't answered. Each time I checked my phone to find no new messages, pain stabbed my heart.

I stopped by the riding ring, remembering the many times Ed had worked with me out there honing my abilities.

Millie trotted out of the darkness to rub my legs. I picked her up and held her against me, pressing my face into her fur before carrying her to the barn. Dex saw me coming and grabbed her crate. Together we got her in. He took her to the back seat of Becca's truck. I flicked on the barn light for a last look around. In the dust where Millie's crate had been, something shiny caught my eye. I bent to pick it up.

Ed's voice recorder.

He must have dropped it when he collapsed during the fire, and it slid under the crate. No one had had any reason to move the animal carrier since.

I pushed play. Nothing. Tried rewind. Nada. It probably needed fresh batteries. Maybe there were some in the house. If not, when we stopped later, I'd get some. Had Ed been talking into it when he collapsed? The thought of what I might hear chilled me. I put it in a bucket I carried for last-minute items and walked back to the store rooms.

We'd already packed up most everything that wasn't nailed down. Saddles and bridles, brushes and buckets, hay nets and leg wraps. I'd put as much as I could in the old trunk, and we'd loaded that into the first stall of Becca's trailer.

I stood staring at the implements, thinking about how these and the ones at Winterlight had kept getting moved.

"You can always use a good pitchfork," Dex said.

I nodded.

Becca started taking them down. "This stuff is expensive. I'll find room. I'll keep them if you don't want them."

Dex and I watched her for a moment, then I grabbed the ones Becca hadn't. Dex's phone buzzed. He pulled it out, read a message, put it back in his pocket.

"Needy client still needy?" I asked.

He smiled. "Why don't we go inside and get some of Penny's coffee before shoving off? We can double check our route, sync our watches and all that."

I wasn't sure I liked how obsessed he'd become with Penny's coffee. "All we need to do is load the horses. We can put coffee in travel mugs and take it with us. We know where we're meeting later. Your GPS works as well as mine."

"I understand you want to get going."

"If you want to hang around, go ahead. Becca and I are leaving."

I followed Becca to her trailer and stowed the rest of the tools. Then, we brought the horses out of the barn and led them in, one by one. Beau and Sasha had always been easy to work with. Though it had been years since they'd stepped foot up a ramp, they followed me in without hesitation.

"Such good horses," I crooned to them.

Dex met us inside the house and had a cup of coffee ready for each of us. *Not* in travel cups.

"I don't know how you take yours, Miss Brannon," he said as he handed Becca a mug.

"Thanks. I can fix it."

I took mine to the kitchen, went through cabinets, found a stash of insulated thermoses, and plonked them on the counter. I poured my coffee into one, handed another to Becca, and turned to Penny.

"Do we need to do anything else in here before leaving?"

Susan and I had already disposed of the perishables when we'd cleaned on Friday.

"Nope." She had Isabella strapped into her carrier. "We're ready."

All three of us turned to Dex. He held up his hands as if at gunpoint.

"I know when I'm outnumbered." He flung is duffle over his shoulder. "Let's go."

It was full dark by the time we pulled out of the drive. A profound sense of relief washed through me to finally be on the road.

We'd gotten about half a mile when another large vehicle came toward us. As we passed each other, I realized it was a pickup truck hauling a gooseneck horse trailer. There were no other horse farms up this road but mine.

"Well, crap," I said.

"Don't tell me we need to go back?" Becca groused.

"I think we'd better."

She swore and complained the whole time she used a neighbor's drive to turn the rig around. I was beginning to like her. I waved at Penny and Dex to keep going, but they followed us.

The first thing I saw as the headlights swept the drive was a black Lab sniffing around the hydrant.

"Dang," I said. "That looks just like my dog."

Becca pulled behind the other trailer. It had a temporary plate as if it had just been purchased.

Becca craned her neck to peer around the side of the other rig. "Hmmm...juicy."

I couldn't see whatever she was referring to. "What does that mean?"

"There's some serious ass eye broccoli coming this way."

I frowned at her, got out and went around the front of the truck saying, "Can I help you?" as I did.

"I imagine you can," a man answered.

My stomach flipped and my heart leapt into my throat.

CHAPTER TWENTY-SEVEN

"Malcolm?"

We fell against one another, holding so tight it hurt. I inhaled what felt like my first ever breath, filling my senses with him, reveling in the press of his body against mine.

"What are you doing here?" I asked.

"God, it's good to see you," he said at the same time. He squeezed me tighter, lifting me off the ground.

Dex and Penny's headlights caught us for a moment. I kept my face buried in Malcolm's neck. Noire ran over and jumped on me. I petted her.

"Good girly," I said.

"I got your message," he said.

I sniffed, realized I was crying. "That was just a couple of hours ago. You didn't get here from Missouri since then."

"True. I left yesterday. But that's not what's important."

"It's not?"

"No. What's important is the answer to your question."

"My question?"

"If I wanted you to stay." He took my head in his big hands, put his nose to mine. "The answer is yes." His voice had gone rough, and he cleared his throat before adding, "A thousand times yes."

My heart felt like it stopped for a moment as if unsure what to do with that information, then it continued, stronger than ever. I blinked at him. The pressure began to build in my chest again.

"Even though I'm difficult?"

"Would I have driven all this way to bring you and the horses home if I wasn't?"

"You've never said…."

He put my head back into the cradle of his shoulder. "I know. I'm sorry. I guess I thought you knew how I felt. How good we are together. How right it feels to spend every day with you, to come home to you. I thought you felt it, too."

"I did—do—but…"

"You were afraid."

I nodded. If I tried to speak, my voice would break.

"Me too," he said.

Someone started clapping. I'd forgotten we had an audience.

"Could one of you explain what the heck's going on?" Becca asked. "At this rate, we'll be fighting the Monday morning commute."

I exhaled a watery laugh and gestured at the truck and trailer he'd driven in. The dusk-to-dawn light had come on, and I could see the truck was blue, the trailer aluminum. Exactly what I'd planned to get when I received the trust fund money.

"What's all this?"

Malcolm put his arm around my waist and walked me closer. "This, my love, is your birthday present."

"My birthday present? This is much too much for that. Even for a thirtieth birthday. That's crazy. You can't afford it." I knew his financials better than he did.

"I've been putting a little extra away for a while, but that's beside the point. I thought you'd say it was too much, so…" He dropped to one knee and took my hands.

This was not happening.

"Viola Parker, will you marry me?"

I found myself on my knees in front of him, my arms around his neck.

"Yes," I said. "A thousand times yes."

CHAPTER TWENTY-EIGHT

"But I'm not making the deadline to finish the one-year contract," I said.

"I already sent the paperwork in," he said.

He'd taken my hand and dragged me inside the barn where we could have a few moments of privacy. Yet, we spoke in hushed tones as if being loud might dispel the haze of euphoria surrounding us.

"I've missed you."

"Me too," I said, "but what do you mean, the paperwork?"

"I asked your parents where to send your glowing letter of recommendation and the confirmation that you worked for me for one full year by the time you were thirty."

"But I haven't."

"Do you, or do you not, still work for me?"

"Not if I'm engaged to you I don't."

"But you did up until a few minutes ago. Today completed the year. That was close enough."

I nuzzled the hollow at the base of his throat. "Was it glowing? Really?"

He kissed my forehead. "Rhapsodic." Another kiss to the tip of my nose. "Luminous." His lips brushed mine. "So incandescent the paper nearly caught fire."

I might catch the barn on fire again if we didn't quit soon. "Ummm. I like the sound of that." Then a thought occurred to me, and I pushed away from him. "What about Martina?"

"What about her?"

"I thought you two—"

He pulled me against him. "Never."

"But she said...she texted..."

"I know."

I pulled back as much as I could, but he wasn't letting me get far. "You knew?"

His face took on a pained look. "It was kind of my idea."

"What? Why?"

He rested his forehead against mine. "I wanted you to be sure."

"You wanted to make me jealous."

"Not exactly. I wanted to give you enough space to think objectively about us. I didn't want you to stay with me because it was easy or convenient or out of any sense of obligation—"

"You talk like you don't know me at all."

He took a long breath, let it out. "You're right. It was me who needed space. I didn't want the reason you stayed to be because you felt pressured. You make my life so much better, and I didn't want to confuse that with simply wanting you." His hands slid to my bottom and pressed me tighter to him. "And I do want you. All the frigging time."

"Is there a better reason?"

"I mean you've made Winterlight more than I ever hoped for. I didn't want to be greedy about that. I wanted you to stay only if it was the right thing for you."

I looked him in the eye. "I want to stay with *you*. Whether that's at Winterlight or someplace else doesn't matter."

He leaned against one of the stalls, and I rested against him. Comforting barn smells surrounded us—hay, shavings, horses. I never wanted to move, but we had to. The horses stomped in Becca's trailer, and I could hear the murmur of the others' voices. Isabella joined the conversation as well. Hand in hand, we went outside.

Penny jiggled the baby. Becca sat in her truck. Dex stood with his hip against the fender of my trailer wearing a wide smile.

"Nearly didn't make it in time," Malcolm said.

"I delayed as long as I could," Dex said. "But these are some efficient and determined women."

I looked from one to the other and tipped my head toward Malcolm.

"Let me guess," I said to Dex. "Your needy client?"

He nodded.

Sheesh. Clearly they'd been in contact the whole time. Someone could have enlightened me, but I was too happy at that moment to be mad at either of them.

We went over our plan again. We had enough people to drive straight through, but horses—and infants—needed frequent breaks.

I wanted to drive my new truck, ride with Malcolm, pilot Penny's car so she would rest, and make Malcolm and Dex sit together so they'd discuss what had made them fight, although it looked like they'd already resolved that. I didn't want Becca to have to be alone, and I hated asking Malcolm to turn around and travel for twenty hours again. What I wanted more than anything was to take him somewhere quiet and disappear together for a good long while.

But I couldn't make all those things happen. Not at the same time, anyway, and not without delaying our departure.

Everyone agreed we should leave as planned.

"Get me some of that coffee," Malcolm said. "I'll be fine."

Penny's strong brew had been fueling road trips for years.

"I'm used to driving by myself," Becca said. "I like it. I transport horses for other people all the time. That's mostly how I make a living. Don't worry about me."

I took her at her word. Malcolm pulled me aside and asked, "Is that Becca Scissorhands? What was your Shakespearean insult for her—the heavy-seated bugbear?"

I winced at my nicknaming creativity. He kissed my cheek, grinned, and climbed back into my pretty new truck. I went with Penny so we could pick up her car, ditch the rentals at the airport, and not have to backtrack.

"Holy crap, Vi," Penny said as soon as the doors shut. "What did you say to him? That's the most romantic thing I've ever seen."

My head floated above my neck like a helium balloon. If it weren't attached, it would float away. The pain in my chest had been replaced by a warm hum. "Yes," I said with a smile that made my cheeks hurt. "I said yes."

"Of course you did. You're not an idiot. I mean in the message you sent him. You did text him, right?"

I nodded. "Not much. Just that I missed him and wanted to stay at Winterlight, if he wanted me to."

"But he was already almost here when you sent it." She sighed. "Wow. He came all this way to get you. What was in the box? Let me see your ring."

"Oh," I said with a glance at my naked hand. "No ring. It was the key fob for my new truck."

"That's not very mushy."

"Maybe not to you. It's perfect for me."

We sipped coffee. Isabella cooed from the back seat. "See," I said, "Issa agrees. She's a smart one."

Penny tsked and shook her head. "He's going to get you a ring, right?"

"It's not about the ring, Penny. I don't care about that."

She stared out the window for a few minutes. We'd reached the highway and merged with the Sunday-night-going-back-to-the-city cars. It was early in the season yet, and traffic wasn't as congested as it would be come Memorial Day.

"Maybe you're the smart one after all," Penny said after a while.

A short time later, she fell asleep. Dex shut the back door as quietly as he could when I picked him up, and she didn't wake.

Via the rearview mirror, I watched Dex gently run the back of one finger over Issa's downy hair. This soft side of Dex really had me stumped. I enjoyed it, but it made me wonder if he had designs on my cousin and her young daughter. He at least was enamored of the baby—the last thing I would have expected of him. But he was soon snoring as well, and I turned my attention to negotiating the highways and bridges that would take us to the other side of Manhattan. I drank all my coffee as well as theirs. Even so, by the time I caught up with Malcolm and Becca at a rest stop in Pennsylvania, I could barely keep my eyes open. We let the horses rest for twenty minutes, Dex took over driving Penny's car without protest from her—telling in and of itself—and I got in with Malcolm.

My new wheels had bucket seats and a center console. For a moment, I longed for the torn bench of my old truck. We'd be able to sit next to each other, he'd put his arm around me, and I'd fall asleep secure in his strength. Instead, I adjusted my seat nearly flat and took in a deep breath of new-car smell. Noire licked me from her perch in the back, then positioned herself so she could rest her chin near my ear. I told Malcolm I loved him—if nothing else, I had to love a man who would drive all that way to come get me and two horses and a cat he didn't need, *and* bring my dog with him—and conked out.

I sit on Wastrel, bareback, no bridle. With his high withers, he isn't the most comfortable horse to ride without a saddle, but I like feeling his warmth through my jeans. Heatless fire presses in from all sides. I'm unable to see anything except the flames, yet I know we are in Ed Todd's barn. I cannot hear Ed or the horses. I'm afraid. I tangle my fingers in Wastrel's mane and urge him forward, but he doesn't move. What does he want me to see?

I hear flapping wings above and wonder if it is the blackbird from the show, the one that flew out of not-Dex's back. Am I on the wrong lead about him? Is this about him and nothing to do with Harry and Ed and the fire?

Finally, we walk forward, Wastrel's shod feet clip-clopping on the aisle's concrete, then soft ground. We leave behind the fire and enter a cloud of thick fog or smoke. The bird keeps pace. I can't see it, but I can hear it. I am muzzy from lack of sleep. The fog is a warm blanket that smells like a gentle rain shower, soothing and soft. I want to nod off. The gentle rhythm of Wastrel's undulating back is like being rocked in a cradle. My eyes close.

The bird flies in my face, startling me. Before us, the fog clears. Winterlight stretches below us as if we are viewing it from the bird's eye. We have never flown before, and although I don't believe I can fall, I clamp my legs tighter. Wastrel swings away from the barn and pasture, over the house, and down to the acres of timber that parade to the river. Wind whips my hair back and drags tears from the corners of my eyes.

The trees are leafing out, but I can see horses and riders galloping single file along one of the trails. Three, no, four. It's not safe to go that fast on that stretch. I know because I could ride those paths in my sleep.

Wastrel drops closer making my stomach flip as if on an airplane experiencing turbulence. The blackbird flits through the branches of a shag-bark hickory ahead of us. We get alongside the group, keeping up without touching the ground, silently gliding through the forest where there is no trail, trees and branches slipping through us. Still, I duck and gasp each time a trunk or limb blocks our way.

At the lead of the running horses, it's me, intently riding Malcolm's big chestnut Selle Francaise, Gaston. His long strides eat up the ground but Becca is closing the distance, her new mare pulling on the reins to catch us. A couple of strides behind her is Emily riding hell bent for leather on Captain. Several horse lengths back, Sandy and Fawn huff and puff to keep up.

This isn't a fun outing. We're being chased. No, we are chasing someone. Two someones twist and turn their mounts through the trees up ahead. Too quick. A switchback into a ravine is coming up fast. At this speed, they'll miss the turn, crash through the underbrush, and tumble down the steep hill.

We need to stop them. But I have no control. Wastrel swerves into the path in front of the other me, and I nearly topple to the ground. But I hang on, and we begin to catch up with the two we're chasing. I can't see the riders, but I recognize the horses. The second is Dex One's mare, Ciqala, her powerful haunches bunching with each stride, her hooves slinging dirt.

In front of him, frothing with sweat from being repeatedly whipped on the side with a riding crop, is the only dark bay at Winterlight.

Cali.

CHAPTER TWENTY-NINE

THE TRUCK EASED THROUGH A DIP, and the change in speed and motion together with the creak of trailer connections brought me out of a deep sleep. Daylight had me squinting when I tried to open my eyes.

"Where are we?" I yawned around the question.

"Truck stop in eastern Ohio."

"That's it? Is Pennsylvania a long-ass state or what?"

Malcolm reached for my hand, raised it to his lips, kissed my fingers. "Yup. I suppose it's just as long going east to west as going west to east, but it doesn't seem quite as bad with you by my side and knowing we're heading home. Even if you have been snoring worse than your dog the whole way."

I jerked my hand out of his. "Have not."

He exited the truck, came around to my side, and slipped my hand into his again as I got out. "You'll need to take over after breakfast."

I squeezed his fingers. "Love to."

He put his arm around my shoulders and pulled me against him. I inhaled contentment.

"By the way," he said. "Happy thirtieth birthday."

"Thank you. Thirty. Such a big, round number."

"The thirties are good. Trust me. And yours are going to be extra good." He kissed the top of my head.

Waking, I'd fallen into a bliss dream. Sleeping, not so much.

Becca pulled up next to us, and Dex and Penny next to her. We waited while she organized Isabella, whose pink cheeks and sagging lids clearly showed she'd just been tugged from dream land like me. She rested her head on Penny's shoulder. I took the diaper bag, and we went in to eat.

"This would be a good place to take the horses out to stretch their legs," Becca said.

I nodded my agreement and took out my phone to send a quick text to Emily making sure all is well at home. I didn't know what the dream meant, and I hoped it wasn't a premonition, but dread roosted in my gut.

My phone dinged, but it wasn't Emily.

Ciao Bella. Buon Compleanno!

Giacomo, wishing me happy birthday. I chuckled.

"What?" Penny asked.

I showed her my phone. She frowned at it. "What does it say?"

"It says 'Hello Beautiful. Happy Birthday!'"

"Oh my God. How could I forget?" She reached for my hand. "Happy Birthday. I had a present for you and left it at home. Darn it."

I leaned my head on Malcolm's shoulder. "I don't need any presents." I texted thanks to my grandfather.

"It's getting thick in here," Becca said.

We ignored her.

"Now, you're an old lady," Penny said.

"You'll be one, too, in a few months." It was what we always said to each other on my birthday.

My phone dinged again.

Glad to know you're on your way home. Happy Birthday baby girl <birthday cake>

That, from my father. I'd barely answered him when one came from my mother.

You made it. Shopping after you get back? <Champagne bottle> <shopping bags> <heart> <heart>

I smiled. But the scary dream intruded on my happiness. We sat in a booth next to the front window. Our vehicles were visible in the truck lot off to the side, but tractor-trailers kept going by. I didn't like not being able to keep constant watch.

"They'll be fine," Dex said.

"What are you worried about?" Penny asked.

I flicked my gaze to her. "Nothing."

Becca clunked down her coffee mug and signaled the waitress to bring more. "You think we're stupid? You've barely taken your eyes off the trailers since we sat down."

"You're sleep deprived," I said.

She gave me a mocking smile. "Are you scorning me, thou currish weather-bitten mammet?"

I wasn't sure whether to be horrified or proud. She'd just called me a snappish old god—or goddess—using the same Shakespearean insults I did.

Malcolm groaned. "Not two of you?"

Dex snorted. Penny's eyes went wide with concern. The old me would have shot a worse insult right back, and the situation would have quickly gotten ugly. Instead, I gave Becca my best smile.

"The fool doth think she is wise, but the wise woman knows herself to be a fool." I was far from a Shakespeare scholar, but I'd managed to memorize a few pithy quotes besides the insults.

"As You Like It," Becca said. "If paraphrased. Good one."

"Not paraphrased," Penny corrected. "She just made the pronouns feminine."

Oh, my dear sis-co. Always and forever on my side. She'd completed a minor in Shakespeare studies in college. That was when my fascination with the bard's words began.

Becca lifted her eyebrows at Penny then turned to me. "I am a tad fore-spent, but that doesn't mean I can't tell you're worried about something or looking for someone."

Having Becca around would be a constant challenge. That could be good. Or bad.

"I have a few hours left in me," Dex said, pulling her attention from me. "If you don't mind, Miss Brannon, I can drive the horses for a while."

"I guess that's all right if everyone else trusts you." She covered her mug when the waitress brought the coffee pot.

Dex gave Becca his best squinty-eyed detective look, but she ignored him. I smiled and held up my cup for the frazzled waitress to fill, delighted to have my family around me and glad the conversation had gone in a different direction. I didn't want to share the dream. But even though it hadn't woken me as they so often did, unease made my belly tighten around my breakfast. The sooner we got back on the road, the better.

I checked my phone. Still no answer from Emily.

We were walking out when a flash of red near the parking lot entrance caught my eye. I must have gone pale because Malcolm took my elbow and asked, "What is it?" He looked in the direction I stared, but the vehicle had already sped away.

"It...I think...no, couldn't be. I'm sure it was my imagination."

Dex had his spidey senses out, I could tell, scanning all the vehicles within range. "What did you see, Miss Parker?"

By the tone of his voice, I knew he'd brook no crap from me on this.

"A red Range Rover," I said. "I'm sure of it. Almost sure. Like the one in the garage at Harry's East Hampton house."

"The one that was at Ed Todd's hooked up to a trailer when we left?" Dex asked.

"Very same," I said, though I didn't want it to be. "Or not. Land Rover probably sold more than one of those in a five hundred-mile radius."

"Not sure I like coincidences like that," Malcolm said.

He, of course, was completely read-in on everything that had been going on.

"What if it is?" Penny asked. "What does it mean?"

I blinked at her. Becca had already started for the trucks. I followed, hoping Dex would field this query.

"Nothing at all," I heard him reassure my cousin. "Just surprising."

"Vi looked scared, though."

I pretended I didn't hear, but could tell Dex had taken Isabella from her by way of distraction.

"Vi's just tired," he said. "After all, Harry was the last one to drive it, and he's in jail."

Penny made some response that indicated her ruffled feathers had been soothed. I walked Noire, then Millie, and fed them. Dex took Beau and Sasha to a grassy area far from the traffic. Becca led her mare in the same direction. Malcolm gave the trailer a quick cleaning, refilled hay nets and offered water to the horses. We were soon back on the road.

Dex drove Becca's truck after some terse instructions from her, and she agreed to ride with Penny so she wouldn't be alone. I thought Malcolm might go with Dex, but he said he'd stick with me.

"I don't like it," he said. "If that Range Rover *is* the one from the Ed Todd's place."

I refused to fuel his worry and considered calling Susan and asking her to check if Baba's vehicle was still at Ed Todd's. But it was Monday . She'd be with her youngest grandson. I wouldn't bother her.

"Get some rest," I said to Malcolm.

He gave me a look but dropped it and put his seat back. Soon, he was snoring worse than my dog.

We'd been driving about an hour when I saw the red Range Rover again, parked at a small rest stop. That could not be a coincidence. I watched in the side and rearview mirrors but couldn't tell whether it got on the highway behind us or not. I called Dex.

"I saw it," he said. "It's following."

"Shit. Who do you think it is?"

"Can't be Harry."

"You think it's Baba?"

I couldn't see him but knew he'd shrugged. We stayed on the line together without speaking. I knew he was thinking, processing all the details we knew.

Could it be Harry? How could he have gotten himself released already? As for Baba, even off her meds, she had no reason to pursue me across the country.

While I waited for Dex to gather his thoughts, I pictured Babette on that Christmas morning when I discovered Cali at their place. She'd called me to say Santa Claus had left a gift for me. I'd expected some extravagant gesture from Harry like several cases of canned whipped cream. But no. Cali stood in a stall wrapped in a red-and-green blanket that had a note pinned to it. Baba, wreathed in smiles and Christmas cheer, had brought me a steaming mug of hot chocolate and left me alone.

That was when I learned Harry had bought Cali for me. The note said he'd gotten her *for a song* after the mare put Becca in the hospital at a show a few months prior. Harry had gone away, he'd written, *to get better*. He'd accused me of being *cold backed*—that I never let anyone stick, especially him —just like the mare, and wished me luck. He said he hoped one day to earn more than my disdain.

Dex interrupted my thoughts. "When we get to Columbus, there's two ways to go around the city. We'll stay on 70. You go north on 270."

"Okay, but—"

"Speed up and get ahead of me. On the northwest side of the city, take 33 toward Marysville then take 42 back down to 70. I'll catch up. Stay alert."

My heart rate kicked up a notch. "Take 270 to 33 to 42 to 70. Got it."

"A few miles after you get back on 70, there's a rest stop. Go there unless you hear differently from me."

"What about Penny and Becca?"

"I'll call them."

I did as he said, glad Malcolm slept through the entire exchange.

My heart still pounded too hard for comfort. Snippets of conversations banged against each other in my head. Harry insisting we belonged together. Dex's questions from the night before—had Harry *always* gotten *everything* he wanted?

He hadn't.

Harry hadn't gotten me.

My body went cold. I turned down the truck's fan and stared through the windshield without really seeing what was in front of me.

Oh, Harry. Surely not. We were friends. Had I hurt him so badly? I'd been oblivious to his feelings for me all this time. I'd had a crush on him when we first met, and we sort of went out a few times, but then I found him in a compromising position with a man, and that was it. We'd continued as buddies, but nothing more.

Or so I thought.

An hour and a half later, I pulled into the rest stop. Malcolm woke.

"I need to pee," I said and hopped out.

He yawned, nodded, and kept sleeping.

Dex brought his rig up next to ours, got out, came over.

"Did you tell me Harry gave you your new phone last year?"

I nodded. "Yes, why?"

"Has it been acting strangely?"

"Can you be more specific?"

He spoke quickly. "Lighting up when you haven't touched it, random beeping noises, shutting down by itself, battery running out when you haven't used it?"

"I guess, but it's always been like that."

"Goddamn it. Get it." With a glance over his shoulder toward the highway, he added, "Now."

I returned to my truck, pulled the device out of the console, gave it to him. He started tapping and swiping.

"What is it? What do you think's going on?"

"I slowed down and blocked the Rover," he said. "You got way ahead. There's no way they saw where you got off."

"So?"

"So, when you got back to 70, they were still tailing you."

I looked around. "What? Where?"

"They got off a couple of exits back. Get your stuff." He handed me my phone. "Take this inside and drop it in someone's bag or pocket."

"A thousand dollar phone?"

"Just do it and get back on the road." He shoved Becca's keys in my other hand. "I'm taking your truck. Hurry."

I grabbed my purse and Noire and ran inside. Once there, I hesitated, scanning the interior for a target. This wasn't a gas station or restaurant, simply a highway rest stop with restrooms and vending machines and that smelled too strongly of disinfectant. Near the water fountain, a young woman juggled a purse along with two small children and a baby in a stroller. It would be easy to slip the phone into one of the diaper bag pockets.

Would I be endangering someone? Why didn't I ask any questions? Dex was ruthless when it came to protecting his own. I pulled up the birthday text messages, read them one last time, then locked the device.

I headed toward the restroom hoping to cross paths with a brawny truck driver. There were several tractor trailers in the parking lot but few people inside. The woman with the kids had already left. A couple of teenaged boys came in. They carried nothing, and their tight jeans already had mobile devices in the back pockets.

Just when I'd begun to think I'd have to ditch the phone in a trash can, a wall of a man exited the men's room. He wore loose overalls, a plaid shirt, and thick boots. A well-trimmed beard covered much of his face and swirling tattoos adorned his solid forearms. Truck driver? Motor cycle guy? Didn't matter. A black leather backpack with the zipper slightly open hung from one thick shoulder. As we passed each other, I slipped the phone inside, then ducked into the ladies room. I locked myself in a stall and tried to calm my breathing.

God help me. What had I done? What was going on? I hadn't heard back from Emily, and as someone who prided herself on not caring about being constantly connected, I suddenly felt isolated.

I used the facilities, washed my hands, splashed cold water on my face.

Tattoo guy lingered at the snack machine, clearly indecisive about what to get. I sat on a bench pretending to clean my fingernails. The teenagers came out, both engrossed in their mobile devices. Noire sat beside me. Her tail thumped the tiled floor when the boys went by, but they didn't look up. After a long moment during which I feared my presence might become awkward, my target's blunt fingers finally stabbed at the number pad of the snack machine.

I patted Noire and started to rise. But no. My prey moved a couple of steps to mull over what drink would go with his bag of Cheetos.

My nervous knee started bouncing. I pressed my hands along my thighs, but it didn't help. Why these places didn't have whipped cream machines was beyond me.

I couldn't wait any longer to be sure he left without noticing my phone. Dex said hurry. This guy would surely get going soon.

When I got back to the horses, Becca's rig sat alone. There was no sign of Dex and Malcolm or my new truck and trailer.

CHAPTER THIRTY

I TURNED IN A SLOW CIRCLE.

They left me?

I had no way of contacting them. Or of being contacted. Cold panic crept up the back of my neck. The breeze chilled my sweaty face.

They left me.

A shiver shook my whole body.

I spun on my heel. Where was tattoo guy? I glanced up in time to see him exit the building, the backpack still hanging open. I fast-walked toward him, trying to calm my unsteady breaths and create a story for how my phone ended up in his bag. But he squished himself into a plum-colored Prius and sped away before I made it halfway across the parking lot.

I reversed and ran for Becca's truck. Noire bounced at my side, thinking this was a fun new game, but I couldn't respond to her.

They'd left me.

I wasn't alone. I had the horses and Noire and Millie. For a moment, I thought to follow tattoo guy's car, but the point of offloading the device was to send our pursuers in a different direction. I think, anyway. It happened so fast. Dex must have found or suspected spyware for him to tell me to get rid of the phone.

How? And by whom? Harry had given me the phone. Why would Harry put spyware on it?

Or drive all the way to Missouri to move my barn implements when I wasn't there?

Or nearly run me over?

Or be following me now?

Had he been the one who shot at me and Dex?

Our pursuers, whoever they might be, could be anywhere. Once again, that swift current sucked at my legs. Had I given any thought to how I might spend my thirtieth birthday, this wasn't it.

I pushed down the clutch, put the truck in gear, and slowly pressed the gas so as not to unbalance the horses. Millie made a plaintive sound. She'd need a break from the crate soon.

Back on the highway, there was no sign of the purple Prius. Nor the red Range Rover. Nor my blue truck and silver trailer. Due west, heavy clouds darkened the horizon. Great. A storm. And we were all headed straight into it.

CHAPTER THIRTY-ONE

THE STORM HIT with the ferocity of a hurricane. First, a powerful headwind tried to push us backwards. Behind it came a short hail storm that at first made me fear we were being shot at again. I ducked but kept a firm grip on the steering wheel, barely keeping us straight and in our lane. Next came a punishing downpour whipped horizontal by the high winds. The late afternoon turned dark and only got darker as afternoon became night. The wipers couldn't clear the windshield fast enough. Tension had my body drawn tighter than a fishing line hooked to a shark. Along with other drivers, I slowed and turned on the emergency flashers. Some pulled off under the overpasses to wait it out.

After a couple of exhausting hours, I got off the highway at a busy intersection where gas stations, fast food restaurants, strip malls, and big-box stores all competed for shoppers.

No sign of the Prius or the Range Rover. Nor had I caught sight of Dex and my new rig or Penny and Becca. Not that I'd been looking all that hard. Driving through the storm had consumed all my attention and energy.

I pulled into the far end of a Walmart supercenter where there was plenty of room, and sat for a few minutes shaking out my tense legs and arms, stretching my cramped back and shoulders, and flexing sore fingers, noting they trembled only a little. I pressed my hands flat over my chest. Surely it wasn't healthy for my heart rate to be so high for so long.

Contending with the storm had left no time for wondering about Harry's intentions. But now all that plowed into me again. And what of Dex taking off with Malcolm like that? Had they really sorted out their fight? Dex had been acting strange the entire trip.

Goosebumps lifted the hair on my arms. My nervous knee started bouncing. My state must have been obvious to Noire. She nudged her nose under my arm and licked my cheek. I hugged her, smoothed her ears, scratched her neck, and felt calmer. The knowledge that Malcolm had brought her to me eased some of the tension. He loved me. Amazing.

But was he all right? Or was he captive of some scheme that had nothing to do with Harry and Ed and whatever the motivation might be behind all that?

I shook myself. This line of thinking did me no good.

I left Noire in the truck and loosed Millie inside the trailer where she could use the pine shavings as a litter box. The horses looked tired and needed hay.

At the moment, I had a more important mission. By the time I got inside the store, I was soaked but didn't care. The sprint had felt good, the movement loosening me up and releasing some of the strain on my body. The temperature had dropped, and the cool rain felt refreshing. The store's air conditioning, on the other hand, immediately made me tense again. I grabbed a cart and blindly plucked a couple of shirts and a package of socks off a rack in the clothing area, grabbed towels as I whizzed through home goods, and snatched up a pair of sneakers before jogging to electronics.

I clipped a metal shelf somewhere around sporting goods, nearly toppled an entire endcap of tortilla chips as I took a turn through the grocery section, then cut off an elderly couple to beat them to a register.

I was out of breath but the checkout girl barely glanced at me and my dripping hair or the towel draped over my shoulders as she scanned my purchases—two packages of pre-sliced apples and peanut butter, a bottle of water, a can of whipped cream, and the cheapest prepaid mobile phone I could find along with the dry clothes. And…what the hell? Somehow, one of those reusable ice pack thingies that go in coolers had ended up in my cart. I was about to say I didn't want it, but it was already scanned and in the bag. I grabbed everything and returned to electronics to get the phone activated and the card of minutes I'd bought loaded up so I could use it.

I flung it all in the trailer's dressing room and took Noire for a walk before drying her off. I donned one of the new shirts—which turned out to be an extra large ribbed camo tank with ruffles—just my style, socks—very fashionable white crews, and shoes—yellow slip-on Tom's knockoffs, and sucked down half a can of whipped cream. Then I sat for a few minutes listening to the rain pound the roof before calling Penny. Hers was the only number I had memorized.

She didn't answer. Of course not. She wouldn't pick up a call from an unknown number anymore than I would. I texted her that it was me. A few moments later, she responded with,

What color was my first bicycle?

WTactualF? I answered. *Pink. WITH TASSELS AND A WHITE BASKET!!!!*

My new phone rang.

"For God's sake," I said.

"Dex said to ask you something to make sure it was you."

The line crackled with interference, which made me suspect someone was listening in. Damn Dex. "Is he there?"

"No," Penny answered. "I haven't…him. But he called…and…you'd lost your phone."

"If I lost my phone, I'd be calling you from the same number because I'd…" I pressed my thumb and forefingers against my eyebrows. She was probably getting only every few words like I was. "Never mind. Where are you?"

"Getting ready to stop…Indianapolis…dinner. Storm…. We…overnight. Isabella needs to get out of the car for a while."

I just loved how everyone carried on without me. What had Dex told them?

"You better not be stripping the gears in my truck," Becca yelled from the background. "Or jerking around my new horse."

Somehow everything she said came through loud and clear. My back teeth clamped together. "Tell her I know perfectly well how to drive a stick, and her horse is fine, as are mine, thank you very much."

"I think she heard you. I'm pretty sure Dex and Malcolm did as well."

The line cleared. "Where are they?"

"I don't know. Driving straight through, they said."

They would.

"Call me when you know where you're going to be," I said. "I'll catch up as soon as I can."

By the time I got back behind the wheel, I was wet again. Not quite soaked through, but I'd tried to get Millie back in the carrier before starting off, and she was having none of it. I left her in the trailer. She knew how to keep out from under the horse's feet, and she'd be happier where she could move around. I left her a bowl of food, and we were off.

Now that I was back in contact and had presumably shaken our pursuers,

I felt more relaxed. Hearing Penny's voice calmed me. The storm was at a lull, but the forecast, according to local radio, called for it to continue. We wouldn't drive out of it until some time tomorrow.

I called Penny back and asked her to text me Malcolm's and Dex's mobile numbers. We'd all exchanged each other's info before leaving. I also asked her to call one of them to give them my new number.

A couple of minutes later, my phone rang. I grabbed it off the seat expecting it to be Malcolm, but it was Penny.

"I called and texted them both," she said.

"Okaaaayyy?"

"I don't know if it is okay. Neither of them is answering."

CHAPTER THIRTY-TWO

MY MIND LOCKED UP, then immediately jumped to the worst possible conclusion.

They'd been in a wreck.

Harry'd run them off the road and they were dead in a ditch.

Harry'd shot them.

Harry'd set my new rig on fire with them in it.

He'd beaten them to death with a stirrup.

I took my foot off the gas and put my blinker on to move into the right lane. I felt like I might throw up. Everything I knew was wrong. I was a terrible judge of character. How could I have trusted and loved someone as evil as Harry all these years? Everyone and everything I cared about was gone because of him.

Okay, several worst possible conclusions.

"Vi." Penny said. "The guys are fine."

I'd nearly forgotten we were still connected. Obviously, not everyone I cared about was gone. Noire kept herself cuddled against me. I wiped my eyes and pressed one hand against my queasy stomach as if that alone could settle it back into place. Now was not the time to lose it.

"I'm sure you're right," I said to Penny with scant conviction. "Text me the address of where you decide to stop. And let me know immediately if you hear from them."

We hung up.

It was the storm, I told myself. They were in a spot where they had no service.

I held Noire close and repeated this idea over and over as I drove and listened to twangy country music. Not my favorite, but the only station that would come in clearly.

Bleary eyed and wiped out, I pulled into a hotel on the outskirts of Indianapolis a couple of hours later. The rain had eased to a steady shower, and driving had become easier for a while. Even so, if it hadn't been time to get off the highway, I would have had to stop anyway.

I hadn't heard from anyone other than Penny letting me know where she and Becca were, and their room number.

Which turned out to be Penny's and *my* room number. Becca wanted to sleep in her truck to stay close to the horses. Fine with me. The place was pet-friendly—not including equines—and I brought Noire and Millie inside.

"I thought you were stopping for dinner," I said.

"Too tired," Penny said around a yawn. "Room service will do. I already ordered you a burger and fries." She stretched out on the bed with Isabella by her side. "And no, I haven't heard from anyone. Do you think—"

"I don't know what to think. I'm sure they're okay, like you said."

I'd texted Malcolm, told him I was worried, and asked him to call me as soon as possible. I usually kept things light between us, but we were engaged now, and dammit, he should let me know what the hell was going on.

I wanted to start reading Ed's diaries but nodded off before the food arrived. We ate in silence, took turns showering, and went to bed.

I closed my eyes but couldn't sleep. Images of a demolished truck surrounded by emergency vehicles kept flashing in my mind's eye. For once, I wished for the oblivion of sleep and Wastrel's familiar, if aggravating, presence. I needed him to help me sort things out, to tell me why I was on the wrong lead.

The air conditioner droned on, then off. Other guests went down the hall making no effort to be quiet. Next door, someone flushed the toilet, then took a shower.

The temperature in our room was comfortable, but I couldn't get warm. Fear and worry skittered relentlessly beneath my skin. I pulled Noire closer. She put her head on my shoulder. I stared at the ceiling thinking I'd rather be sleeping outside with the horses. But I wasn't exactly ready to snuggle up with Becca, so I stayed put.

Some time later, I thought I was dreaming when I opened my eyes to Millie balanced on my chest, her green eyes glowing in the dark. I jumped.

She hooked her claws into my skin and held on. Something brushed against my face. I sat up and turned on the light.

There, on the pillow next to me, a dead freaking mouse. I poked it. Fresh but definitely expired. Noire lifted sleepy lids, then her keen nose started sniffing. I snatched up the rodent before she made a midnight snack out of it and dropped it on the bedside table.

"Christ almighty," I whispered. "What the hell, Millie? Do you conjure these things out of thin air or did you pack a few for the trip?"

Issa started to cry. Penny murmured something soothing and pulled up her oversized T-shirt so the baby could nurse. To me, she hissed, "Can you keep it down? And turn off the damned light."

"Sorry." I snapped off the lamp and looked at the cat with a frown, which I'm sure she could see even in the dark.

Slowly, my eyes adjusted. Street lights lent a dim gleam to the room. Millie stared at me with an unreadable expression, but I got the feeling she was trying to tell me something. I picked up the mouse by the tail muttering, "I thought this was a nice hotel," on my way to the bathroom where I flushed the dead body.

Millie followed, winding around my bare legs, then putting her front feet on the toilet seat to watch her catch swirl away. Noire slid off the bed and followed. I shut the door. The two of them sat side by side, Noire's glossy black coat a stunning contrast to Millie's white. I washed my hands and sat on the edge of the tub, elbows on my knees, fists under my chin, and canted my head at the cat. "I'm awake, now, thanks. What's on your mind?"

Her tail twitched. Her lime-colored eyes met mine. We gazed at each other for what felt like a full minute without blinking.

A thought formed and wriggled its way up from my subconscious. It was born from the notion that Millie had always been an amazing mouser, keeping Ed Todd's barn free of rodents for years.

So…how was it that mice had gotten into the electrical panel to chew the wires and cause the fire?

I stood, suddenly filled with energy and purpose. "Oh my God, Millie, you're brilliant. Thank you." I bent to pet her, and she pushed her nose against my fingers is if acknowledging my sudden insight.

Penny's smart phone sat on the bedside table. I retrieved it and returned to the bathroom. I didn't have anyone's numbers stored in my new phone, and it didn't have an internet browser, but I looked up Susan's number from Penny's phone and soon had what I needed—except for a reasonable time of day to make phone calls. It was two in the morning. An hour later back on the Island, but I didn't think Susan would appreciate her phone ringing this early even for something this important. I'd have to wait until later to call and ask her what I wanted to know.

I sat on the toilet, my knee bouncing with anticipation instead of nervousness for a change. I went back out to the room, got my whipped cream from the mini-fridge, and took my phone into the bathroom as well.

Sitting on the toilet, I took a long pull from the can before waking my device.

No text or voice messages.

Where the hell were Malcolm and Dex? I glared at the screen willing a notification to pop up. I found a puzzle game on Penny's phone and played that for while by way of distraction, but couldn't keep my gaze from constantly checking my own for a message.

Half an hour later, one arrived.

Sorry, my love. Ran into a bit of trouble. We're fine. Let me know where you are when you wake up.

Was he kidding? I nearly slid off the slippery toilet lid as relief swept through me. My thumbs flew over the keys.

Awake. Hotel east of Indy. Where are you? What kind of trouble?

He didn't answer right away, and I'd run out of patience. I grabbed a room key, went to the hallway, and called him.

"You had me scared to death," I said when he answered.

"I know. I'm sorry."

"What's going on? Where are you?"

"We're at a hotel off 70 near…where the hell are we?"

"Budget hotel in Greenup, Illinois," I heard Dex say.

"Oh, good. You stopped. I'm glad. But why haven't you returned anyone's calls?"

"Yeah. About that. We had our phones off for a while and then forgot. And…um…your truck."

I went into the stairwell, ran down two flights as fast as I could without falling, and made my way outside. The night was damp and foggy and smelled faintly of diesel fuel, but it wasn't raining.

"I don't care about my truck. I'm just glad you're okay. What happened?"

Malcolm cleared his throat. "Dex had the bright idea to pull over to the side of the highway, hide in the woods, and see if anyone stopped to look at the rig."

"It was a good plan," Dex yelled.

"Okay," I said. "Anyone, as in whoever was driving the Range Rover?"

"Exactly."

"It worked," Dex yelled.

"Wasn't it raining?" I asked.

"Dex said that would be good cover." Malcolm sounded weary.

"It was," Dex said.

Had the man forgotten he'd been shot two days ago? "Do you have me on speaker phone?" I asked.

There was a beat of silence, then Malcolm said, "Not anymore."

"So, what happened? The Range Rover stopped? Who was it?"

"Not the Rover. After about an hour of sitting in the rain, a dark sedan pulled over. A man got out, not the driver. Before you ask, we couldn't see who was behind the wheel."

He paused. Sounded like he was taking a drink. I wanted to be there with him. To touch him. To see for myself that he was all right. "And?"

"Give me a chance to tell it." He cleared his throat again. "He walked all around, looked inside the trailer. Tried to open the truck, but we'd locked it. He went back to the car, apparently spoke to whoever was inside, then came out and slashed the tires."

"Slashed the tires? Why? You're killing me. Who was it?"

"Yes. I don't know. And we couldn't see his face."

"After all that, you didn't see who it was?"

"It was dark and raining," Malcolm said.

"I didn't have my night vision goggles," Dex said, still eavesdropping on the conversation even though he couldn't hear my side of it.

"We didn't need them," Malcolm said. "We couldn't see him clearly, but he was tall and trim with dark hair, and his left arm was in a sling." He paused, and when he spoke, his voice had gone cold. "Vi, we're sure it was Harry."

CHAPTER THIRTY-THREE

The good news? They were okay.

The not-so-good news? Harry really was the bad guy in all this. I could not accept it. Didn't want to believe it. Couldn't allow myself to deny it.

But who was driving the car he was in? *What* was driving him? Surely it wasn't that he'd never attained the one desire he said he wanted more than anything.

Me.

If that were the case, this wasn't exactly the way to go about achieving that goal. Not that it *was* achievable.

"I might have to kill him." Malcolm had that sharpness in his voice that scared me.

I decided to ignore the remark for the time being. "What do you think happened to the Range Rover?" I asked.

"My guess is they ditched it," he said. "Dex made a few phone calls, got the license plate number, and reported it."

Dex said something in the background I didn't catch.

"Oh, right," Malcolm said. "We made a report about the sedan and the tire slashing as well. But we didn't get the make and model or plate number."

Harry was a hunted man. If he were desperate enough before all this to chase me across the country, what might he do now? *Had* he killed his father? What was he capable of?

I didn't know him at all.

I sat on a wet bench in a small courtyard in front of the hotel and rubbed my tired eyes. "I guess you're waiting there for new tires?"

I'd barely driven my new rig, and it had already been through the ringer.

"Had it towed to a place closer to home," Malcolm said. "We'll stay here until you pick us up."

I hoped he didn't expect me to pay that towing bill. But I'd be very happy to see him. Both of them.

"Can you put Dex on?"

I heard Malcolm say, "She wants to talk to you," in an amused tone, and then Dex came on the line.

"Sorry about your truck."

"Nothing that can't be fixed. Listen, I thought of something, and I'm hoping you can do some research."

"I'm at your service, Miss Parker."

"You ought to be after that stunt. Have you forgotten you were shot all of forty-eight hours ago?"

"Even you said it was only a flesh wound."

I didn't want to let my relief at knowing they were okay transmute fear into anger, but it took a couple of deep breaths before I could speak without sounding exasperated. Anyway, I needed his help.

"I'm calling Susan in the morning, but maybe you can do something in the meantime. The fire at Ed's was deemed an accident caused by mice chewing the wires, right?"

"Not all that uncommon."

"Maybe in other barns, but not this one. Millie kept the place rodent free."

He didn't say anything for a long moment. I knew he'd draw the same conclusion I had. "You think the report was falsified?"

"Is that possible?"

"Sure. The insurance company probably sent its own investigator, and the local authorities would most likely accept his conclusions."

"Can you find out who the investigator was? Maybe ask him some questions?"

"It would be my pleasure."

Dex liked grilling suspects—anyone—a little too much. "Thanks. I'll call Susan in the morning and let you know if she remembers anything useful."

"Miss Parker, I believe we make a good team."

After saying goodnight to Malcolm, I returned to the room. Noire and Millie were both on my bed as far as they could get from each other. Noire had her head on a pillow, and Millie had curled herself into a tight ball near the foot at the opposite corner. My dog's tail thumped when I slid between them. I don't remember closing my eyes.

I am in a deep pine forest. The scent is sharp but soothing, the ground beneath my feet spongey with years of accumulated needles. I am on foot, but Wastrel is near, just the other side of some rough-barked trunks. Muted light slants through the dense branches. Each brush against one releases more of the clean, pitchy smell of pine while my steps free the musty odor of decay.

The space between the trees is tight. No way Wastrel and I could walk side by side. Branches hang so low I must duck beneath them. Wastrel walks through them.

Ahead, the trees thin and we enter a small clearing. At the center grows one towering evergreen. It is filled with glistening black birds who are noisy, the sounds grating and unpleasant. I realize I have seen them before. At Winterlight. What had Malcolm called them?

We walk around the tree. On the other side, the woods are more open, and the pines are interspersed with oaks, hickories, and maples. As one, the birds take flight with a whoosh. I flatten myself against Wastrel's side as they go by us like a winged train. Fast behind them comes the sound of galloping hooves. Two horses are on us before I realize what's happening, their riders pushing them and looking over their shoulders. They brush past us, so close I can smell their sweat, hear their labored breathing, but I have thrown my arm over my face for protection. It could be Cali and Ciqala again, but I don't look until it's too late, can't see the riders. They are being chased.

Then I'm on Wastrel, and we're sliding through the trees. The birds surround us, swooping and diving and calling out in their harsh voices as though egging us on. Their wings brush my face; their bodies bump against Wastrel's neck and shoulders.

The woods end. We ride off a cliff. The birds sail above us and away, so many they blacken the sky.

I surged up and awake, panting and sweating and gulping air as if I'd been drowning.

Sunlight streamed in through a gap in the curtains. Penny bent over Isabella, changing her diaper on the next bed. She glanced at me with a smile, but that quickly faded when she saw my face. "What's wrong?"

I lifted my hand to my chest. "Nothing. Bad dream." I rose, filled a glass with water, drank it down. "There's good news, actually. I heard from Malcolm and Dex last night. They had a little incident with the truck, and it's being towed to Missouri. We're to pick them up somewhere in Illinois."

Her smile returned and color rose to her cheeks. I feared she really was taken with Dex and that wouldn't end well. What if it was him riding his horse in the dream? Why would we be chasing him? And who was riding Cali?

"That is good news," she said. "But what sort of incident?"

"I'll tell you over breakfast."

Soon, we were on the road, Penny driving her car with me riding shotgun, and Becca happily alone in her truck. I spoke to Susan. What she told me put the final nail in Harry's coffin. I had been on the wrong lead about him all along, and Wastrel had been trying to warn me for months.

The last moment of the last dream hit me. Fear had me reaching for the armrest to steady myself. I breathed deeply, then called Dex.

"What did you find out?" I asked him.

"You want the bad news or the worse news?"

"I also learned something awful."

"You go first," he said in a voice that was all business—no trace of the charming and urbane Dex I'd met over the weekend.

"Apparently," I said, "Harry showed up right after the fire and offered to help Susan in any way he could."

"Mighty convenient, but sounds reasonable so far."

"Until you get to the part where he said his father would help hurry along the inspection and insurance payout."

"Which he apparently did," Dex said. "The paperwork was processed very quickly."

I let out a puff of air. Where was I when all this went down? Oh right, that was when my mother and I had been kidnapped by my grandfather's murderous cousin, Benito.

"Why didn't anyone call me?" I asked as much to myself as to Dex.

"It was all taken care of before Ed's will was found and read."

Before anyone knew I was to inherit. That made me feel slightly better. "So, is that the bad or the worse news?" I asked.

"Bad. The worse news is that shortly after handing in his report, the fire investigator was found dead."

I stared out the window for a few moments, gathering my thoughts. "Let me guess. It wasn't an accident."

"Not unless he accidentally beat himself to death with a gold stirrup."

CHAPTER THIRTY-FOUR

NOT ONLY WAS it not an accident, it was another deliberate killing. But if Harry was behind it all, had he beaten himself at the horse show? That seemed beyond the pale even for a drama queen like him. And if not, why hadn't he been killed like his father and the hapless fire investigator? If Harry's beating had been a threat or warning, then was he now being compelled against his will? Maybe by the guys he owed money to? What did that have to do with me?

And what of that cryptic text message from his mother? *Time's up!* Given that my phone might have been hacked from the get-go, was it possible Harry's was, too? Or Babette's? Last I knew, Babette refused to use a cell phone. Could they both be acting under duress?

As we drove along, I had only questions and no answers. I wanted to nap, but the current dream trend didn't feel particularly helpful. Worse, it scared me. Plus, I was too restless to sleep.

We picked up Malcolm and Dex. After stopping for lunch, Malcolm took over driving for Penny, and I got a stack of Ed's notebooks from the trailer. Dex hopped into Becca's truck with her. She gave him a glare, but that, of course, didn't daunt him. Penny slid into the backseat of her car with Isabella.

Ed started his daily writing early in his career when he had only himself and one horse. His entries were sketchy rather than prosy. He noted the date, the weather, how he worked his horse, what feed he was using, if his gelding's bowel movements were normal.

Only a few pages in, it was obvious his main goal at the time was to make connections and find better horses to ride. He competed in every show he could afford and listed those people whose acquaintance he'd made that day and what his or her network was. He was calculated in his pursuit of success. Like me, he worked for anyone who would hire him doing anything so long as it had to do with horses. Within his first year, he'd sold the gelding for a profit and bought two green prospects off the track. He already had his eye on the farm that eventually was his. And later, mine.

He approached the elderly couple who owned the place with an offer they couldn't refuse. He took over the management, moved into the tack room, brought in paying customers, and started making repairs. It worked well for all concerned. A couple of years later, confident the farm would be in good hands, they retired and offered it and all its contents to Ed for less than what any of it was worth.

He was in business.

We were driving beneath the Arch in St. Louis when I found Ed's entry for the first time he saw Babette. His writing style changed, became almost poetic.

On a blustery winter's day out fox hunting, he spied her sitting her horse in the only shaft of sunlight sneaking from behind the clouds. She looked like a queen, he wrote, and rode like an angel. Slim as a shingle, she was, with a tantalizing hint of glossy black hair showing beneath the edge of her helmet.

The hounds picked up a scent and were off before he had a chance to approach her. He galloped his horse as close to hers as he dared and later learned her name from another club member. It was only a matter of time before he introduced himself and they began talking.

I'd seen a few pictures of Ed when he was younger, but always in riding garb, usually wearing a helmet, mostly from far away. Tall and skinny. I supposed he was handsome. I'd just never looked at him that way. Not that it mattered. As Dex had rightly accused a few days before, I'd never thought of Ed as someone who'd had a life before I came along.

"Ed and Babette knew each other for a long time," I told Malcolm.

His eyebrows hiked up. "Significant?"

"Maybe."

I kept reading.

They spent quite a bit of time together, and Ed was clearly in love. As we turned into Winterlight's drive, I read that she had married Alcott Brown. Her parents insisted. She obeyed. She'd never made promises, Ed wrote, but she broke his heart.

I asked Ed once why he never married. He joked that horses were the love of his life. He didn't need more than that.

Everything Ed told me was gospel when I was a kid. I never questioned him, never gave it a second thought. But now I wondered. He'd been in love with Babette. Had she loved him back?

I looked up from reading, feeling car sick from having my head down in the dusty pages of Ed's diaries for so long.

Several cars filled the space in front of the barn. Giacomo and my parents stood in a group with our neighbors, Hank and Clara, as well as Emily, Renee, and Sandy and even Martina. Malcolm's mother, Helen, stood behind Hank and Clara.

"What the heck?"

My father held a sign that said, "Welcome Home!"

My mother held one that said, "Welcome Penny and Isabella!"

Hank and Clara held one up that said "Happy Birthday Vi!!"

Sandy jumped up and down making her sign hard to read, but I'm pretty sure it said, "Congratulations Malcolm and Vi!!!"

I turned to the man beside me, my fiancé. His wavy surfer hair gleamed. A day or two without shaving left an enticingly scruffy stubble on his square jaw. The muscles of his shoulders stretched his T-shirt tight across his pecs. I wanted to jump his bones the first moment we had. But that pleasure was obviously going to have to wait.

"Looks like you've been in communication with everyone."

He smiled, and his blue eyes glinted as if lit from within. My heart did a few extra pitter-pats inside my chest, thumping almost painfully against my sternum.

He took my hand.

Penny leaned forward to look through the windshield. "Wow. That's so nice."

The greeting was crazy over the top, but I had to admit I liked it. And I loved knowing I was finally home.

At the same time, I couldn't shake the apprehension brought on by the latest dreams.

"Your parents look amazing," Penny said.

She hadn't seen Gemma and Adrian since we were teenagers. My parents were only in their late forties and had been international ballroom dancing stars for years. They were fit and trim, and yeah, they looked good.

We got out. There were introductions and hugs and tears and cooing over the baby. Isabella ended up in my mother's arms. I watched diverse and ineffable emotions skitter across her face and knew she was remembering how she'd left me behind as an infant so long ago, feeling anew how much she regretted it.

Noire ran around sniffing everything, peed several times, then went in the barn to get a drink from the bowl by the hydrant.

We'd gotten at least a half hour ahead of Becca and Dex, and they were swinging through the airport for Dex to get his truck, so we had time before she arrived with the horses. I crooked my finger at Emily and Sandy to follow me into the barn and ready three stalls for our new guests.

Once they were at work, I walked the rest of the way down the aisle to the implement wall. Those not in use hung straight and true. I breathed a sigh of relief, then ducked through the fence into the pasture to check the herd.

With all present and accounted for, I stood amongst them, letting their strength and acceptance wash over me. Noire had followed, and she lolled at my feet begging for belly rubs. Cali stopped grazing to come up behind me. She put her chin on my shoulder, slid it to my clavicle, and pulled me back against her chest. I wrapped my arms around her beautiful head, then rubbed her eyes and ears while she nudged my pockets looking for treats.

"Good girl," I said. "You'll have to make do with petting for now."

She gave me a little shove to let me know what she thought of that.

"I'll bring you a carrot later. No complaining. You have all this lovely spring grass."

She pushed against my side. I slid my hand under her mane and scratched her neck where I knew she liked it. She stuck out her nose and her lips quivered with pleasure.

"We'll go for a ride first thing in the morning, okay?"

Cali swung her big head up and down in agreement.

Becca arrived, we put the horses in their stalls, and I put Millie in the tack room for the time being until I had time to get her used to her new digs. We went in the house. Everyone. My mother had arranged a party after all. There was roasted chicken, green beans, potatoes, salad. Pies, of course, from Clara, along with plenty of whipped cream to squirt on top.

At one point, my parents cornered me away from the others.

"We're very happy for you," my mother said. She clasped her long fingers together. "And now we have a wedding to plan."

Uh oh...

My father put his arm around my shoulders. "He asked our permission." He glanced across the living room to Malcolm. "Good man."

"And our blessing," my mother added with a contented smile. "Now, where'd that baby get to?"

Mom wandered off in search of Issa. Penny would no longer lack for help or babysitting. Happy warmth suffused my belly.

Later, right when yawning threatened to overcome me, Giacomo, Penny and Issa all returned to the city with my parents. That freed up the apartment for Becca to stay in, at least temporarily. There was no need for her to continue living in her truck. Emily said Mrs. Erdman, whom she lived with, had another bedroom available and would probably rent it to Becca if she wanted.

Hank and Clara headed home on their Gator. I went to the barn to tidy up the apartment and change the sheets before Becca went to bed. Renee, Helen, and Malcolm walked with me.

"What do you know about birds showing up in dreams?" I asked Renee. I figured if anyone had a handle on the dream significance of an animal, she did. If there was any meaning to it at all. It had showed up often enough for me to wonder.

"Animal totems aren't something I've studied much. Why?"

"A particular bird has been haunting my dreams. It's probably nothing."

"*Your* dreams? They're never nothing, girlfriend."

Renee wished us well again, got in her car and left. I'd seen her and Dex deep in a conversation and wondered what, if anything, was between them now that he might have eyes only for Penny. He and Renee had been friends for a long time, and then more after Renee's husband passed away.

"What kind of bird?" Helen asked.

Malcolm's mother had long, wavy hair, dark blonde, like his, was of medium build, but lithe. Sometimes she reminded me of a fairy come to life. She favored maxi skirts and peasant blouses, and that's what she wore now. Red-polished toes peeped from beneath the hem of her flowing tan skirt. She lived on the other side of the farm by herself, but we visited each other often and had become friends. Soon, she'd be my mother-in-law.

"Grackles, I think," I answered. "Black, but not. That is, kind of shiny, with different colors depending on the light. I've seen them around here."

Malcolm squeezed my arm, said he was going to start getting the apartment ready, and left us alone.

"I'll look it up when I get home and let you know what I find. Sound good?" Helen got in her car and started it.

I knocked on the window. She lowered it. "You think it means something?" I asked

"It always means something," she said, and with a wave, she put the car in gear, and left.

CHAPTER THIRTY-FIVE

MALCOLM and I cleaned up and went to bed. The house was quiet. We weren't. With the perfect spring weather, the windows were open, and I feared Becca could hear us. Hell, Hank and Clara could probably hear us. That led to exaggerated shushing, snorting, and giggling on our parts.

Later, Malcolm slept.

I didn't.

Helen had texted him grackle information for me. She reported that the glossy black birds are a sign to listen to inner messages and look past superficial appearances to see what really is. That I should take courage, let out repressed emotions, and take back that which is mine—to reclaim my power.

That this exactly echoed the cards Renee had pulled for me just a few days before raised my pelt. I was still missing something vital to understanding what was happening. I'd tried to listen to my inner messages, if Wastrel dreams counted. I'd been shown repeatedly that superficial appearances hid the truth of a person or situation. But who or what was the real Harry? I had no idea and knew my judgement to be clouded by wanting to believe him innocent.

I made myself a pot of coffee and dove into the next journal. Here were heartwarming entries about me when I first started taking lessons with Ed. He described in loving detail what he believed to be my supernormal innate talent, drive, and focus—even as a six year-old. It was hard to read. He'd never said these things out loud to me. I had to wipe away tears more than once as the easy exhilaration and pleasure of those days came back to me full force. Losing Ed had ripped a gaping hole in my heart, and it had yet to mend, maybe never would.

He told Babette about me. She retorted that her son, almost the same age as me, was just as good and had more promise. Ed doubted it, at least in his diary. At some point, she brought Harry to Ed to get his opinion, or prove to him that her son was better. Why? What possible difference could it make? Unless she had been in love with Ed and this was her twisted way of letting him know she was hurt, too? Could you ever know what went on in someone else's mind?

I didn't remember ever seeing Harry at Ed's place when we were kids, but it could have been a day when I wasn't there. Those were rare, but I did have to attend school.

Ed was not impressed with Harry. It wasn't clear if he said this to Baba or not. Later in his writings, Ed mentioned that she was careful never to enter Harry in the same division that I was riding in at horse shows. That must have been how Harry ended up exclusively riding hunters, and me, jumpers.

I had been completely oblivious. Ed most likely made sure I knew nothing about it. He wouldn't want to distract me from riding and winning. A sick feeling pricked my belly. What of Harry? Did he know about this strange competition between his mother and Ed? Was Harry compared to me when younger? Harangued about riding more like me? Did he harbor a long-festering hatred of me because of all this?

The thought sat in my gut like putrid meat.

I ran to the bathroom and threw up.

Harry was a good rider. Competent. Calm. Adaptable. There was absolutely no reason to be envious of my abilities, let alone hate me.

Was I being blind? Was I refusing to see past the superficial to what really was? One of the cards Renee pulled said the answers to my questions were within me, but if they were, some aspect of my subconscious was blocking them.

Around three in the morning, I came to the day in the journal when I was assaulted. Ed's handwriting became jagged; his pen strokes had torn the page in places.

The man arrived at the farm under the guise of buying horses. Ed had never met him, but when he introduced himself, Ed knew he was Babette's husband.

He wasn't interested in horses. He got the girl alone. God help me, it was my fault. MY FAULT. I almost killed him with my bare hands. I was too trusting. She's all right, thank God. Maybe she won't remember. I hope she forgets.

I never will.

CHAPTER THIRTY-SIX

ICY FEAR REACHED up and took a strangle hold of my throat. Where had I put Ed's tape recorder? I needed to hear his voice, listen to what was going on the last couple of days he lived.

The trailer. I ran out the front door and down the drive, flung everything around until I found it, then raced back to the house and emptied every junk drawer looking for the right kind of battery. None. Nor in the hall closet or Malcolm's office.

Shit. Fuck. Piss.

How could we not have any AA batteries in the house? I wrote Malcolm a note, jumped in his car, and drove to the nearest all-night Walmart, twenty five miles away.

The tape in the machine was the only one I had. Whoever had broken into Ed's house must have found the others because I looked, and they were nowhere. Then again, he'd hidden the written diaries practically in plain sight. Maybe I hadn't looked hard enough.

I inserted the batteries, hit rewind, then play, and sat in the car and listened.

Another hot one, came Ed's gravelly voice. *Sure could use some rain.* There was a rustling. After that, sound was slightly muffled but I could still understand him—from his front shirt pocket probably. *Oh, it's the twenty fifth of August. Can't forget to say the date, now can I? There's a good girl.*

I closed my eyes. The fire happened the next day.

A clinking metal sound as he put Sasha's halter on. He patted her neck.

Come on, old girl. The stall door creaked open and her feet clip-clopped onto the concrete aisle. *Should have put you out last night but I was too tired after finalizing all the paperwork.*

I turned it off and started driving home. Ed always kept up a running conversation with the horses, just like me. Hearing him, so familiar, so dear, my earlier fear subsided. Next, he would shuffle to the barn to get Beau. I could easily picture him and his routine.

Back on the highway, I hit play again.

Ed continued talking as he haltered the gelding and led him to the field. *She'll find out tomorrow. She won't be happy. But it's the right way to do it. I know that now. She's gotten too unstable, poor thing, and he's, well, him. Now, the boy I had high hopes for, but it just won't do. The drinking and the drugs. No, can't have it. Vi doesn't need that headache.*

I pushed the pause button and began looking for a place to safely pull over. Malcolm would never forgive me if I threw up in his Jaguar.

She had to be Babette. Which meant *he* was Alcott, and *the boy* could be none other than Harry.

I jerked the car to the shoulder, opened the door, and puked until I had nothing left. I sat there for a few minutes, as wrung out as a damp dishrag. Told myself to go home, curl up in the safety of Malcolm's embrace, listen to this with him rather than alone.

What would Babette learn that would make her unhappy? Would it make her unhappy enough to set fire to Ed's barn and kill him the very next day?

I put the car in drive, pushed play, and listened while Ed began cleaning stalls. He hummed to himself, another endearing habit, then said, *Vi, my girl, I sure do miss you.*

I steered right back onto the shoulder, turned the car off, put my face in my hands, and sobbed.

CHAPTER THIRTY-SEVEN

THE NEXT MORNING—LATER that morning for me—Dex came over, and he, Malcolm and I sat around the chrome-legged kitchen table drinking coffee and discussing what we knew. I played them the tape. Ed had started recording the next day and had been at it when he noticed the fire and got the horses out. If he saw who set it, he didn't say.

I thought I'd sobbed out all my tears a few hours before, but they still trickled down my cheeks when I listened again to Ed calmly talking the horses to safety. The last thing on the tape was him coughing and calling Millie. I hated knowing he'd succumbed to the smoke without knowing she was all right.

Malcolm pulled me onto his lap and held me close.

"The paperwork must have been his will," Dex said.

"But it sounds like he changed it and that's what was going to anger Babette," I said. "Why would he have had Babette or Harry in it in the first place?"

"He'd loved her, once," Malcolm said. "Maybe still did after all those years, even if she was unstable."

"Harry said she's bi-polar," I said.

Exhaustion nagged me, but I couldn't rest. I was hyped up on coffee, and that gave me an idea. I stood.

"Where are we going?" Malcolm asked.

Should have known he wouldn't let me out of his sight. "I'm going to find a picture of Harry and take it to that coffee shop in Troy—the Roasted Bean. See if they recognize him."

"What difference does it make?" Dex asked.

"I just need to know if he was here. Know for sure he was moving the tools and that it was him who almost ran me over."

"Will that make you feel better?" Malcolm asked.

"I don't know," I said. "But I need to know."

"What would make me feel better is to punch him in the face," I heard Malcolm say as I went out the door.

That, at least, was an improvement over wanting to kill him.

We'd given Emily the day off. Becca had her mare on cross ties when I went in the barn. I told her we were going into town but I had to get something from upstairs first. I had a box of mementos and personal things on the shelf in the closet that I'd never moved to the house. Shortly, I had what I needed. Downstairs, Becca had put her mare, whose name, I'd finally learned, was Bella, back in her stall. Dex and Malcolm were already in his truck.

"Mind if I tag along? It will give me a chance to learn my way around."

"Sure," I said.

Forty minutes later, we trooped into the coffee shop beneath the tinkle of a bell above the door. The Roasted Bean was as I remembered it—warm and welcoming. The owner—she'd waited on Giacomo the first time I'd been in —sat in an upholstered chair to one side chatting with a customer. From behind the counter, a young girl took our orders. I got a dirty chai tea latte and everyone else ordered what they wanted. While she rung us up, I showed her the picture.

It was of me and Harry at a show after the competition was over. We leaned on the fender of a trailer. The top buttons of our shirts were undone, jackets and helmets off. Harry's signature stock tie had been loosened. We each held up a can of beer and smiled into the camera. Behind us, several blue ribbons hung in the trailer window. It had been a good day, about ten years ago. Harry had changed since then, but not much.

"Ever seen this guy in here?" I asked.

The girl tilted her head. "Wow, cute. No, I'd remember him."

"Let me see," the owner said.

I showed her. She stared at the picture a long time.

"Yes?" I asked.

She shook her head. "I don't think so, but something about him is familiar."

"He's from New York. You would have noticed his accent."

"That's it. There was a woman in here last week. Older. He looks like her.

Something in the chin and nose." She handed the picture back to me and turned to the girl behind the counter. "Remember that lady? You noticed her Fendi handbag."

"Oh, yeah. Expensive." The girl turned from making our drinks and wrinkled her nose. "Friend of yours?"

My heart sank. I hadn't wanted it to be Harry, but I didn't want it to be anyone else I knew, either. "I've known her for a long time," I said, assuming we were talking about Babette. "Why?"

She brought me my frothy, delicious drink. "She acted like she was high on something or upset."

"Upset?"

"She was real jittery," the girl said. She passed Malcolm his coffee. "Ordered tea for here, decided she didn't like it and dumped it in the bus bucket. Had me make a caramel latte, then said she wanted a muffin but couldn't decide which kind, so she took one of each. Once I had them plated, she had me wrap it all up to go and added another tea even though she'd just said she didn't like it. Then ran out like she was late for an appointment."

She gave Dex and Becca their drinks. "Her hands were shaking so badly that she dropped her credit card a couple of times when she was trying to pay. But she gave me a really good tip."

"Do you remember what day that was?" Dex asked. "And the time?"

The girl shook her head.

"Had to be Wednesday," the owner said. "You were off the rest of the week."

"That's right," the girl said with a nod. "It was Wednesday, some time in the morning."

Exactly one week ago. The very same day the black BMW with New York plates nearly side-swiped me and Noire. The same morning Wastrel appeared after being absent for months. I took my tea and sat at the big table where we could all fit comfortably and turned to Dex.

"I don't like being a detective."

"That makes two of us. But rarely is it this personal."

I put my elbows on the tabletop, leaned my cheek on my fist, and stared out the window to Main street. "Why?" I asked no one in particular.

"Has to have something to do with the paperwork Ed mentioned on the tape," Malcolm said.

"Would someone like to explain what you're all talking about?" Becca asked. "Anyone."

I was so tired, I explained most of it, or what we knew and suspected.

High level, left out the parts about Wastrel, but filled in the blanks of what we'd told her and Penny before we left Long Island.

"Wow," she said. "What is it about you that stirs up such strong emotions in people? That's impressive. I'd be happy if someone got half that passionate about me." She took a drink of her coffee. "Not to the point of killing anyone, though. That's extreme."

"Ya think?" I said.

She rolled her eyes and smirked.

Dex slid his card onto the counter. "If you see either the guy in the picture or the woman who was here last week, please call me."

We finished our drinks and returned to Winterlight. Despite my fatigue, I'd promised Cali a ride, and I needed one. Malcolm said he'd go with me, and I looked forward to some alone time with him. We grabbed halters and walked out to the pasture together to get Cali and his horse, Gaston.

They weren't with the herd. They weren't anywhere in the field. They were gone.

CHAPTER THIRTY-EIGHT

IN THE DREAM, we'd been chasing Cali and Ciqala, but Wastrel was often fuzzy on the details. Someone had taken them, I was sure of it. The gates were secure. We ran the fence line to see if there were any places where a tree had fallen across it or a horse could have squeezed through.

We returned to the barn and Malcolm called the police. I called Emily and Sandy. We needed as many hands on deck—or butts in saddles—as possible to track the horses. Dex rallied his team to search the roads for any evidence of a truck and trailer, for the sedan they'd last seen Harry in, or for Cali and Gaston themselves.

Dex would wait for Emily and Sandy to arrive so we could go out looking in two teams of three. Malcolm, me, and Becca would take Miss Bong, Captain, and Bella, respectively. Dex, Emily, and Sandy would take Ciqala, Emily's horse, and Fawn.

Malcolm and Dex quickly worked out a plan to quarter the farm and search the surrounding area. I called Hank and Clara as well as Helen so they could keep their eyes open for anything unusual, and Renee to come hold down the fort at home.

As in prior times like these, Dex made me take his spare handgun. I had yet to use it. Why he always had one eluded me. Malcolm had thrown a western saddle on Miss Bong that had a scabbard, and he shoved his shotgun in it.

"Better to have and not need than need and not have," he said.

I took a deep breath knowing better than to argue but not sure I liked going out loaded for bear.

Becca said she didn't want to know why we were armed, but she pocketed a box knife she kept handy for cutting the strings on hay bales. She also grabbed the reusable ice square thingy I'd accidentally bought at Walmart. She tied it by its handle to the back of her saddle. I'm not sure why she chose that, didn't have time for questions, but admired her resourcefulness.

"You don't have to come," I said to her. "You understand there might be danger."

"Um, yeah, I get that. Are you saying I'm not part of the team?"

We stared at each other. It struck me as an odd thing to ask in the moment and revealed a vulnerability of Becca's I hadn't suspected.

"You are totally part of the team," I said. I strapped on my helmet and led Captain outside. "Make sure your girths are tight."

Malcolm planted a big kiss on my lips and swung aboard Miss Bong. He was fully in super-hero mode. I gave Becca a leg up, got on Captain, and we were off.

There were tracks, but they could have been anyone's. Horses were led in and out of the pasture and ridden on the trails all the time. There was nothing distinctive about Cali's or Gaston's shoes to distinguish their hoof-prints from anyone else's. In other words, we were flying blind as to what direction they were taken. Which was why we went one way, and Dex took his team another. We'd eventually meet somewhere in the middle. In the meantime, we'd keep in touch via cell when we could. Service was spotty in the woods unless you were up on a ridge.

We trotted single file, Malcolm in the lead, and cantered when we could, keeping our heads up and scanning the land in all directions for any sign of them. Noire bounded ahead, stopping to sniff at rocks and clumps of grass and occasionally digging for whatever prize she thought might lie beneath the surface. Then, she'd race to catch up, weave through the horses, and get out front again.

Every fifteen minutes, we stopped to check for messages. At the second check point, Dex called to say one of his men had found what appeared to be an abandoned vehicle on the road east of the farm. It wasn't the sedan he and Malcolm had seen Harry in on the highway. This SUV had Illinois plates and had been reported stolen the day before.

It didn't mean it was Harry and Babette. Damning evidence aside, I held out hope that neither of them were responsible for any of this. Both Cali and Gaston could jump out of the pasture whenever they wanted. Most of the time, they chose to stay put. If they got out, they stuck around the barn where they knew their feed was. Even though this time was different, I was confident we'd find our errant equines wandering in a meadow and bring them home in time for lunch.

By afternoon, I sagged in the saddle and wished I'd brought snacks and water. Lost horses brought me as close to panic mode as I ever got, my crazed dash through Walmart not withstanding. The pistol butt jabbed my back where I'd shoved it in my waistband. The day had grown warm, and sweat stung my eyes. Becca looked hot and tired as well, but alert.

No one had seen anything.

No one complained.

Bella had proved herself a worthy mount for the expedition, easily keeping up with the other two horses who were used to being ridden out, sometimes for hours at a time. She was fit from competition, had a kind eye, didn't fuss. At the horse show, when she'd made faces at Vagrant, it had probably been because she'd been keyed up, and he was a stallion.

We stopped to rest and touch base with the other team at one of the highest points of the farm. The ridge afforded a view across a creek-filled ravine to a sheer bluff on the other side. This was not a part of the huge tract of land we usually rode through, and we hadn't been on an actual trail for an hour or so. Negotiating fallen trees, ducking low branches, and avoiding blackberry bushes made the going slow and exhausting.

Becca rubbed her eyes and kept scanning the woods in the distance.

"Thank you," I said.

She smoothed Bella's mane, smiled slightly but didn't make eye contact when she said, "I know how I'd feel if it were my horse."

I nodded and considered again the message of the grackle. Take courage, Helen had said, and release repressed emotions. Whenever I heard that sort of thing, I immediately thought it was about negativity. That we all needed to release anger and worry and fear. But seeing Becca's shy smile and hearing her soft admission, I realized that the same advice applied to positive emotions like joy, happiness, love. These were feelings I had learned to deny myself and struggled to express.

How much courage had it taken Becca to admit she wanted to train with me, to drop her life and follow me to Missouri, to admit she wanted to be part of my team? She said she'd like to elicit passion in others, but surely her steady nerve was worth more than blazing ardor?

"There." Becca pointed to the bluff.

Malcolm swung his binoculars in that direction. I narrowed my eyes. Yes. Movement. "Is it a herd of deer?"

"It's them." He picked up his reins.

"I can't see," I said. "What are they doing?"

"They're being ridden." He punched in a quick message to Dex and pocketed his phone. "I can't tell by whom, but there are riders on their backs, and they're moving away fast. Let's go."

Malcolm urged Miss Bong down into the ravine, and we followed. Images from the dream flashed in my mind as we descended, the stomach-flipping sense of falling once more gripping me.

"They were going away from the bluff?" I yelled to him.

"As far as I could tell."

He pushed the big mare to move faster than the careful walk she'd prefer to take the steep incline at. In his western saddle, he was more secure than we were in our English ones. I wished I'd thought to use a western saddle, but there was nothing for it now but to grab mane and hold on as Captain began to slide down the hill.

"You okay back there?" I shouted over my shoulder.

"Fine. Don't worry about me."

I'd been about to release some repressed emotions and tell her I liked her when she spotted the horses. As we safely reached the bottom, I hoped I'd have a chance later.

Swollen from spring rains, the creek was both deeper and wider than usual. Miss Bong cleared most of it in one leap and took off to attack the uphill side of the ravine. Captain hesitated. A jumper he was not. But he was brave, and at my urging he plunged into the foamy water and climbed the opposite bank. We took off to catch the long strides of Malcolm's mount, twisting through the tree trunks. Too like the dreams.

I glanced back to see Becca and Bella still on the wrong side of the creek, the mare balking at the rushing water. Becca dismounted and spoke to the horse, then faced forward and confidently led her downstream where it split around a gravel bar. They got across, Becca remounted, and they galloped forward to close the gap.

Malcolm and I were already halfway to the bluff, crossing back and forth at sharp angles to do it. Beneath the leaves and forest litter at the horses's feet there was little soil, mostly gravel and solid rock. The horses scraped and skidded trying to find their footing.

Becca encouraged Bella. "You can do it," she said. "Good girl. Keep going."

At the top of the bluff, a wide trail went off in both directions because we liked to view the river valley below and sometimes drove up here on ATVs. We wouldn't be enjoying the vista today. Once we hit clear going, we'd be flat out.

"Where's Dex?" I yelled to Malcolm.

"Other side of the river," he shouted back.

Meaning the main channel, the one I'd forded on Gaston with Nicky trying to escape JJ almost a year ago. It formed a meandering border along much of the south property line. They wouldn't catch up with us any time soon.

We reached the top. Malcolm yelled, "Ha!" and slapped Miss Bong's neck with the reins. Captain needed no encouragement to bound after her, and I gave him his head. Soon, I heard Bella's hoofbeats and breathing coming fast from behind.

Like the dream, except there weren't two horses right ahead of us.

Coming up, the trail narrowed for a hairpin turn before widening out again. Malcolm sat up, checked Miss Bong onto her hindquarters, swung her shoulders around, and kept going. Captain slowed and drifted to the side. He was fine going straight but lacked the athleticism for even half of a rollback. I took my right hand out to guide him closer to the trees. Too close. The rein hooked over the stub of a branch we'd trimmed when clearing trails during the winter.

The rein pulled taut. I tugged. It stayed stuck. Captain's eye rolled back and his head started to lift. In another moment, he'd be panicked, fighting it.

Before I could figure out what to do, Becca came up beside us, leaned forward, stretched out her fingers, and jerked my rein free. Bella slid between Captain and the tree without bumping either. Becca waved a salute and carried on. Once on the straightaway again, Captain dug in to catch up.

Another turn was ahead, just as sharp but in the opposite direction. Malcolm and Becca were already around it when Captain and I reached that point and nearly ran into their butts.

They'd stopped dead.

At the opposite edge of the clearing in front of them, I saw the reason why.

Cali and Gaston faced us. Babette sat astride my horse, Harry on Malcolm's. Babette held the reins of Gaston's bridle. All of them were wild-eyed and breathing hard. Harry especially.

No wonder. His hands were tied behind his back and his head was in a noose.

CHAPTER THIRTY-NINE

My breathing came harsh and uneven into the silence. Blood pounded my ears. The mingled smells of sweat and fear clogged my nose.

My gaze skipped from Babette to Cali and Gaston, then to Malcolm and Becca, and finally came to rest on Harry.

Babette was decked out in formal hunt attire including a black riding jacket, tan breeches, starched white stock tie. Her left hand held both Cali's and Gaston's reins, her right a pistol. Not a big one, but it could get the job done.

Her feet rested in gold stirrups.

Cali's nostrils flared with each quick breath, and she had cuts on her legs and shoulders. I willed myself not to react, but God help me, the first moment I could, I'd throat punch Babette.

Gaston's sides heaved and sweat darkened his apricot-colored coat. His head hung to his knees. That was good. He didn't need to walk away right now.

Malcolm's eyes drilled a hole through Babette. One hand held the reins, the other casually rested on the butt of his shotgun. Nothing about his demeanor said relaxed. Miss Bong bobbed her head, but all the horses were glad to stop and catch their breath.

Becca also held her reins in one hand. The other slowly undid the knot around the ice square. Bella chewed the bit and looked ready to leap forward.

"Don't do anything to spook the horses," I said out of the side of my mouth. If Gaston moved out from under Harry, he was dead.

Harry wore jeans, barn clogs, a button-down Oxford. No helmet. His dark hair was plastered flat, and his white collar was soaked through.

The rope around his neck looped tautly over a stout oak branch. When I looked into Harry's eyes, I understood how Babette had managed it. He stared into the middle distance seeing nothing. She had him doped up.

I absorbed these details in the span of three heartbeats.

Even though he didn't seem to recognize me, I gave Harry a slight nod, turned to his mother. "For God's sake, Babette, what do you want?"

Her head cocked to one side then the other in an oddly robotic motion. She shifted to one hip as if settling in for a chat. Cali bent one hind leg. Babette tapped my horse's side with her calf, and the mare straightened up. I held my breath, but Gaston didn't take Cali's movements as a signal to step out from under Harry.

Babette was an excellent horsewoman. She'd ridden to hounds for years, and that required a fierce level of dedication and fitness. The fact that Harry had stayed aboard while being led through the woods at a gallop with his hands tied behind his back—high as a kite—testified to what a strong rider he was.

Babette answered me in a calm voice. "That's for me to know and you to find out. All's fair in love and war."

Oh no. We were dealing with Our Lady of Platitudes. I'd have to engage her in verbal battle even though every cell in my body screamed *do something*.

"Isn't it obvious?" she asked.

It wasn't. Not completely. I'd figured out a few things, but I wanted to hear it from her. One detail I was certain of—I'd been on the wrong lead about Babette Brown.

"Perception is reality," I said.

She smiled as if this were a game and countered with, "Patience is a virtue."

One I lacked. "I know you had a relationship with Ed, but married Alcott. Why?"

"I wanted to be rich." She tilted her head again. "We should all be careful what we wish for."

"Ed was in love with you," I said. "You broke his heart."

"God never gives us more than we can bear." She glanced at her hands as if inspecting her fingernails, but they were hidden inside gloves. "Ed was penniless."

"Money can't buy happiness," I said.

Her eyes met mine. "You'd be surprised."

"Everything happens for a reason." I sounded loonier than she did. "Time heals all wounds. Can't we forgive and forget?"

"No. This was meant to be."

Gaston stamped his foot. Harry flinched. With the noose distorting his face, he'd aged a decade. What Alcott said to him slammed into my mind.

I suppose a real father would do that...

It hit me. Jesus. How could I have missed the most critical aspect of this story?

"Everything was fine," Babette said with disgust, "until you showed up."

I jerked my attention back to her.

"Ed wouldn't shut up about you. He couldn't have been more proud of his little protégé if you'd issued from his own loins."

"Did he know?" I asked.

"Know what?" she snapped.

I reminded myself not to agitate her beyond her current state. Which was manic, if I understood anything about bi-polar disorder.

"Did Ed know he was Harry's father?" Her eyes narrowed. She hadn't thought me *that* clever. "The farm was supposed to go to him, wasn't it."

Babette nodded. "Yes, later. At the time, Alcott thought *he* was Michael's father."

Harry hated when his mother called him by his first name. I couldn't tell if he heard. By the rasp of his inhalations, breathing was getting harder.

"Did you send Alcott to prey on me that day?" I asked.

"Remember, that, do you? You shouldn't dwell on the past. You said it yourself. Forgive and forget."

"That kind of thing is hard to forget."

"It is what it is. I knew of Alcott's proclivities before we married." She lifted her shoulders and let out an exaggerated sigh. "I might have mentioned Ed had a cute prospect hanging around."

Twisted, twisted woman. "A dirty barn girl," I said and heard Malcolm's breathing hitch.

Even at ten yards, I could see her eyes contained a freaky gleam.

"Setting Alcott on me didn't work. What was your next ploy?"

"Good things come to those who wait," she sang. "Eventually, I told Ed the truth. He readily agreed to put his son in his will. You'd left to seek your fortune elsewhere. Or follow your bliss? What goes around comes around. Poor Ed. Another woman he loved left him for money."

My face grew hot, and not from fear or exertion. She was right. Ed's vision was failing. He couldn't drive. He told me I should move on. I'd been hurt at first, but taken him at his word. I was good at that. Good at accepting the superficial and not looking deeper, feeling deeper, for what was real. If Ed had been saddened by my leaving, I'd never known. I'd been so clueless.

"It's not like you needed money or land," I said.

"It wasn't about the money," she bit out. "It was the principle of the thing. Michael was his, and he needed to provide for him. Especially after…" She dropped her head back and stared at the sky.

"What happened?" I asked. "Did Alcott guess the truth?"

She brought her splintered gaze back to mine. "Curiosity killed the cat." She laughed at her joke. "I came up with a new plan. A better one. When in doubt, try, try again."

This was Our Lady of Platitudes on freaking steroids. A light breeze moved through the forest, rustling leaves, moving branches. Gaston's head lifted. He'd caught his breath—all the horses had—and might not stand still much longer.

"But then you left the state," Babette continued, her tone full of accusation. "I needed you to come back, marry my son, and run the farm together." She looked Harry up and down. Her face showed no emotion.

"It was you who bought the phone," I said. "You told Harry to send it to me. But first, you made sure you could track my movements."

"Michael's also. It was a two-for-one-deal."

"Harry doesn't like being called Michael. If you cared about him, you'd know that."

"You know nothing about a mother's love for her child."

Captain had been resting one hind leg. He straightened it to cock the other. My gaze flew around the clearing, checking the mood of the others. So far, so good.

"You treated me like your own," I said, "yet you came to Missouri and started moving my tools when no one was at the farm. To what, make me want to leave? Make me think I was crazy?"

She gave me a wicked smug smile. The impulse to punch her threatened what was left of my good sense. I wanted Cali to buck her off but couldn't risk Gaston moving, not yet.

"You almost ran over me and my dog."

"C'est la vie. You needed reminding that everything's better in New York."

"What about when the trunk got moved in the tack room at Ed's? Was that you, too?"

"That was Michael, just as he confessed. It was an accident, but it did get me thinking."

"Thinking you should kill the man you supposedly loved, the father of your son?"

"I needed him to see it was time to give up the farm so you and Michael could have it. What the mind can conceive, it can achieve."

"You started the fire. You killed him." My voice broke.

Something that might have been pain warped her features. "He wasn't supposed to die!"

"You might have killed the horses."

"I knew he'd get them out. But I was so angry when I heard he'd left everything to you. Nothing for his own son. All because of a few bad choices on the part of a young man."

Harry had made more than a few bad choices, but we weren't here to debate that. Malcolm adjusted his seat making his saddle creak. Bella took one step sideways.

"All I had to do was threaten to expose Alcott's obsession with dirty barn girls. He took care of the investigation so Ed would get the insurance money right away. I *did* care about him."

"Did you kill the investigator?"

She rolled her eyes. "Not until after he submitted his report. He asked too many questions."

"And Alcott?"

"He cut me off. That was unacceptable." She blew out a frustrated breath. "No good deed goes unpunished."

Was the good deed that Alcott cut her off, or had she done a good deed by murdering her husband? Gaston began chewing his bit, a sure sign he wanted to get moving, and soon.

"This past weekend, you were still working the marriage angle. Harry said we belonged together."

"Not very convincing, I know. His drug addiction jumbled up his brain."

She took a moment to admire her trussed-up son. His head had begun to slump forward.

"It makes him easy to manipulate," Babette continued. "But poor on follow-through. Even a good beating didn't straighten him up. He needed to try harder."

Clearly, the woman had lost it. "What was the point of hiring someone to shoot at me?"

She made a contemptuous scoffing sound. "It's hard to find good help. They were supposed to scare you into asking for my son's help. So what if they got a little carried away."

The woman had a gift for understatement. "What's going to happen here, Babette?"

"Why, you're going to forget this foray into…" She flicked her wrist as if that explained. Cali flinched. The handgun flopped over and hung from her trigger finger. I sucked in a breath. She looked at the weapon like she'd forgotten it, then palmed it and pointed it at my horse's head. "Into whatever all this is," she finished. "You'll thank me later. Marry my son. Your children will be Ed's grandchildren. Won't that be superb? It would make Ed so happy."

I only needed to convince her to release Harry. He didn't want to marry me any more than I wanted to marry him. I was done exchanging platitudes.

I risked a glance at Becca. She had the the ice block untied. "Can you hit her from here?" I asked softly.

She dipped her chin without looking at me.

"Be ready to shoot that rope," I whispered to Malcolm. He didn't acknowledge me but slid his hand down the shotgun's stock.

Becca, I noticed, sank deeper into her heels and scooped her fingers under the front of her saddle. I'd entered that hyper-vigilant state I'd so often observed in Dex. Every nuance of behavior and color of the scene around me stood out in sharp relief

"If you want Harry to have the farm, he can have it," I said. "Let him go. I'll sign it over to him."

Babette frowned, thrown, I could tell, by this offer.

"No," she snarled. "That's not good enough. It has to be both of you."

I wiggled the reins and tightened my legs, picturing what would have to happen. How Captain had to spring forward so Harry could straddle him if Gaston wasn't there. Captain's ears twitched to attention. For good measure, I took hold of the front of the saddle like Becca had.

"Or what?" I asked Babette.

She yanked Gaston's reins. Gaston jerked his head. Becca gasped. Harry squeezed his eyes shut. He was in there, hearing every word we said.

"That would defeat the purpose," I said too loudly, barely able to think over the pounding of my heart. "I don't believe you'll do it."

"No?" Babette asked. "Then how about this?" She lifted the gun and pointed it between Cali's ears again.

This threat I wasn't so sure about. Hell, I wasn't sure of anything.

"You won't risk it," I said. "The horses will spook. You might get hurt. And if Harry dies, you lose everything. Is that what you want?"

She gaped at me, absorbing my words. Thinking I was getting through to her, I rushed on.

"But you could win, everything. You can have Ed's farm with Harry running it. You should have seen him at the show. He's only gotten better since rehab. You'll have enough blue ribbons to paper the entire house."

She lowered the gun, sat thinking for a moment. I began to exhale. She lifted the gun again, this time pointing it at Malcolm.

My dog chose that moment to rush into the clearing shaking a wriggling raccoon.

CHAPTER FORTY

THE HORSES JUMPED. Babette's gun went off. Cali bolted. Gaston followed. Bella spun after them. Whether with or without Becca, I wasn't sure. Captain scooted sideways. I hung on and kicked him forward, got beneath Harry's flailing legs. But Captain wouldn't stand. The other horses had left. He wanted to go after them. As I tried to steady him, I realized I'd made a fatal error. Captain was a good six inches shorter than Gaston. Harry got his feet on either side of Captain, but it wasn't enough to take weight off the rope. He made horrible choking sounds.

"Put your feet on his back," I screamed.

Harry kicked me trying to find a foothold behind the saddle. Was he too out of it to understand?

Malcolm shouted, "Duck!"

I dropped to Captain's neck. The shotgun blast battered my ears. I heard pellets slinging through leaves followed by a thump, then nothing but air as Captain spooked right out from under us. Vaguely, I was aware Miss Bong reared and pivoted out of the clearing. Above us, a snap. I hit the ground with Harry on top of me. The branch crashed over us in a hail of green.

I crawled out from under him and shoved the branch aside. He was still fighting for breath. Babette had tied the rope in a simple slip knot. The fall tightened it even more. It wouldn't budge. Harry's face turned purple. Frantically, I looked over my shoulder, but we were alone.

Tears blurred my vision as I scrabbled at the rope. Harry's body convulsed once, twice, then his features went slack.

"No!"

In desperation, I put the muzzle of Dex's gun against the rope behind Harry's ear, made sure it was angled away from him, and pulled the trigger, then jerked at the rope. It held. I fired again and again until it finally fell away.

"Oh my God, oh my God." I slapped his cheek. "Harry!" I thumped his chest. "Breathe, goddammit."

He wheezed.

"Okay. You're okay."

Noire ran up and started licking him. I pushed her away. "Not now."

He blinked. His mouth worked but no sounds came out.

"Stay still. Don't try to talk."

"Vi!" Becca rode Bella into the clearing. "Over here. It's Malcolm."

I ran to her she jumped off her horse. Malcolm lay in an ugly heap just around the turn. New fear punched me in the gut. I dropped to my knees beside him.

He groaned. I knuckled my eyes and pushed off my helmet. He rolled over and tried to sit up. Noire came to wash his face as well.

"Don't move," I said.

I ran shaking hands all over him, through his hair, poked and prodded. No blood. "Are you shot?"

He held up one hand. Noire licked that, too. "I'm all right. Just got…the wind…knocked out of me. And," He sat, still chugging air, felt down his leg. "Maybe dragged." He grasped his ankle and grimaced. "That might be broken." He removed his helmet as well. "Is Harry okay?"

"I think so." I glanced in that direction, needed to go back and check on him. "What the hell happened?"

"I fired at the rope just like you wanted. Miss Bong didn't like that."

"None of the horses liked it. The whole branch came down. Captain spooked. I got him over there but he's too short. Then you fired, and we fell. I had to shoot the rope off Harry's neck. Dex gave me his gun." Babbling. Didn't care.

Malcolm stroked his thumb over my cheek. "Deep breaths," he said softly.

I immediately calmed. Worry clouded his eyes. How he beat it back to soothe my battered nerves was beyond me.

"Are you all right?" he asked.

I nodded. "Thank you for saving him."

He slid his hand to the back of my neck, pulled my forehead against his. "We both did."

I wanted to stay like that but turned to Becca. "How did you stay on?"

"I was already chasing the madwoman when he fired. We were halfway to the bluff."

I stood and looked in that direction but couldn't see past the next turn. "The bluff."

"I stopped her," Becca said.

"How?"

"Hit her right in the neck with that ice thing. She's out *cold*." She winked at me.

That jolted a laugh out of me. "Holy crap. What speed were you going?"

"Flat-out gallop."

Malcolm made an appreciative face. "That's a hell of shot."

Becca swung her arm as if winding up to pitch. "Four years of high-school softball, four more in college."

"We'll figure out how to properly thank you later." I turned back to Malcolm. "You and Harry need to see a doctor."

I gave him my hand. He pulled himself up and put his arm around my shoulders. The fact that he didn't argue about a doctor spoke to how much pain he was in. With him hopping on one leg, we went to Harry.

"Becca," I said. "Do you still have that box cutter?"

She brought it over. I freed Harry's hands. He sat, slowly brought his arms around front, flinching the whole time, and rubbed his neck. The skin was raw and torn, beginning to swell. His face was still bruised from the beating at the horse show. His wrists had red welts on them as well.

Malcolm patted his pockets. "My phone's gone."

Did he want to take a picture? "I'm sure it's around here somewhere," I said.

From the other side of the clearing a man asked, "Everybody in one piece?"

Dex. I'd never been so happy to hear his voice. "We're over here," I said.

He dismounted and walked Ciqala to us. Emily and Sandy followed. "Heard a couple of shots. Came as quick as we could."

"You missed the excitement," Malcolm said. He nodded at Becca. "Our newest teammate took out the bad guy with a reusable ice pack."

"Impressive," Dex said. His eyebrows quirked a question at me.

"It was Babette," I said.

Becca put her hands on her hips. "If it hadn't been for Vi's epic platitude smack down, I wouldn't have had time to loosen the knot holding the giant ice cube."

"Perhaps you could lead me to our suspect, Miss Brannon. Let's make sure she's secure."

"Give me your phone, first," Malcolm said to Dex. "I need to call the sheriff. We'll wait here since the road's wide enough for them to drive up."

"Can't we just round up the horses and go home?" I caught up with Becca and Dex.

"Um, hang on." Becca put her hand on my arm. "About the horses."

I stopped and looked at her hand. "What about them?"

"They scattered."

"I expected that."

"Of course." She paused, and I could sense her choosing her words. "After Babette fell off, Cali kept going."

A coil of dread unraveled in my belly. Two cold tendrils threaded into my groin and down my legs making them fragile as a new blade of grass. "She knows how to get home."

Malcolm hopped over to me, grasped my other arm. He teetered. Dex steadied him.

"Vi," Becca said, her tone gentle. "She went over the bluff."

CHAPTER FORTY-ONE

I RAN.

On legs stiff and wobbly with fear and fatigue, I raced for the bluff. I fell twice, once near the prone form of Babette. She looked gray. She might be dead. I'd grieve for her later. Maybe never. I got up and kept going. In my head, the only sound was the word *no*.

Over and over and over.

When I reached the bluff, I opened my mouth to scream *Cali*, but like a bad dream, like Harry, all I could produce was air. I screamed anyway.

Over and over and over.

I didn't see her but found what might be her tracks and let them pull me down the bluff after her, hope trying to elbow aside terror. There was no blood. She probably hadn't been shot. It was less steep here, not a sheer drop. But everywhere I looked, I saw only the potential for death or fatal injury. Each log and shadow became a jumble of torn flesh and tangled legs.

I heard Malcolm and the others yelling for me to wait, they'd help, but I ignored them and kept going. One way or the other, I had to find her.

I didn't.

I tried to search sensibly. To think in terms of grids, to use trees or rock outcroppings as guides so I didn't wander in circles. I lost sight of the tracks but kept going. Sirens squawked in the distance. Someone might have called my name. Sound is funny in the forest, especially when there are high spots and low areas, exposed rock and a breeze. Not long after, a medical helicopter flew over, must have landed somewhere near the bluff, then took off after several minutes. I hoped Harry was on it. Malcolm, too. Babette…not so much.

Shadows lengthened. The low areas grew cool as the heat of the day rose and dissipated. A dehydration headache thrummed beneath my scalp. I began to stumble and lean heavily on each tree trunk I passed. At some point, Noire found me, and I was glad for her company and heightened senses.

I could feel Cali's fear and confusion. Maybe it was my own. We'd been negligent to leave the farm unattended when we didn't know where Harry was, let alone that Babette was involved. Bad enough our absence had allowed the theft of the horses. When we caught up with them, I didn't immediately rescue Cali from her rider. I had a lot of explaining to do.

For the first time, I wondered if Becca had been wrong about what she'd seen. I'd hunted, thoroughly I thought, up and down the bluff and around the base. Not finding Cali dead was a good thing, but finding her would be better. She could be hurt, the reins could have gotten caught around her legs, tripped her. I tried to halt my darting thoughts, but couldn't.

Eventually, I ended up back in the ravine, downstream from where we'd crossed earlier. Knowing the water wasn't drinkable, I rinsed my face, combed fingers through my tangled hair, and sloshed water up my arms. I sat, took off my boots and socks, put my feet in the cool stream, and laid back to rest for a few minutes.

How was it I hadn't crossed paths with any of the loose horses? I hoped the others had better luck. Maybe they'd already found Cali. I'd been stupid and impulsive to take off alone. Story of my life. I'd left behind injured people I cared about. I'd left Malcolm with a broken ankle. Now, they were probably worried about me. I was selfish, thoughtless.

But losing Cali after all this…. Oh sure, I'd survive, but I no longer wished to settle for mere survival.

I would start for home before full dark, get an update, apologize, beg forgiveness, and come back out in the morning. Noire curled up beside me and I stroked her glossy black head. She sighed.

Of course, I fell asleep.

As with many of my dreams, I am enveloped in fog. Unlike the dreams I've remembered since coming to Winterlight, I am alone. Wastrel has always been with me, but not this time. I'm on my own. But that horse taught me to be patient, so I wait. The fog will clear. New understanding will emerge. I will see the way forward.

I am seated cross-legged as if meditating, though that's hardly my thing. Maybe it should be. I inhale the dense mist. It has formed exquisite beads in my arm hair and eyebrows, lustrous as pearls. Each exhalation forms a new cloud, brighter than that which encircles me. Each luminous billow hovers. They contain images that are at first hazy, then clear. Images of an undreamed future.

I see Ed Todd's place, fixed up and busy with horses, ponies, children. The kids are laughing, as well they should be with so many beautiful four-legged creatures to play with. My next breath brings Winterlight to life, also lively with the activity of horses being ridden and cared for.

Elation, triumph, and contentment accompany these pictures. The work is both strenuous and fulfilling. Malcolm is by my side. I do not see him but feel his essence.

How can I be in two places at once?

I inhale the last of the gray fog and now have only white around me. No defining features, no horizon. I let go of the need to understand and wait for deeper meaning to come.

Wastrel is near. As always, preceded by that crazy mix of delicious scents that I hope is what heaven smells like. I wonder if this time, I have joined him there, and that's why all I see is this opaque snowiness.

Unlikely.

As Wastrel's form coalesces in the distance, color seeps into the scene, tans and browns and muted greens. I am perched on a desert sand dune at sunset. The golden light limns hardy shrubs that defy the parched environment to thrive. This can be me, I realize. If I choose, I can put down roots and flourish.

Wastrel comes to stand beside me. From him, I pick up an easy satisfaction, the way he often felt after a good trail ride or schooling session. He paws the soft footing, drops to his knees, then his haunches, and rolls. He always loved a deep sandy patch to scratch his back and polish his coat. After flipping from side to side and back again, he stays put, legs folded underneath his powerful body like a sleeping cat. He puts his head in my lap. I stroke his long nose, his ears and cheeks, and lightly run my palms over his eyes. He emits a long groan of pleasure.

I could sit like this for hours, but my happiness is shattered by the notion that this might be the last time I will ever touch him. Could he be done with me? I put my arms around his neck and cry hot tears into his mane. Yet, if he is gone, I will no longer be dogged by the foul deeds of others, impossibly cryptic clues, obscure visions.

One or both of the futures I breathed into form could be what lies ahead for me. I will wait. And plan. And work.

Wastrel rises and shakes himself, sprinkling me with sand. His warm breath fans over my neck and shoulders as he nudges me with his soft muzzle. He walks away. I touch each of his legs as he goes by, then grab what I can of his silky tail and let it slide through my fingers.

One last time.

CHAPTER FORTY-TWO

I WANT to wake to Cali standing over me. Instead, someone wraps me in a blanket, picks me up, carries me through the woods, puts me to bed. Yet, at the same time, I am still sitting in the desert straining to see Wastrel in the distance. I hear men's voices. They are hushed. I can't make out what they're saying. One might be my father.

Later, I learned it was Dex Two carrying me. He came to help when Dex One called to let him know that I, as well as his horse, Miss Bong, were among the missing. My father was with him. Noire led them to my nearly unconscious form.

My mother and Penny had kept the coffee flowing and took turns cooking for everyone while they had searched on foot, on horseback, on four-wheelers. Even Clara and Hank went out on their Gator.

All looking for me.

I was humbled and chastised. I had never wanted to elicit strong emotions from people let alone feel them. Except for anger. Anger had fueled most of my life. Now that I had allowed myself to feel other emotions—good ones—I knew this was the very best way to live. The only way to truly live.

Once I was secure, and daylight returned, they switched their attention to finding the horses. Against my will, I slept most of the day, unable to hold up my head let alone keep my eyes open. By late afternoon on Thursday, all the horses were rounded up except Cali.

I'd worked hard the past couple of years to earn her trust and I'd betrayed it. I didn't deserve anyone's trust or affection. Yet I had it. I longed to keep it.

There were injuries to attend to, mostly minor, but my mother and Penny wouldn't let me leave the house. The vet came out to check over the horses and treat the wounds that needed stitching. Becca, Emily, and Sandy saw to cold hosing swollen limbs and changing bandages.

My mother forced water and broth into me. My belly was hollow, my head fuzzy. I wandered from the front porch to the back, waiting. I wasn't good at it.

Harry was in the hospital, recovering and detoxing. His mother as well. She'd survived the tiny iceberg thrown by Becca's mighty pitching arm, and somehow managed not to break her neck when she hurtled off my horse's back. Still, she was banged up, sprained, and had a massive contusion on the back of her neck. The doctor said it was a wonder she hadn't sustained a spinal cord injury.

It might have been better if she hadn't lived. The list of warrants for her arrest was long, and she'd be extradited to New York to face the charges as soon as she recovered. Harry might be indicted as an accomplice to her crimes, but we'd all testify he'd been coerced, drugged, and acting in fear for his life.

Malcolm had been treated at the emergency room and sent home in a boot with orders to keep his leg elevated and ankle iced. The fracture was small but needed time to heal. It made him crabby. Misery loves company, and we commiserated over being out of the action, feeling impotent. Fussing over him kept me from fretting over my horse for a few minutes here and there, never for long.

Thursday drained into Friday and still no sign of Cali. I had no appetite. My stomach was full to the brim with a writhing mass of anxiety, apprehension, and foreboding.

Late Friday night, restive from doing a lot of nothing and feeling physically better thanks to my mother's ministrations, I snuck out of the house. In the barn, I scooped grain into a bucket and followed the trail into the woods.

A three-quarter moon brightened the night, but I knew the path well enough to find my way. As I walked, I shook the bucket. My voice had returned.

"Come onnnn," I yelled.

From the pasture, Gaston whinnied in answer. He'd been calling off and on all day. His way of helping bring Cali home. They had become friends over the past few months, almost as close as Beau and Sasha. Then again, food had always been a strong motivator for him, and the sound of the grain bucket always got his attention.

He hadn't gone far when the horses spooked out there in the woods. First patch of grass he came across stopped him. They found him quickly, and he emerged from the fray unscathed.

"Come onnnn!"

Gaston answered again, louder this time. He'd probably run the fence to the farthest back corner of the pasture.

I stopped to take a drink, congratulating myself on bringing a large bottle of water with me this time. I'd stuffed carrots in one back pocket and an energy bar in the other.

"Come onnnn!"

This time, galloping hoofbeats accompanied Gaston's loud neigh. I hopped to the side of the trail as I realized he was coming up behind me. Fast. He went right by. I stepped back out, shook the bucket and yelled, "Hey handsome."

I heard his sliding stop, a sound as distinct as screeching tires. He spun and quickly returned. I gave him a small handful of grain. He tried to shove his elegant head in the bucket.

"Nope. This is for Cali." I pulled the grain out of his reach and patted his muscled neck. "Are you here to eat or help? If all you want is treats, take yourself right on back to the pasture, you big goof."

I started walking again. Gaston followed, whether because of the bucket of grain I carried, the carrots in my back pocket, or out of concern for Cali, I wasn't sure. But each time I yelled *come onnnn*, he added a loud whinny.

Clouds scudded in to play hide and seek with the moon. When it was too dark to see where to put my feet, I rested my free hand on the big chestnut's neck. Now and again, we stopped to listen. Gaston would stand with his ears swiveling back and forth, his huge eyes seeing what I could not.

We startled three deer from their beds and heard the *who-who-who-cooks-for-you?* call of a barred owl. From toward the river, the baying of a roving pack of coyotes sent a shiver snaking down my spine. More than once, underbrush along the trail rustled with movement making me gasp and grab Gaston's mane. Small animals gamboled away from our intrusion into their world. In the wet areas, the chirp of spring peepers and laughing gurgle of leopard frogs drowned out all else.

An hour later during one of our pauses, Gaston pricked his ears intently toward the woods on our right. He nickered softly, a breathy sound that made his nostrils quiver.

No answer. I tried to hear what he did. He took a step off the trail. I did not want to traipse into unchartered territory again, but when he took off at a trot, I had no choice but to run after him. Several people at Winterlight would happily kill me if I gave them another horse to look for.

I tried to grab Gaston's tail, but he was too quick. He skidded down an embankment and gracefully hopped up the other side, quickly getting ahead of me. It took me longer to negotiate the terrain without spilling the grain or snagging my legs in the tangle of deadfall on the forest floor.

The sound of Gaston's feet swishing through the leaves and underbrush stopped, and he snorted a couple of times. Or was that an answering snort?

My heart sped up. I crept along as quietly as I could, straining to see which direction he'd gone, listening hard. It didn't help that the clouds chose that instant to obscure what little light was to be had.

Then, I saw him. He stood in a mossy clearing not much larger than the space of a couple of stalls. Did I count eight legs or was it just my imagination? I didn't want to trust the wave of hope billowing into my chest. When a tail swished in Gaston's face, I knew he wasn't alone.

He stepped back to get nose to nose with her at the same moment the clouds moved on.

Cali.

Not in a bloody pile as I'd feared and imagined, but bathing in a shaft of moonlight, grazing on lichen. My legs turned to noodles, and I sat down hard. She came over and graciously accepted my offer of carrots, then ate the grain. I poured water into the empty bucket. She sucked it up.

Lightly, I ran my fingertips over a scrape on her forearm, the skin beneath the missing hair light against her dark-chocolate coat. A deeper gash crossed her right cannon bone. It still oozed a bit of blood. A cut arced from her chest to her shoulder, the ruched skin along its border silhouetted against the moon.

"I'm so sorry, my beautiful girl."

I reached up to stroke her face. She sneezed in mine, spraying me with dirt and bits of chewed oats and carrots. I laughed through a new flood of relieved tears.

"I deserve that for letting that crazy bitch take you."

She stood evenly on all four legs, didn't appear to be favoring one. The wounds I could see were superficial. Her bridle had come off. The saddle was still strapped to her back though it had shifted to one side.

Of Babette's signature golden stirrups, there was no sign.

CHAPTER FORTY-THREE

One Year Later

ON MY THIRTY-FIRST BIRTHDAY, I paced the driveway of Winterlight East, formerly known simply as Ed Todd's place, impatiently awaiting the arrival of the last and most important person needed for the ribbon-cutting ceremony.

Behind me stood nearly everyone I cared about. Malcolm, my parents, Giacomo. Penny chased after Isabella. Both Dexes were nearby along with Emily, Sandy, and Becca as well as Susan with her husband, a couple of their children and spouses, and several of their grandchildren.

Renee stood close to her new beau. She'd graciously released Dex One from any perceived obligation to her. After seeing him with Penny and Isabella, she said he needed to be with a woman who could give him children.

Even Miko, whose father had recovered, had returned. He and Emily were taking it slow at finding their way back to each other. Martina listened intently to a young man I didn't know. Noire was around somewhere, mostly likely helping to keep Issa corralled.

Hank and Clara had stayed in Missouri to take care of the farm. Helen had sent her best wishes, but demurred at our invitation, saying she didn't like to travel.

Others in attendance included local officials and dignitaries, interested neighbors, and the doctors and staff. All in all over one hundred people stood between the rebuilt pasture fence and refurbished barn with its new indoor arena.

The press had already completed most of their interviews. They shuffled around drinking coffee and rechecking their equipment in anticipation of the perfect photo opportunity.

Which wouldn't happen if a certain someone didn't get here soon.

I turned to Malcolm. "I swear to God, if he's a no show after all this, I'll track him down and beat him senseless. Again."

Malcolm put his hands on my shoulders. "I know how you feel, but that would be counterproductive, not to mention bad publicity." His fingers tightened. "He'll be here. You know how he is. He needs to make an entrance."

So true. Harry hadn't lost his flair and love for the dramatic. Ten minutes later, and twenty minutes late, he rolled up the drive in his new convertible—not a BMW—top down, grinning and waving as everyone applauded.

We got in position, Harry and I both holding the silly giant scissors, and smiled for the cameras. We endured—well, I endured, Harry enjoyed—the clicks and flashes and cheers for about a minute. Then, *snip*, and it was done.

Winterlight East—Equine Assisted Therapy was officially open for business.

Harry and I shook hands with each other. More pictures. We hugged. Laughed. Shared a few secret smiles. We'd been through so much together. He wore a tweed hacking jacket and one of his more colorful stock ties. It covered the scar around his neck. Plastic surgery had repaired the damage done to his nose by the stirrup. He retained his model good looks and easy charm, yet a new air of confidence and authority had settled around his shoulders. The cameras loved him.

A little while later, we moved to the indoor arena to host a catered luncheon. Everyone wanted to talk with us, be seen with us, get a selfie with us. When I could, I shifted the attention to Dr. Rachel Singh, our chief counselor, who never tired of explaining how healing with horses worked, and how we would start by focusing on sexually abused children but intended to grow to treat the challenges of other types of abuse.

Dex Two had volunteered much of his time over the past year to handle the legalities. Martina was head of Technical Services and Support, and her horses would live in a wing of the barn reserved for non-therapy animals. Emily had switched majors from criminal justice to psychology with an equine assisted therapy specialization and would eventually be a therapist. Miko had begun work toward a BS in Equine Administration. He was our barn manager.

Dex One, who had hinted he no longer wanted to be a private investigator, became our entire human resources department as well as the volunteer coordinator. He said detective work and HR were basically the same thing. I told him he couldn't interview prospective employees the same way he grilled suspects. He only gave me a look that said I didn't know what I was talking about. He'd been ready for a change, and when Penny decided to move back to the Island, the opportunity to follow had made the decision easy.

The anger he'd unleashed on Malcolm that day in the barn had been fueled by a fraught combination of unacknowledged envy and midlife crisis. He admitted that when he walked in on us, the embers of discontent had been sparked to a blinding blaze.

Harry was the money man and Chairman of the Board. Alcott had cut off Babette, but he'd never changed his will, if he'd even intended to. Harry got everything, and it was a lot. On top of that ridiculous sum, he'd sold his parents' valuable real estate in East Hampton as well as the city apartment. He invested and managed the proceeds well, finally turning his business degree to good use and discovering a buried talent for finance.

After many lengthy, late-night conversations, we'd agreed that converting Ed's place into a healing facility was the very best use of Alcott's wealth as well as a magnificent way to honor Ed's memory. That it also fully redeemed Harry for his part in Babette's scheme didn't hurt. He was building a new house not far away on a couple of acres along the north shore and had set up a generous trust to sustain our non-profit facility.

One day, in the midst of a planning meeting between the two of us, he'd asked, "Have I finally earned more than your disdain, V?"

The question took me off guard, and it took me a few moments to formulate a response. "I really was that bad," I admitted. "I'm sorry."

"You were as cold-backed as that crazy mare you love. But just like her, you've settled down and warmed up to your handlers." He gave me two flirty winks. "If you know what I mean."

I rolled my eyes. "I've always loved you, Harry, if not all your choices. I understand what drove you, but I hope my approval isn't why you're doing this."

He looked thoughtful for a minute. "No," he said with a shake of his head. "I'm doing it for my approval."

I pulled him into a hug. "You're only beginning to achieve your potential."

His eyes glittered with unshed tears when I released him. He turned away to hide this uncharacteristic show of emotion and our meeting continued.

Harry had magnanimously spent some of his money on a good lawyer for his mother. I would have let her rot. Good defense or not, Babette got life without parole for first-degree murder and manslaughter. She admitted beating Alcott and the fire investigator to death but adamantly maintained she had not deliberately killed Ed, nor attacked her own son. I knew she was responsible for both those acts, however, and I would never forget it.

Malcolm and I had driven to Long Island from Missouri to return Beau, Sasha, and Millie to their home. Beau and Sasha were Winterlight East's official goodwill ambassadors, and I loved knowing that these animals, adored by Ed, were here to get the place started right. Needless to say, Millie was in charge of rodent control, and Susan had found three kittens for the elderly cat to train.

Ed's house had been converted into offices and therapy spaces. I'd done some of the work myself, banishing the bad memories in the process. For now, patients would come for treatment a few hours at a time. Eventually, we would add on to provide for longer stays.

Once the press and official guests had gone home, we cranked up the music for an after-party, but I faded fast. I found a chair and soon dozed into a dreamless sleep. At some point, my mother shook me awake.

"Old woman," she said. "You should go to bed. It's been a long day."

I yawned until my jaw cracked. "You're older than me but you're awake. Last I noticed, you and Dad were still out on the dance floor."

She pulled a chair next to mine, sat, and put her glass of champagne on the table. "I'm not the one who's pregnant."

I shushed her and slipped my hand over my barely rounded belly. We'd told only my parents and Malcolm's mother so far.

"*Now* can I plan your wedding?" she asked.

We'd been so busy the past year making the arrangements for Winterlight East, there'd been no time. Thanks to my trust fund, an indoor arena was taking shape at Winterlight West as well.

I waved a negligent hand at her and stood. "Plan away. Just make sure it happens before November."

"October is a lovely time to get married," she said.

My eyes went round. "I'll be gigantic by then."

Malcolm came up behind me and looped his arms around my waist. His hands covered mine. "You'll be beautiful," he said.

I twisted to look over my shoulder at him and lifted an eyebrow.

"Maybe even more beautiful than usual," he added.

I turned and put my arms around his neck. "Are you tired?"

He gazed down into my eyes. His swam with so much tenderness, I sometimes thought I would drown. But I knew he wouldn't let me. I had the rest of our lives together to show him I loved him as much as he loved me. I'd taken the grackle's lessons to heart, gathered my courage, and let trust rule.

"Wide awake," he said. "Why?"

"Do you mind if we start driving back tonight?"

He took my hand and together, we said our goodnights. We walked through the barn and patted Beau and Sasha. Millie was hiding from the guests, probably watching over everyone from the loft. We loaded Noire in the back seat of my truck, got in the front, turned it around, and headed out the drive.

Dusk had settled, comforting in its smudged warmth. A thin strip of orange hung at the western horizon, barely visible through the trees. The in-between time. Neither day nor night. A place where I'd spent much of my life until two years ago when chance landed me at Winterlight.

A shadow in the pasture caught my eye.

"Stop," I said.

Malcolm didn't question my odd command. He was used to me.

I got out and went to the fence. Wastrel stood on a little rise watching us, his outline fuzzy in the near dark. Unexpected happiness rolled into me. He tossed his head but didn't come over. We looked at each other for a long moment, then he wheeled and galloped away. This, I thought—hoped?—really was the last time I'd see him.

"Goodbye, old friend," I whispered. "Thank you."

I climbed back into the passenger seat and snapped my seatbelt in place. Noire stuck her nose over the console and panted hot breath on our arms.

Malcolm wrapped his big hand around mine. "Everything okay?"

I squeezed his fingers. "Everything is perfect."

"Ready?"

I nodded as my heart swelled. "Let's go home."

End of *Wrong Lead*

ABOUT THE AUTHOR

Long Island native Candace Carrabus spent her formative years in the saddle, just imagining. She still rides horses and writes stories—frequently simultane-ously—and many of these stories are imbued with the magic and mystery horses have brought to her life. She shares a farm in the Midwest with her family, which includes several four-legged critters.

Sign up for her newsletter at candacecarrabus.com

 facebook.com/AuthorCandaceCarrabus

 twitter.com/CandaceCarrabus

 instagram.com/candace_carrabus

ALSO BY CANDACE CARRABUS

FANTASY

Raver, The Horsecaller: Book One

The Roar of Smoke, A Book of the Meldborn

THE WITTING WOMAN NOVELLAS

The Man, The Dog, His Owner & Her Lover

The Good Horse, The Bad Man & The Ugly Woman

Publisher: Witting Woman Works

Cover design by Molly Phipps

ISBN-13: 978-0-9993622-0-4

❀ Created with Vellum

Made in the USA
Columbia, SC
15 December 2018